GALLIPOLI

www.transworldbooks.co.uk

Also by Peter FitzSimons

Nancy Wake: a Biography of Our Greatest War Heroine
Kim Beazley
Nick Farr-Jones
Nene: the Queen of the Magazine Wars
The Rugby War
A Simpler Time
John Eales: the Biography
Steve Waugh
The Ballad of Les Darcy
Little Theories of Life
Tobruk
And Now for Some Light Relief
Kokoda
Charles Kingsford Smith and Those Magnificent Men
Mawson
Batavia
Eureka
Ned Kelly

PETER
FITZSIMONS
GALLIPOLI

BANTAM PRESS

LONDON · TORONTO · SYDNEY · AUCKLAND · JOHANNESBURG

TRANSWORLD PUBLISHERS
61–63 Uxbridge Road, London W5 5SA
www.transworldbooks.co.uk

Transworld is part of the Penguin Random House group of companies
whose addresses can be found at global.penguinrandomhouse.com

First published in 2014 by Random House Australia Pty Ltd

First published in Great Britain in 2015 by Bantam Press
an imprint of Transworld Publishers

A CIP catalogue record for this book
is available from the British Library.

ISBN 9780593074909

Maps and drawings on pp. 68, 280, 570 and 576 drawn by Midland Typesetters

Printed and bound by Clays Ltd, Bungay, Suffolk

Penguin Random House is committed to a sustainable
future for our business, our readers and our planet. This book
is made from Forest Stewardship Council® certified paper.

1 3 5 7 9 10 8 6 4 2

To Charles E. W. Bean, Ellis Ashmead-Bartlett and Keith Murdoch. The first for so skilfully and courageously chronicling many of the events herein; the latter two for their bravery in influencing the course of events.
I dips me lid.

Remote though the conflict was, so completely did it
absorb the people's energies, so completely concentrate
and unify their effort, that it is possible for those
who lived among the events to say that in those days
Australia became fully conscious of itself as a nation.
*Charles Bean, Official History of Australia
in the War of 1914–1918, Vol. I*

History will undoubtedly concede that strategically
the attack on Constantinople is absolutely
sound, and the results of success will be far-
reaching. It is the manner in which it is being
carried out, which is causing all the trouble.
Ellis Ashmead-Bartlett, The Uncensored Dardanelles

I could pour into your ears so much truth about the
grandeur of our Australian army, and the wonderful
affection of these young soldiers for each other and their
homeland, that your Australianism would become a
more powerful sentiment than before. It is stirring to
see them, magnificent manhood, swinging their fine
limbs as they walk about Anzac. They have the noble
faces of men who have endured. Oh, if you could picture
Anzac as I have seen it, you would find that to be an
Australian is the greatest privilege the world has to offer.
*Keith Murdoch to Andrew Fisher ('The Gallipoli
Letter'), 23 September 1915*

CONTENTS

CONTENTS

LIST OF MAPS

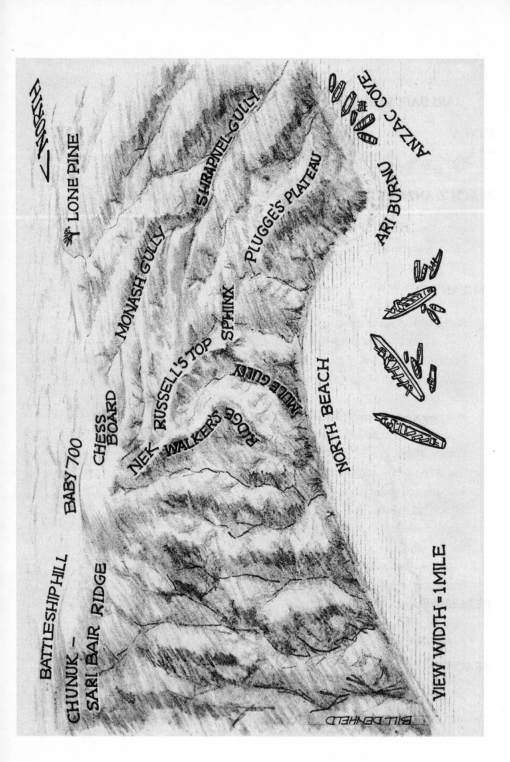

Anzac Cove and Lone Pine, by Bill Denheld

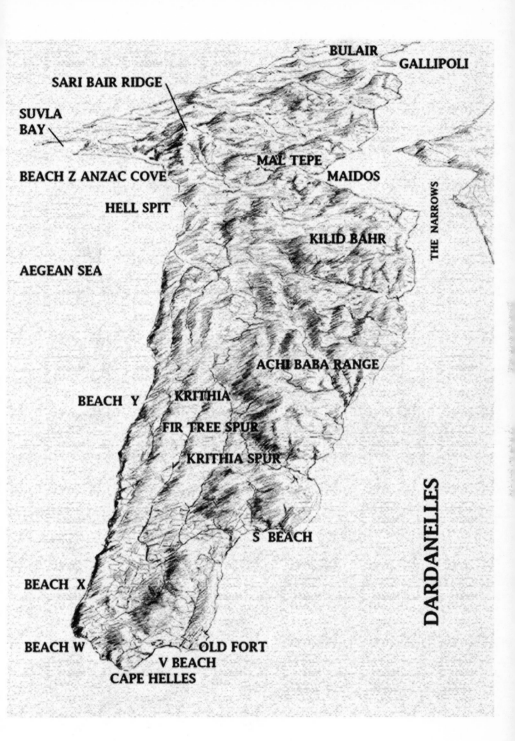

View over Gallipoli Peninsula, by Bill Denheld

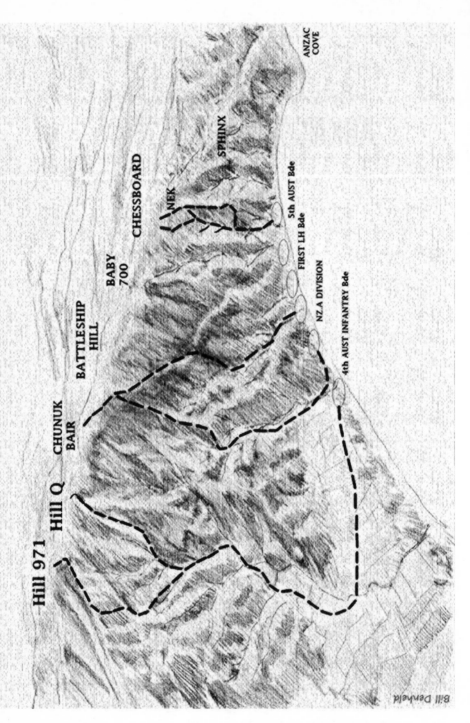

Gallipoli attack lines, by Bill Denheld

BACKGROUND AND ACKNOWLEDGEMENTS

Gallipoli and I go back a long way.

As the youngest of seven kids, born to parents who had returned from serving in the Second World War to carve out a farm in the bush at Peats Ridge – just an hour north of Sydney – the very name 'Gallipoli' resonated for me like no other. A place of extraordinary deeds, of inspiring courage and sacrifice, it made you proud to be an Australian. Knowledge of it went with *being* an Australian. I learned about it at primary school; I heard about it every Anzac Day service up at Central Mangrove RSL; and I frequently thought about it, *at the going down of the sun, and in the morning . . .*

Sure, I was sort of proud of Mum and Dad and their service in the Second World War – Mum as an army physiotherapist, helping rehabilitate the veterans of Milne Bay and Kokoda; and Dad at El Alamein and in New Guinea – but it wasn't as if they had been at Gallipoli, where I knew the *real* action had taken place.

I studied it quite seriously at high school, I read about it on my holidays and wrote an essay on it while at the University of Sydney. My reverence for it blossomed to the point that, as a rugby player living and playing in Italy in the mid-1980s, on my '84/'85 Christmas break, I drove my tiny little Fiat all the way through the Iron Curtain, through Yugoslavia and Bulgaria to first Istanbul, and then of course down to Gallipoli.

Alone – long before visiting these battlefields had become something of a rite of passage for many young Australians – I wandered around, awe-struck at the savagery of the terrain, how the cliffs rose all but straight from the shore, how the trace of the trenches meandered in parallel lines so close together, how some of the gullies they'd fought in and for looked rather more like abysses to my eyes.

Standing on the beach below the spot known as The Sphinx, I noticed a great deal of erosion in the landscape all around, and wondered about it until I suddenly realised. That was not mere erosion, it was the scars of thousands of artillery shells hitting those hills!

At Lone Pine Cemetery, amid all the gravestones marked with such words as **DUTY NOBLY DONE, HE DIED IN A FAR COUNTRY/FIGHTING FOR/HIS NATIVE LAND, A MOTHER'S THOUGHTS OFTEN WANDER TO THIS SAD AND LONELY GRAVE** . . . I noted an epitaph that quite shocked me, going something like **DIED IN A FOREIGN FIELD. AND FOR WHAT?**

Coming back from the battlefield towards the nearest town – Gallipoli itself – I gave three hitchhiking Turkish workers in blue overalls a lift up to the next town, and though the language barrier between us was insurmountable, I was a tad amazed that they seemed extremely friendly, even after I identified myself as – steady, fellas, *steady* – an *Australian*.

Would I be so hail-fellow-well-met with someone from a nation that had come to my shores and killed 90,000 of my countrymen?

No.

I returned home to Australia, proud that I had made my pilgrimage to sacred soil, and then embarked on a journalistic career, covering many subjects but always with an eye out for Anzac Day stories. I was particularly stunned by the reaction I received to a yarn I wrote about a cricket match played on the shores of Gallipoli, even while Turkish shells were bursting all around. Letters, phone calls, people stopping me in the street, expressing their wonder at the Diggers' bravery . . .

Many years on, stories of Gallipoli were still striking so many chords with the Australian people you could play an anthem to it. In the late 1990s, for no reason I can think of, I suddenly started taking my kids to Anzac Day services in town.

In April 1999, I was in my car heading down Sydney's Market

Street, about to turn left onto Sussex Street, to the *Sydney Morning Herald* building, when some highbrow historian on ABC Radio used the phrase 'when the Australians invaded Turkey, at Gallipoli'.

Invaded? Such an ugly, aggressive, non-reverential word! Yes, I suppose, technically, Gallipoli was on Turkish soil – even though it was GALLIPOLI – and, strictly speaking, if you wanted to really get pernickety about it, our blokes didn't really have the Turkish blessing to land on their shores. So, if your measure was hoity-toity historical, then it just possibly could be construed as an 'invasion', so long as you put some monster quotation marks around it. But it sat very uncomfortably with me, and was the first time I had been obliged to think of the whole idea of the landing on Gallipoli shores in less than holy terms. But the more I thought about it as the years passed, the more I drifted into a rather more sober view.

To open my 2004 book on Kokoda, I quoted the words of Paul Keating, shortly after, as Prime Minister, he famously kissed the hallowed ground in New Guinea in 1992: '*The Australians who served in Papua New Guinea fought and died, not for defence of the old, but the new world. Their world. They died in defence of Australia and the civilisation and values which had grown up there. That is why it might be said that, for Australians, the battles in Papua New Guinea were the most important ever fought.*'[1]

Now *that* resonated.

'After all,' I would occasionally note in after-dinner speeches, when feeling brave, 'at Gallipoli, they fought for England and lost. At Kokoda, they fought for Australia and won.'

Other times, I would note, 'How weird we Australians are! After the Germans invaded Poland in 1939, they moved their way through most of the rest of Europe, knocking over army after army, and got all the way to North Africa, still without registering a defeat. The *first time* the Germans were stopped was when they came up against the Australians at Tobruk. Same with the Japanese! After dropping bombs on Pearl Harbor, the Japanese Imperial Army knocked over the Philippines, moved down through the Malayan Peninsula and knocked over Singapore, before landing in New Guinea . . . where they were defeated, for the first time, by the Australians at Milne Bay and then Kokoda. So we have on our national military record that our soldiers were the first to stop the Germans and the Japanese during the Second World War. But when it comes time for a day of military remembrance, we say, "Yes, yes, yes, that was us that stopped the hitherto unstoppable Germans and Japanese, but did we ever tell you about the time we got sent packing by the Turks?"'

There is usually a momentary stunned silence – someone said something *against* reverence for Gallipoli? – before people give rueful smiles and acknowledge it *is* a strange thing.

Broadly, after immersing myself in writing about the Second World War, I came to the view that the whole Gallipoli story was overdone, and that Australia's emotional centre of gravity when it came to our military history had moved forward.

Still, as the Centenary of Gallipoli approached, I found myself on both the Council of the Australian War Memorial and the Anzac Centenary Advisory Board, two institutions where I was exposed to many fascinating angles to Gallipoli I had not previously considered. Again I was given cause to reflect on just what it was all about, what it all meant from the perspective of 100 years on.

I particularly remember a presentation to the Anzac Centenary Advisory Board in early 2013 made by a very learned academic from Monash University, Professor Bruce Scates, where, at our behest, he presented 20 stories about Australians who had fought in the First World War and what had happened to them, including most particularly Hugo Throssell, as part of a broad plan to present 100 such stories to the public. Each story seemed more horrifying than the last, in detailing the appalling consequences of young men dying grisly deaths and leaving behind ruined families.

At the end of his presentation, no one spoke for a good 20 seconds.

Devastating!

'Did . . . uh . . . um, anything *good* happen to anyone?' one of the people around the table asked.

His expression said it all: NO.

'Surely the bad outweighs the good in war,' the good Professor finally replied firmly. 'We can't afford to lose sight of that.'

When someone suggested that the most disturbing cases be cut from the presentations and be replaced with 'positive, nation-building stories', he bristled.

'We owe the *truth* to a generation that suffered so much,' he said. 'And the truth is the effect on most lives was devastating. If you try to make me put a positive spin on it, I shall resign.'

In March 2013, once I'd embarked on a book about it, I revisited Gallipoli and again walked through Lone Pine Cemetery, intent on finding that inscription that had haunted me from 30 years earlier – **DIED IN A FOREIGN FIELD. AND FOR WHAT?** Alas, among the 1167 graves there, I couldn't find it, but I did come across other moving epitaphs, such as that for Private L. J. Dawson, of the 1st Battalion, **OH FOR THE TOUCH OF A VANISHED HAND**, which I quoted in my newspaper column upon my return. It prompted a flurry of correspondence, where readers sent in other epitaphs they had seen at Gallipoli, including one for Trooper Eric Chalcroft Bell, Killed In Action on 19 May 1915, aged 22: **LOVING HUSBAND OF NELLIE, BELOVED FATHER OF EVA, DULCIE & ERICA**.

What, I wondered in my column, became of Nellie, Eva, Dulcie and Erica? The answer, coming from a reader descended from them, was devastating, involving grinding poverty, orphanages and sexual abuse of those daughters.

It influenced the way I wrote this book. I did not want to go down the 'They died for our freedom' path, because however noble the intent of many of them, I have never come across the 'pursuit of freedom' or its like as a motivating factor in any of the myriad letters or diaries I've read, and though 'fighting for Australia' and 'doing my duty' was indeed a frequent refrain, in many cases the bitter truth, as noted by Charles Bean, is they just *died*. Tragically. Too often for not even the gain of one yard of land. Did they even have right on their side?

I happened to be at the Australian War Memorial in 2013 when Paul Keating, commemorating the 20th anniversary of the reinterment of the Unknown Soldier, said, 'The First World War was a war devoid of any virtue. It arose from the quagmire of European tribalism. A complex interplay of nation-state destinies overlaid by notions of cultural superiority peppered with racism . . .'[2]

The more I researched, the more I began to wonder whether it was a fairer summation to say that many were in fact sacrificed on the altar of British Imperialism?

I began the book with these things in mind, though – as with my last book, on Ned Kelly – I didn't want to draw specific conclusions. I wanted to detail *what happened* across the board, not just from ground level with the Australian soldier, but also for the New Zealanders, the Turks, the Brits and other nationalities, the officers and all of the politicians and leaders who put them all there in the first place.

As with all of my books with historical themes, I wanted to make it read like a novel, but fill it with accurate raw detail and perch it on 2000 or so firm footnotes to show that it is nevertheless real. For the sake of the storytelling, I have occasionally created a direct quote from reported speech in a newspaper, diary or letter, just as I have changed pronouns and tenses to put that reported speech in the present tense. I have equally occasionally restored swearing words that were blanked out in the original newspaper account due to the sensitivities of the time. Always, my goal has been to determine the most likely words used, based on the documentary evidence presented.

Trying to bring the Turkish side of the saga to life became problematic in the storytelling when the Turks and Australians used different geographical nomenclature to describe the same landform. To get around this, I have broadly followed Charles Bean, with the most notable exception being '*dere*' – a Turkish word meaning 'gully'. No doubt, for example, 'Sazli Dere' is the name used by the Turks, but the narrative is clearer as 'Sazli Gully', and only rarely did the Diggers and officers themselves use Turkish terms for landforms.

For the same reason of remaining faithful to the language of the day, I have stayed with the imperial form of measurement and used the contemporary spelling. Though the Turks used 'Istanbul' to describe their ancient capital, for ease of narrative told from a fundamentally Anglo perspective I have used 'Constantinople'.

One happy circumstance in doing this book was that the three principal members of the research team I have worked with on so many previous books happened to have particular strengths on this subject.

Libby Effeney lived in Turkey for five years, speaks the language and has strong contacts within the Turkish historical academic community. She was able to visit Turkey on my behalf, finding the nuggets of gold to bring the Turkish side of things to life. A PhD student from Deakin University, her intellect, work ethic, creative nous and drive to get to the bottom of things was invaluable in all facets of this book, and I warmly thank her for all her work, including liaising with the other researchers on specific subjects. She was a joy to work with throughout, combining great professionalism by day with warmth in emails at midnight, assuring me it would all come together in the end. When she becomes a Professor, I will boast of having worked with her. I already do.

Sonja Goernitz is a dual German–Australian citizen familiar with the highways and byways of German historical institutions, and she was able to return to her homeland to winkle out gems from the German side of the equation. She, too, was tireless in her efforts, and I thank her.

My friend of 35 years standing, Henry Barrkman, was living in Dublin for most of the course of writing the book and was able to access the London Archives relatively easily. An angel of accuracy, a demon for detail, his impact on this manuscript was immense. I thank him most particularly for two things: always challenging the accepted version of events until such times as original documentation proved it; and trawling the minutes of the hours of the *days* of endless meetings of the War Council 100 years ago in London, noting who said what to whom and when, to work out how the actual decision to go to Gallipoli was made. All up, a bravura performance.

There were many other valued researchers too, including Matthew

Sheldon, who visited the British Library and the Parliamentary Archives at the Palace of Westminster, Lachlan Dudley, who did general research, and Bryce Abraham, who was particularly expert on the story of Albert Jacka.

I first started working with my professional on the ground at the Australian War Memorial, Glenda Lynch, for my book on Tobruk over a decade ago. In this one, she was as uber-efficient and thorough as ever, a pleasure to work with – as was her fellow researcher at the Australian War Memorial, Jean Main.

I also tapped the expertise of people in particularly specialised fields, and I offer my warm thanks to: Dr Michael Cooper, who helped inform me on the medical aspects of the story; Gregory Blake, for his assistance in all matters to do with firearms and artillery; Dr Kevin Fewster, on the Battle of the Wazza; Hugh Dolan, on the submarine narrative; Keith Quinton, for help with the *Pfalz* saga; Mike Carlton, on the *Emden*; Ashley Ekins, for his expertise on esoterica, including the latest figures on the casualties of the campaign; Berhan Göz, for his excellent research assistance in Turkey; and Dr Mehdi Ilhan from the Australian National University, for help with the Turkish side.

Many of the diary and letter entries you see in this book came courtesy of Noel Boreham, who has spent years at the Australian War Memorial reading and understanding them, and placed his expertise and treasure trove at my disposal. My appreciation, too, to Glenda Veitch of the State Library of New South Wales, who was very helpful throughout, as was Dolores Ho of the National Army Museum in New Zealand.

By the time I had a draft manuscript, Gallipoli expert Dr Peter Williams was extremely helpful in vetting it, spotting errors and providing helpful feedback. Throughout the book, Dr Peter Pedersen was a wonderful source of advice, as were my friends, Australia's most esteemed historian, David Day, and our most esteemed historical writer, Thomas Keneally. I acknowledge the valued input of Tim Sullivan, the Deputy Director of the Australian War Memorial. Elizabeth Brenchley, Mike Carlton and, most particularly, the granddaughter of Hugo Throssell,

Karen Throssell, also provided wonderful advice in their particular fields, for which I thank them. I have used some of the interviews done with Gallipoli veterans for the ABC by Steve Sailah, and thank him for his cogent advice. The Melbourne writer and journalist Christopher Bantick was a great sounding board on many sensitive issues.

As to illustrations and maps, I am once more particularly indebted to Jane Macaulay and Bill Denheld. I make a particular plea that before embarking on this book *you look at those maps and drawings.* Digest them. Refer back to them. It took me a long time to get my head around the landscape of Gallipoli and the Dardanelles, which is why I commissioned so many maps and drawings.

The story of Gallipoli is obviously well-covered ground, with myriad writers having already forged paths for those of us following, trying to understand. While I have a comprehensive bibliography at the end, allow me to particularly salute Charles Bean, who laid the foundation stone for us all, together with his fellow correspondent Ellis Ashmead-Bartlett. As to authors, I also particularly appreciated books by Peter Burness, John Hamilton, Fred and Elizabeth Brenchley, Sir Winston Churchill, Edward Erickson, Martin Gilbert, Oliver Hogue, Robert Rhodes James, Sir Roger Keyes, John Masefield, Robert Massie, Dudley McCarthy, Alan Moorehead, Les Carlyon, Henry Morgenthau, Tolga Örnek, Feza Toker, Christopher Pugsley and Dacre Stoker (who published under his birth name of Henry Stoker). Of them all, I particularly loved the work of Dudley McCarthy, Alan Moorehead and Oliver Hogue, who gave a fantastic insider's account, which I have drawn heavily from; and I was awed by just how comprehensive the work of the late Jill Kitson was when it came to documenting Keith Murdoch's involvement at Gallipoli, and acknowledge my great debt to her labours.

I also thank the families of soldiers at Gallipoli, who allowed me to publish their forebears' words in this book. I thank Associate Justice Mark Derham and his family for allowing me to access Sir Cyril Brudenell White's papers at the Australian War Memorial; Dorothy Hoddinott and Alan Bingham for granting me permission to use the diary of their father, Charles Edward Bingham, as a source; and John Carter and Alison Flanagan for providing me with the wonderful story of their grandparents, Gordon Carter and Lydia Kathleen King.

As ever, my dear friend at *The Sydney Morning Herald*, Harriet Veitch, gave me wise counsel on every part of the manuscript and did the preliminary editing, sorting out tangled sentences, pointing out inconsistencies and placing at my service the extraordinary width of her general knowledge.

I thank all at Random House, most particularly Nikki Christer, Peri Wilson and – *please give it up for!* – Alison Urquhart, for her enthusiasm and support from first discussing this idea over lunch in 2010 to now putting this book to bed. She is my publishing Uluru.

My thanks also, as ever, to my highly skilled editors, Brandon VanOver and Kevin O'Brien, who have gone through the lot with the finest of all fine-tooth combs, like only they possess, and given the whole thing a professional sheen, while Catherine Hill and David Henley proved endless in their patience in the last push.

Thank you, thank you all.

I hope you enjoy it.

Peter FitzSimons
Neutral Bay, Sydney
September 2014

Prologue

A NATION IS BORN

War fell upon the British people out of a clear sky . . . The notion
that the assassination of a foreign Archduke by an outraged patriot
could precipitate them personally into battle and death – that
the son who came home daily from his work in a London office,
or who shook from his eyes the spray of the Sydney surf, would
within a few months be lying with his hair matted in blood on
a Turkish hillside – did not even suggest itself until the tempest
was rushing down upon them in the last few days of the crisis.

Charles Bean, Official History of Australia
in the War of 1914–1918, Vol. I [1]

I suppose that nothing short of such a great international
crisis could have brought together and made bedfellows of
such a queer mixture of human beings – out of workers,
deadbeats, sailors, an odd man or two in uniform, farmers,
a few clerks, stiff collars and a correct cut here, a ragged coat
and unwashed face there. Out of such a weird gathering it
seemed impossible that an army could ever be formed . . . [2]

Sergeant Charles Laseron, 13th Battalion AIF, and former member of
Mawson's Australasian Antarctic Expedition, Diary, 23 December 1914

Who will say that Gallipoli was a failure if from the trials
endured there, and in memory of the unconquerable
spirit of those who died, Australia should have developed
a nationalism based on the highest ideals. [3]

General Sir Cyril Brudenell White

1

Just as pilgrims head to the Promised Land, merchants gravitate to the metropolis and the mightiest oceans attract the greatest of seafarers, so too are there certain spots on earth whose siren call has Emperors, Kings, Sultans, Presidents and Prime Ministers sending their armies and navies from even the most distant of seas, flooding forth on the tides of war to attack with every weapon at hand.

The decades and centuries pass, the Empires rise and fall, but still the soldiers and sailors attack, and still they die . . . until one Empire occupies the spot and the next rising Empire must gird its loins, *stiffen the sinews, summon up the blood*, to try for it once more . . . or be no Empire at all.

In the history of the world, there is no greater exemplar of this blood-drenched phenomenon than the drowned valley of the Dardanelles, the narrow waterway that cleaves the mountainous forms of Europe and Asia on either side. It is an axis on which whole Empires have hung in the balance for 3000 years, an abyss that has swallowed armies and navies whole since the first mass of men took up arms.

A natural crossroads for Emperors embarked on imperialism, just as it is for pilgrims pursuing the path to Jerusalem and Mecca, securing its right of passage has been a rite of passage for Emperors, Kings, Popes, Caliphs, Warlords and barbarians alike. Since the time of the Trojans, all of the Peloponnese, Hellenic, Persian, Roman, Byzantine, Bulgarian, Venetian, Ottoman and British Empires have shed blood to dominate it. Nigh on 1200 years BC, the city of Troy, which lies on the eastern shores of the Dardanelles, was destroyed after being besieged by the Greeks in the Trojan War – an epic of fire and slaughter that was immortalised in Homer's *Iliad*. The Dardanelles is a dreamy place of hazy but hazardous history stretching back to antiquity, where the flowers bloom, the birds sing, the goats bleat and the butterflies float by as the seasons pass and all is a bastion of the bucolic . . . only to regularly and suddenly burst into savagery on a mass scale, causing death by the tens of thousands.

Never, however, was there a battle involving so many men, from so many nations, from so far afield, leaving behind so many shallow graves, as the one that took place there in 1915 . . .

Two old and grand Empires, one at the height of its powers, the other in decay, fought with a ferocity unmatched, before or since. One Empire felt that the fate of the fight for *world* domination rested on the result. The other was in no doubt – the remains of their own Empire were on the line.

So how did federated Australia, a new nation just a decade and a half old, far distant from the centre of both Empires, come to send tens of thousands of her sons to the Dardanelles, and why did they fight with such fury against a people with whom they had no direct quarrel?

Therein lies a tale, which, if you cock your ear to the wind, begins with the sound of many marching bands . . .

—

Coming up Sydney's George Street on this fine morning of 1 January 1901, the day of Federation, when the nation is to be *born*, band after band form part of a grand procession on their way to Centennial Park, where the precious document will be signed.

The pageant proceeds, the crowd cheers – an estimated half a million have turned out for the occasion – and the many Union Jacks wave gaily in the morning breeze.

There is a delirious aspect to it, though not everyone is swept away by it. A writer for the *Bulletin* magazine, whose mood is clearly out of kilter with those around him, is quick to note just who makes up most of the procession. 'Instead of the battling "men and women who really make Australia" there were soldiers and soldiers and soldiers, emphasising the sadness that Australia, the land of peace, has become for British ends a land of war . . .'[4]

Stiff of back, clear of eye, gay in their brightly coloured uniforms, the soldiers keep marching, men from all over the continent, and indeed the world.

But the *Bulletin* writer is adamant. These men, in his view, are 'bred for slaughter, ignorant of personal responsibility, following the fetish "loyalty" blindly, utensils of the privileged classes for the defence of whose prerogative they exist . . . The people gazed fascinated, and cheered – did they know what? And so, with the blare of bands, through the packed streets the pageant passed, with the Governor-General at the tail looking so puny, so wan – as if in his own person he figured the wan and puny basis of the idea of monarchy which he represented.'[5]

But such churlish views really are in a tiny minority on this day to beat all days. In Sydney, you could perhaps count them on the fingers of one finger, as the people continue to roar their acclaim. Within two hours – from the moment that Lord Hopetoun, Australia's first Governor-General, and Prime Minister Edmund Barton and his ministers of State are sworn in, as a choir of 15,000 sings on – Australia becomes a nation.

From the beginning, for most people, having men under arms is a hugely important part of being a nation, second only to having those men 'blooded' in battle, actually fighting for the nation. Back in 1889, the 'Father of Federation', Sir Henry Parkes, had spoken of 'the crimson thread of kinship', the common blood that binds the white people of the colonies to each other, and to the nations of the British Empire. And yet there is also a strong notion abroad in the land that no nation is worthy of the name until that crimson thread becomes a river, shed in the service of that Empire.

It is a culture that grows in the first decade of the century, and nowhere is the reverence for matters military better illustrated than with the arrival on Australian shores of the most illustrious military man in the British Empire.

For did anyone *ever* make a finer entrance to Sydney Town?

As the train bearing Lord Kitchener of Khartoum on his national tour pulls into No.1 Platform at Central Station shortly after 3 pm on this day in early January 1910, there is a flurry of activity on the platform, as delicious expectation crowds forward.

And there he is! The great man – the double row of ribbons and medals on his chest attesting to his bravery over the decades – alights from the train and is instantly surrounded by federal, state and local politicians. A roar goes up from the crowd, kept back by barricades, so loud and powerful it is all but strong enough to rustle the myriad Union Jacks and palm fronds that adorn the arches above the platform for the occasion.

Get back! Get *back!*

'Tall, well set up, and military-looking,' *The Sydney Morning Herald* will describe him, 'Lord Kitchener has a typically British face, florid, with brown moustache, and keen blue eyes.'[6]

Tightly behind him, just as he is always close to him wherever he goes, is his dashing Aide-de-Camp – and perhaps more, for theirs is a bond beyond the mere military – Captain Oswald FitzGerald. (His predecessor in the role, Captain Frank Maxwell, had been sacked on the spot when Lord Kitchener found that he had married while on leave. *Married!* Captain FitzGerald is unlikely to do that, and in fact shares living quarters with Lord Kitchener in London.)

No fewer than 80 policemen escort Lord Kitchener and the attendant Captain FitzGerald to their waiting car, through an honour guard of the metropolitan police who have served in the Boer War and are wearing their medals for the occasion. Next to them – *Attehnnn-shun!* – half a dozen cadets stand at rigid attention, scarcely daring to believe that this icon of the Empire is inspecting them, and even speaking briefly to a lucky, tremulous few . . .

At his very appearance outside the railway station, 10,000 voices roar their acclaim, and there are tens of thousands more on every wall, railing, lamppost and footpath as he makes his way to Government House.

That evening, backed by a coterie of his most senior officers, here is Lord Kitchener again, in Sydney, right now, in front of us privileged few, at this glittering black-tie soiree – filled with such luminaries as the Chief Justice of the High Court, the Archbishop of Sydney, the Defence Minister and the High Commissioner for Australia – at the Town Hall.

Lord Kitchener, freshly appointed Chief of the Imperial General Staff, the Imperial war hero who subdued the Sudanese and bested the Boers in South Africa, has come to our fair shores at the invitation of Prime Minister Alfred Deakin to give us formal advice – vis-à-vis the proposed new *Defence Act* – on just how we can better defend the country to ensure that the British Empire is protected.

You can see by looking at him just why, upon his arrival in Darwin a fortnight earlier, the *Herald* had noted for its Sydney readers that though from a distance he appears a 'mild-looking gentleman, as compared with the ferocious portraits', up close he becomes 'a swarthy, fierce-eyed man of gigantic mould'.[7]

But hush. For here is Sydney Lord Mayor Sir Allen Arthur Taylor, standing to propose the toast to the King – '*The King*', '*The King*', '*The King*' – before formally welcoming Lord Kitchener. 'I must congratulate the British Government,' the Lord Mayor begins, 'for allowing such an eminent peacemaker, whose record is a household word amongst the British race, to come amongst us to advise the Commonwealth Government on the vital question of defence. The liberty we have enjoyed since our birth has been generously provided by a generous mother, therefore we must be prepared to assist to defend our vast continent, and thus strengthen the Empire . . .' *(Loud cheering.)*[8]

The Minister for Defence, Mr Joseph Cook, MP, supports the toast, welcomes their distinguished visitor on behalf of the Federal Government, and notes that they 'have invited Lord Kitchener to give that good advice which he was so well qualified to give with regard to the defence of Australia', and in organising 'the co-ordination of the defensive units of the Empire, and of Australia'.[9] *(Cheers.)*

More toasts to the great man follow from more luminaries, before three cheers greet Lord Kitchener himself, as he rises to respond.

'My Lord Mayor, your Excellency, and gentlemen,' he begins in his stentorian tones, 'I very greatly appreciate the cordiality of your welcome and your kindness in inviting me to this banquet tonight, and I can assure you that I consider it a very high compliment . . .' *(Loud cheering.)*[10]

Oh, what a night we are having. Lord Kitchener! Here in Sydney!

The great man goes on to specify his plans for how the Australian Government should introduce a new national Military Training

Scheme, in order to be able to better defend itself and be of greater service to the Empire.

It will be compulsory for every male citizen and will begin with 120 hours annually of junior cadet training for all lads 12 and 13 years old, followed by senior cadet training for 14- to 18-year-olds – the equivalent of 16 days annually. This, as reported by *The Sydney Morning Herald*, will soon see 'a senior cadet force in the neighbourhood of 100,000. That is the nucleus of the army of the future.'[11] To cater for the officer class, Lord Kitchener recommends – though, coming from him, it is practically a command – the opening of a military college.[12]

While the reaction to these plans is generally positive, this is not universal, and the most outspoken is a body formed in Adelaide, The Anti-Compulsory Military Training League, soon renamed The Freedom League, which bitterly opposes all compulsory military training as a gross infringement of personal liberty. The training scheme is 'picturesque European tomfoolery', while the *Defence Act* is 'wicked, foolish, and wasteful'.[13]

Again, however, such protests are in the tiny minority, and in early 1914 there is another visitor from the British military to Australian shores.

And in the end, it's weird, you know? For, so often in the endless cavalcade of people that public figures encounter, there is nary the tiniest sign that they are meeting the person who will go on to profoundly alter their own lives. No drum roll, no trumpet, no clash of cymbals . . . no sign. It is just another quick handshake and chat as far as the visiting Inspecting General of British Forces, Sir Ian Hamilton, is concerned. It is just some local newspaper chappie – 'Keith Murdoch', I think his name is? – whom he meets after making a public address at the Melbourne Town Hall. Hosted by the Caledonian Society, it is a glittering occasion, attended by 250 distinguished citizens. General Hamilton has come to Australia and New Zealand to inspect troops – to get some idea of their relative strengths – and to try to standardise forces throughout the Empire.

Of the Empire, *for* the Empire, the separate armies must no longer be random pieces of a patchwork but rather be perfectly aligned with each other. They must use the same ammunition and rifles – the .303 Lee-Enfield Rifle SMLE, known to the soldiers as 'Smelly'[14] – and be trained in the same manner, because the idea is to 'make in Australia a territorial division of one grand Imperial army, which could face the world without fear'.[15]

He is extremely impressed with the troops he inspects on his tour, noting that, although 'still very young, they are full of intelligence and grit. On at least two occasions I have seen brigades tested severely, once by heat and heavy marching, the other time by floods and mud. In each case the men made light of their trying experiences, treating them as an excellent joke.'[16]

Before leaving Australia, Hamilton visits the newly established officer-training college at Duntroon, where he talks long and hard with the Commanding Officer, Brigadier-General William Bridges, together with his director of drill, Lieutenant-Colonel Ewen MacLagan.[17] He also sits for a time under a gum tree, chatting with one particular officer who has impressed him with the brilliance of his troop manoeuvres, Colonel John Monash, before inspecting the soldiers and aspiring officers.

Shortly before taking his leave, General Hamilton wishes them all 'plenty of wars and rapid promotion!'.[18]

He is cheered to the echo.

———

The Dardanelles at this point? Few in Australia are giving them any thought. For most people, the Ottoman Empire – whatever and wherever that is – is the most unheard-of thing they've never heard of.

Australia's eyes are on Europe alone, which appears to be dividing into armed camps of opposing alliances – with the 'Triple Entente' of Great Britain, France and Russia leading one group, lined up against another group led by the 'Central Powers' of Germany and Austria-Hungary. This is of some concern, but, as the British Empire has never been stronger, and Australia is puffed-chest proud to be a part of it, there is no doubt whose side we would join in the case of war.

The Ottoman Empire? Even for those who know something of its contours, it is hardly a threat. For, while the sun so famously never sets on the British Empire, quite the reverse is the case for the Ottoman Empire, which is in the darkest shadow of its 500-odd years of existence. Sure, in days of yonder yore, when the soldiers of the feudal armies of Europe were hungry, undisciplined and armed with pikes, Ottoman soldiers were well fed, highly trained and armed with gunpowder weapons, allowing them to straddle three continents. From the Danube to Yemen, from Albania to the northern shores of the Black Sea, and from Algiers to Baghdad, the Muslim Caliphate had covered a fifth of the globe. But those days are long gone, and it is now reduced to just half of its original size.

It has been chipped away at from the outside by the inexorable rise of the European powers, who, by the early 1900s, control 85 per cent of the earth's surface. And it is dissolving from within, as Ottoman subjects, especially its Christian minorities in the Balkans – led by Bulgaria, Montenegro and Rumania – are vigorously chafing at the ties that bind. Greece has already fought and won its independence from Ottoman rule, as has Serbia. In their image, countless other groups all over the Empire are now as rebellious as they are resolved to fight for their own freedom.

For the Europeans, the crux of the 'Eastern Question', which they love to grapple with and debate in their grand parliaments and palaces, is just which of them is to benefit from the inevitable dissolution of their Ottoman neighbours, known far and wide as 'the sick man of Europe'. In 1875, the influential Scottish essayist Thomas Carlyle had written a letter, published in *The Times*, after the particular 'Eastern Crisis' of that year, containing the nub of the matter: 'The only clear advice I have to give is, as I have stated, that the unspeakable Turk should immediately be struck out of the question, and the country left to honest European guidance.'[19]

The phrase 'the unspeakable Turk' resonates, for it so perfectly captures the European view of a shambolic Muslim people. And there are many potential occupiers in line. Over the centuries, Russia has been the Ottomans' most belligerent foe, wresting the Crimea, much of the northern coast of the Black Sea and the Northern Caucasus from their control. And now, with their Orthodox Christian brethren in the Balkans, the Russian Empire is well positioned to swoop in there, too. But Germany and Great Britain – the true powerhouses of Europe – are unwilling to see the Balkans brought under the Russian realm and for the moment have backed the Ottomans against Russian designs, awaiting their own time to pounce.

As the first years of the 20th century grind on, the embattled rulers in Constantinople have managed to keep their proud Empire alive. The Sick Man staggers on, though change is not only afoot, it has boots on and is marching hard, straight at the old guard . . .

On 23 July 1908, a mixed bag of dissidents, intelligentsia, liberal thinkers, and modern military and naval officers, roughly united by a common desire for democratic change – a group known as the Young Turks, led by the Committee of Union and Progress (CUP) – succeed in a near bloodless revolution. The supreme leader of both the state and the entire Islamic community, Sultan Abdul Hamid II, agrees to the Young Turks' proposals to work towards modernisation, so long as he can remain in power . . .

This is followed by a counter-revolution, and then a *counter*-counter-revolution in April 1909 – yes, the Ottoman Empire is now that kind of place – led by powerful Young Turks in the army. The Sultan is deposed, and replaced by his younger and more malleable brother, Mehmed V, while a new Grand Vizier – effectively, the Prime Minister – is instated.

A brief period of relative quiet ensues in the capital, though many continue to foment dissent in the Balkans, which grows more fervent with every passing month. And finally, the conflagration comes. The First Balkan War of 1912 sees a coalition of Montenegro, Serbia, Greece and Bulgaria capturing much of the European Christian territory of the Ottomans – a third of the total European territory and a fifth of its population – with the Bulgarians even advancing to within 30 miles of Constantinople, before being pushed back. It is a swift and devastating blow to the Ottomans, as in the space of just two months they must surrender two of their armies and all of the Christian Balkan states. By the end of the year, the Ottoman Government, now headed by Grand Vizier Kâmil, a man nudging 90 years old, urgently seeks the intervention of the Great Powers, Great Britain and Germany, to save them from disintegration.

The Europeans are not long in penning their demands. The Ottomans are to cease all further military activities and hand over even more territory, including the Holy City of Edirne, which is to be given to the Balkan states. Oh, the humiliation. But do they have a choice? Without the support of the Great Powers, Constantinople itself might fall to the Bulgarians and their Balkan allies. And so, on 18 January 1913, at the Sublime Porte – the seat of Ottoman power in Constantinople for the last 400 years – Grand Vizier Kâmil meets with his Grand Council of Ministers to agree to the unthinkable . . .

The scene is set. With a weak government preparing to haul up the white flag, it is time for the Young Turk leadership – mostly proud, nationalistic Turkish military men hailing from the Balkans themselves – to make a move.

By a twist of fate, three particularly ambitious Young Turks are in Constantinople on this very day and agree to take action. They are led by a fearless firebrand like they don't make them anymore, Lieutenant-Colonel Ismail Enver, who has lately come to public notoriety through his military derring-do. The young, energetically impulsive and aggressively nationalistic officer, with the impossibly upturned moustache – waxed to the point that it would do a candle proud – is backed by the well-liked Talaat, now Secretary-General of the CUP, and Staff-Colonel Cemal, a military man of clout.

For these men, the mere thought of Edirne, and any further part of the Ottoman Empire, being ceded to the Europeans is anathema. They are convinced not only of their moral legitimacy in moving against such a craven surrender but also of their support from a significant portion of the armed forces and the public for so doing.

On this afternoon in Constantinople, these three radical rebels, backed by 40 junior officers and soldiers – all of them armed – bring matters to a head.

Ya Namus Ya Ölüm! Honour or death!

And you can see them there now, on this chilly afternoon.

As Colonel Enver, atop his fine steed, leads his tight band of supporters through the streets to the Porte, one of them pauses to stand atop a step and delivers a speech for all to hear: 'Countrymen! The Government is ceding Edirne. At this moment, the notes are being signed in there. The Turkish nation will never accept this . . . Here is the fighter for liberty, [Colonel] Enver, going towards the *Bab-ı âli* . . . join him. End the administration of incompetents.'[20]

A few fearless souls do, bolstering the numbers of the radicals further. So it is that, just as the Council is about to formalise the shameful deal with the Europeans, the plotters storm into the council chambers and seize control. Enver and Talaat take Grand Vizier Kâmil into his adjoining study and make two very telling points with the muzzles of their guns. One way or another, it is clear that, in a minute from now, either the Grand Vizier's signature or his brains will be on a resignation letter.

Kâmil quickly writes his resignation letter to Sultan Mehmed V: 'Please be so kind as to comprehend with your exalted knowledge that I was, in this respect, forced to submit my humble resignation to the Imperial Presence on the proposal made to me by the people and the military authorities . . .'[21]

But the raid is not without bloodshed. For some of the plotters cannot control themselves and gun down War Minister Nazim and his Adjutant-Major.

Enver and Talaat move quickly. They leave the Porte, pausing only for Colonel Enver to address a growing crowd out the front. 'Kâmil has resigned,' he calls, holding the letter of resignation up for all to see. 'I am now on my way to the Palace. I will inform His Excellency the Sultan. A Government able to defend the nation's rights will be formed.'[22]

Within hours, the Sultan indeed confirms, at Enver and Talaat's behest, that a brilliant general by the name of Mahmut Şevket is now both the Grand Vizier and War Minister. Talaat is provisionally confirmed as Minister of the Interior, while the new strongman Enver decides to stay close to the source of his strength, and remain as Chief of the Xth Corps and its 40,000 soldiers.

Despite a victory for the day, months of tumult follow. In March, the Bulgarians capture Edirne, while in July Grand Vizier Mahmut Şevket is assassinated. All in all, things keep going from bad to worse for the Ottoman Empire, as the army lies in ruin, the Officer Corps is in a constant state of turbulence, refugees continue to arrive from the now Christian Balkan states, and the direction of the whole Empire is entirely unclear.

But, out of it all, one bright star continues to rise in the darkness: Colonel Enver, the pride of the Fatherland!

For in July 1913, during the Second Balkan War, Enver successfully commands the mission to recapture Edirne, a feat for which he has the gratitude of the people. It is also the newly promoted Major-General Enver who decides that to properly modernise the Ottoman armed forces, they need European help. And so, while a British Naval Mission is already helping with the battered navy, he arranges for a German Military Mission to help reform the tattered army. (A German speaker himself, and former attaché to Berlin, this suits Enver's purpose well.) Under the command of the fastidious General Otto Liman von Sanders, the German Military Mission begins to arrive in December 1913.

From their fickle alliances in Europe, the Germans and British tread warily around each other in Constantinople, each eager to gain the allegiance of the suddenly resurgent Ottomans.

Enver's star continues to rise, to the point that, in January of 1914, he is promoted to the rank of General, becomes Minister for War and Chief of the General Staff – making him the political *and* military leader of the armed forces – while his key ally, Cemal, is appointed Navy Minister and given the rank of General. Talaat remains as Interior Minister.

But General Enver's tightening grip on power is not universally celebrated, and many of his detractors, however minor their complaint, are quickly relegated to out of the way places. Even some of his fellow Unionists are sent where their voices are less likely to be heard. One such man, whom Enver recognises as a possible nuisance, is CUP member and Young Turk Lieutenant-Colonel Mustafa Kemal, who has summarily been sent to the Bulgarian capital of Sofia as Military Attaché. Feeling almost banished, removed as he is from the corridors of power, Mustafa Kemal – an independent and nationalistic man of grand ambition, deep reflection and rather regal bearing – becomes ever more frustrated, but for the moment there is nothing he can do.

By mid-1914, Enver's control over what is left of the Ottoman Empire is complete, as he is the most powerful man in the Ottoman Government and armed forces.

And yet, even now, in Australia, there is not the slightest apprehension that the Dardanelles and the Ottoman Empire will become the focus of the entire nation's attention, before 12 months have passed.

How did it all change so quickly?

I told you. Therein lies a tale . . .

Chapter One
A REAL WAR

The Balkans generates more history than it can
locally consume.[1]
A remark attributed to Winston Churchill

And Australia will do her part. Britain is proud of her
colonies, and the colonies are justly proud of Britain. Let
outsiders touch the motherland and they will find her
cubs from all parts of the world will come to the rescue.[2]
Victorian Premier Sir Alexander Peacock

Europe today is a powder keg and the leaders are like men
smoking in an arsenal . . . A single spark will set off an
explosion that will consume us all . . . I cannot tell you
when that explosion will occur, but I can tell you where . . .
Some damned foolish thing in the Balkans will set it off.
German Chancellor Otto von Bismarck at the Congress of Berlin, 1878

10.15 AM, 28 JUNE 1914, SARAJEVO, BOSNIA, A SHOT IS HEARD AROUND THE WORLD

On this bright, shining morning, the heir to the Emperor of Austria,
Archduke Franz Ferdinand, and his wife, Sophie, are in an open-topped
limousine, magisterially gliding down a street in Sarajevo. They are here
on an official visit to this far-flung outpost of the Austro-Hungarian
Empire, all too aware that there is tension in the air, that many Bosnian

Serbs wish the Serbian regions of Bosnia to follow the Kingdom of Serbia and break away from the Empire.

It is the 14th wedding anniversary of their wonderfully happy marriage and both are thrilled to be able to simply sit beside each other, for once, in public. As Sophie was not born a royal, this is not allowed back in Vienna, but here the two can hold hands and there is no one to complain. Their motorcade glides on; the crowds press forward and cheer.

And then it happens . . .

Seemingly from out of nowhere, a young Serb, Gavrilo Princip, trained in assassination by members of the Black Hand movement, charges towards them with a pistol in his hand. Though dying of tuberculosis, Princip is intent on doing his bit for Bosnia before he bows out and . . . he fires two shots.

On the vehicle's running board, bodyguard Franz von Harrach hears the shots and, the next thing he knows, a thin stream of blood has spurted from the Archduke's mouth and splattered his own right cheek. The Duchess rises and cries out to her beloved husband, '*Was ist mit dir passiert?* – What has happened to you?'[3]

And yet, no sooner has she said that than she too reels, bleeding from a terrible wound in her abdomen. Now she collapses onto the floor of the car, with her face between the Archduke's knees.

The Archduke gurgles to his beloved, stricken wife, '*Sopherl, Sopherl! Sterbe nicht! Bleibe am Leben für unsere Kinder!* – Sophie dear! Don't die! Stay alive for our children!'[4]

The bodyguard gathers himself, seizes the Archduke by the collar of his uniform to stop his head dropping forward and asks him whether he is in great pain. Franz Ferdinand answers quietly but quite distinctly, '*Es ist nichts.* – It's nothing.' A pause, and then he repeats the phrase six more times – '*Es ist nichts . . . It's nothing . . . It's nothing . . . It's nothing . . . It's . . . nothing . . . It's . . . . . . nothing . . .*' – ever more weakly, as his face begins to contort. It is almost as if he is really trying to convince himself that repeating it would make it so, but it is not to be . . .

Because only a few moments after he stops saying it, there is a violent choking sound caused by the bleeding. Both he and his wife die shortly afterwards.

Things soon take on a momentum all their own. For it is the strong view of the Austro-Hungarian Empire that the assassination of Franz Ferdinand cannot go unavenged, and at 6 pm on 23 July it gives Serbia a list of ten severe demands that must be agreed to within 48 hours, or else war. The Austro-Hungarian Empire is well aware that Serbian Army officers formed the Black Hand. Together with the National Defence Society, formed by Serbian Government members, it aims to bite off the Serbian pieces of the Austro-Hungarian Empire's Sachertorte. The assassination provides the Empire with the opportunity to stop them once and for all.

Afraid of the consequences of invasion by a much superior force, the Serbian Government agrees to almost all of the Empire's ultimatums. However, Serbia insists that it cannot agree to the demands regarding the limitation of freedom of speech or freedom of the press, nor can it allow Austro-Hungarian agents to participate in the investigation of the assassination. 'Part of your demands we have accepted,' Serbian Prime Minister Nikola Pašić explains in a note to the Austrian Ambassador Baron Vladimir von Giesl. 'For the rest, we place our hopes on your loyalty and chivalry as an Austrian general.'[5]

Austria's reply is not long in coming.

At 11 am on 28 July 1914, Austria declares war on Serbia. That very evening, three of her warships sail down the Danube and fire salvo after salvo of shells into Serbian fortifications at the Zemun-Belgrade railway bridge, just three miles north of Belgrade. So the Serbs wish to fire bullets at an Austrian Archduke? Then Austria will fire *shells* onto the capital of the Serbs!

It is, of course, a catalyst for cataclysm, the one move that makes Europe's two armed camps of complex alliances take up their arms, put on their marching boots and start to move against each other. For with Austria-Hungary declaring war on Serbia, can Russia stand by and see the Serbs, blood of its Slavic blood – its military and spiritual ally – under such outrageous attack?

It cannot.

On 30 July, Tsar Nicholas II orders mobilisation of troops on the Russo-Austrian front, deploying four armies against the Austro-Hungarian frontier, with a total of 700,000 Russian soldiers now on the move . . .

Can Germany stand by and see Russia march on the flesh of its flesh, its greatest ally to beat them all, Austria-Hungary?

It cannot. And it, too, now mobilises.

Britain, of course, watches such events closely, and none more so than the First Lord of the Admiralty – the politician in charge of the British Navy – Winston Churchill.

Yes, yes, yes, the prospect of war is nominally appalling, and Churchill pays lip service to that notion in a note to his wife, Clementine, but, still, he cannot help himself. 'I am interested, geared up and happy,' he writes to her in a letter from the Admiralty. 'Is it not horrible to be built like that? The preparations have a hideous fascination for me. I pray to God to forgive me for such fearful moods of levity . . .

'Kiss those kittens & be loved for ever only by me

'Your own

'W.'[6]

A war! A real *war*! And he, as First Lord of the Admiralty, able to move the fleet around nearly at will!

The next day, the Kaiser of Germany, Wilhelm II, appears on the balcony of his Berlin palace. 'A momentous hour has struck for Germany,' he tells the great crowd. 'Envious rivals everywhere force us to legitimate defence . . . Go to church. Kneel down before God, and ask him for help for our brave army!'[7]

Der Kaiser! Der Kaiser!

30 JULY 1914, SYDNEY, BLACK CLOUDS ON A SUNNY DAY

On this Thursday morning, a young delivery boy cycles his way up the long carriageway, through minutely manicured gardens, rose arbours and orchards, right to the front door of Yaralla, the stunning Victorian-Italianate mansion that lies on the banks of Sydney's Parramatta River.

The honour of his task quite takes his breath away.

For it is here that His Majesty's representative in Australia, His Excellency Sir Ronald Craufurd Munro Ferguson, 1st Viscount Novar, the Scottish laird who is now Governor-General of Australia, has been staying with his wife, Lady Helen, since earlier in the month. The cable the delivery boy is carefully carrying is addressed to him.

The lad's tentative, respectful knock – for it does not demand an answer so much as ever so gently signalling that he is at the door if someone would be so kind as to answer it – is all but instantly answered, and he hands his coded cable-gram over.

The preliminary steps laid down in 1907 by the Committee of Imperial Defence are to be effected immediately . . .[8]

It is the first of three such cables that the Governor-General receives over the next two days. The tall, grey-haired and distinguished representative of the King, later described by his private secretary Bede Clifford as 'essentially kind' but 'choleric',[9] finds that the cables are all from the same source and bear the same theme, once decoded from diplomatic niceties. In London, His Majesty's Government is concerned that it appears as if Europe is sliding towards war, and it is viewed as wise if Australia could begin to mobilise its armed forces, prepare to close its ports to all but authorised shipping and make ready for war. It is the Governor-General's task to communicate this to the Australian Government and gauge just what level of support it might be able to give to the Mother Country.

But therein lies another problem. For the matter is slightly complicated by the fact that, this very day, there has been a double dissolution of Federal Parliament, and Prime Minister Cook has just begun a bitterly fought election campaign, where the wily Labor Opposition Leader Andrew Fisher – twice a former Prime Minister himself – is making more than a little headway against him. This means Cabinet ministers are scattered to their own electorates and so cannot quickly gather. And yet neither the Prime Minister nor the Opposition

Leader leave any doubt as to whom their loyalties are owed.

In Adelaide, Andrew Fisher stands before a large and outspoken delegation organised by the Freedom League, who are opposed to the compulsory sections in the *Defence Act 1909* that include the training of young boys and fining those, such as Quakers, who do not participate in the scheme on religious grounds. In what is to be the first cast of his history-making statement over the course of the election campaign, Fisher makes his feelings crystal clear: 'I am in favour of defending this country with the last man and the last shilling against anyone who would try and take it.'[10]

'But not with boys and youths!' a lady calls out.

'I agree,' Mr Fisher replies tightly in his thick Scottish brogue. His great moustache bristles, perhaps in the manner of a man stopping himself from saying that *he* had worked in the coal pits from the age of ten, and doing a man's work had never hurt *him*. 'I am with you,' the master politician continues. 'I want to train the boys at the best time so that they will be *ready* to fight.'

A shudder moves through the room, together with many, mostly feminine, cries of protest. The horror. The *horror* of preparing young Australian boys to take lives and risk their own in the process. And these women will not be quietened by their menfolk.

Rising to the occasion, Mr Fisher assures the men that it is all right, that he understands. 'We must hear the ladies,' he says graciously.

'Do you see straight-up boys returning from drill?' an elderly lady cries excitedly, as she stands up. Before the Opposition Leader has time to respond, she answers her own question. 'No,' she says, now stooping down, as if under a great weight on her shoulders. 'They are all bundled up like this. Don't take the little boys. Take boys of 21, and I am with you . . .'

Mr Fisher is not fussed. 'I have seen about 15 different military systems,' he replies, 'and taking the soldiers man for man, and boy for boy, I have not seen boys better fitted for military service than the Australians . . . If the burden is too great for the youngsters, it is a matter for the surgeon or the medical man to adjust. Surely they can trust the surgeon!'

'Would *you* trust the surgeon?' a voice cries out, amid much other rumbling and jeering.

Mr Fisher moves to quell the dissent, still trying to be reasonable. 'Then whom would you trust?'

A determined-looking, elderly gentleman rises to his feet, and the meeting falls quiet to hear his words. 'Whom would I trust? Their *mothers!*'

The answer brings great applause and laughter before the meeting descends into accusations against Mr Fisher and recriminations against his party and *all* who would send young men to fight useless wars.

It is so bad that a shaken Mr Fisher tells the reporter of Adelaide's *Daily Herald* after the meeting, 'I have never in my life met a deputation which made such imputations and suggestions of the vilest kind regarding certain men and myself in my life [*sic*].'[11]

The Freedom League is not entirely alone, however, as there is rising disquiet, most particularly among the Irish Catholic working class, with their view put most eloquently by the newspaper of the Political Labor Council of Victoria, *The Labor Call*, which publishes a strong editorial with a pungent point:

It is unthinkable to believe because an archduke and his missus were slain by a fanatic the whole of Europe should become a seething battlefield, and deplorable misery brought upon the people. But there is one thing certain, if such a catastrophe comes to pass that will be the end of war.

It will assuredly end in revolution and the dethronement of monarchs. If the workers of the world federated, like those of this hemisphere, and said we will not fight, then war and swashbuckling is at an end. War is a horror made for the Krupps and Armstrongs of twentieth century civilisation. What glory is there in to-day's warfare? None

whatever; it is only slaughter and carnage . . .
human beings massacred like grasshoppers in a
farmer's wheat field. The days of such antiquated
ideas of killing one another to satisfy a king or a
party are surely numbered. Let those who make
war do the fighting.
Without the soldier, where are the armies?[12]

But these are only the naysayers, while the broad mass of the community remains firmly behind the British Empire, whatever the cost.

And, not to be outdone in what has clearly become a burning election issue (all's fair in love and war), at his own meeting in Horsham the night after Fisher has declared for the Empire, Prime Minister Cook – a former coalminer just like Fisher and every bit as passionate for the Old Country – makes the level of his own loyalty to that Empire clear. 'Remember,' he thunders with outrage on behalf of Britain, 'that when the Empire is at war, so is Australia at war. I want to make it quite clear that all our resources in Australia are in the Empire, and for the Empire, and for the preservation and the security of the Empire.'[13]

Prime Minister Cook repeats that assertion the next day at another meeting, in Colac, and goes a little further: 'There is no use blinking at our responsibilities. If the Old Country is at war so are we. It is not a matter of chance at all . . . All obligations necessary for the defence of the Empire must be placed at the disposal of the responsible authorities whenever they are needed and at whatever time they were called for.'[14]

Hurrah! *Hurrah!* HURRAH!

MORNING, 1 AUGUST 1914, IN LONDON, CHURCHILL CLIPS TURKEY'S WINGS

It is a great day for what is left of the Ottoman Empire. It is the day that Captain Hüseyin Rauf, the Ottoman Empire's greatest naval hero, arrives with his Turkish crew to Armstrong Whitworth's Elswick shipyard at Newcastle-on-Tyne, north-east England, where he is to formally take possession of *Sultan Osman I* – the bigger of the two dreadnoughts that have been built for the Ottoman Navy. The next morning, at 8 am sharp, the crew are to run the Turkish flag up on this powerful nautical beauty and hold a ceremony to mark this highly anticipated occasion.

Turkey has laboured long to raise the 2.3 million lira (some £6 million) to pay for these battleships. Extra taxes have been placed on such staples as tobacco and bread. The previous December, the monthly salaries of all civil servants had been summarily diverted into the ship fund. In every Turkish town and village, women had cut and sold their hair to wigmakers to raise yet more money. Donation boxes had been placed on bridges across the Golden Horn in Constantinople and on the ferryboats traversing the mighty Bosphorus. The purchase of these powerful dreadnoughts from Great Britain has been something that has brought the people of the nation together in difficult times, something that will give them security – allowing them, most importantly, to defend themselves against the Greeks to their west, and to rule the Black Sea and thwart Russian plans to invade their land.

And *what is this?*

For as Captain Rauf is looking out across the dockyard, preparing himself for the pomp and pageantry of the handing-over ceremony, he suddenly notices men in uniform – and not Turkish uniforms – with guns and bayonets drawn, marching towards Turkey's ship. In minutes, these British Army troops of Sherwood Foresters Regiment have made an armed guard around the ship and claimed it for Great Britain.

How is this possible? What has happened? Who has done this?

It is typical Winston Churchill, the First Lord of the Admiralty.

With war ever more imminent, it is ever more obvious that the British Empire will likely be needing every bullet, bomb and battleship it can get its hands on. Churchill had suddenly given the orders for the troops to move in and reclaim the two ships in the name of His Majesty, and now it is done. 'In view of present circumstances,' the First Lord tells the builders of the ships, 'the Government cannot permit the ships to be handed over to a Foreign Power.'[15]

With this requisition of *Sultan Osman* (renamed *Agincourt*), and soon thereafter that of her sister ship *Reshadieh* (renamed *Erin*), Britain can now count on 26 dreadnoughts in the North Sea, against just 17 dreadnoughts for Germany.

And Turkey?

Well, in the final analysis, Churchill doesn't care.

It is not just that Britain is *always* in need of more vessels to rule the waves, as is her God-given right, it is that Turkey is of uncertain alliance in the coming war – for there can be no doubt that war is indeed upon them – and two warships on Turkey's side of the equation could alter the whole balance of power in the Balkans. It is what needs to be done.

While in New York, London and Berlin, the preferred time for serious meetings is in the morning, when all is fresh and clear, in Constantinople the time for meeting is ever nigh at night. Over coffee, whisky and cigarettes, the talk can go into the wee hours as, over the shoulders of those attending, the minarets muse in the moonlight.

Though unaware of the seizure of the Turkish battleships, the Turkish leadership are already engaged in heated debate over whether to join with the Triple Entente – Great Britain, France and Russia – or side with Germany and Austria-Hungary. Should the Triple Entente prevail, would the Dardanelles be given to the Russians? The Ottoman leadership first and foremost want to remain neutral and non-interventionist for as long as possible, not least because their military remains in disarray since the Balkan Wars. But serious negotiations for a *secret* alliance with Germany have been taking place throughout July and are swiftly coming to a head. Yet what might happen to Turkey in the event of Germany losing the war? The deliberations rage, and conditions for an alliance with Germany are fine-tuned.

Still there remains resistance to signing the document . . . until . . . a cable arrives from the Turkish Ambassador in London, informing his masters in Constantinople that the two dreadnoughts that Turkey had paid for have just been requisitioned by the British Government. Embargoed on a whim! Among the weary Ottoman leaders, there is uproar. Disbelief. Confirmation. *Outrage.* Under the circumstances, there is little more discussion.

4 PM, 2 AUGUST 1914, SAID HALIM'S VILLA, HANDS OFF TURKEY

Grand Vizier Said Halim and German Ambassador Baron von Wangenheim meet at the former's waterside residence to write their signatures and their paths to war. Although Turkey has no wish to be *in* the war, the treaty, if signed, will commit the Germans to coming to Turkey's aid if it is attacked. The Ottomans also agree that it will allow the German Military Mission to have 'an effective influence on the general conduct of the army'.[16] Under the circumstances, there is little discussion, and the secret treaty is signed.[17]

Navy Minister Cemal would later explain, 'Germany, whatever else might be said, was the only power which desired to see Turkey strong. Germany's interests could be secured by the strengthening of Turkey, and that alone. Germany could not lay hands on Turkey as if she were a colony, for neither the geographical position nor her resources made that possible. The result was that Germany regarded Turkey as a link in the commercial and trading chain, and thus became her stoutest champion against the Entente Governments, which wanted to dismember her, particularly as the elimination of Turkey would mean the final "encirclement" of Germany. Her south-western front remained open thanks to Turkey alone. The only way in which she could escape the pressure of the iron ring was to prevent the dismemberment of Turkey.'[18]

EVENING, 3 AUGUST 1914, CRY HAVOC AND LET SLIP THE DOGS OF WAR!

Strangely, it is the politeness of the message that is most shocking. For the note presented on this evening by the German Ambassador to France, Baron Wilhelm Eduard Freiherr von Schoen, to Monsieur le President de la Republique de France, Raymond Poincaré, is nothing if not elaborate in its courtesy:

M. le President,
The German administrative and military

authorities have established a certain number
of flagrantly hostile acts committed on
German territory by French military aviators.

Several of these have openly violated the
neutrality of Belgium by flying over the
territory of that country; one has attempted
to destroy buildings near Wesel; others
have been seen in the district of the Eifel;
one has thrown bombs on the railway near
Carlsruhe and Nuremberg.

. . . I am instructed, and I have the
honour to inform your Excellency, that
in the presence of France's acts of
aggression the German Empire considers
itself in a state of war with France in
consequence of the acts of this latter Power
. . .

Be good enough, M. le President, to receive
the assurances of my deepest respect.
(Signed) SCHOEN.[19]

The German Ambassador, according to protocol, also asks for, and receives, his passport and the passports of his senior staff, as they wish to leave Paris immediately, before the actual fighting begins.

France's sole solace, as expressed by the French President soon afterwards to his Chamber of Deputies, is that, 'At the hour when the struggle is beginning . . . [we are] helped by Russia . . . [we are] supported by the loyal friendship of Great Britain.'[20]

At least, he hopes so.

For what will Great Britain do? The newly appointed Secretary for War, Lord Kitchener – backed by Sir Edward Grey – is firm in his insistence that 'if Britain abandons France, it can never again claim the right to be a world power'.[21] The situation is further complicated by the fact that, even before declaring war on France, Germany had delivered an ultimatum to Belgium, demanding free passage for German troops to cross its territory to get to France. King Albert of Belgium had refused outright . . .

AFTERNOON, 3 AUGUST 1914, AUSTRALIA COMES TO THE PARTY

It has taken some time, given the exigencies of the election campaign, but after Governor-General Munro Ferguson's prod of four days earlier to Prime Minister Cook:

Would it not be well, in view of the latest news from Europe, that Ministers should meet in order that Imperial Government may know what support to expect from Australia?[22]

. . . it is organised. Finally, on this chilly afternoon in Melbourne, the caretaker Prime Minister and four members of his ten-man Cabinet are able to convene in Federal Parliament on Melbourne's Spring Street. Their deliberations as to what to do about the request from the British Government do not take long. Shortly after the meeting is over, the Governor-General is quick to send a cable to London, assuring the British Government's Secretary of State for the Colonies of the total fidelity of its most loyal son, and that, in the event of war, Australia is:

PREPARED TO DESPATCH AN EXPEDITIONARY FORCE [OF] 20,000 MEN OF ANY SUGGESTED COMPOSITION TO ANY DESTINATION DESIRED BY THE HOME GOVERNMENT. FORCE TO BE AT COMPLETE DISPOSAL HOME GOVERNMENT. COST OF DESPATCH AND MAINTENANCE WOULD BE BORNE BY THIS GOVERNMENT.[23]

Of course, there has never been any doubt: just as Prime Minister Cook has stated, if Great Britain goes to war, Australia will not only be with her *but also cede control of its forces to Great Britain*. Yet, while loyalty to the British Empire is first and foremost, there are other reasons for Australia to offer to fight. With so many German territories scattered around the Pacific – New Britain, the Caroline Islands, the Marianas, the Marshall Islands, German Samoa and North-East New Guinea, not to mention their major base at Tsingtao in China for the cruisers of the German East Asia Squadron – it is obvious that if Britain goes on to lose the war, Germany will become even more powerful than it already is. And, of course, should Germany *lose* the war, there is every chance that Germany's territories will be ceded to Australia.

For its part, Lord Northcliffe's *Daily Mail* has no doubts as to the rights and wrongs of the affair:

Our duty is to go forward into this valley of the shadow of death with courage and faith – with courage to suffer, and faith in God and our country . . . We must stand together at this hour . . . On us of this generation has come the sharpest trial that has ever befallen our race. We have to uphold the honour of England by demeanour and deed . . . We are standing for justice, for law against arbitrary violence.[24]

2.35 AM, 4 AUGUST 1914, MOVES IN THE MEDITERRANEAN

The matter is more than merely delicate; it is life and death. The previous evening at 1800 hours, Admiral Wilhelm Souchon had been in the western Mediterranean aboard his flagship *Goeben* – a German battlecruiser displacing 22,640 tons, with ten 11-inch guns – in the company of the light cruiser *Breslau*, when he had received a signal bearing stunning news.

Germany is at war with France!

Once he had told his crew, they had started singing and shouting all together, and were so joyous they had even lifted him on their shoulders!

After the declaration of war, he had immediately guided *Goeben* and *Breslau* towards the French North African coast, intent on sinking some French troopships that were taking the Algerian Corps back to defend France. It is at this time that he receives a surprising order from Admiral Alfred von Tirpitz:

ALLIANCE WITH GOVERNMENT OF CUP CONCLUDED AUGUST 3. PROCEED AT ONCE TO CONSTANTINOPLE.[25]

4 AUGUST 1914, HOUSE OF COMMONS, WESTMINSTER, FOR KING, FOR COUNTRY

The atmosphere is electric. Germany had not only declared war on Belgium the day before – for having refused permission for German troops to march across its territory to invade France – but on this afternoon at Visé, Germans are pouring across the Meuse River and into Belgium regardless. 'The Rape of Belgium' has begun.

What now? Will Great Britain honour her own treaties to France and Belgium and join what is certain to be a catastrophic conflagration, or will she remain aloof?

At 3 pm in the House of Commons, His Majesty's Foreign Secretary Sir Edward Grey – a distinguished-looking aristocrat, of rather regal bearing himself – stands to answer that very question. 'It may be said, I suppose, that we might stand aside, husband our strength, and . . . at the end of it intervene with effect to put things right. If, in a crisis like this, we run away from those obligations of honour and interest as regards the Belgian treaty, I doubt whether, whatever material force we might have at the end, it would be of very much value in face of the respect that we should have lost.'[26]

He is answered by tumultuous cheering from his fellow parliamentarians on both sides of the chamber. Britain will honour its obligations.

In a Europe now choked by ultimatums and refusals, overwhelmed by the sound of marching feet, of clanking artillery moving into position, of weeping women and children farewelling their soldiers as they leave, Grey adds his own ultimatum, one he knows to be entirely useless. Germany must respect Belgian neutrality and stand down from its mobilisation or Great Britain will declare war.

German Chancellor Theobald von Bethmann-Hollweg's response is effectively delivered that same afternoon, when he tells the Reichstag that while the German invasions of Belgium are *technically* in violation of international law, the fact is that, '*Meine Herren . . . wir sind jetzt in der Notwehr, und Not kennt kein Gebot!* – Gentlemen, now we are in a state of self-defence, such distress does not know any rules.'[27]

He is met with cheering and applause so powerful that, as the newspaper *Berliner Tageblatt* notes, 'hardly anyone of Bismarck's successors had received the like before'.[28]

Germany is not the only country that can hand over polite notes. For that evening at 7 pm, the British Ambassador to Germany, Sir Edward Goschen, passes the same to the German Secretary of State, Gottlieb von Jagow, informing him of His Majesty's Government's demands that Germany make a commitment by midnight German time to go no further with violating Belgian neutrality. The Ambassador does so even though he knows that, by now, over one and a half million German soldiers massed along that country's western frontier have begun to pour across the Belgian border and, despite fierce resistance, are heading towards northern France, on their way to Paris – they think.

At the same time, Russian soldiers are now flooding west towards Germany, even as the Austrian Army is moving on Serbia.

Whatever final hope Sir Edward has is extinguished an hour later, when, in a private dinner with Chancellor Theobald von Bethmann-Hollweg, the German leader confesses to the British Ambassador, in tears, his astonishment that Britain would indeed go to war with Germany over '*einen Fetzen Papier* – a scrap of paper', represented by the 1839 treaty guaranteeing Belgian neutrality. Sir Edward Goschen carefully explains that because that scrap of paper bears England's signature, her honour is at stake. The two take their leave of each other, most unhappily.

In London, the crowds begin to gather outside Whitehall and Buckingham Palace, in Trafalgar Square and in the Mall. By the evening, with still no word that Germany has backed down, those crowds have turned into cheering masses. They are mostly the common people, but wending their way among them are many men and women in evening dress, wanting to be a part of it, as field guns and ammunition wagons rumble by to great cheering. Men dressed in khaki receive the same acclaim. Our *boys*!

By 6.30 pm, the Victoria Memorial before Buckingham Palace at the centre of Queen's Gardens is simply *black* with people, singing and cheering and hoping for an appearance by the King.

And there he is!

A massive cheer goes up from the crowd as, at 7 pm, King George V and Queen Mary appear on the balcony of Buckingham Palace, accompanied by the Prince of Wales and Princess Mary. They are regaled with a mass throaty rendition of 'God Save the King' and 'For He's a Jolly Good Fellow'. The same scene is repeated at 9.30 pm, as the crowd gets still bigger, and *again* at 11 pm, though by now Princess Mary has gone to bed.

So it is that, after Big Ben has tolled 11 times, for thee, and for hundreds of millions of people across Europe now at war with each other, Prime Minister Herbert Asquith, Chancellor of the Exchequer David Lloyd George, Foreign Secretary Sir Edward Grey and Home Secretary Reginald McKenna sit in complete and morose silence for a full ten minutes contemplating the catastrophic consequences of what has occurred. The three brass chandeliers that provide dim illumination to the men add to the sense of gloom.

Suddenly, a flurry of activity outside, as the First Lord of the Admiralty arrives . . .

'Winston dashed into the room radiant,' Lloyd George would recall, 'his face bright, his manner keen and he told us, one word pouring out on the other how he was going to send telegrams to the Mediterranean, the North Sea and God knows where. You could see he was a really happy man. I wondered if this was the state of mind to be in at the opening of such a fearful war as this . . .'[29]

Outside, as midnight approaches (the crowd unaware of the time difference), there is a change in the air. 'A profound silence fell upon the crowd,' *The Times* would report the next day. 'Then as the first strokes rang out from the Clock Tower, a vast cheer burst out and echoed and re-echoed for nearly 20 minutes. The National Anthem was then sung with an emotion and solemnity which manifested the gravity and sense of responsibility with which the people regard the great issues before them.'[30]

7.45 AM, 5 AUGUST 1914, MELBOURNE, THE FIRST SHOT FIRED

Aboard the German cargo ship SS *Pfalz* – a 6557-ton steamer – anchored at Port Melbourne's Victoria Dock, the captain gives the order to the engine room: '*Langsame Fahrt*. – Slow ahead.'

Slowly now, if a little nervously, given the news out of Europe overnight, the ship heads south out of Port Melbourne and down Port Phillip Bay – ostensibly to head to Sydney, but truly to dash to a South American port. The ship is under the temporary direction of Captain Michael Robinson of the Port Phillip Pilot Service, who remains calm in the growing tension.

Just 30 minutes later, *Pfalz* has crossed the bay to Portsea, where the small pilot boat *Alvina* pulls alongside and an officer from the Examination Service climbs aboard to give a final check of the ship's papers and ensure that all is in order for it to depart Australian waters. All seems fine, and with that flourish of the pen that officers of the Examination Service so often reserve for their signatures on unimportant documents, the papers are signed and *Pfalz* is allowed to proceed.

The officer climbs back down into his boat, and Captain Robinson is suddenly aware of odd scenes of jubilation all around, as the young German skipper, Kapitän Kuhiken – who has just taken over his first command – engages in rounds of handshakes and back-slapping with his senior officers and some equally jubilant German consular officials[31] who have mysteriously emerged from below decks. Odd. In any case, his own pilot boat will soon be here to take him off, once he has got *Pfalz* through the heads.

Only minutes later, the commander of the heads forts, Lieutenant-Colonel Augustus Sandford, is at Fort Queenscliff when he receives a phone call from Major Eric Harrison, the Commanding Officer at 3rd District Headquarters, Victoria Barracks, St Kilda Road.[32]

Great Britain is at war with Germany.

Australia is therefore at war with Germany.

The German ship is trying to get away and must be stopped!

Or *sunk*.

Sandford passes on the word to Major Cox-Taylor, in charge of the Battery Observation and Command Post at Eagles Nest. It is an order the Battery has been half-expecting, given the British ultimatum to Germany. But what their precise move is to be, nobody is quite sure. A warning shot? Or a shot at *Pfalz's* bridge?

Immediately, Sandford calls up the ranks, all the way to the Defence Minister in his parliamentary offices. With the minister engaged in a meeting with the Attorney-General, the head of the department is left to look up an old, obscure book on what, precisely, protocol dictates their next move should be. He finally finds it: a 'heave-to' shot.

The order is relayed back to Sandford and on to Cox-Taylor.

Crisply, Cox-Taylor gives his orders to Captain Moreton Williams, who barks his own commands in turn. In an effort to do this peacefully, Sandford hoists the signal 'STOP INSTANTLY' – a yellow and black quartered flag – on the signal staff atop the fort, even while below his feverish gunners are carefully, oh so carefully, loading a 100-pound projectile into the firing chamber of one of their two six-inch Mk VII guns.

Closely now, the course and speed of *Pfalz* is watched. Will she slow? Will she turn?

Neither! She is heading full steam ahead for the open sea!

And then it happens.

The single roar of the big gun rolls like a ball of dirty thunder over *Pfalz*, followed an instant later by the shriek of an – *INCOMMMMING!* – shell, which crosses the bows of the German ship and hits the water just 50 yards off its starboard quarter, landing with a massive, towering spout of water.

First stupefied, then horrified, those on the bridge turn in the direction from which the shot has come and now see, for the first time, the signal atop Fort Nepean. And yet, for two men, that signal means different things.

For the pilot, Captain Robinson, it means the ship must be instantly turned around – and he in fact gives the order on the engine-room telegraph of 'Full speed astern' – while, for Kapitän Kuhiken, it means *Volle Fahrt voraus!* Full speed ahead!

Briefly, the two men struggle for control of the engine-room telegraph, as they shout at each other. Finally, though, it is Robinson – and, more importantly, the thought of what the next shell amidships might do to them – that wins over Kapitän Kuhiken, and he ceases the struggle.

It is with great satisfaction to those in Fort Nepean that *Pfalz* now turns and moves towards Queenscliff before returning to the examination anchorage, where a naval boarding party arrive. The vessel returns to Williamstown under guard and it remains under watch for the night before the ship is officially interned. Meanwhile, its crew are placed under arrest . . . essentially for being German.

Of course, not all foreigners in Melbourne town are treated so grimly on this auspicious day. For, see there! There is that well-known operatic singer M. Eugene Ossipoff. Laughing, joking, two men lift his – *heaaave!* – hefty form onto their shoulders and march down the street with him as a crowd of a thousand swells around. Compliments to *La France*! We're all in this together and must stick together!

There are cheers for the King and for the government, and then everyone sings the national anthem.

When they get to Flinders Street, however, M. Ossipoff begs off, shouting, 'I think you are mistaken. You are calling me a Frenchman; I am a Russian.'[33]

Close enough!

Early in the afternoon of this same day, 5 August 1914, Lieutenant-Commander Dacre Stoker is just settling down to lunch in the Garden Island Officers' Mess when a high-ranking fellow officer walks in and announces, 'Gentlemen, war was declared on Germany at midnight, English time.'[34]

In the stunned silence that follows, the officer rises to the occasion and fills the void with a very suave, 'Waiter, a gin and bitters, please.'[35]

Stoker is gutted, completely gutted. A war. A *war*? Great Britain is at war, and here he is, stuck on the other side of the world, in Australia? Why, oh why, has he, as a polo-playing Irishman, been so bone-headed as to accept a commission in Australia to command one of their two new, state-of-the art submarines manufactured at the Vickers Armstrong works in Lancashire – *AE1* and *AE2* – when something like this could happen? It is so unfair!

When he had arrived here in Sydney ten weeks earlier, there had been no *clue* that a war could break out, and in the company of the Commander of the *AE1*, Lieutenant Thomas Besant – a softly spoken and highly educated man, beloved by his men – he had had fun.

Back in England, there had been a view abroad, at least in certain sections, that submarines are 'underhanded, underwater and damned un-English',[36] but no such view is apparent in Australia, where they and their 35-man crews, about half of whom are Australian, had been loved from the first.

But now, his comeuppance – they are stuck in Australia, while the war has broken out in Europe. 'The prospect of our ever getting a chance at the enemy seemed utterly remote,' Stoker would record, 'whilst our brethren in the North Sea would, in our imagination, be banging their torpedoes into Dreadnoughts and things every odd hour of the day. We cursed the moment in which we had been lent to the Australian navy. Our self-pity was extreme.'[37]

In fact, however, Stoker appears to be one of the few people in

Australia not absolutely delighted with the news. From that very morning, even before war had been declared, so many men had been laying siege to military establishments such as Victoria Barracks in Sydney and Victoria Barracks in Melbourne – seeking to join up, so as not to miss out – that special staff had had to be put on to take down their names.

Many of the volunteers are members of the South African Soldiers' Association – veterans of the Boer War – eager to give it another go and relive the glory days of charging across the veldt. Others are mere striplings, who do not want to miss out on the fun. A few are family men with steady jobs, who nevertheless feel it is their patriotic duty to sign up. Between them all, the river of men flowing to the recruitment depots soon turns into a flood.

It is with a great deal of pride that Governor-General Munro Ferguson cables London:

THERE IS INDESCRIBABLE ENTHUSIASM AND ENTIRE UNANIMITY THROUGHOUT AUSTRALIA IN SUPPORT OF ALL THAT TENDS TO PROVIDE FOR THE SECURITY OF EMPIRE AT WAR.[38]

The streets of Melbourne abound with the sound of many proud voices singing 'Rule, Britannia!':

Rule, Britannia! Britannia, rule the waves!
Britons never, never, never shall be slaves.

And yet, among the cognoscenti, there really is a fear of what might come. One thought is from the well-known journalist for *The Sydney Morning Herald*, the Bathurst-born but Blighty-bred Oxford graduate Charles Bean. In the wee hours of the following morning, walking home down Sydney's Macquarie Street, the tall and finely featured, bespectacled redhead pauses for an instant, his attention suddenly caught by the formation of the clouds in the moonlight: 'Piled high in the four quarters of the dark sky above, [they] seemed to him like the pillared structure of the world's civilisation, of which some shock had broken the keystones. The wide gap overhead seemed to show where one great pillar after another had crashed as the mutual support had failed; and, as the sky peered through, the last masses seemed to sway above the abyss. The stable world of the nineteenth century was coming down in chaos: security was gone.'[39]

Ah, but for the moment such fears really do remain only in the tiny minority, as recruits continue to flood into the enrolment centres and sign up, most particularly when the papers print the happy news:

His Majesty's Government gratefully accepts the offer of your Ministers to send a force of 20,000 men to this country.[40]

Organisation of the troops now proceeds at pace. Beyond the main body of Australian infantry, there will also be at least a 2200-strong brigade of the Light Horse – highly prestigious mounted soldiers just like the ones who had performed so admirably in South Africa during the Boer War – together with Field Artillery, a probable complement of Army Service Corps and Army Medical Corps. The details are still being worked out, most particularly by Major-General William Throsby Bridges, who has been charged with organising and taking the expeditionary force to England.

It is an astute choice. The 53-year-old had been born in Scotland, educated in England and sent to the Royal Military College of Canada before coming to Australia. He had served the British Army with distinction in the Boer War, and in 1909 had become the Australian Army's first Chief of the General Staff. The rigidity in him courses up from his British bootstraps, runs through his ramrod-straight backbone and into his collar before coming to an uneasy halt on an upper lip so stiff that it is the perfect resting spot for his immaculately trimmed moustaches. As the first Commandant of the Royal Military College at Duntroon in June 1911, it is he who has set the tone for the rising officer class of the Australian Army, he who has trained many of them.

From the beginning, Bridges is heavily assisted in the execution of his task by his highly competent Chief of Staff, Lieutenant-Colonel Cyril Brudenell White, a man so intelligent and organised that no sooner had the war burst upon them than he had taken from his desk drawer mobilisation plans for a hypothetical expeditionary force he had previously drawn up.

Together, the vision of Bridges and Brudenell White is that, while the force they create will be at the service of the British Empire, it is not to be mere support troops from different states, to be sent piecemeal into British Army units, as had happened in the Boer War. Rather, the force will be self-sustaining and remain intact as one fighting body – composed of men from all states, *Australians* all – under his own *Australian* command.

What name can best encompass these two central ideas of a fighting force that is *from* Australia but *for* the Empire?

Why not the 'Australian Imperial Expeditionary Force'?

No, too much of a mouthful.

The 'Australian Imperial Force', then?

Done. And the 'AIF' for short.

Oh, and we'll pay them well.

Though in person the 'grim, reserved'[41] Bridges comes across as being as cold and mean as a night without a shirt atop Kosciusko,[42] on this issue he is generous, and he decides to make the salary an exceedingly handsome six bob a day – better than any other soldiers in the war, and *six* times what the British privates are getting.

The 1st Division of the AIF will consist of three brigades,[43] to be led by the three Macs. The 1st Brigade goes to 35-year-old barrister Colonel Henry Norman MacLaurin, son of the University of Sydney Chancellor (after whom he has been named) and brother of pioneering surgeon Charles. The 2nd Brigade is put under the command of a 47-year-old martinet, Colonel James Whiteside McCay. Most significantly, in charge of the 3rd Brigade, Bridges places Colonel Ewen MacLagan, a fellow Scot and career army officer who had married an Australian woman and settled at Duntroon, to be the director of drill and discipline. As

MacLagan has already demonstrated a capacity to take the raw material of a mass of men and turn them into a disciplined fighting force upon which victory lies, he is the first man picked for the role.

And so Colonel MacLagan, too, sets to, from a couple of back rooms at Melbourne's Victoria Barracks, putting his forceful personality and tireless work ethic into the enormous task of creating a brigade from troops drawn from five states.

Further north, *The Sydney Morning Herald* sets the tone. Beneath the banner headline 'WAR DECLARED', the paper's editorial is nothing less than exuberant:

> **For good or ill, we are engaged with the mother country in fighting for liberty and peace. It is no war of aggression upon which Britons have entered, but one in defence of small nations threatened with humiliation and absorption, if not with extinction; and above and beyond everything our armies will fight for British honour . . .**
>
> **What remains for us at this end of the world is to possess our souls in patience, while making the necessary contributions of time, means, and men to carry on the great war upon which so much depends. It is our baptism of fire.**[44]

Similar passion is evinced in New Zealand, where, at 3 pm, the Governor, Sir Arthur William de Brito Savile Foljambe, 2nd Earl of Liverpool, stands on the steps of the old parliament buildings and – flanked by Prime Minister William Massey – clears his throat to address a crowd now 12,000 strong, who have gathered in great anticipation. After reading out an exchange of cables he has had with His Majesty the King, whereby His Gracious Majesty expresses his appreciation for New Zealand's affirmation of loyalty, he gets to the point.

'Fellow subjects: War has broken out with Germany.'

The cheering from the crowd is thunderous, and then even more so when the Prime Minister calls for three cheers for the King, which leads to a spontaneous rendition of 'God Save the King', followed by 'Rule Britannia'.

'We have no time for speeches,' the Governor concludes. 'I will send [to Britain] the following message: "The Empire will stand united, calm, resolute, trusting in God."'[45]

Hurrah! Hurrah! Hurrah!

There are just a few in the crowd, however, who evince a different emotion and, as *The New Zealand Herald* would report, are 'visibly affected by the gravity of the announcement. A few people, some old men, including one seasoned veteran, were seen with tears trickling down their cheeks, whilst several women had handkerchiefs applied to their weeping eyes.'[46]

Down at the Wairoa, as *The Nelson Evening Mail* would report, 'natives assembled at the Land Court called on Judge Jones to explain the European crisis. They thereupon passed a resolution offering their services to the Government for the defence of the Empire.'[47]

And then something more. After hearing the explanation, this fine body of Maori men conducted a *haka*, a war cry from the ages, for the ages.

If there is to be a world battle, then New Zealand will be there with the best of them.

New Zealand's offer is contingent on its soldiers serving in a combined force with the Australians – something that has been under discussion in case of war since 1912 – but that is no problem, as both Australia and Great Britain quickly agree to it.

6 AUGUST 1914, LONDON, FISHER FIZZES

When the news breaks of *Goeben*'s escape from the clutches of Admiral Milne's British Mediterranean Fleet, no one is more outraged than the irascible Sir John Fisher, the First Sea Lord. A curmudgeonly 73-year-old, around so long that the first Royal Navy ship he'd joined had been wooden and powered by sail – now brought back from retirement to help young Winston Churchill with the Admiralty – he floats the idea that Admiral Milne should be shot. (Shades of Voltaire's famous observation of the English: '*Dans ce pays-ci, il est bon de tuer de temps en temps un amiral pour encourager les autres.* – In this country, it is good, from time to time, to kill one admiral in order to encourage the others.')[48]

Milne, and the Commander of the Fleet's Mediterranean Cruiser Squadron, Rear-Admiral Troubridge, have made a right cock up of things. This is the Admiral who had once infamously declared, 'They pay me to be an Admiral; they don't pay me to think,'[49] and he has now proved the point. *Goeben* and its little sister ship *Breslau* had been heading back east, having completed token sorties against the Algerian coastal towns of Philippeville and Bona, when vessels under Troubridge's command encountered them. War having yet to be declared between Britain and Germany, all Milne could do was to order the tracking of these soon-to-be enemy ships, which somehow managed to give their pursuers the slip before re-coaling in the Strait of Messina.

In the interim, now on a war footing, one First Lord of the Admiralty, Winston Churchill, would have thought it a simple matter of tightly patrolling either end of the Strait and trapping *Goeben* and *Breslau* like ships in a bottle. For reasons best left for Troubridge to explain at his court martial, as a result of a series of miscommunications, poor decisions and pea-heartedness, *Goeben* and *Breslau* had made good their escape, last seen heading east . . .

7 AUGUST 1914, THE WAR CLOUDS DARKEN OVER CONSTANTINOPLE

Over the past week, the people of the Ottoman Empire have greeted each new morning with prayers, followed by the latest news of the war from Europe. For readers of the popular *Ikdam* newspaper, their first intimation of war had been on 29 July, with the headline:

Declaration of War
The Austrian Government declares war on Serbia.[50]

On 3 August, even more unsettling news:

Germany declares war on Russia. France declares war on Germany.[51]

And so each day brings more news of escalating conflict. Chatter outside the mosques, in the barber shops, the bookshops and cafes, on fishing boats, rooftops and street corners is dominated by the rising tensions in Europe . . . as they all speculate on the real question: what is to be the Ottoman Empire's place in all of this?

As news of war slowly trickles east, from the Empire's ancient cosmopolitan centres along rickety, rocky roads leading to the villages of Anatolia and beyond, the tales grow twisted and colourful, and a heightened sense of patriotism begins to mount.

But who, exactly, is our enemy in this chaos? Russia, as always. The Greeks, no doubt. Bulgaria, for sure. But England is our friend in the sea, is she not? And Germany our friend on land, helping our army to reorganise. The French have surely been a help to us too. Can we, a Muslim people, trust a Christian state?

Lively and loud debates rage, fuelled by what little information the people have at hand.

On 4 August, the Minister of War, General Enver, had announced, 'All men between twenty and forty years old: To Arms!'[52] And he did mean all men. Conscription is the order of the day. Men born in 1891, 1892 and 1893 are already under arms. To bolster their numbers, all men born in the years 1875 to 1890 are being drafted as the active reserve. And those born from 1868 to 1874 are drafted as the territorial reserve. In order to bring the army to full wartime readiness, the General Staff estimates it needs some 460,000 drafted men and 14,500 officers, as well as a pool of about one million men available for recruitment should the need arise.

The question of adequate supply of *everything* is fraught. And so, the initial mobilisation order requires that 'when departing for his military service, each conscript needed to bring staples such as bread, dried food stuff and sugar, sufficient to feed himself for five days'.[53]

Through all this, though, the Ottoman leadership officially maintains 'neutrality'.

A neutral call to arms?

An 'armed neutrality', yes.

The men joke about it over coffee and backgammon. The women matter-of-factly maintain that the will of Allah will dictate what is best for the fatherland, and what is best for them. They busy themselves with their children, chores and prayers. *'Allah selamet versin.* – May Allah bring Peace,' they mutter to themselves in the morning as they roll up the family mattresses, sweep the floor, soak the beans, tend the garden, leave the dough to prove and think of their young sons going off to do their rightful duty all too soon.

8 AUGUST 1914, KITCHENER'S MOB MASSES

And now the posters begin to appear all over London hoardings, calling for volunteers for the 'New Army'. They are soon to be referred to as 'Kitchener's Mob', for the facts that the face soon appearing on those posters is that of Lord Kitchener and the men enrolled really are seen by the regulars as an inexperienced, unprofessional mob.

As to those regulars, they have already been formed into a British Expeditionary Force, which on this very day gets its mobilisation orders to depart for France on the morrow. In the words of one of the Highlander troops, their job will be to 'gie a wee bit stiffening to the French troops'.[54] Most are desperately hoping to be given a chance to kill Germans.

EARLY EVENING, 10 AUGUST 1914, CONSTANTINOPLE, A SON HAS BEEN BORN TO US

Another night. Another meeting. This is between Colonel Hans Kannengiesser of the German Military Mission and the Ottoman Minister of War, Enver. Suddenly, there is something of a commotion outside. Someone wishes to interrupt their conversation?

'Lord Kitchener Wants You' recruitment poster, 1914 (AWM ARTV0485)

It proves to be the very pushy German nobleman officer Lieutenant-Colonel Friedrich Freiherr Kress von Kressenstein, who has news that cannot wait, and which – he bristles with righteous authority and glares through his rimless glasses – needs an urgent decision. 'Fort Çanakkale,' Kressenstein says, 'states that the German warships *Goeben* and *Breslau* are lying at the entrance to the Dardanelles and request permission to enter. The fortress asks for immediate instructions to be sent as to the procedure for the commanders of the Kum Kale and Sedd-el-Bahr.'[55]

Enver prevaricates, which is unlike him. He knows he requested *Goeben*, but that was days ago now. Indeed, the Ottoman Military Attaché in Berlin had informed him as early as 3 August that he had been told 'very confidentially' that Kaiser Wilhelm II might agree to

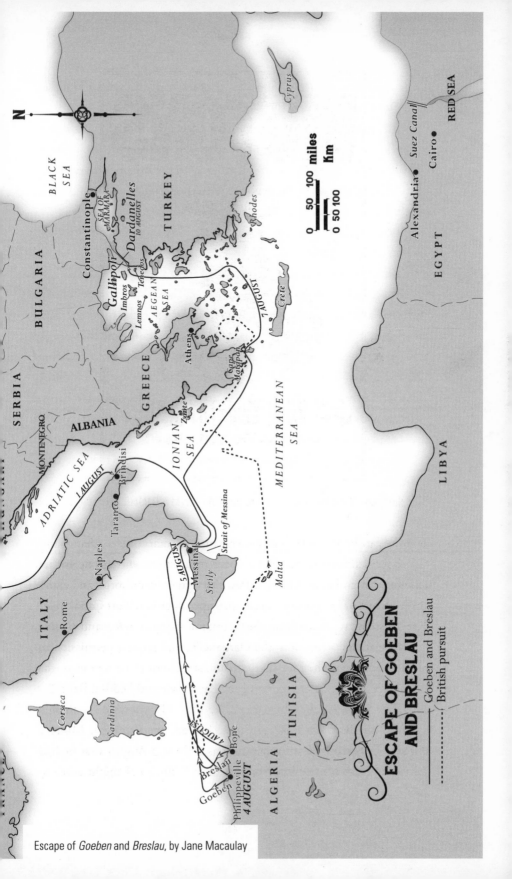

Escape of *Goeben* and *Breslau*, by Jane Macaulay

send *Goeben* to Constantinople and, subsequently, to send it alongside the Ottoman Navy into the Black Sea.[56]

This news had been welcome then, but now that the stakes have risen, with war on the Western Front a reality, his request is problematic. The entry of these ships, in this manner, with the British in pursuit, will surely bring an end to Turkey's purported neutrality and spell war for the Ottomans. And their army is far from prepared.

'I can't decide that now,' he says in rapid staccato. 'I must first consult the Grand Vizier.'

'But,' von Kressenstein insists, 'we need to wire immediately.'[57]

Enver takes a moment to think silently. The British Fleet will not be long in finding the ships where they lie, and if Turkey is to accept them, then it must be done now or never. There is a certain logic to it . . .

(As eyewitness to the moment, German military officer Colonel Hans Kannengiesser would later comment, 'It was a very difficult problem for Enver – usually so quick at arriving at a decision. He battled silently with himself though outwardly showed no signs of a struggle.')[58]

He pauses. He deliberates. Is this the moment?

He draws himself up and says the words, 'They are to allow them to enter.'

Though relieved, the imperious von Kressenstein cannot resist following up. 'If the English warships follow the Germans,' he asks, 'are they to be fired on if they also attempt an entrance?'

A second Rubicon beckons . . . and, again, Enver is reluctant to cross it. 'The matter,' he says gravely, 'must be left to the decision of the Council of Ministers. The question can remain open for the time being.'

'Excellency,' von Kressenstein persists, 'we cannot leave our subordinates in such a position without issuing immediately clearly defined instructions. Are the English to be fired on or not?'[59]

'
. . .

'
. . .

'Yes . . .'[60]

The German cruisers may enter.

The British ship will be stopped.

The Minister for War, General Enver, breaks the news to his Cabinet colleagues of what he has done, referring to *Goeben* with the smiling words, 'A son has been born to us.'[61]

With her forces not yet mobilised, 'neutral' Turkey attempts to disguise this act of war – offering safe harbour for more than 24 hours to a ship of a combatant country – by proposing a sham purchase of the *Goeben* and *Breslau*. Germany agrees, the only condition being that, along with the warships, Admiral Souchon and his crew be drafted into the Ottoman Navy. So both warships will be claimed as Turkish; however, they will still remain firmly under German control. And while the Turks can *announce* their purchase of the ships, no actual sale can be made until the war is over and the Reichstag has approved it.

Genius!

The next morning, the Navy Minister, Cemal, releases an official communiqué, just two sentences long, announcing the news in the newspaper *Ikdam*: '*Osmanlılar!* . . . *Müjde!* – Ottomans! . . . Good news!

'The Ottoman government purchased two German vessels, the *Goeben* and the *Breslau*, for 80 million marks. Our new vessels entered the straits at Chanak last evening. They will be in our port today.'[62]

There is wild acclaim across Constantinople and other big cities. Though they were expecting news of their dreadnoughts from England, the edgy Ottomans are happy to be receiving these two brilliant new ships. And they are due to Constantinople that very day! We must get down to the shoreline to welcome them in.

The Turks have shown the English what they think of their treachery, taught them a lesson and made their navy stronger, all in one!

Ambassador von Wangenheim, meantime, has radioed Admiral Souchon – described by one contemporary as a 'droop-jawed, determined little man in a long-ill-fitting frock coat, looking more like a parson than an admiral'[63] – to tell him the news. Once the German ships get through the heads, they must immediately hoist the *Turkish* flag.

Ach, und noch was . . . And one more thing.

The ships will soon no longer be *Goeben* and *Breslau* but *Yavuz Sultan Selim* and *Midilli*.

Later that morning, the American Ambassador to the Ottoman Empire, Henry Morgenthau – a lawyer from New York turned property speculator – drops in at the German embassy to find his German counterpart, Baron von Wangenheim, beside himself with excitement.

'Something is distracting you,' Morgenthau says. 'I will go and come back again some other time.'

'No, no!' says the Baron. 'I want you to stay right where you are. This will be a great day for Germany!'

A few minutes later, the blessed thing happens. The German Ambassador receives a radio message. 'We've got them!' he shouts to Morgenthau in his thick accent.

'Got what?'

'The *Goeben* and the *Breslau* have passed through the Dardanelles.'[64]

Chapter Two
GETTING STARTED

Otherwise Australians shook their heads when they
saw men of the first contingent about the city streets.
'They'll never make soldiers of that lot,' they would
say. 'The Light Horse may be all right, but they've got
the ragtag and bobtail of Australia in this infantry.'[1]
Charles Bean, Official History of Australia in the War of 1914–1918

13 AUGUST 1914, THINGS CONTINUE TO SHAPE

In Melbourne, in his stone-walled office at Victoria Barracks on St Kilda
Road, General Sir William Bridges is in the eye of the cyclone, personally
calm and considered but making decisions that cause furious activity
around the country as men continue to flood into recruiting depots.

By now, it has been established that existing territorial units will
form the base of the Australian Expeditionary Force, which will
be composed for the most part of volunteers in their 20th year and
upwards. Ideally, while half of the force will have military experience, the other half will be trainees drawn from the universal training
scheme and raring to go. All of them must be at least five foot six
inches tall, with a chest measurement of at least 34 inches around the
nipples to the back.

Initially, the AIF will comprise one large infantry division, the 1st
Australian Division, composed of three brigades, with attendant units,
and one Light Horse Brigade. Where possible, each brigade will be
drawn from a particular state, its battalions from a particular district.

Already, the government has started buying some of the 2300-odd horses thought necessary – most of them 'Walers', a combined breed able to travel long distances in hot weather and go for as long as 60 hours without water, even while carrying a total load of over 20 stone! The government is also calling upon horse owners 'to repeat the generosity shown during the Boer War and donate any horses suitable for military purposes'.[2]

As to the manpower, while recruits are welcome from everywhere, including such institutions as Melbourne's Scottish Union – an umbrella group for Scottish clans and societies located in Victoria – General Bridges is very clear about one thing: 'Kilts could not be allowed. All Australian regiments must wear khaki, the only distinction being the colour of the hat-band . . .'[3]

Oh. And one more thing . . . Upon enlistment, some of the older recruits have the skin on their left chest examined to see if they bear tattoos of either *BC* or *D*. These are infamous old-time British Army tattoos, marking the bearer as either having *B*ad *C*haracter or being a *D*eserter.

In Constantinople, meanwhile, and indeed across the Ottoman Empire, there is all but equal activity as – led by Minister for War Enver and aided by the German Military Mission – there is an enormous effort to get the Turkish Armed Forces battle-ready against the growing likelihood that they, too, will soon be at war. Ammunition is produced and stockpiled, weaponry ordered and training of new recruits commenced with urgency.

This is no easy thing when, as an Empire of 23 million subjects, of whom just over half are Turks, they are 'resource poor, industrially underdeveloped, and financially bankrupt',[4] but at least the Turks themselves don't lack fervour. Despite the fact that the Ottoman Army is still not remotely recovered from the devastation of the Balkan Wars, despite the fact that the country's roads and railways, the telegraph network and the whole national infrastructure are antiquated, especially when compared with their European counterparts, still the army is capable of moving reasonably quickly via the key waterways – the Bosphorus, the Sea of Marmara and the Dardanelles – and it is the first and last that receive the first and last of its men and munitions.

The Black Sea, the Bosphorus, the Sea of Marmara and the Dardanelles, by Jane Macaulay

With Russia, as ever, the most likely threat to Turkey, detachments from the 1st Army Corps are ordered to the shores that lie at the northern end of the Bosphorus, as are torpedo boats. Down at the Dardanelles, the Bulair Battalion stationed near the town of Gallipoli had received mobilisation orders as early as the last day of July, and they are busily engaged in gathering troops and planning 'tough and realistic battle training'.[5]

Just the day before, the 9th Infantry Division's 26th Regiment at Gallipoli had reported its 2nd and 3rd Battalions at war strength. The Division's 27th Regiment have also reported for duty at war strength. Things are moving fast on the Gallipoli Peninsula.

19 AUGUST 1914, THE STREETS OF MELBOURNE THUNDER TO THEIR TREAD

Far and near and low and louder
On the roads of earth go by,
Dear to friends and food for powder,
Soldiers marching, all to die.[6]
A. E. Housman, A Shropshire Lad

Here they come!

Ever and always, there is something magnificent about a large body of young men moving to the same rhythm, and this is a case in point. They are new recruits to the Australian Imperial Force, who have formed up at 9.30 this morning at Victoria Barracks, and are now 'marching' – at least the best they can – to the newly established camp at Broadmeadows, some ten miles away, to the north of the city. For the most part, the 2500 men – the nucleus of four battalions! – are still in the civilian clothes they were wearing when they signed up, but, gee, don't they look magnificent all the same! As they pass by Melbourne Town Hall, heading up Swanston Street, the only thing louder than the volunteer band – who, if you can believe it, are playing bugles and bagpipes at the same time – is the raucous cheering of the people.

And see how the pretty girls glow at them as they stride abreast, their chests puffed out as they gaily wave their hats to all their mates now gazing enviously upon them from office windows and roofs. They are now soldiers of the *King*, don't you know, heading away to *war*, to fight for the *Empire*! And the new recruits are so thrilled about it they all even wave happily at the men already becoming known as the 'Would-to-God-ders' – those many men so often heard to say, 'Would to God I could join myself, but . . .'

But there is no ill feeling at all now.

'It was,' notes the *Age*'s special war correspondent, Phillip F. E. Schuler, 'the first sight of the reality of war that had come to really grip the hearts of the people, and they cheered these pioneers and the recklessness of their spirits. There were men in good boots and bad boots, in brown and tan boots, in hardly any boots at all; in sack suits and old clothes, and smart-cut suits just from the well-lined drawers of a fashionable home; there were workers and loafers, students and idlers, men of professions and men just workers, who formed that force. But – they were all fighters, stickers, men with some grit (they got more as they went on), and men with a love of adventure.'[7]

Finally, at 5 pm, they arrive at their 'camp', if that is what you can call row after row of tents hastily thrown up in dusty paddocks that stretch two miles wide by a mile and a half deep. 'Bedding,' one trooper records, 'was 2 blankets and a waterproof sheet – later came palliasses [mattresses] and straw.'[8]

Their first port of call, even before heading to the 'Mess', is the quarter-master's store, where they are issued with khakis, webbing belts, packs, heavy brown boots and their first slouch hats – which they try on, oh so self-consciously. And then straight to the barbers to have their locks shorn.

Though you're not yet soldiers, not by a long shot, at least you bastards can start to *look* like soldiers.

From as soon as reveille the following morning, the grass in those paddocks starts to grow greener for the blood, sweat and tears those men expend in training . . . before inevitably being killed off altogether and being ground into either dust or mud by the ceaseless tramp of feet. For now the men, in their newly issued kit, begin with – '*by the right, quiiiick march . . . left, left, left, right, left*' – marching practice in their individual companies, and they soon progress to lessons in firing rifles for those few who don't already know how to do it. And then there are endless bayonet drills: how to sharpen it, attach it to your rifle and, most importantly, kill your enemy with it. The tummy is your best go, men – it's a big target, unshielded by any bones that will prevent you driving the blade right through your enemy, and a good strike will almost always prove fatal.

While that is the general thrust, the specifics are a lot more complex, and the man who is the Chief Bayonet Instructor at Broadmeadows,

Captain Leopold McLaglen, is so expert on it he would later write a book so his expertise could be preserved. 'When at close quarters with opponent, his equilibrium may be readily upset, thus placing you in position to deliver "Point". From the cross rifle position force opponent's rifle to his left, dropping your bayonet on side of opponent's neck, your opponent naturally flinches to the right, his rifle being locked by your movement and your own body being guarded. At this moment place left foot at the side of the opponent's left foot, trip his left foot smartly to the left, at the same time forcing your bayonet downwards on opponent's neck . . .'[9]

One of McLaglen's best students would prove to be a young fellow from down Geelong way by the name of Albert Jacka. Young and tough, he has been born and raised chopping wood, and though not a huge man, there is nothing of him that is not muscle, gristle and bone. While others soon tire at bayonet practice – all that shouting and stabbing at bags of straw – Jacka never does. He is 'greased lightning'![10] Light and lithe, Jacka can put four holes in the bag in the time it takes other men to put in one, and already be onto the next bag and the one after that. As a little boy, he had been, his brother would later say, 'very, very bashful, though always ready to fight if anyone picked a quarrel'.[11] Though quite reserved, he intends to be ready to fight.

All of the new recruits now belong to the body of an entirely new order. You see, men, the base unit is a 'section', made up of a non-commissioned officer, like a Sergeant or a Corporal, a Lance-Corporal and 14 'privates' at full strength. Three sections then make up a platoon, commanded by a Lieutenant; four platoons form a company of up to 227, commanded by a Major; four companies form the backbone of your battalion of 1017, under the command of a Lieutenant-Colonel; four battalions make a brigade of 4080; and three brigades totalling some 12,000 plus approximately 6000 supporting 'divisional troops' – artillery, signals, medical, transport (horses and wagons), engineers, etc. – make up the approximately 18,000 of the 1st Australian Division.

In command of a division is not God Himself, but not far off

– usually a Major-General. When you put *two* divisions together with ancillary support units, you have an Army Corps.

As to those men training specifically with the Australian Light Horse, they learn that – unlike the 'beetle-crushers' (*sniff*) of the infantry – they are organised into brigades of about 1700 men each, composed of 546-strong regiments, consisting of three squadrons divided into troops of 32 Lighthorsemen divided in turn into eight sections of four men.

It could get very complicated, and for many of the new recruits the only safe way forward is to snap off myriad salutes at anyone with insignia indicating they aren't of your own lowly rank, and try to work out just what their military status and significance is later on . . .

Together with such skills training, there are frequent, sometimes daily, battalion parades, where the young soldiers have to turn up exactly on time, positively gleaming in their neatness, and then march and manoeuvre around the parade ground like clockwork. They must do such things as 'Forming Fours', whereby, through intricate manoeuvres of fancy footwork and many shouted orders – 'By Sections – Number!', 'Form – Fours!', 'Two – Deep!'[12] – two long ranks of ten men become five short lines of four and permutations thereof in just a few seconds.

Of course, initially, the men are constantly getting it wrong, and of course the Drill Sergeant is constantly growling at the men – '*As you were! As you WERE!*' – particularly once they graduate to the more complex forms such as Fours Wheeling and Forming Sections, but bit by bit it starts to come together.

But woe betide anyone who, on parade, does not have polished boots, shining brass and proper attire well presented. A mere unfastened button is enough for the Sergeant-Major to growl, 'Fall out, number three, and dress yourself . . .' And yes, number three does do that, usually 'with dragging step and unmistakable signs of disgust on his countenance',[13] but it is done.

It is all about imposing a discipline so that, in a battle, the soldier's instinct to obey a command from a superior officer is instant and automatic. In battle, they are told, there are 'the quick and the dead', and this training is about ensuring that they will be quick in both the response to the order and the execution of it. If an officer tells you to turn left, you turn left, *Suh!*; if he tells you to turn right, you turn right, *Suh!*; and if in battle he tells you to advance 50 yards and attack on the right flank, then that is what you do, *Suh!*

And so the training goes on in Broadmeadows as, day after day, new recruits flood in to fill out the expanding rows of tents. With them come the big guns of the artillery units, and, with the arrival of the 8th Light Horse, many horses.

Mostly, it is staggering how quickly a disparate group of civilians can be turned into a fierce fighting force, but not always . . . At the Blackboy Hill Camp in Western Australia, a 29-year-old English-born artist by the name of Ellis Silas is struggling, really struggling, to fit into the military life, as he would confide to his diary:

> Am in camp for three weeks during which time I often break camp to go to my studio to work on my large canvas which I hope to finish as it may be the last I shall ever paint. After the quiet of my studio I find this terrible, life in camp and the uncongenial society of rough Bushmen. They are [however] good fellows and seem to think a lot of me.[14]

And they really do – at least most of them . . . On one occasion, as the whole company is engaged in drilling on the parade ground, Silas becomes distracted by the spectacularly panoramic sunset and how he would paint it, the colours he would use, exactly how he would frame it and . . .

And suddenly this rather frail-looking fellow with the soft hands is standing all but alone at attention in the middle of the parade ground, as the rest of the squad have marched off. The only man left standing with him is the Drill Sergeant, who, to judge by the torrent of foul abuse he is now shouting into poor Ellis's ear, is not very pleased by it.

Meanwhile, other recruits are equally being whipped into shape all over Australia, including at Sydney's Royal Randwick Racecourse, Kensington – where, in the absence of tents, they rough it by sleeping on and under the grandstand benches – as well as in the suburb of Liverpool. In Queensland, they are at Enoggera, in Tasmania at Pontville, and in South Australia at Morphettville.

Everywhere, there is confusion and chaos as the authorities try to organise regular food and accommodation for a vast body of men – let alone put them through training – and most days everything is catch-as-catch-can and more often than not catch-as-catch-can't. Everyone simply must muddle through for the moment, and so they do. The immediate focal point for all the men is to have some level of readiness before the troop ships – first to be gathered in King George Sound, off Albany in Western Australia – take them across the seas to England.

When will this be, exactly? The plan is for late September, which is now just weeks away.

MID-AUGUST 1914, CONSTANTINOPLE, A RUDE AWAKENING

Kahkovah chyortah? What the hell is that?

For, on this otherwise dull afternoon, the cold quiet of the Russian Embassy, which is situated on the banks of the Bosphorus, is suddenly shattered by what sounds like a cross between a dying cat and the fall of Moscow.

The humiliating answer is not long in coming. Out there on the waterway, as close as they can get to the shore without hitting it, are anchored *Yavuz Sultan Selim* (*Goeben*) and *Midilli* (*Breslau*), and there on the deck is a German band playing every instrument as if they have four hands, all while grinning German sailors wearing fezzes sing up a storm in accompaniment!

Deutschland, Deutschland über alles,
Über alles in der Welt,
Wenn es stets zu Schutz und Trutze

Brüderlich zusammenhält.
(Germany, Germany above everything,
Above everything in the world,
When, for protection and defence, it always
takes a brotherly stand together . . .)

The *indignity* of it.

But enough of this fun. Admiral Souchon gives the order to weigh anchor, and the two ships proceed south to parts unknown, their insolent music still floating back to the outraged Russians.

20 AUGUST 1914, THE FALL OF BRUSSELS

It is simply *staggering.*

As the first few German regiments enter the capital of Belgium, there is mostly horror and outrage from the locals, but also stunned amazement. This is, before their eyes, the most feared army on earth. Marching German soldiers. Column after column of them. Thousands of them. *Tens* of thousands of them. HUNDREDS of thousands of them!

For it is extraordinary how they just keep coming, in 'one unbroken steel-gray column', as American journalist Richard Harding Davis would describe it for the *New-York Tribune*. 'Hour after hour passed and there was no halt, no breathing time, no open spaces in the ranks, the thing became uncanny, inhuman . . . It held the mystery and menace of fog rolling toward you across the sea.'[15] For no fewer than *26 hours*, straight.

In Great Britain, the *Daily Mail* whips up public sentiment, particularly after the Germans crush the Belgian town of Louvain a few days later. The attack, as the paper reports, was 'almost incredible in its wickedness . . . [men were] remorselessly shot down by the guards. They drove the women and children into the fields, perpetrating upon them atrocities which cannot be detailed in cold print. They then bombarded the city and destroyed the best part of it in a few hours . . . Germans have been systematically taught by their military to be ruthless to the weak. The Kaiser, a single word from whom would have stopped this riot of savagery, has, on the contrary, done his best to kindle the lowest passions of his men.'[16]

23 AUGUST 1914, IN TOKYO, JAPAN COMES GOOD

In the complex web of alliances and treaties, at least one thing breaks Australia's way. Under the provisions of the Anglo-Japanese alliance first signed in 1902 – renewed and expanded in 1905 and 1911 – Japan on this day declares war on Germany. (After all, Japan has the same interests as Australia in not seeing Germany as a major power in the Pacific after the war, should they win.) For Australia, an immediate and much valued benefit is that Japan agrees to provide its warship *Ibuki* as an escort for the Australian troopships that will soon be heading across the Indian Ocean on their way to England. With the German East Asia Squadron on the loose, there will be enormous danger attached to the trip, and it comes as a great relief that *Ibuki* will be there.

As to when those troopships will be leaving, that is rather problematic. For, while it is one thing to be training up such a fine body of men, it is quite another to safely get them *en masse* over to England, where they will be needed, most particularly after German cruisers have been spotted in the Pacific. Thus, the first steps for the Royal Australian Navy – in order to make the waters safe for the Australian troops to sail on – are to hunt down and eliminate those German cruisers, and to seize the brutes' territories, claiming them for the British Empire.

LATE AUGUST 1914, CONSTANTINOPLE, 'DEUTSCHLAND ÜBER ALLAH'

It is the way of these things in Constantinople. In the cafes and bars, on the boulevards and back streets, you never know who you are going to run into. A case in point is when Turkey's Minister of Finance, Cavid, happens upon a distinguished lawyer from Belgium he knows quite well.

'I have terrible news for you,' the Turk tells him sympathetically.

'The Germans have captured Brussels.'

Rising to the occasion, the Belgian, an enormous man, gives a consolatory hug in return to the Turk. 'I have even more terrible news for you,' he says, nodding to *Goeben* and *Breslau*, anchored just a short distance away on the Bosphorus. 'The Germans have captured Turkey.'[17]

And they really have. With German flags, German staff cars, German advisers and German military officers everywhere, Admiral Souchon installed as the Commander-in-Chief of the Ottoman Fleet and *Goeben* ~~~~~~ bobbing beautifully off the Golden Horn ~~~~~~ not for nothing would the local joke run among the foreign diplomats that they are witnessing a clear case of '*Deutschland über Allah*'.[18]

And, of course, it is not just in Constantinople that the Germans are starting to dominate. Just after arriving in Turkey, Admiral Souchon had, at the request of Enver, cabled Berlin requesting that they immediately send a troop of *das Deutsche Heer*, the German Army engineers and workers, to begin work on strengthening the fortifications of the Dardanelles Straits against an attack from the sea. Under the command of Admiral Guido von Usedom, that troop of 27 officers and 521 other ranks had been quickly despatched – initially arriving in Turkey disguised as factory workers – and had begun work in the last week of August.[19] A large part of their focus is trying to modernise the defences on either side of the entrance to the Dardanelles and, more particularly, the many forts and batteries further north, which stand like ancient sentinels on either shore of the Narrows.

There are two forts at this entrance to the Straits – Sedd-el-Bahr at Cape Helles, on the European shore, and Kum Kale, on the Asian shore opposite, just three miles from the ancient site of Troy. Kum Kale had been built in 1659 and, for most of that time, had had the same sets of cannon, but the Germans have recently been able to install artillery pieces, including several Krupp L/22 guns. Yes, they're old, dating from the 1870s, but they're also powerful. With an 11-inch calibre, they can hurl a 515-pound shell as far as 8500 yards, which is precisely the kind of thing needed to defend the Dardanelles.

Together, the Germans and Turks set to with a will, and Admiral

Souchon is soon able to report to the Kaiser, 'The Turks and especially the Governor in the Dardanelles, Major-General Cevat, who speaks German, are most willing to be taught by us and to allow themselves to be helped.'[20]

1–3 SEPTEMBER 1914, CHURCHILL CHEWS ON HIS CIGAR

Just what are the Turks going to do? It is something that Winston Churchill has been pondering rather intensely of late, since the German battleships had escaped up the Dardanelles. He strongly suspects they will eventually side fully with Germany, and it is against that possibility that, on this first day of autumn, he writes a memo to General Douglas, the Chief of the Imperial General Staff, to inform him that arrangements have been made with Lord Kitchener, the Secretary for War, for the War Office to 'examine and work out a plan for the seizure, by means of a Greek Army of adequate strength, of the Gallipoli Peninsula, with a view to admitting a British fleet to the Sea of Marmara'.[21]

The memo is not well received. Major-General Charles Callwell, the Director of Military Operations and Intelligence at the War Office, estimates that the Ottoman garrison on the Peninsula is likely 27,000 strong, and clearly expresses his view in a memorandum of 3 September that 'it ought to be clearly understood that an attack upon the Gallipoli Peninsula from the sea (outside the Straits) is likely to prove an extremely difficult operation of war'.[22] Referring to a discussion that had taken place in 1906–07, he argues that a successful operation would require at least 60,000 men, 30,000 of whom should be landed in the first instance.[23]

11–13 SEPTEMBER 1914, AUSTRALIA ON THE MOVE

This, then, is even better than playing polo – just possibly even better than romancing a beautiful woman . . .

This is life! This is death!

This is being in command of a state-of-the-art Royal Australian Navy submarine going after Vice-Admiral Maximilian Reichsgraf von Spee's German East Asia Cruiser Squadron – based at Tsingtao in China – that is said to be now lying in Rabaul's German-occupied Simpsonhafen, Simpson Harbour, the ruling city of German New Guinea.

Lieutenant-Commander Dacre Stoker is, of course, in command of the *AE2*, while his superior officer, Lieutenant-Commander Thomas Besant, is in command of the *AE1*, and they are in turn accompanied by HMAS *Australia, Sydney, Encounter, Warrego, Yarra, Parramatta*, a store ship, three colliers and *Berrima*.

All together, the vessels are part of the first military expedition sent overseas by the newly formed country of Australia, and the 2000 volunteers are proudly titled the Australian Naval and Military Expeditionary Force.

Location of Rabaul in relation to Australia, by Jane Macaulay

Alas, Simpson Harbour proves to be clear of German cruisers, meaning that Stoker and his men cannot go into action as they have long been dreaming of. However, after the German Governor refuses to surrender New Britain, 25 naval troops and a party of *Sydney*'s men under Lieutenant-Commander Finlayson are landed at the German gubernatorial capital of Herbertshöhe, on the shores of Blanche Bay, to occupy the island in the name of Australia and the British Empire. Though the Australian forces suffer their first six fatalities in the process, this is quickly achieved.

Two days later, on the afternoon of 13 September, in the main square of Rabaul, the denouement . . .

And oh, the *glory* of it.

For, with all German resistance now ceased, the men of the Australian Naval and Military Expeditionary Force line up in the tropical splendour of Rabaul's main square, a spot superbly positioned to be at the centre of Rabaul's business, administrative and social life – a lush, green space, dotted with palm and mango trees – and command the heights that look down upon the powerful Australian ships gloriously bobbing in Simpson Harbour, a vista of glittering blue surrounded by high mountains.

After the band of the *Australia* has formed up, it is time. While Admiral Sir George Edwin Patey and Colonel William Holmes – resplendent in their naval whites – stand to attention with a rigidity that rivals the central flagpole they are facing, it is Holmes's own son, Lieutenant Basil Holmes, who has the honour of unfurling, then attaching, then hauling up the good ol' Union Jack, while the ships in the harbour unleash a roaring 21-gun salute, 'God Save the King' is sung and three cheers for His Majesty ring out.

Rabaul has now formally been claimed for the British Empire, and it is the Australians what have done it! Let all the villages and villagers throughout New Britain be told the wondrous news and let this document now pasted up all over the newly claimed territory be officially read to them:

All boys belongina one place, you savvy big master
he come now, he new feller master . . . Suppose you
work good with this new feller master, he look out
good alonga you, he look out you get good feller kai-
kai; he no fighting black boy alonga nothing.

You look him new feller flag, you savvy him? He
belongs British, he more better than other feller . . .
British new feller master he like him black feller
man too much. He like him all same you piccanin
alonga him . . . Me been talk with you now, now you give
three good feller cheers belongina new feller master.
NO MORE 'UM KAISER. GOD SAVE 'UM KING.[24]

The joy in Australia at the military victory is unbridled, led by the
Argus, with its huge headlines:

GERMAN NEW GUINEA
NEW BRITAIN CAPTURED
SEAT OF GOVERNMENT TAKEN
AUSTRALIANS IN ACTION
30 GERMANS; 4 AUSTRALIANS KILLED[25]

Though there will continue to be some scattered German resistance, it
does not last long. Australia soon will have control of all German territories in the Pacific below the equator, including Nauru, Bougainville,
New Ireland, the Admiralty Islands and New Guinea, while New
Zealand takes over Samoa.

More problematic than these triumphs, however, is the German
East Asia Squadron that the Australians had been hoping to destroy.
For it will soon emerge that, while Admiral von Spee had taken most of
his cruisers across the Pacific to South America to attack British shipping there, he has left one cruiser, the *Emden*, behind, with an order for
its *Kapitän*, Karl von Müller, to capture and destroy every Allied ship
he can in the Indian Ocean.

14 SEPTEMBER 1914, AT SIMPSON HARBOUR, A SILENT WATCH KEPT

In the meantime, there is nothing for it but for the navy to look elsewhere for the German cruisers and other German ships, starting with the nearby St George's Strait, which separates New Britain from New Ireland.

No matter that the *AE1* has mechanical problems – for one thing, the port-side diesel-engine clutch is broken – today it is her turn to do the patrol, in company with the destroyer *Parramatta*. Stoker, at least amused that the natives have taken to calling the Australian submarines 'Devil Fish',[26] must bide his time with his team in Rabaul Harbour, waiting for their own turn the following day.

At 2.30 that afternoon, the *AE1* and *Parramatta* exchange signals, just as they have been doing all day, when a tropical haze starts to descend. Within an hour, the two lose sight of each other and *Parramatta* returns to base, arriving at Herbertshöhe at 6 pm. The captain of *Parramatta*, Lieutenant 'Cocky' Warren, is surprised that *AE1* is not back yet, and all the more surprised that she does not return that evening. Perhaps she has had engine failure, or has beached herself on one of the many islands that abound all around?

But no. The next day, despite an extensive search by *Encounter*, *Parramatta*, *Warrego*, *Yarra* and the particularly devastated skipper and crew of the *AE2* – knowing there is only 24 hours of oxygen in the submarine if it is still intact – there is no sign of *AE1*. Nor the next day. Nor the day after that.

Lieutenant-Commander Stoker and the crew of the *AE2* are not only worried sick, like everyone else, but also haunted. Wherever their friends on the *AE1* are – and over the months they have all become close to the three officers and 32 sailors, who are, like them, half-British and half-Australian – it could just as easily have been the men of the *AE2*. Are they alive, trapped under the water and slowly, excruciatingly suffocating? Are they all already dead, after some cataclysmic event has sent them to the muddy bottom? Has the submarine exploded after one of the eight torpedoes it carries has detonated? Earnestly, desperately, the men of their sister sub, the *AE2*, scan the waters and the shores for the tiniest sign of debris. They look over the sides, hoping to see a dark shadow that might indicate a blob on the bottom. Something, *anything*. But there is nothing. Stone-cold, motherless *nothing*.

After three days – a good two and a half days after *AE1* would have run out of oxygen anyway – the search is called off.

Lieutenant-Commander Stoker accepts that the men are dead, but he will never stop mourning them. And nor will the rest of the crew members – one of them, Torpedoman John H. Wheat, later dedicating his memoirs to the crew of the *AE1*: 'They lie coffined in the deep, keeping their silent watch at Australia's North Passage, heroes all . . .'[27]

17 SEPTEMBER 1914, OUT OF THE LOOP

Lieutenant-Colonel Mustafa Kemal, now serving as the Military Attaché in Sofia, Bulgaria, is isolated from the major decisions of his government. And he does not agree with many of them.

More than this, he is unsure of the leadership of General Enver, and his move to plunge the Ottomans into war. When he had heard of Enver's appointment as War Minister earlier in the year, he had written in confidence to a member of his party, the CUP, warning of the move: 'Enver is energetic and will want to do something. But he doesn't stop to reflect.'[28]

And now, with the Ottomans plunged into war, this opinion has only strengthened. He writes to his friend, 'This is very dangerous. It is not clear which way we shall head. It is very difficult to keep a large army idle for any length of time. Looking at Germany's position from a Military point of view, I am by no means certain that it will win this war.'[29]

And again, today, he sits to pen a letter to another friend in Constantinople arguing that there is no need for haste, and that they are better off delaying their entry into war. He writes, 'Our comrades will accuse me of pessimism, if the Germans are in Paris by the time you receive this letter. But I don't care.'[30]

Indeed, it is likely for this very reason that General Enver and the Ottoman inner clique would prefer Mustafa to stay where he is for the moment, so that his dissenting voice cannot be heard in the central seat of the government.

But even if Mustafa Kemal doesn't agree with the decisions of the government, he is sure of one thing: he needs to be in the fold, to fight for his country. He cannot be a Military Attaché in Sofia while his country is at war! And he has written to General Enver communicating just that. As he writes to his friend, 'I am yet to receive [Enver's] response. If for any reason they do not want to allow me to return, let them say so clearly and I shall then decide my course of action.'[31]

21 SEPTEMBER 1914, A BLESSING WITH NO DISGUISE . . .

A cry in the night.

And unto them a child is born . . .

In the wee hours of the cool morning, in their home at 11 Cole Street, Elsternwick, a son is born to the newly commissioned Commanding Officer of one of the just formed Light Horse Regiments, Major Alexander Henry White, and his beloved wife, Myrtle.

Like father, like son, the baby is called Alexander White, and he is the joy of their lives from the first, notwithstanding that the 32-year-old Major White transfers from the Victorian Mounted Rifles to the AIF on this day and will soon be busy as never before in training his newly formed 8th Light Horse Regiment at Broadmeadows.[32]

Major White is an officer and a gentleman, kind, resolute, strongly conservative and opposed to all vices, such as drinking, swearing and gambling. He and his senior officers will gather at Broadmeadows and throw themselves into the task of laying the foundation stones for their regiment. Their motto, they decide, will be *'More majorum'* – 'After the manner of our ancestors' – with a badge showing a rearing horse, under the Imperial Crown, flanked by two sprigs of wattle.

Badge of the 8th Light Horse Regiment

For a uniform, of course, they have the usual khaki, but also their many polished leather accoutrements and spurs, together with the famed slouch hat, out of which emerges what will soon become the Light Horse trademark: the emu-feather plume[33] (often claimed by the proud troopers, when asked by curious foreign soldiers, to be 'kangaroo feathers').[34]

There is also something almost undefinable about them, but it is close to an *aura*. As their official historian, H. S. Gullet, would later describe them, they are 'in body and spirit the true product of the Australian countryside . . . the very flower of their race'.[35]

In Sydney on this day, the 6th Light Horse is also coming together. One of their new recruits is 34-year-old *Sydney Morning Herald* journalist Oliver Hogue, who was knocked out in the early rounds of the ballot to become the official war correspondent and so has decided the next best thing is to go to war as an actual soldier, and become an unofficial correspondent, sending back articles and columns to his newspaper under a *nom de plume*: 'Trooper Bluegum'.

Oh, how thrilled he had been, four days earlier, when he was accepted, writing to the love of his life, Bonnie Jean:

September 17, 1914.

My Dearest Jean,

I've got news for you, Honeybunch: startling news potent with grave possibilities for us both . . . Aye, your own heart will have told you I'm a soldier of the King![36]

Indeed! Nothing less than 'Trooper James Bluegum, 333, D Troop, B Squadron, 6th Light Horse Regiment, 2nd Brigade, Australian Imperial Force'.

One last thing, though, before he is truly committed . . . Just as the sun is setting over Sydney Town, and the clouds are all gold and rose and amethyst, he steadies himself. First kissing the Bible, and then putting his hands upon the holy book, he utters the sacred words: 'I, James Bluegum, swear that I will well and truly serve our Sovereign Lord the King in the Australian Imperial Force, until the end of the War, and a further period of four months thereafter unless sooner lawfully discharged, dismissed or removed there from; and that I will resist His Majesty's enemies and cause His Majesty's peace to be kept and maintained; and that I will in all matters appertaining to my service, faithfully discharge my duty according to law. So Help Me God.'[37]

It is done.

'They are a splendid lot of fellows,' he writes to his Jean. 'It's astonishing what a big proportion are moneyed men – sons of wealthy farmers and squatters. The few city men we have are for the most part sons of station folk; and amongst them are bankers, solicitors, journalists, dentists, surveyors, university students and such like. I doubt if anywhere in the Allied armies you could find a regiment in which the rank and file were men of such high average ability and intelligence.

'I know you'll laugh at that, my sweetest. Here I've only belonged to a regiment for a few hours and I'm singing its praises as if we had centuries of glorious traditions behind us. Note the birth of *esprit de corps*.'[38]

This is in spite of, and perhaps in part because of, the hardships they must suffer together: sleeping in stables, doing chores, eating poorly – on a diet that is little more than tough beef, old potatoes and endless bread and jam – being bellowed at, training till they drop. On their third night in the stables, the rain pours on them like an open tap, drenching all their bedding and scratchy army blankets with a flood that is ankle deep.

'Are we downhearted?' comes a jovial cry in the night.

'No!' comes the bantering response from all around.[39]

One bloke tells them that he was not sure whether to enlist or not, and so, on his way to church with his best girl, he'd asked her what her favourite hymn was, knowing it would be one of two. 'If she had said "Abide with Me",' he tells his new mates, 'I would not have volunteered, but she promptly said "Onward, Christian Soldiers".'[40] And so, here he is!

MID–LATE SEPTEMBER 1914, WESTERN FRONT, FRANCE, 'YOU CAN BEND, BUT YOU CANNOT BREAK'

This is warfare as never before seen in history. Yes, there have previously been massive armies, and artillery, and machine-guns, but never on this scale nor with this much *firepower*.

After that first day of crossing into Belgium, *die deutsche Armee*, the Imperial German Army, had barely been stopped, with Brussels falling on 20 August, followed by Luxembourg and the Ardennes.

The Battle of the Marne had begun in early September as five German armies totalling one and a half million men fought all the way to that tributary of the Seine that is the River Marne, threatening to engulf Paris, just 43 miles away. Against them, five French armies and the British Expeditionary Force under Field Marshal Sir John French had fought themselves to a complete standstill, suffering casualties on a horrific scale, with over 80,000 soldiers killed in the first week, making it 155,000 French dead for the first five weeks of the war. The fate of the whole battle had been teetering on the edge, when the cavalry had arrived in unlikely form.

Soldiers of the French reserve, 6000 strong, had turned up at the front in Parisian taxicabs – ever after to be known as *les taxis de la Marne* – helping the Allies to consolidate an unlikely breakthrough that had been made in a gap between Germany's First and Second Armies. For the first time, the Germans had fallen back to consolidate their own position.

Now, with two hugely powerful forces facing each other along a front that is 350 miles wide, and already 150,000 French, British and Germans dead *in just eight days* of the Battle of the Marne, there proves to be only one way to survive. It is John French who is among the first to realise it, during the First Battle of the Aisne, on 14 September, shortly after Germany's new artillery shells – what the men call 'Jack Johnsons'[41] – begin to fall on his soldiers. Fired from six-inch howitzers, the high-explosive black shells are far more devastating than anything the British have seen, and in open country under bombardment, the solution becomes clear.

Dig. Dig. Dig. And then dig some more!

'Throughout the whole course of the battle our troops have suffered very heavily from this fire,' French would report, 'although its effect latterly was largely mitigated by more efficient and thorough entrenching, the necessity for which I impressed strongly upon Army Corps Commanders.'[42]

And, of course, as the British bring their own heavy artillery and machine-guns forward, the Germans do the same – always choosing to build their trenches before open ground, where an advancing force will be most exposed and 'the much greater relative power which modern weapons have given to the defence'[43] can simply cut them to pieces, with machine-guns capable of firing nine bullets *a second*.

With those bullets and shrapnel filling the air like a swarm of angry bees, making both advancing *and* retreating now out of the question, there is only one way to go, and that is down. If you don't get beneath ground level as a live man, you will soon be there as a dead man, and both sides dig demonically. And once you have dug deep, the next thing to do is dig *wide*, to try to dig around the flank of your enemy

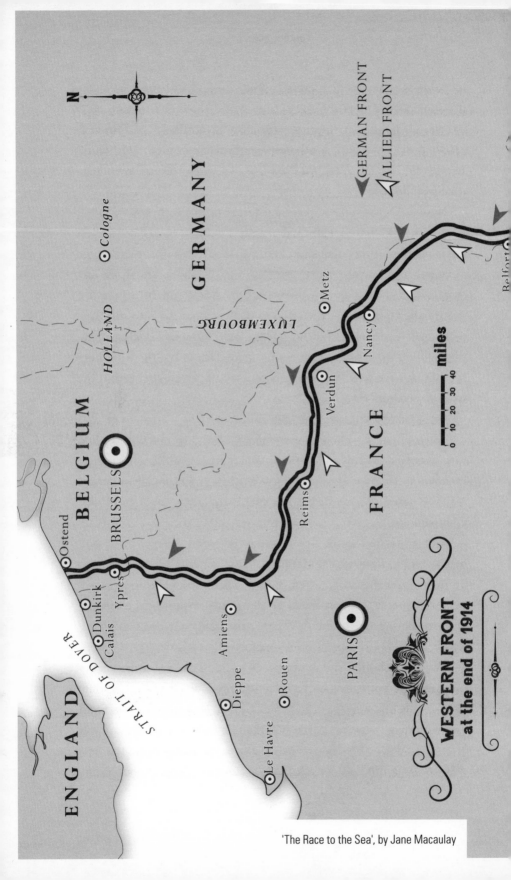

'The Race to the Sea', by Jane Macaulay

and attack from there, 'in order to escape the costly expedient of a frontal attack against heavily fortified positions'.[44] The Allies dig towards the German right flank, while the Germans furiously dig towards the Allied left flank. Of course, all kinds of military manoeuvres are tried to break this nexus but, again, Sir John French notices, 'all ended in the same trench! trench! trench!'.[45]

He establishes a military maxim that will never leave him: 'Given forces fairly equally matched, you can "bend" but you cannot "break" your enemy's trench line.'[46]

And so begins the famed 'Race to the Sea', the parallel lines of trenches anywhere from a mile to 50 yards apart that will eventually extend from Alsace, at the Swiss frontier with France, to the North Sea, separated by a no-man's-land that continues to kill the vast majority of those who venture into it.

In only a matter of weeks, this entirely new kind of battle – 'trench warfare', it is called – takes hold. The old tenets of speed, outflanking and *attack*, of charging cavalry and precisely executed wheeling movements, have been quickly replaced by depth, consolidation and *defence*, interspersed with regular mad charges from both sides, as thousands of men with death-stares as fixed as their bayonets charge to their all but certain deaths, into the teeth of heavily entrenched, chattering enemy machine-guns, backed by heavy artillery, flanked by reams of barbed wire and manned by tens of thousands of soldiers.

Who can possibly win at this type of warfare? No one. But the side that first runs out of soldiers to be killed loses.

21 SEPTEMBER 1914, IN THE EASTERN MEDITERRANEAN, BACK DOWN OFF THE SHELF

For all the downsides of war, the undoubted upside is that promotional opportunities are available for survivors as they never are in peacetime. For, in the furnace of *actual* warfare instead of mere training, there are demonstrations of competence and incompetence, bravery and cowardice – not to mention sheer, brutal attrition – which mean that those on the lower rungs can suddenly rise to dizzying heights that they might never have otherwise dreamed of.

A case in point is Vice-Admiral Sackville Carden, now in charge as the Admiral Superintendent of the Malta docks – 'the final pre-retirement posting of an average undistinguished career',[47] as one writer puts it – when he receives an extraordinary cable, ordering him to take the reins of the British East Mediterranean Squadron, charged among other things with ensuring that the German ships the *Goeben* and *Breslau* don't escape from the Dardanelles.

It is a reluctant appointment of the Admiralty's, with Churchill himself soon to write of Carden to the First Sea Lord Sir John Fisher, the civil head of the Admiralty, 'he has never commanded a cruiser Sqn. & I am not aware of anything that he has ever done which is in any way remarkable'.[48]

The curmudgeonly 73-year-old Fisher, who has just returned to the post of running the Admiralty – a post he had previously held from 1904 to 1910 – finds himself in a moment of rare agreement with the young and flighty Churchill, who tends to drive him mad with his brilliance and his cavalier approach to the fleet. 'Who expected Carden to be in command of a big fleet?' Fisher writes to a colleague. 'He was made Admiral Superintendent at Malta to shelve him.'[49]

But there is no choice, and Carden it is. Never has he had a responsibility like this, but all he can do is answer his country's call and do the best he can.

LATE SEPTEMBER 1914, AUSTRALIA, THE BEAT GOES ON

For all the joy of such actions as the taking of Rabaul and other German possessions in the Pacific, the truth of it is that they are no more than minor skirmishes, whereas what Britain really expects from her loyal sons in Australia is thousands of men, hopefully *tens* of thousands, ready to shoulder arms and come to the Mother Country's aid in the theatres of war in which Great Britain herself is engaged.

And they are not long in coming. From farms, foundries and

factories, from shops and shoemakers, from settlements, towns and villages all over Australia, the young men continue to flood into recruitment depots, and from there to the training camps, where they are poked, prodded, hustled, bustled, shorn, shouted at and ordered about as soldiers have been since time immemorial when the horizon of the near future shows black battle clouds approaching.

There are so many that Lord Kitchener himself has passed on to the High Commissioner in London, Sir George Reid – who has passed it on to the Australian press – his 'special thanks for the splendid help promised by Australia, and hopes and believes that everything will be done promptly and well. He highly appreciates the way in which his scheme has been carried out. He knows the Australian soldier, and knows that he will give a good account of himself. His final words were, "Roll up, roll up."'[50]

At the Rosebery Camp, Trooper Bluegum is in it with the best of them – all of it on foot, despite having joined the mighty Light Horse. As their horses are not yet ready, they drill day after day to master 'the mysteries of sections right, form troop, form squadron, form column', before spending whole days learning how to do rifle drill, to 'stand at ease', 'stand at attention', 'slope arms', 'present arms' and all the rest till their arms ache. And all this before they are even allowed to 'fix bayonets' and practise sticking those bayonets into dozens of 'Germans', who in fact look a lot like suspended bags of straw.[51]

25 SEPTEMBER 1914, DAMN *EMDEN*!

For those contemplating the despatch of 30,000 soldiers across the seas to England, the situation is tense. Two German armoured cruisers, *Gneisenau* and *Scharnhorst*, had been reported in the freshly *former* German colony of Samoa on 14 September, just 1800 miles from Auckland. They are currently 'at large and unlocated'.[52] Meanwhile, in the Indian Ocean, *Emden*, under the command of Kapitän Karl von Müller, has been continuing to send British merchant ships to the bottom at much the same rate of knots as they had previously been happily proceeding along the trade routes. Three days earlier, on the evening of 22 September, *Emden* had made an audacious raid on the harbour of Madras, firing its ten guns on the town and its oil refineries, creating complete havoc and sowing panic before just as quickly making good its escape, with barely a shot fired back at it.

Unleashed in the Bay of Bengal, as reported in the Australian papers, the German cruiser had captured six British ships, 'of which five were sunk, and the sixth sent into Calcutta with the crews'.[53] (Von Müller's treatment of captured crews, it is grudgingly accepted, has been nothing short of gentlemanly – something amazing to find in a modern German man of war, commanding a modern German man-o'-war.) True, *The Sydney Morning Herald* reports to its readers that the headlined **MARAUDING EMDEN**[54] is dangerous and strong, 'but not so strong as the *Sydney* and *Melbourne*',[55] and yet the authorities do not care to take that chance.

If that German cruiser got among insufficiently protected troopships preparing to take the New Zealanders and Australians across the Indian Ocean, the results could be catastrophic.

As a first precaution, on 25 September, *Minotaur* from Britain and *Ibuki* from Japan, which will be escorting the troopships across the Indian Ocean, are directed to continue to travel east across the bottom of Australia after they reach Albany (expected around 1 October) to gather in the New Zealand troopships and take them back to Albany.

Melbourne, meanwhile, is despatched to chaperone the recently departed Queensland troopships into Port Phillip Bay. Here they will harbour until being given the go-ahead to head off west once more, across the Great Australian Bight, to 'the point of concentration' off Albany.[56]

26 SEPTEMBER 1914, THE MOUTH OF THE DARDANELLES BARES ITS TEETH

No, His Majesty's Fleet cannot go up the Dardanelles, but it can hover just off the entrance, and it does so . . . with a vigilance never far from violence. For what is this, now? On this sultry early afternoon, a tiny, one-funnel Turkish torpedo boat has no sooner emerged at the mouth of the Dardanelles, about to enter the Aegean Sea, than it is chased by the British destroyers HMS *Rattlesnake* and HMS *Savage*. Once boarded, it is discovered that it bears German soldiers, at which point the British summarily order the Turkish captain to take them and his vessel back whence they have come.[57]

A Turkish torpedo boat, in its own *Turkish waters*! How can this happen?

It is an informed decision taken by the man who has just been appointed as Commander of British Naval Forces in the Mediterranean, Vice-Admiral Sackville Carden, and it has been approved by Admiralty. For although Great Britain is not at war with Turkey – yet – the Admiralty reasons that, as the Turks have made it clear that Germany has control of their fleet, the consequent risk to the British Fleet is too great . . . and their action is justified.

To Turkish eyes, it is very close to piracy on the high seas. Turkey and Great Britain are not at war, so *by what right* do British captains tell a Turkish captain to do *anything*?

As to the Germans, they, too, take a grim view, and none more so than German Army engineer Oberst Erich Paul Weber – one of the 500-man German contingent that Vice-Admiral von Usedom had rushed to the Dardanelles to shore up the coastal defences – who, as part of the secret treaty signed between Turkey and Germany on 2 August, has military control of the fortifications that defend the Dardanelles. No sooner has he heard of the outrage than he gives the order to close the Dardanelles to all bar Turkish traffic.

Within hours of the Turkish torpedo boat's interception, an additional string of mines closes off the navigation channel, to go with the three lines first laid on 4 August. This fourth string of mines crosses the Dardanelles at its narrowest point, while large signs are put up at the Straits' northern and southern entrances advising what has been done. The lighthouses are switched off. The Dardanelles are closed for business until further notice. Yes, it has been ordered by a German, but in Turkey's name.

As Carden reports to Admiralty on the morning of 27 September:

FRENCH AND ITALIAN STEAMERS NOT PERMITTED TO ENTER STRAITS, THEY REPORT AUTHORITIES HAVE BLOCKED DARDANELLES PERMANENTLY.[58]

Strategically, it has been a brilliant move for Germany, as noted by Ambassador Morgenthau. Driving the crucial wedge between Russia and her western associates has simply required 'ignoring the nominal rulers and closing a little strip of water about twenty miles long and two or three wide! It did not cost a single human life or the firing of a single gun, yet, in a twinkling, Germany accomplished what probably three million men, opposed to a well-equipped Russian force, could not have brought to pass. It was one of the most dramatic military triumphs of the war, and it was all the work of German propaganda, German penetration, and German diplomacy.'[59]

In the days following this bottling up of the Black Sea, the Bosphorus begins to look like a harbour suddenly stricken with the plague. Hundreds of ships arrive from Russia, Rumania and Bulgaria, loaded with grain, lumber and other products, only to discover that they can go no further. There are not docks enough to accommodate them, and they have to swing out into the stream, drop anchor and await developments. The waters quickly become such a cluster of crowded vessels – all with masts and smokestacks – that a motorboat must pick its way through the tangled forest. Initially there is hope that the Turks might reopen the waterway, and for this reason these vessels, constantly increasing in number, wait patiently. Then, one by one, they turn around, point their noses towards the Black Sea and lugubriously start back for their home ports. The Bosphorus and adjoining waters become a desolate waste. What for years had been one of the most animated shipping ports in the world is ruffled only by an occasional launch, or a tiny Turkish caique, or now and then a little sailing vessel.

Most outraged of all is Russia – its major export–import route between the Black Sea and the Mediterranean has been destroyed in one fell swoop. As Russia's north-western ports are frozen over in winter and the Kaiser's fleet is blockading the Baltic, Russia is effectively isolated from major trade. Not surprisingly, that nation's long-held desire to own Constantinople and control the Dardanelles strengthens.

A short time later, in Constantinople, the American Ambassador, Henry Morgenthau, requests and is granted an audience with the Grand Vizier – who leaves a Turkish Cabinet meeting at his call – only to find him a shaking wreck, barely able to get a sentence out, so terrified is he of the whole situation and what is now likely to occur.

Morgenthau's words do not soothe him. 'You know this means war,' says the Ambassador.[60]

The Grand Vizier does not faint outright, but it is likely a close-run thing.

Shortly afterwards, Cavid, the one-time financier from Salonica and now the Minister for Finance, emerges, and his first words to the American Ambassador would stay with the New York man ever after: 'It's all a surprise to us . . .'[61]

It is extraordinary! This most important strip of water in all of Turkey, the key to the defence of the nation, the thing most likely to bring them into the war, and the Cabinet hasn't made the decision to close it!

'I certainly had a graphic picture,' Morgenthau would record, 'of the extremities to which Teutonic bullying had reduced the present rulers of the Turkish Empire. And at the same moment before my mind rose the figure of the Sultan, whose signature was essential to close legally these waters, quietly dozing at his palace, entirely oblivious of the whole transaction.'[62]

27 SEPTEMBER 1914, AND THE WINNER IS . . .

It is one of those things.

While it is the nature of journalism to always try for professional detachment – to coolly observe and not become emotionally involved, even when covering hugely important things such as Federal elections – such detachment proves impossible when an exceedingly smaller election sees the journalists themselves as the key candidates in question.

Such is the case in these last days of September, when the Executive Committee of the Australian Journalists' Association announces who it has elected to become Australia's official war correspondent, to accompany the Australian Imperial Force when it shortly sets sail for Europe. (This is a new concept, born of what has just happened in Belgium, where a single journalist in the thick of the action, Henry Hamilton Fyfe, writing for the *Daily Mail*, has managed to inspire a nation with his tales of British derring-do. Perhaps, instead of chasing journalists away, the answer is to put them cheek by jowl by trowel with the soldiers.)[63]

From a field of 20 applicants, including Oliver Hogue, the final ballot has come down to just two men, both of whom want it very, very badly. One is Melbourne's Keith Murdoch, a highly regarded Federal parliamentary correspondent who had left *The Age* in 1912 to work for the Melbourne *Herald* and Sydney *Sun*, and who is a close friend of the newly installed Prime Minister Andrew Fisher. Yes, the 29-year-old son of a clergyman still has something of a stutter, which he has worked hard to overcome, and truth be told he is not a brilliant writer, but he is accomplished, hard-working and well connected, particularly with the Labor Party, which is where his sympathies lie. And the other candidate is the more bookish-looking fellow, the bespectacled Charles E. W. Bean, the esteemed senior correspondent of *The Sydney Morning Herald*.

Both men realise the obvious: that the war is the story of the day, of the era, the story that most Australians will want to read about, and there is little doubt the position of official war correspondent will be the making of either man.

And the winner is . . . by just a vote or two . . . Charles Bean.

As announced by the Minister for Defence, Senator Sir George Pearce, Bean will be inducted into the Australian Army, given a rank of Captain and paid £560 per annum, together with a corresponding field allowance.[64] The 35-year-old Bean is thrilled; his eyes glisten through his spectacles, belying his otherwise humble demeanour. Murdoch, though, who tends to wear his heart a little more on his sleeve, is devastated, but at least he has the good grace to warmly congratulate Bean.

For all that, official war correspondents such as Bean have a problematic role. They have actually been given a rank in the army, so where do their loyalties lie? To their many readers, who are depending on accurate accounts of what is going on? Or to the armed forces they now veritably belong to? If generals make terrible errors, is it permissible to report that fact? Not according to the army, for it insists that all its official correspondents make a legal commitment to abide by strict censorship rules, which means that not a single word may be published without the army signing it off.

EARLY OCTOBER 1914, BROADMEADOWS, BUT NOT ON A SUNLIT UPLAND

It is a devastating dynamic of human history: while large groups of men without women have an inclination to behave badly, that tendency can be overwhelming when the men are in their early adulthood, when their period of isolation is extended . . . and when they might suddenly come into contact with women once more, after the sun has gone down and they have been drinking. A lot.

By now, as their departure for England seems eternally delayed, the inevitable happens, and more and more reports come in of drunken soldiers on leave of an evening running riot on the streets of Sydney and Melbourne.

As later noted by Charles Bean, 'the delay put a heavy strain upon discipline. Broadmeadows Camp was 10 miles from Melbourne, and officially every soldier was supposed to be in his blankets by 9.30 pm. As a matter of fact, every night both men and officers thronged the streets and cafes in Melbourne until the small hours of the morning. In Sydney, the blueblood Commander of the 1st Infantry Brigade,

Colonel Henry MacLaurin, whose discipline was sterner than that of other brigadiers, arranged a "drive" of some of the streets and secured a large haul of absentees.[65]

The 'six bob a day tourists', as some members of the civilian population derisively refer to them – in reference to their pay, which is higher than the average working man's – are seen to start fights, fall down drunk and worse. And in the Broadmeadows Camp in these dreary days of early October, things start to come to a head . . .

Now, quite what happens to the 'rather good-looking and well-proportioned girl named Hettie Bellingham' inside one of the camp's tents will always be a subject of great contention, but the rumours that swirl initially are devastating enough for what happened 'to be classed as anything from a saturnalia of salacity to an almost inconceivably diabolical outrage'.[66]

All that truly seems to count for many of the soldiers of Broadmeadows is that the BLOODY DISGRACEFUL *Truth* newspaper has gone so big on the whole story, putting it in the public domain for the first time. It also prints 'the super-sensational rumor that A GIRL OF 16 had been plied with liquor and then outraged by about thirty soldiers'[67] and gives the young woman's side of the episode, whereby she asserts that, after going into a tent with a soldier, 'When we had been talking a little while, he went and got me a cup of tea, and after I drank some I DON'T REMEMBER anything more.'[68]

The upshot is that mere 'outrage' does not cover the reaction of the soldiers of the Broadmeadows Camp. There are nigh on 10,000 under canvas here, with precious few officers, and because maybe a few blokes had their way with a willing girl, the whole lot of them have to have their good name slurred? Not without a hard response they won't!

So it is that, on that day, hundreds of them converge on Melbourne proper, whereupon many of them begin to tear down the *Truth* placards promoting the stories. For good measure, they also take the disgraceful rag from the paperboys and start tearing bundles of them to pieces, while the paperboys are threatened not to keep calling out their scurrilous lies about a scandal at Broadmeadow, on pain of a cuff on the ear! Of course, the police are called, and, of course, the soldiers don't back down.

What makes matters worse is that, as crowds form on Swanston and Bourke Streets, which is where most of the action takes place, the broad mass takes the side of the soldiers and urges them to belt the coppers!

Which the soldiers do . . .

Soon enough, a full-blown riot is underway, involving what *The Argus* estimates at 'over 20,000 people'.[69] It is a problem well beyond the capacity of the dozen constables there to do anything about, and reinforcements are urgently called for. In the end, no fewer than 200 police – on foot and mounted – are assembled to confront the crowd, which they do by striking at them 'wildly with their truncheons and handcuffs'.[70]

At the height of the melee, many of the soldiers announce their intent to go to the offices of *The Truth* at La Trobe Street and 'destroy the bloody joint'.[71]

As the crowd surges in that direction, the police on horseback, quickly followed by their colleagues on foot, race to the *Truth* offices and 'form up a cordon in front of the lane leading to the building to defend it, and in this they were assisted by many soldiers who had previously remonstrated with their reckless colleagues'.[72] (But *not* assisted by many of the crowd, who climb up on verandah posts and the like and roar at the soldiers to, 'Give it to the police!')[73]

In the end, the only way to clear the area and re-establish control is for the police on horseback to charge back and forth along the footpath and the roads, bowling the rioters out of their way. By midnight, the crowd has dispersed.

In short, as the weeks pass, the situation for the authorities becomes ever more reminiscent of the apocryphal remark most often attributed to Arthur Wellesley, the 1st Duke of Wellington, after surveying the British troops sent to him in Spain in 1808: 'I don't know what effect these men will have on the enemy, but by God, they terrify me.'[74]

The authorities need to get these men on the ships and get them on their way.

MID-OCTOBER 1914, PERTH, A RIDING REGIMENT RISES

The best thing is that it now looks as if the war is not going to be over by Christmas, as many had feared, and there should still be plenty of fun to go around. Even more men join.

In Western Australia, a squadron of Light Horse had been so quickly filled out with 158 men, it had been decided to raise a whole regiment, composed of 546 officers and men. They begin forming up the 10th Light Horse of the 3rd Brigade at Guildford, a small rural settlement ten miles or so north-east of Perth. Composed of tinkers, tailors, candlestick-makers, not to mention rich men, poor men, beggar men and thieves, together with barristers, auctioneers and graziers . . . they are at least all united by a common ability as horsemen – and in many cases even bring their own horses with them.[75]

Among them are two notable blue-bloods, Ric and Hugo Throssell, scions of a former Premier of Western Australia who, after being educated at Prince Alfred College in Adelaide, have made a big go of it farming the property their father bought for them at Cowcowing in the Western Australian Wheatbelt – even though in the last two years they have faced a severe drought that has somewhat loosened their hold on the land, and the land's hold on them. Selling the horses and stowing the hoes, they had ridden, brothers-in-arms, the 60 miles to Northam to enlist.

Thirty-year-old Hugo – who is in fact the youngest of the 14 Throssell siblings – is the standout member of the new recruits. At school, he had been a brilliant boxer, great runner and captain of the football team, as well as a highly accomplished student. Tall and refined-looking, with the rather ascetic, angular face of a natural aristocrat, albeit with a jaw made of solid granite, he has an easy grace about him and the odd combination of humility and an ability to inspire the men he leads that soon sees him commissioned as a Second-Lieutenant in charge of a troop of 39 men,[76] while Ric has the rank of Corporal. No one is prouder of Hugo than Ric, and indeed the bond between the two is remarkable from the first. As brothers who have been raised together, schooled together, and who then lived together as they worked their farm, the two have decided to head off to war together.

And now they train together, ever and always inseparable, even among the 500 other men, as from sun-up to sundown they gallop, wheel and whirl, under the hot sun on the hard soil that lies by the Helena River at Guildford, before finally retiring to their tents on the nearby grassy slope.

As popular as the friendly Hugo Throssell is, however, the man they all look to, the one in charge of the whole regiment, is 48-year-old Lieutenant-Colonel Noel Murray Brazier, a licensed surveyor and pastoralist from Kirup, as stout a citizen soldier of the Old School as he is in build. (Unlucky the horse that must bear him.) A strict disciplinarian – under his rule, your first offence is your last – the man variously known as 'the Colonel' and 'the Father of the Regiment' has a moustache that bristles rather in tune with his personality, but he is nevertheless loved by the men and loves them in turn.

It is he who is the driving force that has formed them, who believes in them, who had personally recruited many of them by first approaching their fathers, with whom he had worked with distinction in the Boer War,[77] who works them till they drop and then works them some more before, in the evenings, he often holds court in his tent with a pot in one hand and a cigar in the other, among his senior officers.

It is a life he was born to, which he adores. 'Fine looking men,' this son of a Victorian clergyman had recorded in his diary as his first impressions of the first lot of Western Australians on parade, ready to leave the state. 'March discipline only fair. Lump in my throat all the same.'[78]

21 OCTOBER 1914, COMING TO THE POINT OF CONCENTRATION

Another body of fine men is just preparing to leave Victoria on this unseasonably warm day as the first licks of the summer up ahead start to caress the shimmering air at Port Melbourne Pier. There, the Victorian contingent of the Australian Imperial Force start filing up the gangplanks of their many ships and prepare to settle in.

Most importantly, those now boarding include General Bridges and his 1st Australian Division HQ staff, who board the luxury liner *Orvieto*. For the next six weeks, the nerve centre of the whole operation will be in *Orvieto*'s drawing room.

Rather less grandly making his entrance onto the same ship is the gangling figure of Charles Bean – now 'Captain Bean', if you please, of the AIF – Australia's official war correspondent. (And perhaps even writer of the Official History, as Defence Minister Pearce has intimated to him before departure.) It is with quite some emotion that he takes his leave. He gazes through his round spectacles, already coated with a fine salt layer, down upon his father in the madding crowd on the pier – they have broken through the sentries – as the luxurious Orient liner *Orvieto* pulls away, keeping his eyes on him till the last, just as his father is keeping his eyes on him, though the latter also diverts his gaze to the HMAT *Euripides*, on *Orvieto*'s starboard, where Charles's brother, Captain John (Jack) Willoughby Butler Bean – a medical officer with the 3rd Battalion – is also on his way. The whole Bean family are very close, and the Bean boys' mother, Lucy, would also have been there, bar the fact that she did not think she could bear it.

Emerging from Port Phillip Bay, *Orvieto* and its convoy turn west, heading across the Great Australian Bight to gather in King George Sound, Albany, and then start the long haul to conquer the Indian Ocean before heading to England.

25 OCTOBER 1914, OUT OF THE MOUTHS OF . . .

Another Sunday, another bloody compulsory Church Parade at Broadmeadows. It is something so generally dull that, only a few weeks before, four blokes had been lagged for playing two-up in the middle of the sermon! But it does have its moments . . .

On this day, the preacher is just getting to the climax of his sermon when he exclaims loudly, 'You live on bread . . .'

Without missing a beat comes the muffled reply from 2000 throats, 'And jam.'[79]

LATE OCTOBER 1914, 'THE FUTURE OF TURKEY IS AT STAKE'

It has been 11 weeks since the declaration of war. Admiral Souchon, the German officer with the French name and the high Turkish posting, is growing more than merely impatient. He can abide Turkish neutrality no longer and decides to 'cash the blank cheque' sent to him by Berlin on 4 August: 'Concur proposal to undertake operation Black Sea with agreement or against the will of Turkey.' The operational order was, 'Do your utmost: the future of Turkey is at stake.'[80]

General Enver, too, wishes to end the prevarication and pledges support. Turkey's Minister of War issues a secret order:

THE TURKISH FLEET SHOULD GAIN MASTERY OF BLACK SEA BY FORCE. SEEK OUT THE RUSSIAN FLEET AND ATTACK HER WHEREVER YOU FIND HER WITHOUT DECLARATION OF WAR.
WAR MINISTER ENVER[81]

On 27 October, the *Goeben* and *Breslau*, sailing under the crescent moon of the Turkish flag, and accompanied by the Ottoman cruiser *Hamidiye* and other small vessels of the Turkish Navy, sail into the Black Sea for 'manoeuvres'. The Russians are wary of the German–Turkish Fleet and stalk them closely. With the rising of the sun on 29 October, manoeuvres turn hostile.

Over the next two days, the *Goeben* and *Breslau* busy themselves – in the company of a scattering of Turkish warships – firing salvo after salvo of high-explosive shells and sending torpedoes into the Russian ports of Odessa, Sevastopol, Feodosiya and Novorossiysk, in this last sinking 14 ships – including the British-registered steel schooner *Friedericke* – and setting fire to the oil tanks.

All hell breaks loose, with fire, brimstone and explosions aplenty . . . and not simply in the said ports. In response to the stupefied Russians' outrage at this unprovoked attack, Admiral Souchon claims that the Russians had started it.

The Grand Vizier, Said Halim, receives a heavily doctored description of the altercation from the Minister of War, General Enver. Sitting down to read the correspondence, this man who has been so eager to avoid any Ottoman–Russian naval engagement in the Black Sea realises he has been duped. His Empire is set on the path to war thanks to a handful of Cabinet members.

Though war is yet to be declared, thanks to Germany the war has come to Turkey. In a last-ditch diplomatic effort on the afternoon of 30 October, the British, Russian and French Ambassadors to Constantinople give a 12-hour ultimatum to the Turkish Cabinet. The Ottoman Empire is to disarm *Goeben* and *Breslau*, expel its German Admiral and sailors, end secret relations with Germany and become strictly neutral or face the consequences.[82]

Well, then . . .

That evening at the Sublime Porte, an emergency Cabinet meeting is held. It is Talaat Pasha, the Minister for the Interior, who is perhaps the most outspoken. Yes, he is very annoyed at Germany's independent aggression in the Black Sea, but that changes not the position. 'The Entente can give us nothing but the renewal of promises, so often broken,' he insists to his colleagues, 'to preserve to us our present territory. Hence there is nothing to be gained by joining them. And if we refused aid to our German allies now in the time of their need, they will naturally refuse to help us if they are victorious. If we stay neutral, whichever side won will surely punish Turkey for not having joined them . . .'[83]

Therefore, he concludes, Turkey must fight on the side of Germany. Most of the others agree. Turkey will not back down. And there is more to be gained by siding with Germany, against Russia, than with Great Britain.

All of the Entente countries' Ambassadors take the cue, promptly requesting their passports and signalling their intention to leave.

Later that evening, American Ambassador Henry Morgenthau visits his British counterpart, Sir Louis Mallett, who is sitting in his study. Before him is a roaring fire, and in a semicircle around him are large piles of documents, which he is slowly feeding into the flames as secretaries and clerks ferry back and forth replenishing the diminishing piles.

'These papers,' Morgenthau would record, 'contained the embassy records for probably a hundred years. In them were written the great achievements of a long line of distinguished ambassadors . . . [and they] now went, one by one, into Sir Louis Mallet's fire. The long story of British ascendency in Turkey had reached its close. The twenty-years' campaign of the Kaiser to destroy England's influence and to become England's successor had finally triumphed, and the blaze in Sir Louis's chancery was really the funeral pyre of England's vanished power in Turkey.'[84]

The following day, the Ottoman Government declares war on the Entente.[85]

Chapter Three
FAREWELL TO AUSTRALIA

No one will gainsay the intense patriotism of the
Australian soldier. He is perhaps primarily an Australian,
and a lover of all things Australian. This spirit may
be said to dominate his thoughts and actions.[1]
Lieutenant-General Sir William Birdwood,
Commanding Officer of the Anzacs

1 NOVEMBER 1914, FAREWELL TO THE HOMELAND

Every day, for the last five days, it has been the same thing. Rumours
have swirled among the 36 transport ships and their three escorting
warships at anchor just outside the inner harbour of Western Australia's
Albany that, the following day, the first contingent of the Australian
Imperial Force – all 24,000 of them – will be on their way to England,
but the following day has dawned, and nothing has happened.[2] Most
of the movement in and out of the harbour remains just the Norwegian
whalers who have been in operation here for the last two years. At last,
however, the previous evening, solid, confirmed word had been received
of departure on the morrow.

And now, after weeks of delays, dashed hopes and false rumours,
it is actually happening! For with the grey dawn there is a flurry of
activity of tenders and barges among the ships, as all eyes turn to the
flagship of the transports, *Orvieto*, bearing General Bridges and his
staff. Its massive form is illuminated by the red sun rising above a picturesque island out to seaward, bearing a lighthouse sharply silhouetted

against a sky getting a little foggy as the funnels of all the ships pour steam and smoke.[3]

As described by the 'Special Commissioner with the Australian Troops for *The Sydney Morning Herald*', Andrew 'Banjo' Paterson, aboard the troopship *Euripides*, the whole scene is wondrously picturesque: 'The sea is dull, still grey, without a ripple. A vague electric restlessness is in the air. What are those coming out of the inner harbour? Two grim, gliding leviathans, going majestically out to sea to take their places as guardians of the fleet.'

Yes, *Sydney* and *Melbourne* are here and getting into position on the flanks. And the flagship *Minotaur* will shortly lead them out, with *Ibuki* joining them in two days' time.

'There is something uncanny in the absolute silence with which everything is done. They glide past the frowning cliffs, whose feet are awash with the sea, through the long lines of waiting transports, and are soon lost to sight steaming right out into the eye of the sun.'

And now, Banjo, look there!

As the correspondent watches closely, an oily rush of lightly churning water is visible at the stern of *Minotaur*. Her screws are turning.

'At least a thousand pairs of field glasses,' Banjo records, 'are centred on her anchor chain. Link by link it comes in-board, and the leader of the fleet is underway. Noiselessly the great ship gathers speed and moves ahead through the waiting fleet; and, as she goes out, the vessels that are to follow her in line get silently under way and fall in line behind her.'

They are moving.

'As gracefully as a fleet of swans after some great leader, they drop into place and soon are rising to the sea.'

Among all the Australian ships, of course, are the distinctively greyish-black transport ships of the New Zealanders – all of them with all-black funnels – and as the ship of Banjo Paterson streams past, the sailors aboard give their fellows a rousing haka. '*Ake, Ake, Ake, Kia Kaha,*' they cry,[4] all with impressive and synchronised gesticulations, their words translating, Banjo says, to 'we will fight on for ever and ever.'[5]

As opposed to the Australians, a large portion of the New Zealanders are experienced professional soldiers. None more so than Lieutenant-Colonel William Malone, the Commanding Officer of the Wellington Infantry Battalion. A good, God-fearing officer of the Old School, he is a 55-year-old French-speaking farmer turned solicitor turned military officer from Taranaki, who plays the piano like a maestro and yet whose major passion is his wife and three young children from his second marriage back in Stratford, and five older children nearby.

A strong advocate of compulsory training, he had seen this war coming from a long way off and been appointed Commanding Officer of the 11th Regiment Taranaki Rifles in 1911. Despite his age, when war broke out he had immediately volunteered his services for a senior posting and been placed in charge of the Wellingtons, whom he has been training fearfully hard. (The only saving grace for his soldiers is that the 'old man' pushes himself as hard as he does them. And as he is a solid six foot, and hard as nails, no one is much inclined to grumble *too* loudly . . . just to stay on the safe side.) Malone's men are spread among three ships, while the Otago Infantry Battalion, the Canterbury Infantry Battalion and the Auckland Infantry Battalion are spread across another four ships between them.

As Banjo Paterson would note for his readers – published in *The Sydney Morning Herald* some time later, after clearing the censors – 'thirty thousand fighting men, representing Australasia, are under way for the great war'.[6]

In a convoy strung out over nine miles of ocean, they are bound west across the vast Indian Ocean, heading back to the Old Country to be trained on England's Salisbury Plain, to get them in shape to get stuck into the Hun – provided the war is not over before they get there.

Now, while most of the Australians look with lingering gaze to their homeland slowly sinking below the horizon to the east, one man in particular is looking, at least spiritually, to England. Four years earlier at Newcastle, a then 18-year-old John Simpson Kirkpatrick had first arrived on Australian shores. He had liked it so much from the outset that he had jumped ship and spent the intervening years cane cutting and doing station work in Queensland, coalmining in the Illawarra, goldmining in Western Australia, working as a steward, fireman and greaser on vessels around the Australian coast – and even 'waltzing his matilda' from farm to farm in Queensland as a swagman.

Now, with the outbreak of war, the strapping young man has quickly joined up under the name of 'John Simpson' (or 'Jack', as everyone calls him) – to avoid trouble for having previously jumped ship – in the hope, among other things, of getting back to his ageing widow mother, and his sister, at South Shields on Tyne.

Jack's great passion in life, beyond his love for his mother and sister, is animals. No stray dog had ever come into his orbit without getting a pat or a spare bit of sausage if he had one, no cat a caress, no horse a hug. Even now, as he leaves Australia, tucked inside his shirt-front is a baby possum that one of his tent-mates had found in camp and Jack has effectively adopted, feeding and watering it as if it were his own baby. But Simpson's possum is far from the only Australian native fauna now heading west, as many other soldiers have smuggled aboard everything from kangaroos to wallabies to *koalas*, tucked away into great-coats and the like.

As to what part of the army Jack will join, that has been sorted. The muscular 22-year-old with the strong streak of independence is not only physically suited to be a stretcher-bearer but there is something else besides . . . As one of his comrades, Sergeant Oscar Hookway, would later recount, 'He was . . . too human to be a parade ground soldier, and strongly disliked discipline; though not lazy he shirked the drudgery of "forming fours", and other irksome military tasks.'[7] So stretcher-bearer it is, specifically as part of the 3rd Field Ambulance.

3 NOVEMBER 1914, DARDANELLES, CHURCHILL SALLIES FORTH

How to respond to the outrageous German aggression against Russia facilitated by Turkey?

As is his greatest pleasure, First Lord of the Admiralty Winston Churchill orders the British Fleet, which is still lurking with intent off the Dardanelles, to do what British military forces have always done rather well. That is to sally forth to the forts with all guns blazing and give the enemy a 'whiff of the grape', let them know just what they will be up against if they persist with their own infernal bellicosity.

The idea is for Admiral Carden to have two of his battlecruisers, *Indomitable* and *Indefatigable*, together with France's *Suffren* and *Vérité*, sail past the entrance to the Dardanelles at the break of day at just the range where the squadron's guns can reach the forts, fire a few salvos and then retire before the old and ineffective guns of the forts will be capable of making effective reply.

No, war has not yet been officially declared on the Ottoman Empire – at least not by Great Britain and France – but no matter. Winston Churchill simply cannot *wait* to get to grips. Despite the fact that the formal advice of Admiral Sir Edmond John Slade to the First Lord of the Admiralty is directly against such a demonstration – a bombardment of the sea face of the Dardanelles forts offers very little prospect of obtaining any effect commensurate with the risk to the ships[8] – Churchill insists.

And there they are now.

At 4.55 on this sparkling morning, the four battleships move into position, some 13,000 yards from the forts on either side of the entrance to the Straits, and from his command position aboard the bridge of *Indefatigable*, Admiral Carden gives the order. The signal flag to commence operations is unfurled. In an instant, the first gun fires, soon joined by more than 30 others, hurling their heavy 12-inch shells to the forts some seven miles distant.

Yes, four shells are fired back from the forts, but they all fall so short of the British ships that the Turks soon decide not to waste their shells, and stop.

And then it happens. From one of the ships, likely *Indefatigable*, a shell blasts from the muzzle and traces a perfect arc towards the old fort at the entrance to the Dardanelles, Sedd-el-Bahr. For those firing at the fort – which is built of locally quarried stone, sitting 30 yards above the sea and all of 250 years old – there is no reason to expect that this shell will do much more damage than the other shells. That is, while it may shatter a few stones, and even take out a gun if it lands closely enough, it is unlikely to threaten the structure.

Ah, but this shell, *this* shell, somehow has the fort's number on it. By a one-in-ten-thousand shot of shots, it hits the outside wall at just the spot where it is able to penetrate before exploding inside the ammunition magazine, detonating all the shells not yet carried to the guns. To the amazement of those on the ships, the bottom part of the castle explodes before their eyes, causing 'a column of dark grey smoke and debris reaching a height of 300 to 500 ft'.[9] The explosion is so powerful that all ten guns in the castle are taken out of action, and 86 Turkish soldiers are killed – ever after to be known as 'the first martyrs'.[10]

Just ten minutes after the barrage begins, the water-borne squadron withdraws.[11]

Churchill is thrilled with the result, while Constantinople is panicked.

The British are coming! The British are coming!

Once the news hits, many of the well-to-do of Constantinople make evacuation plans, while the common people make plans to defend the city and, whatever else, save its mosques and treasures, not to mention the Sultan himself. To prevent the British Fleet from getting right to the heart of the city, the idea of placing mines in the Bosphorus to protect the Golden Horn estuary is discussed.

Far more practically, down at the Dardanelles, the Commander of the Fortified Defences at Chanak, Major-General Cevat – a man whose soft blue eyes and moonface belie a steely temperament – is energised as never before. 'The bombardment of November 3 came as a warning to me,' he would later recall. 'I understood that I needed to spend all of my time organising our defence arrangements and assigning reinforcements using every means possible.'[12]

In terms of strengthening the defences of the Dardanelles, the Turks are helped immeasurably by German Admiral Guido von Usedom, his special engineers and work troop, as all together they bolster the defences: repairing the forts, building more gun batteries, increasing searchlights and installing 60 mobile mortars and howitzers in concealed positions on both sides of the Straits. Massive mounds of earth are put around all the heavy gun batteries, just as sandbag walls are put around the gun-crew pits and ammunition stores.

The brief attack on 3 November had been exactly what was needed to galvanise the Turks and their German sponsors into bringing the defences of the Dardanelles further towards the modern age. Not for nothing would a later British inquiry into the affair conclude, 'the preliminary bombardment of the outer forts on 3 November 1914 – ordered by the Admiralty without consultation with the War Council – [was] an almost irreparable mistake'.[13]

In London at the time, however, Prime Minister Herbert Asquith – known to his friends as 'Squiff', as a play on his last name and for his fondness of heavy drinking – takes it a lot less seriously. 'The shelling of a fort at the Dardanelles seems to have succeeded in blowing up a magazine,' he writes (as he so often does) to the beautiful 27-year-old aristocrat and socialite Venetia Stanley, 'but that is *peu de chose . . .*'[14]

A small parenthesis here. Yes, it is odd that a 62-year-old British Prime Minister in wartime should so regularly write – sometimes as often as three times a day – to a woman 35 years his junior, but the weird ways of love have never stopped at the door of 10 Downing Street. After the doctor had prescribed separate bedrooms for Asquith and his rather fragile second wife, Margot, in 1907, Asquith had developed what Margot acidly described as a 'little harem',[15] a collection of gorgeous young women he regularly engaged with, of whom Venetia is now the foremost. It is not only Margot Asquith who takes a rather dim view of the whole thing, as no less than Clementine Churchill is appalled to note how the current British Prime Minister frequently peers down women's dresses, while it is the claim of socialite Lady Ottoline Morrell that Asquith, 'Would take a lady's hand as she sat beside him on the sofa, and make her feel his erected instrument under his trousers.'[16] Close parenthesis – with relief.[17]

5 NOVEMBER 1914, AHOY TO THE CONVOY

Day after day, the sun rises, soars high and then low in its searing arc across a sky nearly as blue as the sea all around. To the 20,758 Australians and 8427 New Zealanders aboard the 38 troopships – also bearing 11,294 horses[18] – it almost seems as if their convoy is the only thing that leaves a momentary mark in the eternal blue-ness.

All alone? They certainly hope so – but at least they have some protection against whatever enemy craft might be out there. On the far western horizon, five miles out in the lead, they can see the pillar of smoke that represents *Minotaur*, their key cruiser escort. Not only does the smoke provide the direction for all the other ships in the convoy to follow, and pace, but most crucially *Minotaur* is riding shotgun, its officers scanning their own horizons in every direction for any sign of an enemy force.

To one young soldier, Lance-Corporal Percival Langford, it looks like their very own 'formidable monster . . . with her big guns fore and aft'.[19]

The two pillars of smoke far to starboard and to port equally show where, respectively, *Ibuki* and *Sydney* lie, while *Melbourne* brings up the rear. Most particularly, all officers on the bridges of these vessels are on the lookout for the German cruiser *Emden*, which has wrought such havoc in recent weeks. Armed with two torpedo tubes and a main armament of ten 4.1-inch guns, and skippered by one of the Imperial German Navy's best, Kapitänleutnant Karl von Müller, *Emden* already has two warships and no fewer than 21 Allied merchant ships on its ledger of kills. This includes a spectacular raid just three days earlier on Penang Harbour, where it unleashed shocking destruction, sinking first a Russian ship, *Zemtchug*, and then a French warship, *Mousquet*. Should *Emden* ever get among the Australian and New Zealand convoy, the result would be catastrophic.

In addition to keeping a sharp lookout, lights are extinguished at night and there is a strict rule against throwing any refuse overboard – as it has been established that in one case a cruiser was able to follow such a trail for 100 miles until catching up with the convoy and sinking the ships. It is a precaution that might mean the difference between life and death. For it is on this day that disturbing war news breaks upon the convoy.

Two of von Spee's armoured cruisers, *Scharnhorst* and *Gneisenau*, had engaged with a British squadron off the South American coast in the Battle of Coronel on 1 November, and two British cruisers, *Good Hope* and *Monmouth*, had been sunk. Added to this, for several weeks *Emden* has been rumoured to be near Sumatra. Given the convoy is Colombo-bound, who knows how close *Emden* is now to their current position?

Another bulletin that has been eliciting great comment around the water cart is that, as reported by the Foreign Office, 'Owing to hostile acts committed by Turkish forces under German officers, a state of war exists between Great Britain and Turkey as from to-day.'[20]

Well, that settles that. Aboard several ships in the convoy there had been great discussion a couple of days previously, after *Osterley* had passed at 6.30 pm and given them the news by semaphore that Kingsburgh had won the Melbourne Cup – hooray! – and that Turkey had declared war with Germany. The debate had been whether that meant that Turkey was *for* or *against* Germany? Now they know.

The most urgent query they have now, as expressed by Charles Bean, is, 'Shall we be stopped in Egypt?'[21]

In the meantime, there on the high seas, a more pressing problem is seasickness, which most soldiers are experiencing for the first time, as reported in the *Kan-Karroo Kronikle*, the journal of the troopship *Karroo*:

Sergeant Baker stood at the top of the stairs wearing a look of sorrow.

'What's the matter?' he was asked.

'I ate a little fish for brekker and it's breaking its bally neck to get back in the water,' he gurgled as he made a dive for the rail.[22]

6.25 AM, 9 NOVEMBER 1914, COCOS ISLANDS, FROM *BURESK* TO BERSERK

The Cocos Islands, a former British annexation granted in perpetuity by Queen Victoria to the Clunies-Ross family in 1886,[23] slumbers and simmers out in the middle of the Indian Ocean. Little happens here from one week to the next. But on this morning, something different . . .

A ship is approaching. A *war*-ship.

The man on duty at the wireless station on the high point of the island looks for the reassuring British ensign on the unidentified ship fast approaching. There is none! Feverishly, he taps out a message to all ships in the vicinity:

STRANGE WARSHIP APPROACHING
SOS STRANGE CRUISER OFF ENTRANCE.[24]

In fact, not only strange but also obviously dangerous, as the German warship soon disgorges 'a small steam pinnace with two cutters in tow . . . full of men, who . . . are armed and wear unusual-looking tropical helmets'.[25] There is just time for the operator to send out one other message:

SOS SOS SOS
THREE-FUNNELLED WARSHIP OFF THE
ISLAND, LANDING PARTY IN . . .[26]

before German soldiers from the *Emden* – of course! – led by Kapitänleutnant Hellmuth von Mücke, burst into the radio room. They have come to obliterate this very station just on principle. The operator has no way of knowing whether his signal has been received by anyone.

Less than 50 miles away, the radio operator on *Melbourne* is just passing the time, filling out the logbook after another boring night, when suddenly he hears the famous signal:

. . . ▬ ▬ ▬ . . .   . . . ▬ ▬ ▬ . . .   . . . ▬ ▬ ▬ . . .

SOS! SOS! SOS!

All because a strange warship is approaching the – where is it? – Cocos Islands.

Running now, the radio operator passes on the message to *Melbourne*'s captain, Mortimer L'Estrange Silver, who gives the orders to proceed to the islands at full steam.

Aboard *Orvieto*, Charles Bean immediately realises something is up – a hint of sudden action.

'Look at *Ibuki*,' someone says within his earshot.

Bean turns his head and torso as he unfolds his long legs, almost like a giraffe, and he stands, squinting out to sea from behind his wire frames. And indeed, just ahead, the Japanese ship is racing across the bows of the convoy to join *Melbourne*, smoke billowing from her funnels as never before.

'Aloft at the peak,' Bean would describe, 'planted fair against the black smoke-cloud, flew one huge Japanese ensign. As she passed ahead of the fleet she broke from the mainmast a second great ensign of the rising sun, her battleflag.

'She was moving fast, punching great masses of white out of the dark water and spreading the seas wide on either side of her bluff bows. When she reached the *Melbourne* in the distance, she was seen once to turn and head for the horizon in the direction of the fight. She had signalled, "I wish to go and help *Sydney*." But the captain of *Melbourne* refused the permission requested.'[27]

For Captain Silver has only just realised that *Melbourne* and *Ibuki* have a higher duty, which is to stay with the convoy, protecting its 30,000 troops, sailors and 25 nurses spread over seven ships. Captain John Glossop, on *Sydney*, is ordered to take his light cruiser to find out what is going on.

Just over two hours later, on the Cocos Islands, Kapitän von Müller is relieved to see the smoke of an approaching ship, knowing it must be his collier, the captured English vessel *Buresk*, which is overdue, and . . .

And *mein Gott!* That is not *Buresk*; it is *ein australischer Kreuzer* – an Australian light cruiser![28]

Leaving Kapitänleutnant von Mücke and his men on shore behind
– for there is simply no time – the German skipper gives the orders:
'Dampf auf in allen Kesseln! – Steam up in all the boilers!'

'Anker lichten! – Up anchor!'

'Klarschiff zum Gefecht! – Clear ship for action!'

'Maschine beschleunigt Dampf auf für höchste Geschwindigkeit! – Full
steam ahead!'[29]

Sydney is ten nautical miles off the Cocos Islands, approaching from
the north-east, when, just after 9.30 am, Captain Glossop – with his
glasses fiercely trained on the low smudge of land in the distance – sees
something. There!

Emerging from the smudge now is a tiny dot, billowing black smoke.
It is . . . it is . . . it is a warship! Very likely a German warship, to judge
from the SOS, and very likely that scourge of the South Seas, *Emden*!

As the two combatants close, the German light cruiser four years the
Australian's senior, the question is who will throw the first punch and
when? *Emden's* 4.1-inch guns can go as far as six miles – about 10,500
yards – while the *Sydney's* six-inch guns can reach further, to 15,000
yards. But, under full steam, rolling from side to side on the swell, is it
worth firing from so far, now that the six-mile limit has been reached?

Captain Glossop does not think so, even though his ship is over
1000 tons heavier and so cuts through the swell more easily. He says to
his senior officers, 'I think we had better get a thousand yards nearer
before we fire . . .'[30]

Kapitän von Müller doesn't think so, and at 9.39 am gives the order.
'Feuer frei! – Fire!'

First, Captain Glossop sees puffs of smoke from four for'ard guns on
Emden, and about 15 seconds later he hears a high-pitched whistle, as if
from a train coming straight at them . . . and then all hell breaks loose.

One shell hits the spot on the aft-deck from where the ship's guns
are controlled, grievously wounding many men. Another shell lands
in the most forward part of the bridge and, *without exploding*, first
knocks the cap of Gunnery-Lieutenant Dennis Rahilly off his head,
then destroys the range finder and kills the man in charge of it, before

finally, mercifully, bouncing off the deck and disappearing overboard.[31]

Everywhere now there is blood, screams and moans . . . but very little panic. In fact, the body of the man working the range finder has landed on a 16-year-old lad, Able Seaman Roy Millar, who had been working the telescope beside him – and knocked him out. But look now. He is stirring, under the weight of his dead colleague. Now, pushing the bloodied corpse off him, the lad rises to his feet and says, 'Where's my bloody telescope?'[32]

Picking it up, he gets back to work, training that telescope on *Emden*, eyes peeled for torpedo tracks and doing his calculations as everyone else who has survived gets back to the job at hand.

The gun captain, receiving instructions from fire control, yells to his men: 10,300 yards and closing, 10,200 yards and closing, 10,000 yards and closing . . . The two 'trainers' of the guns peer through their sights with their beady eyes, coordinating with each other – 'Right-a-lot' . . . 'Hair-to-right' . . . 'Mark' – and as the thin wires in both of their sights cross, one of the trainers says, 'Target.' They're on. 'Ready,' they yell to the gun captain.

'*Shoot!*'[33]

One of the early shells from *Sydney* not only destroys *Emden*'s wireless room but also damages her steering, meaning Kapitän von Müller must slow his ship down to re-establish control.

Speeding up once more, *Sydney* continues to pour shells into the grievously wounded *Emden*, though the German cruiser does manage to turn to bring her port guns to bear – a manoeuvre quickly matched by *Sydney*.

After 35 minutes of battle, carnage reigns supreme aboard *Emden*, while catastrophe waits in the wings. By now, *Sydney* has fired over 500 rounds, each bearing just over 13 pounds of high explosives, and while more than a hundred have hit home, the most crucial are those that have damaged *Emden*'s weapons systems. Though the German cruiser has been able to fire many more shells, only 14 have hit . . . of which only five have exploded.

Still, the men of *Emden* have fight in them, and when Kapitän von

Müller gives the order, '*Hol alles raus!* – Everything you can get out of the engines!' they respond immediately.[34]

Alas, even then they can get no closer to *Sydney* than 5500 yards. When word comes that the torpedo room has to be abandoned because of 'a shot under water', the captain knows he has no choice. Much of the ship is on fire, many of the crew are either dead or dying, and as the shells continue to slam into *Emden* and explode, the blizzard of shrapnel continues to cut a swathe through survivors.

'As it was now impossible for me to damage my opponent in any way further,' von Müller would write in his report to the German Admiralty, 'I decided to put my ship, which was badly damaged by gun-fire and burning in many places, on the reef in the surf on the weather-side of North Keeling Island and to wreck it thoroughly, in order not to sacrifice needlessly the lives of the survivors.'[35]

And yet, despite it all, their spirit remains, with one German sailor heard to lead his compatriots in '*Ein Hoch auf das Vaterland!* – Three cheers for the Fatherland!'[36] an instant before a shell lands to blow them all apart.

The air is thick with the choking and burning Lyddite fumes from the exploded Australian shells,[37] and the whole ship would be out of control if not under the hand of a master mariner such as Kapitän von Müller, backed by a courageous and expert crew. At a rate of ten knots, at 11.20 am, the German cruiser hits the reef and comes to a dead stop, of course throwing officers, sailors, wounded men and many, many dead men forward, together with everything else on the ship that is not bolted down. For a split second, there is nothing to be heard but the crashing of the waves against the ship's suddenly exposed hull and the roaring of the engine. Then come the screams, the agonised groans, the cursing and shouting of the surviving crew . . .

Aboard *Sydney*, the dramatic end of *Emden* is met with a great deal of satisfaction: 'She came looking for a fight, and she got it,' Captain Glossop would later tell Banjo Paterson.[38] The skipper now dictates the message that will, on the instant, be sent to the rest of the convoy, and soon all the way back to Australia, where the news creates a sensation:

EMDEN BEACHED AND DONE FOR[39]

For the men on the convoy of ships, who had seen the *Ibuki* and *Sydney* steam off, 'The news went round like wildfire and everyone left off work to cheer. Good old *Sydney!*'[40]

After chasing the *Buresk* to see it also sunk, Captain Glossop gives the order for *Sydney* to head back to *Emden*. They arrive at 4 pm to find that, though *Emden* is beached, she still flies her colours – which he takes as a signal that she has still not surrendered. Thus, just to make sure there will be no further resistance, from a range of 4300 yards aft, Glossop gives the orders for several more salvos to be fired into the stricken German cruiser, which kills and wounds dozens more of the Kaiser's sailors before the national flag is frantically lowered, by Kapitän von Müller's own brave cabin servant, and burned. A white flag is soon seen lolling in its stead.

(As to this tragic loss of yet more life after the battle is well over, it would later be asserted by von Müller in his German Admiralty report – possibly to cover for the fact he had neglected to take his flag down – that the whole affair was 'very embarrassing for Captain Glossop himself and that he had let mainly his first officer determine himself to act in this way'.)[41]

It is over. Now at battle's end, with this settling of accounts, it is time to check that account. The net result of the whole confrontation is that the Germans have lost two ships, 134 men killed and 189 men captured, while *Sydney* has come off comparatively lightly, with many wounded but just three fatalities and one man also likely to succumb to his wounds. As recorded by the first Australian doctor to board *Emden*, 'Men were lying killed and mutilated in heaps, with large blackened flesh wounds. One man had a horizontal section of the head taken off, exposing mangled brain tissue . . . Some of the men who were brought off to the *Sydney* presented horrible sights, and by this time the wounds were practically all foul and stinking . . .'[42]

As a gesture of respect for the gallantry of von Müller – who is the last man to leave *Emden*, and who Charles Bean judges to be 'a gaunt clean-shaven, big-boned sailor, far more resembling an Englishman than a German in both his appearance and his outlook'[43] – Churchill sends a message that he and his officers are allowed to keep their swords. It does not happen, however, because their swords had been lost in the carnage; and von Müller's rapport with the Australian captain remains strained, somewhat, by the firing on his ship after it was beached.

The proprieties of the victor over the vanquished are observed and, while the wounded are given immediate medical treatment, the unscathed survivors of *Emden* are taken aboard *Sydney* and accommodated comfortably upon their words as gentlemen that, on the trip to the Ceylonese capital of Colombo, they will not cause trouble. (A condition that is observed, with the exception of some of the German sailors destroying their crockery and throwing their cutlery out the window. No problem – from that point on, their food is simply slopped on the table and they must eat it with their fingers.)

When *Sydney* again comes within sight of the convoy, Captain Glossop sends his 16-year-old messenger, Ernie Boston, to fetch Kapitän von Müller, saying he would like to see him on the bridge. On his way there, the German comes out on deck and for the first time sees the troopships in every direction.

'Boy,' he says to the underling, 'what is all this?'

'That,' he is told, 'is the [38] transports with the Australian and New Zealand [soldiers, heading to the war].'

The German naval officer continues to stare at all the ships for a full minute, before coming to his conclusion. 'It'll go hard for the Fatherland,' the Kapitän says morosely, 'if all Dominions rally to their England like this.'[44]

A short time later, he is asked what would have happened had he been aware that the convoy of troopships had been so close to *Emden*. Kapitän von Müller is crisp in his reply, first pointing to the cruiser on their port bow. 'I should have run alongside her and fired a torpedo. Then, in the confusion, I should have got in among the transports. I would have sunk half of them, I think, before your

escort came up. I should have been sunk in the end, I expect –
I always expected that.'[45]

As for the men on the convoys, they know that aboard the approaching *Sydney* are the survivors of the *Emden*, 'and, out of consideration for
them, the troops kept silent as the ship passed'.[46]

And the 53 German sailors ashore on the Cocos Islands, with
Kapitänleutnant Hellmuth von Mücke, at the time of the battle? That's
them there, sailing nor' by nor'west in a 70-ton schooner, *Ayesha*,
that they have stolen from some powerful local family by the name
of Clunies-Ross. After watching the battle from the shore, and realising that he and his men would inevitably be captured unless they did
something, Lieutenant von Mücke had had the yacht provisioned with
everything they could quickly get their hands on, and by 6 pm on the
evening of the battle had made good their escape.

In the meantime, Banjo Paterson reports that *Sydney* – the 'idol of
all in this fleet' – came through the line and, though all had wanted to
cheer her, a strict order had been read to all the officers from the flagship: the *Sydney* will pass through the transport about 3 am tomorrow
morning. Owing to the presence of wounded on board her, there will
be no demonstration. As she passes, all ranks will stand at attention and
the bugles will blow the attention.[47]

As to the news of the sinking of *Emden*, it is greeted with acclaim
and celebration throughout Australia, but likely nowhere is there more
pure joy evinced than in the breast of Lieutenant-Commander Dacre
Stoker of the *AE2*, now on the way back from the tour of duty in the
Pacific. Together with the news shortly afterwards that all bar the
light cruiser *Dresden* of Admiral von Spee's squadron had been sunk
during the Battle of the Falkland Islands, it means 'the Pacific was
now clear of enemy ships, and a submarine lying in Sydney harbour
could not claim to be of any useful purpose in the war'.[48] And Stoker
already has an idea of how he might be able to get his submarine
closer to the action . . .

14 NOVEMBER 1914, IN CONSTANTINOPLE, A CALL TO THE FURIOUS FAITHFUL

And so it has come to this.

While Turkey is certainly the 'sick old man of Europe', the sick old man of Turkey is the Sultan and Caliph of the Ottoman Empire, Mehmed V. In his lifetime, this man – proclaimed as a direct-line descendant of the Prophet Muhammad – has seen the power of his throne go from a golden absolute to a tinny facade, entirely dependent on the support of the Young Turks, the militant leaders of the CUP, who actually run the country.

The old man still has his purposes, however, and on this day in the hall of the old Topkapı Palace, where some relics of Prophet Muhammad lie – including a sole strand of hair from Muhammad's beard – he attends a ceremony where the Ottoman Empire's chief religious leader, Esad Efendi, Sheik-Ul-Islam, reads out a fatwah in the Sultan's name allowing for the proclamation of jihad upon the British, French and Russian infidels.

The fatwah judges that, among other things:

> If several enemies unite against Islam, if the countries of Islam are sacked, if the Moslem populations are massacred or made captive; and if in this case the Padishah in conformity with the sacred words of the Koran proclaims the Holy War, is participation in this war a duty for all Moslems, old and young, cavalry and infantry? Must the Mohammedans of all countries of Islam hasten with their bodies and possessions to the Jihad?

> Answer: 'Yes.'[49]

Following on from the fatwah, on 23 November, Sultan Mehmed V decrees as Caliph that the proclamation of jihad should be disseminated through-out the Muslim world – published in all the major newspapers around the Ottoman Empire the following day, through all of Medina, Baghdad, Damascus, Basra and Jerusalem – justifying the Empire's bellicosity:

To my army! To my navy!

. . . The fleets of England and France have bombarded the Straits of the Dardanelles . . .

Russia, England, and France never for a moment ceased harbouring ill-will against our Caliphate, to which millions of Muslims,[50] suffering under the tyranny of foreign dominations, are religiously and whole-heartedly devoted, and it was always these powers that started every misfortune that came upon us . . .

In this sacred war and struggle, which we began against the enemies who have undermined our religion and our holy fatherland, never for a single moment cease from strenuous effort and from self-abnegation.

Throw yourselves against the enemy as lions, bearing in mind that the very existence of our empire, and of 300,000,000 Moslems whom I have summoned by sacred *Fetva* to a supreme struggle, depend on your victory . . .[51]

It is now nothing less than a religious *duty* for no fewer than 300 million Muslims to rise up, rise up, rise up, my children, and throw them out!

24–28 NOVEMBER 1914, ABOARD THE CONVOY, THE NEWS BREAKS

For the 30,000 Australasian soldiers, imbued with the glory of the British Empire, it is nothing less than a duty of membership of this Empire to be answering this call-up.

And it is good, and it is great, and in his cabin on *Euripides* Banjo Paterson composes the words that will soon be sent back (once it passes the censors) to Australia, to be published by *The Sydney Morning Herald*: 'It is strange to look out over the grey sea, not a ripple on the water, the horizon shrouded in haze, and to think of England calling up men from the ends of the earth – to think of these great flotillas . . . of which one is, perhaps, even now behind that haze, all steaming steadily and purposefully towards the goal. Has anything like it ever been seen in the world before? The ends of the earth are called in for troops, the sea is furrowed with keels, and the very air is called into service to carry messages. If anything would cure a man of being a "little Australian", it would be such an expedition as this.'[52]

No more 'little Australians' for them. This is big Australia!

But, have yers *heard?* They reckon the bottle-washer heard it from the Chief Cook, who heard it from the Lieutenant, who heard it from the Navigator, who overheard the Captain telling the Chief Engineer that they had received orders from the Admiralty today that we're *not* going to land in England after all! Nup, instead of being on board for the next few weeks, we're going to land somewhere soon, and maybe train there!

'Everyone naturally quite excited as this means landing under the week,' records one officer, Lieutenant Henry Coe, in his diary. 'The news was received with great enthusiasm by the men who cheered and cheered. This will be ever so much more comfortable for us anyhow as the climate is much more like our own. We need not bother about the cold now.'[53]

On every ship, the news travels from stern to starboard to port to bow and back again in an instant flat, and if the proof is not in the pudding that night, it comes with the crusty boiled potatoes at lunch the next day, when the soldiers receive confirmation that they will be heading up the hundred miles of the Suez Canal before heading west to make a landing in Alexandria and then taken on a train to Cairo.

No one is more relieved than Australia's High Commissioner to Great Britain, Sir George Reid, who has been agitating for this very destination. There has been a dreadful problem with Canadian soldiers behaving badly in the already overcrowded training camp on Salisbury Plain, raising hell in the nearby cathedral city of Salisbury – something Sir George wishes to avoid happening again.

1 DECEMBER 1914, LONDON, LORD NORTHCLIFFE'S TEMPERATURE RISES

The problem?

Real and terrible things are happening on the Western Front, but Lord Northcliffe's journalists are unable to report them accurately in the *Daily Mail* and *The Times*, because the British Government censors won't allow it. American papers report it all accurately, with photographs, and they sell in their thousands, but his papers, and all British papers, are hamstrung from reporting the *truth*.

In great frustration, and rising anger, Lord Northcliffe takes pen in hand and writes to one of the more influential figures of the day, Lord Murray of Elibank, that, 'What the newspapers feel very strongly, is that, against their will, they are made to be part and parcel of a foolish conspiracy to hide bad news . . . English people do not mind bad news.'[54]

EARLY DECEMBER 1914, THE CONVOY GETS CLOSE

And sure enough for the soldiers from Australia and New Zealand, over the next few days it happens before their eyes. First, land appears to starboard, and then to port, and then starts closing in on both sides, a gaping maw of Mother Earth, about to swallow them whole, and they can't wait.

On the blessed night of 1 December, they enter the Suez Canal. Lieutenant Coe records in his diary, 'The marvellousness of it fairly takes my breath away . . . The first part was just like my idea of Venice.'[55] In the moonlight of an impossibly bright and freezing-cold night, he can see 'sentries posted along the banks and then we came to a camp from which we got a good old cheer'.[56]

At the gusty break of dawn, everyone is up and about on deck, and the first camp they can see clearly is an Indian regiment who – framed by the pink desert and the Arabian Hills behind, looking down benignly – have secured themselves in a fort of sandbags and barbed-wire entanglements, and who are wildly cheered, just on principle.

'Coo-ee!' the Australians cry. 'Coo-eeee! Coo-EEEE!'[57]

Goodness gracious me. The Indian soldiers and their English officers swarm from their tents at their call, to roar with laughter and heartily wave back! The men of the British Empire are gathering, and there is an immediate soldierly solidarity between them all, with the Indians smiling and waving in return as these genuine 'ships of the desert' pass by.

And not just the British Empire. On Banjo Paterson's *Euripides*, the response from a French ship they pass, when the Australian band plays 'La Marseillaise', is inspiring, as the anthem is met with 'the frantic delight of the Frenchmen, who cheered and cheered again'.[58]

On they keep moving up the narrow canal, the ship-bound troops fascinated by the steady procession of endlessly interesting things, including many tiny settlements of sad mud huts beside small agricultural patches, where they can see heavily veiled women carrying huge water jars amazingly balanced on their heads, while the turbaned blokes seem to be doing three-fifths of bugger-all as they haul hard on the end of a coffin nail, or kneeling and . . .

And what the hell are they doing *now*? One Australian soldier records his impressions of this soon-to-be-common vision in his diary:

I have just witnessed a tribe of natives paying their tribute to their God the Sun. They looked very funny kneeling and bobbing up and down like a Jack in a box, then they would mutter something to themselves, with their hands up in the air, then nearly knock their brains out with bowing to the sun.[59]

This is *weird*, cobber! Somewhere in the distance, some bastard is wailing. The most amazing thing, though? Aboard *Euripides*, it is the vision of a major town on their northern horizon, complete with spires and big buildings, just kind of floating on the shimmer of the far horizon, seen by all, that nevertheless . . . fades . . . from view as they approach!

Nothing more than a mirage.

'This ghostly desert town,' Banjo Paterson records, 'made more impression on the men than anything that they saw; it seemed uncanny.'[60]

As the troops remain transfixed by this alien world passing them – at the perfect distance to give them the feeling they are simply watching a film at the cinema – the ships' crews labour to navigate this impossibly thin waterway. Lieutenant Coe, aboard the *Shropshire*, notes his vessel twisting in tight turns and at one point even scraping the side of the canal, as well as another boat, the *Ascanius*. It's 'not as wide as the Yarra', he observes, 'barely half as wide indeed'.[61]

Finally, without major damage inflicted, they come to Port Said, at the northern end of the canal. All the ships come roughly together in a wild flotilla, and every soldier who can gets up on deck and exuberantly cheers all the other soldiers on the other ships. As one soldier records, the town 'looks for all the world like a Noah's Ark or a cardboard house constructed by a youngster in its earliest endeavours at house building . . . Everything is the colour of sand. Even the buildings are sand coloured. It is one of the last places I should hope to be stationed in.'[62]

And yet, because Port Said can only cope with unloading two ships at a time, the Australians quickly push on to the bigger port of Alexandria, where a band greets them with a rendition of a new song that has been getting popular of late, 'Advance Australia Fair'. The men then have to make their way through hundreds of young Arab urchins – boys and girls – begging them for baksheesh. Just beyond, hundreds of peddlers and hawkers want to sell them everything from wheelbarrows to cart their gear in, rings and jewellery taken straight from the tombs in the pyramids, an original piece of the cross that Jesus Christ was crucified on, to one of the *actual* 30 pieces of silver that Judas was paid off with. Yours, for just 50 piastres, a little less than half a pound!

Later, one of Trooper Bluegum's cobbers, Trooper Newman, will pay ten piastres for a handkerchief that has on its four corners images of King George, Lord Kitchener, General French and the Commander of the Grand Fleet,[63] Admiral John Rushworth Jellicoe, while all over it are dukes and earls. 'It may be the only chance I'll get,' Trooper Newman says, 'of poking my nose into high society.'[64]

All over the quay are low four-wheeled carts – measuring about three feet by eight feet – attached to what the troops instantly begin referring to as 'Arab stallions' but are in fact donkeys. Well, here are some of *our* animals. Though the koalas and possums smuggled aboard by the Australian troops have perished on the trip over for want of the right food – and at least one of the kangaroos had taken one big jump too many, to finish in the middle of the Indian Ocean – here now is a surviving Old Man Kangaroo, who *refuses* to budge from the wharf. And nor does Old Man particularly care for the large crowd of Egyptians who have gathered to see the newcomers and are now staring with sheer amazement at this *extraordinary*-looking creature.

Open-mouthed they stare, while the kangaroo merely glances at them. (If you've spent six weeks on a troopship with a thousand Australian soldiers, you have pretty much seen it all anyway.) But perhaps they might be worth a closer look? Alas, when the kangaroo takes just a couple of bounds in the direction of the gathered natives, it is met with a melee of madness as, with 'ear-splitting yells, some hundreds of Alexandrians made record time in seeking safety from the "ferocious" beast'.[65] Even the smaller scrub wallabies are viewed as demons in disguise by the natives: 'One fellow the wallaby chased and he dropped all his tomatoes and fairly screamed and called upon "Allah" to save him, for surely he thought the devil was on his track.'[66]

Ah, how the Australians laugh. These 'Gyppos', as they are already referred to, would run away from anything.

Within three hours, the soldiers are on the train, steaming south through the Delta country on the 120-mile trip to Cairo, and the farmers among them are particularly impressed. One soldier records, 'The intense cultivation of the Delta was a great surprise to us.'[67] Others, such as the softly spoken cove from Sydney, Sergeant Archie Barwick of the 1st Battalion, look out the window as wide-eyed as when they had first approached Suez. 'I fairly drank it all in,' he recalls, 'for we were now in the land of mystery and wonderful things.'[68]

'The native villages are most peculiarly laid out,' noted Warrant Officer Frederick Forrest, 'and the method of tilling the land somewhat strange to us Australians. It is quite common to see an ox and a camel, or a camel and a donkey pulling an old wooden plough.'[69]

Wooden ploughs! Just how primitive is this country?

Pretty primitive, cobber. Look over there, with mum, dad, grandma and three kids travelling on two camels, all eating from the same cabbage that they are feeding to the goats trotting along behind . . .

As the soldiers pass, they see 'strings of camels proceeding in leisurely fashion, the riders being Arabs in flowing garments and gaudy turbans or Fez caps'[70] looking, in the words of Charles Bean, as if they 'might have stepped out of the Bible'.[71]

At least, however, the purpose-built siding for the Australian troops just off Cairo Central Station is modern, having been completed only in the past few days. After the men arrive there at 10 pm, the next thing is to transfer their supplies and gear into trams, donkey carts, mule wagons and army transport carts escorted by magnificently uniformed Egyptian Mounted Police, while by the light of the moon they must march off on the road parallel to the tram track, west then south to where their training camp lies, at Mena, ten miles away.

To get there, they must take a bridge across the mighty ribbon of the Nile, and as they approach it – marching behind their band – the Australians pass some yellow plastered barracks where the just-arrived Lancashire Territorials of the 42nd Division are quartered. Woken by the band, those worthies tumble from their bunks and rush across the gravelled parade ground. 'When they found that the troops marching past them were Australians,' Charles Bean would record, 'they cheered, clinging to the railings and waving.'[72]

Hurrah! Hurrah! Hurrah!

Some five miles of marching later, the men catch their first glimpse, and the gasp goes up. The pyramids! I can see pyramids by the light of the moon, pyramids so big their tops poke out above the fog that has settled on the desert floor.

Is it yet one more mirage?

No, mate. The camp for the Australian soldiers lies in a desert valley within coo-ee of the towering 482-foot Great Pyramid of King Cheops and his lesser brothers – and all who see the pyramids are astounded, Bluey, by their sheer *bulk*.

Of course, no tents have been erected for the new arrivals in their camp, nothing prepared, so they simply lie on the soft sand and sleep the best they can – for, in the very words of many a man in those wee hours, it is cold enough to freeze the balls off a brass monkey. Who knew the desert could be so cold at night?

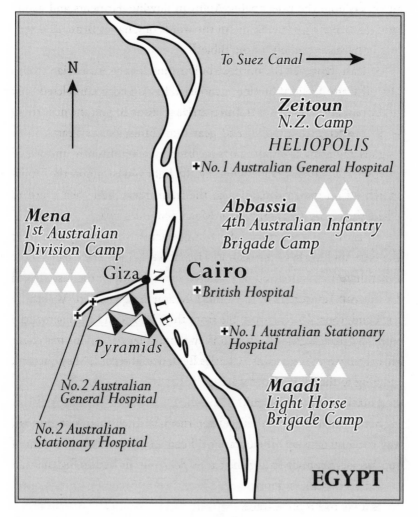

Cairo district army camps and hospitals, by Jane Macaulay

Chapter Four
A MAN WITH A PLAN . . .

Are there not any alternatives than sending our armies to
chew barbed wire in Flanders? Further cannot the power
of the Navy be brought more directly to bear upon the
enemy? If it is impossible or unduly costly to pierce the
German lines on existing fronts, ought we not, as new
forces come to hand, to engage him on new frontiers . . .?[1]

First Lord of the Admiralty Winston Churchill to
Prime Minister Asquith, 29 December 1914

MID-DECEMBER 1914, CAIRO, IN THE SHADOW OF THE PYRAMIDS

For the imperious Sphinx, this is nothing new under the searing sun.

For nigh on 45 centuries, it has gazed indifferently on the sweaty
military men marching before it: on the way to battle, on the way from
battle, preparing for battle. True, these particular men, from Australia
and New Zealand, have come from further away than ever before, and
their battle is set to take place somewhere unknown, but much of the
rest is the same. The men stagger back and forth, they are shouted at,
they curse when they are sure their officers can't hear them, they stagger, they occasionally faint and tumble down to the hot sands below.

Ah! That sand! In an instant, a faint breeze becomes a sandstorm.
'Impossible to keep the sand out,' one young Australian private notes
in his diary. 'Tiny particles found their way through the fabric of the
canvas [of the tent] and in a few minutes there was a yellow layer of

sand over everything. At dinner, the stew looked as if someone was continually shaking a pepper pot over food and you could feel the sand going down the throat. Through eating and inhaling fine particles of sand, hundreds of the men soon developed what was dubbed "The Pyramid Cough!".[2]

For most of the Australian soldiers now settled into the endless line of sandy tents in the desert that is the Mena Camp – while the New Zealanders are in Zeitoun and the Light Horse in Maadi – the strangeness of the environment is soon matched by the sense of time. Is it really only six weeks ago that they left Australia and all that was familiar to them? It now seems so long ago – another world, another life.

For every day starts with reveille at 5 am sharp, the sound of the bugle whipping across the desert sands and through their thin canvas tents before drilling right into their ears.

Up! Up! Up! Rise and shine!

Shine like the scorching sun, which, even early, belts down upon them as they devour a quick breakfast of eggs, and bread and jam. Many of the men are not adapting well to the produce of this strange land and are grateful when, after some time at the camp, some of their food starts arriving from home. As Lieutenant Coe later records, in the rough manner of speaking that breeds freely among the men in the camp, 'We get Australian butter, which is much appreciated. The Arabic butter being too much for our palates. Rancid always . . . We also get Australian eggs, which is a huge boon, as the native eggs taste like a nigger smells which is not nice.'[3] (Less appreciated are the cans of bully beef coming from home, which you practically need a hammer and chisel to penetrate.)

At 7.30 am, they fall in for the first of many inspections and roll-calls for the day. And then to the serious stuff.

Their exercises include digging trenches, attacking a hill under heavy fire, retreats, outflanking opposing battalions and marching in full kit for staggering distances, before marching back again, staggering still more. Yes, they have a small break at high noon for lunch, but when that consists of a small tin of sardines and a small roll of bread shared between two men, it is no wonder one of their favourite marching songs is 'The Brigadier gets turkey / The Colonel he gets duck / The officers get chicken / And think themselves in luck / The Sergeants get their belly full / We watched them through the wall / But all the poor old Privates get / Is one dry roll.'[4] On their marches into the desert, they must look out for big rocks that, between them, they can carry back, paint white and then use to mark out their territory at Mena Camp.

As the always diligent Charles Bean records, often spied with his pad in hand, jotting notes all the while in his mad dash of a scrawl, 'All day long, in every valley of the Sahara for miles around the pyramids, were groups or lines of men advancing, retiring, drilling, or squatted near their piled arms listening to their officer . . . At first, in order to harden the troops, they wore as a rule full kit with heavy packs. Their backs became drenched with perspiration, the bitter desert wind blew on them . . . and many deaths from pneumonia were attributed to this cause.'[5]

Meanwhile, the troopers are equally busy with their own training regime, endlessly taking their horses on long treks through the desert to toughen both horse and rider before making rapid attacks on a designated sand hill three miles away, and dismounting and firing a dozen times, before fixing bayonets and charging, and so on and so forth as the sun blazes down and they can return at the end of the day before the Sphinx that still never blinks at their effort.

As to the signallers, they too are flat out refining their methods of communicating over great distances by use of heliographs and flags – the former using flashes of reflected sunlight to communicate by Morse code, and the latter waving flags in both hands in such a manner that each double movement spells out a letter that another signaller can interpret. And even then, once the men are back in camp, there are frequently night manoeuvres to engage in, charging around in the desert moonlight until as late as 11 pm.

Inevitably under such hardships, strong friendships are formed between the soldiers suffering together, united in their common detestation of the Brass, the beggars and the endless cans of bully beef, known by them as 'tin of dog'. All together, the soldiers are what they sometimes refer to as 'F.F.F.' – 'frigged, fucked, and far from home'.[6]

For the gunners, there is also firing practice, and if the Sphinx is seen to wince at this, it is likely because, at least as local legend has it, just over a hundred years earlier the troops of Napoleon Bonaparte had shot off the Egyptian equivalent of a 'bullseye' – the nose of the Sphinx – while engaged in target practice.

Bit by bit, things start to gel. When the men had started this caper, they had been a motley mix of teachers, timber-workers, carpenters, con men, lawyers, labourers, illiterates . . . and, yes, perhaps a few reprobates and troubled souls eager to take this well-paid opportunity to get away. Now what are they? They are men of the Australian Imperial Force. Over the weeks, a certain *'spray de corpse'* – or whatever that French saying is – grows up between them.

Being Australians, there is always time for levity, no matter how exhausted they are. On one occasion, a company from the battalion of one of the AIF's most famous characters, Lieutenant-Colonel Pompey Elliott, are on the march near Cairo when they pass by a group of hawkers and their donkeys.

Left . . . left . . . left, right, left . . .

At that very moment, a male donkey becomes excited by a nearby female donkey, and the impressive manifestation of that excitement makes the soldiers roar with ribald laughter. Annoyed, the nearest hawker gives the donkey's ear a vicious twist, whereupon the lateral tension of the situation instantly dissipates.

Just a few minutes later, the Captain of the leading company is striding out, closely followed by his Senior Sergeant and the men when – *hulloa!* – here comes a carriage bearing two beautiful Englishwomen.

Company . . . Halt!

As one of the women smiles coquettishly at the handsome Captain, and he returns an enthusiastic salute in kind, a loud but laconic drawl comes from deep within the ranks: 'Twist his ear, Sergeant.'[7]

As for leisure time, there is frankly not a whole lot of it, but sometimes in lunch hours the men have such things as races between 'Arab stallions', with four or five men going up against each other over a circular course, while the rest whoop like madmen[8] – before a fresh batch of soldier 'jockeys' try their luck. Ah, how they laugh!

Another beloved activity is recorded by young Trooper Percival Langford: 'Just along side us are the pyramids. When you read about these things they are not usually retained in the memory, but when you actually see them you don't easily forget. At the very first opportunity we set out to climb the first of them . . . The view from the top is glorious.'[9] From there, they can gaze east at the shining ribbon in the desert that is the Nile River, festooned with the 'white wings gliding up and down [of] the triangular sails of the native dhows'.[10] Some enterprising Gyppos have even set up a small stall at the top, so the soldiers can enjoy the view while sipping on soft drinks and coffee.

Nothing, however, is more popular than taking the quick tram ride into exotic Cairo. Most particularly, they love to visit 'the Wazza', the red-light district. The most cosmopolitan place in an already extraordinarily cosmopolitan city, its narrow, winding streets are filled with Persians, Syrians, Sudanese, Armenians, Turks, Italians, Greeks, Arabs, French and other nationalities from all parts of the world. It is filled with hawkers and peddlers of all kinds, imploring the soldiers to buy their wares and always greeting them with such calls as 'Australi very good, very nice . . . Plenty money Australi . . .'[11] and 'WALKING STICK! Cigarette flag! Cigar, pos'card! B'ery goo-o-d!!! B'ery nice. Australia, b'ery goo-o-d! Baksiesh. Gib it–'alf piastre . . .'[12]

One shopkeeper is insistent: 'Don't go elsewhere to be cheated, Australians. Come here!' While another puts a sign out the front proclaiming to all:

ENGLISH AND FRENCH SPOKEN; AUSTRALIAN UNDERSTOOD.[13]

And the Australians in turn even learn a few words of Egyptian, such as *'saieeda'* for 'goodbye', *'yallah imshi'* for 'go', and, most importantly, *'bint'* for 'woman'.[14] For the most potent attraction of the Wazza is that it is *filled* with them – young women, old women, fat women, skinny women, perfumed women . . . *available* women.

They titter and teeter out from the balconies of the three-storey villas that lean towards each other over the streets, wearing dressing-gowns that tantalisingly flap open. They stand in doorways, they congregate in bars, they coquettishly flutter and flirt and flounce . . . and, most importantly, they root like ginger for as little as five or six 'disasters' (piastres), the equivalent of just a single shilling! And, of course, they want the Australians most of all, because these boys are the best-paid soldiers of all, on six shillings a day – even if one shilling a day is held back on a savings plan – while their British equivalents are on just a shilling. As to the New Zealanders – who prove to be not bad bastards, though it sounds like they trod on their vowels – they are on five shillings, while the French earn the equivalent of two shillings a day and the Indians get approximately a fifth of fuck all.

Helping to make the Australians feel rich, able to toss their money around like drunken sailors, is that they are actually paid in piastres, absurdly tiny coins that don't actually feel like money at all. And why not spend it in the Wazza? While a man can't buy any legal grog in Cairo after 6 pm, at the Wazza the beer flows all day and through the night, and let a man get a skinful of their particularly strong beer and *then* see how he goes resisting these sinful bints.

But still he is not weakening, you say? All right, then let him go to one of the cancan halls, where he can see a dozen or so women dancing totally *naked* – for many of the soldiers, the first nude women they have seen in their lives – and then see what happens! Mate, for just a few piastres, you can *touch* them, you can reach out and feel their swaying buttocks and pendulous breasts, and who can resist that? Not me, and not many.

As Sergeant Archie Barwick writes, 'Once inside these dens unless you have a very strong will, you are done for. They are places of the vilest description where the inmates would sell their soul for sixpence.'[15]

And, yes, maybe these whores are the cast-offs from the Marseilles brothels, in for stints as bints, for a bob a job on their backs in Cairo

. . . before they're also kicked out of here to end up in the whorehouses of Bombay, but so what? Apart from the fat Nubian Ibrahim al-Gharbi, who is the King of the Wazza – a weird one who dresses in women's clothing and wears a white veil – there really isn't much other authority, and you can do what you like. (The one exception to this absence of authority proves to be a beloved Salvation Army chaplain, the Reverend William McKenzie – chaplain to the 4th Battalion, soon to be known as 'Fighting Mac' – who regularly goes to the Wazza to drag drunken Australians out of the brothels and put them on the tram back to camp, before they can disgrace themselves.)

It's not just the alcohol that is intoxicating, though, it is the *feel* of the whole place: the perfume, the pimps, the passers-by of all descriptions, the music, the laughter, the squeals of delight and debauchery, the excitement, the sweet smell of hashish, the bloody fights that take place as you dodge the pools of vomit from other blokes who have gone before you and avoid ever more bints grabbing you by the hand to see if they can drag you upstairs. It's the sheer *thrill* of it, as you go looking for that Upper Sudanese woman they're all talking about, who is as black as the devil's hooves, stands six foot seven inches tall, and bangs like a dunny door in a hurricane!

Mate, you go to the Egyptian Museum if you must and look at your mummies, or search for that ancient sycamore tree in Heliopolis where they say the Virgin Mary rested on her way from Bethlehem to Egypt.[16] Me and the other blokes have no interest in mummies or virgins of any description and are going back up the Wazza to see the brown girls with the rosy red cheeks! And, yeah, I may even have another go on a rancid mattress, with the same bint as last time, but you can keep your sermons. I wanted my first time to be with sweet Annie from back home in Gunning, but it just hasn't worked out like that. If you and I are going to maybe die in battle, I, at least, won't be *dying* a virgin like *you*.

The what?

The venereal disease? Yes, of course there's a bit of a worry about that. Some blokes are pissing razor blades, and others have got the most shocking sores all over their old fella and worse. But I am sure none of that will happen to me.

You say this is why the authorities don't like the Australians heading into the Wazza this regularly – in such numbers, and drinking so heavily – consorting with the whores and so forth? So what? As a species, we Australians are locally notorious for not caring *what* the authorities think.

Not for nothing does the joke soon spread among the other troops camped there that there is an exchange that goes on night after night among the camp sentries:

> Sentry: Halt! Who goes there?
> Voice: Ceylon Planters' Rifles.
> Sentry: Pass, friend.
> [A little later]
> Sentry: Halt! Who goes there?
> Voice: Auckland Mounted Rifles.
> Sentry: Pass, friend.
> [A little later again]
> Sentry: Halt! Who goes there?
> Voice: What the fuck has it got to do with you?
> Sentry: Pass, Australian.[17]

And it's not just the authorities that many of the Australian troops have no respect for. A disdain for the local folk in general is growing wilder each day. For what started as amused wonderment – to watch them run scared from a scrub wallaby, to see that 'they won't work on Friday, they say their prayers in the open. Women are beasts of burden, child marriage, harems . . . ploughs drawn by a camel and a donkey harnessed together'[18] – descends quickly into a clear sense of superiority over them, and their *disgusting* and *backward* ways.

As one soldier later writes of the local women in a letter to his parents, 'The women, when they decide to have their clothes washed, once in 3733 years, simply wade right in and wash the clothes on them, at the same time filling their water jug for drinking purposes.'[19]

Generally, the men in these parts seem very timid, refusing to engage and even running away whenever the soldiers chance across them in the desert.

21 DECEMBER 1914, ANZAC: A LEGEND IS BORN

His name is Lieutenant-General William Riddell Birdwood, a veteran English officer of dapper distinction with long and successful campaigns in India and South Africa on his record, and he has been personally given a dashed important task by Lord Kitchener. That is to weld the Australians and New Zealanders into one comprehensive fighting force, an army 'corps' answerable to one General Headquarters and ruled by one Army Corps Commander – him.

After arriving with his senior staff at the Mena Camp on this morning, having travelled for nine days from his previous base in Bombay, Birdwood sets to with a will. Despite his lack of a soldierly air, and his rather nervous manner – his stammer is pronounced – 'there is no mistaking his perfectly wonderful grasp of the whole business of soldiering'.[20]

Right then . . .

This corps will have at its base two infantry divisions and a mounted division. To bring the New Zealand Infantry Brigade up to the level of a division, the 4th Australian Infantry Brigade will be added when it arrives in Egypt, as will another infantry brigade if it can be assembled. The mounted division will be composed of the 1st, 2nd and 3rd Australian Light Horse Brigades (the 3rd Light Horse Brigade will arrive in March) and the New Zealand Mounted Rifles Brigade.[21]

Commanding the Australian forces, of course, is Major-General William Bridges, while the New Zealanders are under the command of a British officer, a long streak of misery, six foot bloody six of him, General Sir Alexander John Godley.

Together, they will be called the 'Australasian Army Corps', and . . .

And oh no, they bloody well *won't*.

The men from the 'Shaky Isles' – as New Zealand is sometimes known, for its propensity for earthquakes – strenuously object to their own identity becoming lost in a name only two letters different from 'Australian'. (Truly? A lot of the New Zealanders, many of them professional soldiers in the image of Colonel William Malone of the Wellington Battalion, simply don't warm to the loud Australian soldiers with their hard-drinking and wild, whoring ways, and they will *not* be in a corps subsumed by their name. Simply put, at least from the side of the New Zealanders, the tribes of *coo-ee* and *kia ora* are not a natural fit.)

The obvious then beckons.

The 'Australian and New Zealand Army Corps', then?

Yes, that will do. Bridges and Godley are in agreement.

Now, of course, that is rather a mouthful to put in every cable and on every official document, and it is for this reason that, at a meeting in Cairo's swish Shepheard's Hotel – chosen as the Mediterranean Expeditionary Forces (MEF) headquarters – a discussion takes place as to the best code-word for it. The officers do so in a rather disinterested manner, trying out the sound of such names as 'Ausnew', which of course wouldn't do, as the New Zealanders would no doubt complain that their part of it is without a capital letter.

It is then that the lowest ranked man in the room, Sergeant K. M. Little of Feilding in New Zealand, comes up with the bleeding obvious on his notepad. 'Perhaps,' he says to his Major, 'the word the initials form, "ANZAC", would serve?'[22]

At this very moment, a junior member of Birdwood's staff enters the room and the Major offers this as a solution. 'ANZAC!' the junior member says, rolling it around his tongue. 'Hmm, sounds all right. I'll see the General.'[23]

General Birdwood likes it, and it is done. In a similar salute to equality, the New Zealand Infantry Division, which, along with the 1st Australian Division, makes up ANZAC, is soon renamed the New Zealand and Australian Division.

Broadly, the men come to quite like Birdwood and rather enjoy his sheer *English-ness*. He is the epitome of what they had imagined an English officer to be – with a mouth big enough to hold *two* plums. (Not that Charles Bean minds. Having spent his formative years in England attending the same school as Birdwood, Clifton College, he has one plum himself, and the two get on famously from the first.) And yet, despite that, 'good old Birdie',[24] as the soldiers refer to him, is not too bad for a Pommy, and he clearly has much the same affection for them. He is openly admiring of their physical strength, if not always their sense of discipline and innate respect for their English superior officers.

It will be the stuff of unproven legend – but the men love the story either way – that one of Birdie's officers, who wears a monocle, turns out on the parade ground one day to be confronted by hundreds of grinning Australian soldiers, each with a penny in their eye. With some aplomb thus, the English officer takes his monocle, throws it into the air, *catches* it in his *eye*, and roars at them, 'All right, you bastards, let's see you do that.'[25]

They cannot, and he has their respect thereafter.

CHRISTMAS DAY 1914, MENA CAMP, IT'S A BONZA FEELING BEING SHICKERED

Yes, for the Anzacs it is a strange thing to spend the holy day of Christmas in a land not so far from where Jesus was born, only to find that the locals for the most part don't care and actually spend much of their time doing what they do every day, banging their heads in the direction of Mecca, but such is their lot.

However, the soldiers are allowed to sleep in for once, and during Church Parade each man is given a specially embossed tin with an image of Princess Mary on the front – the same gracious lady who has donated this present – packed with a heady mix of confectionery, tobacco and spices.

Whacko!

And then to Christmas lunch . . .

For the occasion, large, temporary sheds are constructed and painted

white by the locals, trestle tables put up, with the whole thing decorated by palm fronds and branches of eucalyptus,[26] and a rough kind
of Christmas dinner served. 'Xmas under the pyramids,' Bert Smythe
writes home. 'Fine romantic for a penny horrible isn't it. Give a man a
dusty taste in his mouth wouldn't it. All things considered, dust, sand,
stew, wind, after dinner [aches], & other misfortunes – our Xmas was
fairly Merry & bright we have all survived the unusual ordeal . . . The
plum puddings that we were issued with, were about as big as a large
orange & were tied up in small pieces of cloth . . .

'We were informed that some of the puddings contained coins. But
I doubt it very much as they were made by niggers. After the food has
been disposed of, we knocked the heads off the wine bottles & we all
got Shickered. It's a bonza feeling being shickered, especially when you
reach the stage of seeing double or in my case fourble.'[27]

29 DECEMBER 1914, CAIRO, BEAN SPILLS 'EM

Just what is the role of an official war correspondent anyway? To whom
does his duty ultimately lie? Is it to the public or to his editors? Is it to
the rank and file of the army that he is covering or to that army's senior
officers, whom he is most directly answerable to, the same men he
depends on for continued access of information? It is a question Charles
Bean has great cause to reflect on, and it is an extremely uncomfortable
one. Particularly on days like today, when on the stairs of Shepheard's
Hotel he is rather brusquely buttonholed by Major-General William
Bridges, the man commanding the AIF.

Bridges asks him to write an article essentially explaining why, as
Commanding Officer, he is about to send more than a hundred soldiers home in disgrace for reasons varying between gross ill-discipline
and having succumbed to venereal disease. 'It is just as well,' Bridges
explains, 'that Australians should have some idea of why some of them
are returning, or else they will probably treat them all, on their own
representation, as heroes.'[28]

In the end, Bean agrees. For one thing, 'One gets very ashamed of oneself writing continually all is well when as a matter of fact all is not well. It doesn't seem fair to the people of Australia.'[29] So why not tell the truth, instead of writing the relatively trivial stories he is about to?

Certain he is doing the right thing, he starts to write the long article on his Corona 3 portable typewriter . . .

```
The last week has been one of some
anxiety to those who have the good name
of Australia at heart [for in Cairo]
certain scenes have occurred . . . which
are already affecting the reputation of
Australia in the outside world.

     I was speaking the other day to one of
the most distinguished men in the British
army. 'They are as fine a body physically
as I have ever seen,' he said. 'But do
all Australians drink quite so much?' The
truth is that there are a certain number
of men among those who were accepted
for service abroad who are not fit to be
sent abroad to represent Australia . . .
who are uncontrolled, slovenly, and in
some cases what few Australians can be
accused of being - dirty . . .[30]
```

Of course, it is not just senior officers and journalists who worry about the number of Australian soldiers going whoring. For many AIF soldiers themselves are gutted by what is going on, and no one more than 32-year-old Private Tom Richards, a 1st Field Ambulance stretcher-bearer. A famous rugby union flanker – both a Wallaby *and* a British Lion before the war – he writes in his diary on 29 December, 'I have not been inside one of those places, but I am told from six to a dozen soldiers are often waiting in one room for their turn. It also shows a terrible weakness in our educational affairs when young men must run this awful risk to get their knowledge of the world and thereby learn to curb their carnal appetite.'[31]

Still, not all of the encounters are sordid. Trooper Bluegum – despite having pledged his love to Jean forevermore – is one soldier completely smitten with a particular woman he has met out on the town in Cairo. 'I will never forget those Egyptian nights,' he would later reminisce, 'and one girl of girls. Tall and stately, like a queen she moved amongst the revellers. The rest of the dancers were just the frame round her picture . . . We danced. Her blue eyes laughed into mine . . . And the world has never been the same world since.'[32]

Somewhere between smitten and *bitten*, he simply cannot get her out of his head.

AFTERNOON, 31 DECEMBER 1914, ALBANY, HITCHING A RIDE

It is a measure of just how confident the Australian authorities now are that the Indian Ocean really has been swept clean of German raiders that on this afternoon, as the second contingent of troops takes its leave of Albany, bearing over 11,000 Australian soldiers and 123 nurses, nearly 2000 New Zealand soldiers and over 6500 horses on 17 transports, it is escorted only by the tiny *AE2*. The submarine is being towed by the armed merchantman turned troop-carrier HMAS *Berrima*, and it is ready to detach at a moment's notice and engage in battle if necessary.

On board HMAT *Ceramic*, one English-born soldier who in civilian life had been an accomplished artist, Ellis Silas of the 16th Battalion of the AIF 4th Brigade, records in his diary, 'A greyish day. Nature is sad. She weeps for us as we steam away close to the great bluffs of the coast of Western Australia. Far away astern of us there are a few specks getting ever smaller – the last sight of Australia – 'tis fitting that the dusk should be creeping on, for it was seven years ago that I saw these same specks of land at the dawn of a glorious day – that was my first view of Australia, the land which has been so much to me, which gave me my great chance in life, which I now leave perhaps for ever.'[33]

By now, at least, Ellis is far more used to his comrades in arms. He judges them to be 'very nice fellows, but rough; if only one of them had a greater comprehension of the right and proper place to use the past and present tenses'.[34]

The mood of *AE2*'s skipper, Lieutenant-Commander Dacre Stoker, by contrast, could not be more joyous across the board. For his idea has worked. After journeying to the seat of the Australian Government in Melbourne, he had obtained an interview with Defence Minister Senator Sir George Foster Pearce and passionately put the view that the best contribution Australia could now make to the war effort was to offer up *AE2* to the Admiralty in London. The Admiralty had subsequently accepted Pearce's 'generous offer with many thanks'.[35] And so now they are on their way.

True, it is a tad undignified to be towed all the way to Port Said behind HMAS *Berrima*, but there is really no alternative on long voyages. The main thing is they really might be able to see some action at last.

Equally pleased is Colonel John Monash, not only the Commanding Officer of the 4th Brigade but also the Commander of the convoy. For days, this citizen soldier of 30 years standing – the one-time dux of Scotch College, from a Jewish German family, boasting three degrees that rest on his towering intellect – has been so frantically engaged in the organisation of getting away that he has fallen ill. But now that they really are on the high seas, the sickness lifts and his spirits soar.

'The fleet at sea is a truly magnificent and impressive sight,' he observes. 'Standing on the bridge of the flagship . . . I can see the whole fleet spread out in regular formation and responsive to every signal as to course, speed and interval. I feel it is something to have lived for, to have been entrusted by one's country with so magnificent a responsibility.'[36]

As to Albert Jacka, the young forest worker from Victoria, he is nowhere so grand as on the bridge of the flagship but rather is right in the thick of the soldiers of the 14th Battalion, in the bowels of their troopship, HMAT *Ulysses*. And not for him, ramblings on the world and his place in it. Just a simple notation in his diary will do him: **Left Albany about 9. A.M. Journeying to Columbo.**[37]

LATE AFTERNOON, 13 JANUARY 1915, 10 DOWNING STREET, NO ... WINSTON ... NOT ... QUITE

The war is not going well, and the sheer exuberance of that evening so long ago in front of Buckingham Palace is now long gone. Now, just six months into hostilities, more than 18,500 British soldiers have been killed in the war, the vast majority of them in France at the hands of the Germans – while the Royal Navy has 4000 dead from ten warships sunk.

The opposing forces entrenched on the Western Front are now in tight deadlock; the frontline is torpid.

And there is a torpor in today's long meeting, which gets heavier and ever more dreary as the meeting goes on. No matter how important the discussion points, a blanket of dreary drowsiness inevitably settles over a gathering many hours in, and this meeting of the War Council at 10 Downing Street is no exception. Instituted by Prime Minister Asquith after war was declared in August, and meeting over the green-baize-covered mahogany table in the Cabinet Room, the Council's putative purpose is to reach quick and momentous decisions by dint of having all the key decision-makers in the one place at the one time. At least, that's the theory.

And yet, truly to this point, it has been the glowering Secretary for War, Lord Kitchener – all moustache, machismo and menace – who makes the key decisions. The nation's most revered soldier, 'Kitchener of Khartoum' does not take kindly to civilians – no matter how powerful they might be politically – telling *him* what should be done on matters of warfare. And this notwithstanding the facts that his is a Cabinet appointment and he is actually filling a civilian post, answerable to that Cabinet.

His attitude gives comfort to those present. 'Everyone felt fortified,' the Secretary of the War Council, Lieutenant-Colonel Maurice Hankey, would later reminisce, 'amid the terrible and incalculable events of the opening months of the war, by his commanding presence. When he gave a decision it was invariably accepted as final. He was never, to my belief, overruled by the War Council or the Cabinet, in any military matter, great or small. All-powerful, imperturbable, reserved, he domi-nated absolutely our counsels at this time.'[38]

On this day, however, there might be a change in the wind. Not only has this, only their eighth meeting in six months, been going since high noon – with only a brief break for lunch – as the shadows have fallen outside and the blinds have been drawn to shut out the winter cold, but the news and the plans are all so depressing. The casualty rate on the Western Front in France continues to be appalling and all for precisely no gain. Exactly as *The Labor Call* had predicted, thousands of soldiers from both sides continue to be 'massacred like grasshoppers in a farmer's wheat field'.[39]

This does not stop Field Marshal Sir John French, Commander-in-Chief British Expeditionary Force on the Western Front – seated right beside Prime Minister Asquith, who is stealing furtive glances at the letter he has just received from dear Venetia – from asking for yet another major offensive. Passionately, this longtime military man, known as 'a fighting general' (his walrus moustache bristles in rough syncopation with his personality), outlines his plans to strengthen the Western Front in key places. He needs 50,000 more men and is keen to break up the new armies such as the Anzacs and put them under existing formations of the British Army.

Asquith says little, and is in fact busy penning his reply to Venetia. Time dawdles in the stale air, as visions come of yet more waves of young men charging to their all but certain deaths. Papers are strewn across the table, and the mood is black. It is now that Winston Churchill, in his capacity as First Lord of the Admiralty, speaks up. A brilliant orator, a persuasive debater, a man with many gifts who feels at his most vibrant when organising those who bear arms, the 40-year-old has astutely waited all this time, until the meeting is at its lowest ebb, before pushing the plan he has been working on for weeks. It is a plan that really will at last outflank the Germans, that will bring the Royal Navy at last into play, that will likely knock out one enemy country while immeasurably aiding an ally country. If it can just be executed properly!

Yes, he wishes to force a passage through the Dardanelles. Once through the Narrows, His Majesty's Navy could steam through the Sea of Marmara all the way up to Constantinople and send salvo after salvo of heavy-artillery shells right into the heart of the densely packed and thinly defended city, until the Ottoman Empire is brought to its knees. Constantinople would fall, as would the Ottoman Government, and the blockade that keeps Russia from sending out its wheat to the world's markets would be lifted.

As he has vociferously advocated, 'An attack on the Gallipoli Peninsula, . . . if successful, would give us control of the Dardanelles and we could dictate terms at Constantinople.'[40]

A fortnight earlier, the War Council had received a personal appeal from the Russian Commander-in-Chief, Grand Duke Nicholas, that Britain make a 'demonstration' against Turkey, 'either naval or military',[41] so that his forces in the Caucasus could be relieved. This would fit the bill perfectly. At stake are the half-million troops of Balkan states – excluding Serbia, now busy fighting off the Austro-Hungarians – who had fought the Ottomans in 1912–13 and are clearly itching to do so again, to grab more of the Ottoman Empire, but who for the moment are remaining neutral until they see which way the war goes. With a forcing of the Dardanelles, those troops might very well come into play.

Churchill doesn't call his own idea genius, but that is certainly his belief – and that notwithstanding the fact that three years earlier he had written a Cabinet memorandum proclaiming that 'it should be remembered that it is no longer possible to force the Dardanelles, and nobody would expose a modern fleet to such peril'.[42] For he is now certain that, by sending 'a comparatively small naval enterprise, directed at a vital nerve-centre of the world',[43] so much could be achieved.

And yes, this *is* a subject he has raised before. At the meeting of the War Council just after Christmas, in fact, he had already made something of a case in a memo to the Prime Minister: 'Neither side will have the strength to penetrate the other's lines in the Western theatre . . . although no doubt several hundred thousand men will be spent to satisfy the military mind on the point . . . Are there not any alternatives than sending our armies to chew barbed wire in Flanders? Further cannot the power of the Navy be brought more directly to bear upon the enemy?'[44] The difference is that this time he actually has a plan to show them, by virtue of a large map of the Dardanelles, and copies of cables he has exchanged with Admiral Carden.

In an instant, the dullness of the day is forgotten. This is *not* like Sir John's plan, to keep throwing lot after lot of 20,000 soldiers at a time at the Western Front, in the hope that the Germans will run out of live soldiers first. Churchill's plan is, potentially, militarily brilliant, quick in results and economic with lives. This is throwing their strongest military asset right at the weakest point of the enemy's defences. 'The whole atmosphere changed,' Maurice Hankey would note. 'Fatigue was forgotten, The War Council turned eagerly from the dreary vista of a "slogging match" on the Western Front to brighter prospects, as they seemed, in the Mediterranean. The Navy, in whom everyone had implicit confidence and whose opportunities had so far been few and far between, was to come into the front line.'[45]

For the moment, the Western Front is mercifully forgotten, as all get to grips with the possibility of sending the might and pride of the British Empire, the Royal Navy, through the ancient thoroughfare of the Dardanelles, right to Constantinople. There is something magical in the very prospect. Constantinople – standing at the veritable crossroads of the world, the place where twain twines, where Asia of the East really does meet Europe of the West, where Russia from the North must pass to get to the Mediterranean in the South – in British hands? Wonderful!

And Churchill has been busy, all right, working out just what is feasible, and arguing his case, in the words of the eloquent Welshman Lloyd George, 'with all the inexorable force and pertinacity, together with the mastery of detail he always commands when he is really interested in a subject'.[46]

A fortnight earlier, gentlemen, on 3 January 1915, the First Lord of the Admiralty had cabled Vice-Admiral Sackville Carden:

DO YOU CONSIDER THE FORCING OF
THE DARDANELLES BY SHIPS ALONE A

PRACTICAL OPERATION? IT IS ASSUMED OLD
BATTLESHIPS FITTED WITH MINEBUMPERS
WOULD BE USED PRECEDED BY COLLIERS OR
OTHER MERCHANT CRAFT AS BUMPERS OR
SWEEPERS. IMPORTANCE OF RESULTS WOULD
JUSTIFY SEVERE LOSS. LET ME KNOW YOUR
VIEWS.[47]

Now, while Carden had replied two days later that in his view the
Dardanelles could not be rushed, he had added:

THEY MIGHT BE FORCED BY EXTENDED
OPERATIONS WITH LARGE NUMBER OF SHIPS.[48]

A week later again, Carden had followed up with his views on just what
would be required – that is, a dozen battleships, three battlecruisers,
three light cruisers, 16 destroyers, one flotilla leader and four seaplanes,
all of them supported by a dozen minesweepers and a score of attendant
craft. He also wants six submarines, as the key hope of them all is to get
the subs through the Dardanelles to the Sea of Marmara, where they
would be able to play havoc with the main line of supply and reinforcement for the Turkish Army on the Gallipoli Peninsula.

Having considered Carden's response, it is Churchill's strong view
'that a plan could be made for systematically reducing all the forts
within a few weeks. Once the forts were reduced the minefields would
be cleared, and the fleet would proceed up to Constantinople and
destroy the *Goeben*. They would have nothing to fear from field guns or
rifles, which would be merely an inconvenience.'[49]

And that is precisely what Churchill thinks should be done now.
Three heavily armed modern battleships and about 12 old pre-dread-
noughts ought to do the job. As a matter of fact, Churchill feels so
strongly about the prospects of forcing the Dardanelles that he has
already committed to the cause the fastest, most thickly armoured and
close to the most powerful warship that Britain has ever built, the just

commissioned and supremely modern *Queen Elizabeth* – classed as nothing less than a super-dreadnought.

Instead of engaging in her calibration exercises in the Mediterranean for no result, she could test out her recently designed eight 15-inch BL MK1 guns and all the rest on the noggins of the recalcitrant Turks. (These are nothing less than the most powerful guns the Royal Navy has ever produced, each one furnished with 100 rounds of high-explosive 1938-pound shells, at a muzzle velocity of 2458 feet per second – 1675 miles per hour – with a range as far as 33,550 yards at 30 degrees elevation. Who better to test them out on than the Turks?)

And Churchill will quickly arrange for the plan of attack to be communicated to the French – together with a request for the cooperation of a French squadron under a French Rear-Admiral – while it is hoped the Russians might provide naval action at the mouth of the Bosphorus at the 'proper moment'.[50]

Enthusiasm for the plan continues to grow. True, Great Britain had tried this before, when, back in 1807, Admiral Sir John Duckworth, in his flagship, *Royal George*, had led seven ships of the line and some smaller vessels through the Dardanelles into the Sea of Marmara – firing hard and being fired upon from the forts and batteries – before reaching Constantinople. Failing to incite the Turkish Fleet to come out and fight like men, after ten days he ran the gauntlet back down through the strengthened defences of the Straits, being fired upon and firing hard, before returning to Tenedos to count his heavy losses.[51]

But in these modern times, surely things will go much better. The Royal Navy has dominated the seas since Napoleon's challenge was met at Trafalgar in 1805, and the possibility of defeat is no more contemplated than the idea that any country in the Muslim world could seriously throw out a challenge to the British Empire, their sea-mines notwithstanding.

Churchill is not strong on exactly how those minefields can be cleared – lying as they do right under heavily armed forts – but hopefully those details can be worked out later. Nor is it precisely clear how the fall of Constantinople will cause those in Berlin to hold up their hands in surrender, but there is something so confident in Churchill's presentation, so compelling about it, that he is able to carry all before him.

For his part, Sir John French is appalled. His men are fighting for their lives on the Western Front and now the War Council wants to put resources into this eastern sideshow? Doesn't Churchill realise that attacking Turkey in this manner would be 'to play the German game'?[52] Far better, in his view, to keep what soldiers there are in Europe proper to, preferably, attack the Germans now occupying the Belgian coast.

Tension is developing between the 'Westerners' and the 'Easterners'. How are the British Empire's precious resources to be shared across the obviously crucial theatres of operation on the Western Front and those existing and emerging in the east? Might achieving victory in the east create a series of circumstances that contributes to breaking the deadlock in the west?

Recorded in the minutes, 'Lord Kitchener, "thought [Churchill's] plan worth trying. We could leave off the bombardment if it did not prove effective."'[53]

As to Prime Minister Asquith, he is generally supportive, though, as he writes in a letter to Venetia in the middle of proceedings, while 'now (4 pm) in the middle of our War Council, which began at 12', he is 'keen to tell you all about it, & see if it meets with your approval'.[54]

In the end, even French gives up and concurs with the now unanimous motion: 'That the Admiralty should prepare for a naval expedition in February to bombard and take the Gallipoli Peninsula with Constantinople as its objective.'[55]

At least one person at the meeting, however – even though he does not have a vote – remains strongly against the proposal. Only a few days afterwards, First Sea Lord Sir John Fisher writes to his one-time protégé, the Commander-in-Chief of the Grand Fleet, Admiral Sir John Jellicoe, informing him that the only way Fisher would support the Dardanelles operation would be if it became a joint military/naval operation, and even then it would need '200,000 men in conjunction with the Fleet'.[56] For without soldiers hitting the shores, how could the navy alone take out the mines and the forts? Sir John just can't see it. Every ounce of his six decades' experience in the navy – which he used to love with filial duty but now adores with a paternal passion – tells him that this is wrong, that disaster awaits. The young, ambitious Churchill may be prepared to wantonly sacrifice ships in the hope of advancing his career, but he, Sir John Fisher, is NOT. (His fondness for writing in capital letters is indicative of the fact that he also tends to speak, and think, in them.)

For now, however, Fisher's caution really does place him in the minority, while Churchill, for one, is simply intoxicated at the wonder of the whole thing. 'My God!' he says shortly afterwards to the Prime Minister's wife, Margot Asquith, at a small gathering at Walmer Castle, 'This, *this* is living History. Everything we are doing and saying is thrilling – it will be read by a thousand generations, think of *that*! Why, I would not be out of this glorious, delicious war for anything the world could give me . . .'[57]

Suddenly, the sound of clinking glasses and light chatter ceases. Taken aback at his obvious enthusiasm for war at a time when so many thousands are dying every week, his audience pauses so awkwardly in conversation that Churchill feels obliged to quickly follow up, not least because Mrs Asquith is an infamous gossip.

'I say, don't repeat that I said the word "delicious" – you know what I mean . . .'[58]

No . . . Winston . . . not . . . quite.

Some time before, Winston's wife, 'Clemmy', had even told Mrs Asquith that 'inventing uniforms is one of Winston's chief pleasures and temptations'.[59]

Yes, he is clearly a brilliant man, but what is also clear is that he is enjoying this war hugely.

MID-JANUARY 1915, AN UNFORTUNATE OUTBREAK

In the past four weeks, no fewer than a thousand men have been hospitalised with venereal disease (VD) – mostly syphilis, gonorrhoea, genital warts and herpes, and God knows what else, though most of them know something is up from the first moment they start pissing razor blades. The sheer number of those afflicted brings 'serious and far reaching consequences and introduced the medical service to its most difficult problem in the war'.[60]

Some men come forward of their own volition; others are found out when they are formed up in companies and submitted to what is known as a 'short-arm inspection', where they must present their penis to an inspecting doctor, and 'skin it back and milk it down'[61] so he can look for pus at the end of the urethra.

Notices are put up in every Mess:

Syphilis and Venereal Diseases

It is well that soldiers should realize that in this country prostitutes are all more or less infected with disease. There is absolutely no control over European prostitutes, and they, unfortunately are the most affected. Soldiers should also realize that in resorting to the company of these women it is not only venereal, syphilis . . . that is to be feared; many other diseases from which soldiers die abroad are directly attributable to infection from brothels, such as smallpox, enteric and dysentery.[62]

How to deal with it? Beyond quarantining the affected and administering injections that would kill a brown dog, while putting them on a course of mercury pills, the next thing is to dock the pay of all those hospitalised, including that part the soldier had allotted to his family, as they are no longer earning their keep. When out of hospital, those with VD have to suffer the humiliation of wearing white armbands. Lectures are also instituted about the physical and moral dangers of consorting with prostitutes. Some condoms are even issued – so thick are they it is debatable whether a nail could get through one, let alone a disease, and as to a screw . . . it gets to be rather beside the point.

Despite this widespread outbreak among the troops, it is so taboo – so shameful! – that few dare to talk about it, even to each other. They certainly leave it out of their letters home, and even their private diaries.

13–15 JANUARY 1915, PORT SAID, FORTUNE FAVOURS THE BRAVE

Nurse Lydia King doesn't believe a word of it, not one *word*, do you hear? Having just arrived in Egypt after the long ocean trip from Australia, the fetching 29-year-old with the full lips and lustrous hair – originally from Orange, via Royal Prince Alfred Hospital in Sydney – is on her way with a contingent of her fellow newly recruited army nurses to look after the men of the AIF, when she decides to have her fortune told by an Egyptian fortune-teller, just for a laugh. And that fortune, this exotic-looking chappie tells her, as he gravely turns over the cards that show her future, is clear: 'You will live to be a bent old woman, walking with a stick. You will be rather deaf but have very good eyesight. Next year you will marry a very nice good man, and have two children.'[63]

Marry next year? Her? Not likely. She is too busy. And the times are too turbulent. She has no idea even where she will *be* next year, let alone who she might be in love with enough to marry, so how could the fortune-teller? 'All this I reckon, bunkum,' she writes in her diary that night,[64] before resuming her journey the next day to Cairo, and thence to Mena Camp, where she and the three other nurses she has been travelling with are to be based.

As ever, she sticks close to her fellow nurse from Royal Prince Alfred Hospital, Ursula Carter, and they have no sooner arrived in this extraordinarily dusty camp than they receive a visit from Ursula's brother, Lieutenant Herbert Gordon Carter of the 1st Brigade's 1st Battalion. He seems . . . a very nice chap. Tall, handsome, with piercing eyes, the strapping 29-year-old has a caring manner about him and is so obviously pleased to see his sister that it is clear he has a very strong family instinct. That afternoon, they all hire donkeys to go all around the pyramids and the Sphinx, and laugh the afternoon away as the sun beats down. When Lydia momentarily falls off her donkey, Gordon leaps off his own in an instant to help her back up. And he speaks French!

Lieutenant Carter? He is himself quite a little taken with 'Nurse King', as he strictly refers to her in his diary. For believing in, and feeling comfortable with, strong women is simply in his blood. Something of a Sydney Grammar blue-blood from a wealthy Sydney family – his father had purchased the girls' school Ascham at Darling Point from its founder, Miss Marie Wallace, and had gone on to become its principal, instituting fewer tea-party-related subjects and more mathematics and natural-history classes – with a First Class Honours degree in Engineering from Sydney University, he is a refined man, but Nurse King's adventurous ways please him. It is no small thing for her and his younger sister to have come on such an adventure to the other side of the world, to potentially put themselves in harm's way to look after Australian soldiers, and just as he has vowed to his parents to do everything to look after Ursula, he instinctively feels protective towards Nurse King too. Apart from everything else, he likes the way the no-nonsense nurse refuses to sit primly on the donkey's side-saddle, the way a lady is meant to, but actually sits firmly astride a proper saddle, as that is the most sensible way . . . even if she does fall off. It feels good to help her up. That evening, he takes the girls to Shepheard's Hotel, where they dine at the table right next to General Birdwood.

LATE JANUARY 1915, COLONEL MUSTAFA KEMAL RETURNS TO ACTIVE SERVICE

The rather distinguished-looking military man, astride his fine horse, now arriving in Constantinople's dusty and bustling Beyazit Square attracts his fair share of attention and more. There is just something about him – his poise, his polish, his *bearing*, his piercing blue eyes and regal cheekbones – that makes the clutch of old men chatting and talking of the day's news turn their heads, as do the young women in their headscarves sweeping the streets, as does the man with the flock of peacocks, yelling his incomprehensible language that every herder must establish between themselves and their flock, and even his young son. Perhaps, too, at a generally lugubrious time, this man is beaming.

For although Lieutenant-Colonel Mustafa Kemal has enjoyed his time in Sofia – not least for the acquaintance of several delightful, educated women in a social life of fancy-dress balls and more European surroundings – he had been honoured and relieved to finally receive a telegram from General Enver's deputy, Ismail Hakki, ordering him to leave Sofia immediately and assume command of the 19th Division.

Colonel Mustafa's constant agitations to be sent back to active duty, to be back among soldiers in the struggle for his country, have finally been answered, and he now approaches the War Ministry through the soaring keyhole archway at its entrance – the very symbol of military power in the Empire – with delight.

Leaving his mount in the courtyard of the grand three-storey Ministry building, he walks up the stairs and through the marble columns to the office of the War Minister himself, the thin and pale General Enver, who has just returned from personally leading an offensive against the Russians in the Caucasus. Only Enver's moustache remains as upturned, waxed and magnificent as ever, while all the rest of him droops.

'You're a little tired?' Colonel Mustafa says.

'No,' Enver replies, naturally defensive around his ambitious colleague, 'not that much.'

'What's happened?'

'We fought – that's about it . . .'

'What's the position now?' Mustafa presses.

'Very good,' replies Enver.[65]

Not wishing to press General Enver any further, Colonel Mustafa turns the conversation to the subject of his appointment: 'You have kindly appointed me commander of the 19th Division. Where is it? And which corps and army is it part of?'

'That's right,' Enver replies. 'If you enquire with the general staff you'll get precise information.'[66]

Sensing that General Enver is deeply preoccupied and exhausted, and even a tad uncomfortable in his presence, Mustafa Kemal takes his leave and soon presents himself to the offices of the General Staff. Entering the bustling room, he announces himself: 'I am Lieutenant-Colonel Mustafa Kemal, Commander of the 19th Division.'

To his dismay, everything is so badly organised that his introduction draws nothing but blank stares. Kemal is embarrassed, being made to feel 'almost as if I was playing a confidence trick on them'.[67]

Within the coming days, he learns that his division is being formed at Tekirdağ, on the north shore of the Sea of Marmara, an area he is familiar with from his days in the Balkan Wars. Quickly, he begins his preparations to join them.

Chapter Five

'THE FATAL POWER OF A YOUNG ENTHUSIASM'

So, through Churchill's excess of imagination, a
layman's ignorance of artillery, and the fatal power
of a young enthusiasm to convince older and more
cautious brains, the tragedy of Gallipoli was born.[1]
*Charles Bean, Official History of Australia
in the War of 1914–1918, Vol. I*

It is my hope that the Australian people, towards
whom I have always felt a solemn responsibility,
will not rest content with so crude, so inaccurate,
so incomplete and so prejudiced a judgement,
but will study the facts for themselves.[2]
Churchill in reply, The World Crisis, Vol. II

28 JANUARY 1915, WAR COUNCIL MEETING

Bloody Winston!

For Churchill starts pushing it again, doesn't he? With other members of the War Council backing Churchill, Sir John Fisher can no longer stand it and breaks his 'obstinate and ominous silence'[3] to vigorously protest.

Now former Prime Minister Arthur Balfour is going on, waxing lyrical about the virtues of such a naval attack on the Dardanelles:

'It would cut the Turkish army in two . . . It would put Constantinople under our control . . . It would give us the advantage of having the Russian wheat, and enable Russia to resume exports . . . It would also open a passage to the Danube.'⁴

Sir John Fisher can no longer bear it. All these things might be true *if* the fleet gets through, but that is simply *not* going to happen. He decides on the instant to resign and is starting for the door when he espies Lord Kitchener looming large off his starboard quarter, closing fast and clearly preparing to engage. *Now.*

Clutching the older man by the elbow, Kitchener pilots him towards the shelter of the bay window, where the two can talk quietly.

Within ten minutes, Sir John Fisher has been warped back into his original berth and the meeting, which has not paused for an instant, continues.

Taking up the cudgels, Admiral Sir Henry Francis Oliver announces that the first shot could be fired in about a fortnight and that ships are already on their way. By the time of the attack, they would have no fewer than 16 destroyers, 24 French and 21 British minesweepers, and other small craft. For a forward naval base they have decided to use Port Mudros on the Greek island of Lemnos (which was taken from Turkey in 1912 and which the Greeks will surrender under 'protest' to retain their neutrality), situated some 50 miles from the mouth of the Dardanelles.

LATE JANUARY–EARLY FEBRUARY 1915, SUEZ CANAL, HERE AT LAST

Those who thought the 'unspeakable Turks' incapable of crossing the Sinai Desert to threaten the Suez Canal have been proven wrong. Yes, the Ottoman Empire has fallen on hard times, but it has enough kick left that it is *still* capable of driving major military forces over great distances, and one of them now stands, threatening the Allied defences at the canal itself, near Ismailia on the west bank.

Hence why Captain Stoker and the crew of the *AE2* are rushing through the canal at a pace of 14 knots instead of the peacetime speed

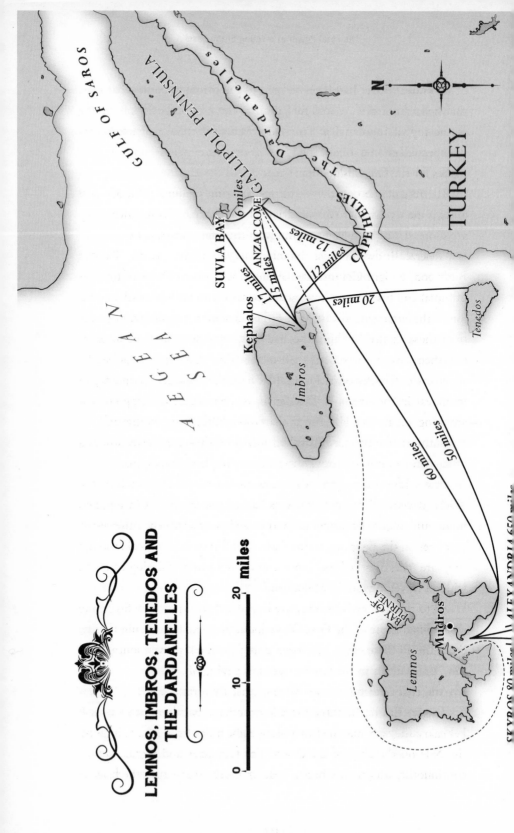

Lemnos, Imbros, Tenedos and the Dardanelles, by Jane Macaulay

of six knots. Stoker had been so keen to get through, come what may, that he had not even waited for permission, despite the risks. Arriving at the top of the canal at Port Said, Stoker is thrilled when 'orders unexpectedly come to join the Fleet off the Dardanelles',[5] and the *AE2* makes for the Greek island of Tenedos.

The rest of the convoy, meantime, bearing Colonel John Monash and his men, push on to Alexandria and then back to Cairo, where they are soon settling into Mena Camp with the other Australians.

General Birdwood (just anointed, if you please, as *Sir* William Birdwood, Knight Commander of the Most Exalted Order of the Star of India) and his senior officers are impressed with both Monash and his men – the latter generally being Australians of more substantive positions than those in the 1st AIF, who had taken a little more time to extricate themselves to become soldiers of the King. And they are physically superb, with Charles Bean noting, 'The huge men who at this time began to appear in the streets of Cairo gave the appearance of being built, if anything, on an even larger scale than those of the first contingent.'[6]

But, just like the 1st Australian Division, they are mostly stunned by their surroundings, though there are a couple of exceptions.

One soldier from Oodnadatta says he is most disappointed by the desert, declaring, 'It's not nearly as bad as the salt plains in my own home run.' Not to be outdone, another soldier says that the compressed carriages on the Egyptian trains make him feel quite homesick, though they are 'certainly a little more comfortable than the dog-boxes in which I travel to work in Melbourne'.[7]

As to the new arrivals, they are impressed with just how fit, strong and trained those of the First Divvy look, for there is no doubt that all the training these coves have been doing for the last five months, and most particularly in the last six weeks, is paying off.

And that training is never more intense than right now . . .

To give the 1st Infantry Brigade experience in night attacks, on 8 February they are marched to a place eight miles from Mena, high up the Nile on the edge of the desert. For four days and nights, almost continuously and with Charles Bean in close observance, the brigade goes through an endless series of sham-fighting and entrenching.

'In the short rushes of the final night attack,' Bean would record, 'the men, when they flung themselves down to fire at the end of each advance, dropped fast asleep. In some cases the next line found them in that state when it came up, and nudged them to go on again.'[8]

And yet the 3rd Brigade is even more impressive. They are engaged in a field day in the desert under their British Commanding Officer, now seconded to the Australian Army, Colonel Ewen MacLagan, when a sudden command is given that requires them to shift from their present location towards where MacLagan and Bean are standing, looking earnestly in their direction as the sun beats down. Two of the battalions are so far away in the desert, just this side of the horizon, that they appear as no more than a few vague dots, treading the silvery line where earth meets sky and mirages are born.

The British officer MacLagan has enough experience to know that at this distance it will be at least 15 minutes before they arrive and . . .

And what is this?

After just a few minutes, the dots thicken, enlarge, take shape . . . They are men. Big men. Running hard, the sweat coursing down their dusty faces in rivulets. They are the 9th Battalion – Queenslanders – coming on strong in a cloud of dust of their own making, like a boom of angry thunder rolling across the desert.

As they run past, Bean looks at his watch and shakes his head in wonder. It has taken them just *eight* minutes.

Only one machine-gun section remains out there . . . and here they are already, hauling their 30-pound Vickers machine-gun, a few of them lugging the even heavier 50-pound tripods on their burly shoulders, others the ammunition. Still others tote different guns as they all keep charging through the deep sand.

'Hurry up! Double up!' cries the officer, and so they do, throwing some of the gear straight into the waiting wagons while being careful with the more delicate instruments.

'Come on!' the officer roars again. 'We can't wait to lower that elevating screw.'

Within a minute the machine-gun detachment has departed, as Bean would describe, 'down the dip, the horses trotting, the men holding on to the carts or running behind – fading fast in their own dust'.[9]

Who knows what kind of action these men will see, but they look fit, strong, well trained and *dangerous*. And MacLagan – a thoughtful veteran who had served in India and the Boer War and is a natural leader of men – has clearly done an outstanding job in training them. (The only soldiers that come close are the men of the Wellington Infantry Battalion, where Colonel William Malone has continued to work them till they drop, weeding out all those not up to his rigorous standards.)

Tragically, other Australian soldiers have been judged at this time as principally a danger to themselves and those around them and, just as General Bridges had warned Charles Bean, are sent packing in disgrace. No fewer than 301 Australian soldiers – many suffering from VD, but 131 guilty of ill-discipline in many forms – are expelled back to Australia aboard the troopship *Kyrra*. Those with VD – mostly gonorrhoea, syphilis and genital warts – are kept in strict isolation. Their pay has been stopped, their pensions cancelled, their families informed of the reasons for their return and their names published in the papers. When they get to Australia, they know they will be kept in 'an isolation camp at Langwarrin'.[10] They, and all the others, will be dishonourably discharged.

8 FEBRUARY 1915, ALBANY, THE 10TH LIGHT HORSE REGIMENT, AMONG THE SEAHORSES

As the hot sun of the long day starts to wane, it is almost time to go. At last, after four months of training, practising their drills, bringing themselves and their horses up to the keenest pitch of fitness, the HQ, together with A and B Squadrons of the 10th Light Horse Regiment, is ready to leave Western Australia and head to Cairo, where in time they will meet the rest of the 3rd Light Horse Brigade.

Surveying them all, their Commanding Officer, Lieutenant-Colonel Noel Brazier, could not be prouder if they were his own sons. Alas, his admiration for the regiment is not universal, and just as *Mashobra* pulls away 'neath the caterwauling seagulls, and all the men are waving to their families, at this poignant moment – *should auld acquaintance be forgot, and never brought to mind* – the newly arrived Second-in-Command of the 3rd LHR Brigade, 49-year-old Brigade-Major Jack Antill, outflanks Brazier and attacks from a totally unexpected quarter.

'This,' he yells, 'is the worst disciplined regiment I have ever seen!'[11]

Now, the Brigadier-Major doesn't slap Colonel Brazier in the face with his glove as he says it, but he just as well might have. Brazier keeps his own counsel – just – knowing that if he allows himself to speak, the torrent of vitriol he has inside will blow like a volcano. But still Antill does not calm and a short time later makes further nasty remarks about Brazier's men.

As Brazier and others in the 3rd LHR Brigade quickly come to understand – though not excuse – this is simply Brigade-Major Antill's nature, just as a bird flies and a fish swims.

Hailing from Picton in New South Wales, Antill has been a professional soldier all his life – he was very likely *born* a soldier – and it is not for nothing that they call him first 'Bull' Antill and then 'the Bullant'. For just like a bullant, Antill is aggressive, military by instinct and exclusively *militant* in his approach to all problems. There is no problem so great that a bigger hammer and a louder voice can't fix in the short term. In all of the brigade there is only one man he defers to – and even then, only just – and that is 57-year-old colonial Frederic Hughes, described with rare dismissiveness by Charles Bean as 'an elderly citizen officer belonging to leading social circles in Victoria',[12] as in, his appointment has absolutely nothing to do with any military acumen he has ever displayed. Though Hughes certainly looks the part of a military man, with a world-class moustache, impeccable uniform and a back so straight it would put a ramrod to shame, he has never actually fired a shot in anger on a battlefield, nor been fired upon. He is obsessed with the form of the military, with no experience of the fury.

And so, while the driving force of the 10th LHR remains Brazier, the man presiding over the 3rd Brigade is the Bullant. As those men will all soon learn, he does not smile, he snarls. He does not converse, he dictates. He wants all the troopers in his brigade to hear him and *fear* him.

The Bullant is, in fact, just the kind of man that Colonel Noel Brazier most detests, and he has done so from the moment he met him . . . to save time. It is a detestation matched only by the one Antill feels for this Brazier upstart.

MID-FEBRUARY 1915, MENA CAMP, THE NEWS BREAKS

Have you blokes seen this? It's that bastard war correspondent, Bean, and he's been writing terrible things about us in Australia. Me dear old mum just sent me a copy, and she is none too impressed. Just read some of it!

Copies of the article coming back to the soldiers are passed from hand to hand, and the outrage grows as they see their names so slurred . . .

WASTERS IN THE FORCE.
SOME NOT FIT TO BE SOLDIERS.[13]

That *bastard!*

Charles Bean – mortified, finding himself crudely insulted by passing soldiers, with even threats that 'as soon as we get into the fighting, you will be shot'[14] – pens an open letter, pointing out that he was really only talking about a small minority. But this does not mollify one Sergeant Westbrook, who is soon widely published in the newspapers back home.

> On Our Critic's Apologies
> . . . So you say you're sorry, Mister?
> We sincerely hope you are,
> And we trust you'll tell our loved ones

In our southern home afar.
So just set your pen a jigging,
Write and never mind the rest;
But inform them all sincerely
We're behaving just the best.
There's a few we know who's throwing
Mud upon Australia's name;
But the rest's not going to carry
All the burden of their shame . . .[15]

Many of the men are sure to pen letters of their own, taking the correspondent down a peg or two. One Lance-Corporal writes, 'I suppose you have read all that rot by his wowsership C.E.W. Bean . . . It would be ridiculous to expect an expeditionary force to be all members of the Y.M.C.A. wouldn't it?'[16] Lieutenant Gordon Carter writes to his parents of such reports: 'The peculiar part is that most of their stories have some particle of truth, but that has been so exaggerated as to be unrecognisable.'[17]

All that Bean can do is keep his head up and console himself in his diary; 'Anyway, my job is to tell the people of Australia the truth.'[18] After all, isn't that what correspondents are meant to do, *come what may?*

16 FEBRUARY 1915, 10 DOWNING STREET, THE WAR COUNCIL MEETS

For three weeks now, Sir John Fisher, along with the majority of the Admiralty, has been agitating for a significant ground presence to be assembled to help the fleet to force the Dardanelles.

Although Kitchener and Churchill continue to believe it possible for the fleet to go it alone, Prime Minister Asquith does not. With the war going as badly as it is, the days of Lord Kitchener's say-so being enough to make something happen are gone.

The following key resolutions of this ad hoc meeting will later be regarded by Hankey as the very decisions 'from which sprang the joint naval and military enterprise against the Gallipoli Peninsula'.[19]

'1. The 29th Division, hitherto intended to form part of Sir John French's Army, to be despatched to Lemnos at the earliest possible date. It is hoped that it may be able to sail within ten days.

'2. Arrangements to be made for a force to be despatched from Egypt, if required.

'3. The whole of the above forces, in conjunction with the battalions of Royal Marines already despatched, to be available in case of necessity to support the naval attack on the Dardanelles [and] the Admiralty to build special transports and [small boats] suitable for the conveyance and landing of a force of 50,000 men at any point where they may be required.'[20]

The key object remains, however, securing that naval breakthrough, and Churchill, for one, is happy that a bombardment of the outer forts is then and there being planned.

7.20 AM, 19 FEBRUARY 1915, THE DARDANELLES HAVE THEIR OUTER DEFENCES TESTED

Following the attacks of the previous years, it is likely that the British Fleet will try to force the Dardanelles again, and so it is no surprise to the Turks on this misty morning when, just before 10 am, *Cornwallis* emerges out of the gloom, accompanied by *Triumph* and *Suffren*, firing from long range upon the forts on either side of the entrance to the Dardanelles that guard the way to Constantinople. Taking advantage of the fact that their guns can fire further than those in the forts, whose range extends no further than 12,500 yards, the three battleships stay off shore with perfect safety, launching salvo after salvo. All those on shore can do is keep their heads down and hope to survive.

That becomes more problematic when at 2 pm the ships close to 6000 yards and the fire becomes more accurate still, but at nigh on 4.45 pm the real test begins. Vice-Admiral Sir Sackville Carden sends *Vengeance*, *Cornwallis* and *Suffren* in to 3000 yards, to get in close

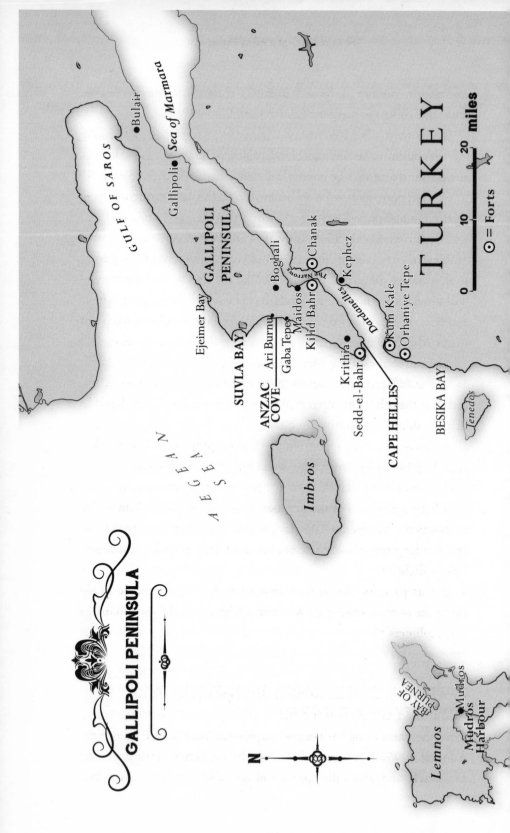

Dardanelles area, by Jane Macaulay

and pour heavy fire on those four forts, while also testing to see just what the Turks are capable of dishing back.

The answer: a fair bit.

That, at least, is the inescapable conclusion of Admiral John de Robeck aboard *Vengeance* after he has ordered the battleship to move even closer to the European shore so as to better inspect the devastating results of their up to 850-pound shells. Suddenly two of the forts, Orhaniye Tepe and Cape Helles, open fire. Clearly, they are *still functioning*.

Nevertheless, *Cornwallis*, which has come in to support *Vengeance*, soon achieves the greatest satisfaction of the day when, after several well-aimed salvos hit their mark, the fort at Cape Helles marked as No.1 explodes, in the words of the *Cornwallis's* gunnery officer Lieutenant Harry Minchin, into 'a perfect inferno, rocks & smoke, flame, dust & splinters all in the air together'.[21]

Beyond that success, though, there is not a lot more to show for the attack as the other forts keep firing, seemingly impervious to the shells that the ships keep pouring onto them.

Although the return fire from the Turks is only spasmodic, it's clear that the guns, unless suffering a direct hit, will remain intact.

At sunset, with the shortage of both light and ammunition, Vice-Admiral Carden withdraws the last of his ships and is firm in his summation: 'The result of the day's action showed apparently that the effect of long range bombardment by direct fire on modern earthwork forts is slight.'[22]

For its part, an official communiqué from Constantinople would claim the only damage done was 'one soldier . . . slightly wounded by stone splinters'.[23]

23–26 FEBRUARY 1915, LONDON, THE FIRST LORD OF THE ADMIRALTY LORDS IT OVER ALL

True, the whole thing has not gone as planned, but the First Lord of the Admiralty, Winston Churchill, is entirely undeterred. Four days after the attack, and now fully apprised of the whole affair, the man who is the principal architect of the whole scheme is holding court among selected guests after dinner at Admiralty House, and he divulges his growing view that to accomplish the scheme it really will be necessary to land a large body of men on the Peninsula.

Over cigars and port, Churchill pronounces himself 'thrilled at the prospect of the military expedition'.

'I think a curse should rest on me because I am so happy,' he exults. 'I know this war is smashing and shattering the lives of thousands every moment – and yet – I cannot help it – I enjoy every second I live.'[24]

At a meeting of the War Council the next day, Lord Kitchener asks, 'Are you contemplating a land attack?'

'I am not,' Churchill replies firmly. 'But it is quite conceivable that the naval attack might be temporarily held up by mines and some local military operation required . . .'[25]

In response, the disquieted Lloyd George asks, is it *really* proposed 'that the Army should be used to undertake an operation in which the Navy has failed?'[26]

'That is not the intention,' replies Churchill. 'I can only conceive a case using the military where the Navy has almost succeeded, but a military force would just make the difference between failure and success.'[27]

Lloyd George is firm: 'I do hope that the Army will not be required, or expected to pull the chestnuts out of the fire for the Navy.'[28]

Of course not, Winston Churchill assures him.

The War Council also looks at sending a force from Egypt, if required.

'Are the Australians and New Zealanders good enough for an important operation of war?'[29] Prime Minister Asquith asks Field Marshal Lord Kitchener.

'Well,' the good Lord replies, 'they are quite good enough, if a cruise in the Sea of Marmara is all that is contemplated.'[30] On the other hand, he adds a little later, the 8000 mounted Australian troops now gathered in Egypt are good enough to reinforce the Dardanelles, but it will still have to be the British troops who do the hard work.

For all that, Lord Kitchener still can't understand 'the purpose for which so many troops are to be used. What are the troops to do, while waiting?'[31]

Lord Kitchener has felt so strongly about it that he reneges on his original decision, peremptorily cancelling the transports to take his 29th Division – perhaps the finest Division in the British Army, just returned from their posting in India and Burma, and other far-flung garrisons – to Lemnos.

It is something that aggrieves Churchill deeply. 'One step more,' he would later recount. 'One effort more, and Constantinople was in our hands, and all the Balkan States committed to irrevocable hostility to the Central Powers.'[32]

But a defeat in the Dardanelles? The consequences are unthinkable.

British prestige would be damaged, risking a revolt in India and even Egypt, thus threatening the Suez Canal.

MORNING, 25 FEBRUARY 1915, MELBOURNE, AWAY AT LAST

It has been a long haul, but now the 8th Light Horse Regiment, recruited exclusively in Victoria, too, is on its way. Over the last five months, under the command of the recently promoted Lieutenant-Colonel Alexander White, the men have trained hard and gelled as a fighting unit, and finally received their embarkation orders.

On this day, as the troopship *Star of Victoria* steams out of Port Phillip, the men of the 8th LHR are peering earnestly at Melbourne Town, but none with more intensity than White, still wearing the locket with the picture of his beloved wife, Myrtle, and baby son, Alexander, around his neck. For unlike most of the others looking towards the shore, he actually has a chance of *seeing* his family, and brings his glasses to bear on the suburb of Elsternwick, where his family home lies.

By God, there is Cole Street! There is his neighbour, Armstrong, and his dog! There – his and Myrtle's lovely house, and there . . . there . . . there . . .

No, alas, he cannot see Myrtle and wee Alex, try as he might. They must be inside, drat it. Still hopeful, White keeps the binoculars trained until Elsternwick falls irretrievably behind and, more than somewhat deflated, he brings his glasses down.

Already well out on the Indian Ocean on this day, aboard HMAT *Itonus*, Hugo Throssell is impatient to catch up with the rest of the West Australian 10th LHR, the first contingent of which had left 11 days before.

Though hugely disappointed at being left behind, and missing his brother Ric, whom he has rarely been away from his whole life, Throssell at least understands the reason for it. His desperate hope is that he won't miss out on the action.

28 FEBRUARY 1915, IMBROS, LIKE A BIRD ON A WIRE

General Birdwood does not like it, not one bit.

Having been commanded to confer with Vice-Admiral Carden – based aboard *Inflexible*, now anchored in the lee of Greece's island of Imbros, just 14 miles from the mouth of the Dardanelles – Birdwood has journeyed there from Alexandria aboard HMS *Swiftsure*. His first concern is the horrible weather – the freezing cold, the thick mist, the low, heavy clouds – which means the ship can make no more than four knots.

More worrying still is Carden's lack of confidence that the Imperial Fleet will be able to do what it had been charged to do: force the Dardanelles. Most pointedly, it is his insistence that he 'must have troops to land and seize any position from which it might be possible to dislodge the Turks by the guns of the Fleet'.[33]

By which he means, of course, Birdwood's troops. But Birdwood is far from convinced that any such move is advisable, and less so when he boards *Irresistible* with his close friend and Carden's second-in-command, Admiral John de Robeck, and journeys as far up the Dardanelles as possible to have a look at the ground they might have to fight on. Of course, they cannot get farther than just beyond Morto Bay, around one mile inside the mouth, before the shells fall so thickly – from guns

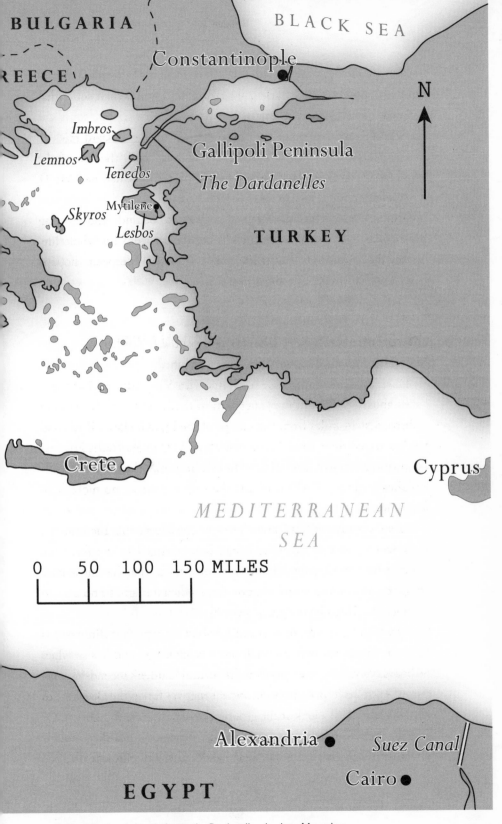

Gallipoli Peninsula in relation to the Dardanelles, by Jane Macaulay

unseen – that they have to withdraw. Beyond that, the weather continues to be appalling.

'In weather like this,' General Birdwood asks his friend, 'could the
Navy really land and maintain troops ashore?'

The Admiral's answer is firm. 'No. The small craft would soon be
smashed to pieces on those open shores.'[34]

A landing could be manageable with harbours, but there aren't any.
It all gives General Birdwood a great deal to think about. A bare beginning should have been to consult weather records before even starting
operations in this area, but it has not been done. Orders are dictated
from London by people consulting maps alone, with no appreciation
for local conditions.

And if the Navy Admirals themselves have no confidence in maintaining his troops ashore, how could anyone else? Yet, there appears
to be no stopping London, who are intent on this all going through,
whatever the cost.

It is a worry all right . . .

28 FEBRUARY 1915, MENA CAMP, 3RD BRIGADE ARE ON THE MOVE

It is a worry all right. It remains classified information, not to be
discussed openly, but there is no escaping the fact that 3rd Brigade are
packing up and moving out of Mena Camp. It seems they have been
selected for the supreme honour of undergoing some kind of special
training, somewhere, as a possible prelude to making a landing on an
enemy shore. Does this mean that the 1st and 2nd Brigade are going
to miss out? Like all those being left behind, the newly promoted
Captain Gordon Carter of 1st Battalion, 1st Brigade certainly hopes
not! Everyone has continued to train hard, and as the weeks have
passed they have become ever more eager to test themselves in an
actual battle.

As the 3rd Brigade march out in the afternoon, they do so to the
cheers of the Australian soldiers of the 1st and 2nd Brigade, and the

music provided by a combined band of the 1st and 3rd Battalion. Gordon Carter cheers with the best of them, but he still needs cheering up when they are gone; the camp seems so barren without them. And what better thing to cheer himself up than to take his sister 'Fuff' and her friend Nurse King out for another donkey ride round some of the native villages? By this time Nurse King is his friend, too, and though they are not 'courting', really, the two still manage to see each other whenever they are both off duty – going to dinner and dancing, visiting the zoo, riding on the scenic railway, climbing the pyramids, taking the donkeys 'Sphinxing', going for drives to the delta. For her part, Lydia King is impressed. 'Had dinner at Shepheard's,' she records in her diary. 'Gordon was in a very confidential mood, he is just a nice brother. I like him immensely; we spent about two hours at dinner and went out in the garden for a while, and watched the dancing . . .'[35]

For his 30th birthday, she gives him a lovely khaki tie, and he looks ever so smart.

4 MARCH 1915, THE WAR COUNCIL MEETS AGAIN

On this morning, Winston Churchill receives two telegrams from Vice-Admiral Carden in the Dardanelles, informing him that although bad weather has 'moderated operations', his latest estimate of how long it will take to get through to the Sea of Marmara, excluding bad weather, is just 'fourteen days'.[36]

In the meantime, at least all the forts at the entrance to the Dardanelles are 'practically demolished'.[37]

Having appraised the situation, Birdwood cables Kitchener, stating his contrary opinion, that 'it must be very doubtful if the Navy could force a passage unassisted, and . . . any military operations in their support must be of a major rather than a minor character'.[38] If it comes to a mass landing of troops, he believes Cape Helles will be the best spot.

Lest Birdwood get the wrong idea, Kitchener's reply on 4 March is stern:

> . . . THE CONCENTRATION OF THE TROOPS
> AT THE ENTRANCE TO THE DARDANELLES
> IS NOT SO MUCH FOR OPERATIONS ON
> GALLIPOLI PENINSULA AS FOR OPERATIONS
> TO BE SUBSEQUENTLY TAKEN IN THE
> NEIGHBOURHOOD OF CONSTANTINOPLE.[39]

But Birdwood insists. *He* is not looking from maps. *He* has personally surveyed the ground with his looking glass, and his cable to Lord Kitchener on 5 March is pointed:

> I AM VERY DOUBTFUL IF THE NAVY CAN
> FORCE THE PASSAGE UNASSISTED . . .
> THE FORTS THAT HAVE BEEN TAKEN UP TO
> THE PRESENT HAVE BEEN VISIBLE AND VERY
> EASY, AS THE SHIPS COULD STAND OFF
> AND SHOOT FROM ANYWHERE, BUT INSIDE
> THE STRAITS THE SHIPS ARE BOTHERED BY
> UNKNOWN FIRE.[40]

And when Lord Kitchener *still* tries to argue the point, Birdwood is unbowed, replying promptly on 6 March:

> I HAVE ALREADY INFORMED YOU THAT I
> CONSIDER THE ADMIRAL'S FORECAST TOO
> SANGUINE, AND I DOUBT HIS ABILITY TO
> FORCE THE PASSAGE UNAIDED . . .[41]

Another thing that worries everyone is the seeming inability of the British minesweepers to make any real headway in clearing a passage through the minefields. On the first three days of the month, they have made three night-time forays, coming under heavy fire each time. They are forced to turn tail – all without destroying a *single* mine.

6 MARCH 1915, CAIRO, WHISTLING IN THE DARK

And what's this now? As dusk falls on Maadi Camp, a curiously melodic but piercing whistle is heard. Heads pop out of tents and gaze at the source: a strapping member of the Light Horse who is striding up and down each row. With each few steps, another whistle.

And now a shout.

In his tent, Ric Throssell has been penning a letter home when he hears the very whistle he and his brother would use to get each other's attention from a distance on their farm at Cowcowing. He puts his head through the tent flap, and sure enough, it is Hugo, just arrived from Australia with the last contingent of the 10th Light Horse!

Ric returns the piercing whistle, and on the instant, Hugo turns.

'Ric, old man! Is that you?' Hugo roars as the two come together and embrace, Hugo thumping his older brother on the back. 'How are you? It's great to see you.'[42]

8 MARCH 1915, DARDANELLES, THE SEEDS ARE LAID

Slowly. Carefully.

With infinite caution, beneath a dim half-moon, the tiny Turkish minelayer *Nusret* gets about its business.

It is the graveyard hours – right on the cusp of being very late at night and very early in the morning – and the darkness is helped even more by the thick fog that has so propitiously rolled in. To even better disguise their presence from enemy scouts, the Turks have painted the sides of the ship black, a change from its usual battleship grey.

Captain Tophaneli Hakki, along with the Commander of the Mine Group, Captain Hafız Nazmi, is on a sacred mission, one so important that he has to ignore the fact that he had a heart attack just a few days earlier. With just 26 mines left in the Turkish armoury, it has been decided to lay them all here, in Erenkeui Bay, parallel to the shoreline. It had not escaped the notice of the Commander of the Forts, Major-General Cevat, that in their previous attacks in February, the British Fleet had often used this widest part of the Straits – about five miles from Asia to Europe – as a spot to turn around.

Despite the darkness and fog and light rain on this night, the few lamps the Turkish sailors use are shielded by blankets held up so that the light travels no further than those working with the mines. *No one*, no enemy spy who might chance to be on the shore, must know of this minefield.

Now, given that each mine is capable of sinking a battleship, let alone their own tiny vessel, the key for the men is not to activate them before they hit the water. Thus, the last act before submerging them, accomplished by the Chief Engineer, is to pull a pin situated on the topsides.

The upper half of each contact mine is studded with hollow lead knobs, known as 'Hertz horns', and inside each one is a glass vial filled with sulphuric acid. Should the hull of a ship come into contact with the knob, it is crushed, breaking the vial and releasing the sulphuric acid, which runs down a tube into a lead–acid battery, which lacks precisely that acid to generate an electrical current. The instant the acid hits, a current detonates the tightly packed explosive within the mine.

After each mine is carefully picked up off the deck by the steam-driven crane and lowered gently over the side and into the sea, it is quickly followed by the anchor and steel cable that will secure its position at whatever depth is required, and then that position is carefully – oh so carefully, my friend, Mehmet – noted on the map, recording the bearings of the drop to key landmarks. Ideally, the mines lie in a line, like an underwater curtain drawn in front of invading ships.

Well before dawn, allowing *Nusret* plenty of time to get away, it is done. The 11th line and the final 26 mines are laid in a north–south direction, 100 yards apart, a mile off the Asian shore. There they bob in the current, giant sacs containing the seeds of destruction for whichever vessel hits them, about two and a half fathoms below the surface. Just let any British vessel move through those waters and they will surely be destroyed.

It is with some satisfaction that, upon *Nusret*'s return to base, Major

Hafiz reports on their sacred mission: the enemy did not detect us.[43]

Allah be praised.

10 MARCH 1915, AT LAST, A BREAKTHROUGH

Finally, the cables from General Birdwood persuade the great man. If he says that the Dardanelles cannot be forced unaided, then Lord Kitchener feels he must take Birdwood at his word and – given that the situation on the Eastern Front in Russia appears to have calmed – on this day he makes his announcement to the War Council.

'I feel,' he says, 'that the situation is now sufficiently secure to justify the dispatch of the 29th Division.'[44]

Victory for the Easterners over the Westerners!

And so the word goes out. The 29th Division is finally fully mobilised, and the transports bearing them, which could have and should have left on 22 February had Kitchener not intervened, now prepare to leave on 16 March.

Perhaps foremost in the troops of the 29th are the 1st Battalion of the Dublin Fusiliers, 1100 strong, billeted at Torquay. It is with great relief that they finally receive the call-up, peppered with sanguine regret at leaving their fine hosts. Before departure, their Commanding Officer, Lieutenant-Colonel Richard Alexander Rooth – a 49-year-old graduate of Sandhurst who has been with the Dublin Fusiliers for 30 years – hands the regimental colours to Torquay's mayor, for safekeeping.

So highly regarded are the 29th Division that just a couple of days later they are even presented, at his request, to His Majesty King George! Formed up along the London Road in Warwickshire, this mighty force of 19,000 Regular Army veterans stretches no less than two miles, each man a model of military decorum, with closely trimmed moustaches, ramrod backs, pressed uniforms and shining boots. Their artillery gleams, and their perfectly groomed horses whinny in seeming unison. Not for nothing would one staff officer say of them, 'never has there been such a division'.[45]

And that certainly appears to be the view of His Majesty, as, with his entourage, he slowly rides his royal steed Delhi along the road in front of his soldiers, inspecting them. While the soldiers, of course, must show no emotion, and can only come to rigid attention as their Sovereign passes, His Majesty is under no such constraints and positively beams as he gazes down upon them. This 'splendid body of men',[46] as he refers to them, after they have done a march-past eight-abreast, are no less than a credit to the British Empire. They are the finest troops in the land and, likely, the world.

LATE AFTERNOON, 11 MARCH 1915, ABOARD *INFLEXIBLE*, TENSION MOUNTS

Anchored near Tenedos, Vice-Admiral Carden can barely stand it. Another morning, another cable from Winston Churchill pressing him to ever more action. Yes, the First Lord of the Admiralty is polite about it, but this one is particularly pointed:

WINSTON S. CHURCHILL TO VICE-ADMIRAL
CARDEN: TELEGRAM
11 MARCH 1915 ADMIRALTY
1.35 PM
SECRET AND PERSONAL
YOUR ORIGINAL INSTRUCTIONS LAID STRESS
ON CAUTION AND DELIBERATE METHODS,
AND WE APPROVE HIGHLY THE SKILL AND
PATIENCE WITH WHICH YOU HAVE ADVANCED
HITHERTO WITHOUT LOSS . . . THE
RESULTS TO BE GAINED ARE, HOWEVER,
GREAT ENOUGH TO JUSTIFY LOSS OF SHIPS
AND MEN IF SUCCESS CANNOT BE OBTAINED
WITHOUT . . . WE DO NOT WISH TO HURRY
YOU OR URGE YOU BEYOND YOUR JUDGMENT,
BUT WE RECOGNIZE CLEARLY THAT AT A
CERTAIN PERIOD IN YOUR OPERATIONS YOU

WILL HAVE TO PRESS HARD FOR A DECISION, AND WE DESIRE TO KNOW WHETHER YOU CONSIDER THAT POINT HAS NOW BEEN REACHED . . .[47]

What to do? For the moment Carden does nothing, bar worry himself sick.

Sick.

12 MARCH 1915, LONDON CALLING

Life is not a symphony. It does not flow, rise and fall, all as part of a rhythm whereby every moment is connected to the next by genius, man's or otherwise. Sometimes, extraordinary turning points in a man's life have no preamble, no hint, no hum, no nothing. It all just happens.

On this morning, General Sir Ian Hamilton is simply getting about his business at the Horse Guards – being Commander-in-Chief of the Central Force, charged with defending His Majesty's Kingdom – when, just as the chime of Big Ben is sounding ten times in the distance, an orderly arrives. The Secretary for War, Lord Kitchener, wishes to see him at the War Office.

The orderly does not have to add 'now'. With Kitchener, a summons is always immediate, and it would be unthinkable to protest that you have something else on. He is *Lord Kitchener.* He wishes to see you. *Now.*

As Kitchener's spacious office – amazingly sparse for such a powerful bachelor, who nevertheless likes collecting porcelain and adores flowers – is just a short distance away, it is only a brief time after being summoned that Lord Kitchener's faithful Aide-de-Camp, Captain Oswald FitzGerald, delicately ushers Hamilton into the great man's presence.

The 62-year-old Hamilton knows his superior well and, despite the fact that Kitchener is less than three years older, admires him deeply. Both men are longstanding career army officers and served in the Boer War together, where for a time Hamilton had been his Chief of Staff.

Kitchener does not even look up; he simply continues writing upon a notepad on his desk, for all the world as if he is still alone. Finally, he utters the words that, if they *were* in a symphony, would no doubt come with a clash of cymbals: 'We are sending a military force to support the Fleet now at the Dardanelles, and you are to have Command.'

The most powerful officer in the British Armed Forces resumes writing his memo without another syllable uttered or even a glance in Hamilton's direction.

Other men might have required written instructions to assume command of the Mediterranean Expeditionary Force, but given that Kitchener's word is law, there is no need.

But what is Hamilton to do, exactly? Kitchener does not say.

And so Hamilton, perplexed, pauses.

Finally, aware that this most senior of his underlings is still here, Kitchener looks up and says, 'Well?'

'We have done this sort of thing before, Lord Kitchener,' Hamilton replies. 'We have run this sort of show before, and you know without saying I am most deeply grateful, and you know without saying I will do my best and that you can trust my loyalty – but I must say something – I must ask you some questions.'[48]

Kitchener's frown and shrug in reply says it all: if you really must. But at least he does provide real information.

Hamilton will be leading some 30,000 Australian and New Zealand troops, a good mob already under the command of General William Birdwood, together with the 19,000 men of the British 29th Division under Major-General Sir Aylmer Hunter-Weston – who have at last been despatched two days before; the Royal Naval Division with 11,000 sailors turned soldiers under Major-General Archibald Paris; and a French contingent about 17,000 strong under Hamilton's old war comrade General Albert Gérard Léo d'Amade. All up, Hamilton would have about 80,000 men at his command, of whom at least 60,000 would be able to bear a rifle and take their place in the firing line.

Such talk starts to stir something deep within Kitchener. His huge moustache quivering as he speaks, the great man now gets up from behind his desk to start pacing the room and begins to wax lyrical as to the tremendous military opportunity that awaits Hamilton.

Why, with just this one clever strategic thrust, they might be able to swing the wavering Bulgarians and Rumanians to the side of the Allies!

'But,' says Kitchener to Hamilton with an airy wave of the hand, 'I hope you will not have to land at all. If you *do* have to land, why then the powerful Fleet at your back will be the prime factor in your choice of time and place.'[49]

Kitchener's vision for the use of Hamilton's troops is clear. They are not really a force of invasion to neutralise the guns, rather a mopping-up operation to be unleashed *after* the fleet has secured the Dardanelles, to round up the devastated Turkish troops before pushing on to take Constantinople.

Perhaps, Hamilton wonders, some submarines could help?

Kitchener agrees entirely but insists on the singular, not plural.

'Supposing,' he says, 'one submarine pops up opposite the town of Gallipoli and waves a Union Jack three times, the whole Turkish garrison on the Peninsula will take to their heels and make a bee line for Bulair.'[50]

Now, Winston Churchill has passed on to Kitchener that he is desperate for the General to leave within hours and has put on a special train ready to leave that afternoon. However, Kitchener is more circumspect, saying that there is 'no need to hustle'[51] as Hamilton must have enough time to get himself organised. In fact, he can have until tomorrow afternoon.

(At least in that time, Hamilton's Chief of Staff, General Walter Braithwaite, may be able to throw together a senior staff to help Hamilton.)

Typically, Hamilton's instructions are the Lord's alone. There is no input from the War Council, the British Cabinet, or the Cabinets of any of the dominions from which many of the soldiers come, like the Australians and New Zealanders.

He is Lord Kitchener. *He* decides. *He* has decided.

MORNING, 13 MARCH 1915, OFF THE DARDANELLES

No, the *AE2* has not seen action yet, but surely they are close. And it is stupendous to be here, based in Port Mudros on the Greek island of Lemnos with the rest of the Eastern Mediterranean Squadron and going out on daily surface patrols like this one.

Today, they are patrolling off the mouth of the Dardanelles, ensuring that no Turkish or German vessel comes out to launch a raid. As usual, Stoker spends much of his time working out the possibilities of taking his sub right up the Dardanelles, under the minefields, and doing what the British surface fleet has so far proved incapable of – getting through to the Marmara Sea and creating havoc.

True, the officers of the Royal Navy claim that 'the feat is impossible'[52], but Stoker is not so sure.

Yes, the navigation would be tricky, as would the minefields and avoiding the artillery in the forts. The current at the Narrows is a nightmare – with the fast surface current from the Sea of Marmara to the Aegean, countered by an equally strong undercurrent coming back – thought to be between one and five knots, swirling against them and constantly throwing them off course. And it is also true that one French sub – *Saphir* – has already come to grief trying to accomplish it.

But Stoker still thinks it might be possible. The key, he decides, is to go in darkness and spare the batteries by using the engines to go as far along the surface as possible before diving under the minefields and bringing the periscope up again around Chanak, to get their bearings. After a final dogleg around Nagara Point, the Straits widen out again and things will hopefully become easier and safer.

It could be done!

Stoker is sure of it and, as a matter of fact, so sure that he soon writes it down in memo form and sends it off, via his friend Lieutenant-Commander Charles Brodie, who works with Carden's Chief of Staff, Commodore Roger Keyes. Until recently, Commodore Keyes had run the Submarine Service and is said to be something of a man of action who might be open to supporting a daring attempt.

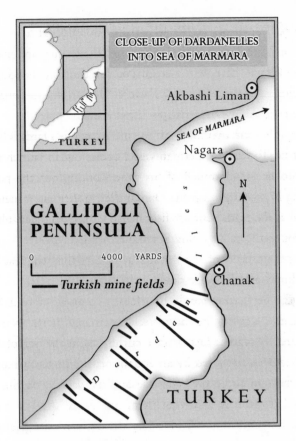

The dogleg at Nagara, by Jane Macaulay

'The feat could be performed,' Stoker respectfully assures him, 'if one exercises the greatest possible care in navigation.'[53]

AFTERNOON, 13 MARCH 1915, LONDON, HAMILTON TAKES HIS LEAVE

Typical Kitchener. After a frantic 24 hours of preparation, Hamilton now comes to say farewell to head off on the most important military operation of his career, and yet there is nothing in Kitchener's manner that acknowledges the scale of the task that has been set him. Hamilton matches the tone, and, as he will later describe it, says, 'good-bye to old K. as casually as if we were to meet together at dinner'.[54]

As Hamilton picks up his cap from the desk to take his leave, Kitchener says, 'If the Fleet gets through, Constantinople will fall of itself and you will have won, not a battle, but the war.'[55]

Erm, yes . . . quite.

There is little time, however, to reflect on such portentous words as the far more important task is to get to Charing Cross Station in time for the 5 pm special train on standby to take Sir Ian to Dover, in the company of the 13 officers who have so hastily been thrown together to form his HQ staff. As recorded in Hamilton's diary, they 'still bear the bewildered look of men who have hurriedly been snatched from desks to do some extraordinary turn on some unheard-of theatre. One or two of them put on uniform for the first time in their lives an hour ago. Leggings awry, spurs upside down, belts over shoulder straps! I haven't a notion of who they all are.'[56]

And, yes, Hamilton has always known that he is on an important mission, but that fact is highlighted by the presence of none other than Winston Churchill *and* his wife, Clementine, waiting there on the platform to see them off, in the company of a few 'dazed wives'.

A word, if you will, General . . .?

In crisp tones, First Lord of the Admiralty Churchill urges Hamilton to make haste, once in the Dardanelles, to land on the Peninsula whatever troops he can get his hands on, as quickly as possible. It is imperative the Turks have no more time to build their defences, don't you see?

(If Churchill is appearing desperate, it is because he is. He needs some success in this venture that he has sponsored from the outset, and he needs it quickly. For Churchill is now, in the words of Prime Minister Asquith to his wife, Margot, 'by far the most disliked man in my cabinet . . . He is intolerable! Noisy, long-winded and full of perorations. We don't want suggestions – we want wisdom!'[57] Only success in the Dardanelles will prove he has the latter.)

No, First Lord of the Admiralty, he doesn't see it like that at all.

Hamilton sees that it is his duty to do *exactly* as Lord Kitchener has asked: wait until the crack 29th Division under General Hunter-Weston has arrived.

Perhaps mercifully for General Hamilton, there is little time to discuss it, for with the locomotive hissing its steamy impatience and the conductors hovering, wanting these highly esteemed passengers to nevertheless get *'All aboooooard!'*, there are many hurried handshakes, familial embraces and wishes for a safe journey and a good result. Then, at last, just after General Hamilton kisses his wife, Jean, goodbye, the train pulls away.

Yes, such partings are always emotional. But, of them all, it is the most experienced man of the lot, Hamilton, who appears the most affected.

'This is going to be an unlucky show,' he says morosely to Captain Cecil Aspinall, his General Staff Officer, beside him in the carriage. 'I kissed my wife through her veil.'[58]

Soon enough, London falls behind in the backward night, and for the first time in 24 hours Hamilton has the luxury of a small time of reflection on the task ahead.

All else being equal, they are just four and a half hours from Calais, where another special train will be waiting to take them to Marseilles, where HMS *Phaeton* will rush them east across the Mediterranean Sea to the Dardanelles.

But do we have our intelligence reports?

Yes, indeed.

It will be Hamilton's claim – later heavily disputed – that at the time of his departure the sum total of all the intelligence he could gather about the likely field of battle was contained in the tiny manila folder he now carries with him. It comprises: a report on the defences of the Dardanelles, written in 1908; a very rough map drawn up in 1908, based on a French survey from 1854 for the purpose of the Crimea War; and a 1912 handbook on the Turkish Army.

LATE EVENING TO EARLY HOURS, 13–14 MARCH 1915, KEYES TRIES TO OPEN THE DOOR

This time, maybe they can do it. This time, beneath a sliver of moon, all the minesweepers are now manned by naval volunteers. They should have the backbone for the task of clearing the minefields from the Dardanelles.

After yet one more debacle two nights earlier, when the minesweepers had turned tail and fled as soon as they had been fired upon – there have now been seven minesweeping attempts for no mines destroyed – Carden's Chief of Staff, Commodore Roger Keyes, has now become heavily involved in reorganising and re-energising the whole effort. (This is typical of him. As a child growing up in India where his father had commanded the Punjab Frontier Force, Keyes is reputed to have announced, 'I am going to be an Admiral,'[59] and kept up his energy towards that goal ever since.)

'It does not matter if we lose all seven sweepers,' he tells the new recruits. 'There are twenty-eight more and the mines have *got* to be swept up.'[60]

The plan this time is to get the seven minesweepers, protected by the cruiser *Amethyst*, the battleship *Cornwallis* and several destroyers, through the minefield and then have them turn and work their sweeps – the always strong current behind them – on the way back down.

And yet . . . things seem . . . quiet.

Perhaps a little . . . *too* quiet?

No sooner is the pod of British vessels right in the middle of the minefields than the silent darkness is sliced by a dozen searchlights from the shore, then shattered by the all-too-familiar sound of artillery. Shells start to rain around the ships, sending up great water spouts. From both shores, flashes momentarily illuminate the hillside, soon answered by the return flashes of explosions from *Cornwallis* and the other ships. Meanwhile, the captain of the 3000-ton cruiser *Amethyst* bravely positions his ship to draw fire away from the minesweepers.

With far more resolution than has been shown previously, the tiny vessels keep pushing through the minefield. Unfortunately, at the turning point above the field there are just two trawlers still capable of operating, at which point the shells landing around them become so concentrated that it would have been nothing more than suicide to remain, and they start to retreat hastily.

At just this moment, *Amethyst* suffers two direct hits, killing 22 men, with many more critically wounded. So devastating is the explosion that the bodies of the dead, chiefly on the mess deck, are blown into so many pieces that the remains have to be collected in sacks and an attempt made to work out which parts went with which. Three men have been killed on other boats.

Some mines have indeed been culled, but the sober truth remains: the minefield barrier is essentially undiminished and remains as much a killing field as it ever was.

At least the British know one thing: with their best efforts, they cannot get the job done in this way. Though Keyes himself remains undaunted, Carden reluctantly decides on a change in tactics – a change as stark as the difference between night and day. Henceforth, he will send the sweepers into the Kephez minefield in bright sunshine only, after the forts that have been so hammering them are themselves bombarded.

Carden is devastated by the number of men lost in the engagement, and his feelings are little salved by a cable from Winston Churchill the morning after the failed attack, in reference to the *previous* failures:

I DO NOT UNDERSTAND, WHY MINESWEEPERS SHOULD BE INTERFERED WITH BY FIRING WHICH CAUSES NO CASUALTIES. TWO OR THREE HUNDRED CASUALTIES WOULD BE A MODERATE PRICE TO PAY FOR SWEEPING UP AS FAR AS THE NARROWS . . . OPERATION SHOULD NOW BE PRESSED FORWARD METHODICALLY AND RESOLUTELY AT NIGHT AND DAY. THE UNAVOIDABLE LOSSES MUST BE ACCEPTED. THE ENEMY IS HARASSED AND ANXIOUS NOW. TIME IS PRECIOUS . . .'[61]

Chapter Six

TESTING THE WATERS

Arthur Balfour: 'Consider the casualties. There must have
been nearly 10,000 men lost in these engagements.'
Lord Kitchener: 'Eight thousand seven hundred at Neuve
Chapelle, but it isn't the men I mind. I can replace the
men at once, but I can't replace the shells so easily.'[1]
Conversation recorded in the diary of Frances Stevenson,
4 April 1915

15 MARCH 1915, DARDANELLES, A TALE OF SMOKE AND SEWER PIPES

Driving along the road that lies by the sparkling Dardanelles on
this gorgeous spring morning, the host of the American Ambassador
Henry Morgenthau, Major-General Cevat – the Turkish Commander
of the Fortified Defences at the Dardanelles – points out with great
pride the minefields across the Narrows, now boasting no fewer than
400 mines.

Ah, but, Ambassador, you have not heard the best part. For many
of these mines – blocking the Russians from coming south and
the British from coming north – have come from the Russians
themselves!

With great gusto, Major-General Cevat tells the man from New
York how every day at the Black Sea entrance to the Bosphorus,
Russian destroyers release mines, hoping they will float downstream
to blow up Turkish ships – or even one of the German warships – and

how, every day, Turkish and German minesweepers 'go up, fish out these mines, and place them in the Dardanelles'.[2]

With every passing week, the defences of the Dardanelles are getting stronger.

The Turkish General goes on to outline the situation of their forts' guns, their recently acquired mobile howitzers and a number of other innovations. On that note, he summons forth a Sergeant, who leads the Ambassador over to a contraption that is no more than an elongated section of sewer pipe. But, as the excited Turks begin to explain, it is so much more than that. Communicating by telephone with those operating the howitzers, the Sergeant is quite capable of discharging this sewer pipe, filled with useless gun powder, at exactly the same time as the howitzers, and so attract – courtesy of the 'conspicuous cloud of inky smoke'[3] – at least his fair share of the ships' shells. The proof is the heavily pockmarked ground all around the Sergeant's faux gun, and Morgenthau is proudly told that the whole ludicrous contraption had attracted no fewer than 500 useless shots.

Lunching back at the Major-General's headquarters, Cevat and Ambassador Morgenthau are joined by three high-ranking officers, including Admiral Guido von Usedom, the man most responsible for strengthening the Turkish defences using German know-how. Most striking to Morgenthau is the officials' total confidence. 'What they seemed to hope for above everything,' the American would note, 'was that their enemies would make another attack.'[4]

They simply cannot wait – and the bigger the attack, the better.

One eager German pines for one thing above all else. 'If we could only get a chance at the *Queen Elizabeth*!' he declares, referring to the mightiest ship in the British armada.

Ah, but this is still not enough for one of the other military men as the wine continues to flow, and Ambassador Morgenthau ever after recalls his exact words: 'If the damn fools would only make a landing!'[5]

15 MARCH 1915, TENEDOS, 'THERE IS A TIDE IN THE AFFAIRS OF MEN, / WHICH, TAKEN AT THE FLOOD, LEADS ON TO FORTUNE; / OMITTED, ALL THE VOYAGE OF THEIR LIFE / IS BOUND IN SHALLOWS AND IN MISERIES . . .'[6]

And sometimes life's flood heads in the wrong direction, the back-rushing midnight waters filled with disaster after disaster . . .

It is not quite clear whether 57-year-old Vice-Admiral Sackville Carden is suffering from nervous exhaustion, an explosive ulcer or the consequences of a 'beastly suet and treacle pudding' he had eaten the day before.[7] Regardless, the upshot is the same.

After a sleepless night drowning in the horrors of the responsibilities of war, taking 80,000 men and over 200 vessels into the jaws of hell that lead to the murderous minefield – a plan that runs directly contrary to his desires – his aides find Carden that morning simply incapable of functioning. All he can get out in his highly disturbed state is that he simply cannot go on.

The Admiralty is advised, and, with relief on both sides, Carden is relieved of his command. He is replaced by Rear-Admiral John de Robeck – now promoted to Acting Vice-Admiral – a 52-year-old veteran of the Royal Navy.

Having raised his flag aboard *Queen Elizabeth* at Tenedos, de Robeck reviews Carden's plan for the attack. In 48 hours' time, three lines of British and French battleships – Lines A, B and C – will enter the Dardanelles, each wave in its turn and at an ever closer range, bombarding the intermediate forts and batteries either side of the Straits. Once these are neutralised, minesweepers will be sent forward to clear the waters, allowing the battleships to progress, if all goes well, all the way to Constantinople.

Despite having an uncommon old-world courtesy about him, Admiral de Robeck commits to the audacious plan to force the Dardanelles by navy alone. (Privately, de Robeck shares the view of all his senior officers: it would be much 'better to have a combined operation', with the army making a landing. The problem is he has never been 'consulted as to whether it was the right way to do it or not'.)[8]

In fact, even many of those who have been consulted are against the one-dimensional attack. One who has watched the Dardanelles campaign with rising concern is War Council Secretary Lieutenant-Colonel Hankey, who writes to Prime Minister Asquith on 16 March:

From the point of view of the War Council the situation as regards the attack on the Dardanelles is far from clear . . . As recently as the last meeting the War Council were informed by the First Lord that the navy still hoped and expected to get through the Dardanelles without the assistance of military forces. Now, however . . . the employment of a considerable land force is contemplated . . .

It must be remembered that combined operations require more careful preparation than any other class of military enterprise. All through our history such attacks have failed when the preparations have been inadequate, and the successes are in nearly every case due to the most careful preparation beforehand . . . It must be remembered also that one of the greatest advantages to be obtained from this class of operation, namely, that of surprise, has been lost . . . It is suggested that the War Council ought to cross-examine the naval and military authorities on the extent of the preparations . . .

Unless details such as these are duly thought out before the landing takes place, it is conceivable that a serious disaster will occur.[9]

Prime Minister Asquith?

He does indeed ask Lord Kitchener about one point raised – has a scheme for a land invasion been worked out? – and is satisfied when Kitchener responds that he has insufficient information on the subject, and such matters 'must be left to the commanders on the spot . . .'[10]

Then he gets back to writing a note to lovely Venetia.

MID-AFTERNOON, 17 MARCH 1915, TENEDOS, HAMILTON PARKS HIS PHAETON

Yes, it has been a frantic trip, but what a destination!

General Hamilton and his senior staff are pacing the quarterdeck of the sleek cruiser *Phaeton*, looking out upon the sparkling, impossibly blue waters of the Aegean Sea, when the captain suddenly turns the wheel to starboard and they steam through the white-cliffed heads of Tenedos Harbour, where the vista that meets their eyes is like manna from heaven.

For here, in this lovely wilderness, as one senior officer would recount, 'the bristling, threatening world of a British battle fleet burst upon our astonished view . . . As we paced the tiny quarterdeck of HMS *Phaeton*, throbbing from stem to stern, who thought of failure? Not the Chief, certainly.'[11]

18 MARCH 1915, DARDANELLES, MONSTERS IN THE MIST

And so it has come to this. After all the meetings, all the cables, all the prevarications and posturing, all the deep poring over maps and compilation of battle plans, on this morning, when the fog of war is both metaphorical and real, 12 British and four French battleships weigh anchor at 7 am. From their base at Tenedos, they soon get up a full head of steam and begin their assault on the Dardanelles. Glory be to the Empire, and let us see if we can put the fear of God and old England into the hearts of the heathens!

Along with *Inflexible*, the up-to-the-minute pride of the fleet, *Queen*

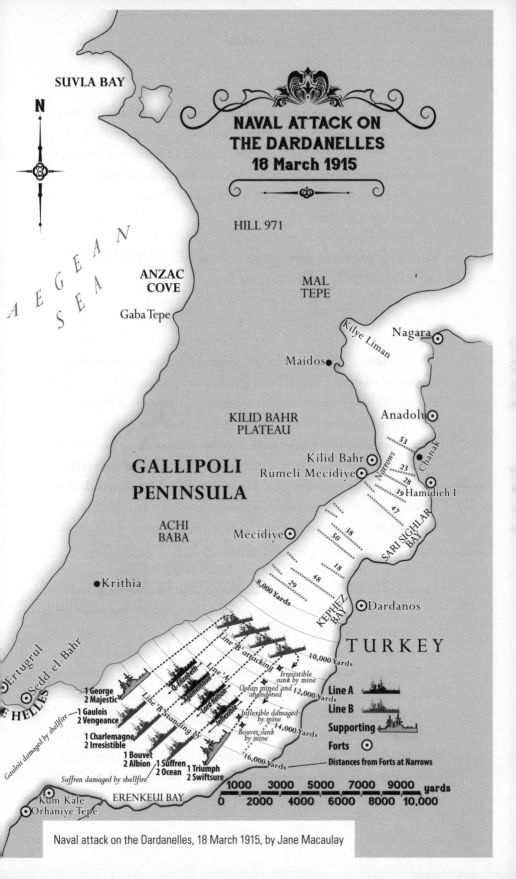

Naval attack on the Dardanelles, 18 March 1915, by Jane Macaulay

Elizabeth, glides imperiously at the head of the flotilla, the tip of the spear. Her guns are bristling, her superstructure is shining, and upon her bridge Acting Vice-Admiral John de Robeck's jaw is set.

The other battleships, formidable in their uniform grey garb, settle into their positions a little to the aft of their leaders' starboard and port, each one attended by a patrol boat assigned to go just in front and ward off any floating mines. Bringing up the rear are the vital minesweepers.

Surely the only entities unimpressed are the weary white peaks of Asia – peering down upon the aquatic cavalcade as they pass – having seen this all before, so many, many times.

—

As the morning mist starts to lift, a young Turkish soldier, looking out from an observation post at the top of a hill just south of Kum Kale, sees something. Definite shapes are emerging. Ships! *War*ships!

It is nothing less than the '[Imperial] Fleet making manoeuvres . . .'[12] Barely daring to believe his eyes, he watches carefully as the fleet turns and starts to charge towards the opening of the Straits! He immediately picks up the telephone and sends out the word: the infidel attack they have been so long preparing for has finally arrived.

News of the oncoming armada quickly spreads among the Ottoman ranks. Orders are barked and bells are rung. Officers and troops rush to their positions. As they do so, 'the sound of the morning's call to prayer, *Allahu Ekber*, rises up into the sky,'[13] reminding each soldier of the solemn duty before them. Even at the cost of their lives, they are to defend their homeland, in the name of Allah.

The Turks are relying foremost on the mines to defend them from a major incursion into the Straits, but the 14 old forts that line the waterway, boasting 82 guns in fixed positions, also have an important role to play. Just back from them are the 230 mobile guns and howitzers that are to aid them.

A little south of Kilid Bahr Castle, the 15th-century fortress standing across from the town of Chanak, the commander of the Rumeli

Mecidiye Fort, Captain Hilmi, calls for his men, now huddling together for warmth, to gather. After issuing his orders, the commander adds, 'No one will bother with the dead and wounded. If I die, walk over me, and just pass. And if I get wounded, pay no attention. I will do the same with you. Those who will replace the wounded and the dead have been determined. Don't expect any rewards in war. This, I will not and cannot promise.'[14]

Among the men walking away purposefully from the commander is Corporal Seyit, a tough, bald, squat timber chopper, renowned in his nearby village for his great strength. He is in command of one of the L/35 Krupp Fortress ten-inch guns. Under orders from Captain Hilmi, they are all to hold fire until the ships are within range. And then they are to unleash hell.

—

The hungry maw of the Dardanelles appears before Admiral de Robeck and the fleet, a maw that has swallowed whole tens of thousands of fighting men before them and never even bothered to spit out the bones. Yes, this is it, the entrance to the channel, a relatively narrow 4400 yards from east to west. It will be here that the first of the Turks' defences may now lash out at them.

Once through the mouth of the Straits, the fleet must continue to shrug off the cannons in the flanking forts and, more significantly, survive the fire of the many mobile howitzers the enemy has set up along both shores (under the watchful eye of their German comrades). About five miles in, the surviving battleships will reach the widest part of the Dardanelles – four and a half miles from shore to shore and just enough width for the ships to turn around – which continues for some three and a half miles before narrowing again. Fourteen miles from the entrance, the fort town of Kilid Bahr is reached on the western shore and Chanak on the eastern shore, and the 'Narrows', in their true sense, begin – just 1600 yards across at the thinnest point and continuous for five miles.

Beyond that, the Narrows widen again to a distance of four miles, until the town of Gallipoli on the western shore marks the beginning of the Sea of Marmara. If the ships can just reach that point, they can go all the way to Constantinople, 200 or so miles to the north-east. (True, it is expected that *Goeben*, *Breslau* and the rest of the small Turkish Navy will be waiting for them in the Sea of Marmara, but ideally the British ships will arrive in sufficient numbers to simply overwhelm the lot of them.)

Of course, it is the Narrows that is the true obstacle, and most particularly the five lines of mines that the British know lie across it.

Leading the way, *Agamemnon* enters the mouth of the Dardanelles, flanked by *Prince George* and *Triumph*, even as the destroyers and minesweepers soon move forward to clear any mines that might lie in their way. *Queen Elizabeth* follows them all, sticking close to the European shore.

Once Admiral de Robeck has his Line A battleships correctly positioned, he orders the hoisting of the signal flag 'Carry on' at 8.15 am.

Let the hostilities commence.

Among the gun crews beneath the turrets, each Lieutenant flicks the switch. A low buzz fills the air, indicating the circuit is now alive. All is tense and so quiet that they can hear the waves slapping against the side of the ship . . . until the calm is shattered by two rings on the fire gong . . . 'Stand by!'

Then another ring . . . 'Fire!'

'The air in the gunhouse, suddenly compressed then released by the great mass of the gun, was rent at the same time by the noise of the explosion. Before the reverberations had died away the gun's crew, with febrile activity, were reloading.'[15]

———

As are the Turkish artillery and howitzer crews lining both sides of the Dardanelles. With the infidels now in view, the bugleman blows his horn and all the companies engage in a finely focused frenzy of activity. Some bring shells, others open the breeches and calculate the

GUN TURRET
BL 15 Inch/42 Naval Gun

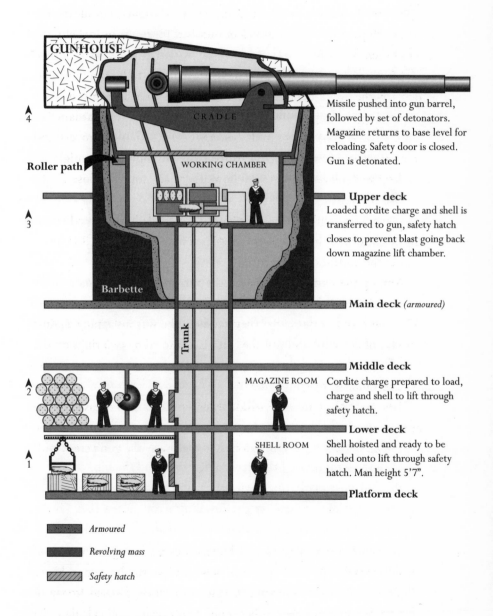

GUNHOUSE

CRADLE

4

Roller path

WORKING CHAMBER

3

Barbette

Trunk

2

MAGAZINE ROOM

SHELL ROOM

1

Missile pushed into gun barrel, followed by set of detonators. Magazine returns to base level for reloading. Safety door is closed. Gun is detonated.

Upper deck
Loaded cordite charge and shell is transferred to gun, safety hatch closes to prevent blast going back down magazine lift chamber.

Main deck *(armoured)*

Middle deck
Cordite charge prepared to load, charge and shell to lift through safety hatch.

Lower deck
Shell hoisted and ready to be loaded onto lift through safety hatch. Man height 5'7".

Platform deck

Armoured

Revolving mass

Safety hatch

Gun turret, by Jane Macaulay

ranges, while still more strain at pulleys to put the charges into place. Everywhere the men's faces are lit up with the special fervour reserved for those engaged in nothing less than a holy war. Above the shouted commands and the sounds of the shells being rammed into breeches and the breechblocks slamming shut, all that can be heard is the sing-song chant of the leader, intoning the same prayer Muslims have used before battle for all of the last 13 centuries: *'Allah is great, there is but one God. And Mohammed is his Prophet!'*[16]

There!

Just after 11 am, puffs of smoke are spotted coming from the back of the fort at Kum Kale on the Asian side of the Dardanelles entrance, to be shortly followed by a rolling boom and . . . spouts of water appear some 500 yards in front of the first ships.

To the fore, in the first wave of attack, Line A, is *Queen Elizabeth* – bearing the flag of Admiral de Robeck – together with *Agamemnon*, *Lord Nelson* and *Inflexible*.

In the next wave, Line B, just over a mile behind, is the French squadron, comprising *Gaulois*, *Charlemagne*, *Bouvet* and *Suffren*, with the British battleships *Prince George* on the port side and *Triumph* to starboard, riding shotgun. (*Majestic* and *Swiftsure* are to relieve these two covering ships in due course.)

Biding their time before they enter the fray, waiting just outside the Straits, are the ships making up Line C – *Vengeance*, *Irresistible*, *Albion* and *Ocean* – which will relieve the ships in Line B. *Canopus* and *Cornwallis* are held back in reserve.

With the fleet now into the Straits proper, it is the Turkish mobile batteries that do most of the spasmodic firing, and though some of the shells find their mark, the howitzers are too far away to actually bring concentrated fire to bear on the invading naval force. They are like boxers circling in a ring, throwing wild haymakers at arm's length.

But now, the field guns and mobile howitzers of the Intermediate Defences unleash a few glancing blows on the leading line of British ships, even as those ships launch their own salvos upon the forts at the Narrows.

Just before noon, Captain Hilmi stands at the head of his command post at Rumeli Mecidiye Fort, thinking hard. Though the enemy ships are not quite within reach of his guns – and his orders remain not to fire until they are – there is no doubt that his fort is within *their* range. Several shells have already knocked out some of his guns and killed several of his brave men.

They must at least try to strike back.

'*Ateş! – Fire!*' he yells to his battery officer.

'*Ateş!*' comes the reply through the megaphone, down the line, to the surviving soldiers manning the guns.

Just as they have trained to do for so long, the men are a-whirl with action. These massive guns are much like the guns on the English battleships now cruising in front of them, with one key difference – there is no hydraulic assistance to raise the shells into the shell cradles. Instead, the shells are lifted by hoists. Then they are rammed by mechanical and physical force into the breech before the breechblock is shut.

Upon hearing the captain's order, the men fire and a massive explosion roars forth – BOOOOOM! The gun recoils and a shell flies out of the muzzle towards *Queen Elizabeth* and . . . and within seconds . . . falls uncomfortably short.

The Turks rush up to the platform, remove the expended powder bags and swab the barrel for embers. A new shell is hoisted up and the process repeated.

As they are doing so . . . BOOM! Another giant German shell bursts forth. Again, no luck.

What the shots do achieve, however, is to draw significant retaliation from the fleet, which had hitherto been shooting blind (and often at the inky cloud of a decoy sewer pipe gun). But now, as the sound echoes and the smoke drifts up from Rumeli Mecidiye Fort, they have a set target.

As Captain Hilmi would recall, 'Because I started to shoot alone, nearly all the ships turned their fire on my fort.'

Within minutes, the battery is 'smothered in smoke from all the shells that landed . . . The artillery sergeants could not even see the sea, let alone their targets.'[17]

—

On the ships, it soon becomes apparent: the barrage of shells upon the forts is working, and the firing from the closest forts upon the British Fleet is falling . . .

On them once more.

Oh Lord.

Time and time again, just when it appears that a fort is taken out of the battle, suddenly its guns roar once more, and the ships are again under attack. Whether it is a Turkish ploy or the gunners are scrambling to regroup, the reason for their temporary silence is not clear. But the result is the same. For from one minute to the next it is never clear to the fleet just where the next shells will be coming from.

Now at midday, Admiral de Robeck judges it the right time for the French squadron to move further up the Straits, supported from behind by *Queen Elizabeth* and company.

The scene, as Winston Churchill would later describe it, is one 'of terrible magnificence. The mighty ships wheeling, manoeuvring and firing their guns, great and small, amid fountains of water, the forts in clouds of dust and smoke pierced by enormous flashes, the roar of the cannonade reverberating back from the hills on each side of the Straits, both shores alive with the discharges of field guns; the attendant destroyers, the picket-boats darting hither and thither on their perilous service – all displayed under shining skies and upon calm blue water, combined to make an impression of inconceivable majesty and crisis.'[18]

Around 1 pm, the line of French ships is coming into range of the Intermediate Defences – and this time it is the Turkish guns that take a toll as one shell hits *Gaulois* in its heart. So quickly does the grievously stricken ship take on water that all it can do is begin to retreat, and later beach herself outside the Straits. Both *Agamemnon* and *Inflexible* are also badly damaged, though both remain operational.

The fire coming from the mobile howitzer batteries on the shores continues to worry the mighty ships. Whereas the forts present obvious targets, and it is easy to see where their guns are positioned, who knows where the howitzers *are?* For the most part they are well secreted, and even if the ships are able to draw a bead on them, it is an easy matter for their commanders to whip the buffalo teams into action – yes, a team of buffalo is used to pull the howitzers – to change positions and keep firing from a new position.

Suddenly, just after 1.15 pm, *Suffren* shakes with a shattering roar as smoke billows and alarms go off. And the ship shakes again. And again! Several heavy shells land in succession, exploding with a blast of flame and seething shrapnel that knocks out a gun turret and incinerates the crew inside. Worse, a molten piece of debris falls into the port magazine, and the flames and burning gases are soon spreading. The explosion of the entire ship is imminent. With many of the communication systems down, it is simply not possible for the men to get a firm direction on crucial decisions. The ship begins to list under the weight of water flooding in, fire rages between decks, and men stumble and scream in agonies untold. The junior quarter-master who is responsible for the ammunition store most likely to blow, François Lannuzel, just 23 years old, reacts. All those who can must leave the store immediately, he orders, so he can face this alone.

It is obvious that the magazine needs to be flooded to douse the flames that threaten to detonate all the shells at once, and yet he does not have authority to do that.

And yet, it is obvious they will explode.

And yet, if he floods the magazines, all the injured men still in there, incapable of leaving, will drown.

And yet, if he doesn't do it, everyone will die anyway!

. . .

. . .

There *is* no answer to the last.

He smashes the glass cover over the relevant sea valve with his fist, turns the mechanism that opens it and, with blood pouring from his hand, races up the ladder and closes the watertight trapdoor behind him. Devastated by what he has done, and still unsure, he runs through the smoke and finally finds his superior officer, Commander Petit-Thouars. 'I hope I haven't overreached myself,' he yells over the tumult of battle, 'but seeing that the *Suffren* was in grave danger of explosion I've just flooded the magazine without orders.'[19]

(He hasn't overreached. French Rear-Admiral Émile Guépratte hails him a great hero, and subsequently Lannuzel is decorated with the *Croix de Guerre* and *La Médaille du combattant.*)

Suffren can fight on!

—

The choking, dusty air in the Turkish forts is filled with the screams of dying men, mixed with the low rumble of prayers to Allah. Nearly all is carnage and chaos, a blizzard of blood in most of the gun pits, human gore splattered on the walls. And even those few guns that are still firing are starting to run dangerously low on ammunition.

In Rumeli Mecidiye Fort, still subject to heavy shelling, several men are dead and over a dozen wounded. Those who can carry on do so. For half an hour, the battery officer has been incapable of commanding after a large stone dislodged by an exploding shell hit him in the back, but again he has taken the reins – only for a piece of shrapnel to destroy his megaphone and two of his teeth, and tear off a piece off his tongue. And *still* he keeps going.

Corporal Seyit is huddled with a comrade next to his gun. It is technically inoperable, the auto-loading gear damaged. But through it all, they continue to heed the orders of their commander: *'Ateş! – Fire!'*

—

Some two and a half hours after the battle has begun, just after 1.30 pm, it appears that the naval force has tamed the Turkish forts. The roar of fire has become a meek, spasmodic trickle. Seeking to capitalise on the enemy's weakness, Admiral de Robeck gives the order for the French wave to retire from the second line so that the third wave of British ships, Line C, can come into play. At 1.43 he calls forward the minesweepers, and these worthy vessels with their courageous crews begin trawling back and forth, operating in pairs, dragging 500 yards of heavy, serrated cutting wire between them. If all goes well, the tandem trawlers will catch the mooring cables and sever them, sending the mines to the surface.

Meanwhile, the French ships *Suffren* and *Bouvet* begin a slow turn *à tribord*, to starboard, making use of precisely that small indent in the Asian shore that is Erenkeui Bay to allow themselves good space. *Charlemagne* and the ailing *Gaulois* turn to port and make their way back down the European shore.

Suffren has successfully turned without incident, despite the damage, and *Bouvet* follows fast in its magnificent, frothy wake. Having just passed the British line, *Bouvet* suddenly shakes like a shot dog, an instant before a huge volume of billowing, reddish-black smoke shoots up from under her, now pouring forth from the starboard for'ard bow. And she is *listing*.

Before the shocked eyes of all observers, the French ship keeps keeling over ever further until she is more than 90 degrees from perpendicular and her masts go into the water.

Less than two minutes after one of the *Bouvet*'s magazines has exploded deep within its bowels, Captain Rageot shouts out to his crew, '*Sauvez-vous, mes enfants!*'[20]

Tragically, only 66 of his men are able to heed his command before, just a few seconds later, the ship 'slithers down like a saucer slithers down in a bath',[21] taking Captain Rageot and over 600 of his brave sailors to a watery grave some 30 fathoms below.

—

It is just after 2 pm. Suddenly the sea is filled with drowning sailors. On the European shore, Captain Hilmi believes it is the shells fired by his own men that have struck the mortal blow on the *Bouvet*.

He immediately gives the order: *'Ateş kes!* – Cease firing!'

The same command is clearly given by other battery and fort commanders, for as French ships race in to pick up what *Bouvet* survivors they can, no shells are fired on them until the men are safely aboard.

They have done it! They have actually *sunk* one of the enemy's big ships!

The battle rages on.

—

Just on 4 pm, a new ship enters the Dardanelles. It is *Phaeton*, bearing General Hamilton, who that morning aboard the vessel had completed his reconnaissance of the Gallipoli Peninsula.

Now, of course, General Hamilton wishes to have his first close-up look at what he would later recall as 'the dream of my life – a naval battle! Nor did the reality pan out short of my hopes. Here it was; we had only to keep on at thirty knots; in one minute we should be in the thick of it; and who would be brave enough to cry halt! The world had gone mad; common sense was only moonshine after all; the elephant and the whale of Bismarckian parable were at it tooth and nail! Shells of all sizes flew hissing through the skies.'[22] Hamilton watches closely as *Queen Elizabeth* moves slowly backward and forward up in the neck of the Narrows, firing all the while, as her attendant 'men-o'-war [were] spitting tons of hot metal at the Turks'.[23]

As far as he can see and hear, the forts are silent in reply, and yet behind them the concealed batteries continue to pour in their defiance. The minesweepers are steaming back and forth, specks in the vastness, dwarfed by the towering spouts of water and spray that rise up all around from falling shells, and here now is the *Inflexible*, some 250 yards away and heading out of the Straits. Hamilton observes closely 'her wireless cut away and a number of shrapnel holes through her tops and crow's nest'[24] – and then it happens.

Inflexible is hit! It shudders and shakes, and as the shocked Hamilton watches on, it quickly begins to list.

'My blood ran cold. For sheer deliberate awfulness this beat everything. We gazed spellbound: no one knew what moment the great ship might not dive into the depths. The pumps were going hard. We fixed our eyes on marks about the water line to see if the sea was gaining upon them or not.'[25]

Again, one of Lieutenant-Colonel Geehl's expertly laid mines has done its deadly work – all within some 50 yards of where *Bouvet* had disappeared – and the first explosion kills 29 sailors.

Still, *Inflexible* manages to stay afloat, though clearly lying heavily in the bows and listing to starboard. With just enough thrust from her engines, she is able to get away and head back towards Tenedos. The *Phaeton* and other cruisers attend her closely.

Just three minutes after *Inflexible* takes her near-mortal blow, *Irresistible* also hits a mine, killing 18 men, and her crew is quickly ordered to abandon ship.

The remaining ships continue to pour fire onto the forts and, sure enough, Rumeli Mecidiye Fort suffers a direct hit.

—

Several minutes after the shell lands on Rumeli Mecidiye – causing shrapnel, flying shards of rock and screams – Corporal Seyit sits up from where he has passed out. All around him, through the smoke and dust, strewn around their damaged gun, he sees the dismembered bodies of his friends and remembers his commander's words from that morning: 'No one will bother with the dead and wounded.'[26]

At that instant he looks hard through the haze in front of him and sees his slender comrade, Ali.

'We have 14 martyrs and 24 wounded,' Ali yells to him. 'It is just you and I left standing.'[27]

Seyit stumbles to his battery's rampart and looks over it. The infidel ships are still there, *still* firing on their land. And now he notices something else. One of the artillery shells remains intact.

'Come, Ali,' he says. 'Help me get this shell loaded onto my back.'

Ali, knowing that the shell is some 300 pounds, looks at him in complete disbelief – it will take at least *four* men to lift it.

'You can't, Seyit,' he says flatly.

'Let's give it a try, at least.'[28]

And merely a try it is, for, as it is covered in grease, they cannot get a grip. After rubbing their hands in the dirt, they make another attempt, even as the roar of the enemy artillery goes on, and this time, *this time*, they manage to hoist it on Seyit's back.

Slowly, carefully, straining with every fibre of his being, Seyit begins to shuffle towards the stairs leading up to the gun, two yards above the ground. He grunts, he groans, he *continues to climb* – Ali suffering every step of the way with him, as he sees the pain his friend is going through – and on reaching the top of the stairs Seyit manages to actually get the shell in the gun, which, despite being damaged, might still be able to fire.

Taking approximate aim, Seyit pulls the firing mechanism and the cannon roars.

It will be the stuff of cherished – if disputed – Turkish legend ever after that it is this shell that also strikes a significant blow.

—

Whether by mine or shell, it is not clear, but just after 6 pm – near the same spot where *Bouvet, Inflexible* and *Irresistible* have come to grief – *Ocean* is now decisively hit, with the resultant explosion destroying the ship's capacity to steer, reducing the magnificent battleship to an abandoned hulk doing figure eights on the Dardanelles as the Turkish gunners pour fire onto her . . .

All is mayhem and madness, and with discretion the better part of valour, de Robeck gives the order and the signal to withdraw is hoisted. Battered and bloodied, and entirely stunned that the Turks have been able to give them such a mauling, the once imperious Imperial Fleet, along with its French allies, turns tail and leaves the Dardanelles. And yet, perhaps not as stunned as the Turks themselves . . .

—

Whatever happens, Captain Mehmet Hilmi could not be prouder of his men. Descending from his lookout post, he now walks among the brave soldiers, many of whom are severely wounded – even the battery officer has stayed till the end, despite having part of his tongue cut off by shrapnel.

'I talked to them like a father talks to his son,' Hilmi would later recall. 'It was heartbreaking. Their wounds were very serious, but they didn't want to grieve me, so they spent their last effort trying to hide their suffering.'[29]

Of all the forts, the Rumeli Mecidiye has sustained the most casualties: 12 dead and 30 wounded.

Watching the enemy ships finally retreating through the Straits, the Chief of Staff of the Fortified Defences, Major Selahattin Âdil, takes a deep breath.

'As night began to fall . . .' he would later recount, 'our hearts [were] full of gratitude and thanks to Allah for assuring our people this important victory.'[30]

Meanwhile, the Commander of the Mine Group, Captain Hafız Nazmi, who had been out on the silent mission to lay the last auspicious row of mines at Erenkeui, is ecstatic that their plan has worked. He sits down for the first time that day and writes a diary entry with far more emotion than his usual cursory note: '. . . ships hit the mine; the mines we lay at Erenkeui!'[31]

At fortress command's headquarters, the officers line up to congratulate their Commander, Major-General Cevat. There is a feeling of deep reflection in the room as the men come to terms with the victory – the victory for their people, their fatherland. '*Şahıslar gelip geçici, millet daimidir.* Individuals come and go, but a People is forever.'[32]

After the moment passes, the Turks realise how much they have to do. First, they must determine the number of casualties and take stock of the state of their defences. With communications down, they are in the dark about how they have fared on the ground. They must not delay. Tomorrow could bring more attacks. Long through the night and into the next day, the Ottoman officers and soldiers work to repair the damaged guns and redistribute ammunition. Overall, the Turkish defenders have been fortunate, incurring just 29 fatalities and 68 wounded.[33]

After everything has calmed, in a tired stupor late that night, Captain Hafiz Nazmi takes out his diary and notes, 'Thanks be to Allah no great damage was done to our forts.'[34]

—

The same cannot be said of the Allied ships, nor of their Commander the next day after a sleepless night. With only 12 of the 18 warships that had gone into battle still capable of re-entering the fray, the 'somewhat depressed' Admiral de Robeck refers to the events of previous day as a 'disaster',[35] and is even surprised that he has not been sacked.[36]

General Ian Hamilton is also shocked and has no hesitation in making his feelings known to Lord Kitchener in a cable:

I AM BEING MOST RELUCTANTLY DRIVEN TO THE CONCLUSION THAT THE STRAITS ARE NOT LIKELY TO BE FORCED BY BATTLESHIPS [ALONE]. THE ARMY'S PART WILL BE MORE THAN MERE LANDING OF PARTIES TO DESTROY FORTS, IT MUST BE A DELIBERATE AND PROGRESSIVE MILITARY OPERATION CARRIED OUT AT FULL STRENGTH SO AS TO OPEN A PASSAGE FOR THE NAVY.[37]

The answer from Lord Kitchener in London is not long in coming:

YOU KNOW MY VIEW THAT THE DARDANELLES PASSAGE MUST BE FORCED, AND THAT IF LARGE MILITARY OPERATIONS ON THE

GALLIPOLI PENINSULA BY YOUR TROOPS ARE NECESSARY TO CLEAR THE WAY, THOSE OPERATIONS MUST BE UNDERTAKEN.[38]

So it is all coming back to the army.

The commander of the Anzacs, General Birdwood, is not in the least surprised. He strongly puts to General Hamilton his view that the Royal Navy has 'shot their bolt'.[39] It is obvious to him that they will not be having another go. There is now no time to lose in getting ready for a landing.

For his part, Admiral de Robeck's Chief of Staff, Commodore Roger Keyes, is outraged at the lack of resolution shown by his superior officer. It is his overwhelming view that the Turks are now vulnerable, that the fleet must go in again, and quickly, as soon as the strong wind now blowing abates. But nothing he says or does can convince the only officer who can make such a decision on the spot, Admiral John de Robeck, to do so.

Very quietly, it is Keyes' strong opinion that from the moment of losing the three battleships, de Robeck had 'ceased to exist' as 'a fighting admiral'.[40]

On his side, Churchill is so sure de Robeck *will* attack again shortly that he quickly despatches the battleships *London* and *Prince of Wales* to join *Queen* and *Implacable*, which are already on their way.

10 AM, 22 MARCH 1915, LEMNOS, ENTER, A MAN WITH A PLAN, PULLING A CHESTNUT OUT OF THE FIRE

General Hamilton, Admiral de Robeck, General Birdwood, General Braithwaite and the Base Commander at Lemnos, Admiral Rosslyn Wemyss, are in deep conference in a private wardroom on *Queen Elizabeth*, moored in Mudros Harbour on Lemnos, and dealing with a difficult task. Once again, they must determine how to force the Dardanelles, as London is demanding with ever greater urgency.

Again, they wrestle with the key problem, as later characterised by

Admiral Wemyss: 'The battleships could not force the Straits until the mine field had been cleared – the mine field could not be cleared until the concealed guns which defended them were destroyed – they could not be destroyed until the Peninsula was in our hands, hence we should have to seize it with the Army.'[41]

From the first, de Robeck is outspoken on that very view.

'I am quite clear,' he says to his army confederates, 'that the Navy cannot get through without the help of all your troops.'[42] Well, then . . .

Generals Hamilton, Birdwood and Braithwaite exchange looks. With an agreement beforehand to say nothing for or against land operations until the sailors abandon the idea of forcing the passage by ships alone, it is clear their worst fears are realised. Up front, the navy men have asked for the army's assistance.

The five military men turn to the task of planning one of the largest amphibious invasions in history. As General Hamilton would later record in his diary, *The sailors want me to pull this particular chestnut out of the fire.*[43]

Quietly, General Hamilton is distressed by just how much there is to organise. '[Had I been a German general,]' he would later comment, 'plans for a landing in Gallipoli would have been in my pocket – up-to-date and worked out to a ball cartridge and a pail of water.'[44]

Not only does Hamilton have no such plan, he does not even have a full staff to advise him on logistics at the most basic level: Where will their fresh water supply come from? How will the wounded be evacuated? Where will they *land*?

And of no small importance, just how many Turkish soldiers would be defending the Peninsula? The intelligence estimate is that there may be as many as 40,000, with perhaps another 30,000 above Bulair and an undetermined number of divisions on the Asian side. It is possible that the 75,000 men the Allies are about to throw into the fray could be taking on 100,000 soldiers.

As to when to land, Hamilton's temptation is to cede to the urging of his old friend General Birdwood – who, in his diary, he refers to as, 'Little Birdie, now grown up into a grand General'[45] – that they go immediately with the troops they have, so as to forestall the strengthening of the defences that the Turks are now clearly engaged in.

But against that, it is Hamilton's view that it will be better to wait for the arrival of the 29th Division – even though, because of Kitchener's own wavering about whether or not it would be required, the 29th is still three weeks away. So Hamilton feels he cannot give his assent to a quick assault. The meeting breaks up and the Admirals and Generals make their way back to their own quarters, each with his own thoughts as to what their chances of success in three weeks' time will be.

One thing that has given Admiral Wemyss a little confidence in the last few days is the vision of all the different soldiers by the shores of Mudros Harbour, 'a curious medley, French uniforms of every description mingling with our khaki . . .

'The differences in national character come out very strongly when brought so close together in such a small space; but all have one thing in common, a good-tempered gaiety which is pleasant to see . . . Through all this motley crowd there is a continual stream of perspiring Australians carrying huge loads of stores and pushing improvised carts. They are magnificent specimens of the raw material of humanity. I think I have never seen finer.'[46]

General Hamilton quite agrees. At ten the following morning, he and General Birdwood land on the foreshores of Port Mudros to inspect some of the 1st Australian Division's finest troops – the 9th Battalion of the 3rd Brigade – all of them trained to a high peak by their Commanding Officer, Colonel Ewen MacLagan.

As an exercise, the Commander-in-Chief of the Mediterranean Expeditionary Force asks the Colonel to have his men carry out a practice attack on yonder row of windmills – massive, old-fashioned, 30-foot wheels with 20 arms, each arm bearing triangular sails – and though to Hamilton's eyes their military tactics don't particularly shine through, there is no doubt that these men of the 3rd Brigade 'are superb specimens'.[47]

(This is in rather stark contrast to Charles Bean's impression of some of the British troops. 'The Territorials have not our physique,' he would report, 'and some of the Lancashire regiments seem to be composed largely of mere children.')[48]

A short time later, General Birdwood has a quiet word with Colonel MacLagan and tells him to begin training his men to land quickly on shore and secure a beachhead. 'The landing-places chosen,' he says, giving a broad hint, 'should resemble those at the toe of the Gallipoli Peninsula. The men are to be practised at communicating information in battle, and at carrying a very full load.'[49]

No, of course nothing is locked in yet. But that is the way things are starting to look.

23 MARCH 1915, DARDANELLES DILLY-DALLIES

Can it really be true?

Is it that the British Fleet will *not* try once more?

Have we Turks wrought a great victory?

Though scarcely daring to believe it, both the Turkish and German military leadership is slowly coming to that conclusion.

In the considered estimation of the German naval attaché, Admiral Guido von Usedom, 'The whole affair gave the impression of groping round without a plan . . .'[50]

It appears extraordinarily timid of the Allies, and General Enver would later say, 'If the English had only the courage to rush more ships through the Dardanelles, they could have got to Constantinople, but their delay enabled us thoroughly to fortify the Peninsula, and in six weeks time we had taken down there over 200 Austrian Skoda guns.'[51]

And many more things, as well.

For if the British are not going to force their way through by ship, it's obvious they must come by land. And so steps must be taken, urgently.

23 MARCH 1915, THE ADMIRALTY, DE ROBECK DISAPPOINTS

Rarely in this war has Winston Churchill been more appalled. Just when he is expecting the fleet alone to finish the job it has started in the

Dardanelles, he receives a cable from Admiral de Robeck, now referred to by Churchill as 'De Row-Back',[52] informing him that, after meeting with Generals Hamilton and Birdwood on *Queen Elizabeth*, the Royal Navy does not wish to make another attempt to force the Dardanelles until the middle of April, and then only in tandem with a major force of the army landing on the shores of Gallipoli.

'I read this telegram with consternation,' Churchill would later recall. 'I feared still more the immense and incalculable extension of the enterprise involved in making a military attack on a large scale.'[53]

Immediately, Churchill drafts his proposed reply, and then convenes a meeting of the Admiralty War Group, essentially the senior officials of the Admiralty and key advisers. With some vigour, he proposes that Admiral de Robeck be instructed:

TO PERSEVERE METHODICALLY BUT RESOLUTELY WITH THE PLAN CONTAINED IN YOUR INSTRUCTIONS . . . AND THAT YOU SHOULD MAKE ALL PREPARATIONS TO RENEW THE ATTACK BEGUN ON 18TH AT THE FIRST FAVOURABLE OPPORTUNITY . . .

WE KNOW THE FORTS ARE SHORT OF AMMUNITION AND SUPPLY OF MINES IS LIMITED. WE DO NOT THINK THE TIME HAS YET COME TO GIVE UP THE PLAN OF FORCING DARDANELLES BY A PURELY NAVAL OPERATION.[54]

The First Lord of the Admiralty is met with 'insuperable resistance'.[55] Now that the two men 'on the ground', de Robeck and Hamilton, have decided on a joint operation, Admiralty has no choice but to go along with their views.

'What more could we want?' Sir John Fisher asks plaintively, clearly thrilled at Admiral de Robeck's decision. 'The Army *were* going to do it. They ought to have done it all along.'[56]

Bereft, Churchill considers resigning, but convinced that would only make matters worse, he decides to stay. In the subsequent Cabinet meeting on this day, he announces with 'grief' the refusal of the Admiral and the Admiralty to continue the naval attack, reporting that for the moment it must be abandoned.

Lord Kitchener, however, rises to the occasion, and simply says the army will 'carry the operations through by military force'.[57]

And that's it.

There is no further discussion, either within the Cabinet or the War Council.

The beginning of a campaign that will see one of the greatest invasion forces ever assembled, involving 80,000 soldiers and over 200 ships, is committed to, as Churchill notes, by 'the agreement of the Admiral and the General on the spot, and the declaration of Lord Kitchener . . . No formal decision to make a land attack was even noted in the records of the Cabinet or the War Council.'[58]

How, in the space of just a few days, has the plan gone from the navy forcing the Dardanelles alone to the soldiers now essentially doing it alone, simply transported there by the navy?

Exactly.

It has just . . . sort of . . . happened.

This key decision falls in a period of over nine weeks when there is no meeting of the War Council in London. And, as a later inquiry would acidly note, 'We think that before such operations were commenced the War Council should have carefully reconsidered the whole position. In our opinion the Prime Minister ought to have summoned a meeting of the War Council . . . We think this was a serious omission.'[59]

As it happens, however, the Prime Minister is as busy as ever on this day, as every day, writing to that fragrant beauty Venetia all the news of what has gone on in Cabinet:

News from the Dardanelles is not very good, there are more mines & concealed guns than they ever counted upon: and the Admiral seems to be rather in a funk.

At the time, the man who feels perhaps most wretched about it all is Churchill. 'Why turn and change at this fateful hour and impose upon the Army an ordeal of incalculable severity?' he records. 'An attack by the Army if it failed would commit us irrevocably in a way no naval attack could have done. The risk was greater; the stakes were far higher.'[60]

But he feels there is nothing he can do. For better or worse, for triumph or tragedy – and he fears the latter – things have taken on a momentum all their own.

24 MARCH 1915, CONSTANTINOPLE, 5TH ARMY – ACTIVATE!

After the attacks of 18 March, General Enver is not too proud to admit that his approach to defending the Straits has been too tame, and so he sends word to the Chief of the German Military Mission, General Otto Liman von Sanders, that he is to wait in his office – the Minister of War is coming to visit.

Arriving a short time later, the flamboyant General explains what he needs from his German counterpart. General Enver is so convinced that the British will now attempt a land invasion on the Dardanelles that he has decided to create an army formation directly responsible for its defence. General Enver would now like General Liman von Sanders to relinquish control of the 1st Army in Constantinople and take charge of the newly activated 5th Army on the Gallipoli Peninsula, in order to prepare them for what is surely coming.

General Liman von Sanders assents at once and makes preparations to leave Constantinople the following evening.

For the first time since the war began, Liman von Sanders feels happier. For months he has been agitating his supervisors in Berlin to recall him to Germany so that he can see action on the front, and now it looks as though the front is coming to him.

In many ways the 60-year-old – described by a colleague as 'a tall, stern, military-looking man, very self-contained, quick in decision, clear in his orders, scanty of praise, sharp in reprimand and in following up a decision once taken'[61] – has been born for the task. For the last four decades his life has been dedicated to matters military, and he has proved to be so good at it that just the year before he had been promoted to General. In 1913, he had become the Commander of the newly established German Military Mission to Turkey and was assigned the task of bringing the Ottoman Army into the 20th century – something he had already achieved a great deal of success in.

The key thing he must do now, he decides as he heads to Gallipoli on a fast ship, is work out where to place his forces, consisting of no fewer than 65,000 men.

As General Otto Liman von Sanders disembarks from his vessel at the port of Gallipoli on the morning of 26 March, he looks up at the 'pronounced mountainous terrain with precipitous ridges, the slopes of which are rent by deep ravines and shaft clefts'.[62] He considers the sparse natural cover – 'a few lone pine woods, a few bushes on the banks of the creeks and [deep ravines]'[63] – and appreciates the amount of work before him.

He is met with a warm handshake from Brigadier-General Esat, the Commander of the Army's 3rd Corps, who is wearing the black wool cap known as a kalpak, a signature of many Ottoman officers. Liman von Sanders has worked with General Esat before and holds him in high esteem, a quality officer that the German knows he can trust to command troops.[64]

General von Sanders and his entourage are ushered to their new accommodation – a house formerly occupied by the French consular agent. After the Allies' flight from the Empire, looters had taken much of the furniture, leaving the General two rooms, with a round table and a wall mirror. Beds and other such creature comforts are to be borrowed from someone in town . . .

Von Sanders receives his assignment just two days after General Hamilton, and these two implacable foes have roughly the same amount of time to prepare.

Chapter Seven

THE SKY LOWERS

You are just simply eaten up with the Dardanelles
and cannot think of anything else! Damn the
Dardanelles! They will be our grave![1]
*First Sea Lord Sir John Fisher in a message to First Lord of
the Admiralty, Winston Churchill, on 5 April 1915*

Time presses; K. prods us from the rear: the Admiral
from the front. To their eyes we seem to be dallying
amidst the fleshpots of Egypt whereas, really, we
are struggling like drowning mariners in a sea of
chaos; chaos in the offices; chaos on the ships; chaos
in the camps; chaos along the wharves . . .
Sir Ian Hamilton's diary entry for 5 April 1915, Alexandria[2]

It's too wonderful for belief . . . I had not imagined Fate could be
so kind . . . Will Hero's Tower crumble under the 15-inch guns?
Will the sea be polyphloisbic and wine-dark and unvintageable?
Shall I loot mosaics from St Sophia, and Turkish Delight and
carpets? Should we be a Turning Point in History? Oh God!
I've never been quite so happy in my life I think. Never quite so
pervasively happy; like a stream flowing entirely to one end.
I suddenly realize that the ambition of my life has been – since I
was two – to go on a military expedition against Constantinople.
*English poet Rupert Brooke, a soldier with the Royal
Naval Division, upon hearing the destination[3]*

LATE MARCH 1915, GALLIPOLI PENINSULA, A FORCE IS UNLEASHED

The Hun is not at the gate, the Hun is *everywhere* – in the barracks, at Cape Helles, at Gallipoli, on the roads between, surveying the lie of the land. General Liman von Sanders roars at his underlings in much the same manner as he roars back and forth across the Peninsula in his staff car, on horseback and even on foot – with speed, force and urgency – as well as being ferried back and forth between the Asian and European sides of the Sea of Marmara. He and his entourage of officers, in turn led by the extremely energetic Brigadier-General Esat, cover 'hundreds of kilometres' in the first couple of days alone, and it feels as if 'there are not enough hours in the day'.[4] Together, they are trying to banish something of the natural lassitude that lies over this ancient land. With the failure of the British Fleet to force the Dardanelles, it is obvious a landing of troops is the likely next option, and von Sanders and Brigadier-General Esat are insistent that the Turkish troops – *Schnell! Schnell! Schnell! Çabuk! Çabuk! Çabuk!* – get themselves and their weaponry ready to meet them.

Troops are sent on long marches and made to do endless training drills to improve their toughness and mobility – including practice marches at night to different beaches considered likely landing places. Munitions are stockpiled in strategic spots. Boats are assigned to suitable ports in the Straits to expedite the movement of troops. The paths and goat tracks that criss-cross the Peninsula are turned into actual roads by labour battalions. Soldiers are trained to be snipers; they learn how to throw grenades for maximum effect. The sentries on the coast are trained to report instantly the first sign of any invasion, and Liman von Sanders is particularly insistent that phone lines are put in to allow them to do so. Defensive trenches are dug just inland from where an invading force might land. Though short of resources across the board – from building materials and tools to artillery and ammunition – local innovation helps make up for it.

Turkish soldiers place torpedo heads tight by landmines, to blow up when the mines do, and strip the local garden fences of wood and wire to augment their meagre stock. At some particular places on the coast, the lapping waters of the Aegean are laced with barbed wire – stripped from farmers' fences – stretched out and hidden just below the surface. With every passing day, the defences of the Gallipoli Peninsula get stronger.

Positions, everyone! The enemy will soon be here!

'The important question,' von Sanders would reminisce, 'was where the hostile landing should be expected.'[5]

He and Brigadier-General Esat identify the most likely landing places, focusing on the lower tip of the Peninsula around Cape Helles, the coast on either side of Gaba Tepe – though this is deemed unlikely by many – or further north around the vicinity of Bulair. The other place of concern is on the Asian shore around Kum Kale, and, after great rumination, von Sanders places one-third of his forces there.

Only by concentrating the forces in central inland positions and enabling them to quickly get to the spot where the British land will the Turks be able to stop them. So, they would be much better off holding the majority of their forces back, 'sending only the most indispensable security detachments to the coast'[6] itself.

Lieutenant-Colonel Mustafa Kemal's 19th Division, meanwhile, is ordered to wait in reserve, headquartered inland at the village of Boghali.

Though von Sanders recognises in Mustafa Kemal the mark of a fine officer, he is wary of the young man's forthright manner. His posture is a little too handsome, his bearing a little too regal, for one yet to truly prove himself in war. On their first meeting, General von Sanders had asked the former Military Attaché to Sofia his opinion on why the Bulgarians had not sprung into action to help the German–Ottoman alliance.

'Because they are not convinced that Germany will win,' Mustafa Kemal answered.

'And what do you think?' asked von Sanders.

'I agree with the Bulgarians,' replied Mustafa Kemal, with a sparkle in his watery blue eyes.[7]

This is not the only issue that Mustafa Kemal has with his superiors' decisions. After being stationed on the Peninsula for the better part of the Balkan Wars, he is convinced that the Allies will attempt to land on the southern end of the Peninsula, not at Bulair or Kum Kale.

For now, Mustafa Kemal is powerless to convince the brass above him, and he must obey the order to march his troops to Boghali. The village sits some four and a half miles directly north of Maidos and four miles to the east of Ari Burnu. At this time of year, the mulberry trees dotted generously around the village are blossoming, and chickens scuttle along the narrow streets between wonky stone houses.

Even before the Allied naval attacks on the Dardanelles had started, Liman von Sanders' respected colleague, Admiral Guido von Usedom, had inspected the Peninsula. He had arrived at Gaba Tepe, along with a cadre of top brass, including the Commander of the 3rd Corps, Brigadier-General Esat, and the Commander of the 9th Division, Lieutenant-Colonel Halil Sami, and their attendant staff.

Together with Lieutenant-Colonel Şefik, Commander of the 27th Regiment, which was stationed at Ari Burnu and had been assigned the task of defending and fortifying that stretch of coast, the men climbed to the top of the promontory at Gaba Tepe – a post that is already well fortified, with troops entrenched, an artillery battery in place and other gun emplacements nearby. It is not far from an extraordinary natural rock formation that looks like the famed Great Sphinx of Giza, and they are able to garner a view of the coastline stretching north and the terrain leading up to the ridges from the beach below.

Peering down the steep incline, which extends all the way to the beach, they contemplate just how an invading force would fare trying to storm ashore here. Some of the soldiers with them are commanded to toss grenades down the slope, and they all watch the explosions closely. *Devastating.*

Soon enough, Colonel Şefik, as commander of the men responsible for defending this stretch of the shore, speaks for the Turks: 'A landing here is not possible without them also capturing the ridges extending from Ari Burnu.'

'We have determined,' a German officer agrees, 'that it is very shallow along the coast. The terrain is very steep and unsuitable for a landing. In the first place, the enemy would have to land at Gaba Tepe and then spread along the line of the ridges behind Ari Burnu in order to capture the area.'[8]

And so the discussion ends, the high brass believing that in the unlikely event the enemy lands on this part of the coast, it will probably be at Gaba Tepe, not Ari Burnu. As a consequence, only one battalion of some 800 men is left behind to defend the coastline stretching from Gaba Tepe to Suvla Bay in the north.

LATE MARCH 1915, ALEXANDRIA, NO QUARTER IN THE QUARTER-MASTER'S STORE

So how does one move 75,000 men from one continent to another, in the middle of the night, equipped to fight, capable of both defending and attacking, of staying for the long haul if things go badly and yet still with the capacity of pushing on to Constantinople if all goes well? And all of it when they are *still* without an administrative staff to see to the thousands of details that might make all the difference between a successful mission and a shambolic one?

It is a very good question, and one that General Hamilton and his staff struggle with every day. The first thing to do is make lists, lists, lists . . . and then make some more. And then you have your individual brigades form up lists:

Signposts 30, White paint 20lb, Black paint 5lb, Casks water 20, Tents 8, Latrine flags 17, Shovels 10, Lamps red 6, Lamps green 6, Lamps white 23, Flares with tow 70, Flare fuel gals 70, Cask wine 56 gals . . .[9]

The wine? Apparently for the officer class, an accompanying slip of paper notes:

Major Stuart explained there was a small
shortage in the wine casks & perhaps in a few
of the other articles but the best had been done
under the circumstances.[10]

The whole thing is of course a logistical nightmare, unprecedented in scale and degree of difficulty. In the words of one contemporary writer, 'They were going to land on a foodless cliff, five hundred miles from a store, in a place and at a season in which the sea's rising might cut them from supply.'[11]

Come to think of it, they will also need hundreds, no, *thousands* of Union Jacks with which to wrap bodies before they are committed to the deep. And yet neither General Hamilton nor his senior officers can expect any sympathy from Kitchener of Khartoum, who has already cabled his concern to Hamilton about the mooted 14 April landing:

I THINK THAT YOU HAD BETTER KNOW AT ONCE THAT I REGARD ANY SUCH POSTPONEMENT AS FAR TOO LONG.[12]

Which is as may be, but General Hamilton can only do so much. He and his staff must simply soldier on while still oft yearning wistfully for the simpler times . . .

On the second-last day of the month, the Commander-in-Chief spies a well-built but agile and distinguished-looking officer with a distinctive, bushy moustache beneath his large nose. It can only be Colonel John Monash! General Hamilton cocks his head to one side and says, 'Well, Monash, when we sat under a gum tree together twelve months ago [at Duntroon], we didn't think, either of us, we should meet again so soon.'[13]

Monash happily agrees, but, always a man of empathy, feels for Hamilton – he clearly looks as if he has the weight of the world on his shoulders.

1 APRIL 1915, WEST OF MECCA, BY THE RED SEA, BEWARE BEDOUIN BANDITS

It has been the most extraordinary journey of their lives. After the destruction of *Emden* in mid-November, Kapitänleutnant Hellmuth von Mücke and his small command of 50 sailors on the Cocos Islands have been travelling, trying to make good their escape. Initially in the Clunies-Ross schooner *Ayesha*, von Mücke has led his men all the way through the Dutch East Indies, across the Indian Ocean and into the Middle East, stalked by death all the way, starved, nearly dead of thirst, ambushed, betrayed, shot at, nearly sunk and lost.

Still, they have managed to keep going and now are on a trek through the desert, just one more night's march from Jeddah, where a 300-strong garrison of Turks is apparently expecting them. True, this is particularly tough country and there are meant to be so many gangs of robbers about that the locals call this area the 'Father of the Wolf',[14] but now, the long night's journey nearing its end, the German officers' thoughts are turning more to their next meal, when . . .

A piercing whistle shatters the dawn, followed by heavy, sustained rifle fire. They are under attack! Rallying his men, von Mücke rushes forward and for the moment at least they are able to get partial cover, first behind their camels and then the nearest sand dunes as they get their weapons out.

How many of them are there?

The answer is appalling. As the sun rises a little more, the Germans can now see that the sand hills just in front of them are *black* with Bedouin bandits, at least 300 of them. All armed, all firing.

Despite the dire situation, von Mücke and his men react with calm vigour. Almost as one, they fix their bayonets. What now?

Von Mücke is just trying to decide when he hears a voice: *'Kapitänleutnant! Kapitänleutnant!'*

He looks over to see it is an 18-year-old sailor, one of their youngest.

'Was gibt's denn? – Well, what is it?' he asks.

'Geht's bald los, Herr Kapitänleutnant? – How soon are we going at it, Sir?'

'*Was denn?* – At what?'

'*Na, stürmen!* – Why, at storming the enemy . . .'

The worthy von Mücke pauses for an instant, reflects, and then takes instant action. '*Stimmt! Du hast recht.* – Exactly! You are right,' he roars, getting up. '*Sprung auf, Marsch, Marsch!* – Up! Charge, charge!'[15]

And charge they do. With a great cheer, Kapitänleutnant von Mücke leads his men in a mad dash, straight at the Bedouins . . .

EVENING, 1 APRIL 1915, MENA CAMP, NO BULL

Hold your horses, Bluey. Something's going on. The word is getting around. A Major of the Army Corps staff has journeyed from Cairo to Mena Camp to see General Bridges behind closed doors, and as he leaves, a jovial Bridges is heard to say, 'Well, thanks for bringing us good news. That's the most cheerful thing we've had happen to us for a long time.'[16]

And now, suddenly, all further leave for officers has been stopped.

It can surely only mean one thing: we're going to get a fight at last.

And it is dinkum, all right.

A group of Australian officers and their men, who had just been about to head off on a weekend at Luxor, 450 miles to the south, are recalled to the Camp from the station. Another group, who had been out having a picnic on the Nile, return to the wharf to find their smiling Colonel waiting for them.

It's true. It's really true!

Ah, the excitement it causes among the officers. The cheers. The songs. The back-slapping! No, no one knows where they are going – the Dardanelles are rumoured, but who knows? – and no one particularly cares. Though for the moment they must keep it to themselves, the main thing is that after all these months they might see some action, actually get to test themselves and their men against the enemy. In the time that remains before they have to march to Cairo, to catch a train to Alexandria, to get on ships that will take them somewhere, most officers busy themselves writing letters to loved ones.

Not the staff of the AIF 1st Division, however. Late into the night, in the dim glow of a single light bulb, they wade through paperwork and put out embarkation orders.

GOOD FRIDAY, 2 APRIL 1915, CAIRO, A POX ON BOTH YOUR HOUSES

There is madness in the air.

A plague of locusts, of biblical proportions, descends on Cairo, sent by God for those who have sinned, are sinning, and will sin. Millions, *trillions* of them – huge yellow, brown and black locusts – enough to black out the sun, to blow the eardrums, to crawl over every single thing and devour every bit of green life from leaves to corn to grass. Enough to make a man think that hell has risen from the earth. They eat the trees, they swarm over the soldiers and the Gyppos alike, their wings like 'whirring wheels',[17] bashing out their own mad frenzy. Oh yes, there is *madness* in the air, and it goes for hours. You see, when the locusts finally leave, the madness does not . . .

Beyond this visitation from the nether world, something is up in the soldiers' world. Practically all the troops at Mena Camp are having the day off, but by mid-afternoon the word spreads: everyone must begin to prepare. They are going to be on the move on the morrow, embarking for a place unknown . . .

Hopefully, to begin a battle! After all this training, all this hard slog, at last they are going to be able to test themselves. There is enormous excitement among all the men, but for those lucky ones who already have leave on this day and are already out on the town, it is doubly so. At bloody least they will have one last night to have a last drink before the stink and blow off some steam. Not for nothing do many start singing, *'There'll be a hot time in the old town to-night . . .'*[18]

Head back to camp and start getting ready? Not on your nelly, mate. We're already out, and we're not moving. For if we are at long last about to see action, what better thing to do right now than *stay* out on the town, do a bit of carry-on, and carry on? And, of course, what better place to paint the town red than the Wazza, ever and always a magnet for us men of restless disposition.

So it is that by 3 pm on that sultry afternoon, several thousand Australian and New Zealand soldiers are milling around the Wazza, a fair proportion of whom are already as full as two boots. How things go bad from there never becomes clear, though Charles Bean will at least record, 'some New Zealanders who had picked up certain diseases in a particular street near Shepheard's Hotel seemed to have made up their mind to go and pay the house back for what they got there.'[19]

What is certain is that many of the soldiers have anger in their bones – and sometimes on their penises – towards the whole area. Their problems with the place include having bought liquor that had been watered down, having been 'mobbed & robbed',[20] outrageous overcharging that would make a bushranger blush, and, most particularly, whores giving them VD.

Whether this anger is exacerbated by a group of the men discovering a pimp pissing in a vat of beer that they have been drinking from, no one is sure, though it is a story that will subsequently circulate. An even stronger story, though of equal uncertainty, is that one of the English soldiers has discovered his long-lost sister in one of the brothels and is now freeing her by force, assisted by the Australians and New Zealanders. Or maybe the initial anger comes from one of the women rejecting a Maori because his skin is too dark. Or a publican calling a Maori a 'nigger'[21] . . . Perhaps it is just everything.

Whatever the catalyst, the result is a fighting force of drunken men, ready to leave for a battle that may take their lives in the near future, congregated in a spot where they have a grievance against many locals – and the brake in their brains that in normal circumstances might make them pull up this side of wild and dangerous is not working.

So why not rough up the pimps a little and destroy a few of the whorehouses?

You bloody reckon?

I bloody reckon, *yesh*, I do!

Just before 5 pm, those many people wending their way through the streets are suddenly stunned to see burning mattresses hurtling down from the upper floors of the whorehouse at Number 8, Darb al-Muballat. This is followed shortly by clothes and bedding fluttering through the windows, and heavy furniture, chairs and shutters shattering as they hit the pavement.

Down below, other Australian and New Zealand soldiers join in the fun and soon throw the smashed furniture and all the rest onto the burning mattresses to get a proper bonfire going. Now angry Egyptian men are shouting – not all of them pimps bleeding from the nose and mouth – bints are screaming, and many, many soldiers are laughing, enjoying the high hilarity of it all. Look, this destruction is not worth having got the pox for, but it is something all right, and also great relief from the sheer tedium of the last few months.

And look at how all the greasy Gyppos run at this first sign of trouble. One smack in the mouth and all the fight goes out of them. If the Australians and New Zealanders are heading for the Dardanelles – as has been rumoured of late – the Turks will likely be just the same.

So too, with the first of the Egyptian police who arrive on the double.

'Finish the bastards off!'[22] the soldiers cry as they round on them, only to see the Gyppo police run, too.

Not so the men on the town 'picket' – an officer, a corporal and a dozen soldiers assigned to enforce army discipline in situations exactly like this – who suddenly arrive to try to get these rioting soldiers out of the whorehouses, where they continue to raise hell and lower the boom.

The picket, comprising South Australian and Victorian soldiers from the Australian 9th Light Horse Regiment, must dodge the falling debris, rush up the stairs and grab every soldier they can get their hands on to bring them down to the street.

No fewer than five of the rioters are formally arrested, and would have been dragged away to the 'Calaboose' had the mob of soldiers not become an angry beast with a mood all its own. They storm the picket, grab their weapons and throw them on the fire. Four of those who are arrested are freed, and the picket has no choice but to beat a retreat and call for help, most particularly when, as later recounted by Charles Bean, 'the officer of the picket was hit heavily on the hand by a big New Zealander who was holding a staircase'.[23]

In short order, 30 British Military Police – the much hated 'red caps', who, in the words of Bean, are 'always a red rag to the Australian soldier'[24] – arrive on horseback, brandishing loaded pistols. Ah, but if the authorities now have their reinforcements, so too do the Australians have 'reinstoushments',[25] as they call them, and more of their own arrive from all corners as the word spreads. The red caps are confronted by a mob, now some 3000 strong, who only take one look at them before throwing a deluge of bottles and stones – whatever comes to hand – as the fires continue to rage, the women keep screaming and the filthy pimps who have not yet escaped keep getting belted for their trouble and . . .

And WATCH OUT!

A *piano* comes crashing down onto the street from the roof – the soldiers couldn't fit it through the window.

In the growing emergency, the Captain of the Military Police orders his men to draw their pistols from their holsters.

'If you don't disperse,' he calls to the rioters, 'I will order them to fire!'[26]

Do your worst, Sonny Jim.

As the mob still doesn't disperse, finally the British officer gives the command – 'Fire!' – and his men do just that, albeit over the heads of the mob, as he has also quietly commanded.

When the rioters still don't disperse, he orders his men to fire *into* the mob at leg-level, and four or five men fall down wounded, enraging the mob further and causing the Military Police to withdraw . . . just in time for the Egyptian fire brigade to arrive and turn their hoses on the flames and the mob itself . . . only to have their hoses cut, their faces belted and their fire truck pushed into the flames. Oh, and the rioters find the heavy nozzles of the hoses useful as battering rams to break down doors and smash ever more windows, while a mob of Maori do a full-blown *haka* in front of the roaring flames.

There is madness in the air tonight and Trooper Bluegum, for one, is enjoying it hugely, knowing it to be fully justified. After all, the publican called the Maoris 'niggers'!

'Well,' he would explain, 'who can blame the New Zealanders for resenting it, and who can blame the Australians for siding with the New Zealanders? Who touches them touches us.'[27]

Now looting breaks out, and more armed troops are called for, while the mob sets fire to a Greek tavern that has also been guilty of overcharging and now must pay the price. The flames roar, the smoke billows, the mob is triumphant. And yes, the vast majority are spectators only, with only a handful of soldiers doing the damage, but no matter. It is such fun!

By 7 pm, a second fire truck has arrived, this one with an armed cavalry escort, and at least a little headway is made in having the fires put out, if not the fire in the mob.

Finally, a whole battalion of Lancashire Territorials arrive with *rifles* and bayonets fixed. Their officer gives the order, and in an instant his men form up the same way they had against the whirling dervishes in the Sudan.

The back row stands, the middle row kneels, and the front row lies down – all with their rifles aimed.

Again, the officer gives the mob fair warning and . . . this time . . . *this time* . . . it works.

(After all, who really can argue the toss when staring at an entire wall of muzzles pointed straight at you? They are *not* suicidal.)

By 10 pm, a rough semblance of order is restored. But what a night they have had! Yes, four rioters have been wounded and 50 arrested, but so what?

They have proved they are fighters and have shown one thing for sure – they care as little for authority they don't respect as they do care for each other as cobbers. Even cobbers they haven't actually met yet. And while they had all arrived in Egypt as Victorians and Queenslanders and Tasmanians and Aucklanders and Wellingtonians, all of that has now been lost. Now, they're far more Australians and

New Zealanders – if not quite yet one united body of *Anzacs*. Most of them have come to fight for the King and the British Empire, but this has nothing to do with that.

The attitude is all in the image of what happens when, in another event much later, one rioter is told to keep the peace in the name of the King and replies, 'Oh fuck the bloody King; don't stop my men, let them pass.'[28]

And yes, there will be some outcry in Australia when details of the riot become known, but, mercifully, some hugely reputable newspapers, such as Melbourne's *Truth* – which had previously been so hard on the soldiers for what had happened at the Broadmeadows Camp with that 16-year-old girl – are now honest enough to point out where the blame truly lies: with the prostitutes.

'Certain happenings in Egypt,' the paper delicately raises the subject, 'have lately tended to give more prominence to [those arrested for riot] but it is only fair to point out that in many of those cases the fault did not lie on the side of the victim. The immorality of Cairo is noted from one end of the world to the other, and "soliciting" is reduced to a fine art among the lewd women of that city, so that resistance to their nefarious methods is a difficult problem, even with men whose morality would be absolutely unimpeachable under fair conditions. The women of Cairo specialise in the manufacture and sale of cigarettes, into certain of which a substance known as embrogras is mixed. It is also induced into drinks of any kind, and the result of its consumption is an uncontrollable desire, to which the Cairo women readily lend themselves . . . Brothels are in abundance, and the harlots are in no wise wanting in enterprise, but try to force poor, innocent Australian boys into their houses of ill fame. Shame.'[29]

So they had it coming!

One of many who does not think like that, however, is the 1st Battalion's Captain Gordon Carter, who is appalled. He had known the Wazza to be an 'awful hole' from the first and only time he had visited it, and had certainly not wanted to spend his last evening there. (Rather, he'd gone to see his sister, Fuff, and Nurse King. And then, being an educated, sensitive soul, he'd retired to read his volume of Shakespeare comedies. 'It's wonderful,' he writes to his parents, 'the enjoyment you can get from reading the old chap over and over again.'[30] Nurse King describes him in her diary as 'a very nice boy really'.)[31]

Another who feels much the same about what has happened at the Wazza is Ellis Silas, who personally is nothing less than 'ashamed' of the rioters after he hears what has happened.[32] But at least there are plenty of things to keep both men, and all of the Australian soldiers, busy in the aftermath.

They must pack up, strike their tents, stow their kits, pack their wagons – take their surviving pet kangaroos to the Cairo Zoological Garden – and start marching. They leave something else behind of significance. Not long after their arrival at Mena, the officers had banned the troops from climbing the Sphinx and one of the more unstable pyramids after one man had been killed in a fall. Nevertheless, as a young private records in his diary just before marching out, 'one daring individual' had managed to climb up the pyramid and plant 'a small Australian flag on top where it still fluttered when we moved away'.[33]

In the space of three days, from 3 April onwards, nearly all of Mena Camp empties out.

With high spirits still abounding, most of the Anzac soldiers begin singing as they march out – and they don't stop until they get all the way to Cairo Central Railway Station.

Sadly, the Australian Light Horse in Maadi Camp are not required to join them, though they live in hope that they may be required. Colonel John Monash would record that when the time came for his own 4th Brigade to leave, 'Thousands of Territorials, and Australians and New Zealand Light Horsemen, many weeping with regret at not being allowed to come, gathered around to give us a royal send-off . . .'[34]

The lucky ones who are going, however, pile into the packed carriages at Cairo Central and begin their journey to Alexandria, where troopships await to take them to a destination still unknown.

'I'll bet this much,' Sergeant Archie Barwick of 1st Battalion would record in his diary, 'that a finer body of troops never left Cairo than the old 1st Div. Every man was as hard as nails & trained to the hour. I was one of the smallest men in our Battalion – that will give you an idea of what they were like, & every man was cocksure of himself, of being able to beat any man, be he Turk or German, & frightened of nothing with legs on it . . .'[35]

Ah, but there are scenes of poignancy, too, as when brothers part. On this evening, Captain Jack Bean is hurriedly leaving for the Dardanelles with the 3rd Battalion when Charles Bean finds him and helps him pack. Before the two take their leave of each other, Jack gives his younger brother a couple of tablets of morphia, against the possibility that Charles might get badly hurt.

'Hope you won't need them,' Jack says softly. 'But you never know.'

'Thanks,' Charles replies as he slips them into his pocket. 'I'll be careful . . . You never know.'

And now, as the 3rd Battalion marches out, it is time for the brothers to take their leave of each other. As Jack climbs upon his horse and slowly takes up his position behind the last of his marching comrades, Charles walks alongside him for a way.

Finally, however, it is time.

Jack reaches down to shake his brother's hand.

'Well, so long, Chas,' Jack says quietly. 'I'll be watching out for you when you come.'

'Yes. I hope I won't be far behind you,' Charles Bean replies. 'So long, Jack . . . Take care of yourself.'

Jack rides on. Charles stands there, staring, as his brother recedes in the darkened distance.

And now, another quiet voice beside him.

'That brother of yours,' says a fellow officer of the 3rd Battalion, who has watched the whole scene, 'is the kindest man I have ever known.'[36]

And so they continue to leave, including Captain Gordon Carter of the 1st Battalion, with one close observer of the whole parade being Nurse King.

'The whole of the 1st Brigade left us starting about 4 p.m.,' she records in her diary. 'It was a dreadfully sad day to think we may never see some of our pals again. Went to bed very sad indeed.'[37]

In Alexandria, cabs await to take the arriving Anzacs from the station through the teeming streets – hey, look at those girls walking around without veils, quite unlike Cairo – to the harbour. And what a spectacle!

'There are,' Colonel John Monash of the 4th Brigade would record when his own time for leaving came, 'literally hundreds of large steamers, warships, transports, troopships, colliers, store ships, hospital ships, water ships, supply ships, repair ships, depot ships, Egyptian, French, British, Australian, and even two of the USA squadrons which visited Australia.'[38]

Where are they going? No one is *officially* sure, and certainly *not* the captains of the ships, who have sealed orders, only to be opened once they leave Alexandria Harbour. (In fact, in some quarters the whole thing is such an open secret that a number of captains don't even bother opening those orders.)

5 APRIL 1915, MUDROS, 3RD BRIGADE TO HAVE THEIR MATES' BACKS

You bloody beauty. It is all very top secret and must not be discussed, but on this Easter Monday, the 3rd Brigade, who have been training at Lemnos for the last four weeks, receive 'official intimation' that they will be the first troops to secure a beachhead on the Gallipoli Peninsula and provide cover for those who are to follow. As recorded at the time, this wonderful bit of information is received by the troops like 'a bit of roast meat to a starving man'.[39] They jump upon it and now begin to practise – full kit on their backs – disembarking, discarding the kit and charging forward to get to whatever defenders there might be, and from the beginning they are expecting plenty.

10–12 APRIL 1915, INTO LEMNOS, A GATHERING OF THE FAITHFUL FLEET

What a pleasure it is! After two days steaming in cramped conditions across 570 nautical miles of the Mediterranean, on this day dozens of troopships from Alexandria carefully make their way through the pale blue waters of 'the Aegean Sea, amid the islands famed in Grecian [history]'.[40] The sun is shining benignly, the air is fragrant, and off to the east on the second day they can see the peaks of the Island of Rhodes, whose historical glory they can contemplate for a couple of hours before they finally come to the minefields that guard the entrance to the glorious and protected Mudros Harbour on Lemnos.

One man sitting on deck notes in his diary as they approach, 'The haystacks and medieval looking windmills all looked so peaceful and remote from the world that it gave one's eye a shock to look upon the line of huge battleships stretched across the harbour mouth.'[41]

On the wider arms of the harbour, the soldiers can see beautiful farms dotting the foreshores, boasting cows and sheep on lush pastures, 'thick with little red flowers and yellow flowers and some sort of blue lupin',[42] rising up to distant, towering green hills that come complete with snowy peaks. It is all such a visual relief after so many long months in the desert. And yes, there by the shore are a few fetching peasant girls too, with the most wondrous olive skin imaginable – the first European women many of the soldiers have seen for months. (At least outside the Wazza . . .)

And yet, as the soldiers' ships continue steaming up the harbour, soon enough the men see them: *hundreds* of transports, warships, torpedo craft, trawlers and white hospital ships with green bands around them, with lighter craft buzzing around on the translucent waters. Most ships flutter the flags of France, Russia and Britain. The scene is colourful, a regatta with soldiers on passing ships cheering each other, ships' horns going off and people on shore waving.

Higher up, they can see the picturesque villages of Lemnos winking down upon them from the surrounding hills.

This then is apparently to be the staging point – everyone is saying their destination seems likely to be the Dardanelles, some 60 miles away, and hopefully they'll launch in just a few days. Apparently, there will be as many as 80,000 gathered here within a day or two. In the meantime, it is for the lucky ones to get ashore and stretch their legs, do some training exercises, as tents around the foreshore rapidly turn the harbour into a small town of hospitals, administrative centres and recreational facilities.

And here now, on 12 April, the Atlantic liner SS *Minnewaska*, bearing the commanders and senior officers of the Anzacs, led by Generals William Birdwood and Harold Walker. Wonderfully for Charles Bean, he is accompanying them – by the skin of his teeth only – due to the loyal support of General Bridges, who had intervened at the last minute to secure permission for the Australian correspondent to cover the Australian landing. Yes, he will still have to wait for permission to file like the (*sniff*) already accredited British journalists, but it is victory enough just to be here.

And Bean has had an amazing trip, appreciating like few others the glory of the waters they have traversed, made famous by Homer's epic poems the *Iliad*, on the Trojan War, and the *Odyssey*, about Ulysses' voyage home following the fall of Troy. Gazing westward, Bean can even see the island of Patmos, where the Book of Revelations is said to have been written, the white town capping the hill like snow, and the great 1000-year-old monastery crowning all.[43]

Within an hour of *Minnewaska* anchoring at Mudros, a boat is sent for the Generals and they are being welcomed onto the one-time passenger liner HMT *Arcadian*, where they meet General Sir Ian Hamilton and his rather prickly Chief of Staff, General Walter Braithwaite. Braithwaite has nearly finished his 'operation order' for the landing and now gives Birdwood and his senior officers their first look at this detailed plan.

Hamilton's vision is for a multi-pronged attack, aiming his sharpest prong, the 29th Division, which has arrived in Port Mudros just the day before, at the southern tip of the Peninsula at Cape Helles. This will give the Brits the best chance of retaining naval gunfire support, as it can fire on that tip from three sides. On the first day, 12 battalions, comprising 14,000 soldiers, will land across five beaches, codenamed S, V, W, X and Y Beaches, with the first and last beaches protecting the flanks of V, W and X, where the main thrust would come at 5.30 am, following a half-hour bombardment from the fleet.

The key attack point will be V Beach, and it is here that approximately 2800 troops of the 29th Division will be unleashed.

How to get so many soldiers ashore quickly? This too has been worked out: when in Rome, do as the Romans do. When just across the waters from the plains of Troy, do as the Trojans had done, not with a massive hollow horse filled with soldiers, but with SS *River Clyde*, an old steam collier that can beach itself and have 2000 British soldiers pour out specially cut sally ports in its side. Meanwhile, a small steam hopper, *Argyll*, would position itself parallel to the shore between the collier and the beach, to make a bridge for those soldiers to pour across and be into the battle in a matter of minutes! The job of all soldiers so landed – in full daylight, to avoid confusion with the admittedly difficult exercise, and allow time for naval gunfire, which would be impossible in the dark – will be to quickly work their way up the Peninsula. Their first day objective will be to take the hill of Achi Baba, which overlooks the Peninsula tip and is six miles from V Beach.

The French, meanwhile, are to make a diversionary landing at Kum Kale on the Asian shore before re-embarking to hold the eastern area of the Helles sector.

'Hints have been thrown out that we are asking the French cat to pull the hottest chestnut out of the fire,' Hamilton would note. 'Not at all. At Kum Kale, with their own ships at their back, and the deep Mendere River to their front, d'Amade's men should easily be able to hold their own for a day or two – all that we ask of them.'[44]

Meanwhile, transports containing the Naval Division will make a demonstration off Bulair, high in the Gulf of Saros, where their aim will be 'to make as much splash as they can with their small boats and try to provide matter for alarm wires to Constantinople and the enemy's Chief'.[45]

As to the Anzac landing, that in the thinking of General Hamilton 'will be of the nature of a strong feint'[46] – an attack secondary to the main one, designed to confuse the enemy as to where to place his precious defensive resources – though, if all goes well, it might even 'develop into the real thing'.[47] Where precisely?

Having examined the coast from the bridge of *Phaeton*, Hamilton's views have already been confided to his diary and are substantially unchanged now.

From Bulair down to Suvla Bay, 'the coastline is precipitous; high cliffs and no sort of creeks or beaches', meaning that a landing there would be 'impracticable'.[48] As to Suvla Bay, it does boast 'a fine harbour but too far North were the aim to combine a landing there together with an attack on the Southern end of the Peninsula. Were we, on the other hand, to try to work the whole force ashore from Suvla Bay, the country is too big; it is the broadest part of the Peninsula; also, we should be too far from its waist and from the Narrows we wish to dominate.[49]

All things considered, it is a spot on the western coast of the European arm of the Gallipoli Peninsula, Gaba Tepe, just south of Suvla Bay, that seems best.

'I mean we could get ashore on a calm day if there was no enemy. Gaba Tepe itself would be ideal, but, alas, the Turks are not blind; it is a mass of trenches and wire.'[50]

Between Gaba Tepe and Cape Helles, the coast consists of cliffs from 100 to 300 feet high, though here and there Hamilton could see sandy strips at their base. There is much discussion about whether it would even be possible to land men, but his view is clear.

'I believe myself,' he would confide to his diary, 'the cliffs are not unclimbable. I thoroughly believe also in going for at least one spot that seems impracticable.'[51]

Gaba Tepe is that.

In the darkness just before dawn, it will be the job of the first troops of the 3rd Brigade ashore to push forward and capture all ground between the shore and the Third Ridge, about a mile inland, so securing a large beachhead on which the other Brigades can securely land.

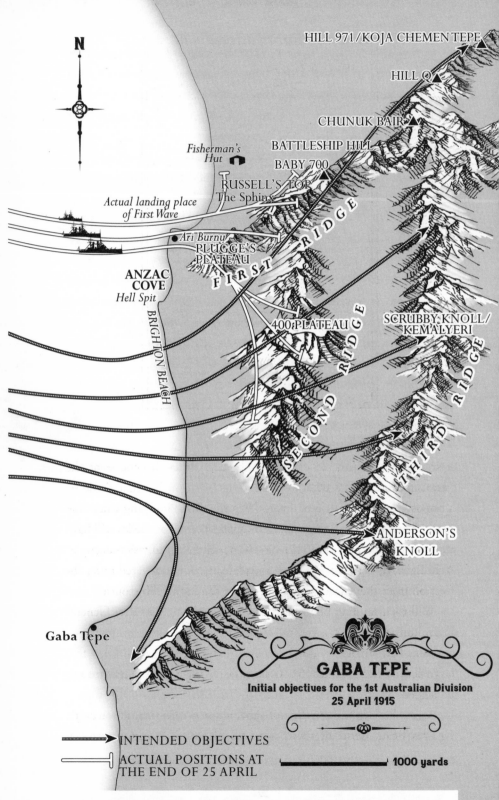

N

HILL 971 / KOJA CHEMEN TEPE

HILL Q

CHUNUK BAIR

BATTLESHIP HILL

BABY 700

Fisherman's Hut

RUSSELL'S TOP
The Sphinx

Actual landing place of First Wave

Ari Burnu
PLUGGE'S PLATEAU

ANZAC COVE
Hell Spit

FIRST RIDGE

400 PLATEAU

SCRUBBY KNOLL / KEM'ALYERI

BRIGHTON BEACH

SECOND RIDGE

THIRD RIDGE

ANDERSON'S KNOLL

Gaba Tepe

GABA TEPE

Initial objectives for the 1st Australian Division
25 April 1915

INTENDED OBJECTIVES

ACTUAL POSITIONS AT
THE END OF 25 APRIL

1000 yards

Intended objectives and actual positions for Anzacs, 25 April 1915, by Jane Macaulay

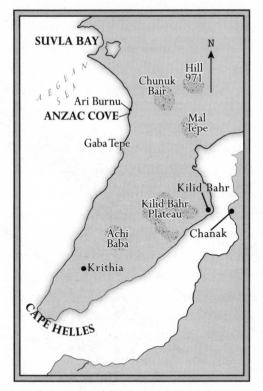

Kilid Bahr Plateau, by Jane Macaulay

It may even be possible to push right across that backbone of the Peninsula and make it the four miles to the Narrows, but that would be a bonus. The key thing remains to keep the Turks guessing where the main thrust will be, so that the 29th Division on Cape Helles will have the best chance of winning the day. (Once the 29th Division occupies Achi Baba, the Turkish forces on the plateau can be squeezed into submission from the Anzacs to the north and the 29th to the south.)

Will their landing be a surprise? Unlikely. Just a day after General Hamilton and his staff arrive in Mudros Harbour, a German spy plane, a Taube, had flown over them at a great height, clearly examining this large fleet assembling just 60 miles from the Dardanelles, but that can't be helped, what?

As to the local inhabitants of Port Mudros, they include, records Charles Bean, 'some of the quaintest looking old Turks I ever saw

– regular Sinbad-the-sailors; every third man was the pirate of the fairy books and yet they say they are most very kindly good-natured old folk – all the Europeans who live amongst them seem to like the Turks.'[52]

What chance that it will be kept from the Turks themselves that just off their shores one of the greatest armadas ever formed is gathering for an invasion?

Buckley's and none . . .

Particularly when all through Alexandria and Port Said the comings and goings of all the ships and their destinations are covered in the Egyptian press, when all of the procurement of the massive amounts of supplies needed is impossible to keep secret, when, as Hamilton's General Staff Officer, Captain Cecil Aspinall, would later report, 'one of Sir Ian Hamilton's Staff received an official letter from London, sent through the ordinary post, and addressed to the "Constantinople Field Force".'[53] It gets worse. Hamilton is 'somewhat startled'[54] in his Cairo hotel to read in the *Egyptian Gazette* over breakfast an article naming the Gallipoli Peninsula as the landing site!

So it would seem, frankly, highly unlikely that the Turks don't know they are coming. All they can do now is hope for the best – and rely on the fact that the Turks won't know specifically where they are to land.

General Birdwood makes his headquarters aboard *Queen* and wastes no time in briefing his two Divisional Commanders. General William Bridges, in turn, is quick to assign the key role of being the first force to storm the beaches to the 3rd Brigade under Colonel MacLagan. Bridges has total faith in MacLagan and his men – even if there are some Turkish trenches providing resistance in parts, they should still be able to penetrate and occupy most of the key high ground on the ridge that descends from Chunuk Bair to Gaba Tepe.

AFTERNOON, 13 APRIL 1915, A FIRST LOOK AT THE FATAL SHORE

It is time to actually have a look at the coast they must storm, and on this sunny morning General Birdwood and Admiral Cecil Thursby – the man charged with getting the Anzacs ashore – are aboard *Queen*,

Colonel Ewen MacLagan (AWM H12187)

looking closely at the strange shoreline just a mile and a half off their port bow as they steam south. With them is the Commanding Officer of the 3rd Brigade, Colonel MacLagan, and, like them, he is not only disguised in blue dungarees and appropriate headgear to make it appear that they are no more than simple sailors, but he is also peering intently at the coast through his glasses. At one point, the spies can see the white houses and minarets of two villages on the Suvla Plain, but for the most part all they can see are unfriendly hills rising sharply from the shore, covered with dark scrub . . . but criss-crossed by freshly dug trenches. They can even spy some barbed wire on the shoreline, glistening in the sun.

After looking at this same area a month earlier, General Hamilton had cabled Lord Kitchener that this place 'looks a much tougher nut to crack than it did over the map . . .',[55] and they feel much the same now.

Colonel MacLagan examines it closely through his glasses. It is a spot, just north of Gaba Tepe, which they know contains three manned Turkish trenches, although they can see no sign of the soldiers yet. Much worse, though, is the other thing they know from their reconnaissance, which is that there is a huge body of Turks just behind the ridges. All up, it does not take MacLagan long to reach his conclusions.

Certainly it is a supreme honour that it is his 3rd Brigade, judged to be the best of the lot, that has been given the task of hitting the enemy shores first, to provide covering fire for the battalions to follow, but it is MacLagan's strong view from the first, and he says so, that against a heavily entrenched enemy, the task is simply 'too big for a brigade'.[56]

Nonsense, Birdwood and Thursby assure him. They have every confidence in the capacity of him and his men. Colonel MacLagan is simply being pessimistic.

But MacLagan is not swayed. Privately he is already forming the view that it will be more advisable to secure tactical points much closer to the beach than the unrealistic objectives further inland on the plan that has been handed down to him from on high.

Once returned from their reconnaissance trip, the key officers get down to tin tacks on the actual specifics of the landing, and the wardroom of *Minnewaska* is soon filled with large vertical maps upon which white discs on pegs (each representing a ship) are moved around. Which ships carrying which things – be they soldiers, artillery, horses, ammunition or supplies – are put in the right order until some rough semblance of organisation is imposed.

16 APRIL 1915, PORT MUDROS, JUST TO SEE HER ONCE

Like many of the men, Captain Gordon Carter of the 1st Battalion is excited and a bit fearful all at once.

'Your object,' Birdwood has told him and his men directly a few days ago, 'is first to force a landing on the Gallipoli Peninsula and help the navy to force the Dardanelles, after which our mission is Constantinople and then perhaps on to the German flank through Austria.'

'Sounds very nice but will take some doing,' Carter had sagely noted in his diary afterwards.[57] Over the last few days, he has been training his men hard in getting from ship to boat to shore with themselves and their gear intact – 'the oarsmen were rather crude at first but soon settled down to it'[58] – including doing night drill. In the course of it, he had even met General Sir Ian Hamilton, 'who spoke very nicely and encouragingly'.[59]

What he most wants to do now, however, before the attack begins, is to see Nurse King, who has sent him a lovely note via a launch from her newly arrived hospital ship SS *Sicilia*, which he can see over yonder, about two miles away. Unfortunately, by the time he manages to get permission to leave his own ship and hitch a ride to hers, he has missed her – she and other nurses had been invited for a tour of the *Agamemnon*. Devastated, he returns to his own ship. If only he could see her, *once*.

Lydia King feels the same, upon her return.

17 APRIL 1915, BY THE DARDANELLES, FROM OUT OF THE CLOUDS

Lieutenant-Commander Charles Brodie has never felt worse.

His friend Lieutenant-Commander Dacre Stoker had suggested to Commodore Roger Keyes that the Dardanelles could be forced – and the Sea of Marmara exploited – by a courageous Commander in a submarine. Such an attempt had been made the previous night by the only available Commander courageous enough to try: Brodie's identical twin brother Theodore in his sub *E15*. There has been no communication since, and now Charles Brodie is on a reconnaissance flight in a Farman two-seater biplane above the Dardanelles, looking for a sign . . . with a terrible sense of foreboding. He and Theodore have always had an almost telepathic sense of how the other is faring, and he strongly senses disaster before . . .

He sees something!

Just inside the mouth of the Dardanelles, he sees on the Asian shore at Kephez Point what appears to be a grey straw lying at right angles to a small beach, with a curious black line . . . Oh God, no, it is billowing black *smoke* . . . It is, of course, the *E15*, and it has been beached. His twin brother is surely dead, just as he had felt. (And, in fact, after the war, he would learn that Theodore had indeed been lying dead in the conning tower, cut in half by a Turkish shell.)

God.

Following Stoker's plan, Theodore had taken the *E15* as far as possible in the darkness before diving. Somehow, however, when surfacing again, the *E15* had been caught by the treacherous currents, causing it to beach right 'neath the guns of Fort Dardanos, which had finished it off – and Theodore Brodie with it. Six of his crew have also been killed.

Oh *God.*

(Lieutenant-Commander Dacre Stoker hears the news on the day the *AE2* is to set sail from Malta, where the submarine is undergoing repairs after losing an argument with a large ship. He is shattered.)

17 APRIL 1915, GALLIPOLI PENINSULA, DEAR MOTHER, I DO NOT NEED NEW UNDERWEAR

The soldiers of the Ottoman 19th Division, stationed in reserve at Boghali on the Gallipoli Peninsula, have been training and conducting endless manoeuvres under their severe commander, Lieutenant-Colonel Mustafa Kemal. Though they are weary, their morale is high, and the men often take time to enjoy the beautiful spring days and the crops of yellow and pink wildflowers that are springing up by the slowly trickling streams that mark the depth of the gullies.

On this day, a bright, young soldier, Hasan Ethem, who has left his last year of law school in Constantinople to fulfil his duty to country and Allah, writes a letter to his beloved mother.

> *Glorious Turkish mother who gave birth to four soldiers! I have received your letter while I was sitting under a pear tree in a greenish meadow. I felt the joy to be in a holy mission, here.*
> *My God! The only intention of those soldiers is*

to prove your glorious name to the British and the French. Bless this honourable intention. Sharpen our bayonets and destroy our enemies . . .

This is the most beautiful place of the earth.

Dear Mother, I do not need new underwear. I still have my money. God Bless You.

Your Son

Hasan Ethem

17 April 1915[60]

18 APRIL 1915, LEMNOS, MOVEMENT IN THE HARBOUR

Something is going on, and there are eyes everywhere, watching.

The local residents of Mudros Harbour are not told what, but their port is busy as never before. Hour after hour, day after day, more troopships arrive, filled with soldiers, and the ships have no sooner dropped anchor than the training begins.

Time and again, a whistle blows and then the soldiers are seen – in full kit, carrying their rifles – swarming down the ships' sides on wildly swinging rope ladders and then rowing to the shore and scrambling out. Others do the same, while also bringing artillery and horses.

And again. And again. And *again*.

One keen observer is General Hamilton, who, after watching the Australians in action, is quick to record his thoughts.

'These Australians,' he writes, 'are shaping into Marines in double-quick time and Cairo hijinks are wild oats sown and buried.'[61]

The men are so good that General Hamilton gives the order for the training to stop.

With good weather, allowing all the supply boats to get about their business in the harbour, they can leave within two days. True, medical arrangements to get wounded men back off the beaches have not yet been organised, but his staff will hopefully be getting to that shortly.

19 APRIL 1915, LEMNOS, CAN HE BE SERIOUS?

Charles Bean is becoming anxious, and it is has nothing to do with the prospect of being under fire, but rather the likelihood that he won't be in the thick of it. *Still* he has received no permission to accompany the troops when they go. All he has is a letter from General Bridges' General Staff Officer, Major Thomas Blamey, requesting that the English officers grant that permission.

Grasping that letter, Bean now boards *Arcadian*, looking for General Hamilton's Chief of Staff, Major-General Walter Braithwaite, whose every utterance to underlings – like a certain P. G. Wodehouse character – has an impatient *what-is-it?* about it.

'I am rather surprised, Bean,' says Braithwaite, 'that Blamey has asked for you to have the same facilities as the English pressmen. It was perfectly understood that you were allowed to come here only on the condition that you write nothing at all, nothing at all.'[62]

'The order was not "nothing at all",' the Australian correspondent carefully corrects him, 'it was "nothing at all until sanctioned". I had supposed that when arrangements were made sanctioning English pressmen I also would be sanctioned. I have simply come to find out.'[63]

'I know nothing about any sanction being given. We have had no word at all about you, Bean. On the other hand the English pressmen have come here properly accredited.'[64]

'Well then, the condition in the order "until sanction is given" meant nothing?'[65]

'Look here!' Braithwaite snaps. 'I have no intention of entering into any argument with you about this. As far as I'm concerned the order meant exactly what it said – that you can write *nothing until sanction is given* . . . And you might keep it in mind, Bean, that we have no reason to suppose that sanction will *ever* be given.'

While it is not quite true to say that Charles Bean 'storms off', he is at least a very black thundercloud heading south.

AFTERNOON, 21 APRIL 1915, LOOKING OVER THE BEST LAID PLANS OF . . . MEN

On a cold, wet and windy day, the departure of the armada has had to be delayed. Colonel Ewen MacLagan takes the opportunity to go through the plans one more time so that all of the senior officers of 3rd Brigade can be locked into what the overall landing plan is and what their own role will be.

He is aided by a pointing stick and a large wall map divided into small, numbered squares.

Now, we of the 3rd Brigade are landing first. We are in two waves of 1500 and 2500 soldiers respectively. Our job will be to eliminate whatever Turkish resistance we find, securing the beaches for the next two waves, before moving inland to secure the three main ridges of the Sari Bair Range, securing the Third Ridge furthest inland being one of the first day's main objectives.[66]

With all going well, all of 3rd Brigade will be ashore by around 5 am, and, snapping at our heels, nine transport ships will in turn move forward, carrying the 2nd and 1st Brigades of 8000 soldiers. Half these men would be landed by the battleships' tows, the other half by the seven destroyers' tows, and we should have 12,000 men ashore by 9 am.

Once the entire 1st Australian Division is ashore, the New Zealand and Australian Division will begin to land in transports, and by nightfall we should have 20,000 men on the Peninsula. Our overall goal is to push across the waist of the Peninsula, cutting off the lines of communication and avenue of retreat for the Turkish forces at Cape Helles. Once across to the European shore of the Dardanelles, the aim is to neutralise the howitzer batteries and forts that have been preventing the minesweepers from doing their work. At the same time that the Anzacs make their landing, the British forces, led by the 29th Division, will be making their landing at the bottom tip of the Peninsula at Cape Helles, and the French on the Asian shore of the Dardanelles at Kum Kale – the last as a feint to confuse the defenders as to where the real thrust of the attack is coming.

All clear?

All clear.

Now, if we can just get some clear weather, we can clear off and be on our way!

MORNING, 23 APRIL 1915, MUDROS, THE SUN SHINES UPON THEM

It is exactly the kind of day the British have been waiting for. One for the ages, *of* the ages. As the sun rises over ancient Troy to the east, the fine mist over Port Mudros clears to reveal the waters to be a 'blue jewel'[67] with barely a ripple as birds flit hither and thither through the masts and around the funnels of so many ships, while the hills of Lemnos beam back upon these soldiers and sailors gathered here from so many corners of the earth.

For this, one of the largest invasion flotillas ever assembled, one could not have hoped for better weather to launch on the Dardanelles, and General Hamilton has no hesitation in giving the order to proceed.

Out in Mudros Harbour, no fewer than 200 ships of various classes – all painted black to suit the night where they must move by stealth – take on soldiers and last-minute supplies. They are ships showing flags from all over the world – Australia, France, Russia and Great Britain, most notably – and they are heading for one spot. The Dardanelles.

From barges, quays and small boats, the soldiers continue to file up the gangplanks, carrying their newly greased rifles over their shoulders. On their backs are freshly filled, heavy packs containing cans of bully beef, Maconochie's soup and jam, together with hard biscuits. Already encumbered enough, before the battle they will be issued 200 rounds of ammunition, enough to last them two days, ideally. All up, including their water bag, the whole pack weighs an amazing 70 pounds – that's five stone! For now, they are quickly directed to various parts of their allotted ships to fill every room, every bit of deck space and, more often than not, every nook and cranny. All is nearing readiness to launch . . .

Aboard *Queen Elizabeth*, however, Admiral de Robeck remains nervous.

What more can they possibly do to help ensure the success of this already highly risky enterprise?

And now he recalls the conversation he had earlier that month with Lieutenant-Commander Dacre Stoker, the captain of that Australian submarine *AE2*, who had said that forcing the Narrows *was* possible. If so, this could change everything. A sub in the Dardanelles and beyond could wreak havoc, seriously interfering with the Turkish supply lines.

Yes, two submarines have already been lost, but the possible prize is worth the risk.

Along with the stricken submarine *E15* the previous December, hadn't 26-year-old Captain Norman Holbrook, together with a crew of 12, pulled off one of the great military feats of the war to date when their Royal Navy, petrol-driven, ten-year-old submarine, *B11*, successfully entered the Dardanelles undetected? Once 'in', hadn't the-little-sub-marine-that-could destroyed the troopship *Mesûdiye* – anchored near the Turkish minefield just four miles south of Chanak in Sari Sigla Bay – killing 37 Turks before turning tail and beating a successful retreat? (For his courage and skill, Holbrook would be awarded the Victoria Cross just a fortnight later. As to faraway Australia, the reception of the news is so great that a tiny town in southern New South Wales changes its name to Holbrook. That sounds so much better, under the circumstances, than its previous name of . . . Germanton.)

So, it *is* possible.

Admiral de Robeck sends once more for the captain of the Australian submarine.

'An interesting psychological moment,' Stoker records in his auto-biography as a tiny steamboat takes him towards the flagship now towering over him. 'When one's heart is set on a thing, it is not often that it comes within grasp . . .'[68]

Off the steamboat, Stoker is met by none other than the Admiral's Chief of Staff, Commodore Roger Keyes, and taken immediately to Admiral de Robeck, who is impatiently waiting for him.

Well, Stoker, the Admiral asks in his clipped tones, are you still convinced you can get through the Narrows?

Yes, sir, I am.

And are you willing to make the attempt?

Yes, sir, I am.

But are you *sure* the whole thing is possible?

Stoker is, and he warms to the theme of his dream once more – how he could wait off the mouth of the Dardanelles until the moon set, then enter very slowly on the surface, being careful not to create the wash that would make the sub noticeable, and so preserve battery power by not submerging until they got to the first minefield.

The Admiral, though hanging on every word, seems far from convinced – but he also makes clear that, because the prize would be so great, he is sorely tempted to give the order for it to be attempted.

Finally, he makes his decision. Go for it. Try to take your Australian submarine under the minefields.

'If you get through,' he tells Stoker, standing up to indicate that their meeting is over, 'other boats will immediately be sent to follow.'

You must leave in two hours.

Yes, sir!

'If you succeed,' de Robeck tells Stoker by way of farewell, shaking his hand with uncharacteristic warmth, 'there is no calculating the result it will cause, and it may well be that you will have done more to finish the war than any other act accomplished.'[69]

With these words ringing in his ears, *singing* in his ears, Stoker takes his leave, the steamboat carefully making its way through a harbour that is now more frantic than ever with vessels going this way and that, their bow waves forming endless rippling criss-crosses that mirror the zigzagging that so many of them must do to make their way through.

Certainly, most of the boats bringing soldiers and supplies from the shore are naval ones, but among them are many 'strange beautiful Greek vessels . . . under rigs of old time, with sheep and goats and fish, for sale'.[70]

Aboard the battleship *Queen*, General Birdwood wishes to have a few words with as many of his Australian troops as he can muster.

'Remember,' he tells them most importantly, and with some gravity, 'the eyes of the whole world will be on you Australians, to see how you fight.'[71]

One more thing, men. The reason you were all paid with Turkish currency yesterday is so that once you have won the battle of the beaches and are on your way to Constantinople, that money will give you something to live off. But there is to be 'no haggling in the villages you pass through as all the prices will be fixed'.[72]

Around and about him as General Birdwood speaks, the loading of men, munitions and all the rest goes on, the seriousness of what they are embarking on in strict contrast with the gaiety of the day itself and the natural beauty of the scene.

The first to leave in the mid-afternoon are the troopships of Great Britain's 29th Division, which weigh anchor and move to the outer harbour of Mudros.

'No such gathering of fine ships has ever been seen upon this earth,' contemporary poet and writer John Masefield would recount, 'and the beauty and the exultation of the youth upon them made them like sacred things as they moved away.'[73]

As they leave, the soldiers on the other ships getting ready to leave on the morrow crowd the deck.

In the celebrated words of Masefield, 'They cheered and cheered till the harbour rang with cheering. As each ship crammed with soldiers drew near the battleships, the men swung their caps and cheered again, and the sailors answered, and the noise of cheering swelled, and the men in the ships not yet moving joined in, and the men ashore, till all the life in the harbour was giving thanks that it could go to death rejoicing.'[74]

And it goes on, the combined throaty hurrahs of thousands of men floating across the waters, gathering volume as it goes, hitting the shore to go still higher as all those on land join in.

'It broke the hearts of all there with pity and pride: it went beyond the guard of the English heart. Presently all were out . . . and the sun went down with marvellous colour, lighting island after island and the Asian peaks, and those left behind in Mudros trimmed their lamps knowing that they had been for a little brought near to the heart of things.'[75]

The 29th travel to their goal with the last words of their Commanding Officer, General Aylmer Hunter-Weston, still stinging in their ears. Not only must they land and secure the beaches for the other troops to follow, but they must occupy Achi Baba, the small mountain overlooking Cape Helles, *by the afternoon* of the landing.

As the sun begins to set over the western hills of Lemnos – 'Just like a stage setting,' one soldier would record, 'with the lovely deep red-coloured orb disappearing between the purple hills and dainty rose pink sky . . .'[76] – three more transports filled with soldiers of the 29th Division slowly steam out of the harbour and make for their designated rendezvous point at an anchorage north of Tenedos. Their ultimate destination, one of five beaches at Cape Helles. They are followed by the ungainly collier *River Clyde*. Its specially constructed sally ports on each side, together with the nest of sandbags on the front deck – through which are poking Vickers machine-guns purloined from the Royal Naval Air Service Armoured Car Squadron – give it a rather odd appearance as it tows a steamhopper and four lighters (flat-bottomed barges that can be rowed ashore, designed to carry as many as 40 men). Sticking close is *Euryalus*, bearing Admiral Wemyss, followed by *Implacable* and *Cornwallis*. All, so far, is going according to plan.

As two pigeons fly above the armada, a soldier comments, 'Doves of peace',[77] but it seems unlikely . . .

Aboard HMT *Suffolk* in Port Mudros, Lieutenant-Colonel James Lyon-Johnston now takes the opportunity to, for the first time, tell his men of the 3rd Brigade's 11th Battalion just where it is that they are going and what it is that they are likely to be facing. Gathering the soldiers in the waist of the ship, with many men even climbing the rigging to better hear his every word, he begins.

'Boys,' he says, 'we have been instructed, along with the 9th and 10th Battalions, to form a covering party for the Australian landing on the Gallipoli Peninsula . . . The position of honour has been assigned to us in being thus chosen as vanguard for one of the most daring enterprises in history.'

He pauses momentarily, watching the effect of his words wash over the men, the knowledge that they have been accorded the greatest privilege of their lives . . . lives that may very well end in just a few hours.

'Boys, the General informs me that it will take several battleships and destroyers to carry our brigade to Gallipoli; a barge will be sufficient to take us home again!'[78]

Oh, how they cheer.

Gallows humour – perhaps their own gallows – but there is no doubt they really do keenly appreciate the honour.

A message is then read to them, from General Hamilton.

Listen up, men . . .

GENERAL HEADQUARTERS,
Soldiers . . . of the King.
Before us lies an adventure unprecedented in modern war. Together with our comrades of the Fleet, we are about to force a landing upon an open beach in face of positions which have been vaunted by our enemies as impregnable.

The landing will be made good, by the help of God and the Navy; the positions will be stormed, and the War brought one step nearer to a glorious close.

'Remember,' said Lord Kitchener, when bidding adieu to your Commander, 'remember, once you set foot upon the Gallipoli Peninsula, you must fight the thing through to a finish.

'The whole world will be watching your progress. Let us prove ourselves worthy of the great feat of arms entrusted to us.'

IAN HAMILTON, General[79]

For his part, on the eve of the eve of this momentous battle, General Hamilton receives a message of his own from Lord Kitchener:

My best wishes to you and all your force in carrying to a successful conclusion the operations you have before you, which will undoubtedly have a momentous effect on the war. The task they have to perform will need all the grit Britishers have never failed to show, and I am confident your troops will victoriously clear the way for the Fleet to advance on Constantinople.[80]

Chapter Eight

THE LANDING ('*SILAH BAŞINA! –* TO ARMS!')

... Cease your preaching! Load your guns!
Their roar our mission tells,
The day is come for Britain's sons
To seize the Dardanelles[1]
William Allan, MP for Gateshead

Death grins at my elbow. I cannot get him out of my
thoughts. He is fed up with the old and sick – only the
flower of the flock will serve him now, for God has started
a celestial spring cleaning, and our star is to be scrubbed
bright with the blood of our bravest and our best.[2]
General Sir Ian Hamilton, diary entry

In no unreal sense it was on the 25th of April, 1915, that
the consciousness of Australian nationhood was born.[3]
*Charles Bean, Official History of Australia
in the War of 1914–1918, Vol. II*

DAWN, 24 APRIL 1915, LEMNOS, NEVER SEND TO KNOW FOR WHOM THE BELL TOLLS; IT TOLLS FOR THEE . . .

Today is the day for the bulk of the Anzacs to get moving. After all
these months of training, *finally* they are about to engage in battle.

The mood of the men is a startling combination of tension, excitement and, yes, fulfilment. After all the hard slog, the hoping, the waiting, it really is about to happen. They are about to be tested in battle!

As the soldiers of the 1st Brigade wake, the view from their portholes is dark and the mood tense. They are the first due to leave, and after a'gulping down their standard breakfast of porridge, stew, bread and jam, and taking their last swig of tea, they collect their packs and parade on deck.

Moving out in an orderly fashion, they climb down from their ships one by one, plonking themselves into the rowboats that are waiting for them below. They are then taken to the four arranged transports, the oars leaving whole loaves of bread and other discarded foods wobbling in their wake. The stink of the harbour is rancid.

Bound for the Bay of Purnea, on the north side of the island of Lemnos, they are underway by the time the sun comes up, following the *Minnewaska*, which also contains several battalions, including that of Captain Gordon Carter. At the prow of that mighty vessel, the Lieutenant gazes longingly at the shadowy bulk of the SS *Sicilia* as she passes, saddened that he still has not been able to see Nurse King. Unbeknownst to him, she is awaking at this very moment, and his is the first ship she sees from her porthole. She prays that Gordon will be all right, whatever happens.

Meanwhile, the men of the 2nd Brigade are the next due to go. After inspection on deck, many of them sit down to write letters to their loved ones. One such letter-writer is the intrepid, fresh-faced, 20-year-old Lieutenant Alan Dudley Henderson. He has just been made a Platoon Commander, which is a far cry from his everyday vocation as an accountant. Due to land in the Second Wave of troops, he is excited to at last be approaching departure and slowly begins to write:

very soon we will have started to do what we came away for and have waited so long to do. While you are in church tomorrow thinking of us, we may be needing all your prayers as it is either going to be a hard fight or an easy walk in, but everything is ready and everyone quietly confident of success. It is going to be Australia's chance and she makes a tradition out of this that she must always look back on. God grant it will be a great one.[4]

Nearby, aboard *London*, Captain William Annear – who is due to be among the first to land – commits to paper a simple instruction:

```
11TH BATTALION.
IF I GET BLOWN OUT I DESIRE THAT MY WRISTLET
WATCH, FIELD GLASSES AND SOVEREIGN PURSE AND
CONTENTS BE FORWARDED TO
     MISS NELLY BERRYMAN,
     GENERAL POST OFFICE,
     HOBART, TASMANIA.
     (SIGNED)
     W.R. ANNEAR,
     CAPTAIN,
     11TH. BATTALION.
     24.4.15.
```
[5]

At a little after midday, the 2nd Brigade, together with the two Indian Mountain Batteries, each armed with six ten-pounder breech-loading screw guns, leave the harbour and also head to the Bay of Purnea, ready to move on towards the Dardanelles at midnight.

By the early afternoon, it is the turn of the 3rd Brigade, who, led by Colonel Ewen MacLagan, are to hit the beaches first, to act as a covering force for those who will follow. The bulk of them (2500) are aboard four transports, from where they will transfer to the seven destroyers at 11 pm, while the 1500 of the first landing wave will board the battleships *Queen*, *Prince of Wales* and *London*, which will lead them in.

Aboard *Prince of Wales*, General William Bridges has one more shot at cheering up MacLagan before he walks up the gangplank onto the destroyer HMS *Colne*. 'Well, MacLagan,' says Bridges, with a sparkle in his eye and merriment in his voice, 'you haven't thanked me yet.'

'Yes, sir, I do thank you for the great honour of having this job to do with my brigade,' the Colonel replies. 'But if we find the Turks holding these ridges in any strength, I honestly don't think you'll ever see the 3rd Brigade again.'

'Oh, go along with you!' says Bridges, laughing heartily.[6]

Shortly after 1.30 pm, the magnificent flagship of the fleet, *Queen Elizabeth* – universally known as 'Lizzie' – weighs anchor. Magisterially gliding, she heads for the impossibly blue waters beyond the murky harbour's entrance. Again, the cheering from the Anzacs, British, Indians and Frenchmen aboard the myriad minion battleships, cruisers and troopships is deafening. They clap and shout, jump, chant and sing.

Onward, Christian soldiers!

There is a spirit of magnificence in the air, of the battle knell, of the ringing clarion call through the ages that men have answered to take up arms against their foes. And with a ship as glorious as this at their head – *Rule, Britannia! Britannia, rules the waves!* – how could they go wrong?

With big Lizzie cutting her path towards the glassy sea, the ships form up into their assigned positions. Overhead, the sun is eclipsed at flickering intervals by a seaplane, which drones and swoops back and forth, looking for any sign of German submarines.

The Anzacs are also on their way, with *Queen* – bearing General Birdwood and his senior staff – in the lead, closely followed by *London* and *Prince of Wales*. On the back of many ships, troops have scrawled signs in large letters:

CONSTANTINOPLE
OR BUST
ON TO THE HAREMS
BRING ON YOUR TURKISH DELIGHTS[7]

Sundown that day could not have been more perfect, a golden orb sinking beneath the western horizon, and splashing pink and purple hues onto the sky-blue canvas as it does so. In the Bay of Purnea, the troops of the 1st and 2nd Brigades, who have been waiting on their transports for most of the afternoon, are mesmerised by the sky in the west when they see movement on the horizon. Five of their warships are moving east towards temporary anchorage at Imbros, which is within sight of the Dardanelles. The mighty 3rd Brigade is on its way!

The men watch silently, exchanging grins and glances that belie their trepidation. As Charles Bean aboard *Minnewaska* notes, the ships pass 'gradually across the skyline, trailing a long streamer of smoke, until the night closed over them'.[8]

Watching their brothers and mates sail off, and knowing they are soon to follow, they are more solemn than they had been in the jubilations of a few hours earlier. There is a difference between 'bravado' and 'bravery', and the latter is more quiet by nature. Who knows what sunrise will bring, and just how many of them will be there to see it?

That is certainly the feeling aboard *London*, where English war correspondent Ellis Ashmead-Bartlett – a distinguished veteran of the Boer War and now a legend of Fleet Street for the six wars he has so dashingly covered – dines with Australian officers of the 11th Battalion of the 3rd Infantry Brigade in the wardroom, the very men due to be among the first ashore. 'Everyone,' the *Daily Telegraph* correspondent would carefully record, 'feigned an unnatural cheerfulness, the wine passed round, not a word was said of what the morrow might bring forth, yet over the party there seemed to hover the dread angel of death . . .'[9]

This, mind, is all in marked contrast to the English military leadership whom Ashmead-Bartlett has been interviewing in recent weeks. For this supremely well-connected eldest son of Conservative MP Sir Ellis Ashmead-Bartlett – who had been educated at Marlborough College along with war poet Siegfried Sassoon – is at least the social equal if not superior of the high military brass, and his unfettered access to them has given a clear impression: 'It did not appear to me

. . . that either the General or his Staff realised the terrible gravity of the enterprise on which they were now embarking . . . It seemed to me they rather regarded the Expedition as a kind of glorified picnic, and that the main consideration was the fact that they had an independent command to exercise which was extremely pleasing to their *amour propre.*'[10]

On each ship after dinner this night, a church service is held, followed by hymns, including particular favourites 'Nearer My God to Thee', 'Stand up for Jesus', 'God Be with You Till We Meet Again', as well as, of course, 'God Save the King' and 'Auld Lang Syne'.

—

On the Gallipoli Peninsula too, that angel of death looms, even if most of the Ottoman soldiers don't yet know it. The soldiers of the 1st and 3rd Battalions of the 27th Ottoman Infantry Regiment are completely exhausted. After spending the previous night in training manoeuvres around Gaba Tepe, their officers have insisted they now march through the night to their camp at Maidos.

As the watery moon begins its long journey across the sparkling heavens, the young men want nothing more than to be lying in their tents, dreaming of their loved ones. But all they can do is keep marching.

And they are not the only Ottoman soldiers on the move. On this day, the Minister for the Interior, Talaat, signs an order that is nothing less than a death warrant for many of the Empire's Armenian population. Long have the Armenians – whose homeland is right next to the Russian border – been held in suspicion by the ruling Turks, and long have they been repressed because of it. In the extremities of these times, however, when it has become apparent that some Armenians have joined the Russians fighting against them, repression tips over into something far more murderous.

'With the discovery of the bombs,' the circular reads, 'and the Ottoman Armenians' joining with the Russian forces by forming voluntary regiments against the Ottoman State, it has become evident that these committees . . . incite upheavals in the regions and threaten the

Ottoman Army . . . Consequently, the government has taken measures to . . . arrest the leaders and the members of the committees, of the people who have taken part in the activities, of the Armenians who are well known by the police forces, gathering of the suspicious people in an area in the towns so as to prevent their escape, launching of searches for weapons in suitable places have been found appropriate.'[11]

The Turkish Ottoman leadership will no longer abide a seditious enemy from within, not while they are being threatened on all sides from without. Turkey for the Turks!

With the approval of General Enver as the Ottoman Army Commander-in-Chief, the final orders of Talaat are distributed. The round-up is not confined to just Armenia. For, on this same day in Constantinople – a day to be later known as 'Red Sunday' – some 250 Armenian Ottoman notables and intellectuals are arrested. Most will soon be executed as part of a general purge of the Armenian population.

MIDNIGHT, 24 APRIL 1915, TENEDOS, FISH IN A BARREL

A rumble in the night, a swish of propellers, ripples of suddenly swirling water and there is movement in the bay at the northern side of Tenedos.

Leading off are the three transports bearing the soldiers of the 29th Division who will storm W and V Beaches and Morto Bay, closely followed by *Euryalus*, bearing Admiral Wemyss, *Implacable*, *Cornwallis* and *River Clyde*. They are followed by tugs pulling floating piers, which will be used to unload supplies once the beachhead is established. The battleships must be in place before dawn, ready to begin their bombardment. The French, meanwhile, leave from the southern side of Tenedos.

Perhaps most tense are those aboard *River Clyde*, the collier earmarked to ram the shore and disgorge over 2000 of the 29th's finest soldiers on the Turkish defenders. On the lowest deck, the men lie cramped up against each other, thankful at least for the warmth of the bodies next to them. One man, feet numbed by the cold, crawls half-asleep to a spot near the engines. He coils up and drifts off, only to wake to 'a heavy sea boot . . . planted firmly on my face'. Most of the men are only pretending to sleep anyway. An officer sits up at a makeshift table made from 'two lime barrels and a few rough boards', with a cigarette in one hand and a pencil in the other. He jots in his diary, 'sitting on board after trying to snooze with head on a big box . . . but too uncomfortable for anything, so whipped out my "bookie" and scribbled; light bad, only an oily lamp with glass smoked black, and nearly 20 feet distant. Queer scene altogether . . . Sunday is just ten minutes old, and the ship's screw has started – we are off!'[12]

WEE HOURS, 25 APRIL 1915, CAST OFF AND DRIFT ASTERN

Bearing the bulk of the First Wave's 3rd Brigade now transferred to their care, the seven destroyers' screws turn languidly, as the black silhouettes of the flotilla bearing the Anzacs now approach the rendezvous point off the shores of the Gallipoli Peninsula.

Just a little back from the main flotilla, the Australian submarine *AE2* is also making its careful way. An attempt to go through the Dardanelles the previous evening had had to be abandoned after the 'foremost hydroplane shaft coupling' broke.[13] But, mercifully, Rear-Admiral John de Robeck is allowing Stoker to make another attempt. 'Try again tomorrow,' he had said. 'If you succeed in getting through there is nothing you could possibly want that we won't do for you.'[14]

This time, however, the orders are different. Yesterday, the hope had been that the sub would make it through the Narrows into the Sea of Marmara and then attack the shipping bringing supplies to the Turkish troops. Now, as the sub would be in operation when much of the fleet would be lying off the entrance to the Straits, it is crucial that the Turks be prevented from floating mines down on the current, which might see the Allies lose ships as they had done on 18 March. Commodore Roger Keyes, de Robeck's Chief of Staff, had told Stoker, 'In fact, generally run amuck at the Narrows – if you get there.'[15]

If you get there? Stoker had burst out laughing. But the rest of it had been no laughing matter. For the order – and Stoker well knows it – means that he and his men are unlikely to come back. While it would be one thing to get through the Narrows to the Sea of Marmara and hunt like a fox for the fat rabbits of supply ships – for preventing the Turkish defenders getting resupplied easily by sea is the key aim – it would be quite another to hunt in the tiny alley that leads to the rabbit nest itself. There, the submarine risks being the rabbit in the search-lights, while all the forts, patrol boats, cruisers and destroyers would be able to bring concentrated fire to bear.

'If you searched the whole world over,' Stoker would write, 'I doubt you would find a much more unpleasant spot to carry out a submarine attack than this Narrows of Chanak. Half a mile wide, with a cur-rent of 3 to 5 knots, it is certainly not an ideal place for manoeuvres in a comparatively slow-moving and difficultly turned submarine. Also, the thought that we ourselves might meet one of those floating mines hardly added to the entertainment the day was likely to provide for us.'[16]

Carefully, slowly, the great battleships continue to steam towards the Turkish shore. For those soldiers awake above decks, all that can be seen is the slightly darker blobs of the other destroyers. Some men take up their 'mandolins, guitars and banjos' to play and sing with a gather-ing chorus, which withers into silence as the night grows older. Some men talk quietly, careful not to wake those who have snatched a final sleep. Face to face with their mortality, the men abandon nicety and share astounding stories and 'home truths' with each other, divulging secrets they never knew existed.[17]

At 1 am, there is a stirring among the men as, even though asleep, they become aware of a change in the rhythm of the ship's engines, which slow to nearly nothing. They are here, at the designated rendez-vous point, just five miles from the spot where the men are to land. Across all the ships, those soldiers remaining asleep are woken – 'Come on, lads, have a good, hot supper, there's business doing'[18] – and given a hot meal of (they knew it!) bully beef and bread, washed down by the second-greatest Australasian restorative of all: a cup of piping-hot tea. On some of the ships, the men are given a tot of rum to settle their souls and warm their spirits.

Aboard *London*, the soldiers have hit it off with the sailors – so much so that the sailors have 'renamed Port and Starboard as A and C after the two Australian companies on board'.[19] Ellis Ashmead-Bartlett wanders around the mess deck with his notebook, observing the soldiers wolfing down their meals, while their officers dine in the wardroom. Yes, perhaps the Last Supper for some, but the Australians are 'as calm as if about to take part in a route march'.[20]

At 2 am, right on schedule, the hissed order goes out on deck to *'Prepare to man the boats . . .'*, even as the men eating their meals below hear the command ringing down the ladder-ways: *'Fall in!'*[21]

And so they do, taking their rifles and their packs, climbing the ladders and forming up into companies by going to their assigned squares on the deck, each of which has a large painted number on it. From the derricks, the ships' boats are now lowered, and rope ladders thrown over the side, while the ships turn parallel to the shore to shield sight and sound from those who may be carefully watching and listening . . .

'With only a faint sheen from the stars to light up the dramatic scenes on deck,' Ashmead-Bartlett observes closely. 'This splendid contingent from Australia stood there in silence as the officers, hurrying from group to group, issued their final instructions. Between the companies of infantry were the beach parties, whose duty it was to put them ashore. Lieutenants in khaki, midshipmen – not yet out of their "teens" – in old white duck suits dyed khaki colour, carrying revolvers, water-bottles, and kits almost as big as themselves, and sturdy bluejackets . . .'[22]

Now in all but complete darkness – even smoking is banned – the Australian soldiers get their rifles on their shoulders and, with their hearts in their mouths, climb onto the swinging rope ladders that dangle into the boats below, only barely bobbing in water so calm that it is 'like a sheet of oil'.[23]

There in the light mist, four midshipmen and one coxswain await in the boat below, whispering respectfully to the lightly growling officers on high how many more they can take – it is up to 40 soldiers to a boat, taking some 40 minutes to load – until one gives out the much-awaited last whisper, 'Full up, sir!'[24]

Very well, then.

'Cast off and drift astern,' comes the next command from the shadowy figure on high.

In the boats – amid all the boxes of ammunition, picks, shovels, sandbags and wire-cutters, among other things – the soldiers of the 9th, 10th and 11th Battalions shiver. They have been told not to wear their great-coats, for they are too cumbersome and it is thought their exposed white skin will help them to keep track of each other once on the shore.

The three battleships begin to tow their four steamboats and attached boats carrying a total of 1500 soldiers in this, the first lot of the First Wave:

∧	∧	∧	Battleships
∧ ∧ ∧ ∧	∧ ∧ ∧ ∧	∧ ∧ ∧ ∧	Steamboats
∧ ∧ ∧ ∧	∧ ∧ ∧ ∧	∧ ∧ ∧ ∧	
∧ ∧ ∧ ∧	∧ ∧ ∧ ∧	∧ ∧ ∧ ∧	Towed boats
∧ ∧ ∧ ∧	∧ ∧ ∧ ∧	∧ ∧ ∧ ∧	

—

At 2 am, just as the Australian troops are preparing to launch their boats, two Turkish soldiers are sitting in their observation post on a ridge above Ari Burnu, the very spot that the companies of the 3rd Brigade are approaching. Both local boys, Idris from Boghali and Cemil from Gallipoli, they chat quietly, smoking and occasionally taking up their binoculars to scan the western horizon, far out across the moonlit waters, where there is nothing but . . .

Bismillah . . . Bu ne? My God . . . what is that?

What?

There! THERE!

And now Cemil can see it too.

Way, way out, in the sliver of silvery light where the sky meets the sea, they can see distinct shapes. *Ship*-like shapes!

Ingiliz! Ingiliz! There are ships! Many, many ships! English soldiers are just off our shores!

Immediately, the two sentries report to the Company Commander.

Captain Faik, Commander of a company of 250 soldiers in the 27th Regiment, is sleeping in his dugout on the Second Ridge when a sentry from his reserve platoon bursts in and awakens him. *Ingiliz! Ingiliz!* The observation post has spotted 'many enemy ships in the open sea!'.[25] Captain Faik immediately rises and surveys the sea using his own binoculars. *Aman Allahım!* Oh, Allah!

There they are, all different sizes, bobbing in the moonlight a fair way offshore. He can't tell if they are moving or still, but they are definitely there in force.

Quickly, he gets his Battalion Commander, Major Ismet at Gaba Tepe, on the telephone and reports what he has seen.

'There is no cause for haste,' the Major's voice crackles back down the line.[26]

For now, Captain Faik is to continue watching closely and report back. *Peki, Komutan.* Of course, Commander.

Racing to his observation post, the captain tries to steady his raggedy breathing as he again brings his binoculars to bear and . . . this time there is no doubt about it. The ships are a great mass now, *dozens* of them, and they are much closer, heading straight for the shores right in front of where he is now standing.

With some trepidation, Captain Faik phones straight through to divisional headquarters near Maidos. He reaches Lieutenant Nuri and reports what he has seen.

'*Telefon başından ayrılma* – Hold the line,' Nuri replies. 'I will inform the Chief of Staff.'

It is an agony. With every second that passes, the ships are coming closer and will no doubt soon be disgorging enemy soldiers, but Captain Faik waits until Nuri returns.

'How many of these ships are warships,' he asks, 'and how many are transports?'

'It is impossible to distinguish what type of ships they are in the dark, but there are *many* of them.'[27]

The conversation ends there and, for a moment, Captain Faik sits on the ridge above the quiet cove, alone, looking out at the approaching fleet in the fading light of the setting moon. They are closer still, fading into darkness as the moon begins to set . . .

At the same time that the men of Turkey's 27th Regiment's 2nd Battalion are being woken up and called to arms, the 1st and 3rd Battalions are just bunking down for the night at their camp at Maidos, some six miles to the south-east. The men, under the vigilant eye of their Regiment Commander, Lieutenant-Colonel Şefik, have finally finished their long march back from Gaba Tepe.

Spent, they soon fall into the sleep of the dead and the dead exhausted.

2.30 AM, 25 APRIL 1915, OFF THE DARDANELLES, LIKE AN ARROW IN THE NIGHT

Slowly, oh so carefully, the *AE2* – after leaving HMS *Swiftsure*, which has been towing it – powers along on the surface into the jaws of hell, represented by the entrance to the Dardanelles Strait. The sea is as cold, flat and dark as black glass, the only ripples upon it forming a perfectly symmetrical and sparkling phosphorescent arrow in the moonlight, with the bulbous black bow of the *AE2* at its tip.

Ahead, searchlights from the shore criss-cross the waters. For the moment, *AE2* sticks closely to the European side of the Straits, slip-slip-slipping along at just a little over three knots, hoping to keep engine noise to a minimum and to stay away from those searchlights for as long as possible.

For all that, so strong is the moonlight, it seems scarcely believable that every fort on the Dardanelles is not there and then a hive of activity, bringing their guns to bear on *AE2*. 'Each time,' Stoker would recount, 'as a beam of light touched the *AE2* with brighter and yet brighter finger, one held for the instant one's breath, lest the steady sweep, arrested for a moment, would show a suspicion of our shadowy presence.'[28]

That thumping?

Not mines.

Just their collective hearts.

Miraculously, however, they remain unspotted.

3 AM, 25 APRIL 1915, SECOND RIDGE, THE FIRST ROAR OF THE TEMPEST

'*Silah başına! SILAH BAŞINA!* – To arms! TO ARMS!'

Captain Faik is roaring now, jolting his soldiers of the 4th Company from their slumbers.

Grunts in the night. The shouts go on.

'*Silah başına! Silah başına!*'

Dazed, the young Turks of Captain Faik's reserve platoon now rouse themselves. Sitting up with their feet dangling out of their tents, they try to pull on their heavy boots in the pitch-black night, and the stark truth begins to dawn upon them: *perhaps this is it*, their actual baptism of fire. As nearly all of them are farmers drawn from the local area, just as their ancestors had been back to antiquity, they have taken talk of invasions to their shores with their mother's milk, just as they too have passed it on to their own small children. And yet, still it is shocking that it can all be happening *right here, right now*, as whistles blow, officers run, and the shouts continue that they all must find their guns and come, come quickly! Taking their standard-issue bolt-action Mauser rifles, they slip out of their tents and button up their khaki jackets as they assemble with their comrades, many of whom are childhood friends, to receive their orders. Their hour has come.

The 70-odd men of Captain Faik's second platoon, meanwhile, are positioned down in the trenches stretching along the First Ridge, above the shoreline at Ari Burnu. They are entrenched in places soon to be known to the Anzacs as Plugge's Plateau and Hell Spit. The Commander, Sub-Lieutenant Muharrem, has just told his men – all peering out like owls from their positions – to wait silently as the boats continue their approach.

Among the men, in a trench at the southern end of the line, is

Private Âdil, recruited from a nearby village. He had been asleep when the Corporal on sentry duty had begun to yell, 'There's something unusual! Get up!'[29]

Taking his rifle and creeping to a bluff that has a clear view of the cove below, the shepherd turned soldier had strained his eyes and, soon enough in the half-light, begun to see it all clearly: many, *many* ships approaching the shore, *filled* with armed soldiers.

—

Slowly, slowly now, their powerful engines just purring, the bristling battleships move in towards the shores of the Gallipoli Peninsula, and for the first time the men can see the barest silhouette of the Turkish hills, behind which the sun will soon be rising.

At 3.30 am, just two and a half miles from the shore, it is time. Aboard *Queen*, Rear-Admiral Cecil Thursby speaks into the wireless and gives the order to proceed.

To the steamboats now, officers loom and hiss down, 'Get away and land!'[30]

Those in command of the steamboats now open their throttles to full steam ahead . . . the ropes to the boats behind jerk tight . . . and off they go at six knots.

Farewelling them on the decks above, lines of sailors at the railings give them a 'silent cheer',[31] taking off their caps and waving them around in the traditional manner while also whispering barely audible imprecations to give the Turks what they bloody well have coming to them.

The steamboats continue chugging slowly for the shoreline. The tumbling throb of their engines booms out across the sea and, strangely, seems to soon deliver back a light echo-o-o. But there are not meant to be any cliffs close in front of them? Still, the sound, stark in the otherwise silent night, envelops the shivering soldiers in the boats, who take what comfort they can from the distraction.

And there is comfort behind, too, as all of the steamboats continue to be slowly followed by the battleships, anxious hens following up on their chicks. For the soldiers in the boats – mere corks on the ocean – it is somehow heartening in the now lightening darkness to see enormous silhouettes hovering near.

But it cannot last long . . .

For, as the seabed inevitably rises to meet the shore, the ships can hover no more, and for those on the decks of the battleships gazing forward, the most visible thing ahead is the few sparks flickering upwards from the funnels of the steamboats, together with just a dim phosphorescence coming from the bow waves of the boats, aquatic fireflies that give up the ghost in an instant.

It seems stunning to Ashmead-Bartlett that these men who 'six months ago were living peaceful civilian lives begin to disembark on a strange and unknown shore, in a strange land, to attack an enemy of a different race'.[32] To the eyes of the Englishman, the steamboats with their boats in tow look like 'great snakes' as they sneak their way forward in the dimness.

In those boats, there is still no talking, no smoking, no nothing. Just waiting, each man nursing his unloaded rifle. Colonel MacLagan does not really want them wasting bullets until it is full light, and nor does he want them to make a lot of noise, insisting that they must do the business with the bayonet. Many of them are now continuing to sharpen those bayonets, while others sit quietly and shiver, most from the cold, others from nervous excitement or outright fear as to what they are about to face. To their ears, the noise of the engines of the steamboats ahead sounds as if it would wake the dead, but still there is no sign of anything from the shore – neither light nor fight.

Aboard *London*, Ellis Ashmead-Bartlett raises his eyes from the boats to the hills of Turkey ahead. All seems in darkness, though in the nervy state of those on the ships, 'the stars above the silhouette of the hills are frequently mistaken for lights'.[33]

Aboard the destroyer HMS *Ribble*, which is soon to tow in the second instalment of the 3rd Brigade, similar scenes have been taking place. As the last tepid gleam of the moon disappears, Lieutenant-Commander

Ralph W. Wilkinson in *Ribble* leans over the bridge and passes the word to his charges. 'Lights out, men, and stop talking. We're going in now.'[34]

Soon enough, the destroyers move forward, pulling the tows with them.

'And thus in the darkness and in silence,' as Captain Ivor Margetts of the 12th Battalion would later recount, 'we were carried towards the land which was to either make or mar the name of Australia.'[35]

As Charles Bean, aboard *Minnewaska*, continues to watch closely, staring to the east where the boats have disappeared, the first sign of the coming dawn is the growing distinction of the hills the Australian soldiers are approaching. Suddenly, from that lumpy and grumpy dark horizon out to the right shoots skyward a single, hazy finger of light . . . which no sooner lazily tickles the heavens above . . . *as a thousand Australian hearts miss a beat* . . . than the searchlight disappears again.

Bean looks at his watch by the light of a struck match. It is 3.45 am.

—

For *AE2*, it could never last.

On the bridge of his 180-foot submarine, just after 4 am, Lieutenant-Commander Dacre Stoker first sees a flash of fire to the west, then an instant later hears the whistle of an approaching shell, just before he hears 'the broken swish of the shell as it hurtled past'.[36]

Time to go.

'Prepare to dive,' Stoker orders crisply into the brass voice tubes that lead from the conning tower to the sub proper below.

So well trained are they, his submariners never have to be told twice, but under this circumstance they positively leap into action. Executive Officer Geoffrey Haggard presses the button on the console three times, causing the hooter to emit three shrill blasts throughout *AE2*, while in the roaring engine room, aft, where twin 12-cylinder diesel engines drown out all other noise, a red light flashes for extra warning. And now the engines cough and then stop, just as the two large electric motors, powered by battery banks of 224 cells, burst into quiet life to take over the sub's propulsion. Stoker and his officers clear the bridge, and the upper and lower lids of the conning tower are firmly shut, as are the exhaust pipes of the engines.

All secure, Stoker, now in the centre of the control room, gives the order: 'Dive the submarine. Open 1, 2, 3, 4, 5, 6, 7 and 8 main vents. Ten down, 40 feet and back to 22 feet.'[37]

Four sailors reach overhead and open spigots on the main ballast tanks. Air can be heard escaping as the tanks fill with cold seawater, making the bow quickly sink, while the propellers powered by the two electric motors start to drive the sub lower. All else being equal, the batteries will be able to keep the sub moving at ten knots for an hour, or five knots for five hours, before she will have to resurface to charge them again with the diesel motors. For the moment, *AE2* stays at a depth of 18 feet, meaning the periscope can still keep an eye on what is happening on the surface.

—

Among the senior Australian officers on the boats still being towed to the shore by the steamboats, there is confusion just after 4 am. In their briefings, they had been told to expect to see ahead of them a flat, sandy beach, giving way to 150–200 yards of flats. But from what they can see in the dimness of the now near shore, there is nothing like that. Instead, the lightly gurgling white water just ahead looks to be practically at the foot of massive hills, one jutting knoll of which looks all of 200 feet high.

'Tell the Colonel,' Flotilla Commander Charles Dix hisses, 'that the damn fools have taken us a mile too far north!'[38]

True or not, it is too late now to alter course. Some 75 yards from the shore, the boats are let loose from the steamboats, and the four seamen allotted to each boat take up the four oars and begin hauling – no easy task in such heavy vessels.

And *stroke*. And *stroke*. And *stroke*. Floating phantoms on the water, gliding to their goal . . .

'The Landing', by Ellis Silas (AWM ART90807)

And then it happens. A single shot rings out in the silent stillness . . . as nerves jangle and soldiers instinctively hold their rifles closer. Is it a random shot in the dark, or something else?

'Look at that!' hisses a son of South Australia, Captain Raymond Leane, in one of the forward boats, now approaching the Turkish shore.[39] Against the ethereal glow of the eastern sky, on the clifftop, stands the ghostly silhouette of a man . . .

An uncertain, enquiring voice rings out, in a foreign language.

Perhaps 20 seconds later come flashes of rifles in the distance as a volley of shots whistles over them. 'Hullo!' an Australian soldier calls. 'Now we're spotted.'[40]

And then, just as rain follows drizzle, and storms oft follow rain, it begins in earnest. Fire is furiously *poured* upon the foremost boats by a platoon of 70 Turks, with the bullets beginning to splash in the water very close. But there is no panic. Some Australian soldiers are even heard to sing a few snatches of the popular song 'This Little Bit of the World Belongs to Us' as the fire upon them gets heavier.[41]

'They want to cut that shooting out,' one soldier notes wryly, 'somebody might get killed.'[42]

And then one of the men in the first boats *is* killed, slumping forward with a bullet through his head, with some parts of his brain splattering those behind with a sickly wetness. And then another man groans and slips sideways, as oars are splintered and boats suddenly holed.

Such groans, gurgles, death rattles and impacts are accompanied by the surprisingly melodic hum of bullets soaring overhead, and the staccato rhythm being kept by the bullets splashing into the water all around them. Private 'Combo' Smith of the 11th Battalion looks up and quips to Lieutenant 'Snowy' Howe, 'Just like little birds, ain't they, Snow?'[43] The entire boat rocks with the soldiers' laughter, despite themselves.

Notwithstanding the shots now raining on them, if all goes well, it is possible they will be in Constantinople by nightfall.[44]

—

It is Private Âdil and the other men of his platoon – dug in on the ridge lying directly above where the enemy is landing – who are the first to fire upon the Australians.

Meanwhile, Captain Faik is still at his observation post up on the Second Ridge behind them, and the 50-odd men of the reserve platoon are primed for further orders, rifles in hand. They are not long in waiting, as the engagement escalates and rapid gunfire begins to pour over them, coming from some of the steamboats armed with machine-guns.

Immediately, Captain Faik orders most of the platoon to occupy the trenches on the plateau above the northern end of the cove, a place the Anzacs will come to call Russell's Top. He also sends two sections, of nine lads each, down to reinforce the trenches closest to the beach.

He then writes a report to Major Ismet at Gaba Tepe, that 'the enemy is about to start landing at Ari Burnu. I am going with my reserve platoon to our emplacements at that location.'[45]

The enemy ships are now even closer, and there is no doubt that the invaders will shortly land.

—

And here they go. Just ten yards away now . . .

'Make a landing where you can, lads,' an officer roars, 'and hold on!'[46]

As soon as the bows of the first boats touch the Turkish shore at around 4.15 am,[47] the first of the Australian soldiers of the 9th and 10th Battalions of the 3rd Brigade jump into three feet of water and begin scrambling forward on the slippery round stones beneath their boots, eager to get onto the crunchy, gravelly beach ahead, which extends only about 20 yards . . . still looking for the 200 yards of open land they know awaits them before they get to the first steep incline.

But it's not there! There is just this small beach tucked into near cliffs, from the top of which a 'fierce rifle-fire',[48] a 'perfect hail of bullets'[49] is now sweeping over them.

As they stagger forward, their clothes and backpacks suddenly heavy with water, many of their rifles are soon choked with sand and gravel. The first men on the 'beach' – though Bondi on a blistering day it ain't – are joined by the soldiers of the 11th Battalion, who have landed a little to the north. Together, they help each other – 'Here, take off my pack, and I'll take off yours'[50] – while they furtively look around.

Nothing of the topography looks the way it is meant to, and in the hurly-burly of landing, all of the platoons have got mixed up – all while bullets from on high continue to be a menace.

Some lucky ones manage to get shelter behind a rough sandbank, while others have been landed in spots where there is no protection at all on the sandy slopes. Among them, Major Miles Fitzroy Beevor, Commander of A Company, 10th Battalion, is having a particularly tough time. He had planned to get to the beach first to organise his men – who call themselves his 'Little Lambs', as in 'anywhere that Beevor goes his lambs are sure to follow'[51] – but as he jumps from his boat, the water comes right up to his neck. Finally stumbling onto the shore, he sees a group of men coming towards him and, unsure whether they are friend or foe, scrambles forward and draws his service pistol, shaking the water out of it as he goes, before going to ground and waiting.

When they are just ten yards away, he jumps up and challenges them, only to hear the reply, 'Brigadier, 3rd Brigade and staff.'[52]

Ah. It's Colonel MacLagan. Beevor sneaks his pistol back into its holster, giving the Commander his name and unit. But MacLagan is disturbed. He marches up to Beevor, grabs his arms and whispers hoarsely, as if trying to contain his alarm, 'Beevor, we've landed in the wrong place!'[53]

Aware of this, and drenched to the bone, Beevor offers a laconic reply: 'I know that, sir . . . but we are here now – my men are assembling a bit further up – will you please give us orders what to do.'[54]

It is the common question, all along the beach.

'What are we to do next, sir?' another soldier asks a senior officer, as the rifle fire from above continues to press the need for rapid decisions.

'I don't know, I'm sure,' comes the uncertain reply. 'Everything is in a terrible muddle.'[55]

But one officer, who with his men has been among the first to land, even ahead of MacLagan, is particularly quick. 'Fix bayonets, lads,' he sings out, 'and up we go.'[56]

Just as they have been trained, as they have done so many times in Australia, in Egypt, and more recently at Lemnos, the soldiers fix bayonets with one smooth movement.

Click.

And now they form into a rough line and – *'Forward!'*[57] – marching as to war, charge at the first enemy trenches, just 50 yards away from where they have landed.

As they charge, the roar goes up from dozens of Sons of the Southern Cross: 'Come on, Australia!'

'Australia for ever!'

'Come on, boys!'

'Give it to 'em, boys!'[58]

The men of the 3rd Brigade push forward. (And they are lucky, in fact, not to have been landed precisely on the selected spot, as the closer proximity of the Turkish artillery on Gaba Tepe would have been even more devastating.)

4.30 AM, 25 APRIL 1915, ABOVE THE LANDING SPOT, SHOTS IN THE DARK

Terrified, but still resolute and determined to do their duty come what may, Private Âdil and his fellow soldiers continue to frantically fire down on the beaches where the boats are now landing in force. It appears that an entire army corps is being disgorged onto their treasured soil.

In the face of this swarm of foreign invaders, these white faces in the gloom, who keep climbing no matter how many fall, it appears the Turks will have no choice but to relinquish their trenches on the First Ridge before their opportunity for retreat is cut off. Already, machine-gun bullets are kicking up dirt-spurts all around and whistling past their ears. All is confusion. All is terrifying. But this does not dissuade Private Âdil and the rest of the dwindling Turkish platoon from continuing to fight, isolated and facing successive waves of advancing enemy soldiers.

Those soldiers eventually get to the lip of their hill, at which point the brave Turks race back to their next defensible position – anything with cover – and defend from there, before moving further back again, looking over their shoulders as they go. The situation for the Turks is desperate, but at least reinforcements are on the way. They think. Major Ismet had received Faik's last report of the situation at Ari Burnu, and he has passed word on to the Commander of the 9th Division, Colonel Sami, headquartered at Maidos:

> 24/25 April 1915.
> Place: Gaba Tepe
> To the Commander of the 9th Division,
> I am receiving reports from the Company Commander that the enemy has landed a group of soldiers at Ari Burnu. The Commander has given the order to drive the enemy back. He will present information as it comes to hand.
> Commander of Gaba Tepe Region
> Major Ismet[59]

Soon after, Major Ismet orders the men of his artillery battery to open fire with the Mantelli gun that is stationed in one of the artillery fortifications at Gaba Tepe. Capable of three rounds per minute, this three-and-a-half-inch gun is soon raining down shrapnel shells and high-explosive shells, causing devastation on the beaches within a radius of some 25 yards from wherever they land.

———

MacLagan, still on the beach with Beevor and his Little Lambs, is recovered somewhat from his initial shock at 'such a complete upsetting of his carefully laid plans' and is now 'sizing up the situation'.[60]

Okay, Beevor, here's what you and your men are to do: 'As soon as your company is assembled, extend it into line and move straight up the heights in front, clearing out any of the enemy who might be in your line of advance. Then, as soon as you reach the top, swing your left flank around, and move southward, clearing the ground as you go.'[61]

Yes, Sir!

MacLagan then adds, 'Move a considerable distance, but not too far, to the South. Select a defensive position facing inland and dig in.'[62]

Beevor relays the order to his men – 'who were in splendid physical condition' – and they begin to move 'up the heights with a will and eager for fight'.[63]

Only a few body lengths up the cliffs, MacLagan yells out from the beach: 'Beevor, get your men to give a cheer.'

Turning, amused, Beevor does not have time to pass on the order when 'such a roar came from along the line of "Beevor's Little Lambs" as must have given the Turks in the vicinity an idea of the kind of lads who were invading their territory'.[64]

Another soldier who is climbing at a different spot, Private Basil Wilmer, the son of a Reverend from the town of Carrick in Tasmania, would later report their 'awful climb, the cliffs being quite 300 ft. high and almost perpendicular, sandy, and covered with low, thick scrub' and that 'the air above seemed full of a swarm of angry bees'.[65] Near the top, two of his comrades either side are shot almost simultaneously. Private Wilmer stops to check on one of them, an old soldier named Batt, but the old fellow waves him away, saying, 'Don't mind us, lad; go on and give it to them hot.'[66]

All around, the Australians are forming their first impressions, with one Australian soldier later quipping, 'it was bloody poor farming country'.[67]

Aboard *London*, Ashmead-Bartlett suddenly hears a cheer coming back over the waters, an indication that perhaps there is a first victory – likely a trench taken. Indeed, just as Ashmead-Bartlett has guessed, the trench on the top of the 300-foot-high Plugge's Plateau that begins the First Ridge, from where the men of Faik's second platoon have finally fled, is at last conquered.

And all of it by bayonet – giving to the Turks, in the words of Trooper Bluegum, 'just what Brutus, Cassius, Casca and the rest gave Julius Caesar'.[68] For *still* the Australians have not paused long enough to fire.

Among those in the lead, which is typical of him, is 40-year-old Captain William Richard Annear, of the 11th Battalion. A fine man and a natural leader, he had been among the first to volunteer for overseas duty, which had led him to be at this time, in this place, coming over the lip of a hill with a few of his men to find himself atop a tiny plateau.

Minute by minute, for Bean, and for the soldiers in the Second Wave of tows, the eastern horizon continues to lighten ever so slowly until, as the official correspondent describes it, there appears 'a brightening sky and a silken, lemon-coloured dawn breaking smooth grey behind the hills'.[69] Strangely, those hills look a lot higher than he imagined from the briefing he had been given, but perhaps that is just the early-morning light playing tricks.

———

At the northern end of the cove, higher up, above the Anzacs on Plugge's Plateau, Captain Faik has wasted no time in ordering his men to '*Ateş!* – Fire!'

Having now betrayed their positions, Captain Faik and his soldiers come under heavy fire themselves from one of the steamboats, clearly aiming at the flashes of the Turkish rifles. Still, most of the Turkish soldiers are able to keep firing, and certainly some of the invaders appear to be falling, but whether that is because they are shot or are taking cover is impossible to tell. What is certain to the Turks – 'Help us, Allah!' – is that their fire is in no way slowing the boats, or the men, who are landing in even greater force. And the *Ingiliz* soldiers are now climbing towards them.

Across the Peninsula, the word is getting out. Although the Turkish soldiers in these parts have grown used to the sound of artillery fire coming from the Straits, this is different for those stationed on the eastern side of the Peninsula. This time, the firing is not from the direction of the Straits at all. It is coming from the west, from the direction of Gaba Tepe. And it sounds heavy.

Despite his exhaustion, the noise wakes the astute Lieutenant-Colonel Şefik, Commander of the 27th Battalion headquartered at Maidos, who has only been asleep for what feels like a millisecond. Alarmed, he leaps from his sleeping mat and gets on the telephone. Reaching the division's switchboard, he is put through to the communication post at Gaba Tepe. 'Is the sound of artillery fire coming from your side? What is going on over there? Is something the matter?'

'The enemy is landing troops at Ari Burnu.'

'Any threat to Gaba Tepe?'

'No. Nothing so far.'[70]

After hanging up, Lieutenant-Colonel Şefik immediately gives orders to his Battalion Commanders and the Commander of his machine-gun company: 'Assemble your men, call them to arms. They are to carry only combat gear. Have them distribute the men's bread rations, and hang feed bags on the animals. When everything is ready, report back to me.'[71]

Within minutes, a camp that had been all but fast asleep is a flurry of furious activity as the battle cry is sounded.

To arms!

To arms!

268

Chapter Nine

'MIDST THE THUNDER AND TUMULT

I think I am about done – thank God men of my
temperament are few and far between – I am quite
satisfied that I'll never make a soldier; a thousand
pities to have been born an artist at a time like
this – I do wish I could take War in the same spirit
with which my comrades face its horrors.[1]
Ellis Silas

4.30 AM, 25 APRIL 1915, NUDGING 'NEATH THE NARROWS

In *AE2*, all has fallen near as silent as the grave, bar one thing . . .

As the submarine makes its way through a veritable forest of mooring wires for the deadly mines above, it starts to scrape against them,
making the most unearthly screeching of metal on metal. The obvious
risk is that, should a wire get caught, it will very quickly drag the mine
down to the submarine, where it will instantly explode.

All the men can do, however, is keep going . . . their hearts in their
mouths . . . prayers on their lips . . . as they call upon the heavens to
allow them to *make it through*.

As to where exactly they are headed, that is a very good question.
It is now infeasible to rise up to periscope level, as they would almost
certainly hit a mine, so all they can do is proceed blind and . . .

And what is *that*?

Something is bumping along the side of their submarine! It starts for'ard on the port side and keeps regularly banging all the way along the side of the sub. No one speaks, for there is nothing to say, with each small bang risking a big BANG.

And then there is another bang, on the starboard side.

'For several minutes,' Stoker would later recount, 'we all listened to it in uneasy silence before it broke away, tapped along the side, and followed the rest of our enemies astern.'[2]

They're *still* alive.

4.35 AM, 25 APRIL 1915, ABOVE THE LANDING SITE, UPWARD EVER UPWARDS

As Beevor and his Little Lambs continue their silent climb, they are given what Beevor calls in his diary their first 'sample of the ingenuity of the Turkish Sniper in camouflaging himself'.[3] A number of those snipers, it seems, have planted themselves in Turk-sized holes that reach just up to their armpits, leaving their shoulders and arms free. 'To their bodies, back and front, were lashed branches of the local scrub, as well as to their arms. This did not prevent them from using their rifles freely.'[4]

When one of them takes a pot shot at Major Beevor, and misses, one of the Australian soldiers trots over to where he has seen the spurt of flame and has a 'good look at Friend Turk who is pretending to be a bush as hard as he can'.[5] Instantly, the Australian switches grips on his rifle, turns it into a club and then brings it down so hard on the Turk's head that his rifle butt breaks clean off, and blood momentarily spurts from the soldier's head just before he dies with a snapped neck.[6]

Beevor's Little Lamb has just done something that in civilian life would have sickened him, seen him arrested and made him an outcast. But now – in this strange state of warfare – he feels satisfied, and quickly resumes his place in the line, a hero to his comrades.

After walking just a few minutes more, another soldier rushes over to Major Beevor and says quietly, 'I say, Sir, there's a bloody Bull Ant biting my leg, may I stop and pull him out?'

Sir agrees, and the soldier grounds his rifle, unbuckles his belt and shoves his hand down his trouser leg. In an instant, a nigh-beatific smile breaks out. 'I say, you fellows,' he calls in a voice hoarse with excitement, 'I've got a bullet through my leg.'

Positively delighted, he buckles up his belt and starts to hop along with his company. The *thrill* of it!

5 AM, 25 APRIL 1915, OFF CAPE HELLES, A BEHEMOTH GLIDES FORTH

On the bridge of *Queen Elizabeth*, moving north from Cape Helles towards the spot where the Australians have landed, officers whisper to each other so that the tinny voices coming up the brass pipes from the bowels of the warship can be properly heard. General Sir Ian Hamilton, positioned beside a notably nervous Admiral John de Robeck – for the responsibility of what they are about to do weighs heavily on him – brings his ear to the wind. They are still six miles off the spot where the 2nd Brigade are preparing to land when – *there*, can you hear it? – the rolling boom of artillery fire comes from behind them. Clearly, the bombardment of Cape Helles has begun.

General Hamilton is pleased. 'The Turks,' he would write, 'are putting up some fight.'[7]

And not just at Cape Helles. For as *Queen Elizabeth* closes on Gaba Tepe, they start to see the puffs of shrapnel shells bursting over the water. And listen now, as Hamilton says, as 'the patter of musketry came creeping out to sea; we are in for it now; the machine-guns muttered as through chattering teeth – up to our necks in it now'.[8]

The glory of it! 'Would we be out of it?' Hamilton will exult. 'No; not one of us; not for five hundred years stuffed full of dullness and routine.'[9]

By 5.35 am, the rattle of small arms seems to have lessened, and ahead those on the *Queen Elizabeth* can see boatloads of soldiers still pushing for the shore, while on the hills others are swarming upwards. 'Even with our glasses they did not look much bigger than ants,'

Hamilton says. 'God, one would think, cannot see them at all or He would put a stop to this sort of panorama altogether. And yet, it would be a pity if He missed it; for these fellows have been worth the making. They are not charging up into this Sari Bair Range for money or by compulsion. They fight for love – all the way from the Southern Cross for love of the old country and of liberty. Wave after wave of the little ants press up and disappear. We lose sight of them the moment they lie down. Bravo! Every man on our great ship longs to be with them.'[10]

As impressed as he is, for General Hamilton 'the main battle called'.[11] Admiral de Robeck has made it clear that he will take Hamilton wherever the Commander-in-Chief pleases on this oh so crucial day, and the General, of course, chooses to leave the feint and go back to the spot where he hopes the true killer blow on the enemy will be struck: Cape Helles, 13 miles to the south.

5.30 AM, 25 APRIL 1915, LANDING SPOT, CRASHING WAVES ON THE SHORE

And now here comes the Second Wave of Australians – battalions of the 2nd Brigade, the first of whom are landing on the beach. With daylight, they can see from the first that there has been a mistake in navigation. They are stunned to see a rocky outcrop staring down upon them that looks remarkably like a larger version of the Sphinx they thought they had left behind outside Cairo.

'You want to dowse that camera,' a Victorian is firmly told by a fellow soldier, 'because there'll be trouble [and] you'll be court-martialled.'

But the Victorian refuses as he furiously clicks away. 'This,' he says firmly, just before they land, 'is going to be the greatest day that Australia ever knew.'[12]

—

With the sun now up, Captain Faik and the men of his company realise the full horror of what they are facing.[13] Before them, thousands of foreign soldiers are storming towards their shores and up their hills.

Though Faik's men fight with determination, they soon hear distant booms, and then large shells begin to rain down on their positions. It is the battleships – *Triumph, Majestic* and *Bacchante* – firing heavy broadsides, and shell after shell pounds into the hillsides where the Turks are reported to be most heavily concentrated. Every time a shell lands, huge plumes of earth, smoke, shrapnel and – very occasionally – Turks are sent skyward. Mostly, however, the shells from the ship – designed to devastate other ships and not targets in mountainous terrain – do little damage as their horizontal trajectory sends them ineffectively over the top of the trenches.

Not so the Turkish howitzers. Just as General von Sanders has planned, these shells are primed to come down from on high, with the shell cap on the nose turned clockwise to just the right degree so that each is timed to explode some 50 yards above the ground, sending shrapnel out over a wide area on the exposed beach. As the Turkish Forward Observer holds his binoculars in one hand and his field telephone in the other, he is able to direct the fire superbly to create maximum devastation, wiping out as many as ten men at a time, many times.

—

Charles Bean, watching from the *Minnewaska*, is entranced by these shells: 'on the face of a small promontory aft two miles of the south of us [Gaba Tepe] is a brilliant pinpoint flash. Some seconds later a curious whizz through the air . . . the long drawn out whizz sinks down and down in scale. There is a flash high in the air . . . Then a bang and the whine of a shower of pellets sprayed as if from a watering can, the whip up of another circle of sea below and another white fluffy cloud slowly floating overhead.'

A man standing near the journalist marvels, 'So that is shrapnel.'

Another calls out over his shoulder, 'Look mate, they're carrying this joke too far – they're using ball ammunition'[14]

The Mantelli gun, in the battery at Gaba Tepe, is firing on the southern part of the beach as well as at the steamboats with their tows approaching the shore, and the results are devastating. These boats simply sink with bubbles of red: 'looking down at the bottom of the sea you could see a carpet of dead men'.[15] When one destroyer comes too close to the shore to unload its troops, artillery fire is directed onto it, and the warship soon has huge streaks of red falling down its grey-painted side.

Through it all, the brave seamen manning the steamboats continue to ferry their charges back and forth, despite being subjected to more fire than the soldiers, who only have to face this most vicious of barrages once. In some cases, the seamen do not have time to clear their boats of those shot on the last shuttle to shore, and the newly embarking soldiers simply have to walk over their fallen comrades – who have paid the ferryman – and even sit on and by the dead bodies.

As the soldiers land, those who have succeeded in dodging the blizzard of shrapnel on the beach start running up the gullies, where again man after man is cut down. The air is filled with the whistles and explosions of the shells, the whizz of bullets, and the screams and groans of the men in the middle of the whole mess.

And yes, some of the newly arrived soldiers are also taking their toll on the retreating Turks, but the problem is that many of these soon-to-be martyrs, instead of just doing the right thing by lying down and dying, are crawling into the six-feet-high shrubs that abound on the higher ground and, with their last breaths, becoming devastatingly effective. As all but unseen snipers, assisted by their still unwounded comrades, they exact a heavy toll on the arrivals.

There is only one way to get them out. 'Five rounds rapid at the scrub in front,' comes the command from a subaltern.[16]

And when that doesn't stop the snipers, from on high comes the next order: 'Fix bayonets!' And chaaaaarge!

Private Basil Wilmer is there to report of 'the satisfaction of seeing our lads beating the scrub, when about half a dozen Turks broke cover and fled, with the Australians cooee-ing and yelling after them. The enemy threw away rifles, equipment, and some even tore off their coats, and cast them off, but it was no good. Our chaps were too slick, and bayoneted them one after the other with great glee.'[17]

In the middle of the throng, one huge Queenslander of the 9th Battalion, Sergeant Edwin Burne,[18] a farmer in civilian life, becomes an instant legend among his few surviving mates, and then well beyond, when he is seen to bayonet a Turkish soldier through the chest and simply pitchfork him over his shoulder like a bale of hay. 'The Turks were higher up than we were,' he would modestly explain, 'and I suppose that is how I was able to throw one of them over my shoulder.'[19]

And yet, while fortune favours the brave, sometimes misfortune can devastate the bravest of them all . . . and now . . . *a Turkish bullet comes from one of the defenders and drills the captain through the head* . . . killing him instantly. Captain William Annear is among the first of the Australian officers to be sent to his grave.

For the shaken Australian soldiers with him, there is only one thing to do. Keep going.

Now they are atop the First Ridge, of course, their goal is to take the next ridge, all of 400 feet high, but therein lies a significant problem. While the first law of aggressive acts is that in compact unity lies strength – individual fingers may hurt, but clenched into a fist they damage, just as stones may sting, but formed into a rock they can kill – the landscape they are now crossing makes that impossible. Between them and the next ridge is an impossible tangle of gullies, ravines, sheer cliff faces and all but impenetrable undergrowth, not to mention a constant rain of bullets from the retreating Turks. It is inevitable that what was a compact unit of 50 soldiers soon becomes five groups of ten, less those who have been shot, and soon enough many groups of three and less. They press on regardless, the best they can.

For the instructions of General Birdwood and his senior officers have been clear for the last month: 'Keep going at all costs! Go as fast as you can!'[20]

And so they do.

6 AM, 25 APRIL 1915, BOGHALI, A DUTY TO DISOBEY

At his small house, Lieutenant-Colonel Mustafa Kemal, the Commander of the 19th Division, is awake, ear cocked to the west.

Guns. Big guns. And *not* his own Turkish guns – for there are none that big in that direction. The long-awaited invasion; it must have begun.

He immediately telephones General Esat in Gallipoli, who informs him that what is happening is as yet unclear, and for the moment he must simply wait further instruction. An independent and most earnest officer, Lieutenant-Colonel Mustafa Kemal does that, but still orders 'all the troops to prepare themselves for mobilisation'.[21]

And then he continues to wait . . . and wait. With no order arriving, he gives one of his own. His mounted company is told to ride 'in the direction of [the highest spot of the Peninsula, Hill 971] in order to obtain information about the situation'.[22]

Finally, at 6.30 am, Mustafa Kemal receives partial confirmation in a report from the 9th Division Commander at Maidos, Colonel Halil Sami. Yes, the enemy is landing at Ari Burnu, and the invaders are beginning to swarm up and over the first of the ridges that overlook the shore there. But their Commanders, it seems, are not panicked, thinking this landing likely a feint. 'It is demanded that you send one of your Battalions to oppose the enemy,' Sami says casually, passing on the order.[23]

But Lieutenant-Colonel Mustafa Kemal disagrees. He has understood from the first the strategic importance of the high ground of the Sari Bair Range, and now that it has been confirmed that the enemy has indeed landed in that area and is heading towards it, albeit over very difficult country, it seems highly unlikely that it is a mere feint.

It is with that in mind that he takes it upon himself to order his whole 19th Division to mobilise. Most particularly, the 57th Regiment and the 72nd Regiment are to head towards the high peaks that overlook the whole invasion area, at all possible speed. (It is an enormous risk for him, personally. His job is to keep his forces in reserve, until ordered to move by his Corps Commander, and if it so happens that

that order comes only to find that Lieutenant-Colonel Mustafa Kemal has taken his men other than where they are truly needed, his career would be over.)

He now heads out with the division's crack 57th Regiment and a battery of mountain guns towards Hill 971, which overlooks the spot where the enemy has landed. Following them are the men of the 72nd Regiment. Desperate to see for himself exactly what the situation is, Mustafa Kemal – riding, as ever, tall in his saddle – takes a cabal of senior officers and goes on ahead of them.

6.25 AM, 25 APRIL 1915, HELL AT HELLES

At Cape Helles, the five separate British landings on the five designated beaches are each meeting entirely different fates. The forces of the Lancashire Fusiliers, landing on the spot designated Y Beach, have encountered almost no resistance at all – there is time to wade ashore and then have a spot of tea. As to *River Clyde*, however, and the 2000 predominantly Irish soldiers that lie within, that is another story.

For it is just before 6.30 am that the 4000-ton collier bursts through the entrance of the Dardanelles and arrows straight for V Beach, a sandy strip 300 yards long that forms the orchestra pit of a natural amphitheatre. Smoke hangs heavy over the beach from the pre-landing shelling, which has been going on since 5.30 am, though that barrage has caused few casualties among the Turkish defenders. That much is evident from the moment they devastatingly open fire on the 700 soldiers of the 1st Battalion, Royal Dublin Fusiliers, being towed in boats by steamboats alongside *River Clyde*.

And now, the collier itself beaches and – after heroic work to get a rough kind of bridge in place – the sally ports burst open, and the first of the Irish soldiers come bursting through.

Just 75 yards back from the beach, Sergeant Yahya's 26th Regiment has been patiently waiting for this moment. He drops his arm: '*Ateş!* – Fire!'

As 100 rifles and the four machine-guns – all of them German, water-cooled, state-of-the-art Maxims – fire a furious fusillade at the courageous soldiers of the Royal Munster Fusiliers of the 29th Division, the Turkish defenders are soon joined by another nearby infantry company, making it around 300 rifles in total firing on those coming ashore. 'They were literally slaughtered like rats in a trap,' one *River Clyde* officer would recount.[24] For every man who makes it to shore, at least three are cut down on the way.

Of the two companies of Munsters that keep coming from *River Clyde* – 500 soldiers in all – only 150 survive the landing, and for the moment sanity makes a rare appearance, and a temporary halt is called on further soldiers emerging. As to the covering force of Royal Dublin Fusiliers in the open boats, of the 40 men in the first vessel that reaches the shore, only three are able to get out – not including their Commanding Officer, Lieutenant-Colonel Richard Alexander Rooth, who is one of the first shot. They stagger up the beach, bleeding heavily.

Only 300 survive the landing unscathed. In the words of one Turkish officer, Mahmut Sabri, 'not one of our soldiers' bullets was fired in vain. In fact in many cases one bullet accounted for several of the enemy . . .'[25]

Dead bodies begin to wash up on the shore, their hands all too frequently reaching for the solid land, their legs bobbing in water red with blood. As one of the *River Clyde*'s officers would recall, 'I never knew blood smelt so strong before.'[26]

The Turks keep firing their bullets and shells, keep adding to the bloody carnage. Mahmut Sabri would recall, 'Ertuğrul Bay [V Beach] was packed with enemy corpses like fish piled on top of each other.'[27]

—

Back at Anzac, Captain Faik's certainty that they are pushing the enemy back is beginning to fade when he feels a searing pain in his groin. Looking down at his wound, he knows he can't lead his men anymore. After handing the command over to Sub-Lieutenant Muharrem, Captain Faik is evacuated.

Private Âdil, meanwhile, is retreating further and further back from his initial position on the shoreline, towards the Third Ridge. The Turks are in desperate need of reinforcement.

Just before 6 am, Colonel Şefik's men had finally been ordered to 'proceed to the Gaba Tepe sector and hinder the enemy's attempted advance between Ari Burnu and Gaba Tepe, throwing those that have made it inland back into the sea'.[28] After an hour and a half's marching at the double, they arrive at the southern slopes of the Third Ridge.

Approaching along a gully behind the ridge, they come across a wounded soldier who says, 'The enemy are close up ahead.'[29]

'Even better!' the Commander replies. 'The earlier we meet with them the better.'

They then march towards a spot just to their north, overlooking 400 Plateau to the north-west, and are ordered to 'keep your eyes peeled, in every direction'.

Şefik rides out in front with his Battalion Commanders. Now arriving atop the knoll, he surveys the land in front of him through his binoculars. 'Just as the wounded soldier had said we saw enemy soldiers at close range . . . they were visible on 400 Plateau . . . But thanks to the scrub it was impossible to discern where exactly their soldiers had advanced to, nor where their left flank was.'[30]

But this is not the best spot from which to command his men. Telling them to hurry, he rides further north, to a spot high up on Third Ridge, directly east from where the enemy have landed. Enemy fire is becoming more frequent, and though Şefik can't yet see them, he knows the invaders are advancing onto the Third Ridge from the movements in the scrub, which catch his eye. Surveying the land closely, the Turkish Lieutenant-Colonel thinks hard about what his next move might be.

—

At around 6.45 am, atop Plugge's Plateau, right next to the body of Captain Annear, it is obvious to Colonel MacLagan that he must make

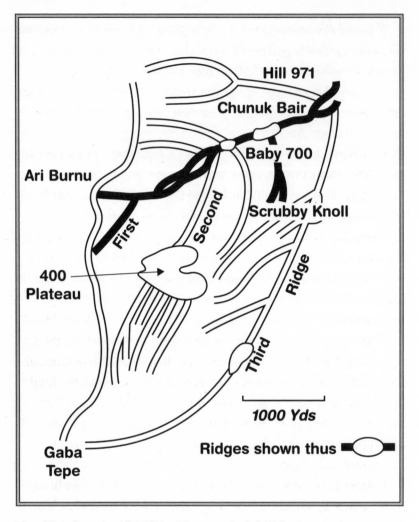

Map of First, Second and Third Ridge, after a map by C. E. W. Bean

quick and important decisions. Though his men of the 9th and 10th Battalions have already pushed on to the Third Ridge, the question is where to now direct the men of the 11th Battalion, who have just arrived on the plateau. The plan had been for them to go straight to the Third Ridge but he has just received word from 400 Plateau, via a signaller bearing a message, that large numbers of Turkish troops have been sighted on the Third Ridge opposite, presenting a serious threat to his right flank.

It seems obvious to him that it is more important to secure the heights immediately in front of them, along the Second Ridge. And so he orders the men of the 11th Battalion to forgo the Third and rush to points along the northern end of the Second Ridge, all the way to the hill known as Baby 700 – for its presumed height of 700 feet[31] – on the Sari Bair Range.

He follows this up by sending orders forward to the men of the 9th and 10th to halt their advance at the Second Ridge and dig in. The Third Ridge to the east, and Battleship Hill, Chunuk Bair and Hill 971 to the north will just have to wait . . . for the moment, at least.

Given the Anzacs have all been landed too far north, it is almost certain that their right flank – where the Turks have men in reserve near Gaba Tepe – is inherently weak, and so that flank must be reinforced.

Scrambling up onto the plateau is Lieutenant-Colonel Harold Edward 'Pompey' Elliot, with his men of the 7th Battalion, the first of the 2nd Brigade to hit the ground running. As per his instructions, Elliot is now planning to send his men forward to secure the heights of the First Ridge to the north-east. But, much to his surprise, Colonel MacLagan orders Elliot to take his men and dig in to the *south*. A disciplined officer, Elliot obeys the order of his senior without question and immediately departs.

Colonel James Whiteside McCay, Commander of the 2nd Brigade, comes ashore amid the ever-growing chaos of the Second Wave's landing a little before 7 am. On the beach, he allows himself a brief sigh as he looks at the terrain that looms ahead of him. Along with his Brigade-Major, Walter Cass, he makes his way to a break in the ridge in front of him, a place that is soon to be aptly dubbed Shrapnel Gully. Not long after entering the gully, he turns left and begins to climb up to a higher point – Plugge's Plateau – to ascertain the situation, so he can send a precise order back to his men, who are still plonking awkwardly off the boats.

As he starts the climb up, he sees Colonel MacLagan coming down. MacLagan informs him that he has intercepted Elliot and sent him and his battalion south, 'because the right was being threatened with being turned in'.[32] MacLagan then issues the command, 'I want you to take your whole brigade off to my right.'

Colonel McCay, who has a growing reputation for questioning all manner of orders – not to mention a healthy sense of sarcasm – responds, 'I was ordered to take it off to the left. It is a bit stiff to disobey orders first thing.'[33]

'I assure you,' says MacLagan, 'my right will be turned.'

Still not convinced, the 2nd Brigade's Commander retorts, 'I had better go forward and have a look.'

'There is not time.'

So McCay strikes a quick compromise: 'Will you assure me that the left will be all right and the right will be turned if I do not do this?'

MacLagan does not hesitate: 'I assure you it is so.'

As if to cast their agreement in stone, McCay replies, 'I accept that assurance.'[34]

McCay orders his men to assemble on the beach and get ready to move south, absolved of any blame thanks to a firm word of assurance between officers – should this direct contravention of orders turn out badly, and the left flank be turned, the fault lies solely with MacLagan. He and his men move off.

A quarter-century earlier at the Westward Ho! school in Dover, Colonel MacLagan had been close friends with one Rudyard Kipling, among whose most famous poetic lines would be, 'If you can keep your head when all about you / Are losing theirs and blaming it on you / If you can trust yourself when all men doubt you, / But make allowance for their doubting too . . .' Right now, MacLagan has kept his head, while many others are losing theirs, and he will indeed be blamed for the decision he has taken, as others doubt him. But at the time, he feels he has no choice. In his view, if they go after the Third Ridge as planned, they risk losing everything.

Approaching 8 am, Lieutenant-Colonel Şefik is ready to order his men to spread along the Third Ridge and engage the advancing enemy. The 1st Battalion is to attack from the southern flank and along 400 Plateau, while the 3rd Battalion is to take the enemy's centre, pushing them back down the Second Ridge and into the sea whence they came. As for the right flank, from Baby 700 and beyond to the peak of Hill 971, he will need Colonel Mustafa's reserve division for that. He simply does not have enough men.

Before going ahead, he sends a report to 9th Division headquarters:

To: Command of the 9th Division, Maidos.
Time: 7:55
1. The enemy have occupied the ridges at Arı Burnu.
2. I am launching an offensive on the ridges between Kocadere and Ari Burnu.
3. I implore you to despatch the 19th Division quickly to [Hill 971].
Commander, 27th Regiment
Mehmet Şefik[35]

Steward. Another cup of tea . . .

—

Aboard *Euryalus*, around the corner just off W Beach at Cape Helles, General Sir Aylmer Hunter-Weston is so far removed from the *Clyde* carnage that at 8.30 am he orders the main force to begin landing at V Beach, whereupon most of them are slaughtered too – with 175 fatalities in a matter of minutes. At 9 am, another company makes the attempt to make it from *River Clyde*, with exactly the same devastating result. At 9.30 am, a company of Hampshires emerges, also to be shot to pieces without ever setting foot on the shore.

Meanwhile, just off Y Beach in *Queen Elizabeth*, General Hamilton had already seen that the landing there had met such minimal resistance that all of the landing group are ashore without a problem. Now seeing just how catastrophic the landing at V Beach has been, Hamilton – against the counsel of his Chief of Staff, Major-General Walter Braithwaite, who thinks it a breach of military protocol – signals Hunter-Weston: Would you like to get some more men ashore on Y Beach? If so, trawlers are available.[36]

To Hamilton, it is obvious that when there is huge resistance in one section of the front, and little on another nearby section, you must push forward hard where there is little resistance, to *at least get your men ashore*, at which point those men could launch an attack on the flanks, and quell the resistance there too.

Hunter-Weston? He does *not* see it like that at all. In fact, he doesn't even bother replying.

Staggeringly, though General Hamilton himself has been watching the whole thing, it is not until 10.21 am that he again signals to the prickly Hunter-Weston: Not advisable to send more men to V Beach. We have 200 on shore unable to progress.[37]

Fifteen minutes later, the answer comes from Hunter-Weston: Admiral Wemyss and Principal Naval Transport Officer state that to interfere with present arrangements and try to land men at Y Beach would delay disembarkation.[38]

Instead, the rest of the men designated to land at V beach are diverted to land at X Beach, where just hours before a bloody ambush similar to the one at V Beach had befallen the Lancashire Fusiliers, though by now it is reasonably safe.

As for the landing of the French on the Asian side of the Straits at Kum Kale under General Albert d'Amade, it is also initially barely opposed, and the taking of the ruined old fort and village the only Allied objective so far successfully achieved. But for the French, it is all rather beside the point. They have not landed in enough numbers to actually move north against the other forts on the Asian side of the Narrows, and because General von Sanders has correctly judged their landing as a feint – committing just one of his five divisions to keep them in check – all the French can do is wait until boats come to take them to the other side of the Dardanelles, where the real action is.

Shivering aboard *Minnewaska*, Charles Bean continues to gaze earnestly towards the shore in the now strong morning light, trying to discern what is happening, when he sees it.

'Suddenly – from high up on the further hills there twinkled a tiny white light – very brilliant . . . Then minutes later someone sees men upon the skyline . . . through the telescope you can see them, numbers. Certain ones are standing full length, others moving along them, others sitting down apparently talking . . . They are Australians! They have taken that further line of hills – three ridges away you can see them: the outlines of men on the further hills; men digging on the second hill; and the white flags of signallers waving on the ridge near the shore.'[39]

—

After two quick looks through the periscope during the night, now Lieutenant-Commander Dacre Stoker again brings *AE2* to a depth of just 20 feet, to take stock in daylight of just where they are. Stoker whispers to his attentive crew, 'Ten up . . . keep 20 feet . . . time for a fix.'[40]

He is amazed to see that in fact they are just off the town of Chanak, well past the minefields and somewhere near the mid-point of the Narrows, just below the part where the body of water resembles a dogleg. The early dawn light gives a strangely beautiful quality to the damaged port. Stoker calls the bearing while Lieutenant Cary fixes the sub's position on the chart in elegant dashes of red crayon.

The first sign of what is to come, however, arrives just a minute after the periscope has surfaced – for that sight is precisely what the many Turkish sentries are looking for with their glasses – and shells from both sides of the Narrows now come pouring down upon the Australian submarine, sending up huge spouts of water all around.

Keeping calm regardless, for at their depth there is no real risk to the submarine even should a shell drop right on top of them, Stoker examines the enemy port, looking for targets, and even has the sangfroid to note that 'around the top of the periscope the water, lashed into white spray, caused a curiously pretty effect, but added little to the ease of taking observations'.[41]

Inside the sub, there are spasmodic *whumps*, as shells explode on the surface, as well as what sounds oddly like gentle hailstones on the roof, as the shrapnel from the shells floats down. Time to 'run amuck', as he had been commanded?

Exactly. For that is what *AE2* has come to do, and right there is the perfect prize: a fat Turkish battleship, from which mines might be dropped.

Stoker is acutely aware that his crew rely on his judgement. They watch his every movement. He is the all-knowing captain, the only one who has the privilege of looking through the periscope to the world above this steel tube. 'We are approaching the Narrows,' he says, 'about one mile.' Some captains prefer not to inform the crew – but that is not Stoker's approach. 'Target range 600 yards . . . a Turkish battleship . . . Prepare bow tube.'

The order is passed by word of mouth to the forward torpedo room. The outer cap is opened and seawater fills the tube. Not a word is spoken that does not need to be spoken.

'Port 15 steer 320. Dead slow.'

Helmsman Charlie Vaughan confirms the change in course. 'Steer 320, aye aye, sir.'[42]

Actually, no. For now, from behind the battleship comes a cruiser, *Feihh i Shevist*, heading straight for them – either to ram the periscope or drop mines across the bows – and Stoker instantly changes plans. Bringing his bow around so that the torpedo is perfectly positioned to hit the cruiser, he awaits his moment to fire.

500 yards . . . 400 yards . . . 350 yards . . . 325 yards . . .

Lieutenant-Commander Stoker keeps calling off the distance calmly. 'Three hundred yards . . . Standby . . . standby . . . fire bow torpedo.'[43]

The order to fire is shouted into the forward torpedo room. The Torpedoman's mate pulls down on a lever that releases an explosion of compressed air into the tube behind the torpedo, forcing it out in a flurry of bubbles. As it exits, the torpedo's internal motor is ignited and the compact but powerful engine engages its tiny propeller and sends the weapon in a straight line towards its target at a speed of some 35 knots.

Suddenly sensing danger, Stoker stops watching the torpedo's wake and instead swivels the periscope in a quick arc. There on the port side . . . a *destroyer* intent on ramming! Stoker instantly gives his next order: 'Red Green 270 close. Destroyer . . . emergency dive . . . 10 down . . . keep 70 feet.'[44]

The orders are confirmed and, only an instant after they have submerged, they hear it . . .

'Amidst the noise of [the enemy cruiser's] propellers whizzing overhead, was heard the big explosion as the torpedo struck.'[45]

Bullseye!

Alas, if the torpedo has caused the immediate devastation that Stoker thinks it has, it means that right in front of them right now there will be either the sinking cruiser or the mines it has dropped or both, which is why he immediately gives his next order: 'Point to starboard.'[46] Three minutes after that danger has passed, he tries to get back on the straight and narrow of the Narrows. Stoker walks across to the chart table, where Lieutenant Cary has marked their progress in red crayon. 'Port 5 steer 010.'[47]

But now another problem. Helmsman Charlie Vaughan can no longer read the gyrocompass. It has been tripped off its axis by the explosion. 'Very good,' says Stoker. 'Steer by magnetic compass.'

He remains calm but knows they are in trouble, for the magnetic compass, near so much metal, is notoriously unreliable. The devastating denouement does not take long, for the submarine is effectively blind amid terrible swirling currents and . . . with a sudden crash, the sub hits the banks of the eastern shore.

Oh . . . Jesus and Mother Mary . . . have *mercy*.

From six fathoms down, the sub quickly slides up to just a fathom below the surface, meaning the whole bridge and conning tower are now above water. And still it gets worse. For when Stoker puts up the periscope once more and swivels it around, he is confronted with that acute blackness that is the blackness of the muzzle of a cannon looking straight back at you, and it suddenly fires! All of it is so instantaneously confronting that Stoker jumps backward.

The sub has hit the bottom directly below the guns of one of the ancient forts that stand on the shoreline. 'With the boat apparently fast aground,' Stoker would later recount, 'and a continued din of falling shell, the situation looked as unpleasant as it well could be . . .'[48]

Aghast, Stoker looks through the periscope and reports to the crew that, 'The sea is one mass of foam caused by the shells firing at us.'[49] And yet, even in the midst of catastrophic misfortune, every so often Lady Luck can still wink at those whose pluck she admires . . .

For so close is *AE2* under the fort that the angle is too steep for the guns to fire down upon it.

Stoker stands like a rock in the control room. Whatever else, he must project calm. 'Full astern,' he orders.

A senior sailor at the main switchboard on the port side of the control room, standing a few feet from Stoker, instantly complies. 'Full astern, aye aye, sir.'[50]

There is a grinding sound but no movement. Clearly, the propellers are cutting into the muddy bottom, but Stoker does not care. 'We have to get off,' he says grimly, 'whether the propellers get damaged or not.'[51]

They keep going, rocking back and forth.

'Full ahead.'

'Full ahead, aye aye, sir,' the sailor confirms, twisting the dial on the glowing panel in front of him in the opposite direction. Every movement is measured.

'Up half ahead.'

Then, 30 seconds later, 'Group up full ahead, sir.'

Stoker waits. They all wait.

They can all hear the twin screws thrashing the water.

There is tiny movement.

'Geoffrey, please pump ballast to the aft tanks.'[52]

The Executive Officer, Geoffrey Haggard, passes the order, sending three seamen to switch the pumps into action and open valves that send water through overhead pipes from the bow to the rear of the submarine, causing her to be heavy aft. Like a seesaw, one end has a tendency to sink with the extra weight.

'Reverse motors. Group up full astern.'[53]

This time, deliberately unbalanced, the submarine is pulled backward into deeper water by her twin screws.

They are still alive!

Soon at a depth of 70 feet, Stoker has her 'on the port propeller, helm hard a-port',[54] with their nose soon pointing for the open sea and safety. And yet, to continue on that course would be against orders. They have been told to run amuck, and successfully torpedoing one cruiser does not quite qualify. No matter that they can hear the endless swish of angry propellers from the ships roaring back and forth on the surface looking for them, Stoker now tries to turn the sub back up the Narrows, making allowance for the four-knot outgoing current and . . .

And BANG! Now they have hit the western, European, shore, where else but 'neath another Turkish fort, this time at a depth of just eight feet!

Up periscope, for a 360-degree swivel, of which 300 degrees is pure horror . . . and the rest . . . wonderful. For there is the fort firing down upon them; a gunboat closing fast and blazing hard; several destroyers firing broadsides; and . . . a 'clear view up the strait showing that if we could only get off we were heading on the correct course'.[55]

A-whump . . . a-*whump* . . . a-WHUMP.

There are perhaps few things more terrifying than being in an exposed submarine hearing, as Able Seaman John Wheat would recall it, 'the shells striking the water and bursting outside',[56] but at least the Commander does not seem to feel it. And at least this time, the cursed current, which to this point has been a nightmare to deal with, now offers a surprising bouquet to providence by swinging the boat's stern around to port and bringing the bow angled down, at which point Seaman Albert Knaggs would confide to his diary, 'We could hear inside the boat the shrapnel dropping on us like a lot of stones.'[57]

Still they are alive, however, and they might have a chance to get off, after all!

'Group up all ahead, both motors,' Stoker crisply commands.[58]

The twin electric motors whirl, the propellers thrash and the submarine shakes heavily under the strain, as the shells above find their range – A-WHUMP, A-*WHUMP*, A-WHUMP. But again, miraculously, four minutes after hitting the bank, there is movement. *AE2* is slipping back down the bank, admittedly with a terrifying grinding noise coming from both propellers and then two massive bumps from something unknown hitting the sub . . . but they'll take it.

Dacre Stoker's plan of conserving battery power, however, has been swept aside by the two calamities. Worse, seawater is found seeping into the bilges. If seawater makes contact with the batteries stored under the decking, then chlorine gas will fill the submarine and everyone on board will die very quickly, choking on the fumes, with their skin, eyes and lungs burning as they asphyxiate. (A torpedo would be kinder.)

Whatever else, at least the submarine is now submerged. On the surface is certain death in the darkness, whereas 'neath the waters of the Dardanelles it is only likely.

'Five degrees downward, make your depth 70 feet,' Stoker commands,[59] as *AE2* continues to move up the Straits to the Sea of Marmara. Hopefully.

—

On the shores of Gallipoli, the Anzacs continue to be devastated by shot, shrapnel and shell. As to quelling the latter, Charles Bean would be quick to note, 'the ships' guns, upon which Churchill had counted with such complete assurance, were so useless in such a situation that they had almost ceased to fire'.[60]

The problem is that Australians and Turks are so mixed up now it is impossible to tell which is which, and the ships risk killing their own if they fire on any but the most distant targets. Yes, the covering force has some red and yellow flags to indicate their position, but the problem is that those flags are also a target for the Turkish artillery. A further problem is that it is impossible for those in the ships well offshore to determine just where the Turkish artillery is.

The one shining light in this dark tale is the armoured cruiser *Bacchante*, whose Captain Algernon Boyle, in response to the urgency of the situation – and the difficulty of spotting where the Turkish artillery is – guides his ship right to the point that it nudges the shore, gets a bead on a particularly troublesome small battery upon Gaba Tepe and, for the moment, manages to silence it.[61]

'I can never speak sufficiently highly of the navy,' General Birdwood would note, 'from admirals down to able seamen. The whole Anzac Corps would do anything for the navy . . . Our men were devoted to those ships and their crews, and will always remember the British Navy with admiration and devotion.'[62]

Aboard *London*, as with all the other battleships, two things keep coming from the shore. The first is requests for artillery fire, in those areas the Turks are fiercely defending – and it is for this reason that most of the battleships now lie parallel to the shore, as they fire in broadside after broadside.

And the second thing coming from the shore is boats of terribly wounded soldiers, arriving in an endless stream of blood. The one fully equipped hospital ship, *Gascon*, is quickly filled to capacity, as are the two transports catering for the lightly wounded, and it is soon for the other ships to take the wounded on and cope the best they can.

'As usual, with the start of all British expeditions,' Ashmead-Bartlett would record, 'the medical arrangements were totally inadequate to meet the requirements of the hour. Optimism had minimised our casualties to the finest possible margin, but the Turks multiplied them at an alarming rate. Apparently there was no one in authority to direct the streams of wounded to other ships where accommodation could be found for them, and many were taken on board the warships.'[63]

Finally, however, a clear order: the wounded are to be taken back to

'Boarding the Hospital Ship', by Ellis Silas (AWM ART90793)

the empty transports whence they came, where as many doctors as can be spared will also be sent, and the ships can take them back to Egypt.

General Bridges remains stunned. Having stepped ashore at 7.20 am – accompanied by his Chief of Staff, Lieutenant-Colonel Cyril Brudenell White – he had found all over the beach dead and dying men. All had been chaos and confusion. Shrapnel raining down. Not a single officer there to greet or brief him. No one in charge.

At General Bridges' headquarters, being constructed just back from the beach, a worrying series of messages from a flaky and clearly receding frontline are waiting for him. MacLagan reports they are being *heavily attacked on the left* (5.37 am), another message reads *3rd Brigade being driven back* (6.15 am), and then another recent and urgent one from MacLagan says, *4th Brigade urgently required* (7.15 am).[64]

What to do?

Why, get to the frontline, of course. With that in mind, Bridges and Brudenell White had immediately started climbing the ridges on the southern end of the shore, seemingly oblivious to the bullets and shrapnel whizzing all around. On the way, they had passed a Battalion Commander who – under the extreme circumstances of the angels of death having been flapping their wings all over him for the last two hours – had fallen to pieces. He was quite 'unstrung'. Bridges had no sympathy and, as recorded by Brudenell White, was 'coldly contemptuous'.[65]

(And yet, the shattered Battalion Commander is not alone. Inevitably, in the face of the slaughter, the spirit of some men is not equal to the extraordinary task set them, and some 'stragglers' will later be found congregating in the gullies.)

As Bridges and his Chief of Staff continue, outraged Turkish bullets start to kick up dust all around. Not happy about it at all, Brudenell White suggests they keep moving and get to a position with more cover, but – almost as a point of honour, it seems – the General ignores him. Not for him, taking shelter from mere bullets. He is of the Old School that thinks being afraid of bullets only attracts the beggars.

Miraculously, General Bridges and his Chief of Staff now reach the top of the First Ridge, only to find some more soldiers – again, not at all unreasonably – taking cover from surprisingly strong Turkish fire. 'For God's sake,' the General roars. 'Remember that you are Australians!'[66]

And so they do, ignoring the dangers and pushing forward once more.

Chapter Ten

BETWEEN THE DEVIL AND THE DEEP BLUE SEA

There are a lot of bush-whackers, copper-gougers, etc. from the Cloncurry district in the 15th Battalion and I believe they are the finest of all soldiers, fearing nothing and as full of dash and endurance as man ever was. I am inclined to think they make it too willing bayoneting and killing, when mercy should be shown and prisoners taken . . . There is no doubt that our men are hard and even cruel.[1]
Lieutenant Thomas James Richards, MC, 1st Field Ambulance

A kangaroo-shooter from the Kimberley country threw a bomb at a Turkish trench only fifteen yards away, and the cries of 'Allah, Allah', told him that his aim was true. He turned to his mates and remarked casually, 'That's the first man I've killed without getting into a heap of trouble.'[2]
Trooper Bluegum

9.30 AM, 25 APRIL 1915, HEIGHTS OF THE SARI BAIR RANGE

The dapper military man in the Turkish uniform lightly jumping from his horse is a study of relief and exhaustion.

After a journey of nearly two hours, Lieutenant-Colonel Mustafa Kemal finally stands tall, chin up, shoulders back, atop the 850 foot high summit of Chunuk Bair, the second highest point of the Sari Bair

Range and the Gallipoli Peninsula, with a small group of his senior officers. The exhausted troops they have been travelling with are some ten minutes behind, as they have been allowed a brief rest, while Mustafa Kemal races ahead to try to spy the enemy.

When he arrives, his worst fears are realised. Not only are the waters below completely filled with British warships and transports, together with many small boats crammed with soldiers pushing into the shore, but just down the slope he can now see Turkish soldiers hurrying up towards him, clearly retreating from the smaller hill they had been assigned to defend, just in front of Chunuk Bair, known to the Allies as 'Big 700' and later as 'Battleship Hill'. Away in the distance, Mustafa Kemal can see the enemy soldiers coming after them, completely unopposed.

'It meant,' he later recalled, 'the enemy were nearer to me than my own troops! And if the enemy were to advance to the position at which we were standing, my troops would find themselves in a very difficult position.'[3]

Indeed. If the enemy captures these heights of the Sari Bair Range, they will control the whole area, making it nigh on impossible to dislodge them.

Mustafa Kemal – at least as he and many others will tell it ever afterwards – reacts as instantly as he does instinctively. After sending an orderly racing back to bring his 57th Regiment forward at all possible speed, he races down the slope to meet the retreating Turkish soldiers. 'Why are you running away?' he yells at them.

'*Efendim düşman!* – Sir, the enemy!' they reply.

'Where?'

'Over there,' they say, pointing to the hill they have just abandoned and the soldiers now clearly visible, pursuing them.

'You cannot run from the enemy!'

'We have got no ammunition left.'

'If you haven't got any ammunition, you have got your bayonets!'[4]

The Turkish soldiers are trapped. Behind them, swarming thousands of enemy soldiers. In front of them, one furious and very senior Turkish officer. On balance, they'd rather face the enemy . . .

'*Süngü tak!* – Fix bayonets!'[5]

Done.

'*Yere yat!* – Now lie down on the ground!'[6]

They lie down on the ground, their rifles thrust forward, their bayonets glinting in the sun. What will the soldiers pursuing them do, when they see this mass of men with their rifles pointing straight at them? Will they come en masse, in which case the all but defenceless Turkish soldiers will be slaughtered and Chunuk Bair taken irretrievably, or will they react . . . as if they are about to massacred by a rain of Turkish bullets?

It does not take long.

For as Mustafa Kemal watches closely, just moments after his Turkish soldiers have dropped down . . . so too do the pursuing soldiers.

The defenders have won some precious time.[7]

—

And here come the New Zealanders! In the first boat approaching the shore is the handsome doctor, a veteran of the Boer War, Lieutenant-Colonel Dr Percival Fenwick, of the New Zealand Medical Corps. As a steamboat goes slowly past them, heading the other way, one of the sailors calls to Dr Fenwick, 'The Australians have got ashore and are chasing the Turks to Hell.'[8] Every man within earshot lets out a raucous cheer.

In the boats around Fenwick are the first soldiers of the Auckland Battalion – many of them highly trained professional soldiers who have spent their adult lives preparing for this moment. They are no sooner ashore than they are charging forward and quickly climbing to support the Australians.

—

On the left flank of the Turkish defence, the troops of the 27th Regiment's 3rd Battalion, under the command of 30-year-old Major Halis, have started the fight.

The well-loved Commander – nicknamed Blind Halis for a shrapnel wound he had received to his right eye during the Balkan Wars – is in the thick of it from the first, exhorting his men to ever greater and more courageous efforts. His soldiers are mostly of ill-educated farming stock from local villages, while he is a military professional who can speak five languages, but still he has the knack of inspiring his men in battle, no matter the carnage. And carnage it is, with a terrible casualty rate all around. A third of his soldiers have been killed or wounded by 9 am, but still they keep firing, praying for reinforcements.

On the far right flank, Lieutenant Ahmet Mucip of the battalion's 12th Company, though only 20 years old, has just taken command of the company after his own Commander had been shot. Following the orders of Major Halis, he guides his men to the top of a ridge that overlooks the sea . . .

Reaching the crest, they fall to their bellies in the scrub and look down.

There!

They are now able to get a good look at the enemy who are climbing the other side: the *Ingiliz*!

For most of the soldiers, it is the first time in their lives they have seen this curious race up close. They are big, lithe and remarkably fair-haired. And there are so *many* of them. Lieutenant Ahmet's eyes grow wide. He looks to the left and right flanks of those climbing, hoping to see an end, but he cannot. The line is never-ending. 'I felt,' Ahmet Mucip would recount, 'as if my chest was about to burst . . .'[9]

But the strange thing?

Even though the *Ingiliz* are climbing with such difficulty, even though they must know they are likely to soon come under attack, they are somehow advancing with great confidence. And they must be stopped.

'Soldiers,' Lieutenant Ahmet Mucip says quietly, 'advancing at the same speed as me, quickly and quietly.'[10]

Ahmet Mucip and his men break cover and, in an instant, attacking from the high ground, open rapid and hellish fire upon the advancing enemy, chopping them down like wheat, though the *Ingiliz* are soon firing back and their dead ones are quickly replaced by reinforcements. A savage battle breaks out, and around him Lieutenant Ahmet can hear groans and death rattles as his men are hit. Many of the merely wounded are shouting to Allah as they shoot, 'paying homage and preaching revenge for the martyrs who, in resistance and prayer, had departed this life'.[11]

The carnage among his own men is great, but they are still holding their ground when Major Halis arrives. He has been shot, and is bleeding, but remains for as long as he can to organise the defence, before giving the Lieutenant his final command: 'Do not withdraw from your positions. The only case for retreat is if you send a messenger with the news that you have all died. I will send reinforcements as quickly as possible.'[12]

With the help of a young private, Major Halis retreats. As he loses sight of his Commander, Lieutenant Ahmet Mucip once again feels the weight of responsibility return, as if he is the only man left standing to defend the homeland. But he reminds himself, 'Is it actually like this? No . . . A small part of the homeland has been left in my custody, and with this comes the hearts, souls and assistance of these gutsy, fighting Mehmetçiks . . .'[13]

—

The first troops of Turkey's 57th Regiment catch up to their Commander at Chunuk Bair around 10 am. His men must attack the enemy now coming up towards Battleship Hill.

And to his men, Colonel Mustafa's verbal order is the stuff of legend. 'I don't order you to attack,' he is said to have told them, 'I order you to *die*. In the time which passes until we die other troops and commanders can take our places.'[14]

(Certainly, however, a written order is less prosaic: I do not expect that any of us would not rather die than repeat the shameful story of the Balkan War. But if

```
there are such men among us, we should at once lay
hands upon them and set them up in line to be shot.)15
```

—

With the arrival of the 57th, the tone of the battle for the marauding Anzacs changes, as heavier punishment than ever pours and roars
down upon them – withering fire and a shellacking of shrapnel from
the highly trained and committed soldiers and gun crews now occupying the high ground along the First Ridge.

It is true, they are not much to look at, these Turks, with their mostly
slight frames covered in rag-tag uniforms, but that is not the measure of
them. For their bravery is beyond all doubt, and even beyond all reason,
as waves of them charge at the Anzacs, shouting – what is that word,
again? – 'Allah! Allah! ALLAH!'

No matter that the first wave is cut to pieces, the second wave comes
on, running over their own dead and dying.

'Allah! Allah! ALLAH!'

How can these bastards be so unlike the Gyppos? Back in Cairo,
you'd only have to raise your hand to a Gyppo and he'd cower away
from you, but the Turks are not like that at all. The Anzacs not only
have the fight of their lives on their hands, they are fighting *for* their
lives, and many are losing as soldier after soldier is cut down.

'Well, lads,' one officer says to his men, as yet one more wave of
Turks starts to charge at them, 'we are in a very tight corner but we'll
die back to back. Fix bayonets.'16

Like the Australians, the Turks realise the importance of the high
ground from the first, and one particular hill – Baby 700, two summits
below Chunuk Bair – is fought for like a football in a rugby game. No
sooner would one side have it than the other would swarm all over it to
wrench it from them, whereupon they are the ones who are attacked.

And now, just before 10.30 in the morning, here is the intrepid,
tall and red-headed figure of Charles Bean, staggering ashore in his
squelching boots, holding a camera and earnestly taking shots of the

scenes on the beach and surrounding hills, before turning to take shots of the men landing behind, as shrapnel sprays all around them. Forget that. The important thing is to capture the moment, to record scenes for posterity that he will be able to expand on with words. Words such as these:

> The sight of the hills . . . made one realise what our men
> had done . . . The place is like a sandpit on a huge scale –
> raw sand-slopes and precipices alternating with steep slopes
> covered with low scrub, pretty dense; a tallish hummock at
> the north end of the beach and another at the south end . . .
> It was a curve of sand about half a mile long, between the two
> knolls. Between them high above us ran back a steep scrub-
> covered slope to a skyline about 300 feet above us. One or two
> deep little gullies came down the mountain-side, each with a
> little narrow, winding gutter in the depth of it, about as deep
> as a man – not more than five or six feet wide and more or less
> covered in low scrub – splendid natural cover against shrapnel
> whether it came from north or south.[17]

Soon enough, he makes his way to the spot where General Bridges' HQ is now constructed – a rough dugout covered with canvas, scraped into the side of the slope in a gully up from the beach. This will be the only sure place to get information on the whole of the battle, and, after throwing his heavy backpack down, Bean sticks close to the HQ from the moment General Bridges gets to work and starts receiving messages from the ridge beyond by telegraph over wires that the signallers had so courageously laid down under heavy fire.

The mood is tense as Bridges continues issuing orders, occasionally being forced to shout over the sound of rifle and machine-gun fire, not to mention the booming sound of artillery from the ships rolling across the waters and bouncing around their gully. From the first, it is clear that the whole battle is in the balance. From everywhere on the frontlines, it seems, as recorded by Bridges' Chief of Staff, Lieutenant-Colonel

Brudenell White, 'urgent requests were coming in all day for reinforcements – urgent demands from every unit that went up. We even had requests from company commanders who had lost their battalions: We cannot hold on unless immediately reinforced.'[18]

Sometimes, Bridges obliges, sending whatever he can; other times, he sends back a terse message: 'Tell them they've got to stick it.'[19] For he cannot send forces he does not have. All he can do is remain calm, weigh the situation and give what support is possible.

Around and about the HQ, a steady stream of wounded men limps past. Not far away, Bean can see 'about half-a-dozen poor chaps . . . lying there dead'.[20] Things are grim all right. When General Bridges sends his General Staff Officer, Major Thomas Blamey, up to the top of the soon-to-be-named Shrapnel Gully to give him a report on the situation, Blamey is not long in returning, to describe it as 'Very ticklish . . .'[21]

What would make a big difference, and is desperately needed, is for howitzers to come into play, but the landing force have none with them, and the 18-pound field guns, with their flat-trajectory shells, are not suited to the mountainous terrain. All that can be landed in the short term, in the late morning, is the first of two Indian Mountain Batteries, boasting light guns, designed to be dismantled and moved up to high terrain. Manned by Sikhs and Punjabi Muslims – the only Allied Muslims on the Peninsula – the six dismantled guns are soon being hauled by a string of mules 'up through the steep Scrub'[22] to a point on the 400 Plateau, where they are reassembled and soon firing.

Captain H. A. Kirby trains his guns on the Third Ridge in the direction of Scrubby Knoll shortly before noon and starts firing the ten-pound shells on the Turks. Their guns are small compared with the Turks' – the heaviest of which can hurl shells of 80 pounds – but they are a start, their first land-based artillery.

As the sun pushes high in the sky, Colonel Mustafa Kemal has a rough idea of just what he and his men are facing. The invaders have landed what appears to be more than eight battalions, on a front about a mile wide, and have penetrated as far as Battleship Hill in the north, and along the ridges in front of the point on the Third Ridge to be known as Scrubby Knoll, a little over a mile from the shore. And yet, so rough is the country between the shore and Scrubby Knoll, so determined the defenders, that the invaders are incapable for the moment of breaking through. Worse for them, they are even struggling to hold onto the land they have won and are beginning to pull back. And they are not the only ones. For, under continual Turkish fire, the Allied transports and battleships have been forced to pull back offshore and out of range. As a result, 'not an infantryman has landed on the beach' since 12 pm[23] – the by now exhausted Anzacs have no reinforcements. The small number of artillery pieces that were coming ashore has also ceased.[24]

As Private Herbert Reynolds of the 1st Field Ambulance, who is seeing the scale of destruction firsthand, scribbles in his diary, 'only two Indian mountain batteries are ashore and we are badly in need of artillery support, everywhere the enquiry is being made along the front "Where is our artillery?" . . . there appears to be no sign of us pushing through to our objectives without them.'[25]

In the extremity of the battle going on all around, not only are men lost from their companies and battalions but inevitably there is now little concern as to whether one is an Australian or a New Zealander. When high up on the Second Ridge, a New Zealander suddenly has his entire foot blown away by a bullet or piece of shrapnel and is seen hopping forward, calling out, 'For God's sake, don't leave me!' On the instant, a young Australian jumps up and says, 'Come on mate, get on my back,' and the two are soon heading back down the hill, *Anzacs* truly together at last.[26]

Captain Gordon Carter? To his amazement, high on the Second Ridge, he has not yet been shot dead. He had landed as part of the Third Wave that morning, and they had immediately received orders to reinforce the firing line, at which point the chaos and carnage had begun. Pinned down by 'terrific enfiladed fire from shrapnel, rifle and machine gun',[27] they had lost their Commanding Officer, Captain McGuire, early with a bullet to the abdomen, leaving Captain Carter nominally in charge, but it is rather beside the point. For his soldiers, like most Anzac soldiers, are now scattered everywhere, and for as long as three hours all they can do is hope to survive by hugging the earth as hard as they can, as men get shot all around. Captain Carter is 'thoroughly scared'.[28] But now what? As the fire upon them eases a little, dozens of men around him make to retire in disorder.

Oh no, they *don't*.

Standing up and shouting at them, Carter imposes some rough order and manages to rally them, as they press forward.

'I give you full credit for this, my Father and Mother,' he later writes to his parents, 'for the action came quite spontaneously and was not the result of any thought. It gave me a great deal of confidence and I felt fairly right from then . . . I kept getting hold of all the scared chaps about and sending them up.'[29]

A little later, he finds another '150 men under a wounded Captain retiring. I could not stand this so made the men rally and found the firing line on the right flank.'[30] Extraordinarily, even in the madness of it all, he still wonders about Nurse King, hoping she is out of harm's way. (She is, almost. Aboard the *Sicilia*, about to take in their first lot of wounded, she and her fellow medical staff are close enough to the action that '[we] can hear the *Queen Elizabeth* firing and each time our boat trembles like anything'.)[31]

———

In a curious combination of calm and great energy, Colonel Mustafa Kemal moves among his troops, just back from the firing line, encouraging, directing, pushing his men forward in what seems like a lull in the fire upon them. Clearly it can't last, however, as the enemy continues to land its forces, and Mustafa knows that there will likely never be a better time to hurl the enemy back into the sea than right now. And so, from Chunuk Bair, he prepares for a mass attack in earnest, ordering more than 30 artillery guns to prepare to commence an intense, unified bombardment of the enemy lines, particularly concentrated on the two areas he aims to hit hardest – Baby 700 and 400 Plateau – while bringing forward all reserve infantry and getting them into position.

NOON, 25 APRIL 1915, HE LIKES TO BE, UNDER THE SEA, WALKING ON EGGSHELLS

Still alive. Even if it feels like only just. After dodging seemingly every torpedo and picket boat in the Narrows, and having several narrow escapes, Captain Stoker had decided at 8.30 that morning that discretion was the better part of valour, and the best thing for the submarine to do would be simply to lie on the bottom of the Dardanelles until the madness overhead had dissipated, and night-time could return to again give them the cover they needed. And so they had nestled on the banks of a small bay on the Asian shore, at a depth of 70 feet.

How to breathe at that depth, with no intake of fresh air?

Exactly.

The only answer is: the best you can. With 35 men in such a confined space, it is no easy matter, for the air is stultifying, having already passed through the lungs – and worse – of all of them, and all of it thickened by the choking diesel fumes that have not yet had a chance to escape, even though *AE2* is now running solely on battery power. And yet, that is still not the worst of it. Overwhelming even those fumes is the stench from the toilet in the forward torpedo room, otherwise recognised as two covered buckets: one for liquids, the other for . . . solids. Both those buckets had tipped over when *AE2* had slid down the first sandbank, and their contents now sluice around with the bilge under the deck planking.

Gawd help us all.

After observing the Sabbath by having a gathering near the periscope for Sunday prayers . . . *Oh Heavenly Father, bless us for* . . . the men sleep as best they can, but it is little enough. What they mostly do is wait, occasionally tense as the roar of engines above signals that they are still being searched for, with boats passing overhead every 15 minutes or so. Just after noon, something hits hard against the starboard side, for'ard – a grappling hook, perhaps – and the whole sub crew is instantly awake and ferociously focused. Again, however, it goes quiet, and all they can do is lie there, gasping for heavy breath, wondering if they will ever see the sun again.

As tough as their situation is, however, they inevitably wonder how those storming the beaches on the Peninsula are faring . . .

—

For the Anzacs, the best they will be able to do now is to hold onto the Second Ridge.

And it appears they are doing a good job of it. For Lieutenant Ahmet Mucip is still commanding his company on Mortar Ridge, but his line is disintegrating and many of his soldiers are now martyrs. However, a battalion of the 57th Regiment has arrived in the gully behind to provide reinforcement. Allah be praised!

Whether the Anzacs can keep holding on is touch and go, especially if the men, taken over by herd mentality and furphies, simply start retreating of their own accord. Major Beevor, still holding the firing line at Wire Gully, has already dealt with this situation once today . . . and now, it seems, it's happening again. He is convinced it is the clever enemy, who are 'using all sorts of subterfuges to undermine the morale' of the Anzacs.[32]

He is making his way back to the line from Battalion HQ when he sees 'a number of men . . . pouring down the slope at the double'. Stopping them, he demands, 'Who has instructed you to leave the Firing Line?'

Several answer at once, saying the word had come from the right that 'every man was to make his way to the beach independently and as fast as he could'.

Tricky buggers!

He tells the men, 'This is nothing but a dirty German trick. I am in charge of the Firing Line . . . no such orders have been given.'[33]

The men immediately turn on their heels and follow Major Beevor back to the line.

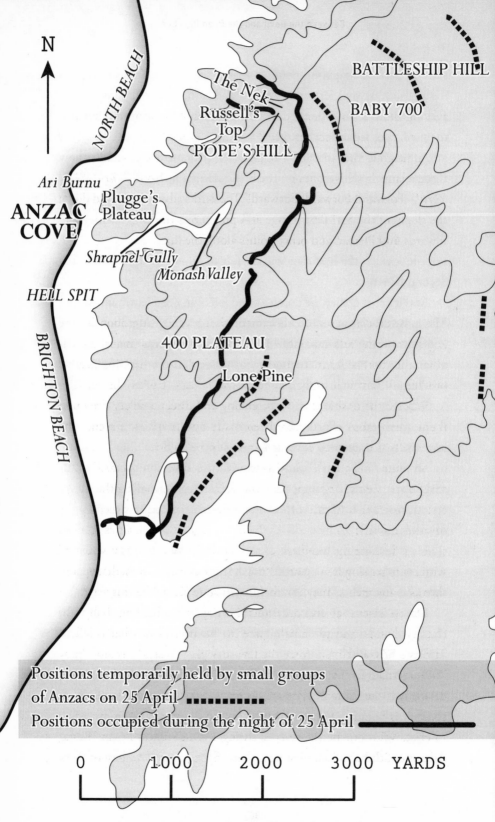

N

NORTH BEACH

The Nek
Russell's Top
POPE'S HILL

BATTLESHIP HILL

BABY 700

Ari Burnu

ANZAC COVE

Plugge's Plateau

Shrapnel Gully

Monash Valley

HELL SPIT

BRIGHTON BEACH

400 PLATEAU

Lone Pine

Positions temporarily held by small groups
of Anzacs on 25 April ▪▪▪▪▪▪▪▪▪▪▪
Positions occupied during the night of 25 April ▬▬▬▬

| 0 | 1000 | 2000 | 3000 | YARDS |

Troop positions, 25 April 1915, by Jane Macaulay

—

Having allowed time for the destructive forces of his decreed bombardment to take full effect (at 400 Plateau, it is reported that the dead are 'almost all torn apart by shrapnel'),[34] Lieutenant-Colonel Mustafa Kemal launches his counter-attack all along the front. '*Yürü! Yürü! Yürü!* – Forward! Forward! Forward!' The Turks advance seaward down the slopes of the Sari Bair Range at 4 pm, across the Legge Valley and towards 400 Plateau and other points along the line.

—

The most crucial battle on this tortured and torrid afternoon is here and now on the hill marked as Baby 700 on the Anzac maps. As it is obvious to both sides that whoever possesses the commanding heights of Chunuk Bair will in fact command the area – having the capacity to both see the positioning of the enemy and direct artillery fire upon them – enormous efforts have been made by the Allies to secure the lower hills as a stepping stone to capturing the higher.

So numerous are the Turkish troops now, so extraordinarily committed are their charges on the now devastated Anzac frontlines, the serious risk is that Mustafa Kemal will indeed succeed in sweeping the invaders into the sea by dark. As the battle rages, the casualties on both sides are devastating: hundreds of men are killed or grievously wounded with every passing hour. Should the Anzacs evacuate immediately and save as many men as they can, before Mustafa Kemal has his way?

On no fewer than five occasions this day of the landing, Baby 700 changes hands, and yet, finally, late in the afternoon, what is left of Turkey's 57th Regiment force the few surviving Australians atop Baby 700 to retreat. In the madness of all the fighting, some soldiers seem to disappear. One instant, they are there; the next, they are gone. With some, it is because they take direct hits from a shell and simply cease to exist. With others, the story is stranger. One such is Private Edgar Adams of 8th Battalion. First he is there, fighting with the best of them as the Turks charge, and then he is gone. A quick search is conducted, but no trace of him is found . . .

As the battle continues to teeter on the point of disaster for the attackers, their only consolation is, with the Turkish guns trained mostly inland, the transports and boats have been able to resume landing troops and materiel. The bulk of the New Zealanders are now beginning to arrive, including the first companies of Lieutenant-Colonel William Malone's Wellington Battalion, which begin to wade ashore from about half-past four in the afternoon.

Likely the most courageous men on the day bear no arms at all. They are the stretcher-bearers, men with 'SB' marked in brassards on their arms. One stretcher-bearer who stands out for his particular bravery under fire is Jack Simpson of the 3rd Australian Field Ambulance Australian Army Medical Corps. Even though the men on either side of him as he had landed at the tail end of the 3rd Brigade were shot dead – and indeed 16 of the unit had become casualties in the boats before even landing – still Simpson had quickly got to work and begun ferrying wounded men back to the shore. And he and many others have been at it all day since.

Down at the beach, Lieutenant-Colonel Dr Percival Fenwick is hard at work attending to the 'numbers of wounded lying [at the Clearing Station] close to the cliff waiting to be sent off to the ship. Every minute the number increased . . . Violent bursts of shrapnel swept over us, and many wounded were hit a second time. Colonel Howse . . . was packing boats and barges with these poor chaps as fast as possible, but the beach kept filling again with appalling quickness . . . The shrapnel never ceased . . .'[35]

By late afternoon, there are no fewer than 700 of them there, waiting to be put on barges and, adding seasickness to injury, towed by steamboat to whichever ships will have them.

As hard as the steamboats towing barges are working – because with rumour of withdrawal in the air, clearing the beach is done in earnest – still they can make no headway in reducing the net number of wounded coming off the beach. Each time they return from the ships, there are a hundred more there, with further hundreds waiting to come down from the heights after nightfall, when it will be safer.

As some of the shattered remains of what had been a fine fighting force as recently as 12 hours ago comes aboard his ship, *London*, Ashmead-Bartlett can witness for himself dozens of men with bloody stumps where their arms and legs used to be, soldiers with their intestines spilling out onto the deck as they are lowered down, men screaming in agony . . . and many, many death rattles of men mercifully breathing their last, *straining* for the blessed relief of sweet oblivion. From those still able to talk, Ashmead-Bartlett at least begins to take notes, gathering information on just what has happened.

Likely nowhere are things as grim as aboard the quickly overwhelmed hospital ship HMT *Armadale*, where the Chief Medical Officer, Dr Vivian Benjafield, has been stunned by the task his people face. With the aid of untrained privates and non-commissioned officers, the medical personnel conduct amputations, tie off arteries, suture dreadful abdominal wounds, try to stabilise those suffering from compound fractures of the skull, and all the rest. By lunchtime, *Armadale* has had 150 grievously wounded soldiers on board, and has had to rip out tables and turn the Mess into a makeshift ward. Can they cope with more?

They *have to.*

Even with the dead being quickly buried at sea, soon the ship is so lacking in space – with now 850 severely wounded men on board – that Benjafield has no choice but to refuse a boatload of severe cases, as his people simply won't be able to get to them. Many such boatloads are reduced to going from ship to ship, begging for the captains to accept their passengers into their makeshift triages.

Things are so desperate that one ship, *City of Benares*, which has just been cleared of a cargo of mules, is pressed into service, while *Lutzow* still has 160 horses on board when it is obliged to take on the wounded and 'the veterinary surgeon is said to have been the sole medical officer for her 300 patients until a naval doctor was sent to help him [the next day]'.[36]

Aboard the ships, the remainder of the New Zealand and Australian Division are preparing to land, and their number includes Signaller Ellis Silas, who, in the late afternoon, is with his 16th Battalion in the bowels of their troopship receiving their final instructions from Captain Eliezer 'Margy' Margolin. The captain talks of the 'impossible task' they face, of their 'probable annihilation' and yet also expresses his confidence that the 16th Battalion will meet the challenge.

As recorded by Ellis Silas, the men 'joke with each other about getting cold feet, but deep down in our hearts we know when we get to it we will not be found wanting . . .' But after Margy's speech, no one is under any illusion. 'For the last time in this world many of us stand shoulder to shoulder. As I look down the ranks of my comrades I wonder which of us are marked for the land beyond.'[37]

Silas is not long in finding out, as just 30 minutes after this last address, he, as part of Colonel John Monash's 4th Brigade, is stepping ashore at Gallipoli while all the while it is 'raining lead'. Though wide-eyed with horror at the spectacle of dead and dying men on the beach, he is stunned at the courage of all those survivors around him. 'It was a magnificent spectacle to see those thousands of men rushing through the hail of Death as though it was some big game – these chaps don't seem to know what fear means – in Cairo I was ashamed of them, now I am proud to be one of them though I feel a pigmy beside them.'[38]

There is little time for reflection, however, as all of these last troop arrivals of the day must be rushed forward to support those in the frontlines, in the case of Silas's 16th Battalion digging in at a spot to be called Pope's Hill, where the men already there are only just holding on under severe counter-attack. There is a real fear that, despite having landed about 15,000 Anzac soldiers by this time, the Anzacs are about to be overwhelmed and an ignominious withdrawal announced.

Silas starts climbing the hills with the rest of his fellows, shocked by all of the noise, the savagery and the sheer bloodiness of this new world. Unable to find any of his fellow signallers in the confusion, he sets to on his own initiative. 'Now some of the chaps are getting it – groans and screams everywhere, calls for ammunition and stretcher bearers, though how the latter are going to carry stretchers along such precipitous and sandy slopes beats me. Now commencing to take some of the dead out of the trenches; this is horrible; I wonder how long I can stand it.'[39]

As the sun begins to sink just behind the purple haze of Imbros – soon to send up exquisitely beautiful streamers of gold into the sky – so the first serious artillery is landed. With a cry of 'Look out! Make way!',[40] a single gun of the 4th Battery Australian Field Artillery is brought to the beach on a barge, unloaded and hitched to a team of horses. They immediately take the strain and start to pull it into position up a steep path to a knoll near the southern end of the beach, as the many wounded soldiers cheer. Even those wounded soldiers passing in a boat headed for the hospital ship muster the energy to cheer and sing out at the sight of the gun, 'They want Artillery!'[41]

An attempt had been made earlier in the afternoon to emplace two field guns. But as no suitable location had been found for them in the highly precipitous country, and with rumours of re-embarkation then circulating, they were disappointingly soon re-embarked. So this gun is particularly welcome. Time to give the Turks back some of their own.

And indeed, with just its second shell, just after 6 pm, the gun appears to silence the Turkish gun on Gaba Tepe that has been devastating those on the beach all day. (Under heavy fire, *Bacchante* had had to withdraw at noon.) As was immortalised in the unit's War Diary, 'A gun's flashes were observed on Gaba Tepe and engaged and no gun fired from the same place again.'[42]

The silencing of this gun is a relief, but only a small one, as death continues to rain down upon the Anzacs. On this devastating day, across the Gallipoli Peninsula, thousands of soldiers, attackers and defenders alike have gone to an eternity of darkness. For those still alive, their most earnest desire is for the darkness of just this one night to descend, hopefully to offer *some* respite.

—

When that darkness at last blessedly comes, it is not simply the Australians and New Zealanders who are relieved at the possibility of a pause. The most senior officer left standing of the 3rd Battalion of the 27th Regiment of the Ottoman 5th Army, Lieutenant Ahmet, would later recount, 'Hundreds of British boys were lying on our land never to open their eyes again. These boys with clean-shaven and endearing faces were curled up in their blood-stained uniforms. Their sight aroused in us feelings of both revenge and compassion . . .'[43]

On balance, however, it is the desire for revenge for this invasion of their land that wins out, as the Turkish soldiers continue to fight strongly. (The non-Turkish soldiers . . . not so much. The men of the 77th Arab Regiment, for example, who are only here because they have been dragooned by their Turkish masters, start to drift away in the darkness and have to be rounded up once more, threatened with their lives from behind if they don't face up to what is in front of them.)

Finally, though, as Lieutenant-Colonel Şefik of the 27th Regiment is reconnoitring to ensure there is no gap in the firing line between his regiment's right flank and the left flank of the 57th Regiment to the north, he suddenly hears strange sounds close by. 'We realised,' he would later recount, 'that these were the sounds of English conversations.'[44]

The invaders are dug in that close to their own lines. After such a day as the Turks have had, can they possibly get their surviving men, as exhausted as they are, to attack once more? No. Lieutenant-Colonel Şefik can see that his own men are too exhausted to go again. Yes, there will continue to be attacks from now, some serious, but for the moment the best thing is to dig in where they are.

The Anzacs come to much the same conclusion, and the basic footprint of the combatants on the Gallipoli Peninsula starts to be carved out in roughly parallel lines. Broadly, it sees the forces of Lieutenant-Colonel Mustafa Kemal's 19th Division – into which Lieutenant-Colonel Şefik's 27th has now been absorbed – controlling the heights, while the devastated invaders are just down from there, furiously digging in and firing back.

And yet the Turks, too, have paid a heavy price on the day. Those soldiers at whom Lieutenant-Colonel Mustafa Kemal had roared that morning 'I don't order you to attack, I order you to *die*' had for the most part done exactly that. It is likely that not more than 200 of the 800 soldiers who had started the day can still hold a rifle and fire it. Of the 200 men in Captain Faik's company who had been manning the trenches closest to the spot where the Anzacs had landed, there are only ten left. Private Âdil is alive, along with just ten or so men of his platoon. But those who are left are still fighting strongly, and are supported more than ever by the fresh reinforcements that keep arriving.

—

Though offshore, Ellis Ashmead-Bartlett is one who already has a fair idea of just how appalling the whole situation is. All day now, the steamboats have been going back and forth to the shore ferrying supplies to – and, since noon, the wounded from – the beaches. Their reports are catastrophic, their cargo worse . . .

Things are going badly. The number of mortalities and casualties is horrifying, and the southern end of Anzac Beach is piled high and spread wide with both. In terms of casualties, things are now so much worse than they had been in the morning, which was appalling enough. While sporadic enemy fire harries the beach throughout the day, the enemy's afternoon bombardment of the Anzac frontline is devastating, killing many more men with every passing minute. And now it gets even worse, as Mustafa Kemal launches a ferocious counter-attack and the Turks control the high ground once more, with the Anzacs clinging to the cliff edge by their fingernails . . .

And what now for Charles Bean? Here are some fellows from Jack's 3rd Battalion who – oh God – seem to be unaccountably quiet around him, even averting their eyes. Has something happened to JACK?

Yes . . . but it could have been worse. Colonel Neville Howse – the Chief Medical Officer of the Australian 1st Division, temporarily in charge of clearing the hills of the wounded and bringing them down to the beach for evacuation – tells Bean that Jack stopped a bullet about

4 pm, but he had not collapsed. 'I don't think the bullet hit any important part,' he tells Charles. 'It was still in – but I don't think it hit the intestine. He has been taken off on a hospital ship . . .'[45]

As it will be recorded in the 3rd Infantry Battalion War Diary on this evening, *Captain JW Bean wounded in execution of his duty attending a wounded man under heavy fire.*[46]

Charles is proud, but worried, but relieved, but worried again about how their parents, and most particularly their mother, will take the news.

At 7 pm, Colonel MacLagan comes down from the firing line to see Bridges. 'Well, old pessimist,' Bridges laughs, in that always confident way of his, 'what have you got to say about it now?'

'I don't know, sir,' MacLagan answers gravely. 'It's touch and go. If the Turks come on in mass formation . . . I don't think anything can stop them.'[47]

Bridges stops laughing immediately. Is it really possible that his fine forces are about to be swept back into the sea whence they came? If so, withdrawal has to at least be a possibility, but he refuses to countenance it . . .

At Cape Helles, the situation is at least as bad for both the British and the Turks, with 3000 casualties for the attackers, and some 1500 Ottomans killed and wounded. For that cost, the British have advanced – and the Turks have conceded – no more than 1000 yards from the shore, and their first day's objective, Achi Baba, is almost as far away as it ever was, glaring at them in the distant moonlight, furious at their folly.

9.45 PM, 25 APRIL 1915, DARDANELLES, THE BLACK THING FROM THE DEEP SURFACES

First there is a ripple on the otherwise dead calm of the Dardanelles, somewhere north of Nagara and south of Gallipoli, then a swirl, and now a rushing of water as a massive black bulb breaks the surface. The *AE2* is at last emerging from the deep after a long, suffocating day on the bottom. It is one thing to have got through the Narrows, but in many ways even more important to get word through to High Command that they have done so, that it *is* possible.

'It was of the utmost importance,' Stoker would recount, 'that we should get into communication with the admiral and tell him that the most difficult part of our task was accomplished. Whether any other submarine should be risked would depend on the success or failure of our attempt, so he must know as quickly as possible that we had practically succeeded.'[48]

Stoker pens a quick note to this effect, advising Admiral de Robeck of their triumph – even as the hatch is thrown open and glorious fresh air rushes in, to be greedily inhaled by all – and hands it to Able Seaman William Wolseley Falconer. This worthy now huddles at his tiny station behind *AE2*'s wardroom and starts frantically tapping away at his largely experimental Marconi wireless telegraph, 'the damp aerial wire throwing purply blue sparks as the longs and shorts of the call sign were flashed'.[49] Falconer occasionally adjusts his headset to make sure that he will instantly be able to hear a response.

But there is no reply. *No reply!*

Desperately, knowing the importance of the message, Falconer keeps tapping, but soon enough Lieutenant-Commander Stoker must make a decision. Even more important than getting the signal through is surviving, and every minute they stay on the surface is another minute of risk.

Reluctantly, Stoker gives the order to submerge once more. 'This wireless failure,' he would later recount with considerable understatement, 'was a very great disappointment.'[50]

9.45 PM, 25 APRIL 1915, ANZAC BEACH, THE FOURTH ESTATE ARRIVES

And who, then, is this strangely elegant man stepping ashore from a steamboat and carefully picking his way through the carnage on the beach? In khakis and rakish green, it is Ellis Ashmead-Bartlett, whose hallmark has always been to be in the thick of the action. On this evening, after waiting all day, he is at least glad to be ashore.

What is most shocking, however, is the 'indescribable confusion' he finds among a unit of men that just that morning had been superbly well organised and healthy. 'The beach,' he would later describe, 'was piled up with ammunition, stores . . . among which lay dead and wounded, and men so absolutely exhausted that they had fallen asleep in spite of the deafening noise . . . It was impossible to distinguish between the living and the dead in the darkness.'[51]

All he can discern in this dark fog of war are ethereal, ghost-like groups of men dazedly moving back and forth, as they exhaustedly head back to, or stagger from, the firing line. It is chaos, and catastrophic chaos at that, with the only semblance of calm being found in a tight group of men, all of them with caps, standing a small way off.

Officers. Generals.

Ashmead-Bartlett carefully approaches and gets close enough to recognise one of them as General Birdwood. Though they've not met, the war correspondent recognises him from the many photographs he has seen. He is just about to delicately announce himself, however, when an officious Australian voice rings out.

'Who are you? What are you doing here?'

'I . . .'

'Seize that man, he's a spy.'

Instantly, the correspondent is surrounded by soldiers, and it is all he can do to get out, 'I am Ashmead-Bartlett, the Official War Correspondent attached to the Expedition.'

Do you have an official pass?

Not actually, no. Just a kind of unofficial one, penned by an officer on the ship.

Not good enough.

'How do I know you are what you say you are?' roars the Australian Colonel. 'Does anyone here know this man?'

A gruff voice comes from the darkness. 'Yes, I do.'[52]

It proves to be a boatswain who has ferried the journalist here and there over previous months, who knows that whatever else he is, he is not a spy. It proves enough to save him from being 'executed on the spot', and to his great relief Ashmead-Bartlett is released.

Not that he can go anywhere particularly. Heading up into the hills in the darkness is out of the question, and Birdwood's Chief of Staff soon tells him that he cannot go back on the steamboat either, as it is the only boat ashore and it will shortly be needed for an urgent despatch. Just what that despatch will consist of he is not told, but he receives a fair clue, not just by the dead and dying men all around him but also by a very excitable Beach Officer Commander who rushes up and says, 'Do not send your boat away, whatever you do. We have to go round all the transports and get them to send in their boats. It is impossible for the Australians to hold out during the night, they are being too hard pressed.'[53]

Ashmead-Bartlett is stunned. Really? Just 18 hours after landing and they are contemplating first extricating all the soldiers from the crazy mix-up of gullies and hills – where they are nose to nose with the Turks – and then evacuating them?

Apparently.

That tiny glow of light by the bit of canvas shelter you can see in yonder gully, just back from the shore – a tiny chirp of cheer in the blackness, with death, destruction and chaos reigning all around? Therein lies a story, and in this case appearances are deceptive. For here are gathered the two highest ranking officers at the landing place, Major-General William Bridges and General Sir Alexander Godley – Commanders of the Australian 1st Division and New Zealand and Australian Division – both imploring General Sir William Birdwood, who has just come ashore in response to their desperate wirelessed request, to give the orders to *evacuate*.

Yes, Sir William, things really are that bad.

As the sound of rifle and machine-gun rolls over them, interspersed with the regular boom of artillery, exploding shells and the moans of dying men, they continue to give Birdwood their best estimates of the situation. It is not simply that the Anzacs have lost many men – which may run to as high as 4000, one-quarter of the total landed – it is that the Turk is fighting far harder than the Allies could have possibly imagined. And yes, the Turks have suffered some 4000 casualties themselves on the first day, but now fresh battalions are being rushed forward to replace the fallen, just as Colonel Mustafa Kemal had foreseen.[54]

As to the Anzacs, there are precious few reserves to go in where they are falling in the frontline, which is no more than half a mile from where they now meet. Morale, which had been so high upon landing, is in as short supply as water, and there are growing fears that the Turks will launch another major assault on the morrow and force their withdrawal.

Far from being able to quickly march on Constantinople, as they had naively hoped, the Allies will be lucky if they can survive the *night*.

Birdwood, shocked that his worst nightmares now seem to be coming true, and yet still reluctant to acknowledge defeat of the Australians only 20-odd hours after they had landed, resists. General Bridges asks to have a quiet word with him and insists that, whatever happens, a decision has to be taken *tonight*, for the sake of the men. Birdwood relents partially . . .

He decides to couch his message to General Hamilton in stark terms. As General Godley writes it all down on the back of a white signal form, the machine-guns continue to chatter and the sound of men screaming and dying in the near distance is heard, even as shells continue to explode across the night sky, sending flickering light across his newly scrawled words:

> Both my divisional generals and brigadiers have represented to me that they fear their men are thoroughly demoralised by shrapnel fire to which they have been subjected all day after exhaustion and gallant work in morning. Numbers have dribbled back from firing line and cannot be collected in this difficult country. Even New Zealand Brigade which has been only recently engaged lost heavily and is to some extent demoralised. If troops are subjected to shell fire again

tomorrow morning there is likely to be a fiasco as I have no fresh troops with which to replace those in firing line. I know my representation is most serious but if we are to re-embark it must be done at once.
Birdwood[55]

One thing General Godley neglects to do, strangely, is to designate who, specifically, the note should go to, causing yet more confusion on this already catastrophically chaotic day . . . Nevertheless, it is handed to the Naval Commander of the steamboat that brought Ashmead-Bartlett to the shore, who now rushes back to his boat with the journalist in hot pursuit.

'Go to the battleship *Queen*,' the Commander yells at his men – and, sure enough, the contours of the massive battleship are picked up after a short run and the note handed over.

'What is our next move?' Ashmead-Bartlett asks him.

'We've got to go to every transport in turn,' the naval man grimly replies, 'and order them to send in their boats immediately to bring off the Australians.'[56]

And so from ship to ship they go in the darkness, with the Commander using a megaphone to have the crew roused to 'hold her boats in readiness to send them ashore at a moment's notice'.[57]

—

Most of the Turks, up in their trenches on the ridges and gullies of this rugged triangle of land, continue the fight, even as a gentle drizzle sprinkles over them. Some men lie, exhausted, trying to sleep 'nose-to-nose with the Australians, and all the more awake because of it'.[58] Though they are tired and sore, at least their bellies are full, for many of them have collected and supped on the trail of loot that has dropped out of Anzac kits or been pilfered directly from the now dead cold Anzac bodies.

—

Midnight.

In his Master Cabin aboard the *Queen Elizabeth*, moored off Cape Helles, General Hamilton is fast asleep, after what has been a very tiring day. Yes, perhaps he could have stayed awake, waiting for more news from the shore, but there would have been little point. He knows the losses to have been heavy, and also that there is a good chance that if the Turks can get reinforcements in time they may even throw the Allies into the sea. But as he has confided to his diary, 'I feel sanguine in the spirit of the men; sanguine in my own spirit; sanguine in the soundness of my scheme. What with the landing at Gaba Tepe and at Kum Kale, and the feints at Bulair and Besika Bay, the Turkish troops here will get no help tonight. And our fellows are steadily pouring ashore.'[59]

Sometimes, however, even those who are sleeping the sleep of the dead and the dead exhausted must answer to the world of the wide awake and alarmed, and so it is that, not long after midnight, General Hamilton is awoken by the shouts of his Chief of Staff, Major-General Walter Braithwaite.

'Sir Ian! Sir Ian!'

Wh . . . wha . . . *what* is it?

'Sir Ian, you've got to come right along,' Braithwaite is continuing to roar, 'a question of life and death – you *must* settle it!'[60]

Given that Braithwaite has never acted like this in their long relationship – he is usually as deferential to Hamilton as he is dismissive of underlings – Sir Ian now comes instantly awake and, with his 'British warms' over his pyjamas, is soon hurrying after Braithwaite down the narrow corridors to the dining saloon, where a spontaneously formed Council of War awaits him.

Hamilton takes one look at the faces of the senior officers awaiting him – led by Admiral de Robeck, Rear-Admiral Thursby and Commodore Roger Keyes – and knows, as 'a cold hand clutched my heart', that things must be every bit as grim as Braithwaite has suggested.[61] And those men look at him, momentarily shocked to see the always impeccable English General with suddenly tousled hair and his dressing-gown draped across his shoulders.

After Hamilton reads the note from Birdwood out loud, in silence he then slowly turns to these, his most senior officers, and asks, 'This is a difficult business . . . What are we to do about it?'[62]

A round-table conversation ensues. Can it really be as bad as those on shore are saying it is? Can those fine young men they farewelled just this morning really now be a shattered force? It seems almost impossible to believe.

Hamilton's most pertinent question is to Rear-Admiral Thursby, who has been responsible for getting the men on the shore and would now be responsible for getting them off. He asks him about the logistics and the time required for any evacuation.

'It will take the best part of three days to get that crowd off the beaches,' Thursby gravely replies.

'And where are the Turks?'

'On top of 'em.'

'Well, then,' Hamilton continues, seeking expert counsel on the matter before them, 'tell me, Admiral, what do you think?'

'What do I think? Well, I think myself they will stick it out if only it is put to them that they must.'[63]

Well, then, they must!

Commodore Keyes is particularly strong on this theme, saying if they can just hold on for two or three days, much of the pressure will be 'relieved by the southern force moving up [from Cape Helles]'.[64]

Against that, there is no doubt that the situation is perilous in the extreme, and Keyes' enthusiasm for staying is not remotely backed by the others. The conversation swings back and forth, with the fate of 20,000 men riding on their decision . . .

Just outside, Lieutenant-Commander Charles Brodie – who has still not recovered emotionally from flying over the stricken *E15* on the morning of his twin brother's demise – is guarding the door like a lion before its lair, when one of the junior ratings rushes up with an urgent message that has come straight from the signals room.

With an obvious glint in his eye, knowing the importance of what he is about to present, he shows Brodie not only who the message is for – the Commander-in-Chief – but also, far more significantly, who it is *from*.

'AE2.'

The Australian submarine.

Frantically, Brodie snatches the message and reads it. It is from Lieutenant-Commander Dacre Stoker. *AE2* has got through the mine-fields of the Dardanelles, and even through the Narrows. *And*, the crew has already sunk a Turkish ship!

Never mind that Brodie has strict orders from Commodore Keyes that the meeting is not to be interrupted under any circumstances; this cannot wait. Braving a glare from Keyes that would peel steel, Brodie bursts through the door without knocking to interrupt the meeting and is even strong enough to speak over Keyes' protestations, urging him to come outside with him to read the cable he has just received.

And, of course, once Keyes reads it, he too realises its significance and practically runs back into the meeting to advise the others. *AE2!* It has got *through*, he tells them in a loud voice.

'Tell them this,' he suggests to Hamilton, nodding towards the troops on shore. 'It is an omen. An Australian submarine has done the finest feat in submarine history and is going to torpedo all the ships bringing reinforcements, supplies and ammunition into Gallipoli.'[65]

The news is of course greeted with enormous excitement and great acclamation. With some flourish, thus, Hamilton finishes writing his message and reads to the gathering from the piece of paper he has in his hands:

> Your news is indeed serious. But there is nothing for it but to dig yourselves right in and stick it out. It would take at least two days to re-embark you, as Admiral Thursby will explain to you. Meanwhile the Australian submarine has got through the Narrows and has torpedoed a gunboat at Chanak. Hunter-Weston despite his heavy losses will be advancing tomorrow which should divert pressure from you. Make a personal appeal

to your men and Godley's to make a supreme effort to hold their ground.

(Sd.) IAN HAMILTON.

P.S. You have got through the difficult business, now you have only to dig, dig, dig, until you are safe. Ian H.[66]

After patting Hamilton on the back for the stout-heartedness and warrior nature of such a message – good old Hamilton, showing a lot of pluck when it is most needed – Keyes heads out the door with the message in his hands, to tell Brodie the news.

'It's done the trick,' he says.[67] Stoker's message has come just in the nick of time, providing the fillip of positive news they needed to keep the Anzacs on site.

It takes some doing, but, by 2 am, just as a gentle rain starts falling on the battlefield, Admiral Cecil Thursby is able to land, and he personally puts Hamilton's note in the hands of General Birdwood. They are staying. They are committed. They must dig in, hold on and strike back.

It has been a long, murderous day and night. And soon enough, just as the men on both sides had been praying for the night to fall, it is not long before they are praying for the dawn, a sunrise that many of them never thought they would see. The most significant sound that Charles Bean – who has already dug his own hole just back from the beach – can hear in the night is the sound of shovels scraping out furrows and then whole trenches. As the men dig – their rifles with bayonets still fixed, ready for action at a moment's notice – the cold rain increases in intensity, drenching them all to the bone.

Chapter Eleven

'ANGIN' ON, LIKE CATS TO A CURTAIN

Of course it was Hell, but you must remember we
had been on that transport more or less for weeks,
we were ripe for any sort of action. We could have
been painting Cairo pink if we had been there,
so we painted Gallipoli scarlet instead . . .[1]
Private Harold Cavill

Had a darn good sleep and got up at about 6 am, and
issued rations to the chaps. Then the shrapnel began
and it hailed around about us and hit everything
around me but myself. We deepened our sleeping
place about three feet, but it was not deep enough.[2]
Captain Dorian King, 3rd Battery, Australian Field Artillery

26 APRIL 1915, THE MORNING AFTER

Good God, the sheer *horror* of it all.

While on the day of the landing there had been little time to comprehend the ghastliness of what was happening all around you – because
you were too busy adding to it – the sun rises this morning on a scene
of such horror that those still alive to see it have the images burned into
their brains forevermore.

As New Zealand journalist-turned-soldier William John Rusden

Hill makes his way up a gully that had been bitterly fought over the day before, he can barely credit, or stomach, what he is seeing: 'Dead, nothing but dead men. New Zealanders, Maoris, Englishmen, Australians, and Turks. Hundreds upon hundreds of them, lying in all sorts of attitudes, some hardly marked, others mangled out of all hope of recognition and swarming all over – the flies.'[3]

Most extraordinary is how men who have survived to see this new day, still so fresh to war, have already been hardened by the battle. As one Australian private records, 'At first the shrapnel had me shivering and the hail of bullets made me duck, but I'm all over that now. I think I hugged the earth closer than I ever hugged a girl. Now it gives me a sort of blood-curdling satisfaction to shoot at men as fast as I can; and a bayonet charge is the acme of devilish excitement.'[4]

—

On this same morning, under heavy machine-gun fire, Colonel Fahrettin, the Chief of Staff of the Ottoman 3rd Corps, struggles his way to the top of the Third Ridge, where he knows Lieutenant-Colonel Mustafa Kemal is temporarily headquartered. And now, in a sheltered place of relative calm, here is Lieutenant-Colonel Mustafa Kemal, standing on a stream bed, just behind Scrubby Knoll on the ridge line.

Colonel Fahrettin, an old friend, is greeted warmly, and they embrace and kiss twice. The two are a study in contrasts. Mustafa Kemal is handsome, with eyes of steel blue and high cheekbones to rival an ancient Egyptian queen. Military in bearing from top to bottom, he is a man of regal posture who looks like he was *born* to lead. Colonel Fahrettin, on the other hand, with his droopy left eye and ill-defined chin, looks nothing of the kind, as highly respected an officer as he is. Both have had sleepless nights, but whereas Mustafa Kemal looks as fresh as the morning dew, Colonel Fahrettin is crumpled.

After Mustafa Kemal has stated his needs, Fahrettin asks, 'Will your headquarters always be here? What is the name of this place?'

'Yes,' he replies with that calm tone and sparkle in his eye that inspires good faith and confidence in his comrades. 'For the time being.' He adds with a laugh, 'Does a gully have a name?'

Colonel Fahrettin smiles and says, 'Yes, yes . . . all right . . . It could be called *Kemalyeri* [the Place of Kemal], for example?'[5]

Lieutenant-Colonel Mustafa Kemal smiles back and nods.

Kemalyeri it is. They embrace once more, and Kemal watches quietly as his friend mounts his horse and begins his ride back to headquarters at Maidos. From the near distance, the combined roar of artillery and machine-gun fire is intensifying again.

—

Such is the way of warfare. Isolated actions are now taking place across the frontline while both sides gird themselves for another big thrust – the Turks to push the Anzacs into the sea, the Anzacs to break through at last. In an effort to do so, the first priority of the Anzac officers is to gather up the men whom Bean delicately refers to as *stragglers* – soldiers who had collected on the beach the previous afternoon and evening – and put them back into the line.

I have heard their number put at anything from 800 to 1000, Bean writes in his diary, choosing his words carefully, even crossing one word out when he decides it is too inflammatory. *Many of them came down with wounded men. This is an offence in war, but few realised it at this early stage. The helping down of wounded did not really begin until about 4 or 5 pm. Then it began to reach serious fair proportions – 6 men came down with one wounded officer.*[6]

For the 4000 men they have lost, the Anzacs have gained an area about a mile deep into the Peninsula, at its furthest point, and about a mile and three-quarters wide. They now continue digging their way around the perimeter, an effort soon matched by the Turks, who are also furiously hurling dirt.

(A lot of the digging on the Anzac side is for wells, as the lack of water is becoming a drastic problem – though at least *the troops had fortunately found a certain amount of water in 1 big gully which started from the sea just to the right of the beach hill*[7] – while the sanitary men are digging latrines.)

At this point, just who is besieging whom is not clear. What is clear, with the arrival of more machine-guns and artillery on both sides (the Anzacs' howitzers are now, thankfully, beginning to be landed), is that anyone who tries to cross the no-man's-land between the two nascent frontlines will not last long. The Turks' position on the higher ground overlooking the Anzacs gives them an overwhelming advantage. The difficult task before the Australians and New Zealanders is to shift the Turks and their artillery off that high ground and continue their push inland to cut off the Turkish forces on the tip of the Peninsula.

The one thing that gives the Anzacs solace in the face of the unrelenting attacks is the shells from 'Lizzie' whistling over their heads and landing on the bonces of the Turks opposite. From 5.30 am, she has been there. True, it is only occasionally that the flat-trajectory shells find their mark on the entrenched Turks, but it is something. There is a loud explosion, an eruption of flame, smoke and dust, and then there is a crater with dismembered body parts all around. More coordinates are passed by field telephone down to GHQ on the beach, and more shells are fired, dealing old Harry to the Turks.

Watching closely, it is something that gives General Hamilton a great deal of satisfaction, at a time when there is precious little to be found elsewhere: 'The explosion of the monstrous shell darkens the rising sun; the bullets cover an acre; the enemy seems stunned for a while after each discharge. One after the other [the guns of *Queen Elizabeth*] took on the Turkish guns along Sari Bair and swept the skyline with them.'[8]

And just let the Turks mass too tightly in one spot, ready to mount an attack where they could be seen by the Anzacs, and it does not take long for Lizzie – Gawd bless her cotton socks – to sort them out, too.

It is all so encouraging that the grand ship stays there until 8.30 that morning, as Hamilton would observe, 'smothering the enemy's guns whenever they dared show their snouts. By that hour our troops had regained their grip of themselves and also of the enemy, and the firing of the Turks was growing feeble.'[9]

Alas, not for long, for as Lizzie moves off to Cape Helles, the Turkish artillery, having survived the ship's guns, returns in numbers. For the Anzacs, the only way to maximise their chances of survival is to dig ever deeper. And while more of their artillery is being landed and trained on the Turkish trenches, it remains the devil's own job to keep the supply of shells coming at the rate they're being fired; each shell has to be laboriously hauled up from the beach to wherever the guns are situated.

Most of the shells being carried up meet the wounded coming down, in a gully that has seen so much Anzac traffic – and therefore enemy fire – it is given the name 'Shrapnel Gully'.

Right in the midst of this dreadful hell of flying bullets, screaming men and shells exploding all around is Ellis Silas, half-amazed that he is still alive after so many have fallen around him. Despite the horror of it, somehow his artist's eye is entranced by the fact that still 'the birds are chirping in the clear morning air; and buzzing about from leaf to leaf, placidly going about its work, is a large bee – to think of what might be makes me weep, for fighting is continuing in all its fury'.[10]

He is fatalistic about what lies ahead.

'Our signallers have been nearly all wiped out – I suppose I'll get my lead pill next. It has been now a ceaseless cry of "Stretcher bearers on the left" – they seem to be having an awful time up there – one poor fellow has just jumped out of his dug-out, frightfully wounded in the arm; I bound it up as best I could, then had to dash off with another message.'[11]

Oh, those stretcher-bearers. In just the last day, they have made their reputation forevermore by their extraordinary bravery under fire. While everyone else is digging in and hugging mother earth as if their life depends upon it – because it does – the stretcher-bearers must walk bolt upright and go to where the wounded soldiers lie in no-man's-land or on the frontlines. Then they must carry them back to dressing stations or right down to the beach, before journeying back again through the same hell. Of course, these heroes are killed in droves, but still they keep going.

'Field Dressing Station', by Ellis Silas (AWM ART90794)

'Whatever fantasies they or their families had held about them being safe behind the lines,' Ellis Silas would record, 'disappeared with the first scream of "Stretcher bearer!"'[12]

Captain Gordon Carter has long since lost all his own illusions about any glory being associated with warfare, and though he had survived the previous night all right – despite the Turks launching three attacks on his position – it is touch and go now. They have again pressed forward only to be pinned down by heavy rifle fire from the front and deadly machine-gun fire from the right flank. Now he is practically sucking dirt, his arms spread wide as he flattens himself, aware that machine-gun bullets are just '2 or 3 inches over me'.[13]

To this is added the shrapnel, which begins to cut into the Australian soldiers. 'This was too much for the men – they retired and I'm sorry to say a great many broke into a rabble.'[14] Nevertheless, by forging forward, Carter and another officer, together with a few men, manage to find some cover, and by 'the shouting of Cooees we managed to get most of them to return to what was really a safe position, unget at able by shells. The men dug and made themselves more secure and we got the position strengthened.'[15]

At Cape Helles, the same chaotic situation reigns as the day before. Some 12,000 soldiers have been landed. They are dug in, and they are holding. The British officers on the ground are catching their collective breath rather than seizing the opportunity to press home any advantage they might hold in certain locations.

One of the biggest of Hamilton's myriad worries is Y Beach. At 9 am, he is handed a message: 'We are holding the ridge, till the wounded are embarked.'

Hamilton is stupefied. Why 'till'?[16] The Turkish main line is several miles away. Why, in accordance with the Cape Helles plan, are the troops not bearing down on the enemy?

Thirty minutes later, at Hamilton's request, Admiral de Robeck has positioned *Queen Elizabeth* off Y Beach, where they can see *Sapphire*, *Dublin* and *Goliath* lying inshore and a steady trickle of British soldiers coming down the hills, some of whom are being ferried out.

But there are none going *up* the hills.

'I disliked and mistrusted the looks of these aimless dawdlers by the sea,' Hamilton would record. 'There was no fighting; a rifle shot now and then from the crests where we saw our fellows clearly. The little crowd and the boats on the beach were right under them and no one paid any attention or seemed to be in a hurry.'[17]

Watching them mill about aimlessly, he clenches his fists in rising frustration. He has come up with this scheme, and he still believes in it, but in all his planning with his senior officers, 'no one doubted that once our troops had got ashore, scaled the heights and dug themselves in, they would be able to hold on: no one doubted that, with the British Fleet at their backs, they would at least maintain their bridge-head into the enemy's vitals until we could decide what to do with it'.[18]

He would like to take a hand, call his commanders on the shore to account, give them orders of his own, but he is persuaded against it by his senior officers on the grounds that he does not know all the facts.

So he does nothing.

27 APRIL, ON A BRIGHT WARM DAY, THE ANZACS ARE JUST HOLDING ON

Constantinople has never been so far away. From the day they landed, that great city has been the Anzacs' ultimate destination, but now it seems far from certain that they will even be able to hold on *here*. This thunderous morning, as the shells continue to rain down upon them, it seems the spot bearing most of the Turkish attack is Walker's Ridge – behind the Sphinx, on the First Ridge. It is here that the 1st Brigade's 2nd Battalion, who have been fighting all but continuously since the landing, is very lightly dug in among the bushes, with little cover. They are commanded by Lieutenant-Colonel George Braund, who in civilian life had been the Member for Armidale in the New South Wales Parliament.

What is making matters particularly precarious for them is that overnight the Turks have dug themselves into a trench in the bushes on the slope in front, far too close for comfort. At 8 am, it takes one bayonet charge by one company to clear them and take the trench. True, the Turks quickly launch a counter charge and take it back, but after Braund reinforces the first company with another 30 soldiers, they are able to wrest it back again.

As the morning wears on, the situation becomes ever more perilous and Braund's 2nd Battalion is only just able to hold on until midday, when they are reinforced by the worthies of Colonel William Malone's Wellington Battalion, led by the man himself.

All together they dig in under the heavy fire now coming from the Turks on Baby 700.

The invaders are multiplying and moving forward once more? Colonel Mustafa Kemal *cannot* allow them to stay there, whatever the cost. At 2.30 pm, he sends successive blocks of his soldiers charging at them.

The first Braund knows of it is when his soldiers in the forward trenches come running back, yelling, 'The Turks are coming in thousands.'[19]

And so they are, rushing down Battleship Hill. Can nothing stop them?

Frantically, a request is signalled, asking for naval artillery to plaster Battleship Hill, and the devastating barrage begins just in time.

'As the dust of each explosion cleared,' Bean records, 'the Turks could be seen running around, dazed, like ants on a disturbed nest. For a few minutes scarcely anything of the hill was visible except a low-lying curtain of green smoke.'[20]

By the time the smoke clears, it is obvious that the Turkish advance has been broken. They have now gone to ground and are digging in once more.

Side by side, the Australians and New Zealanders keep firing, and though their own casualties are fearful, and they have to retreat from their most advanced positions on Russell's Top, they are able to hold a line across Russell's Top from where they can see across to their right to the 16th Battalion on Pope's Hill.

By the time the 2nd Battalion is withdrawn, they have lost just under half of their number to casualties, as Bean would report: '16 officers and 434 men killed and wounded.'[21]

And yet, as Bean would also chronicle, there was a legacy.

'Day and night Australians and New Zealanders had fought together on that hilltop. In this fierce test each saw in the other a brother's qualities. As brothers they had died, their bodies lay mingled in the same narrow trenches; as brothers they were buried. It was noticeable that such small jealousies as had existed between Australians and New Zealanders in Cairo vanished completely from this hour. Three days of genuine trial had established a friendship which centuries will not destroy.'[22]

For the pinned Anzacs in the frontlines, supplies are becoming ever more difficult to come by. So many of the tortuous supply routes – up gullies and across exposed ridges – are now under heavy fire.

At least, General Hamilton is thinking of them, sending a message on this day:

WELL DONE, ANZAC. YOU ARE STICKING IT SPLENDIDLY. TWENTY-NINTH DIVISION

HAS MADE GOOD PROGRESS, AND FRENCH DIVISION IS NOW LANDING TO SUPPORT IT. AN INDIAN BRIGADE IS ON THE SEA AND WILL JOIN ANZAC ON ARRIVAL.[23]

In fact, it is the sticking they are doing with their bayonets that is perhaps having the biggest effect, and on the afternoon of the 27th they need to do exactly that. In Archie Barwick's 1st Battalion at Quinn's Post, the Turks are now so close that the Lieutenant orders the men to prepare to charge.

'Fix bayonets, men.'

They fix bayonets.

'Charge!'[24]

They charge.

With a war whoop, they are up and out of their trench and charging straight at the Turkish trenches.

'I don't remember much about it,' Archie would confide to his diary, 'but I can recollect driving the bayonet into the body of one fellow quite clearly, & he fell right at my feet & when I drew the bayonet out, the blood spurted from his body.'[25]

The next thing Archie knows, somehow they are back in the trench they started from, with just half the men who had charged out. The rest are dead or wounded.

Such is the way of this war that Archie has the time neither to grieve for those who are gone nor to reflect on the fact that he has just *killed* a man – put his bayonet right through him and sent him from this earth. Of course, the Turks soon mass again and the Australians must continue to defend their position. If not for the artillery shells now landing on the Turkish positions, they would once again have been in great peril.

Still, the Turks mass once more.

'The officer in charge collected all the spare men he could find, & we got ready again, at a given signal over the boys went, the Turks did not wait this time, but [ran] off for their lives, I had the great luck to get another unspeakable this time, I was hot foot after him, & he tripped & fell & before he could rise I had the bayonet right through him, & he died without a struggle, it seems an awful thing to say I know killing men like that, but I know there was no prouder man on the peninsula than my humble self that night . . .'[26]

Late that afternoon, when the Turks threaten to break through at a spot called Steele's Post, it again falls to Colonel Henry MacLaurin and his 1st Brigade to stem the breach. Since MacLaurin and the 1st had relieved Colonel MacLagan and his exhausted 3rd Brigade the day before, the fighting has been fierce. MacLaurin's right hand, Brigade-Major Francis Duncan Irvine, first heads up to Steele's Post to have a look at the position, and though snipers are firing bullets all around and he is warned he must take cover, Irvine stands on his dignity.

'It's my business to be shot at . . .'[27]

Two minutes later, he is.

Dead.

Ten minutes later, MacLaurin comes to survey the position and is telling others to be careful of the snipers when a shot rings out and he, too, is 'shot from the same point . . . shot dead'.[28]

Colonel MacLaurin is later buried near where he dropped, his men marking his grave with a simple wooden cross.

MORNING, 28 APRIL 1915, FIRST BATTLE OF KRITHIA

At Cape Helles, General Hunter-Weston has decided that it is time to break out and go once more after their objective of the first day – the small village of Krithia that lies on the southern slopes of the high hill of Achi Baba, and then the summit itself. Once they occupy that position, they will be able to lob shells with fearful accuracy on most of the other Turkish positions on the Peninsula, including the forts along the Narrows that they have come to neutralise in the first place. Once again General Hunter-Weston, himself a late riser, eschews anything so prosaic as a dawn attack, and so it is nearly three hours after dawn – at

8 am – that a rather desultory naval bombardment begins. The French and British soldiers sally forth a short time later.

That exhausted look among many of the soldiers? For many of them, the orders had come as late as 2 am, with officers and troops woken in the dead of night to be told that in six hours they would be fighting for their lives.

Alas, just as the Anzacs had found at 'Anzac Cove' – Trooper Bluegum writes home, 'Anzac Cove gets its name from Australian New Zealand Army Corps. Rather cute, isn't it? Sounds indigenous too.'[29] – although the Turkish defenders' bullets and shells are bad enough, the most shattering enemy they face is the terrain.

What had looked so clear on the map proves to be three major gullies parallel to their line of advance, interspersed with a mass of ravines that soon split them all up, breaking their line and making them easy pickings for the dug-in Turks, who can now fire on them from all angles.

Can General Hunter-Weston – known as 'Hunter-Bunter' to his jolly chums – do something to restore order?

No.

Secure on a hill just inland from Cape Helles, behind V Beach, Hunter-Weston is too far away to exert any control at all, and in this battle the Allied soldiers are essentially leaderless on a grand scale. Officers of individual units do their best, but there is no chess master moving his pieces against the skilled and organised Turkish resistance, and there's not even a secure means of communication between GHQ and the frontlines.

In the face of courageous Ottoman counter-attacks – all of them led by senior Turkish commanders who, following Ottoman military custom refined over 500 years of martial endeavour, are right in the thick of the battle and capable of instant direction – for the most part the invaders prove incapable of holding on even to the ground they have won. By 6 pm that evening, General Hunter-Weston has to acknowledge that his plan has failed, and the attack is called off.

No fewer than 13,500 Allied troops have attacked on the day.

By nightfall, 3000 of them are dead or wounded. Ground gained? About 600 yards.

It is going to be a long way to Constantinople.

29 APRIL 1915, MELBOURNE'S FEDERAL PARLIAMENT, THE NEWS BREAKS

Order! Order! On this crisp and crowded afternoon, the Prime Minister would like to speak. And so Andrew Fisher does, keenly aware that the news he is about to impart will be warmly greeted.

'Some days ago,' he begins, the first speaker of the day, 'the Australian War Expeditionary Forces were transferred from Egypt to the Dardanelles. They have since landed, and have been in action on the Gallipoli Peninsula. News reaches us that the action is proceeding satisfactorily. I am pleased to be able to read the following cablegram received to-day from the Secretary of State for the Colonies: "His Majesty's Government desire me to offer you their warmest congratulations on the splendid gallantry and magnificent achievement of your contingent in the successful progress of the operations at the Dardanelles."

'To this the following reply has been despatched through His Excellency the Governor-General: "The Government and the people of Australia are deeply gratified to learn that their troops have won distinction in their first encounter with the enemy. We are confident they will carry the King's colours to further victory".'

Hurrah! Hurrah!

But will the Prime Minister tell us more detail? *Who*, exactly, has landed? How did the battle go? Casualties?

If only the Prime Minister could.

Sadly, he has no choice but to tell the truth, trying to hide his extreme frustration the best he can.

'We are not in possession of information relating to the actual force that has been transferred which would be of any value to relatives here,' he says sadly. 'We cannot say what part of the Australian forces has been sent, and what has not. We have twice within the last forty-eight hours asked for this information, and we have asked, too, to be allowed to make public the whole of the information of which we are possessed . . .'[30]

And even the following day, though Fisher can report to the house that he has received a telegram from the King – 'I heartily congratulate you upon the splendid conduct and bravery displayed by the Australian troops in the operations at the Dardanelles, who have indeed proved themselves worthy sons of the Empire'[31] – he has no further news.

'Our information on the subject is not materially greater than that which has been made available to the public,' he admits. 'We have invited the Imperial Government more than once to supply us with all details as soon as they can . . . whatever our feelings may be, we must, I take it, stand by what they consider the necessities of the war.'[32]

Privately? Fisher is ropeable. Even as Prime Minister of Australia, he cannot be privy to the manner in which Australians are being used? And the results of their actions?

Outrageous.

30 APRIL 1915, SEA OF MARMARA, THE END IS IN THEIR SIGHTS

What an extraordinary six days for those aboard the *AE2* since entering the Dardanelles! It has been filled with a number of narrow escapes, a great many frustrations as torpedo after torpedo has misfired or outright missed, but also a few triumphs.

For the pure fun of it, at one point they had surfaced next to a group of Turkish fishing boats and hoisted a large ensign, and had been thrilled to see the fishermen supplicating the heavens to spare their lives before frantically heading to shore. There, they tell tales of the gigantic submarine – '*Tahtelbahiri gördük!*' – loose in the Sea of Marmara, which had been the point of the exercise all along.

And the day before, they had been stunned to come across another British sub, *E14*, which – now that Stoker and his men had demonstrated that it *was* possible to go through the Dardanelles – had been ordered to follow suit and create its own havoc.

Stoker had begged the commander of *E14* for torpedoes, but the sub's skipper, Commander Edward Courtney Boyle, had declined, saying they needed those torpedoes themselves, and had further ordered him to meet up at this spot 24 hours hence, which is why Stoker is here now . . . on the surface, looking in vain for their sister sub.

———

Coming the other way, heading north, is a Turkish torpedo boat, *Sultanhisar*, under the command of Kaptan Riza, who, by the by, is having a very bad couple of days. One of *Sultanhisar*'s tasks is to ferry no less than General Liman von Sanders from his quarters in the town of Gallipoli back and forth to Maidos every day, but on this day – when General von Sanders had been late – Riza had obeyed the orders of senior Turkish officers to take the wounded instead. Luckily, the Turkish captain had arrived back just in time for von Sanders' arrival at the dock at Maidos.

The German general, though, was having the worst of days, what with the Brits bombing the town of Maidos to hell and back. So when he learns from the young Turkish captain that they have an unscheduled stop to pick up a boat on their way to Gallipoli, he quickly becomes carpet-biting mad – as only a commanding German officer can.

'A General cannot be kept back from his way for a boat. You Turks are all the same. You don't know your duty!' he'd yelled at the stunned Ali Riza.[33] And the rage didn't stop there, for now Riza and his vessel and crew have been sent back to Constantinople to be replaced by another.

Good – Riza would rather not see von Sanders again in the near future.

Still, while he is on his way, he is eager to see if he can find the submarine everyone is talking about. He diverts to the waters around Karaburun Point at the high end of the Dardanelles Straits to have a look.

And there is something now.

It is a black vessel, very low in the water, that just *might* be a submarine, and Captain Riza quickly orders his crew to squeeze the last possible knot out of their old tub so they can investigate.

—

Stoker sees the torpedo boat all right and quickly gives the order to dive, just as he has done hundreds of times before without a problem. The saddle ballast tanks are filled with seawater, the hydroplanes take on a five degree downward angle and the twin screws drive the submarine into the sea. This time, however, *AE2* no sooner slips beneath the surface, its bow heading down, than something goes radically amiss. Without Stoker giving a command or anyone working a control, the sub suddenly flattens before heading up at such a steep angle that everything not bolted down – including the crew – is sent flying.

Stoker stays calm but is a blur of movement, furiously pulling levers to diving rudders and giving orders to get the water ballast back into the for'ard tanks so it will sink again.

Alas, their sub continues to rise like a whale bursting for air and breaks the surface 1200 yards from *Sultanhisar*, which is now closing fast.

—

'*Ateş! Ateş!* Fire! Fire!' Captain Riza roars as the two sailors manning each of the tiny pom-pom guns on both sides of the bow frantically load their shells. It is the crew on the port side who have the best shot, and the gun-layer hurriedly turns the brass wheel to bring the gun onto the target of the hulking black mass emerging from the depths ahead. He peers carefully along the open metal sights and fires.

Not even close.

And nor is *Sultanhisar*, which is the problem.

Captain Riza speaks into the brass voice tube and demands of his Chief Engineer maximum possible speed.

Getting nearer, Captain Riza thinks of his twin torpedo tubes. There could be no more marvellous method of sinking the hated submarine than with the might of a Turkish torpedo. Once within range of 1000 yards, he turns the wheel and swings *Sultanhisar* suddenly to port, upsetting the gunners, who are still firing to no effect.

Once the word comes from the bowels of the boat that the torpedo is primed and loaded, with great excitement Captain Riza shouts, '*Ateş!* – Fire!' With the detonation of the old-fashioned gunpowder charge in the torpedo tube – no modern compressed air for them – *Sultanhisar* shudders and shakes, and then . . . with the gurgle of a barely strangled vomit, out pops the sick torpedo, half-in and half-out of its tube. Only a portion of the charge has ignited. The force of the rushing water dislodges it, and it slowly sinks to the bottom.

—

'We must get under again at once,' Stoker says calmly, and this time *AE2* responds instantly as the for'ard tanks are filled. In fact, it responds too well – instead of being a whale bursting for air, the submarine is now closer to a heavy spanner, hurtling down towards the seabed. Stoker gives orders for them to level off, but it is obvious that something is seriously wrong. The sub is losing control and keeps going down.

Urgently now, Stoker orders the water pumped from the for'ard tanks, which should bring the bow up, but *nothing works*. The depth gauge keeps registering the gravity of the situation, that gravity is making them sink like a stone: 40 feet . . . 60 feet . . . 80 feet . . . *100 feet* . . . and now there is nowhere left to go on the gauge. The submarine is simply not designed to withstand the water pressure this deep. Next, Stoker orders the ballast tanks blown empty with compressed air, despite knowing this will cause the loss of what little control he has of depth. After all, he wants *AE2* to remain submerged, but not at crush depth. There is a screeching sound, as air gushes into the ballast tanks at high pressure – the system is not designed to vent main ballast at anything like this depth . . .

Is this what happened to *AE1*? Is there some design fault that suddenly sends the sub straight to the bottom? Are they facing their last seconds alive before the hull is crushed and the water rushes in?

Stoker has one last card to play . . .

'Group up full astern both motors,' he calls, and in an instant it is done. The diesel engines roar, the propellers whirl anticlockwise, not a word is heard . . .

Within moments, they will know if they will live or die.

And now a voice rings out. It is the coxswain: 'She's coming up, sir!'[34]

And so she is! All eyes turn to the depth gauge as the needle now comes back the other way. They are heading back to the surface, and now at huge speed . . . where they know a torpedo boat awaits them. The submarine has gained buoyancy as high-pressure air expels the remaining seawater from the ballast tanks. *AE2* is behaving like a cork released at depth. Again, Stoker tries to arrest this mad ascent by flooding the tanks, but the *AE2* continues to rise.

—

There it is! Aboard *Sultanhisar*, the splendid vision of the submarine again coming up from the depths, exploding through the surface in a spray of water and bubbles. Captain Riza trains every gun he can upon it and heads full throttle forward, even as another Turkish gunboat approaches. A black, cigar-shaped thing explodes through the surface in a spray of water and bubbles . . . and the whole upper portion of the submarine is now exposed. The Turk's boat 'fires for all she is worth'.[35]

—

Inside *AE2*, the Executive Officer, Lieutenant Geoffrey Haggard, looks through the periscope and is aghast: 'The torpedo boat is making ready to ram us!'[36]

Suddenly, however, *AE2* again responds to Stoker's commands.

One more time, it hurtles downward at 'a terrible speed and at an awful angle',[37] even faster and steeper than before. Stoker has once again filled both ballast and for'ard tanks in an emergency measure. With the sub tending towards the vertical, everything goes flying once more – 'eggs, bread, food of all sorts, knives, forks, plates, came tumbling forward from the petty officers' mess. Everything that could fall over fell; men, slipping and struggling, grasped hold of valves, gauges, rods, anything to hold them up in position to their posts.'[38]

'Full speed astern,' Lieutenant-Commander Stoker orders, remarkably quietly under the circumstances.[39]

The engines roar back to life, but this time it has no effect. And beyond the calm he has projected to the crew, Stoker's private thoughts are rather less sanguine. 'In heaven's name, what depth are we at? Why do not the sides of the boat cave in under the pressure and finish it?'[40]

Still there is no panic – all the crew who are not gazing with stricken eyes at the sides to see if they are about to cave in look to Stoker.

Movement! She's coming up again!

This time, there is no stopping her. *AE2* bursts to the surface stern first, her motors roaring – there is no resistance to the screws now that they are out of the water – at much the same moment that three shells from *Sultanhisar* hit in quick succession. Hot metal fragments buzz and bounce across the confined space of the sub, even while the submariners fall to the ground, holding their ears against the deafening noise. Smoke pours from the engine room, some water floods in, and unknown to those inside, a torpedo just misses them.

'Finished! We are caught!' Stoker realises.[41]

And it could get worse. The distant gunboat keeps firing on them, even though they are clearly crippled. Miraculously, however, the torpedo boat that has slayed them now moves into the line of fire, protecting *AE2* from the gunboat, and blows its siren, indicating firing must cease.

Further resistance is useless, and Stoker has no hesitation in giving the order. 'All hands on deck.'[42]

It is over.

By Captain Riza's account, 'The British flag was slowly pulled up the mast. The sailors began to wave their shirts and their hats as they came down from the conning tower to the deck . . . *AE2* was slowly sinking and the sailors, one by one, were jumping into the sea.'[43]

Commander Stoker, however, along with Executive Officer Haggard, is still inside the sub, opening the main vents to send *AE2* to the bottom – even the seacocks are opened to speed the process and deny the Turks and Germans any chance of salvaging her and getting hold of the design of this most modern of weaponry. Haggard turns to his captain and says with a shrug, 'Well, time to pull the plug.'[44]

The flotsam and jetsam of their quotidian lives – books, clothing, eggcups and the like – float on the rising water, which is now up to Stoker's knees.

A cry from above: 'Hurry, sir, she's going down!'

Stoker has just seconds to get out, or go down with his ship.

In the wardroom, Stoker is just about to heed the warning when he suddenly notices his private despatch case, which, among other things, contains some money. Given he is likely to be a prisoner for some time, that will be useful. With seconds to spare, he runs over, grabs it and then scrambles up the ladder to the conning tower. As he makes his way onto the bridge, the water is just two feet from the top. The submarine is about to sink . . . forever. Only its stern is still above water, and standing on it, waiting for their skipper, is a half-dozen crew. With him now safe, they dive into the sea to join the others swimming through the frigid water over to the enemy torpedo boat.

Stoker steps off the edge of the conning tower and into the water a foot below. He has just made it.

—

No more firing now. To Captain Riza aboard *Sultanhisar*, it is obvious that the crew of the submarine have surrendered and his boat moves in to pick them up.

'Finally, there was only the captain left,' he would recount. 'He was refusing to leave his ship and was saluting the British flag. This demonstration of patriotism moved us immensely. We all saluted the British flag which was by now floating in the water.[45]

Forthwith, Captain Riza calls his men to order on deck and says, 'My sons. The reward for your zeal and perseverance is the taking of this submarine . . . But now the war is over. Hostility has come to an end, for now your mission is humanity. I am sure you will carry out this mission in a bold manner befitting a Turkish soldier . . .' And with that, the crew of the *Sultanhisar* begin to haul the sailors of *AE2* from the waters and courteously welcome them aboard. Turkish sailors hold out trays with glasses of water.

'*Lütfen bu suyu içiniz.* – Please, drink some water.'

Ali Riza steps forward to meet Stoker, who is approaching him in his sopping-wet white uniform, and speaks in heavily accented English. 'I am Senior Captain Ali Riza.'

'I am Lieutenant-Commander Stoker.'

'Never mind the loss of your submarine. Welcome aboard.'

'Thank you.'

'Things like this happen in war. I was hardly expecting to fight with and capture a British submarine.'[46]

AE2's officers are taken to a cabin aft, to be given dry clothes, while the crew are taken to the forward mess deck and have their wet clothes sent up on deck to be dried.

In just a few minutes, they have gone from being enemies fighting a bitter duel to the death . . . to fellow men of the sea, observing the traditional duty to look after each other in distress.

2 PM, 30 APRIL 1915, MUSTAFA KEMAL DECIDES

It is time to settle this.

The invaders have been here for nearly a week now, and though a great many of them have been killed, still more boatloads keep coming. Two days earlier, the first two of four battalions of Royal Naval Division marines had begun to arrive. Still wet behind the ears, they nevertheless provide 'immense relief'[47] to the Anzacs, especially the 1st Brigade on MacLaurin's Hill and the 3rd Brigade on 400 Plateau.

With 'five fresh battalions'[48] at his own disposal and their line of trenches fast developing, it is time for Lieutenant-Colonel Mustafa Kemal to launch a third and final counter-attack. He calls his senior officers together into his headquarters at Kemalyeri. The officers sit with their legs crossed – *a la turca* – in a semicircle around him, notepads on their knees, pencils in their hands as they jot down the thoughts of this man, their leader, who the day before had been awarded the Ottoman Order of Imtiyaz (Distinguished Service) for his part in the defence of Ari Burnu.[49]

'I am convinced,' Mustafa Kemal says, looking around at his men with his piercing blue eyes, 'that we must finally drive the enemy opposing us into the sea, even if it means the death of us all. Our position compared to the enemy's is not weak. Their morale has been completely broken. He is ceaselessly digging to find himself a refuge. You saw how he ran away when just a few shells dropped near his trenches . . . I cannot accept anyone among us who would rather see a repeat of the embarrassment of the Balkan Wars than die. If you feel there are such men [in our ranks], then let us shoot them with our own hands.'[50]

And so his order to the men who are going into battle the next day is very simple: 'Every soldier who fights here with me must realize that he is in honour bound not to retreat one step. Let me remind you all that if you want to rest, there may be no rest for our whole nation throughout eternity. I am sure that all our comrades agree on this, and that they will show no signs of fatigue until the enemy is finally hurled into the sea.'[51]

1 MAY 1915, MAYDAY, MAYDAY, MAYDAY AT ANZAC

At 5 the next morning, the first day of May, the Turks start to rain shells down on the Anzacs, and the men advance.

The fighting rages all day, men 'fighting nose to nose'[52] on every front. But the Anzacs' defence is insurmountable. The Turks are ultimately forced to retreat, if they can. In the end, though this attack has been better coordinated, the result is the same as just four days earlier. The moment has truly passed for Lieutenant-Colonel Mustafa Kemal to drive this stubborn invader back to the sea . . . and so trench warfare sets in.

—

On the side of the Anzacs, the situation is grim. After just one *week*, half of the AIF's once-proud 1st Australian Division is either dead or wounded.

Where can the Generals find the manpower they need, quickly, to keep their toehold on the Gallipoli Peninsula secure? After calling up those men who had been left behind as fatigue parties on the transports, as well as the replacements for the Australian and New Zealand battalions in Cairo, there is really only one fighting force left that can be called on, and Generals Bridges and Birdwood decide they have no choice. They will have to ask some of the 1500 men in each of the 1st, 2nd and 3rd Light Horse Brigades and New Zealand Mounted Rifles Brigades – all still in camp in Cairo – to leave behind their horses and come to Gallipoli as the 'beetle-crusher' soldiers they once derided. Perhaps a beginning might be to ask for '1000 volunteers to reinforce temporarily the Anzac Infantry'.[53]

True, Bridges and Birdwood want to break the Light Horse Brigades up and send them out piecemeal to bring shattered infantry battalions up to strength, but the Commanding Officers of the Light Horse won't hear of it. They have joined up together, trained together, and now they will fight and, if necessary, die together.

Back in Cairo, the men of the Light Horse are beginning to hear the first of what has gone on at Gallipoli during their visits to some of the wounded who have made it back to the military hospitals. Trooper Bluegum is one who goes from bed to bed, gathering in the stories, listening avidly as soldier after soldier – many of them still in their uniform, slit by bayonet, caked in blood, covered with their own and others' gore – talks of the horror of the landing, the shells, the shrapnel, the deaths, the killings.

'One Turk in a trench shot my pal on my right and a chap on my left,' a soldier tells him, 'then when we got right into the trench he suddenly dropped his rifle and put up his hands. I reckoned that wasn't fair, so I jammed my bayonet into him.'[54]

Most in the hospital, however, are there because all the damage has been done to them.

'My legs are tattooed prettier than a picture,' a Queenslander tells him, talking of the barbed wire he'd encountered in the shallow waters by the shore, 'and I've a bit of shrapnel shell here for a keepsake, somewhere under my shoulder.'[55]

Another recounts, disgustedly, of being shot just about the instant he'd landed. 'Fancy ten thousand miles and eight months' training all for nix,' he spits out. 'Landed at 4 am. Shot at three seconds past four. Back on the boat at 5 am.'[56]

Bluegum hears of groups of Australian soldiers simply blown apart by shells landing among them, of severed heads rolling down hills, of men crawling along without legs.

Of course, upon hearing the stories, the men of the Light Horse have one principal reaction. They want to go – are *desperate* to go – and support the 'beetle-crushers'. Yes, the Light Horse would love to take their Walers, but as soldiers of the King they are prepared to leave the horses behind and serve as required.

'Can you wonder,' Trooper Bluegum would recount, 'that the Light Horse wanted to get a move on and make a start for the front? Can you wonder that when we heard of the terrible list of casualties which were the price of victory, and when we saw our men coming back – many of them old friends, with their battle-scars upon them, we fretted and fumed impatiently? . . . We could stand it no longer. Our boys needed reinforcements, and that was all we cared about. They must have reinforcements.'[57]

Colonel Granville de Laune Ryrie, Commander of the 2nd Light Horse Brigade, gets word to General Birdwood: 'My brigade are mostly

bushmen, and they never expected to go gravel-crushing, but if necessary the whole brigade will start to-morrow on foot, even if we have to
tramp the whole way from Constantinople to Berlin.'[58]

Colonel Sir Henry George Chauvel of the 1st Light Horse Brigade
and Brigadier-General Andrew Hamilton Russell of the New Zealand
Mounted Rifles make similar offers. They *insist* on going.

2–3 MAY 1915, TIME FOR THE ANZACS TO BREAK OUT

While it is oft said of newborn babies that they only really 'start to
look like themselves' a week or so after the trauma of birth, the same
is true, oddly enough, of battlefields in trench warfare. For while the
perimeters of the Anzac battlefield had been as fluid as they were primitive on the first day, changing with the ebb and flow of the cataclysmic
clashes, now they are broadly static, battle-worn . . . and getting deeper
all the time. Both sides keep digging furiously their roughly parallel
trenches around the approximately 1000-acre footprint of the Anzac
occupation.

All the dirt so furiously flung onto mounds in front of the trenches
is moulded into solid parapets that face the enemy. The soldiers create
'loopholes' in the parapets – narrow vertical openings through which
they can fire their rifles. On both sides, the frontline firing trenches
are often dug in zigzags or with boxed recesses, so that if an enemy
captures one end, they can't simply fire a machine-gun down a straight
corridor to capture the lot. The more sophisticated trenches have 'firing
steps', large ledges cut into the side of the trench that the soldiers can
stand upon as they are firing and use to propel themselves up and over
when the time comes. Branching off from those main trenches in all
directions are 'saps', trenches initially built forward into no-man's-land
to allow the soldiers to better observe (or even hear) the enemy. These
may be developed to use in an attack. Then there are the communication trenches, used for everything from supplying the for'ard ones and
connecting tiers of trenches to allowing platoons to get into and out of
the frontlines safely.

Back from those trenches are the 'dugouts', effectively small caves and hollows that the men have fashioned, allowing them shelter from the weather and, more importantly, the shrapnel. From some of these dugouts, the men can look out on the Aegean Sea – when the mists lift it presents a sparkling blue vista – and there, just a few horizons over, is the island of Imbros. Close to the shore, there is always a flurry of vessels going to and fro, keeping the men ashore supplied, the whole thing a vision splendid.

But near to them, on land? Not so calm . . .

Terrain that used to be low shrub on solid ground is now more often 'a ploughed and shrivelled waste of broken water-bottles, bayonets, fragments of bombs, barbed wire entanglements shattered and shattered again . . . battered rifle butts and the shreds that were once human clothes'.[59] Ever and always, there is a constant traffic of men in the hills, mostly bringing supplies up and too often taking wounded and dead bodies down. (Of the latter, most have been shot through the head, as that is the most frequently available target for the Turks, poking up above the trenches – and most of the bodies are missing brains, as at such short range the bullets usually scoop out the lot.)

Thus, a week in, Gallipoli really is starting to look like itself.

All of the main positions now have – or soon will have – names that indicate at least something of the horror of what goes on there: the Bloody Angle, Dead Man's Hill, Sniper's Nest, Hell Spit, Casualty Corner, Valley of Despair and Shell Green – a rare fleck of green field now holed all over by the Turkish shells.

Shrapnel Gully leads into Monash Valley, and it is at the end of this valley that the most dangerous Anzac posts are found, most of them with curiously benign names, despite the fact that they have seen the most bloodshed: Quinn's Post, Pope's Hill, Courtney's Post, Steele's Post, the Nek.

Their distinguishing feature is that they are all so close to the enemy trenches that the combatants can usually hear each other *talk*, and often throw bombs at one another.

There is no more dangerous spot in Anzac than the one named after

Major Hugh Quinn of 15th Battalion, the unit that first held it. Quinn's Post lies at the northern end of the Second Ridge, 800 yards below Baby 700, the hill that gazes out upon Monash Valley and sits 'over Anzac like a tyrannical parent'.[60] It is the most advanced easterly position in the entire Anzac line and the spot where the Australian and Turkish trench systems come closest to touching. It is just ten yards away from the Turks in some parts. To make things even worse, the post is situated in a 40-foot dip, and Turkish snipers gaze down upon it from three sides . . .

'In the Trenches, Quinn's Post', by Ellis Silas (AWM ART90798)

Just five yards directly behind the Anzacs is the precipice of Monash Valley. Quinn's is therefore the key to the defence of Shrapnel Gully and Monash Valley, and if it is lost, the Turks would likely break through to the heart of the Anzacs and the entire front would then be lost.

Baby 700 is bedecked with three tiers of Turkish trenches, giving their elevated artillery and snipers the capacity to fire on most of the aforementioned posts, together with the precarious supply line that wends its way through Shrapnel Gully and Monash Valley.

The entire left flank of the Anzac perimeter is overlooked and threatened by Baby 700.

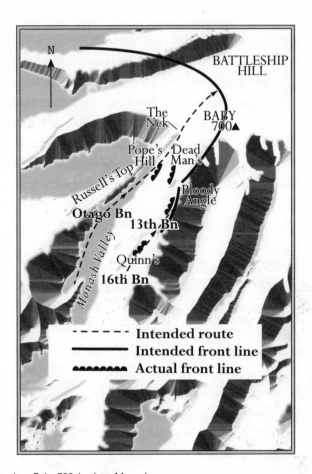

Failed Attack on Baby 700, by Jane Macaulay

Now, a week in from the landing, Generals Birdwood and Godley decide that the New Zealand Brigade, commanded by Colonel Francis Johnston, and the Australian 4th Brigade under Colonel John Monash must, at all costs, capture Baby 700.

At 2.15 pm on the afternoon of 2 May, Godley tells Monash of the plan and the 4th Brigade's place in the scheme of things.

In a few hours' time, at 7 pm, the land-based artillery and naval guns would start a bombardment on the Turkish trenches on Baby 700.

That barrage would lift at 7.15 pm, moving to the hills farther up the Sari Bair Range, and at that instant the attack would start.

Baby 700 will soon be theirs.

Now, no matter that Colonel Monash is a man who was not only born confident but has also always managed to project that confidence onto others – he does not like this particular situation at all. *Not at all.* A careful, logical engineer of some brilliance in civilian life, he likes considered, ordered approaches to problems, and this is quite the opposite. He is receiving his orders just five hours before the attack is meant to start, with entirely insufficient numbers of men for the task, against a heavily entrenched, armed and supplied enemy who would be expecting their attack. This is what he later calls the 'Churchill way of rushing in before we are ready, and hardly knowing what we are going to do next . . .'[61]

Still, he must follow orders just as his men must, including Ellis Silas, who, once he hears that they are to charge from a trench straight at the enemy, immediately worries:

> *I wonder how I shall get on in a charge, for I have not the least idea how to use a bayonet; even if I had, I should not be able to do so, the thing is too revolting – I can only hope that I get shot – why did they not let me do the [stretcher] work? I have told the authorities often enough that I cannot kill.*[62]

And now Ellis has to run a message and very nearly gets killed by snipers, in part because he is not moving fast enough.

'Run for it, you damned fool!' Captain Eliezer Margolin shouts. And now all the men join in: 'Run, Silas, *run for it!* The snipers will get you!'[63]

Strangely, Ellis – whose mouth now seems almost permanently set in an expression of tight horror, as if always trying not to scream, just as his once soft hands are now nearly always clenched fists – doesn't particularly care to run, finally reasoning that if he is destined to die on this day then there is likely little he can do about it. Besides which, he is simply tired of never being able to move about with freedom.

At 6.30 pm, just as the setting sun lights the top of the hill that is their goal with a curious hue of rose and gold, it is time for the 4th Brigade to get into position.

The plan is for them to climb the steep side of Bloody Angle and start their rush on the crest at 7.15 pm, once the bombardment on the Turkish positions stops. For now, things are remarkably quiet.

Ellis Silas's 16th Battalion is in the middle, flanked on the left by the 13th Battalion and on the right by the 15th Battalion. Ellis himself has a stricken, uneasy look on his face as he awkwardly cradles his weapon in his soft hands that are far more suited to wielding a paintbrush.

And now the naval barrage starts, the loudest and most intense they have ever heard, hopefully raining down hell on the Turks. The Australian soldiers stand on the firing step and wait, straining, 'tense, expectant, like dogs in the leash, every muscle strained for the moment of attack – a few whispered orders, the tightening of buckle and strap – the stealthy loosing of the bayonet from its scabbard'.[64]

Just before 7 pm, the barrage stops, and Lieutenant Cyril Geddes of the 16th Battalion looks at his watch. All around him, the Australian soldiers wait, hanging on his words. 'It is 7 o'clock, lads,' he calls. 'Come on, lads, at 'em!'[65]

And with a cry they go, scrabbling out of the trenches, trying to scramble upwards, gripping soil that comes away at their touch.

Instantly, and exactly as Monash has feared, his men come under withering fire as tier after tier of well-protected Turks in their trenches on Baby 700 pour heavy rifle and machine-gun fire onto his men, joined by the Turkish soldiers at Bloody Angle, who together with their furious fusillade of bullets also roll bombs down upon the Australians.

The carnage is fearful. Ellis Silas survives, despite having to go back and forth as a messenger, seeking more ammunition to be sent up to those on the frontline:

In a very few minutes the gully at the foot of the hill was filled with dead and wounded – these poor lumps of clay had once been my comrades, men I had worked and smoked and laughed and joked with – oh God, the pity of it. It rained men in this gully; all round could be seen the sparks where the bullets were striking.[66]

And who should be strutting around in the middle of this hell on earth? It is none other than General Godley, and he wishes to speak to Ellis. 'Your puttee's undone, young man . . .'

'Yes, sir, that's all right,' Silas replies. 'I'll soon fix that up, but for God's sake, take cover. You'll be killed.'[67]

General Godley does not. Like many of the Generals, it is a point of honour not to show fear; he thinks it bad for the men's morale. Someone must show themselves to be fearless on the day, and it is just as well that it is the senior officers.

Godley refuses to move until Ellis does up his puttee. Then, just as he is about to go, he suddenly puts his hand to his cap and chuckles. A bullet has split it. 'That was a pretty near thing,' he laughs.[68]

In all the madness of the battle, of death and devastation happening all around, one man in particular stands out. It is Simpson, and he is – can you believe it? – using a donkey to ferry the wounded from the frontlines back to the dressing stations, frequently under fire.

Just where he got the small donkey is never quite clear, only that he loves it, and the trusting donkey seems to love him. Simpson leads the donkey up to the highest part of Monash Valley, whereupon he would 'leave the mule just under the brow of the hill and dash forward himself to the firing-line to save the wounded'.[69] The work of Simpson and his donkey is outstanding enough to be mentioned in despatches 'for conspicuous gallantry'. Colonel Monash himself would write of the duo, 'They worked all day and night . . . and the help rendered to the wounded was invaluable. Simpson knew no fear, and moved unconcernedly amid shrapnel and rifle-fire, steadily carrying out his self-imposed task day by day, and he frequently earned the applause of the personnel for his many fearless rescues of wounded men from areas subject to rifle and shrapnel-fire.'[70]

As a young lad growing up in South Shields in the far north of England, Simpson had worked at Murphy's Fair – hence his sometime nickname among the men of 'Murphy', just as his donkey is variously known as Murphy or Duffy, to keep things confusing[71] – giving donkey rides to children for a penny a pop from sun-up to sundown, and his touch with the donkeys is sure because of it. As the only place to find fodder in these climes is with the 21st Kohat Indian Mountain Artillery Battery, who have brought many bales for their own mules, there to haul the big guns of the hills, that is where Simpson makes his base at night. He is substantially left to his own devices. The Indians call him '*Bahadur*', meaning 'brave'.[72]

Having become separated from his own AMC unit, he has simply taken it upon himself to proceed on a roving commission regardless, and so obviously valuable is his work that no officer tries to intervene or re-establish control. The result, in the words of one soldier, is that Simpson is 'the only man on the peninsula . . . under no one's immediate command'.[73]

But never have Simpson and his donkey been so busy as on this night. The battle goes on and the 4th Brigade continues to push forward, despite it all.

Picking his way among his wounded and dead comrades, Ellis Silas looks up to see Sergeant David Caldwell, badly wounded but still full of spirit, coming down the other way.

'My!' he says cheerfully, 'but they're willing up there.'

And here now is another man, a mate, waving a bloody stump where his right hand used to be.

'God, but I've done my duty,' he calls sadly. 'Is that you, Silas, old chap; I've done my duty, haven't I?'[74]

Yes, mate, you've done your duty.

But there is little time to care for him. For now, with all the rest, Signalman Ellis Silas endeavours to keep going, while the next wave into battle start singing 'Tipperary' and 'Australia Will Be There':

Have no cause for fear!
Should old acquaintance be forgot?
No! No! No! No!

Australia will be there!
Australia will be there![75]

Against all odds, the 16th Battalion manages to get into the first trench five yards from the crest of the Bloody Angle and use their bayonets to clear it of Turks.

What is most desperately needed now is *support*, so they can hold onto this new, hard-won position.

Where, oh where, are the New Zealanders who are meant to be attacking the Turks from the flanks to take the pressure off the Australians?

Not even at their starting line. It is the worst of all possible outcomes, for not only are the New Zealanders unable to assist their Australian comrades, but now the whole of the higher reaches of Baby 700 is spitting death at all who approach. Any chance of reaching their objective has disappeared.

And now the clearing stations are receiving the first of the grievously wounded, a bloody flow that simply does not stop.

'They kept coming just like the first day,' the diary of Lieutenant-Colonel Dr John Corbin would record. 'Dreadfully wounded and mangled, arms and legs shattered, heads crushed in, chests and abdomens, a most hateful procession . . . No chance of giving anaesthetics . . . view to get them to the ships without delay. The men today are more badly injured and all are in a fearful state of dirt, sand, dried blood, caked and smelly . . . truly this is a dreadful war . . . more like wholesale murder.'[76]

Some one and a half hours after they had been meant to get there, the Otagos finally arrive, and yet they've no sooner come over the lip of the ridge than they are confronted by terrible fire from the Turks on Baby 700. No fewer than half of the brave Otagos are either killed or wounded.

None of this is known to General Godley, who has retreated to his own well-protected dugout some 500 yards away. From there, he decides the time is right to have a company of soldiers from the

Canterbury Battalion attack across the Nek. The result: 46 soldiers and two officers killed.

In the valley below Baby 700, in a moment of rare respite after near-continuous battling since the landing, Captain Gordon Carter tries to grab some precious rest.

'The rattle of musketry was deafening and continued all night,' he records. 'I felt very anxious and could not sleep much – sometimes our rifles seem to have ascendancy and sometimes theirs.'[77]

Idly, he wonders what Nurse King is doing, if she is safe.

And she is, broadly, albeit in appalling conditions.

Offshore, her hospital ship SS *Sicilia* is now full to cracking, and she finds herself tending to no fewer than 250 patients with the help of one Australian orderly and an Indian sweeper as the flickering lanterns throw a ghostly light over 1915's answer to Dante's *Inferno*.

'I shall never forget the awful feeling of hopelessness on night duty,' she would record. 'It was dreadful . . . Shall not describe the wounds, they were too awful . . .

'Night duty is rather weird – going around in the dark and peering at everyone, not switching on the light unless absolutely necessary and doing the dressings here and there that were very necessary and then hearing someone groan or call "Nurse!" Some of the boys were delightful – dying to get well and go back to "get their own back", as they say.'[78]

The Australians of the 4th Brigade who have secured the most advanced trench manage to hold on through the long night against sustained Turkish counter-attacks, and maybe could continue to hold it. But in the first place, no reinforcements reach them, and secondly, just after 5 am by terrible mistake the Allied artillery opens up and the shells land on the very trench the Australians are holding.

The whole attack is a shambles. Not even able to hold onto the ground they have won, the Australians are forced to retreat, and they find themselves back where they started less than 24 hours earlier – less 338 of their number, who now lie in eternity. The New Zealanders have had 262 killed.

On 3 May, accompanied by Major Thomas Blamey, Charles Bean makes his way towards where the battle has taken place. And what Bean sees appals him, for there are *hundreds* of Australian dead.

'The whole face of the cliff of the nearer hill which yesterday was covered with bushes is today bare, and along the top of it our dead can be seen lying like ants, shrivelled up or curled up, some still hugging their rifles, about a dozen of them. The face of the further plateau is also edged with our dead.'[79]

Under the circumstances, he is not surprised to find Monash in his dugout, far from his normal self.

'They've tried,' Monash says morosely, 'to put the work of an Army Corps on me.'[80]

From a starting turnout of some 3600 for his 4th Brigade, Colonel Monash now has just 1770 men capable of picking up a rifle and fighting.

'Monash seemed to me a little shaken,' Bean would confide to his diary that night. 'He was talking of "disaster".'[81]

No doubt.

'The Snipers', by Ellis Silas (AWM ART90804)

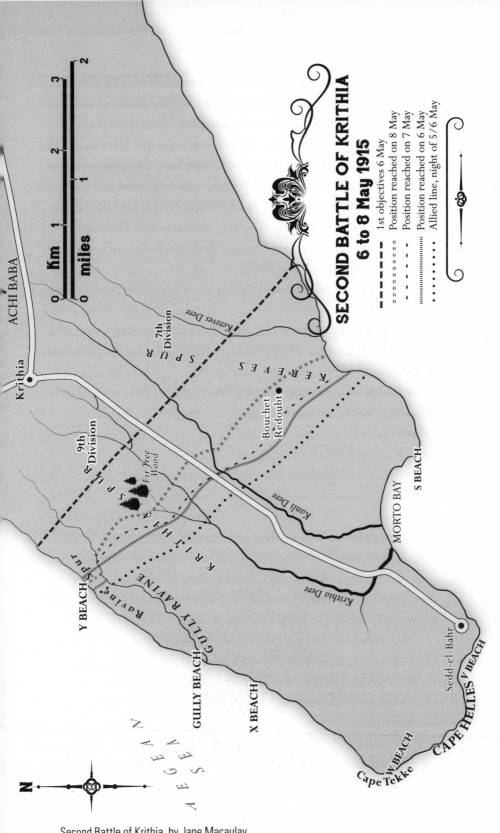

Second Battle of Krithia, by Jane Macaulay

6 MAY 1915, THE SECOND BATTLE OF KRITHIA TAKES PLACE

Though a naturally sunny soul, General Ian Hamilton is becoming desperate. Coming up to two weeks since the landing, his troops are pinned down at both Anzac Cove and Cape Helles. The two forces are not even close to joining up, and none of the strategic objectives designated for the first day has yet been achieved. Most particularly, the high ground of Achi Baba, seven miles inland from Cape Helles, is now defended by heavily entrenched Ottoman forces. That objective remains three and a half miles distant, and it has taken several thousand British and French lives to achieve even that.

But hopefully, on this morning, there will be a breakout at Cape Helles. Under the command of General Aylmer Hunter-Weston, the Empire's forces will once again attack Achi Baba, but this time, *this time*, his brigade of the 42nd Division will be bolstered by an Indian Brigade, together with the 2nd Australian Brigade and the New Zealand Infantry Brigade – the two brigades that remain the most intact after the landing and subsequent fighting. They have been brought over from Anzac, now that the situation there has become at least a little more stable. He will have 25,000 soldiers in all.

At Hunter-Weston's insistence, his forces will begin their attack at 11 am – a curious hour, given the enemy will see them from the first – with the aim of being in possession of the town of Krithia by mid-afternoon and in control of the whole hill of Achi Baba by dusk. Just why the result this time should be any less disastrous than last time he does not explain, and though General Hamilton has *grave* misgivings . . . he feels he must let his old friend Hunter-Weston have his head, what?

Even though Hunter-Weston and his senior staff still have no idea how many defenders there are, where their artillery is situated and even where the Turks are concentrated, the principle is to jolly well allow the Commander to run his own show, and so General Hamilton does.

General Hunter-Weston, however, has few fears. That morning, Ellis Ashmead-Bartlett visits with him in his bombproof shelter near

Lancashire Landing, and the General is kind enough to show the journalist his plans, pointing out the enemy's position on maps and detailing what he and his troops intend to do.

Yes, despite the disasters so far, the General is bubbling over with confidence. 'We will take Krithia this afternoon,' General Hunter-Weston says firmly, 'and possibly Achi Baba. But if there was no time for both, I will ensure we take Achi Baba tomorrow.'[82]

The English correspondent, however, notes in his diary, 'I quite fail to see on what his optimism is based.'[83]

And so it begins, shortly afterwards, with Ashmead-Bartlett watching closely, amazed to be able to witness the battle in its entirety across the substantially open fields that lead to the slopes of Achi Baba, where the Turks are dug in.

'The whole scene,' he would record, 'resembled rather an old-fashioned field day at Aldershot than a modern battle. The Commander-in-Chief had, in fact, his troops under his eye, just as Wellington and Napoleon had them at Waterloo.'[84]

After a very weak barrage on where the Turkish positions are thought most likely to be – weak because the British do not have enough shells – the British and French forces advance in skirmish order across much more broken terrain than they had been expecting, whereupon the well dug-in Turks simply lob artillery shells on them. As to the Turkish soldiers in the forward trenches, they appear soon enough, using state-of-the-art German machine-guns to send such a hail of lead into the attackers that a sparrow could not survive in it, let alone one man, let alone 10,000 men.

The results on this day are so disastrous, with over 1100 casualties – for 400 yards gained – that after less than an hour the attack is called off.

Back at GHQ on HMT *Arcadian*, General Hamilton is still absorbing the disastrous news when a cable arrives from London in response to his request on 4 May that he and his forces urgently need more artillery shells to be sent out.

THE AMMUNITION SUPPLY FOR YOUR FORCE WAS NEVER CALCULATED ON THE BASIS OF A PROLONGED OCCUPATION OF THE PENINSULA. IT IS IMPORTANT TO PUSH ON.[85]

What to do?

General Hunter-Weston has not graduated from the Royal Military Academy for nothing. Why, they will do the same thing the next day – albeit with even *less* artillery support, as by now artillery shells are close to catastrophically low.

This time, the battle goes for three hours before it is called off, and there are a further 1250 casualties.

What to do?

Order *another* attack.

And this time send in the Anzacs.

Chapter Twelve

ANZACS TO THE FORE

Digger 1: One of these days we'll be standing at
the corner of Hay and Barrack streets and a motor
tyre will burst close by, and the people around will
be wondering why we're lying on our stomachs.
Digger 2: And, when a barmaid opens a bottle of
soda we'll all be down under the counter.[1]
A conversation between two West Australian Diggers,
as the bullets fly and the shrapnel shrieks

8 MAY 1915, ACROSS AUSTRALIA, THE NEWS BREAKS

Have you seen it?

There is a story in *The Sydney Morning Herald* by an English chap,
Ellis Ashmead-Bartlett, and he says our chaps have performed *magnif-*
icently in the Dardanelles:

AUSTRALASIANS
GLORIOUS ENTRY INTO WAR.
HISTORIC CHARGE.
BRILLIANT FEAT AT GABA TEPE.
. . . They did not wait for orders or for the
boats to reach the beach, but sprang into the
sea, formed a sort of rough line, and rushed
the enemy's trenches. Their magazines were
uncharged, so they just went in with cold steel . . .

The Australians found themselves facing an
almost perpendicular cliff of loose sandstones,
covered with thick shrubbery. Somewhere about
half way up the enemy had a second trench,
strongly held, from which poured a terrible fire on
the troops below . . .

Here was a tough proposition to tackle in the
darkness, but these colonials were practical above
all else and went about it in a practical way.
They stopped a few minutes to pull themselves
together, get rid of their packs and charge their
rifle magazines. Then this race of athletes
proceeded to scale the cliffs, without responding
to the enemy's fire. They lost some men, but
didn't worry, and in less than a quarter of an hour
the Turks were out of their second position, and
either bayoneted or fleeing . . .

. . . There has been no finer feat in this war
than this sudden landing in the dark and the
storming of the heights, and above all, the holding
on whilst reinforcements were landing.

These raw colonial troops in these desperate
hours proved worthy to fight side by side with
the heroes of Mons, the Aisne, Ypres, and Neuve
Chapelle.[2]

The account is read in many papers around Australia and creates a sensation. Our boys! We *Australians*. We've shown the lot of them. And all
this praise, coming from an *Englishman*.

In a country whose formal foundation just a decade and a half earlier had been a matter of rather dull speeches and resolutions, where
there have been no revolutions, where blood had yet to be shed in the
name of the nation . . . the news is devoured with joy.

The article is cut out and pressed in heavy books for preservation, and thereafter stuck gingerly into scrapbooks. Schoolchildren must sit up straight as it is read to them, while congregations give glory to God, as pastors and priests use it as the basis for sermons. It is revered as confirmation that Australia is not only a real country but, as *The Sydney Morning Herald* puts it in an editorial entitled 'THE GLORY OF IT', also 'a changed people'.[3]

In Ballarat, they add a new verse to 'God Save the King':

> God save our splendid men!
> Send them safe home again!
> Keep them victorious,
> Patient and chivalrous,
> They are so dear to us:
> God save our men.[4]

Not to be outdone, Banjo Paterson, Australia's greatest poet, writes a poem to celebrate the occasion:

> We're All Australians Now
> . . . From shearing shed and cattle run,
> From Broome to Hobson's Bay,
> Each native-born Australian son,
> Stands straighter up today . . .
>
> The old state jealousies of yore
> Are dead as Pharaoh's sow,
> We're not State children any more
> We're all Australians now . . .!
>
> The mettle that a race can show
> Is proved with shot and steel,
> And now we know what nations know
> And feel what nations feel . . .[5]

No doubt about it. Almost as one, Australians revel in what is happening in Gallipoli – talk about it, sing about it, rhapsodise about it – and many grown men are sick with envy at those who know the glory of being there.

Overall, few are more impressed than Keith Murdoch, with the magnificence of both the Australian effort and the writing – though it does make him wonder if he shouldn't go there himself, if not as a journalist, then as a soldier, just as his younger brother Ivon is about to do.

When Prime Minister Fisher reads the article, he is proud, though more troubled than ever. For, despite repeated requests to His Majesty's Government, *he* has found out only a few hours before everyone else much of the detail of what has happened. It is not right – and he is deeply aggrieved by it, not to mention embarrassed.

Meanwhile, the Anzacs on the Peninsula are oblivious of the accolades being thrust upon their deeds. Should they have heard some of the things being said of them back home, elevating them up to the glory of gods, many would have laughed. Surely there is nothing noble about wearing the same pair of underpants for over two weeks? Or sleeping in a hole in the ground, using your dirt-encrusted hands as a pillow? Or spending your 'relief' time – hours spent away from the death of the firing line – continually digging latrines, 'trench digging and sapping or carrying water and provisions up the hill'.[6] And, of course, then traipsing the waste of thousands of men back down again on your return journey?

No, far from feeling heroic, many of the men are simply trying to cope, fighting for their lives, barely surviving this brutal environment. They're teaching themselves to adapt, to block the constant and infernal noise, to accept that every single day *in this place of wrath and tears* they will lose a mate. The heart is a stubborn thing, though, and as mates continue to be lost, the men turn to each other more and more, to shoulder the burden that such loss leaves behind. And with each man buried, the bond between the survivors thickens and grows more precious.

In a hell so dark, even the faintest rays of light can be seen. Simple, singular rays of delight. One being that a semblance of a routine is emerging for the men. Now that supplies are arriving, and quarter-masters' stores and kitchens are set up, they begin to have *things*! Stuff they'd never known they held so dear. A fork! A toothbrush! TOBACCO!

Tobacco day is set for Tuesday, and it lifts the men to think of it: 'we each got half a tin of light capstan and 2 packets of cigarettes and a box of matches'.[7]

They also get a daily issue of rum. It's a modest issue, yes, but it's better than a poke in the eye with a burned stick. As one Digger later confides to his loved ones, 'This rum is a Godsend, because the throb of a man's life runs so low here just now, it is essential to give him some artificial stimulant to keep his heart out of his boots and somewhere above his stomach.'[8]

MORNING, 8 MAY 1915, GALLIPOLI PENINSULA, AN IMPOSSIBLE TASK

At 10.30 am, the first of the forces at Cape Helles – including the sol-diers of the New Zealand Brigade – move off. The Aucklanders are in the centre, flanked by Colonel William Malone's Wellington Infantry Battalion on the left and the Canterburys on the right. They are among ANZAC's finest, and . . .

And they are simply cut to pieces. For what does any of their training count when they are sent into a trap of scything shrapnel and withering machine-gun fire in which a bee would struggle to survive, let alone a soldier? Even those not killed on the instant must go to ground and then try to scrape shelter beneath it. Colonel Malone survives but is devastated at what is happening to his men, of whom, as ever, he is fiercely protective. *Damn* Hunter-Weston.

For the other troops, it is even worse, and though the 'Pig Islanders', as they are also sometimes called, have claimed another few hundred yards, this is practically the only advance shown for the morning.

For General Hunter-Weston, there is only one thing to do, and he gives the order at 3 pm.

The survivors of the New Zealanders – who, as recorded by Malone, 'got forward about 1,200 yards and within 200 to 400 yards of the Turk trenches'[9] – must attack once more at 5.30 pm. There is to be nothing different to the way it had been done in the morning. Simply up and charge at the enemy trenches. Colonel Francis Johnston, Commanding Officer of the New Zealand Infantry, vigorously protests that such an order can 'only lead to the destruction of my force', but he receives no satisfaction.[10] Orders are orders.

Far from intervening to put a stop to it, General Hamilton, who has established headquarters above W Beach, gives an order of his own, commanding that the *whole* line, `reinforced by the Australians, should on the stroke of 5.30 fix bayonets and storm Krithia and Achi Baba.`[11]

The 2568 soldiers of the 2nd Brigade[12] who had been transported down to the Cape by sea and held in reserve must move up on the right flank of the depleted New Zealanders, and together they will push through the British frontline and attack Johnny Turk in his trench.

The first that the Australian command in Brigade Headquarters knows of it is at 4.55 pm, when, just before they are about to have a refreshing chai, a message is handed to Major Walter Cass from Albury ordering the 2nd Brigade to attack at 5.30 pm. The message is staggering.

Charles Bean, recently having received his formal accreditation as a war correspondent, has scrambled to be given permission 'to come off with the 2nd Brigade'[13] and would report, 'This message, received at such short notice that it was doubtful whether it was humanly possible to comply with it, flung an infantry brigade of the A.I.F. for the first and only time in the earlier years of the war into an ordered attack across open country.'[14]

Major Cass immediately sends out runners to the battalions, advising that they must be ready to move on just *one minute's notice*, before going, message in hand, to find Colonel McCay. An hour later, McCay, Cass and a handful of officers are sitting in their dusty trench, about to write the order for their brigade, when the field telephone rings. McCay takes the phone in hand.

Composite Division Commander General Paris has another request from General Hamilton. 'Have you any bands with you?' enquires Paris, hopefully. (General Hamilton likes bands to help make a bit of a display as they attack, so as to encourage their French Senegalese brethren.)

'None . . .'

'Well, have you any colours?'

'No . . .'

'You have bayonets, at any rate,' Paris asserts, noting again that Sir Ian Hamilton – after the soldiers have finished charging two miles across open country in the face of entrenched enemy armed with machine-guns and artillery – would like them to use this weapon as much as they can.

'I do not even know,' McCay replies, 'if it will be possible to carry out the order in time.'

'It has got to be done,' Paris says flatly, before hanging up.[15]

Colonel William Malone of the Wellingtons attempts to debate the sanity of the orders with his own Commander.

'You must push on,' Colonel Francis Johnston responds,[16] in the curiously clipped tones of one who, though born in New Zealand, had been educated in Britain, including at Sandhurst.

Typical. Malone has no respect for Johnston and it is not simply that Johnston is an alcoholic. It is that he is too cavalier with the lives of Malone's men. 'He seems to resent my asking for information,' Malone records in his diary, 'and for [my] not too readily allowing my men to be plunged ahead without reconnaissance and information . . . He says I am more bother to him than all three other Commanding Officers together. They say yes to everything and seem to blunder along but I am not seeking popularity, only efficiency.'[17]

For now, Malone has no choice but to obey his superior's orders. Within minutes, the New Zealanders are forming up at the frontline. The Australians are also forming up in a natural undulation in the field, 1000 yards behind the frontline. The Anzacs know they will soon be down to tin tacks as the bullets and shrapnel fly. (See the map

'Second Battle of Kritha' in the previous chapter, page 359.)

Up ahead, across flowery fields full of daisies and poppies, is open country with a sprinkling of trees and olive groves, which leads to a pleasant slope that terminates in the peak of Achi Baba. At the base of this hill, at left, lies the small village of Krithia, surrounded by what appear to be windmills.

Just as the ferocity of the sun is beginning to ebb for the first time, the big guns of the Allied ships offshore begin pounding Turkish positions, and, as described by General Hamilton, 'fifteen minutes later the hour glass of eternity dropped a tiny grain labelled 5.30 pm 8.5.1915 into the lap of time'.[18]

The instant the barrage stops, amid the clarion call of bugles and the beat of martial drums, a whole crop of glittering bayonets suddenly sprouts from the ground, followed by wave after wave of men bursting forth in an upwards and onwards charge, through the palls of yellow, green and white smoke that cover the lower slopes of Achi Baba.

Down the line, Lieutenant-Colonel Robert Gartside leads his own Australian soldiers of the 7th Battalion forward, calling, 'Come on boys, I know it's deadly, but we must get on,'[19] only to be all but instantly riddled across his abdomen with machine-gun bullets.

Onwards, Christian soldiers, marching as to war, and a real war it is.

As Bean would describe it, 'It was as if the universe was a tin-lined packing case, and squads of giants with sledgehammers were banging both ends of it, and we tiny beings were somewhere in between. The echoes were reverberating away to Achi Baba, and back again.'[20]

To his amazement, Bean finds himself loping forward in the prow of the attack, near Colonel McCay and some of his senior staff, together with half a dozen signallers. As they are tramping heavily up through the incline's low gorse bushes, the fire becomes so intense that one young Australian soldier on Bean's left holds his shovel up in front of his face.

A trench filled with the Lancashire Fusiliers – them again! – appears in front of the Australians, providing a place for a quick breather before the word comes once more: push forward!

Suddenly Bean sees a young man who has been shot just 20 yards or so in front of him, trying to crawl back. As soon as he makes to go out and save him, McCay orders him to stop. 'I must,' Bean replies,[21] his voice filled with Victorian virtue, before rushing forward and, with difficulty as great as the danger, dragging the soldier back to relative safety.

'Look here, Bean, if you do any more of these damn fool actions,' McCay roars, 'I'll send you straight back to Headquarters.'[22]

Still, perhaps it has inspired the Colonel, too – that this thin, bespectacled and completely unsoldierly man has done such a heroic thing – for now, with a rueful smile, Colonel McCay says, 'Well, Bean, this is where I suppose I have to do the damned heroic act.'[23]

'Now then, Australians!' McCay yells to his soldiers as, clutching his revolver, he hurtles up and over the parapet like a man 20 years his junior. 'Which of you men are Australians? Come on, Australians!'[24]

The Turkish defenders draw beads on them from their well-established trenches 600 yards ahead and unleash such a fusillade of fury that the first ranks out are quickly cut to pieces. No matter, the next formation charges forward, and then another and then another. Each time they charge forward, the cry of 'Come on, Australians!' rings out.

'It was great to watch them as they went,' Bean would recount, 'absolutely unaffected by bullets . . . Their faces were set, their eyebrows bent, and they looked into it for a moment as men would into a dazzling flame. I never saw so many determined faces at once.'[25]

On the left, men of the 29th Division are soon pinned down and able to progress no further than 200 yards from their starting point. And, of course, they too are decimated, just as they had been on the first day of the landing when, as Ashmead-Bartlett would recount, General Hunter-Weston had told them that 'they must occupy Achi Baba at all costs that afternoon. Apparently he left the Turks out of his calculations.'[26]

The New Zealanders fare a little better as they are sent over broken ground that offers some cover. Yet, after taking one Turkish trench with bayonets, their advance too is halted by such heavy enfilading fire and shrapnel overhead that they are – exactly as Colonel Malone knew they would be, DAMMIT – torn apart, and the survivors must dig in.

General Hamilton, observing from a safe spot between W and X Beaches, would later record that 'a young wounded Officer of the 29th Division said it was worth ten years of tennis to see the Australians and New Zealanders go in'.[27]

No matter their bravery, there can only be one result: death and devastation. All the survivors can do, like the others, is go to ground less than 1000 yards ahead of their starting point.

All that Hamilton can do as the sun falls is send a message to his men to dig in where they now find themselves, and hope that they will be able to hold off the counter-attacks, which will inevitably come.

Most devastated are the Senegalese, the French colonial troops. Referred to by General Hamilton as 'niggy wigs' and 'golly wogs',[28] they are the Allies' equivalent of the Arab regiments fighting for the Ottoman Empire. There by force not faith, they are possessed of fear not fight, and on this occasion they have to be practically lashed into position by officers of the French Foreign Legion pointing machine-guns and flashing their bayonets at them from behind. Their blue uniforms, too, shine brightly in the sun, and the terrified Africans go forward to the inevitable result.

'They were getting mowed,' one Digger, Bill Greer, would recall years later. 'They were mowing them down. I never saw such slaughter. That was the native troops. The French couldn't care less.'[29]

When darkness falls and the battle at last ebbs, Bean follows the signalling wire forward, in search of McCay. Passing many dead and dying men on the way, after 200 yards he does indeed find the Colonel alive in a forward trench – along with one lone signaller. Though glad to see him, McCay again calls the journalist a 'fool!!!' – the pointed pertinence of those exclamation marks being provided by the three bullets that snap past Bean's ears at the time – before adding sadly, 'They set us an impossible task.'[30]

The soldiers of Victoria's 2nd Brigade – Fitzroy, Euroa and Yarrawonga's finest sons – have been slaughtered. Of 2500 soldiers, 182 are dead, 539 wounded and 335 missing – over 1000 casualties in less than an hour – likely blown to bits with nary a body to bury. The New Zealanders have lost a third of their number, with 120 killed, 517 wounded and 134 missing – the last of whom, experience had tragically proven, would soon be found to be dead. As to the 29th Division, they have lost 1500 soldiers on the day, while the French have lost 812, most falling in front of a single Turkish trench.

In the course of three days, Hunter-Weston's forces have suffered 6200 casualties, three times more than the Turks. And for what? Not even 950 yards of ground.

Disappointed, Hamilton has dinner with his senior officers aboard *Arcadian*. What to do next? How to crack this Turkish nut that does not appear to want to be cracked? No one – least of all Hamilton – is quite sure. Nothing has worked so far.

Pass the port, there's a chap.

On the lower slopes of Achi Baba, hundreds of grievously wounded men lie among the dead, waiting, waiting, waiting for succour that never seems to come.

Charles Bean – having once again judged his duty to help save lives as higher than his duty to merely chronicle events – is nothing if not busy. Moving around in the darkness at considerable personal risk, he assists in guiding what few stretcher-bearers there are to where they are most needed, and ferries water back and forth to the lips of men whose very souls are crying out for it. There are *hundreds* of them, all around, crying for help, for doctors, for their mothers. Out of the night, a feeble voice is heard, asking for a stretcher-bearer.

'You won't see them tonight, my boy,' comes a rather cheerful reply from a passing messenger from HQ, 'they're rarer than gold.'

There is a wounded pause, and then the faint voice from the dark comes back: 'You might let us think we will.'[31]

Bean keeps moving among the men, doling out the water and making each can he carries go as far as possible by asking each man not to have too much. 'Each fellow took about two sips and then handed it back,' Bean would faithfully record. 'Really you could have cried to see how unselfish they were . . .'[32]

At one point, encountering a signaller shot through the stomach and groaning in agony, he reaches for the two tablets of morphia his brother Jack had given him in case of emergency.

'We are now on our last legs,' Hamilton records in his diary. 'The beautiful Battalions of the 25th April are wasted skeletons now; shadows of what they had been. The thought of the river of blood, against which I painfully made my way when I met these multitudes of wounded coming down to the shore, was unnerving. But every soldier has to fight down these pitiful sensations: the enemy may be harder hit than he: if we do not push them further back the beaches will become untenable. To overdrive the willingest troops any General ever had under his command is a sin – but we must go on fighting to-morrow!'[33]

As to General Hunter-Weston, while it might be expected that he would be equally downcast at what has happened . . . not a bit of it. At a later point in the campaign, when he would be asked how many casualties he had suffered, his answer would come close to defining the 'Butcher of Cape Helles', as he would also become known. 'Casualties?' Hunter-Weston snaps. 'What do I care about casualties?'[34]

In the here and now, nigh everyone else does care, however. 'For the first time,' Ashmead-Bartlett records, 'an atmosphere of depression settled over the army at Cape Helles. Up to the evening of May 8th there still remained a slight ray of hope in the minds of the men that something definite might yet be accomplished. Now that hope had fled.'[35] Far from the Allies being able to take Krithia or Achi Baba, things for them are now so bad that, as the disgusted Ashmead-Bartlett notes, it is 'necessary to construct a defensive line to hold off the Turkish counterattacks until reinforcements could arrive'.[36]

For the whole day after the battle, Ashmead-Bartlett remains on board *Implacable* trying to compose a cable that will capture the events of the last three days. And yet . . .

'It is,' as he would confide to his diary, 'heartrending work having to write what I know to be untrue, and in the end having to confine myself to giving a descriptive account of the useless slaughter of thousands of my fellow countrymen for the benefit of the public at home, when what I wish to do is to tell the world the blunders that are being daily committed on this blood-stained Peninsula. Yet I am helpless. Any word of criticism will be eliminated by the censor . . .'[37]

For the moment, however, all he can do is write something that *will* pass the censor.

9 MAY 1915, AUBERS RIDGE, HELL IN ONE DAY

Alas, things are no better on the Western Front, where on this day the forces of Sir John French launch a mass attack on heavily entrenched German positions at Aubers Ridge, in the far north of France. Using defective intelligence and a complete lack of surprise, against a numerically superior force who are armed to the teeth and with enough ammunition stockpiled to sink a battleship, the results are nothing short of catastrophic, with Great Britain suffering 11,000 casualties on this *single day.*

Who is to take the blame? Sir John himself is convinced that it lies with his masters in London, who had not supplied him with sufficient high-explosive shells of the right type, capable of destroying the German machine-gun positions, barbed-wire entanglements and fortifications before the British advance. His anger is exacerbated when, only shortly after the battle is over, he is told he must send no fewer than 20,000 shells straight to Marseilles, where fast ships are waiting to take them on to the Dardanelles, for use in *their* campaign.

In London, when he hears of it in his spacious and elegantly appointed office in Fleet Street's Carmelite House, Lord Northcliffe can stand it no longer. More than not having an adequate supply of the right kind of shells, it is obvious to him that Britain has the wrong kind of *leaders* . . . The Prime Minister, Herbert Asquith, and the Secretary for War, Lord Kitchener, are simply not up to it. And as for Winston Churchill, he is the one responsible for the Dardanelles debacle draining much needed munitions from France.

Something must be done, and Lord Northcliffe is just the man to do it.

Sari Bair Range, by Jane Macaulay

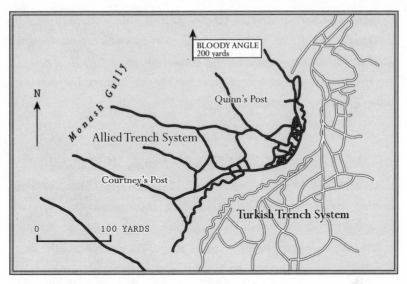

Quinn's Post–Courtney's Post trench system, by Jane Macaulay

EVENING, 9 MAY 1915, HOLDING ON AT QUINN'S POST, 'THE HOTTEST CORNER OF GALLIPOLI'[38]

'Men passing the fork in Monash Valley,' Charles Bean would quote a soldier saying of Quinn's Post, 'used to glance at the place . . . as a man looks at a haunted house.'[39]

The problem is not only that the Turkish trenches are so close but also that they are higher. It means that lobbing bombs on the Australians is de rigueur, and Australian heads that appear for even a moment above the parapet are fair game, good sport.

As General Hamilton would write, after an inspection, 'all the time from that fiery crestline which is Quinn's, there comes a slow constant trickle of wounded – some dragging themselves painfully along; others being carried along on stretchers. Bomb wounds all; a ceaseless, silent stream of bandages and blood. Yet three out of four of "the boys" have grit left for a gay smile or a cheery little nod to their comrades waiting for their turn as they pass, pass, pass, down on their way to the sea . . . Men live through more in five minutes on that crest than they do in five years of Bendigo or Ballarat.'[40]

Despite repeated Turkish attacks against this vital position, the Australians cannot be moved, sticking to their guns even if for great sacrifice. How, then, to achieve the breakthrough?

One Turkish officer has an idea, and on this evening his men start to dig. Quickly. Quietly.

EVENING, 9 MAY 1915, THE NEWS BREAKS IN MAADI CAMP

At Maadi Camp in Egypt, where the Australian Light Horse have been training since 8 February 1915, they call it The Stadium – a very glorified name for what is little more than a rough ring of sand, surrounded by some ropes, where boxing matches are put on to entertain the men.

On this evening, they have got through the preliminary bouts and now move to the main event, where, sadly, an ex-middleweight champion of Ireland by the name of Bonsoll just manages to – with extraordinary *luck*! – get the best of Private William Cameron from Queensland, winning on points over the regulation ten rounds.

Still, you know it is fair because the decision is given by the referee, who is none other than the 2nd Light Horse's Colonel Granville Ryrie. And now, through all the cheering, the Brigadier wishes to be heard. He is going to speak! Is he going to say what they all hope he is going to say? Confirm the rumours that have been swirling for the last few days? The Stadium instantly falls silent, waiting to hear their beloved Commanding Officer.

The 'Old Brig' – an enormous man of no less than 15 stone 10 pounds, who sleeps beneath a dingo skin and keeps a boomerang under his bunk – pauses before he speaks. 'Lads,' he starts out, in his stentorian tones, 'this is the first chance I've had of addressing you since our mates fixed bayonets in earnest over yonder, and I want you to join me in three cheers for our gallant comrades in the Infantry, the men who made the world ring with their deeds on the 25th of April, and who are now hanging on and in dire need of help.'

Hip-hip! HOORAY! *Hip-hip!* HOORAY! *Hip-hip!* HOORAY!

'Now then,' he resumes, when at last the tumult dies down. 'I know that you're all anxious to give them all the help you can, and I can tell you tonight on the best authority that it won't be many days before we are alongside of them.'[41]

This time, the noise near raises the canvas roof as the pent-up emotion of months of waiting pours out. The men throw their hats in the air, pound each other's backs, pump each other's hands and roar themselves hoarse.

You heard him. The Old Brig said it. We are going to Gallipoli! The cheering is so long and so strong that, as Trooper Bluegum would record it, 'the residents of Maadi, when they heard it, thought peace had been declared!'.[42]

Nothing could be further from the truth, and things move quickly from here. Just 36 hours later, the Light Horse receive their formal orders, and on the morning of 12 May, Brigadier-General Frederic Hughes of the 3rd Brigade posts a Special Brigade Order, detailing who will be going to Gallipoli and who will remain behind to look after the horses – some ten per cent of the Brigade.

And there really is a sting in the horse's tail.

For the effete Brigadier Frederic Hughes and eternally rambunctious Brigade-Major Jack Antill, the opportunity is too good to miss. You see, who better to leave behind in charge of those who remain than the ever troublesome Colonel Noel Brazier, who has been in all but open warfare with the Bullant since the day they had left Fremantle.

It is with barely restrained glee, then, that the Bullant posts a Special Brigade Order:

> Lieut Col N. M. Brazier will take up the duties of Camp Commandant and will superintend the instruction of the details remaining in Camp and the care of the horses when the Brigade moves out.[43]

Ah, the Bullant. A military man to the core of his being – obsessed with military hierarchy and his own rather high position in it – he has a chin like a clenched fist, and a voice that would put a cracking whip to shame. He is born to be superior to underlings, and regards Colonel Noel Brazier as one of the more uppity of that breed, who must be put down for his own good. Had the two found themselves in any other situation than the military, they would likely have asked each other to step outside to settle this, but in the military there is no *outside* outside to go to. For the moment, at least, Brazier – notwithstanding that his eyes flash lightning – must bite his tongue.

For the moment . . .

Among those assisting Colonel Brazier will be Lieutenant Hugo Throssell, 'left in charge of 150 men and 550 horses', as the younger man would note in his diary,[44] as he grinds his jaw – which has a slight under-bite – back and forth and side to side out of frustration and sheer disgust.

Throssell does what he can to alter this bitter fate, up to and including badgering senior officers to change the orders and offering money to colleagues to swap with him, but nothing works. No amount of money would convince these men to forgo the privilege of going to Gallipoli, and he finally realises that, for the moment, he just must cop it. Hugo is, by the recollection of a comrade, 'the most disgusted man in Egypt'.[45]

The one man who might argue the toss with him is Colonel Brazier, who also pours his angst into his diary, after everyone else is tired of hearing it: 'Oh Lord. How rotten are things in general. Nothing looks right.'[46]

Just 72 hours after receiving their orders, the 3rd Light Horse Regiment would head off without them, with the farewell words of Mr Hopkins, President of the Citizens' Committee of Cairo, still ringing in the regiment's ears. 'God bless you,' he had said. 'God help the Turks if you get at them with the bayonet.'[47]

They just can't wait to get to Gallipoli. Think of the glory!

DAWN, 11 MAY 1915, ANZAC COVE, AT THE GOING DOWN OF THE SUN, AND IN THE MORNING . . .

Oh, the sheer bloody agony of it. The death, the destruction, the devastation of a once-fine regiment. For, as the exhausted and bloodied sun struggles to get over the Sari Bair Range of the Gallipoli Peninsula this morning, it is witness to a typically catastrophic scene.

There in a godforsaken trench – oh, yes, it is – is a small gathering of shattered soldiers, staring into the middle-distance as they gather around a sergeant reading out a list of names in the roll call.

Private Brockman?

. . .

Private Byrne?

. . .

Private Holdsworth?[48]

. . .

And again and again, as Ellis Silas would note, the reply is 'a deep silence which can be felt, despite the noise of the incessant crackling of rifles and screaming of shrapnel . . .'

Pausing, the sergeant draws a line through each of those names with a quiet, sad sigh and moves on to the next. All that is left is 'a thin line of weary, ashen-faced men; behind us a mass of silent forms, once our comrades – there they have been for some days, we have not had the time to bury them'.[49]

—

Meanwhile, on this day, the Turks are welcoming a most distinguished guest at Kemalyeri. It is no less than General Enver, the Ottoman Minister of War, who has come to pay Lieutenant-Colonel Mustafa Kemal a visit.

For, just over a week earlier, in the midst of battle, Colonel Mustafa had gone over the heads of General Esat, and most certainly General von Sanders, and penned a few – not only controversial but scathing – thoughts to his Minister and ultimate Commander about the situation at Anzac:

I had earlier explained to you the special importance of this sector as compared with all other sectors . . . But Liman von Sanders . . . did not know either our army or our country, and did not have the time to study the situation properly. As a result, his dispositions left the landing sites totally unguarded and facilitated the enemy landings. I urge you strongly not to rely on the mental ability of the Germans, headed by Von Sanders, whose hearts and souls are not engaged, as ours, in the defense of our country. I believe that you should come here in person and take over the command as the situation requires.[50]

And now General Enver is here, though only for a temporary visit.

The two greet each other with the customary kisses, as if nothing is amiss between them, as if Kemal has not laid a most serious charge against his Commander, Liman von Sanders (a plea that, ultimately, General Enver chooses to ignore). They soon retire and discuss other matters – such as how to push these enemy infidels back into the sea – over coffee and numerous cigarettes.

12 MAY 1915, FURPHIES IN FLEET STREET

The news is good!

Printed in London newspapers, and indeed around the world, the cabled report of the fantastic success of the assaults on Krithia are devoured by millions in the Allied countries.

TURKS LOSE 45,000 DEFENDING STRAITS

ALLIES CAPTURE HEIGHTS

Lines of Trenches on Krithia Hills are Carried at Points of Bayonets

May 11. – The allied troops on the Gallipoli Peninsula are continuing their advance, according to an Athens dispatch to the Exchange Telegraph Company. They are reported to have occupied important positions in spite of the desperate resistance offered by the Turks, whose total losses are estimated at 45,000 men. The hospitals in Constantinople are said to be so crowded that wounded are being sent to Konieh in Asia Minor.

Our troops, with conspicuous spirit and courage, carried at the point of the bayonet several lines of trenches on the heights in the neighbourhood of Krithia.[51]

Meanwhile, at Anzac, the 1000-odd men of the greenhorn 1st and 2nd Regiments of the 1st Light Horse Brigade have arrived, followed by the New Zealand Mounted Rifles the next day. The 2nd Light Horse will be stationed at Pope's Hill – 'a long, razor-backed hill forming an isolated post between two gullies which form the head of Monash Gully'[52] – while to the 1st falls the dubious honour of assisting in the defence of Quinn's Post. As the 2nd LHR climb in worried wonderment, wending towards their lofty post, they cross paths with the weary forms of the descending soldiers of the 15th, who are clearly so exhausted they can barely speak.

'What was it like up there?' a goggle-eyed greenhorn asks.

'You may,' replies a vague veteran, 'get a few bombs . . .'[53]

13 MAY 1915, DARDANELLES AND LONDON, TOO HOT IN THE KITCHENER

One minute the 17-year-old battleship *Goliath* is there, moored just inside the mouth of the Dardanelles on the European side, and the next – after a Turkish destroyer creeps out of the Straits in the wee hours and successfully launches three torpedoes straight at it – well, the next it is heading to the bottom, taking 570 sailors with it.

Following the disaster, Sir John Fisher in London has an urgent meeting with Winston Churchill, where he expresses his very strong view that he is in total agreement with a request just received from Admiral de Robeck that *Queen Elizabeth* must come home. For the consequences of losing the pride of the fleet are unimaginable.

To add to their worry, a German submarine has been spotted off Gibraltar heading east, and there is a strong suspicion it is on its way to the Dardanelles.

As Churchill would recount, First Sea Lord Sir John Fisher 'wished at all costs to cut the loss and come away from the hated scene. I was bound not only by every conviction, but by every call of honour, to press the enterprise and sustain our struggling army to the full.'[54]

And yet, outnumbered and outflanked, Churchill reluctantly agrees to bring the mighty warship back to British waters. After all, two 14-inch-gun 'monitors' – shallow-draft armoured shore-bombardment vessels – *Stonewall Jackson* and *Admiral Farragut*, have just been commissioned and it is the view of the First Lord of the Admiralty that if they are sent with two other battleships out to the Dardanelles, they will be sufficient to replace *Queen Elizabeth*.

But who is to tell Lord Kitchener?

Churchill and Fisher decide to do it gently. The following evening at the Admiralty, Winston Churchill sits at one of the octagonal conference tables, with Lord Kitchener on his right, Sir John Fisher on his left, and many other senior officers filling up the rest of the table . . .

It's about *Queen Elizabeth* . . .

The news does not go down well.

'[Kitchener's] habitual composure in trying ordeals left him,' Churchill would later delicately recount, 'and he protested vehemently against what he considered the desertion of the army at its most critical moment.'[55]

In response, however, Sir John Fisher – who has never seen a tantrum he does not want to throw – works himself to an even greater fury. 'The *Queen Elizabeth* will come home,' he says with great force, 'and it will come home tonight, or I will walk out of the Admiralty here and now.'[56]

But Kitchener does not appear to care what Fisher thinks, as his own fury flares.

Ultimately the decision on *Queen Elizabeth* does not rest with either Kitchener or Fisher but with Churchill. It is soon clear that this pride of the fleet will indeed be coming home, and it is Kitchener who walks out in high dudgeon and heads back to the living quarters he shares with his Aide-de-Camp, Captain Oswald FitzGerald, who can hopefully help to calm him. (And he can do that. Sir George Arthur would write in his memoirs that 'Ossy' FitzGerald 'had rooted himself deeper than anyone else in K's affections, [a man] to whom K opened all his heart and from whom no secret, official or private, was at any time hid'.)[57]

14 MAY 1915, LONDON, EGGS THROWN AT KITCHENER OVER SHELL SHORTAGE

This is not just another meeting of the War Council. This is a meeting – the first formal meeting of this body since 19 March despite all the momentous happenings on the war front – where there is to be a reckoning of accounts. Yes, back in January, this same gathering had, in the main, been more than merely enthusiastic at Churchill's championed plan to outflank the enemy by sending the fleet up the Dardanelles, but now things are different.

While success has many fathers and failure is an orphan, catastrophic failure can be an absolute *bastard* . . . and the entirely isolated Churchill is made to feel like one. Still, his humour on this morning may be said to be marginally better than that of Kitchener, who had realised he was under heavy attack from Northcliffe's principal, if not principled, newspaper, *The Times*. It takes direct aim at all those responsible for the organisation of this war, and no one answers more to that description than he does, the Secretary for War:

NEED FOR SHELLS

---◆---

BRITISH ATTACKS
CHECKED

LIMITED SUPPLY THE
CAUSE

A LESSON FROM FRANCE

'The want of an unlimited supply of high explosive was a fatal bar to our success.'

It is to this need that our military correspondent, in the message we print below, attributes largely the disappointing results of the British attacks in the districts of Fromelles and Richebourg on Sunday...[58]

On page eight of the newspaper, Military Correspondent Lieutenant-Colonel Charles à Court Repington makes clear to the *Times'* well-heeled readers that there exists a 'shell crisis'. And the editorial on page nine leaves no doubt as to where the blame lies:

British soldiers died in vain on the Aubers Ridge on Sunday because more shells were needed.
The Government, who have so seriously failed to organize adequately our national resources, must bear their share of the grave responsibility. Even now they will not fully face the situation.[59]

And you wished to say, in our meeting of the War Council, Lord Kitchener?

The Secretary for War's eyes glitter as he loads. Churchill will later note to Asquith he has never seen him 'in a queerer mood – or more unreasonable'.[60]

Kitchener fires. He wishes to begin his remarks to the War Council by savaging Churchill for the fact that he has acquiesced in the disgraceful request by Admiral de Robeck on 12 May to withdraw *Queen Elizabeth* because of fears that it would be torpedoed by the Germans. This has left his army without its most crucial support. 'When the Admiralty proposed to force the passage of the Dardanelles by means of the fleet alone,' he thunders, 'I doubted whether the attempt would succeed, but was led to believe it possible by the First Lord's statements of the power of the *Queen Elizabeth* . . .

'Although I doubt whether the fleet alone could force the passage, I never for a moment thought it possible that, if the army were employed on the Gallipoli Peninsula to help them, the Admiralty would withdraw the principal naval unit on which they and we relied . . .

'I do not know what the proposed replacement of the *Queen Elizabeth* by monitors a month hence may enable our forces to achieve, but I greatly doubt whether they will be even as successful as the *Queen Elizabeth* was.'[61]

His fury, in short, has not remotely abated overnight, nor has it improved since reading *The Times*, and he doesn't mind who knows it. He is still Lord Kitchener, and he is deeply aggrieved. And nor does he want to hear Churchill's brilliant, blathering blandishments now, about how, in fact, the fleet on the Dardanelles would be bigger than ever.

'The effect of the withdrawal of the *Queen Elizabeth* on the Near East,' the good Lord says, stabbing his finger in a manner that is uncharacteristic for the fact that usually just a quiet word from him on anything is enough to settle the matter, 'will be very bad. It will be taken as the first sign of the abandonment of the enterprise, and as the first of many withdrawals. I fear it might even involve the risk of a rising in Egypt . . . I would like to withdraw from the Dardanelles if it were practicable, but unfortunately we cannot afford to do this.'[62]

Perish the thought.

'We have lost over 15,000 men,' Churchill points out, 'and the French over 13,000. If the operation is not carried through, it could be said that a disaster has happened to this country.'

And yet, while Churchill might have expected some support from First Sea Lord Sir John Fisher, who has helped to bring this crisis to a head, it is not to be. No matter that he is not a member of the War Council but only there as an adviser, Fisher feels no compunction in rounding on his nominal master, after at least noting that while the Dardanelles had been conceived first as a naval campaign, then a combined campaign, it is now mostly a military campaign, so it is right to withdraw *Queen Elizabeth*. Clearly, however, what Sir John Fisher really wants to say is this: 'I have been against the Dardanelles operations from the beginning, and the Prime Minister and Lord Kitchener know this fact.'[63] He clearly wishes to note to the entire gathering that he has always predicted it to be a disaster, and now, here you have it, it *is*.

'This remarkable interruption,' Churchill would note, 'was received in silence.'[64]

The mood is, in Churchill's words, 'sulphurous', and the gravity of the situation escapes no one. Should they pull out? Should they simply acknowledge the truth of it: that the Turks have put up a fight far greater than the Allies had ever imagined; that the soldiers of the British Empire are being slaughtered and the whole plan was wrongheaded from the beginning?

This is the tacit view of Foreign Secretary Sir Edward Grey, and the basis of the rather more outspoken demands of Lloyd George, but here Churchill is on stronger ground in vociferously arguing against that course of action. Having lost so many men already, to pull out now would make the country feel that a complete disaster had taken place, rather than embrace the current feeling, that though there have been many sacrifices, it might still be worth it. This view receives support.

Perhaps most cogently, to evacuate just three weeks after having landed 75,000 men would be an acknowledgement that the War Council had got the plan tragically wrong, and the enemy had got it right. And any such evacuation might see the Balkan nations turning to the newly powerful Germans as their true friends. Far better for the War Council to stand its ground and send reinforcements to replace those who had been lost – around 5000 men have been killed in this first three weeks, and 12,000 wounded – and even send in more troops to achieve a critical mass to crack the nut.

For the moment, no firm decision is taken, but that fact alone means that whatever small chance there is of evacuation is put back indefinitely. In the meantime, it is decided that what is most urgent is to get more information from their key man on the ground, General Ian Hamilton, and it is with this in mind that, after the War Council meeting is over, Kitchener cables Hamilton:

THE WAR COUNCIL WOULD LIKE TO KNOW
WHAT FORCE YOU CONSIDER WOULD BE
NECESSARY TO CARRY THROUGH THE
OPERATIONS UPON WHICH YOU ARE ENGAGED.
YOU SHOULD BASE THIS ESTIMATE ON THE
SUPPOSITION THAT I HAVE ADEQUATE FORCES
TO BE PLACED AT YOUR DISPOSAL. [65]

Upon receiving the cable, Hamilton is very quietly underwhelmed, as he would confide to his diary. For nothing in the problem he is now asked to solve has anything to do with the problem he was sent out to solve: 'At first the Fleet was to force its way through; we were to look on; next, the Fleet and the Army were to go for the Straits side by side; today, the whole problem may fairly be restated on a clean sheet of paper, so different is it from the problem originally put to me by K. when it was understood I would put him in an impossible position if I pressed for reinforcements.' [66]

His response, nevertheless, is as clear as mud:

ON THE ONE HAND, THERE ARE AT PRESENT
ON THE PENINSULA AS MANY TROOPS AS THE

AVAILABLE SPACE AND WATER SUPPLY CAN
ACCOMMODATE.

ON THE OTHER HAND, TO BREAK THROUGH
THE STRONG OPPOSITION ON MY FRONT WILL
REQUIRE MORE TROOPS. I AM, THEREFORE,
IN A QUANDARY . . . MOREOVER, THE
DIFFICULTY IN ANSWERING YOUR QUESTION
IS ACCENTUATED BY THE FACT THAT MY
ANSWER MUST DEPEND ON WHETHER TURKEY
WILL CONTINUE TO BE LEFT UNDISTURBED
IN OTHER PARTS . . .

IF, HOWEVER, THE PRESENT SITUATION
REMAINS UNCHANGED AND THE TURKS ARE
STILL ABLE TO DEVOTE SO MUCH EXCLUSIVE
ATTENTION TO US, I SHALL WANT . . .
TWO ARMY CORPS ADDITIONAL IN ALL . . .

I BELIEVE I COULD ADVANCE WITH HALF
THE LOSS OF LIFE THAT IS NOW BEING
RECKONED UPON, IF I HAD A LIBERAL
SUPPLY OF GUN AMMUNITION, ESPECIALLY
OF HIGH EXPLOSIVE.[67]

To make matters worse, the troops on the Peninsula are quickly being stripped of more of their key naval support, as Admiral de Robeck continues to heed the sinking of the *Goliath* and the German sub heading east as portents of an attack. To escape this likelihood, he orders half of the fleet's battleships to go back to Lemnos and Tenedos.

They are quickly followed by General Hamilton, who decides he and his senior staff would be much safer, not to mention more comfortable, on the island of Imbros rather than aboard *Arcadian* off W Beach.

Anzac Cove soon has only two battleships supporting it with artillery fire, instead of four, while Cape Helles goes from seven to four.

15 MAY 1915, GALLIPOLI, BRIDGES CROSSES TO THE OTHER SIDE

With the objectives of the landing as far away as ever, just as it is in Cape Helles after the two battles of Krithia, the question arises: what is the next step? For General Birdwood, the answer is obvious. There must be a third landing at Suvla Bay, to the north of Anzac. With this in mind, he now gives strict orders that no attacks should be made in that direction. 'I wanted,' he would later recount, 'to let the Turks think that we entirely ignored it.'[68]

They must focus meanwhile on holding on at Anzac Cove, and Birdwood remains impressed by the quality of his troops, and particularly the Australians, who embody, he will later exult, 'all the finest qualities with which man is endowed . . . tenacity of purpose . . . resource and initiative . . . indomitable valour . . . inherent and ardent patriotism and love of country . . .'[69]

Everything, in short, bar the first blooming clue as to formality and to their own position in the lower orders of the military hierarchy. Many years later, in a BBC interview, Birdwood will tell of how on one occasion at around this time he was confronted by an Australian soldier on the beach at Anzac Cove, who asks, 'Are you Birdie?'

'I am.'

'Good,' says the Digger. 'I want to complain about inferior bloody material.'

With which, he pulls out one of the admittedly highly problematic grenades the soldiers are issued with, pulls out the pin, and to General Birdwood's horror throws it down near him just a second before it . . . explodes.

Shrapnel flies past his ears and even cuts his leggings! No, none of it actually draws blood, but he remains stupefied at the inconceivable thing that has just happened. And yet, before he can react, the Australian soldier beats him to it.

'Gawd, Birdie,' says he, pushing his hat to the back of his head and putting his hands on his hips, 'that is the first bastard that's gone off this month.'[70]

This capacity of the young Australians to speak truth to power both shocks and awes General Birdwood. He would later tell a story to some fellow Generals about the time he had been getting near a dangerous spot on the slopes of Gallipoli, where there was no protection from the whizzing bullets, and a sentry had called out to him, 'Duck, Birdie; you'd better bloody well duck!'

'What did you do?' the Generals, appalled at the sentry's presumption, asked.

'What did I do?' Birdie replies. 'Why, I bloody well ducked!'[71]

Some officers, however, are simply not like that. It is a point of honour with them not to show fear, not to duck when other men duck, not to mind bullets buzzing around them like angry flies, but to demonstrate at all times as much contempt for the enemy's angry shots as they have for their own safety.

And General William Bridges is very much in this mould.

On this morning, Bridges is with Brudenell White and a medical officer, Captain Clive Thompson, heading up Monash Valley, when they come to a notably dangerous spot for snipers' bullets. A wall of sandbags provides some protection, but not enough. An officer who comes across them there tells them they must take extra care around the next corner, as, 'I have lost five men there today.'[72]

For once, General Bridges appears to take heed, and – for the first time any of them can think of – actually breaks into a run to get past. At the next hotspot, near Steele's Post, the General does the same and runs around a corner.

Suddenly Brudenell White and Thompson hear a commotion. They race ahead to find soldiers kneeling over someone. It is Bridges, and blood is gushing from the middle of his right thigh, where his femoral artery has been blown open. In an instant, Captain Thompson removes his belt, pulls it around the thigh just higher than the wound and applies all his strength to stop the flow.

'Another five heartbeats and he must have died there and then,' Brudenell White will later tell Bean.[73]

But even with the bleeding now stemmed, it is obvious that Bridges' survival is going to be touch and go – and they must get medical help immediately.

'Don't have me carried down,' Bridges manages to gasp. 'I don't want to endanger any of your stretcher-bearers.'

'Nonsense, sir,' Thompson replies, 'of course you've got to be carried down.'[74]

Bridges is soon in the hands of the stretcher-bearers, accompanied by the deeply shocked Brudenell White and Captain Thompson. There are no more shots fired at them, and they have the impression the Turks have spared them. 'The Turk was a gentleman,' would become one of the gentle Brudenell White's favourite observations.[75]

Down on the beach, and then in the hospital ship, they try, they really try to save him. But with such a wound, with so few facilities and such potential for gangrene to set in – which is precisely what happens over the next two days – there is always going to be little chance.

And Bridges knows it. But there is one positive thing, despite it all. 'Anyhow,' he says to the doctor dressing his wound, '. . . anyhow, I have commanded an Australian Division for nine months.'[76]

Three days later, aboard the hospital ship *Gascon*, heading back to Egypt, Bridges dies . . . only a short time after the news comes through that he has been knighted by George V.

General Birdwood's Chief of Staff, Brigadier-General Harold 'Hooky' Walker, a British officer of the Indian Army, takes over temporary command of the Australian 1st Divvy, as it is known, until a replacement can be named.

As it happens, a change of command is in the wind in many places . . .

15 MAY 1915, LONDON, FISHER DRAWS A LINE IN THE SAND

Finally, Fisher can bear it no more, and on this day – the day after the heated War Council meeting – he sends Churchill a letter of resignation:

First Lord

May 15, 1915

After further anxious reflection I have come to the regretted
conclusion I am unable to remain any longer as your colleague . . .
I find it increasingly difficult to adjust myself to the increasing
daily requirements of the Dardanelles to meet your views – as you
truly said yesterday I am in the position of continually veto-ing your
proposals.

    This is not fair to you besides being extremely distasteful to me.
    I am off to Scotland at once, so as to avoid all questionings.[77]

And he really would have gone, too, except that, shortly after-wards, Lloyd George runs into the grim-faced Fisher in the foyer of 10 Downing Street and is told of what he has just done.

Why on earth?

'Our ships [on other seas],' Fisher tells him, 'are being sunk while we have a fleet in the Dardanelles which is bigger than the German Navy. Both our Navy and Army are being bled for the benefit of the Dardanelles Expedition.'[78]

Lloyd George, of course, tries to change Fisher's mind, but all the Munitions Minister can get him to agree to is to delay making a public announcement for 48 hours, to allow the government the time it needs to organise itself to limit the political fall-out.

And Churchill, too, tries to talk him out of such drastic action, writing him a soothing note. But Sir John Fisher is over the whole thing, and Churchill in particular, and writes in his reply letter:

YOU ARE BENT ON FORCING THE
DARDANELLES AND NOTHING WILL TURN
YOU FROM IT – NOTHING. I know you so well!
. . . You will remain and I SHALL GO . . .[79]

And go he does.

15 MAY 1915, AUSTRALIA, SOME MORE REPORTS, WITH BAYONETS FLASHING

It has taken a long time to pass the censors, but at last, on this day, the report of the landing by the official war correspondent Charles E. W. Bean is published in *The Sydney Morning Herald*, and around the country. It confirms the heroism already recorded by Ashmead-Bartlett and is devoured across Australia, again, not least by Keith Murdoch:

> ... When all is said, the feat which will go down in history is that first Sunday's fighting when three Australian Brigades stormed, in face of a heavy fire, tier after tier of cliffs and mountains, apparently as impregnable as Govett's Leap. The sailors who saw the Third Brigade go up those heights and over successive summits like a whirligig with wild cheers, and with bayonets flashing, speak of it with tears of enthusiasm in their eyes.
>
> ... Australian infantry, and especially the Third Brigade, have made a name which will never die.[80]

True, the prose is not quite as florid as that of Ashmead-Bartlett's account, but that is simply the nature of the man.

'Bean!' the English journalist would note of his Australian contemporary's far more factual style. 'O, I think Bean actually counts the bullets.'[81]

EVENING, 17 MAY 1915, ANZAC COVE, ANZACS FEELING UNDERMINED

Quinn's Post is holding on, but only just.

'Quinn's looked the most desolate spot on earth,' Bean would record, no doubt while counting bullets. 'Not a blade of green is left there, the place is scorched to the bone, the pink and brown earth lies bare, tumbled this way and that with trenches – with the desolation of a deserted mining camp.'[82] No mining camp, however, *ever* saw this many explosions, as Quinn's continues to be blasted by artillery and bombs, causing variously plumes of dust, rivers of blood, small white bomb-clouds hanging low like mist or 'an ugly black puff going straight up, like that of a railway engine'. If it is a really big bomb, Bean notes, it sometimes emits black smoke 'like that of a small volcano. These explosions often lifted the earth, red, yellow or black, in dense little clouds – shot fragments of wood, cloth, earth, ten or twenty feet into the air . . . An intermittent stream of wounded came out, some with frightful wounds.'[83]

Something *is* going on. While up there a few days back, before being relieved by the Light Horse, Private Joseph Slack of Australia's 15th Battalion was one of many who had been sure of it. For well over a week now, there have been rumours that the Turks are digging tunnels towards Quinn's – perhaps to put a bomb under them and blow them out of their position – and the rumours have been so persistent among the Anzacs that New Zealand engineers have worked to sink three shafts some 15 feet deep so that men can go down there and *listen* for the sound of any tunnelling coming towards them.

The 15th and 16th Australian Battalions contain men with considerable mining experience, from places such as Charters Towers and Mount Morgan in Queensland, and the goldfields of South Australia and Western Australia. They are disinclined to depend on others for evidence on which their lives depend, so they carry out their own investigations.

Lying on his stomach this night, in an extension of a small trench adjoining his own, soldier Slack can hear exactly that. There it is again, 'the steady, persistent, muffled knocking of the enemy's picks'.[84]

Slack calls for his Sergeant-Major, who also hears it, as does his Company Commander, and many men of his company. These men are in no doubt: 'Jacko is getting under us.'[85]

And yet what can they do?

Seemingly, very little.

18 MAY 1915, ANZAC COVE, ENOUGH IS ENOUGH

Something is wrong, and Ellis Silas knows it. Two days earlier, he had written in his diary, *I think if I am here much longer my reason will go – I do not seem able to get a grip of myself and feel utterly crushed and unmanned*,[86] and it has only got worse since. He cannot concentrate, has no desire to eat, is on the point of tears all the time, and his greatest fear is that in the heat of battle he will *bungle a message and perhaps cause the loss of the lives of many of these brave fellows*.[87]

He has hoped to get wounded, to take his own feelings out of the equation, but, extraordinarily, it has not happened. And last night he had gone 'quite off my head'. Clearly his nerves are shattered, and his Commanding Officer, backed by the medical officer, insists that he must be evacuated to have a complete rest. There is no resentment. Colonel Pope tells him he is sorry to see him go, as 'you have done some valuable work for us', while Captain Eliezer Margolin says, 'Yes, Silas, old chap, it's about time too, you're not cut out for this kind of thing. I hope you will get into the [Army Medical Corps] as you always wanted to do.'[88]

And with that, Silas is withdrawn, making his way from the front-lines on a route that used to be just a dusty track exposed to snipers but is now magically transformed into a road up to 12 feet deep, constructed over the last fortnight or so. It takes him to the clearing station, from where he is put on a hospital ship to take him back to Cairo. He is still compos mentis enough to help as an orderly on the ship, trying to keep the seriously wounded alive long enough to get to a hospital. And yet, upon his arrival at that hospital, he collapses completely, wandering into a delirium where he again imagines himself to be signalling in the horrors of Gallipoli . . .

In the next bed, another soldier, in his own delirium, is singing a series of comic songs, which, while amusing other patients in the ward, drives Silas madder still. He nevertheless manages to record of his ward:

Here as elsewhere Death stalked – four of my comrades passed out within a few hours of each other – an inert

mass covered with the Union Jack is borne away —
thus, one by one, they passed into the Infinite, leaving
behind a name that shall ever ring glorious.
*   As I look into the distant future when the sound of*
guns is but an echo of the past, in grand array shall
I see the spirits of these my comrades marching past,
who in the greatness of their souls have handed to
future generations a fuller, deeper meaning of the word
Patriotism.[89]

Some of the other men of Monash's 4th Brigade are coping a little better than Ellis and the hundreds of other men who have been carried down the hill and loaded onto steamboats. Instead of being shocked by the constant hail of shells that mar their new life in this alien place, they have made a game out of it. As Colonel Monash himself records, 'We have been amusing ourselves by trying to discover the longest period of absolute quiet. We have been fighting now continuously for 22 days, all day and all night, and most of us think that absolutely the longest period during which there was absolutely no sound of gun or rifle fire, throughout the whole of that time, was ten seconds. One man says he was able on one occasion to count fourteen, but none believed him. We are all of us certain that we shall no longer be able to sleep amid perfect quiet, and the only way to induce sleep will be to get someone to rattle an empty tin outside one's bedroom door . . . the noise is much greater at night than in the daytime.'[90]

18 MAY 1915, PLEASE, SIR, I WANT SOME MORE

'It is never difficult,' the most celebrated English comic novelist of his day, P. G. Wodehouse, would famously write, 'to distinguish between a Scotsman with a grievance and a ray of sunshine.'[91]

There is as little confusion when it comes to Kitchener when he is displeased – which is mostly – and it is rarely clearer than in his communications this morning with General Hamilton, who two days before has had the colossal temerity to ask for more troops – *two* more Army Corps at minimum, to replace the men lost! – to break the impasse. Kitchener tersely responds:

I AM QUITE CERTAIN THAT YOU FULLY
REALIZE WHAT A SERIOUS DISAPPOINTMENT
IT HAS BEEN TO ME TO DISCOVER THAT MY
PRECONCEIVED VIEWS AS TO THE CONQUEST
OF POSITIONS NECESSARY TO DOMINATE
THE FORTS OF THE STRAITS, WITH NAVAL
ARTILLERY TO SUPPORT OUR TROOPS ON
LAND, AND WITH THE ACTIVE HELP OF
NAVAL BOMBARDMENT, WERE MISCALCULATED.
 A SERIOUS SITUATION IS CREATED BY
THE PRESENT CHECK, AND THE CALLS FOR
LARGE REINFORCEMENTS AND AN ADDITIONAL
AMOUNT OF AMMUNITION THAT WE CAN ILL
SPARE FROM FRANCE . . .
 I KNOW THAT I CAN RELY UPON YOU TO
DO YOUR UTMOST TO BRING THE PRESENT
UNFORTUNATE STATE OF AFFAIRS IN THE
DARDANELLES TO AS EARLY A CONCLUSION
AS POSSIBLE, SO THAT ANY CONSIDERATION
OF A WITHDRAWAL, WITH ALL ITS DANGERS
IN THE EAST, MAY BE PREVENTED FROM
ENTERING THE FIELD OF POSSIBLE
SOLUTIONS.[92]

Chapter Thirteen

THE TURKISH OFFENSIVE

The Australians at Anzac hold the most extraordinary
position in which any army has ever found itself,
clinging, as they are, to the face of the cliffs. Roughly
the position consists of two semicircles of hills, the
outer higher than the inner. They are extremely well
entrenched and cannot be driven from their position
by artillery fire or frontal attacks . . . The Turks are
entrenched up to their necks all round them.[1]
Ellis Ashmead-Bartlett, The Uncensored Dardanelles

Their beauty, for it really was heroic, should have been
celebrated in hexameters not headlines . . . There was
not one of those glorious young men I saw that day
who might not himself have been Ajax or Diomed,
Hector or Achilles. Their almost complete nudity, their
tallness and majestic simplicity of line, their rose-brown
flesh burnt by the sun and purged of all grossness
by the ordeal through which they were passing, all
these united to create something as near to absolute
beauty as I shall hope ever to see in this world.[2]
*Compton Mackenzie, novelist and member of
General Hamilton's staff at Gallipoli*

18 MAY 1915, FROM ABOVE ANZAC COVE, ATTACK OF THE WILD TURKS

Mustafa Kemal is restless, roaming . . .

He has just received word that Brigadier-General Esat – under order of General Enver and General Liman von Sanders – will be taking more hands-on control of the recently formed Northern Group and moving into the headquarters at Kemalyeri. Yes, the name will remain, but Colonel Mustafa Kemal is to move his 19th Division headquarters to Battleship Hill, where he will command the northern sector of the Northern Group. And one more thing . . .

General Enver has made clear after his visit to the Peninsula that nothing less than the infidels being pushed off the Turkish homeland is acceptable to the government in Constantinople.

The objective of the attack, *regardless of losses*, is really quite simple: 'Attack before day-break, drive the ANZAC troops from their trenches, and follow them down to the sea.'[3]

With 30,000 soldiers secretly amassed in the preceding days and suddenly on the charge, they should be able to dislodge the invaders, who cannot number more than 20,000. After all, they only need to break through at one strategic point – say, Quinn's Post – and the rest of the Allied defences should fold in on themselves.

God help the Anzacs, because Allah won't.

—

Among the Anzacs, on this morning of 18 May, it is noted: for some reason the Turks are not firing at them today. No bullets, no constant explosions of shells all around. You can hear the birds singing.

(Well, mostly anyway. In the mid-morning, a flock of storks is unwise enough to fly over the Australian trenches, at which point furious firing skyward breaks out. Two of them fall in positions where they can be recovered by the Diggers, meaning a welcome change from bully beef tonight.)

But then the silence returns.

And something else is odd. Walking around the trenches that afternoon, General Birdwood notices a lot of movement in the Turkish lines.

Could they have something planned? His senior officers agree it is likely. Even though the Allies have only been on these shores for a little over three weeks, they already recognise that anything out of the ordinary is usually a prelude to an attack. And as this is *so* out of the ordinary, perhaps it is a big attack. As a precaution, General Birdwood orders reserves to come forward and be in position to move quickly if required.

Their suspicions are confirmed when a pilot of the Royal Naval Air Service flies over the Peninsula at a safe height and sees 'two of the valleys east of the ANZAC line are packed with Turkish troops, densely crowded upon the sheltered slopes'.[4]

But it gets worse. When a second plane is sent up to confirm the report, its pilot not only sees the same masses of troops but also spots four steamers unloading even *more* soldiers on the European shore of the Dardanelles. Reports roll in throughout the day, bringing news of 'considerable bodies of mounted troops and guns'.[5] Just what on earth are the Allies about to face? Against the 17,500 men the Anzacs can muster, it looks as though there must be 40,000 of the brutes about to come at them. Can it really be that bad?[6]

They are not long in finding out.

On the Anzac perimeter, at 5 pm, the air is suddenly filled with a distant boom, closely followed by a whistling sound, before a weird screeching comes in an ever higher crescendo and then . . . a massive explosion. And then another, and another, and another. More shells than ever before start falling, 'chiefly on the Australian line from the Pimple northwards to Courtney's'[7] . . . And it is not just those at Anzac Cove who can hear it. Off the coast, the next contingent of the Australian Light Horse are arriving in their transports and crowd the decks, transfixed by the 'rumbling of heavy artillery'[8] that rolls over them. As they get closer, they can see 'the intermittent flashes of the guns'[9] in the gathering dusk. They won't be able to land tonight, but even this small glimpse of action is enough to:

Stiffen the sinews, summon up the blood,
Disguise fair nature with hard-favour'd rage;
Then lend the eye a terrible aspect;
(Shakespeare, *King Henry V*, Act 3, Scene 1)

They cannot *wait* to land.

Just before 5.30 pm, it happens. Behind the Turkish trenches closest to Courtney's Post, three Turkish soldiers load a howitzer and follow their strict routine, their Sergeant shouting, '*Hazirol!* – Ready!' and then, '*Ateş!* – Fire!'

An instant later, the howitzer erupts and the shell heads skyward, a searing streak of flame, before lobbing towards the Australian lines. Of course, the Turks have no idea exactly where it will land, only that it will be right among those who had been raining exactly the same kind of devastation on them.

Carter is organising the soldiers in his trench to get into better sniping positions, willing the barrage to stop. Even over the sound of so many other exploding shells, he now hears a whistling, getting louder, screeching now, squealing . . . *Is this it?* . . . He involuntarily stiffens his whole body, as if that might save him. The shell lands just a few yards away, and explodes . . .

In his dugout, Bean records that the sound of Turkish fire is so overwhelming that it has 'grown to a roar like that of a great stream over a precipice'.[10]

As his position is close to the signals office – the communications nerve centre for all of Anzac Cove – he heads over to seek more information. The office is doing exactly that as he arrives, checking with all the brigades and their battalions on the frontline. All bar 2nd Battalion have reported that, despite the unprecedented barrage, everything is under control. Bean waits, as they all do, for an operator to track them down.

Soon a report comes crackling down the line: all is 'OK'.

'Tell him I wanted to know,' Brigadier-General 'Hooky' Walker says, 'whether in view of the firing there is anything to report.'[11]

'He says it's only the Turks firing.'[12]

Barely worth mentioning when you put it like that. Just after midnight, Bean goes back to bed.

Nevertheless, because of the air intelligence that the Turkish troops are massing, all soldiers on the frontline at Anzac are instructed to 'stand to arms at 3 am'[13] instead of the usual 3.30 am.

The strangest thing? Despite the horror of what the men are experiencing as still the barrage grows in intensity, more than a few soldiers are struck by the vivid wonder of what they are witnessing.

'The scene during this shelling was a wild but beautiful sight,' Archie Barwick would recount. 'A mass of bursting shells, our own & the Turks' & as they burst they threw out different coloured flashes, some golden some pink, yellow, blue, dark & light red & all different shades from the different sorts of explosives they were using.'[14] It is all more spectacular than the fireworks on Empire Day back home!

Suddenly, however, it stops and there is a strong sense that something big is about to happen.

Everyone ready?

Among the four divisions of Turks, the soldiers crouch, waiting for the bugle to sound.

Among the Anzacs, there is a last-minute check of ammunition, bayonets and rifles. Everyone knows that there will shortly be a rush at them – the only thing yet to be determined is just how big it will be.

And suddenly a piercing bugle call cleaves the night.

From the Turkish trenches come thousands of voices crying *'Allah! Allah! Allah!'*, and here they come, spectres rising from the ground in front, and then suddenly looming large as the first wave rushes towards the Anzac trenches . . .

And, *now* . . .

The shout goes up, the triggers are pulled, and the night is filled with the chattering roar of dozens of machine-guns and thousands of rifles, together with the boom of the mountain guns, followed by the screams and groans of mown-down Turks.

Bizarrely, even above such uproar and agony the strangled sounds of Turkish bands playing martial tub-thumpers can also be heard as whole lines of Turkish soldiers continue to run forward with calls of 'Allah!'.

It is slaughter, pure and simple. With such a mass of men coming at them, at such a close range, the Anzacs in the frontline simply cannot miss, and most bullets find a billet in a Turk. Soon the succeeding waves of attackers tumble over the bodies of the dead men who have gone before.

So fearful is the damage being done by the Allied frontline soldiers that those behind plead, 'Come on down and give us a go . . . I'm a miles better shot than you.'[15]

When that doesn't work, in one trench so crammed that not everyone can get up on the fire-step, one bloke behind and below is heard to offer '5 quid to any of youse who will give me your spot'.[16]

As to Allah, no one has the least sympathy for either the deity or the men who are endlessly shouting his name. They continue to charge forward, 'Allah! Allah! Mohammed! Allah!'.

'Yes,' an infantryman roars as he shoots the Turkish soldiers down, 'you can bring them along too!'[17]

As the Turks continue to charge, the Australians can even sit on the parapets to make themselves more comfortable as they shoot. It is all just so 'dead easy – just like money from home'.[18]

The heaviest of the Turkish attacks are around 400 Plateau, Quinn's and Courtney's Post. The last is held by the 14th Battalion, but, after throwing bombs into a trench bay, one mass of Turkish soldiers actually captures a part of it. For the Australians, for the whole of Anzac Cove, the situation is now critical. The trench *must* be recaptured, and quickly.

The man on the spot is none other than Private Albert Jacka, the wiry 22-year-old timber worker from Wedderburn, Victoria, who is in a firing bay right where the Turks have broken through. As the emergency escalates, Lieutenant Keith Crabbe from the 14th Battalion HQ rushes up, only to be shouted at by Jacka to stop – if he comes any further, he will be killed by the Turks around the corner.

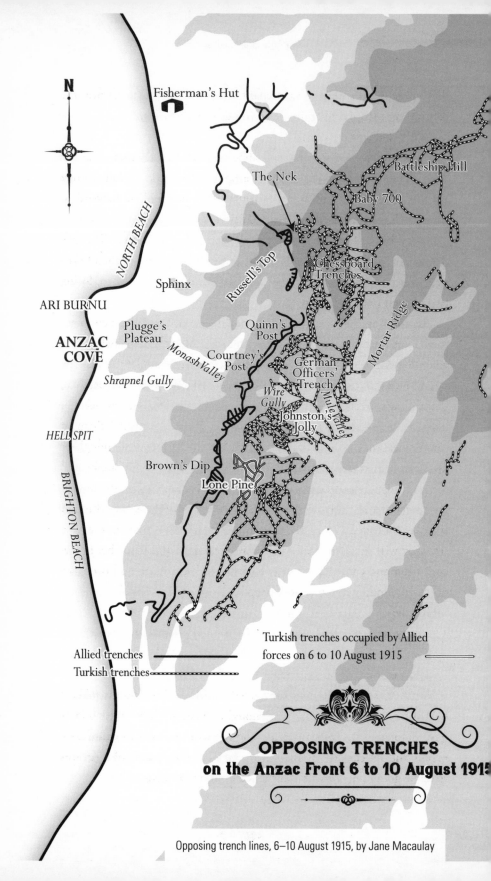

Opposing trench lines, 6–10 August 1915, by Jane Macaulay

'If you are given support,' Lieutenant Crabbe shouts to Jacka over the continuing cacophony of fire, 'will you charge the Turks?'

'YES!' Jacka shouts back.[19]

As confident as Lieutenant Crabbe is of Jacka's abilities – he has always been a soldier who'd sooner a fight than a feed, a donnybrook ahead of a drink – still he sends four Australian soldiers forward to support the Victorian in the zigzagging trenches.

Jacka himself gives the call and then takes the lead. The five Australian soldiers rush forward and, through brutal use of their bayonets, put paid to the first lot of Turkish soldiers they come to, losing two of their own in the process.

Regrouping, Jacka and Lieutenant Crabbe decide on a new plan, their faces illuminated by the flickering light of exploding shells, their voices having to rise above the continuing onslaught. It will later be said of Jacka that he was 'strong, completely confident, entirely fearless, bluntly outspoken, not given to hiding his light under a bushel . . . likely to be overlooked by his superiors, until it astonished them in some emergency',[20] and this is just such an occasion. For though of lower rank, it is Jacka who commands. At his suggestion, Crabbe and the two surviving soldiers will feint an attack at one end while he will try to get at the Turks from another angle, working his way through the maze of trenches to a point he and Crabbe know. Then, at the time set, they will throw bombs where the Turks are thought to be. In the confusion and carnage, the waiting Jacka will climb up and over into no-man's-land, race across and jump back among the Turks.

Ready?

Ready.

Go!

In an instant, Jacka is gone . . .

Some 45 seconds later, at the agreed count, Crabbe and his soldiers hurl their bombs and wait. Sure enough, an instant after their bombs have detonated – exploding close enough to the Turks to cause confusion and let carnage reign – they can hear the sounds of a furious struggle going on, with several shots and many screams.

Among the Turks, Jacka is a blur of movement, a whirling dervish with the bayonet in the manner that the Chief Bayonet Instructor at Broadmeadows, Captain Leopold McLaglen, had taught him so well. Alternating between using the tip of his bayonet to knock theirs out of the way, and thrusting it forward, Jacka rips and tears, parries and thrusts, all the while expertly dodging their attempts to get *him*. First one Turk goes down, and then another, and then another, and then . . .

And then, for the other Australians who have been listening to the screams of the struggle, all is calm . . .

When Crabbe cautiously ventures forward 15 minutes later, just as the first glimmers of dawn appear around 5 am, it is to find Jacka surrounded by dead Turks and the Australians those Turks have previously killed.

The face of the Victorian is flushed, an unlit cigarette dangling from the corner of his mouth. He has his gun trained on three terrified Turks, their shaking hands raised in surrender.

'I managed to get the beggars, sir,' he says, nodding towards the seven Turkish soldiers he has shot and bayoneted.[21]

'I am going to recommend you for a Victoria Cross,' the stunned Lieutenant Crabbe replies.[22]

Elsewhere, the furious battle goes on as the Australians keep firing at the oncoming Turks, working the bolts of their rifles as fast as they can, while other lads feed endless canvas belts of bullets into the chattering machine-guns.

For no less than an hour, the waves of Turks keep coming, only to fall before the withering fire.

'*Saida*, goodbye,' one Digger yells as he despatches yet another Turk. 'Play you again next Saturday!'[23]

At last, the tide turns. Instead of rushing forward, the Turks begin to pull back to their own trenches, pursued by a furious fusillade of fire all the way.

And what is this? From out of the Turkish trenches now leaps a Mohammedan priest, 'his white robes flying in the gentle breeze, calling on his men to charge in the name of "*Allah* God"'.[24]

Soldiers of the King, laden with packs weighing up to 70 pounds, drawn up before the landing that will be made good by the help of God and the navy. (Courtesy State Library of Victoria)

Turkish shells burst in the water close to Australian Army boats off Ari Burnu. (AWM H03569)

'Are we downhearted?' The mascot cat of the battleship HMS *Queen Elizabeth* located off the shores of Gallipoli Peninsula strolls light-heartedly along one of the 15-inch guns. (AWM G00250)

Boats filled with soldiers, having been towed close to shore by steamboats from the battleships and destroyers, make good their landing at Anzac. (AWM J03022)

The Sphinx towers over the 1st Anzac Corps headquarters, located just back from the beach at Anzac Cove. (COURTESY STATE LIBRARY OF VICTORIA)

A soldier's welcome from a respectful distance for the ever-popular Lord Kitchener, who visits Anzac on 13 November 1915. (AWM H10354)

Waiting for the man (Lord Kitchener) to arrive at Anzac, 13 November 1915. (*Left to right*) Brigadier-Generals Napier Johnson (NZ Field Artillery Brigade), Russell (NZ Mounted Rifles), Monash (1st Division AIF 4th Brigade), Francis Johnson (NZ Light Infantry), Stephenson and Antill (3rd Australian Light Horse Brigade). (AWM G01325)

Colonel Mustafa Kemal (Ataturk, fourth from left), with officers and staff of the Anafarta group, of which he was given command in August 1915. (AWM P01141.001)

General Otto Liman von Sanders, Commander of the Ottoman Fifth Army responsible for defence of the Gallipoli Peninsula, was the son of a Prussian Jewish nobleman. (AWM J00200)

Gallipoli was a cross to which Winston Leonard Spencer Churchill, First Lord of the Admiralty (1911–1915), nailed himself. (PHOTO BY KEYSTONE-FRANCE VIA GETTY IMAGES)

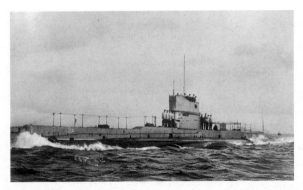

The submarine *AE2* on its way to the Dardanelles. (Photo courtesy State Library of Victoria)

'At the going down of the sun and in the morning we will . . .' have a cup of tea. A silhouette against the skyline of a soldier pouring an early morning cup of tea on the beach at Anzac. (AWM G00588)

Keep your hair short and the lice at bay. Note well-established dugout in background. (AWM J02604)

A communication trench, either on 400 Plateau or near Bridges' Road, around May 1915. Note the men sleeping on the floor of the trench, and the hole dug into the side of the trench used for storage or as a place to sleep. (AWM P02667.013)

Home, sweet home. (AWM P02647.012)

Summer has hit and there is torpor in the air; the heat shimmers as the sun shines. (AWM P02649.032)

In the quarter-master's makeshift store at Anzac Cove, the walls are made of boxes of corned beef. Rows of either petrol or water cans are in the foreground. (AWM P02648.030)

A cricket game is tentatively staged by the 'Die Hards' at Shell Green on 17 December 1915 to trick the dumbfounded Turks into thinking it business as usual for the languid colonials. (Courtesy State Library of Victoria)

'You have only to dig, dig, dig, until you are safe!' (Courtesy State Library of Victoria)

General Birdwood (behind) gets a fix on Johnny Turk's trenches just 30 yards distant. (AWM G00572A)

Lance-Corporal Beech's invention, the periscope rifle, utilised by a soldier of the 2nd Light Horse Regiment, probably at Quinn's Post, while his mate to the right checks the results with a trench periscope. (AWM H10324)

Machine guns, invaluable for providing covering fire during Allied attacks, were increased from two to four per battalion in August 1915 under Minister of Munitions Lloyd George. (Courtesy State Library of NSW)

'Straight of limb, true of eye, *steady and aglow*.' (Courtesy State Library of NSW)

Having been rested at Lemnos, the battle-hardened 7th Battalion heads back to Anzac. (Courtesy State Library of Victoria)

Hugo Throssell of the 10th Light Horse Brigade survived the disastrous August charge on the Nek to lead a heroic attack on Hill 60, for which he was awarded the Victoria Cross. After the war he committed suicide. (AWM A03688)

'Pass me the pepperpot, I know he's in there somewhere!' Turkish snipers went to great lengths to successfully camouflage themselves and pick off Anzacs undetected. (It is possible this image was staged on Lemnos.) (AWM G00377)

A cup of water for a wounded foe. An Anzac brings succour to a Turk. (Courtesy State Library of Victoria)

He ain't heavy, he's my brother. Note in the distance can be seen North Beach, running north towards Suvla. It is probable this image was staged, however it re-enacts a frequently seen scene. (AWM G00599)

A wounded soldier being operated on at Gallipoli before either returning to the front or, as is likely, having been stabilised, evacuated by hospital ship (or similar) to Lemnos or Cairo. (Courtesy State Library of Victoria)

A blindfolded Turkish Army envoy is led to General Birdwood's Headquarters to negotiate the armistice to bury the dead, which took place two days later on 24 May 1915. (AWM A05615)

One of more than 20 Allied cemeteries at Anzac. (Courtesy State Library of Victoria)

Turkish soldiers' bones and skulls. The Turkish Army is estimated to have suffered almost twice as many deaths (86,692) as the Allies (43,921). (AWM H11907)

War correspondents, Australia's Charles Bean (front) and Britain's Ellis Ashmead-Bartlett, on the island of Imbros. (AWM A05382)

'Trooper Bluegum', Oliver Hogue's dugout at Anzac. Several portraits of a woman and one of Lord Kitchener are hanging on the wall. (AWM A02353)

Keith Murdoch outside Charles Bean's dugout during his visit to Anzac Cove. (AWM A05396)

British Royal Navy battleship HMS *Cornwallis* firing a broadside at Turks in the mountains at Suvla Bay. *Cornwallis* was the last ship to leave Suvla Bay during the evacuation on the night of 19 December 1915. (AWM H10388)

Evacuation of the wounded from Anzac Cove on barges, seasickness adding to the injured men's woes. Those able to stand or sit were transported on the steam launch *Keraunos*. (AWM C02679)

Chipper to the last, General Sir Ian Hamilton departing for England after the failure of the operations at Gallipoli. (*Left to right*) Commodore Roger Keyes (Chief of Staff to Admiral de Robeck), Admiral John de Robeck (Commander of the Naval Forces in the Dardanelles), General Sir Ian Hamilton (Commander-in-Chief of the Mediterranean Expeditionary Force) and General Walter Braithwaite (Chief of the General Staff, Mediterranean Expeditionary Force). (AWM H10350)

Happily ever after: Lieutenant Gordon Carter and Nurse Lydia King, who married in 1917.

No doubt this fellow is big on religious ceremony, but at least one Australian soldier does not stand on any ceremony at all. He simply lines up the priest and pulls the trigger, dropping him immediately. Still, Trooper Bluegum would report, 'He was a brave man and rose twice only to go down each time.'[25]

—

Yes, a tragedy to have a non-combatant so slaughtered, but Colonel Mustafa Kemal realises the importance of such holy men among the common troops. Though not a man of religious conviction himself, most of his troops are, habituated to kneeling to pray five times a day towards Mecca. Colonel Kemal would even write to a female friend, Corinne, that the soldiers' 'private beliefs make it easier to carry out orders which send them to their death. They see only two supernatural outcomes: victory for the faith or martyrdom. Do you know what the second means? It is to go straight to heaven. There, the *houris*, God's most beautiful women, will meet them and will satisfy their desires for all eternity. What great happiness!'[26]

Also shot on this morning is Turkish soldier Hasan Ethem, the law student who had written so lovingly to his mother the month before, expressing his confidence that Allah would prove his 'glorious name to the British and the French'.[27] Now dead in a ditch.

—

Offshore, the horseless horsemen of the 2nd Light Horse Regiment climb high into the rigging of their transport ships and gaze at the Promised Land: Anzac Cove!

In this near-darkness, it almost looks like a volcano that has received a great shotgun blast – it is now belching flame and fire from a dozen places at once. What look like toy ships offshore are firing back at the enraged mountain, drawing more high spurts of dust in the upper reaches.

Before disembarking, Colonel Granville Ryrie gathers the men to give them one last collective talk. 'My only fear,' he begins, 'is that you will be too impetuous. Your comrades who have gone before have made history. Their courage and dash and their invincible charge on a well-nigh impregnable position will be a theme for historians throughout the ages. Their only fault was – they were too brave. They were ordered to take one strongly fortified line of trenches and they actually took three.'[28]

Concluding, the Colonel says, 'If I get back to Australia and some of you fellows don't, I know I shall be able to tell your people that you fought and died like heroes. If you get back and I don't, I hope you will be able to tell my countrymen that Colonel Ryrie played the game.'[29]

And here they come again. In mid-morning, the Turks launch more attacks, though for the most part these offensives seem to have a lot less force behind them, perhaps in part because – emotionally and physically – it is hard for a man to run powerfully at his enemy when the ground between is covered with the dead and still-dying soldiers who have already tried to do exactly that. And all the harder still when, in broad daylight, the charging men present such easy targets.

So now, instead of the men charging out and shouting 'Allah! Allah! Allah!', most of the shouting is coming from the Turkish officers behind them who are threatening to shoot their soldiers in the back if they don't face up to be shot from in front. It is *pitiful*. Sometimes the Turkish soldiers even emerge from their trenches without rifles, in just twos and threes, only to be immediately shot down. The heads of the next lot of reluctant Turks soon appear, 'the dust whipped up by the Australian and New Zealand machine-gun bullets following them in small clouds along the parapets'.[30]

While the Turks are being slaughtered in devastating numbers, inevitably the Anzacs, too, are losing men. In rare pockets, there is actually some penetration.

In one area, known as 'the Pimple' – a bulging offshoot of the key Australian post of Lone Pine – the fighting is so fierce that Lance-Corporal William Beech from the 2nd Battalion races away to get reinforcements.

Elsewhere, the calls go out: 'Stretcher-bearer, left! Stretcher-bearer, right! Stretcher-bearer, forward! STRETCHER-BEARER!'

And, of course, John Simpson Kirkpatrick and his donkey are right in the middle of it from the first, risking shot and shell to take wounded man after wounded man back down to the dressing station. As ever, when warned of the danger he is in, Simpson replies with a dismissive wave, 'My troubles!'[31]

As to his worthy donkey, the soldiers love him. These days, there are no more jokes about 'Arab stallions'. The sturdy little beasts are capable of traversing these cruel hills, carrying unimaginable burdens, and 'Simpson and his donkey' are already legendary for getting to the spots where many others fear to tread.

Usually Simpson would have breakfast about halfway up Shrapnel Gully, but with the huge attack on there is none ready.

'Never mind,' Simpson calls out to the cook as he passes. 'Get me a good dinner when I come back. I'll be back soon; keep it hot for me.'[32]

The battle grinds on, with the Turks' officers continuing to push their soldiers forward to entirely useless sacrifice, proving that military madness is not the privileged purview of the Allied Commanders alone.

By around 10 am, the worst of the fighting comes to an end, though a steady stream of wounded keeps coming down Shrapnel Gully. They include a man being carried by the donkey, but where is Simpson, aka 'Murphy'?

Where is Murphy?

Quickly, a troop goes out to look for him, only to find him some 200 yards up Shrapnel Gully, lying on his back with a bullet in his heart.

As subsequently recorded in the 3rd Australian Field Ambulance War Diary:

Owing to heavy machine-gun fire in SHRAPNEL Gully three patients were re-wounded in transit & three casualties occurred amongst Bearer Division. No 202 Pte J. Simpson shot thru heart. Killed, while escorting patient.[33]

The troops who know him are devastated.

'Where's Murphy?' a soldier of the 1st Battalion asks shortly afterwards.

'Murphy's at heaven's gate,' the sergeant replies, 'helping the soldiers through.'[34]

Up at the Pimple, Lance-Corporal William Beech returns and is horrified to find five of his comrades shot through the head. One of them, Sergeant Higgins, has obviously died because he had risen above the parapet to have a quick shot. Taking a periscope to sneak a quick peek, the Lance-Corporal and Private John Adams are shocked to see hundreds of Turks massing. Obviously, if they lift their own heads and rifles to shoot at them, they will last no longer than a couple of seconds.

Crying out with anger, Beech spits out the words, 'To think we can see so many Turks and we're unable to fire at them.'[35]

And it is in such an extreme circumstance as this that the gentle muse of inspiration alights on Beech's shoulders, prompting him to think out loud: 'I could attach a periscope to a rifle and fire it from undercover . . .'[36]

Though on the Anzac side there are 160 dead and 468 wounded from this battle, those figures pale in comparison to their enemy's losses. Of the 42,000 Ottoman soldiers who have engaged in the attack, no fewer than 3400 dead lie in no-man's-land, while a devastating 6700 have been wounded.

(Inevitably, in death and wounds, the two sides come together. Just offshore aboard *Sicilia*, Nurse Lydia King – infinitely relieved not to see Gordon among those being offloaded from yet another bloody stretcher – will shortly write in her diary: 'Anchored off Anzac near Gaba Tepe where our Australians are . . . Another busy day but it is just great being with our own again . . . I have two wounded Turks in my ward. They are very dirty and smelly.')[37]

Seeking to capitalise on the devastating loss, the Anzacs arrange for interpreters to call out in Turkish that the best thing the Turks could do now would be to surrender, something that achieves no result whatsoever. It clearly takes more than 10,000 casualties over just a few hours to make these Turks lose faith. Later, when a message asking the Turks to surrender is thrown into the nearest trenches, the reply is all but instantaneous: 'You think there are no Turks left. But there are Turks, and Turks' sons!'[38]

And you know what, cobber? Maybe they aren't such bad bastards after all.

As Charles Bean would note, 'After the terrible punishment inflicted upon the brave but futile assaults all bitterness faded. Moreover, seeing the dreadful nature of the wounds inflicted by their own bullets at short range, the troops were less ready to believe – as they had done previously – that the wounds of their own men were caused by "explosive" bullets. The Turks had displayed an admirable manliness. When, by order of the intelligence authorities, interpreters called out to them that they would be kindly treated if they surrendered, the invitation was frequently answered by a bomb or a bullet.'[39]

The Diggers *like* that attitude, and recognise in the Turks' aggressive obstinacy . . . themselves.

And something else, while we're at it. It has become clear that the Turks are careful not to send artillery shells onto hospital ships marked conspicuously in white and green paint with the Red Cross,[40] and brilliantly lit at night. And they oft do the same for stretcher-bearers. (It is thought more likely that poor Simpson was felled by a stray bullet or piece of shrapnel, rather than specifically targeted.)

'From this morning onwards,' Bean would note, 'the attitude of the ANZAC troops towards the individual Turks was rather that of opponents in a friendly game.'[41] One Anzac would recall, 'They tried to drive us into the sea . . . They were a very brave enemy . . .'[42]

From this morning on, in London, Lord Kitchener knows that he, specifically, is the target of a campaign being mounted by Lord Northcliffe to have him removed from the position of Secretary of State for War. On this morning, the editorial of the *Daily Mail* could not put it more clearly:

. . . Men died in heaps upon the Aubers Ridge ten days ago because the field guns were short, and gravely short, of high explosive shells. LORD KITCHENER must bear his share of the responsibility, because against much wise advice he insisted upon keeping in his own hands the control of questions with which the War Office was far too preoccupied to deal.

Shrapnel has great and valuable uses, but for smashing up the formidable entrenchments of the enemy it is not much more use than sprinkling them with a watering can.

Among all parties there is a feeling that the Government requires to be reconstructed and strengthened . . .[43]

Back at the Pimple on this morning, a different kind of man from Beech might have just accepted that there was nothing he could do about Turks killing his comrades, but, being a very practical man, he is determined to do something about it. *Now.*

Living out the Australian axiom that there is 'no problem so great that enough elbow grease and fencing wire can't fix it in the short term', Beech quickly sets about constructing something he has just thought of, an invention that just might give the advantage back to the Diggers. Taking a .303-calibre Lee-Enfield rifle, he constructs a timber frame made of broken boxwood, fencing wire and elbow grease, then reconnects them in the shape of a right angle – with angled pocket mirrors at the top and bottom. The top mirror looks directly along the sights of the rifle, while the bottom mirror is positioned to catch its reflection. Later, to those nosey parkers who will wonder what the hell the contraption is, he will have a standard reply:

'I'm tired of fightin' Turks; I'm goin' to play them at cricket.'[44]

Now, by putting the end of the frame that holds the rifle to his shoulder *below* the parapet, by virtue of the mirrors he can still aim along the sights. With a string on the trigger, the whole thing can be operated in comparative safety.

In the late morning of that same day, after the firing has calmed down, Major Thomas Blamey, the 1st Division Intelligence Officer, accompanied by Charles Bean, is visiting the front trenches of the Pimple when he notices an amazing thing. There in a trench, two Diggers are working away, 'engrossed with a framework of broken box-wood and wire, attached to a rifle . . .'[45]

But what is it?

'An arrangement so that you can hit without being hit,' Beech explains with more deference than he has mustered for others.[46] (It is one thing to mouth off at a nosey parker, and quite another to mouth off at *Major* Nosey Parker.)

And it works! When Beech puts his shoulder to the stock of the rifle, he is able to stay well below the level of the parapet, take careful aim, and fire.

Major Blamey is seriously impressed. And all the more so when, after testing, the contraption is found to be accurate at up to 300 yards.

That evening, in that twilight hour when there is oft a tacit agreement between the two sides to stop for tucker, John Simpson Kirkpatrick is laid beneath the sod, a simple cross put above his grave.

'If ever a man deserved a Victoria Cross,' Padre George Green, the army chaplain who conducted the funeral, would later say, 'it was Simpson. I often remember now the scene I saw frequently in Shrapnel Gully of that cheerful soul calmly walking down the gully with a Red Cross armlet tied round the donkey's head. That gully was under direct fire from the enemy almost all the time.'[47]

The truth?

There have been many brave stretcher-bearers at Gallipoli to this point – perhaps many as brave as Simpson – but none of them will come close to capturing the imagination the way Simpson and his donkey have. While Simpson is deeply respected by the Diggers at Gallipoli, by the time the story gets back to Australia and is endlessly repeated, it takes on a grandeur that, on a good day, can put the rising sun to shame.

And his donkey?

At least as legend would have it, the worthy animal is taken over by an Indian officer, who, from the first and ever after, looks after it like a silkworm.

In the meantime, after this major battle of 19 May, things really are different at Anzac Cove. Bean is not far away from the frontlines at half-past eight one morning when, from one particular section at Quinn's, something suddenly comes sailing from the Turkish trenches and lands just beyond the Australian parapet.

GET DOWN!

From long experience, the Australian soldiers know that it is most likely some kind of bomb . . . yet, strangely, there is no explosion. Very carefully, the sergeant closest to it takes a close look through his telescope. It seems to be . . . some kind of . . . package?

In fact, waving hands appear from the Turkish trenches, and then even a head pops up.

It seems the Turks are inviting them to have a closer look at the package? And now an Australian head goes up, and then another Turkish head, and soon many Turkish and Australian heads are lined up above the parapets.

Suddenly, even before the sergeant can give permission, the soldier next to him has jumped over the parapet, round the rolls of barbed wire, and darted out to bring back the package.

No shot is fired. Just grinning Turks, waving. *Go on, you Australians, open it!*

Oh so carefully, the soldier does exactly that as his mates crowd around.

Inside is a small packet of cigarettes, together with a pencilled note, scrawled in bad French:

A Notre Herox Ennemis. [48]

For their part, the Diggers have enough schoolboy French between them to translate: 'To our heroic enemies.'

Who would have thought it? Those kind bastards! And a quick smoke reveals them to be slightly better than the 'camel dung' cigarettes, as the Anzacs called them, that they'd been reduced to smoking in Cairo.

What can the Diggers send them in return? Perhaps a couple cans of bully beef . . .?

And so the two cans go sailing over the parapets and are quickly gathered up by the Turkish soldiers. What, the Diggers wonder, will they make of it?

It does not take long before they have an answer. Another message comes from the Turks, wrapped around a stone:

Bully beef non[49]

No to the awful bully beef. Do the Australians have anything else? The Diggers throw some sweet biscuits and a tin of jam, which are soon replied to with more cigarettes, more kind notes.

Notre Cher Enemi.

Femez A Vee Plessir.

(Bush French for 'take at your pleasure'.)

Finally, though, after 45 minutes of such pleasantries, it is time for the day's work to begin – trying to kill each other – and after one of them waves with both hands and shouts, *'Finis!* – Finish!' they all know they must get back to it.

Quickly, heads on both sides go back down and the bombs start sailing back and forth once more.

20 MAY 1915, AN ILL WIND

Typically, it is Ellis Ashmead-Bartlett who gets wind of it first among the correspondents. With both Cape Helles and Anzac Cove at an effective stalemate, all either side can do is pour in even more men to hold what terrain they possess. General Hamilton is planning some kind of fresh 'breakout', something to definitively break the stalemate, using what Ashmead-Bartlett describes as 'the old army reinforced by two fresh divisions. The idea is preposterous and can only lead to a fresh massacre of the innocents. How strange this attitude of mind, namely, to risk your army and endanger your country rather than worry Kitchener for the right number of troops and guns!'[50]

And the truth is, even with those reinforcements, Ashmead-Bartlett has no confidence that the Allies can make headway. For him, so far the whole affair has been a debacle, and as he had confided to his diary the night before, 'I feel certain the Military Authorities out here are concealing the truth from the Authorities at home and that they will not tell them the real facts about the situation because they are afraid they will be withdrawn altogether and then good bye to K.C.Bs, K.C.M.G. and all the other damned Gs and Peerages they have in mind. But this is only playing with a great question when the whole safety of your country is at stake. But our leaders in the field are very little men. That is the trouble.'[51]

And now they want to have a breakout and attack the Turks? It is *sure* to lead to disaster.

'I went to bed in despair.'[52]

MORNING, 21 MAY 1915, LONDON, SOME MAIL FOR YOU, LORD KITCHENER

Another day, another attack on Lord Kitchener, this time written by Lord Northcliffe himself and put in the mass circulation *Daily Mail* beneath a headline:

THE TRAGEDY OF THE SHELLS: LORD KITCHENER'S GRAVE ERROR

Lord Kitchener has starved the army in France of high-explosive shells. The admitted fact is that **LORD KITCHENER ORDERED THE WRONG KIND OF SHELL** – the same kind of shell which he used largely against the Boers in 1900. He persisted in sending shrapnel – a useless weapon in trench warfare . . . The kind of shell our poor soldiers have had has caused the death of thousands of them.[53]

This proves to be merely Lord Northcliffe's opening remarks . . .

Yes, there is a reaction – a strong one. Many people are outraged at such an attack on such a national icon as Lord Kitchener – a servant of the people, who has risked his life for the Empire on so many occasions! – and there is significant fall-out. Copies of *The Times* and the *Daily Mail* are burned on the floor of the London Stock Exchange.

Several important advertisers flee and, practically overnight, circulation of the *Daily Mail* falls from 1,386,000 to 238,000.

But Lord Northcliffe simply does not blink.

'I mean to tell the people the truth,' he tells his chauffeur, 'and I don't care what it costs.'

He says much the same to his panicked staff: 'I don't care. What I wrote was true. Our men out there are being killed because there are no shells to smash the German defences. I'm determined that they shall have them.'[54]

23 MAY 1915, CONSTANTINOPLE, VON MÜCKE'S RETURN FROM HELL

Kapitänleutnant Hellmuth von Mücke can barely believe it. Their staggering journey over six months has taken them all the way from the

Cocos Islands on *Ayesha* (the yacht they had stolen from the Clunies-Ross family), across the perilous Indian Ocean (dodging British ships all the way), through to the Dutch East Indies and into the Middle East. The angel of death stalked them closely, flapping her wings in their faces when they had been attacked by 300 Bedouins as they approached Jeddah in the Kingdom of Hejaz.[55] By charging, they had managed to scatter the natives, killing 15 of them, with only one of their own men wounded in the process. And now, after another seven weeks of perilous trekking through the farthest reaches of the Ottoman Empire, they are at last approaching its heart – Constantinople.

Their train is even now pulling into the ancient city, where the Chief of the Mediterranean Division, Admiral Wilhelm Souchon, has honoured them by arriving at the station with his senior staff.

On catching sight of the Admiral, von Mücke barks a few brief commands, at which point his men instantly line up, snap to attention and salute – proving to their Kapitänleutnant 'that the brigand existence we had led for months had not destroyed our military trim'.

Lowering his sword before his superior officer, Kapitänleutnant von Mücke stares straight ahead in the best military fashion and says, 'I report the landing squad from the *Emden*, five officers, seven petty officers, and thirty-seven men strong.'[56]

He then takes their war flag – complete with its stunning red, white and black colours, with iron cross and eagle – which they have brought with them all this way, clicks his heels, bows and presents it to the Admiral.

Reporting for duty, *Herr Admiral*.

(As later noted by German writer R. K. Lochner, back in the Fatherland, 'the safe return of this part of *Emden* crew aroused a storm of joy. Mücke was the hero of the day, he was enthusiastic, and his men were welcomed everywhere. The onward journey from Turkey via the Balkans and Austria to Germany became a triumphal procession.')[57]

Not far away, at the same station – and indeed, at many stations all over Constantinople – yet more soldiers are readying to head south to the Gallipoli Peninsula, via a trip to a nearby port.

'All of us who left Constantinople for Gallipoli,' one Turkish soldier would later reminisce, 'had already heard of the hellish fighting that destroyed thousands of lives in a matter of hours. Because most of those who went were reported dead almost immediately, those getting ready to leave kissed and embraced their families with great affection. They showed their love and care for each other probably for the last time. I kissed my mother the same way, and she cried constantly as I left her. I didn't want to upset her more, so I didn't tell her we were going to the front-line at Helles.'[58]

24 MAY 1915, AT ANZAC COVE, SMILING MAY YOU GO AND SMILING COME AGAIN

It has taken some time to organise – with negotiations begun after the 1st Brigade's Colonel Owen had waved the flag of the Red Cross – but on this day it happens. A truce has been negotiated. From 7.30 am onwards, soldiers on both sides are instructed to stand down – no guns fired, no bombs thrown, no grenades, no artillery. An amazing silence falls upon the trenches.

Colonel Fahrettin, the Chief of Staff of 3rd Corps and the Turkish officer who led the negotiations for the ceasefire, would recall, 'There was a deep silence and the enemy ships were all of a sudden out of sight.'[59] For the first time in weeks, men can hear the lapping of the Aegean Sea, even after the dawn. After some heavy rain overnight, a soft mist slowly rises from the gullies and settles over the trenches . . .

On the beach at Gaba Tepe, right by the tangle of barbed wire that marks the beginning of the path of no-man's-land that winds its way for two miles all the way around Anzac Cove – up valleys, through gullies, across plateaus and back down through bluffs before coming out on the beach again – two groups of Turkish and Anzac officers, each accompanied by 50 soldiers carrying sticks bearing white flags, assemble.[60] All of the Anzac soldiers are given two packets of cigarettes, of which one is designated to be given to their Turkish counterpart.

The officers shake hands while the bristling soldiers survey each other warily . . . though at least the gift of cigarettes helps warm things a little. And then they start off, before, as described by journalist Compton Mackenzie, 'the smell of death floated over the ridge above and settled down upon us, tangible, it seemed, and clammy as the membrane of a bat's wing'.[61]

At least a light, almost cleansing rain begins to fall. Heading up the Second Ridge, the group keeps going till it comes to the first lot of corpses. A pairing of white-flag men are left there to mark the 'middle line' of no-man's-land, while the rest of the group moves on.

According to the terms of the truce, the soldiers from each side are to come out of the trenches and bury their men on their side of the line, while taking enemy corpses to the middle line for the other side to bury. Enemy rifles are also to be returned, albeit with their bolts removed.

And so it begins, progressively, through all of no-man's-land. Tentatively at first, and then with growing confidence, the Anzacs and Turks rise from their trenches and slowly walk towards each other, scarcely believing that this is possible, that they could really be upright in no-man's-land without being shot to pieces.

These men from countries on opposite sides of the planet continue to walk towards each other – over the corpses of their fallen friends, their brothers, the enemies who they have shot – until they are face to face.

This is Johnny Turk up close? He looks . . . he looks . . . well, frankly, a bit like we do. Darker, certainly, and smaller, sure, but instead of the sneering half-humans the Allies had been expecting, the image they have conjured up over the weeks, they are *men* . . . just like them.

And the Turks clearly feel much the same. They had been led to believe that the Anzacs are cannibals and have started to call them 'White Gurkhas'.[62] But they don't look so much like cannibals as . . . well . . . young, fair-faced, wide-eyed boys. As for the newly arrived Light Horsemen, though, the Turks are quite surprised by their get-up and have already started to make them the butt of a few jokes. It seems they are quickly coming to the consensus that 'the men with the fur round their hats are not as good as fighters as the Australians'.[63]

The first thing is to quickly look for any signs of life among the thousands of bodies, and occasionally there actually are some, with those survivors rushed away by the stretcher-bearers. But before long, both sides are heavily engaged in the real task at hand: burying their dead. (Not all join in, to be sure, with one Australian soldier exclaiming, 'I don't mind killing, but I bar burying the cows!')[64]

While the smell of the dead in the trenches has been awful, here it is overpowering, gut-wrenching, nauseating, and more than a few men on both sides sink to their knees and throw up. There are only two basic ways of coping with the stench. One is to take some of the wool soaked in antiseptic proffered by the Turkish Red Crescent men – the equivalent of the Red Cross, with the symbol changed for religious reasons – and stuff it up your nostrils, though this method needs to be constantly renewed.

The other way is to smoke, and on this day even non-smokers are seen puffing away while burying soldier after soldier beneath the sod. One Australian Digger looks down to see 'squelching up from the ground on either side of my boot like a rotten mangold the deliquescent green and black flesh of a Turk's head'.[65]

He sees an entire parapet made out of dead bodies.

Despite the gravity of the situation, however, there is still some levity when at one point some Turkish soldiers burst into laughter as their Australian counterparts hold up cigarettes and call out *'Baksheesh!'*.[66]

Before long, they are all exchanging cigarettes with their 'enemies', and even exchanging pleasantries. One Turkish soldier offers his considered and clearly heartfelt view to his Australian counterpart: 'English good – German no good.'[67]

But back to work.

The bodies that have been lying there for four weeks are the worst; they are black and bloated, and mostly only identifiable by the identification discs around their necks. The major problem with these bodies is that they tend to break up as you move them. You can be left holding an arm or a leg, as the tissues burst apart and the gases escape, emitting a stench that can bring even a strong man low. But at least the lack of identification helps hide the horror of what you are doing.

When it comes to the more recent corpses, there is no hiding it: these are clearly men – *mates* – whom you'd often known for months, whom you'd joined up with, trained with, travelled with and fought alongside. And many a man is seen to weep as he finds a beloved friend, a brother, a brother-in-arms, whom he had last seen charging forward, only to finish here as this decomposing mess, with an agonised expression on what remains of his face – his death grimace.

On their side, the Turks are doing it even tougher. To begin with, there are so many more of their dead – as many as 10,000 by one, likely exaggerated, count. In the words of a Turkish captain talking with British intelligence officer Captain Aubrey Herbert, a speaker of the Turkish language who had been instrumental in arranging the truce, 'At this spectacle even the most gentle must feel savage, and the most savage must weep.'[68]

Inevitably, the middle line soon proves to be very blurred, as neither army particularly cares where it is. They just concentrate on getting the bodies buried, usually under about only half a foot of soil. Yes, there might be a problem should the rain become heavy and wash that soil away, but for now they have no choice. There are simply too many bodies to worry about burying them deeper.

Soon enough, there is even more fraternising. 'After lunch,' Fahrettin would recall, 'it started to get more crowded and the men of the Australian–New Zealand Corps started to teach our soldiers English words.

'One of the first words they taught us was "ANZAC", which was the name given to their group of soldiers. And it was at that time that we first really met these charming and good-humoured people.

'"Are you English?" one Turkish soldier asked.

'"No, we aren't English. We are Australian and New Zealanders . . ."

'When we asked, "Why are you in this war?" they answered, "The English are our brothers. Our religion and our culture are one and the same."

'At every opportunity, the ANZACs showed that they liked our soldiers' attitudes and actions. Within a short amount of time, sympathy grew up between the two sides. The Anzacs would rip buttons and badges off their uniforms and give it to our soldiers as a memento, and would ask for something in return. Because the buttons on our uniforms were hidden, our soldiers looked for something else to give them, one soldier finding a small coin which he handed to the man across from him. They gave each other chocolate and sweets and began to talk with each other using sign language . . .'[69]

One Australian soldier, amazed at the sheer contours of a particularly gigantic Turkish soldier, pulls out a tape measure and asks if he can measure him. The Turk laughs and graciously concedes to the request.

He was a bloody GIANT, I tell you!

In many areas where the Turkish dead are thick and the Australian dead more scattered and quickly buried, the Australians take advantage of the lull and go down to the ocean. By 2 pm, one soldier would record in his diary, 'the sandy stretch of beach reminded one of Cronulla or Maroubra, so numerous were the bathers & as the day advanced it became so thick I had grave fears of the trenches in case of treachery'.[70]

Charles Bean takes the opportunity to visit the most dangerous place at Anzac, the most forward, exposed position – Quinn's Post – and is shocked, not just by the obvious precariousness of the position, and that his tall figure has to bend particularly low to stay safe . . .

'In one trench there is an archway such as you often find, left to avoid enfilading fire, I suppose. It is not four foot – scarcely three foot – thick; but in it is a dead Turk. His boot and his fingers of one hand stick out from the roof as you squeeze your way under.'[71]

And Bean is not the only one taking advantage of the truce to have a stickybeak at things he would not otherwise get close to. A number of the Turkish 'soldiers' edging close to Anzac lines are in fact Turkish officers in the uniforms of their men . . . and one of the Australian 'privates' is none other than General Birdwood![72]

By 4 pm, most of the men are back to their posts, as the time is drawing close for the truce to be over. By 4.17 pm, the white-flag men are retired, after first shaking hands with their counterparts.

Captain Aubrey Herbert chaffs the Turks he is with, saying, 'You will shoot me, tomorrow.'[73]

'God forbid!' they cry back in chorus, laughing and cheering. 'We will never shoot you.' And now a group of Australians go to shake hands with the Turks: 'Goodbye, old chap. Good luck!'

'Oghur Ola gule gule gedejekseniz, gule gule gelejekseniz,' the Turks reply.[74] 'Smiling may you go and smiling come again.'[75]

It is with some regret, then, that the two sides take their leave of each other, shaking hands and waving goodbye as, one by one, they climb back into their trenches, all on the strict understanding that it will be 25 minutes before the battle resumes.

A strange kind of hush now falls over Anzac Cove. There is wonder at what has happened on this day, and even exuberance at this break-through of humanity that they have all been privileged to be a part of. There is desperate sadness at the things they have seen, the once-cherished friends they have buried. And there is real melancholy: now that the armistice is over, they must once again take up arms and kill or be killed by the very men with whom they had been sharing cigarettes just a few minutes earlier.

At 4.45 pm, a single shot rings out, followed shortly afterwards by another, and then a burst of a machine-gun, and then another, and then a bomb explodes.

It is on again.

25 MAY 1915, OFF CAPE HELLES. FOR ELLIS ASHMEAD-BARTLETT, DIFFERENT DAY, SAME OLD STORY

> I went ashore at 10 a.m., to visit Hunter-Weston. He told me there would be another attack in a few days' time, and once again he was quite confident of taking Achi Baba. I am getting tired of this old, old story.[76]

25 MAY 1915, A POLITICAL CRISIS IN LONDON

With the extent of the debacle in the Dardanelles now becoming ever more apparent to both the public and the political class, it is inevitable that someone will have to pay the piper, and who better than the man who has championed the campaign all along: Winston Churchill? That certainly is the view taken by the shaken Prime Minister Asquith. On this day, he does a deal with the Conservative Opposition whereby they will form part of a Coalition government that retains him as PM but sees the end of Churchill – a one-time Conservative himself before defecting to the Liberals in 1904, so he has it coming – as the First Lord of the Admiralty.

'I am finished,' Churchill tells the Prime Minister when advised that he will have to leave the Admiralty, 'finished in respect of all I care for; the waging of war.'[77]

Asquith would have liked to rid himself of the troublesome Kitchener, too, but while it is one thing for Lord Northcliffe to have shed three-quarters of his readership by attacking the Secretary of State for War, the newly formed Coalition cannot yet afford to lose the same number of votes by doing the same.

So for the moment, it is Churchill who suffers alone.

'I'm finished,' he repeats to his great friend, Herbert Asquith's daughter, Violet Bonham Carter.[78] Standing alone by the edge of a manicured lawn by a river, he appears to her 'like Napoleon on St Helena'.[79]

There can surely be no way back from here. And yet he will prove to be not the only one with a sinking feeling on the day . . .

25 MAY 1915, OFF GABA TEPE, *'SEHROHR AUSFAHREN!* – UP PERISCOPE!'

In the German submarine *U21*, Kapitänleutnant Otto Hersing can barely believe his luck. Only just arrived off the Dardanelles, he has no sooner passed at a depth of 70 feet beneath the steady humming of the many patrol craft on the surface and put up his periscope than he catches sight of the old 12,000-ton British battleship *Triumph*, firing broadside after broadside on Turkish positions on Gaba Tepe. (In fact, it is trying to wipe out a gun known as 'Beachy Bill', which has been playing hell with the troops lately. Entirely untroubled by the attention, Beachy Bill is in turn trying to lob shells onto the English battleship.)

Clearly, the Gunnery Officer in *Triumph*'s tower is aided by an observation balloon floated from the deck of nearby HMS *Manica*, with two officers in the basket able to correct the fall of shot.

Ja, there is a protective ring of destroyers around *Triumph*, but that is not an insurmountable problem. The most promising thing is that to improve its accuracy on the Turkish positions, *Triumph* is at anchor, presenting a stationary target.

Oh so carefully, Kapitänleutnant Hersing at his command station in the conning tower with his watch officer by his side – both of them tingling with anticipation – gives out order after order down the voice tube in his crisp, cool manner as he tries to manoeuvre the submarine into the perfect position. Down below in the submarine proper, no one else speaks apart from those relaying his orders forward.

'We were groping,' as Hersing would later recount, 'towards a deadly position – deadly for the magnificent giant of war on the surface above.'[80]

Finally, at 12.25 pm on this gorgeous day, he feels they are there.

'*Sehrohr ausfahren!* – Up periscope!' he commands.[81]

And there it is, only 300 yards away – easy prey.

'Never had an undersea craft such a target.'

They have a clear line of sight to *Triumph*'s midships, which means that – barring torpedo nets that may be in place – there is also a clear way through for at least two of the six torpedoes he is carrying. The key now will be speed of action, to get the torpedoes away before their periscope is spotted.

'*Erster Torpedo fertig, zweiter Torpedo fertig* – First torpedo ready, second torpedo ready!'[82]

Time stands suspended. No one breathes. No one moves. All eyes, all ears are on Kapitänleutnant Hersing. The word comes back from the Torpedo Gunner's Mate that all is in readiness.

'*Rohr eins – los!*' Hersing commands, his heart leaping to hear his own words. 'Torpedo one – launch!'

An instant later, by the subsequent German account, '*das Boot wie ein nasser Hund* – the boat shakes itself like a wet dog'[83] as the six-yard-long torpedo bursts forth with a sudden rush of expelled air and tears along at the rate of 35 knots. It is with great satisfaction that he sees 'the tell-tale streak of white foam darting through the water',[84] and he's so enthralled that he leaves the periscope up.

The torpedo continues to roar towards its target. On its front is a tiny brass screw that winds down as the torpedo passes through the water, arming it some 100 yards from the moment of expulsion – far enough away that it cannot detonate close to the submarine that has launched it.

Now Hersing consults his stopwatch. In 18 to 20 seconds, there will be an explosion or . . . nothing . . . in which case he will know the torpedo has hit one of the heavy steel mesh torpedo nets the Allies have been using to try to protect their ship, or missed entirely. Still no one speaks. All wait with him in the tight, closed atmosphere.

Nine seconds . . . eight seconds . . . three . . . two . . . one.

Suddenly, through the periscope he sees a huge cloud of smoke leap out of the sea amidships on *Triumph*, then the sub is hit with the sound and vibration of, first, a 'dry, metallic concussion and then a terrible, reverberating explosion'[85] – WHAM! – as if Neptune has hit the hull with a huge trident.

At this close range, at a speed of 35 knots, the torpedo has gone straight through the torpedo nets and hit *Triumph*'s hull, igniting the switch on its activated tip and detonating the 350 pounds of TNT instantly.

As it happens, General Birdwood is right on the spot at the time, aboard the minesweeper *Newmarket*, and has his glass trained on *Triumph* at that very moment. To his horror, a huge column of water suddenly bursts up from her side.

'By God, she's hit!' he calls to the skipper beside him.[86]

And badly at that . . .

On *U21*, there is the beginnings of a cheer, which Hersing instantly stifles, and then the entire crew clearly hears the sound of the *Triumph*'s internal bulkhead collapsing: dreadful cracking and creaking noises as air and seawater fight for entry and escape through the same jagged hole.

The stricken *Triumph* begins to list heavily to starboard.

'Down periscope!' Kapitänleutnant Hersing orders.[87]

Mission accomplished, *U21* immediately glides down to the depths while, topside, both the thrilled Turkish and horrified Anzac soldiers watch, mesmerised, as the list on *Triumph* becomes even more pronounced, going all the way to 45 degrees from horizontal after eight minutes. Crew members fall or jump into the sea, and small boats race to gather them in. The Turkish artillery, which had initially been shelling the stricken ship, now stops to allow the rescuers to do their best.

After 12 minutes, the ship capsizes, 'her green bottom upwards in the sunlight. The crews on the neighbouring ships stood to attention as she made her last plunge down to the bottom through clouds of smoke and steam.'[88] Seventy-one men go to the bottom with her.

—

With *Triumph*'s sinking, the complexities of keeping the soldiers on the Gallipoli Peninsula suddenly multiply. In an urgent crisis meeting held that afternoon on HMT *Arcadian* between General Hamilton and Admiral de Robeck, the thrust for the overall commander is obvious: 'Our nicely worked out system for supplying the troops has in a moment been tangled up into a hundred knotty problems.'[89]

The major fear for the Allies, of course, is that the German submarine is still lurking in their waters, about to strike at any moment, and it is for this reason that *Arcadian* has two old merchantman ships lashed to each side as torpedo buffers.

After the meeting is over, Admiral de Robeck appears to take the view that discretion is the better part of valour and, aboard *Lord Nelson*, with three French battleships in close attendance, zigzags his way back to the safe port of Mudros.

26 MAY 1915, ANZAC COVE, FROM REVELATION TO REVOLUTION, ONCE MORE UNTO THE BEECH, DEAR FRIENDS, ONCE MORE

Major Blamey has moved quickly – so quickly that on this day the inventor of the periscope rifle, Lance-Corporal William Beech, leaves the trenches and comes down to the beach so he can convert a workshop already producing periscopes into a veritable factory for producing periscope rifles en masse. ('All the looking glasses have been taken off the ships,' Percival Fenwick notes in his diary, 'and are being cut up into small squares to make periscopes.')[90]

And within days of starting the factory, Beech is promoted to the rank of Sergeant.

It is all so successful that 'Birdie' will soon write to the Governor-General of Australia, affirming:

```
Our complete moral superiority over the Turk
is partly due to the very clever invention of
a man named Beech, who produced a periscope
rifle. When we got here we denuded the
whole of our transports of their looking-
glasses and made up some 2000 periscopes on
our little beach. This man then made a very
simple device. The result is the Turk only
sees the muzzle of a rifle coming over the
parapet without anything behind it to shoot
at - and we understand from prisoners that
he dislikes it intensely.[91]
```

Mind you, it does take some getting used to. On one occasion, a well-loved soldier by the name of Bill Blankson[92] has his first go at using a periscope rifle after a notably hard fortnight of digging trenches without rest. In that time, he had neither washed nor shaved, so perhaps he is far from his best when he looks through the scope.

And what does he see? What does he see, our Bill, with his first look? It would kill a brown dog . . .

His first vision is of a filthy big Turk staring back at him, *glaring* at him, right through the other end of the periscope!

With a cry, Bill leaps back, grabs his rifle and prepares to jump the parapet and fight the brute to the death.

The others grab him.

Settle, Bill, *settle*! You haven't been holding the periscope close enough to your eye, you silly coot, and instead of seeing the landscape ahead you have just seen your *own* ugly mug in the lower mirror!

(The problem with the upper mirror, as it turns out, is that it would 'flash with the sunlight and they'd fire and smash the mirror . . .')[93]

Others, however, go better at it – and none better than an Australian from the Queensland Light Horse by the name of Billy Sing, a fellow with a Chinese father and an English mother. See, there's just something about Billy and his powers of concentration; his passion for killing Turks is extraordinary. Grabbing a steel plate with a small loophole in it from one of the ships, he builds it into the parapet of one of the high trenches. Now, with the bloke beside him acting as a spotter, they wait, for hours if necessary.

There! The spotter has seen movement at a weak point in the Turkish defences, where the hat of a tall Turk or the top of a bayonet can be seen moving along at a steady pace. He alerts Billy, who has his own periscope rifle aimed on the Turkish loophole that the soldier will pass in five seconds.

Five . . . four . . . three . . . two . . . one.

Billy squeezes the trigger and a crack rings out. From the enemy trenches, a cry, a death rattle, the sign of the rifle being flung into the air.

And that is another notch on Billy's rifle.

At other times, he sees a Turkish head bob up for a sneak peek, and he knows that a man who would do that once will inevitably do it again. Billy just waits and waits and waits . . . for *hours*. There! *Crack!*

Another notch.

In response, of course, the Turks bring down furious artillery fire, but Billy and his mate just move on, going to another loophole, and do the same thing. Over time, they will claim to have killed no fewer than 100 enemy soldiers.

Not that everyone believes the claim, mind. One day, General Birdwood is doing his rounds and, after chatting with Sing, asks a man in another sniper's post, 'How many Turks have you got so far?'

'I have never even *seen* a Turk, far less shot one,' the soldier replies gruffly.[94]

'And what do you think of the 63 currently claimed by Sing?'

'Some fellows are better liars than others!'

General Birdwood agrees but adds, 'If every man would really take the same interest as Sing and get even one-tenth of his successes, we should be in Constantinople next week!'[95]

So successful is the periscope-rifle factory that another factory producing jam-tin bombs is soon established beside it. Those Diggers too crook to take their place in the frontline sit in a circle and carefully pack the old jam tins, which are in plentiful supply, with as much explosive as they can fit, before jamming in every bit of hard metal they can find – old cartridge cases, bits of barbed wire, finely cut-up scrap metal and even pebbles. With a short fuse added and a ciggie in your mouth, or a 'slow match' by your side – a sandbag rolled up and tied tightly with twine and lit at one end to smoulder, ready to flare when blown upon – those in the trenches have a new weapon for their arsenal to supplement the scanty and rather ineffective grenades with which they have been supplied.[96] On average, you have four and a half seconds between lighting the fuse to explosion, and the skill is to be able to time your throw so it explodes as it lands.

Though the jam-tin bomb is considered something of a joke at first, it is soon obvious the Turks don't find it funny at all, as many of their soldiers are killed and maimed. The Anzacs start to take the device more seriously.

The factory, which at one point keeps 54 soldiers busy, is soon producing 200 bombs a day. In fact, it is so successful that up at Pope's the Diggers again improvise and build a massive catapult, with arms, as one Digger would describe it, 'six feet high, shaped like a "V" and the arms had very strong elastic and it was wound back by a winch and had a leather sack at the end in which one of our jam tin bombs was put in'.[97]

That thing could hurl bombs so far that you had no idea who they hurt or maimed, but gee it could be fun to send them hurtling in all directions. The Turks or bombs, do I mean? Both.

The Turkish bombs are exclusively thrown by hand. About the size and shape of a cricket ball – and so called 'cricket ball bombs' by the Diggers – their fuses come out the top, and the Turks are able to light them simply by rubbing the fuses on their trousers or on some phosphorus pinned to their tunics.[98]

In truth, it is extraordinary how blasé both sides could get, hurling such things back and forth, with Trooper Bluegum noting that before throwing their own grenades or bombs, the Diggers would often cry, 'Are you there, Abdul? Well, here's *baksheesh*.' Or maybe, 'Here you are, Mohammed, here's a Christmas box.'[99]

And when a Turkish grenade would come back in reply, or even to open their own innings, the Australians would nod sagely in the manner of vendors in 'Gyppo' markets and say, '*Maleesch*', or 'Ver' good, ver' nice . . .'[100]

On a good day, they can love it. On a bad day, they die.

Apart from devising bomb contraptions and attending to the relentless chores attendant to the upkeep, watering, feeding and cleaning of thousands and thousands of men, the Diggers in Monash Valley and all over the Peninsula are trying to carve out and cosy up their bivouacs so they have a place to call home. As Colonel Monash notes, 'The allusion is to the wonderful sticking properties of this Corps. The Turks have been trying to scrape us off for over four weeks, but we still stick fast.'[101] They live in noisy, crowded – and increasingly filthy – conditions and under the constant hail of fire. A man needs, after all, a small patch to lay his slouch hat and call his own.

Colonel Monash himself writes, 'We manage to make ourselves fairly comfortable in our bivouacs. My home is a hole in the side of the hill, about 6' x 7' and 4' deep. The sides are built up with sandbags and the roof consists of three Water Proof sheets lashed together. Biscuit boxes serve as tables, chairs, cupboards and other furniture. I have my valise to sleep on, and get a daily bath out of a canvas bucket with a sponge; and at rarer intervals a dip in the sea . . .'[102]

But he, Brigade Commander no less, is of course staying in the royal suite of dugouts, and most men survive in even smaller and far more rudimentary hovels. One man later writes home, 'I have laid out my bed, 1 oilsheet, 2 blankets and an overcoat for a pillow. I haven't many oil paintings on the wall, but I'll tell you what is there. First a dirty towel – dinkum dirty – none of your half and half business about it, then a Haversack containing two razors, 3 toothbrushes (toothpaste – nil, use salt instead, a "housewife" I think they call it, but it's certainly not the kind of housewife I sometimes dream of . . .), a hairbrush . . . tin of dog, packet of biscuits . . . Above my head like a beautiful chandelier hang a pair of boots . . .'[103]

It may not be much, but for the Diggers who have been here a month now with scant news from their loved ones fretting in their true home of homes, this little patch is their castle.

EVENING TO EARLY MORNING, 26–27 MAY 1915, BOTTOMS UP

There is trouble brewing, and Ellis Ashmead-Bartlett knows it.

With the sinking of *Triumph* the day before, everyone is on edge – and for good reason. If a German submarine can sink such a battleship, it can likely bring ruin to *any* ship, and in all likelihood it will be Ashmead-Bartlett's own HMS *Majestic*, anchored 500 yards off W Beach at Cape Helles.

It is for this reason that he decides to do two things on this evening. The first is to help the captain drain the ship of the last of its champagne reserves – it is better that they, rather than the fish, drink it – and the second is to sleep on the deck that night, on a comfortable mattress he has had brought up from below.

Ashmead-Bartlett wakes suddenly at sun-up the following morning.

Something is just not right.

'What time is it?' he asks the sentry nearest him on the deck of *Majestic*.

'Six-fifteen, sir,' the sentry replies.

Harrumph. That is way too early for a gentleman of the press to be awake, so he goes back to sleep.

Twenty-five minutes later, however, England's finest war correspondent is awoken by heavy, running footsteps – on his chest, among other things.

'What's the matter?' he calls after the departing figure.

'There's a torpedo coming!'[104]

So he had been right.

With a massive *whump*, the torpedo hits *Majestic* on the port side, and the ship all but immediately starts to list in that direction.

It obviously does not have long to stay afloat.

'Then,' Ashmead-Bartlett would later write, 'there came a sound as if the contents of every pantry in the world had fallen at the same moment, a clattering such as I had never heard, as everything loose in her tumbled about.'[105]

Ashmead-Bartlett is not shocked, despite *Majestic* threatening to turn turtle at any moment. More than anything, he admires his own prescience at suspecting this was going to happen all along. Still a little hung-over from all the champagne so wisely consumed the night before, he now hangs over the side and soon drops down, bouncing off a part of the failed torpedo net and into the water. Within minutes, he is able to swim with many of the other sailors to clamber aboard one of the many boats that have been sent to their aid.

The journalist is mercifully clear when – in full view of thousands of cheering Turks in the hills and shocked Allied soldiers on the toe of Cape Helles – *Majestic* gives up the ghost. With a final shake of her upturned stern, she heads to the bottom of the Aegean Sea, taking 40 souls with her.

The *Majestic* is the third Allied ship sunk in the Dardanelles in the past two weeks.

Within a day, Ashmead-Bartlett is heading to London to have a quick break and replace all the wardrobe and writing materials that he has lost in the sunken ship. Still a little shocked by his narrow escape the day before, he steals the biggest lifebelt he can find from *Fovette*, and, clutching it tightly as his only piece of luggage, heads up the gangplank of the cargo ship *Baron Ardrossan*, which is to depart shortly.

'What are you carrying that belt for?' the captain asks wryly.

'So I don't sink to the bottom of the Mediterranean if we get hit,' the journalist explains.

'Don't you worry about it,' the captain says, waving a dismissive hand. 'I've got eleven hundred rounds of 12-inch ammunition on board as ballast, and if anything strikes us we shall go up so high that the only thing which could help you would be an aeroplane.'[106]

With a sigh, Ashmead-Bartlett abandons the belt and makes his way to his quarters.

Commodore Roger Keyes, for one, is not sorry to see him go. 'He is a most unpleasant person,' Keyes writes to his wife, 'but an able writer. All his reports go through me, and they are accurate, but he takes a most pessimistic view and has tried to send two or three impossible telegrams which we and GHQ stopped.'

Though Ashmead-Bartlett has gone, Keyes has ensured that others will 'strictly censor his stuff'. Yes, even in London, 'he won't be allowed to publish anything about the Dardanelles uncensored'.[107]

In the wake of the twin sinkings, Admiral de Robeck institutes quick measures to prevent another disaster, including removing the last of the big battleships and supply ships from the Dardanelles. The former will now only return to provide artillery cover for special operations and will be meantime based in Mudros, protected from submarines by a boom across the harbour entrance. So too the supply ships. From now on, their supplies must be placed on smaller, insignificant ships in Mudros and sent to Anzac Cove and Cape Helles from there, those crafts making trips of 60 miles instead of the previous 3000 yards.

For his part, de Robeck now bases himself on the yacht *Triad*, something so small that surely no sub would bother to torpedo it.

'What a change since the War Office sent us packing with a bagful of hallucinations,' Hamilton soon writes morosely in his diary. 'Naval guns sweeping the Turks off the Peninsula; the Ottoman Army legging it from a British submarine waving the Union Jack; Russian help in hand; Greek help on the *tapis*. Now it is our Fleet which has to leg it from the German submarine; there is no ammunition for the guns; no drafts to keep my Divisions up to strength . . .'[108]

Things are grim and getting grimmer.

In the absence of the big ships, all that is left are light cruisers and destroyers. What had started as a joint operation now appears to be army alone. It is hard not to feel abandoned.

As General Birdwood would later recall, 'Not one of us failed to realise how absolutely dependent on the Navy we were, day and night, for everything. Our many landings, our covering-fire, supplies – for all these the Navy was indeed, as an Indian would say, "Mah-Bap", or our mother and father.'[109]

28 MAY 1915, IMBROS, BACK TO FRONT

It had been a close-run thing. The howitzer shell that had landed just a few yards from Captain Carter nearly killed him. Luckily, however, it had fallen into the soft earth of the parapet, which absorbed much of its impact, and Carter had come back to consciousness with no feeling in his legs and no ability to see. A few more seconds and he realised that his legs were merely buried, and the lack of vision was caused by the smoke. His men had dug him out and the smoke had cleared. He was hurt, yes – the shell had landed so close that the right side of his face had been burned, his right ear deafened and his right leg badly bruised, while the blast had also removed much of his clothing – and he had had to be evacuated here, to the hospital at Imbros, to recover. But now, after just a few days, he feels stronger and is eager to get back to Anzac. His only regret is that in his brief time in hospital he has been unable to see, or even track down, Nurse King.

In the wee hours of the following morning, he rejoins his men back in the old trench and finds his nerves are very shaky, but after an hour or so he settles down and is even able to snatch some sleep before dawn.

'From looks of things here,' he writes in his diary, 'I anticipate that this job should be thru' in about a month from today.'[110]

3.30 AM, 29 MAY 1915, ANZAC COVE, A BAD BLOW-UP

All is in readiness. After weeks of preparation, of carefully digging tunnels out from the Turkish trenches towards the Australian positions at Quinn's Post, the soldiers of Turkey's 14th Regiment have reached a spot right *under* their enemy. Despite the fact that the Anzacs have recently woken up to it, the Turkish engineers have been able to lay one of the tunnels with charges.

And now it is time. With all of the soldiers of the 14th Regiment in the frontline opposite Quinn's not only forewarned, but with their rifles and bayonets at the ready, and their front foot on the fire-step ready to launch, the Turkish captain takes the two wires in his hands and with some satisfaction slowly brings them together, gazing resolutely forward at the enemy trenches bathed in the ethereal light of the full moon.

In an instant, the ground at Quinn's simply erupts with a muffled roar from the bowels of the earth and a searing flame shoots so far skyward that the low clouds above glow red. Turkish soldiers and artillery unleash a blizzard of bullets and shrapnel on the front trench in an attempt to kill any number of the 350 men of Australia's 13th Battalion, together with 100 10th Light Horse Regiment troopers currently stationed there and not taken out by the initial blast. The Turkish soldiers charge forward, eager to capitalise on the chaos and take over the position.

—

For the Australians in nearby trenches and below in Monash Valley, the air is filled with the screams of their comrades in the darkness and a red glow coming from the direction of Quinn's Post. All they can do is push towards it in the darkness, dodging the body parts as best they can and hoping to stem the breach.

Meanwhile, the Turks are charging towards what used to be the Australian positions, throwing bombs ahead of them and using their bayonets to finish off dazed survivors.

'The first thing that some of the stunned Australians on the flank of the explosion heard, on coming to themselves,' Charles Bean would recount, 'was the sound of gruff voices close to them speaking in an unknown language.'[111]

Australian it ain't.

And those who try to go beyond it are soon cut down by the Anzac defence-in-depth, just as, once the confusion has lessened a little and the first streaks of dawn allow the Australians in adjoining trenches to see clearly, they are able to bring devastating fire on those Turks now trying to cross no-man's-land to support their pals.

Shortly after the explosion, the 15th Battalion prepare to counter-attack and retake Anzac's most precarious Post.

Meantime, Lieutenant Terence McSharry of Brisbane – who had been just back from Quinn's when it blew up – is taking action of his own. After racing to a dugout where he knows a supply of jam-tin bombs is kept, he grabs a dozen and lights a candle, which he places inside a tin to keep it from blowing out. As some of the survivors come staggering back, he calls, 'Come on, Australia!'[112] which rallies them. He sallies forth with two men to get into a position where he can throw the bombs at the advancing Turks. They get there just in time to see a Turkish officer heading down a trench to his right, leading a dozen soldiers.

'The leader was advancing confidently,' Charles Bean would report, 'but those behind him . . . seemed to be without enthusiasm, peering through the half-dark.'[113]

The instant the Turkish soldiers see the dim figures of McSharry and his men, they duck their heads, but their officer is made of sterner stuff and instantly brings his pistol to bear, firing off a shot before McSharry can duck and . . . blows his hat off.

And now it is the Australians' return of serve. McSharry and his men light their bombs and lob them over to where the Turkish heads have ducked down. Screams shatter the night. In all of the confusion, the Turks in the main trenches higher up the hill throw their own bombs in the same direction, not realising they are killing their own men. Just one of those Turkish soldiers makes it out alive.

It is the beginning of an intense battle that lives up to Quinn's Post's reputation as the most dangerous location at Anzac. The fight rages for five hours, and by the time Quinn's Post is finally retaken, 33 Australians have been killed.

Another day, another brutal fight where they have lost many good men and suffered many terrible casualties. And yet, and yet . . . on this day there is something both impressive and different under the sun.

The first thing Colonel John Monash notes is how well his men perform under the severe pressure of bombardment and a full-blown attack.

'To a stranger,' he writes to a friend, 'it would probably look like a disturbed ant-heap with everybody running a different way, but the thing is really a triumph of organization. There are orderlies carrying messages, staff officers with orders, lines of ammunition-carriers, water-carriers, bomb-carriers, stretcher-bearers, burial-parties, first-aid men, reserves, supports, signallers, telephonists, engineers, digging-parties, sandbag-parties, periscope-hands, pioneers, quartermaster's parties, and reinforcing troops, running about all over the place, apparently in confusion, but yet everything works as smoothly as on a peace parade, although the air is thick with clamour and bullets and bursting shells and bombs and flares.'[114]

What touches him amid it all is something he would later describe as being to 'the eternal credit of Australian soldiers'.

For after they had retaken some temporarily lost trenches, it was only to find 17 Turks left behind. Under the circumstances – for the Australians had lost many of their own on this day to these men, and their blood is up – Monash would not have been surprised to see all the Turks killed on the spot. Instead, an interpreter was sent for and these enemy soldiers were persuaded to surrender.

Still, to the General's amazement, there is more.

No sooner had the Turks been disarmed than 'our boys crowded around them with water bottles and biscuits which they devoured ravenously, and then gave them cigarettes, and all the while lines of stretcher-bearers were carrying past our dead and wounded. Gallantry can surely touch no higher pinnacle.'[115]

Yes, Gallipoli is an inhuman bastard of a place, but, despite it all, from both sides there are stunning moments of humanity that shine through . . . At least for the Turks and the Anzacs, as no such rapprochement occurs with the Germans. One is even heard to shout across the trenches in his thick accent, 'Come on you – kangaroo-shooters!'[116]

Nor are German aviators seen to be any more likeable all of a sudden. While the Turkish artillery seems always to be mindful of hospital ships, one day a German plane flies right over a hospital ship and drops an enormous bomb that only misses by 50 yards or so. The medical officer of the 6th Light Horse Regiment is so outraged – he knows better than anyone just how many desperate cases there are aboard that ship – that he momentarily loses his equanimity. He hurls a brick at the enemy lines, just on principle, before explaining himself to the bemused soldiers: 'I wear the Red Cross, so I cannot fire at them, and they are not supposed to fire on me.'[117]

How they long to kill Germans.

31 MAY 1915, ANZAC COVE, A FATE THAT SPLITS THE DIFFERENCE

Despite this new-found warmth between the two sides, there is no relenting in the ongoing danger.

On this hot morning, Trooper Ernie Wiggins is in his dugout when two of his mates call for him to come outside and join them.

Ernie, an English-born Queenslander, ain't interested – okay, you coves? A more careful man than the other two, he just momentarily puts his head out and calls back, 'Not yet, the shrapnel hasn't stopped.'[118]

At that very instant, a shell explodes and a piece of shrapnel screams precisely between the other two and neatly bisects Ernie's head. Kills poor ol' Ernie stone motherless dead, it does. Too right, it does.

Just another day in the life – and many deaths – of those making war at Gallipoli.

Chapter Fourteen

SUMMER SETS IN

During June and July the strength of the troops visibly
declines. The great frames which had impressed beholders
in Egypt now stood out gauntly; faces became lined,
cheeks sunken. [You could spot new reinforcements] by
their sleek complexions, new clothes and fat on the ribs.[1]
Sergeant Ken Stevens, 11th Squadron, Auckland Mounted Rifles

To Let: Nice dugout on the skyline.
Owner leaving for Field Hospital.[2]
*Advertisement appearing in the June edition of the Diggers' hand-
drawn newspaper circulated on Gallipoli, 'The Dinkum Oil'*

Cover with earth just after you rise,
To keep down disease and lessen the flies[3]
Notice over latrine at W Beach, Cape Helles

EARLY JUNE 1915, MERCURY RISING ON GALLIPOLI PENINSULA
. . .

In western Turkey in summer, the sun does not shine so much as *beat*.
The breeze falls away, the clouds disappear and, for those fighting in the
trenches below, there is no respite. What little greenery on the hills that
has survived the battle so far turns brown, and every exploding shell
brings clouds of dust that linger and choke, as do the endless bullets.
Dead bodies – and since the armistice hundreds more have by now

gathered in no-man's-land – fester within hours, bringing a stench that overwhelms both armies. In the heat, they tend to bloat like whales, and soldiers from both sides fire at them to release the gases.

Those bodies and the open latrine trenches provide the perfect breeding ground for the flies that are already there in their billions, 'from the size of a pin's head to great bluebottles that are so bloated they can't fly'.[4] They get in your mouth, under your arms, into every open wound they can find, and, as one Digger sums it up in a letter home, 'they are far worse than the Turks'.[5] On the plus side, the flies do add a touch of much needed protein to the soldiers' diet, as god knows 'you could not eat without eating flies'.[6] Bully beef with a crunchy fly crust. Strawberry and fly jam on hard oatmeal biscuits. Salty fly-studded bacon, washed down with sweet fly-swilling tea. They are simply everywhere, in swarms.

'Maggots are falling into the trench now,' one Digger, Ion Idriess, would recount of his experiences. 'They are not the squashy yellow ones; they are the big brown hairy ones. They tumble out of the sun-dried cracks in the possy walls . . . A lot of the flies flew into my mouth and beat about inside . . . I nearly howled with rage . . . Of all the bastards of places this is the greatest bastard in the world.' The horrors never stop: 'A dead man's boot in the firing possy had been dripping grease on my overcoat, and the coat will stink forever.'[7]

Now installed on Imbros in the largest tent, General Hamilton has problems of his own with the flies, as he would soon record in his diary: 'These Imbros flies actually drink my fountain pen dry!'[8]

Lice and fleas are also a scourge. The men call them 'grey backs' and 'moovies', and they infest their clothes and sheets. Just like the damn flies, they are 'impossible to get rid of'.[9] It is not uncommon to see men 'sitting outside their dugouts with nothing on, hunting through their clothes for these and having "louse competitions" to see who can catch the most'.[10]

It is not just the Diggers on the Peninsula who are affected. Ellis Ashmead-Bartlett, taking a break from the front on the island of Lesbos, would complain that he had not slept a wink all night, for the fleas. Strange, replies Bean, he had not been troubled by them? 'Ah, but you see, Bean,' replies the suave English journalist, 'even a flea cannot bite a bone.'[11]

On the Gallipoli Peninsula, simple scratches don't heal, quickly turning into festering, suppurating ulcers that remind some of the Australian scourge known as Barcoo Rot. These ulcers, warm and wet, are the perfect place for flies to lay their eggs. Diarrhoea, caused by dysentery spread by the flies and fleas – known by the Diggers as the Gallipoli Gallop or Turkey Trot – runs rife. By the second week of June, with the mercury rising, it is so bad that, for the first time, more men a day are evacuated from Anzac Cove for sickness – around 80, to increase to 140 by the end of the month – than for battle wounds. As one man notes, 'we let the louse do what the Turks could not'.[12]

The overflowing latrines? As ever, they are just shallow trenches, three feet by one foot, and two feet in depth, which the men straddle. According to one Digger, 'The stench was indescribable and the flies . . . the toilets were just a trench dug in the ground with a piece of timber across it and two biscuit tins at the end.'[13]

The resultant scenes are appalling, with one Digger, Joe Murray, recounting in a letter, 'My old pal, a couple of weeks ago he was as smart and upright as a guardsman. After about ten days to see him crawling about, his trousers round his feet, his backside hanging out, all soiled, his shirt – everything was soiled. He couldn't walk. My pal got a hold of him by one arm. I got a hold of him by the other. We lowered him down next to the latrine. I don't know what happened but he simply rolled into this foot-wide trench, half sideways, head first into the slime. We couldn't pull him out, we didn't have any strength and he couldn't help himself at all. We did eventually get him out but he was dead, he'd drowned in his own excrement.'[14]

Of course, dysentery's bedfellow is dehydration, and, under such conditions, plentiful water would have been most helpful, but there is little – the vast majority of it has to come in by ship from as far away as Egypt and Malta – and the Anzacs are limited to just half a gallon per man per day, a tenth of the natural need of a soldier in the field.

What can you do with it? Most use it for drinking, for just staying alive, expending no more than a thimble's worth for anything else such as shaving and washing, let alone washing out the dixies (large, oval cooking pots) or one's mess tin, in which the disease-spreading flies feed and breed. As to washing their clothes, some men use a thimble of phenyl – usually used as a drain cleaner – while others 'have systematic hunts for foreign bodies in clothing'.[15]

As summer starts to blister, water becomes an ever greater issue. At least the way the story would go, when one particular soldier is seen to be staring glumly at the water in the bottom of his pannikin just doled out by his Sergeant, the senior man growls at him, 'Well, what the 'ell you looking at?'

'Nothing,' replies the private, 'just wishing I was a bloody canary.'[16]

(Back at Broadmeadows Camp in Melbourne, there had been a man named Furphy who emptied the sanitary cans and carted away the waste.[17] According to one Anzac, Furphy 'always had some rumour as to the date of the sailing or destination'. And Furphy was 'always wrong',[18] but his name lived on, as it had quickly become shorthand for the wild rumours that he started. Rumours and gossip were such a part of the Anzacs' daily life that there were even furphies about Furphy. One rumour was that the term originated at the Mena Camp in Egypt, where the most popular place in camp to meet and exchange news and gossip had always been around the water carts branded 'J. Furphy and Sons'.)[19]

The men are exhausted. Exacerbating the exhaustion is the fact that every morning now, from 3 am till 5 am, every man has to stand to arms, ready for an attack, and even when they do sleep, it is with their clothes and boots on. In fact, active duty is welcomed by most, as once relieved from the frontlines the fatigue work begins: trudging water and other supplies up hills under the heat of the sun and the maelstrom of constant shelling. As one soldier writes in his diary, 'I can tell you it's no joke climbing the hills with a load. It takes the stuffing out of one – but there is no stuffing to take out.'[20] And another notes, 'it's like stopping work to carry bricks'.[21]

By now, the days of having your puttees done up are long gone, and the soldiers are frequently shirtless, protected from the sun only by the shadow thrown by their slouch hats, while their once long pants have been cut down to shorts that are now little more than rags, all too often with holes in the back so the dysenteric discharge has somewhere to go.

In fact, men walking around in 'shorts' – which are naturally to become an iconic Australian male fashion item – are displaying something of a cutting-edge invention, born to be worn in the trenches at Anzac. Colonel John Monash claims his own part in sparking the new vogue in a letter to his wife: 'We allow the men great freedom in dress – I started it and the others followed. You know what "Shorts" are? They are Khaki overalls, cut down so as to finish four inches above the knee – like a Scotsman's trews. These worn with short underpants . . . look really well – the leg showing from two inches below to four inches above the knee, and soon getting as brown as the face and hands. I have dressed like that for some weeks, with khaki shirt and no collar or tie. Even Godley dresses the same now and all the other Brigadiers also. It is a very comfortable kit, especially for climbing hills. As to the men, well – they wear the same kit as the above, but no shirts, no puttees, and no socks, so you see there is nothing left but the boots and trews, and so they go about in the sun all day, and are already blacker in the skin than our Turks or Hindu muleteers.'[22]

Despite the heat, the flies, the sickness and the general exhaustion, there is more hard physical work being done at Anzac Cove than ever. For, in the immediate wake of the Turkish tunnelling beneath Quinn's Post to blow it up, of course General Birdwood has ordered the Anzacs to reply in kind. The call has gone out for soldiers and officers experienced in mining to come forward, and a posse of them is soon formed up into a special unit with the specific task of tunnelling towards the Turkish trenches. Most of the work is proceeding from Quinn's, Pope's and Courtney's – with 260 soldiers in all slaving like demented moles.

Beyond that, there is a continuous program of trench improvement, as the Anzacs continue to dig as if their lives depend upon it . . . because they do.

The sun beats down, the bullets fly, the shells burst, the boats filled with sick and wounded soldiers continue to head away . . . and the Diggers dig. For it remains a triumph of the human spirit that, no matter how agonising the circumstance, how hell-like one's place on earth, an ability to adapt can still manifest itself. So it is with many of the soldiers at Gallipoli at this time, who, unaccustomed as they were, are now world authorities in things they never previously imagined. Most have developed the golden ear of an orchestra conductor, as one Digger writes with wonder to a friend: 'The different sounds of bullets, shells, etc., we are now experts in.' He advises, 'There is the sharp crack of the bullet overhead, with a "ping" when it hits anything. There is the nasty, unfriendly swish of one that passes close to your ear. Then there is the "crackle" of a machine-gun, changing to a mournful disappointed "whisp whisp" when the bullets get closer. Lastly, there is the cheerful whistle of the shrapnel shell well overhead, and at which we all used to duck (we don't now, we know they're safe). It's the vicious brute that is just past you as you hear it that makes you take cover in case there's another following it.'[23]

Oh, and that 'whiz bang'? That, my friend, is the shellfire from a Krupps field gun. There, can you hear it? *Whizzzz* . . . BANG! It sounds just like that.

Only a short time after landing, the men had even been able to recognise the individual booms of the major Turkish cannons and given them names. 'Beachy Bill' comes from somewhere up on Gaba Tepe, and it focuses its fragments mostly on the landing beaches, while the roar of 'Farting Annie' and 'High Velocity Archibald' rolls to them from the Suvla plain a couple of miles to the north, and 'Lonely Liz' appears to be coming from a gully to the south. Playing havoc with the men at Helles, from across the way near Kum Kale, is 'Asiatic Annie'. And then there's a 'most vicious little gun called "Pip Squeaker"'.[24] (This is one of the many disadvantages of the Anzacs. All their land artillery fire comes from very clearly defined places, easily visible to observers, whereas the Turks can with impunity position their own artillery anywhere within range and usually on the lee side of the hills facing the Allies, making them nigh impossible to hit.)

Under such circumstances, it is never difficult to tell who the new blokes are – the reinforcements who intermittently arrive from Cairo – as, apart from having recognisable uniforms and even some flesh on their bones, they tend to throw themselves to the ground at the first sound of attack, to the roars of laughter from the others.

And there is also the matter of the local lingo and their lack of comprehension. For even though the veterans have only been here a short time, already their experience has been so intense, and unique, that new words have appeared in their vocabulary that nigh on everyone understands. See, the Turkish enemy is not just that, he is more colloquially known as 'Abdul', 'Jacko' and 'Johnny Turk'.[25] The highly ranked officers who sometimes – but not often – visit from Imbros are 'base wallahs'. Of these, none are worse than the 'brass hats', so highly ranked they have red tags on their lapel and around their caps, and they are ever and always impeccably turned out and accompanied by their 'bum-brushers', otherwise known as batmen. The Diggers, meanwhile, must hold up their trousers with an 'ANZAC button', otherwise known as a nail, while most men enjoy the distraction of 'coffin nails', otherwise known as ciggies. They all hate 'ANZAC soup', which is a massive hole formed by the explosion of a shell now polluted by a corpse, but they'll take a 'Tin of Dog' – that's bully beef – if you've got one. Those who have been merely wounded sometimes get an 'Aussie', an injury bad enough to be sent back to Australia, and a 'Blighty' if you're packed off back to a hospital in the Old Dart.

(The truth? In the horror of it all, such a wound is so coveted by some men suffering the trauma of war that they do it to themselves, 'generally gunshot wounds to the left hand'.[26] The penalty for being found to have done this is to be court-martialled and sentenced to several months' imprisonment, usually on hard labour.)

The killing, on both sides, goes on.

The Third Battle of Krithia on 4 June delivers the same result as the first two, with little ground gained for another 6500 British and French soldiers killed and wounded. The Turkish counter-attack, to recover a few hundred yards of ground on a short front, sees 6000 Turks killed and wounded.

7 JUNE 1915, LONDON, A COMMITTEE OF ITS VERY OWN

A pall of devastation hangs over the entire Peninsula, and for General Hamilton at this time, the only good news is that back in London it appears the 'Easterners' are winning their own war for control of the levers of power.

For, despite having been stood down from his position as First Lord of the Admiralty, Winston Churchill has remained busy and has circulated a treatise to fellow Cabinet Ministers pointing out that while no number of extra divisions added to the 24 already in France will affect the profound stalemate on that front, just three New Army Divisions – raised in large part by adherents to Lord Kitchener's famous poster – added to General Hamilton's forces of eight divisions already on the Gallipoli Peninsula would make all the difference. 'It seems most urgent,' he insists, 'to try to obtain a decision here and wind up the enterprise in a satisfactory manner as soon as possible.'[27]

Quite.

And at the first meeting of the Dardanelles Committee – the name given to the reorganised and enlarged War Council – on 7 June, Churchill so pushes his plan, backed by Kitchener all the way, that the Committee agrees.

So it is that, on this same day that General Hamilton surveys the vast human wreckage of Hunter-Weston's latest disastrous effort, he also receives a cable from Lord Kitchener:

WE ARE SENDING YOU THREE DIVISIONS
OF THE NEW ARMY. THE FIRST OF THESE
WILL LEAVE ABOUT THE END OF THIS
WEEK, AND THE OTHER TWO WILL BE SENT
AS TRANSPORT IS AVAILABLE. THE LAST

OF THE THREE DIVISIONS SHOULD REACH YOU NOT LATER THAN FIRST FORTNIGHT IN JULY.[28]

Three fresh divisions. *Another* 50,000 soldiers. And this to go with a division of Kitchener's New Army that has just arrived in Cape Helles. (True, the latest arrivals are less soldiers than badly undertrained civilians wearing the uniforms of soldiers, led by officers who either went to the right school or are of the Old School and have been recalled from retirement, but at least they provide some of the manpower that Hamilton so desperately needs.) All up, Kitchener's cable means Hamilton will have 140,000[29] fighting men in the Dardanelles. With that kind of manpower, it really should be possible to crack the Turkish nut, and discussion among Hamilton and his senior officers in their new quarters at Imbros immediately refocuses on how best to do this, how best to break out of their confines at Cape Helles and Anzac Cove, crush the Turks and push to Constantinople.

MID-JUNE 1915, IN CAIRO, A BOB IN, AND THE WINNER SHOUTS!

It's been a month now, and still there is no sign for Lieutenant Hugo Throssell and Colonel Noel Brazier, or for the detachment left behind of the 10th Light Horse, that they will be required to rejoin the regiment in Gallipoli – and they can barely stand it.

Are they really to suffer the humiliation of being stuck in Cairo when all the fighting is going on? When will they get the cable calling for them? Here at the Maadi Camp, it is a very dull, tedious existence waiting for news.

To break that tedium, sometimes Hugo goes into town with fellow soldiers, where, as ever, they make an enormous impression on the locals, who regard the emu plumes on their hats with awe and call them 'the Kings of the Feathers'[30] – though they don't always believe the claim that they are 'kangaroo feathers'.

In town, the Australians frequently play a betting/drinking game once called 'Selling a horse for a dish of eggs and herrings', which starts when the cry goes up, 'A bob in, and the winner shouts!'[31] Every man then puts a 'bob', a shilling, into the middle of the table and whoever wins a simple game of chance – with everyone taking a number and trying to 'sell a pony'[32] – has to buy a round of drinks for everyone at the table, before pocketing anything left over . . .

It all helps pass the time until they can get to Gallipoli, which is where they all desperately want to be.

MID-JUNE 1915, LONDON, THE JOURNALIST RAISES A STORM

Back in London, Ellis Ashmead-Bartlett is nothing if not busy. After arriving on 6 June, he has spent the time writing up the Dardanelles campaign to date, buying the supplies he needs to return to Gallipoli – pads, pens, a typewriter, leather shoes, fine clothes and toiletries – and fending off the many, many people who wish to see him to discuss what on earth is going on out east and how it has all gone so wrong.

There are, in fact, so many people that Ashmead-Bartlett decides to restrict himself to seeing Cabinet members only, and the officials of the War Office and the Admiralty. They include Winston Churchill, with whom he dines on 10 June, in the company of Winston's mother, Lady Randolph Churchill, as well as the Duchess of Marlborough and several others.

And yet this is not the Winston that the journalist had known so well. The old Winston had been glowing, garrulous, brilliant, oratorical and, above all, confident that he had all the answers. This Winston is bruised, battered, hurt, harried, vulnerable, pasty white, much older and sombre. There is only one thing that fires him up, and even then it is only nearing the end of the dinner: the lack of resolution displayed by the navy to see his Dardanelles plan through. The words tumble out, the fury rises, along with the sense of abandonment, of waste.

And to whom is he addressing his remarks?

Why, to Ashmead-Bartlett's amazement, they are directed across the table to his aged mother. Assuming what is clearly a familiar position for her, she sits quietly with an interested expression as her brilliant and adored son lectures her on just where the Dardanelles campaign had all gone wrong and how it was everyone else's fault. For you must understand, Mother, that 'the battle of March 18 had never been fought to a finish and, had it been, the fleet must have got through the Narrows'.[33]

Ashmead-Bartlett listens attentively, knowing it to be 'the most appalling nonsense', as he records in his diary. 'This is still the great obsession of his mind, one which he will never get rid of. He seemed to feel little or nothing for the brave fellows who had lost their lives in his ill starred enterprise . . .'[34]

And yet, such is the way of things that, when the ladies retire – with rather unseemly haste, once Winston pauses for a moment – it is the English journalist himself who becomes the target. 'You,' he accuses, 'have come home to run down the expedition and to crab it, and to talk about it before a lot of stupid Society Gossips. You have turned the whole thing to ridicule just for the sake of making a story out of it.'[35]

While it is possible Ashmead-Bartlett resembles this remark, he also resents it. 'I was as keen as everybody to see it through,' he insists, 'if only it was handled in the right manner.'[36]

With the journalist's tacit confirmation that he had no problem with Churchill's plan *conceptually*, and that the problem lies with those *executing* his plan, the wounded politician at last dismounts from his natural position atop his high horse and tells Ashmead-Bartlett he will facilitate a meeting with the Prime Minister so he can tell him that, personally.

And sure enough, at 1 pm the next day, Ashmead-Bartlett receives a message from Winston to meet him at Downing Street, and shortly thereafter this shining member of the Fourth Estate finds himself sucking deep on the rarefied air of the most 'sacred Council Chamber' in the land, 'where, for two hundred years, all great decisions which have made or marred us have been taken',[37] the Cabinet Room.

For over an hour, the two of them see Prime Minister Asquith together, with Winston laying out the maps he has brought with him so that he and Ashmead-Bartlett can present the plan they had worked out the previous evening. Their passionate view is that the best way forward is to land a major force north of Bulair. Yes, that's it – cut the Peninsula off at its very neck and you are in a position to emplace guns and block all the supply lines (sea and land) to the 140,000 Turkish soldiers in the south. The key, for Ashmead-Bartlett, is that by doing so you 'force the Turks to leave their carefully prepared positions in the south, and meet us on ground of our own choosing'.[38]

Impressed, Asquith reaches out towards the map with his elegant finger and places it over Bulair, blotting out the Peninsula's neck. He nods, saying, 'It seems to be the only natural thing to do.'[39]

Clearly, both the Prime Minister and Churchill have learned more from talking truth with Ashmead-Bartlett about what is actually going on over there than they have through reading all of the reports of General Hamilton put together.

'I wish you would draw me up a short and concise memorandum on the whole situation,' the Prime Minister tells Ashmead-Bartlett as the younger man takes his leave, 'and let me have it some time this evening. There is a Cabinet Council tomorrow, and I would like to have it by me. I would also like you to be present to answer any questions which may be put to you.'[40]

How quickly things have moved! From being unable to tell the truth of what is happening at the Dardanelles to being invited to Cabinet. He even dines that evening with Winston's replacement as First Lord of the Admiralty, Arthur Balfour, who questions him closely on the whole campaign, with a particular view to naval operations.

When Ashmead-Bartlett tells Balfour that the military men on the ground often fail to tell the truth to their masters at home, Balfour sighs and says, 'Yes, I find the greatest difficulty in getting all the information I require. I hope you will tell them out there that they need not be afraid of me. But I do not know about my predecessor.'[41]

The following day, at the Cabinet meeting at 10 Downing Street, the war correspondent's memo is presented, as he waits outside. After detailing how the rest of the positions are stalemated, with no prospects of breaking out, the memo comes to the key point, which is that, with all of the Turkish defences of the Dardanelles now strengthened, 'it is a fundamental error to assume any longer that, if we are able to occupy the southern extremity of the Peninsula so as to embrace Kilid Bahr and the European shore of the Narrows, we have opened the gate to Constantinople for the Fleet'. Further, the situation at both Cape Helles and Anzac is a stalemate. Therefore . . .

Ashmead-Bartlett proposes that a force of five divisions could do the job:

> Once firmly established and entrenched
> across the neck of the Peninsula, the
> campaign is at an end. The Turkish Armies in
> Gallipoli could not hold out for ten days.
> They have no reserve of supplies on the
> Peninsula.[42]

And who could be put at the prow of the attack?

Ashmead-Bartlett is clear:

> I would not advocate using troops now
> at [Cape Helles] and Anzac for this new
> movement, but it might be desirable to take
> off the Australian brigades and place new
> formations in their trenches.
>
> These Australians, who have been brought
> up to strength, are now experienced and
> extremely good in enterprises which require
> dash and initiative.[43]

But all of this is details. What is important is that the thrust be well directed and supported:

```
In conclusion, once you get astride the
peninsula the campaign is won. You have only
then to clear the minefield and get your
fleet through to Constantinople.⁴⁴
```

After 90 minutes of deliberations, a leading Liberal comes out to ask Ashmead-Bartlett a few questions, followed by none other than . . . Lord Kitchener.

The war correspondent is a little shocked, expecting someone of stature, of grandeur, of either menacing or magnificent presence. But no, the man in person evinces 'nothing . . . to inspire either fear or awe', and the correspondent's primary impression is of a man whose 'skin is red and rough'.⁴⁵

The Secretary for War asks a few questions, mostly concerning the route of Turkish supplies onto the Gallipoli Peninsula, which Ashmead-Bartlett is happy to answer. Then the moustachioed one questions the correspondent closely about the position of the troops at Anzac and Cape Helles.

The younger man is insistent in pressing the point that it is 'out of the question to hope to storm either Krithia or Achi Baba, and would only lead to useless slaughter . . . I would back my opinion on this point against all the generals on the spot . . . At Anzac the Dominion troops are in the position of an army holding a closely invested fortress from which they could not even make a successful sortie owing to the nature of the ground, and the fact that everywhere our lines are commanded by the higher hills occupied by the Turks.'⁴⁶

'Yes,' the Secretary for War replies, 'they seem to be absolutely held up at Anzac, and lost very heavily in the last attack, but don't you think they might get on a bit and seize that hill?'⁴⁷

Too risky, Ashmead-Bartlett replies, as the approaches to the heavily defended hill are so steep and bare, and so lacking in any kind of cover.

Could the Anzacs not then move south of their position and take 'Achi Baba in reverse?'.⁴⁸

Ashmead-Bartlett is stupefied. 'Any such move is out of the question until Gaba Tepe is taken to allow the Australian right to push forward,' he replies, trying to hide his amazement at the sheer, numbing ignorance of the question, 'and it would also be necessary for our left flank at Helles to advance considerably.'[49]

'But why did they give up Gaba Tepe?' Kitchener asks.

'They never held it.'[50] Can this be *possible*? After six weeks of reports from the Dardanelles, most of them from General Hamilton, Kitchener clearly does not have the first clue about key aspects of the campaign.

'To avoid the difficulties of the Bulair landing,' Lord Kitchener goes on, 'is there no other point between Anzac and Bulair where we might get across?'[51]

'I have never heard any other spoken of,' Ashmead-Bartlett replies, 'except, of course, Suvla Bay . . .'[52]

MID-JUNE 1915, EASTERN ANATOLIA, LIKE JACKALS ON RABBITS

It is the tramp of the dead. As the Ottoman Empire's war on those who would attack it externally continues, so too does it continue to destroy those it perceives as its internal enemies, most particularly the Armenians. On the orders of Talaat, not just leaders but now mere members of the Armenian community are led away, never to be seen again.

On this day, some 25,000 of them have been expelled from their town of Erzincan and marched to the south, to a destination unknown. All they are told is they can take with them only what they can carry.

In the middle of one grief-stricken group tramping along, escorted by gendarmes holding guns, and some soldiers, is an 18-year-old youth, Soghomon Tehlirian. When the war had begun, he had been studying engineering at the German University in Constantinople, only to be first conscripted into the army and then expelled back to the family home he has now been expelled *from*. As he plods forward with his crying mother, two sisters and brother, there would seem to be no worse hell than this, and they can only hope that the father of the family, who has been taken away, is still alive . . . when it happens.

Suddenly the gendarmes turn their guns on them and start robbing them, soon joined by a mob of Turks. One of his sisters is pulled down and raped, and after his mother cries 'May I go blind!'[53] she is shot dead before him, even as his other sister is also raped. All is madness and mayhem, screams and grunting. When his brother tries to help his sister, a soldier cleaves his head open with an axe. Tehlirian rushes forward, only to be smashed in the side of the head himself. Much later, he comes to consciousness in the darkness, beneath the body of his brother and surrounded by the bodies of everyone else in the group, including his family. The corpse of his mother is lying face-down, just a little way away. He has been left for dead.

Even in Gallipoli, something of such atrocities is heard of by the Anzacs, with Percival Fenwick noting in his diary, '[General] Enver paid a hurried visit to Anzac, and advised the Turks to blow our trenches up. He then hurried back to Constantinople and, we are told, shot a lot of Armenians, as he could not shoot Australians. There must be some excitement in being Head Man in Turkey. One can shoot anyone you happen to dislike.'[54]

MID-JUNE 1915, ANZAC COVE, BEAN'S FULL OF 'EM

All right for some. While Ashmead-Bartlett is swanning around London and the like, Charles Bean continues to count bullets and gather the information he needs for both his articles and the Official History. 'I was sniped at twice today looking over the parapets,' he faithfully records in his diary,[55] adding to his bullet tally.

When not wandering the trenches, or fighting the flies in his tent, or racing to the latrines to outrun the inevitable results of having a bad case of the 'Gallipoli Gallop', Bean is also working on a project called 'Dinkum Oil', a new trench newspaper that has won wide acclaim and popularity after just one issue:

News:

A wounded sniper captured the other night proved to be a lady from a Turkish general's harem. Since this occurred many men have been anxious to go out looking for snipers.[56]

THE ADVERTISEMENT

Full Private wishes to buy Guide Book to London. Places safe from Zeppelin to be marked with a cross.

Wanted – Some nice girl to stroll with on the Engineer's new pier.

Lance-Sergeant would exchange a grand dugout piano for three tins of Maconochie's rations.

Section Commander requires pair of good field glasses to find his men when there is shrapnel about.

Man with good memory would like the job of taking messages from the troops to friends in Cairo.[57]

Bean is also thrilled to receive a couple of letters from his brother, Jack,[58] now recovering in Alexandria, dated over a month before. It is crazy, and deeply frustrating, how long it takes for mail to arrive – and it is the cause of widespread angst at Anzac Cove.

Charles Bean gets back to work, sorting through his notes and trying to understand the whole situation as completely as he can. It is not as if, however, he and even the troops themselves don't get some respite. For now that summer has hit and there is torpor in the air, even the Mohammedans on the other side sometimes take a break from mounting attacks, and occasionally things fall so quiet that all you can hear is the endless buzzing of flies.

The most interesting activity for the Anzacs is swimming in the Aegean Sea, and one Sunday morning at this time, Charles Bean counts no fewer than 404 men bathing, while there are a lot more than that just quietly sitting on the beach half-dressed and basking in the sun, enjoying the tiny let-offs from being in the frontlines or doing fatigue duty. By now, a lot of them, he notes, as Monash had, 'are much darker than the Turks'.[59]

For all that, there is still a great deal of risk, as inevitably the Turks start to fire shots and shells at the distant bathers now so tightly packed in the waters. Back home, on sunny Australian beaches, the call would often go up, ''Ware shark!' Here, it is, ''Ware shell!'[60]

Bean is down at the shore a couple of days later when a shell explodes and a man emerges from the water with his arm hanging by a thread. He wears a stunned expression, not screaming or shouting, but simply holding the near severed arm with his other hand.

In a similar situation in, say, Bondi, with a man emerging from the sea from a shark attack, the waters would have been instantly cleared. But this is Gallipoli. Everything is different here. So he lost his arm, so what? They all see worse on a daily basis, and as there is nowhere on Anzac Cove that is free from the shells, they may as well be here as anywhere. So, yes, a few blokes get out of the water after this fellow loses his arm, but not everyone, and there is no panic. Some men swim further out than Bean has seen before, and watch, uninterested, as 'machine-gun bullets . . . drop into the water between them and the shore'. One officer, Major Henry Tiddy, finds the scene slightly amusing, noting in his diary one day after the beach had been shelled yet again, 'fun of the world to see hundreds of naked men making for cover'.[61]

And so the men continue to swim, day by day – even initiating some Turkish prisoners into the joys of surf-bathing – all of it with the full support of General Birdwood, who often has a dip himself. Yes, he is urged to stop the men bathing, but he refuses outright. 'I felt,' he later explained, 'that their spirits would suffer if, in all that heat, they could never get a wash, and I myself was bound to admit that I would rather be knocked out clean than live dirty!'[62]

In fact, Birdie is garnering a lot of respect from the Anzacs, for his continued presence on the frontlines. As a young private writes home to his family, 'General Birdwood was round here the other day. He is a cheery smart little man with a pleasant word for everyone. "Well, lad," he said, "have you shot any Turks this morning?" Of course saluting is all done away with.'[63]

And, despite his rocky start with the men, so too is Charles Bean! As one soldier writes home of the man once thought widely to be little more than a prudish wowser, 'He may have made mistakes but he is quite the most conscientious man on Gallipoli. Lots of the war correspondents are getting their tales from the hospitals but Bean is up on the firing line all the time.'[64]

Detail from 'Bathing under Shell Fire', by Ellis Silas (AWM ART90795)

18 JUNE 1915, BATTLESHIP HILL, READING THE LIE OF THE LAND

Another man who has not left the frontlines since the beginning is the newly promoted *Colonel* Mustafa Kemal. Exhausted, with the sparkle in his blue eyes now turned a dull grey, he stands atop Battleship Hill on this hot afternoon, gazing over the rough and rugged terrain of the Peninsula, from Suvla Bay, just out of sight to the north, down towards Cape Helles in the south. He is ruminating on the growing tension he is experiencing with the Commander of the Northern Group, General Esat, who is just about to arrive with his Chief of Staff, Colonel Fahrettin.

Just that morning, Mustafa Kemal had received a new order from his worthy Commander: Lieutenant-Colonel Wilhelm Wilmer has been appointed Commander of the Anafarta region, which will extend from Ejelmer Bay as far as Sazli Gully and Rhododendron Ridge . . . When necessary, your division is to help them.[65]

To Mustafa's eyes, the order is sloppy, leaving a very blurred line between what should be two very distinct areas of command: his area to the south and Wilmer's to the north. This makes them all vulnerable to an offensive at the obvious point of Rhododendron Ridge, a spur on the west side of Chunuk Bair, leading right to its summit.

And yet, when Esat and Fahrettin join him, they do not see what he sees. With the Peninsula now sitting like a map before them – so intricately bumpy, so complex that 'features of the terrain are easily confused with shadows'[66] – Colonel Fahrettin quips, 'This terrain could only be navigated by guerrillas.'

General Esat turns to his younger, self-assured colleague, Colonel Mustafa, and asks, 'Where will the enemy come from?'

Without hesitation, Mustafa points in the direction of Anzac Cove and traces a line north along the coast all the way towards Suvla Bay, saying as he does, 'From here.'

'All right,' General Esat responds, 'for the sake of argument, what if they do come from there? From where will they then make their move?'

Without hesitation once more, Mustafa Kemal lifts his arm and traces a line from the northern end of Anzac Cove inland along the Sazli Gully, all the way up Rhododendron Ridge to the highest point of the Sari Bair Range at Hill 971, saying, 'They will advance through here.'

General Esat laughs and pats the earnest Colonel Mustafa on the shoulder. 'Don't worry . . . they will not come through there.'

Mustafa Kemal realises that he will not have his position taken into practical consideration by command and sees no reason to prolong the debate. Instead he defers to General Esat, saying, 'Allah willing, it will occur according to your estimations, Sir.'[67]

—

Just 2000 yards away, effectively at the bottom of the hill on which they stand, General Birdwood and his Chief of Staff, Lieutenant-Colonel Andrew Skeen, have continued to refine the draft of a plan that General Hamilton has already shown a great deal of interest in, what Birdie describes as 'a sweep around my left flank'.[68]

With just one more division, he has told Hamilton, he will be able to 'seize and hold the high crest which dominates his own left'[69] – the hills of the Sari Bair Range. By sending two forces out beyond the perimeter on its poorly defended northern section at night, they could push along the beach and then turn east, to come at Sari Bair's high points of Chunuk Bair and Hill 971 from behind. If they could seize them in the night, they would not only be able to see the Narrows at last but also enfilade the Turkish trenches opposite the ANZAC trenches.

With those positions held, there would be few spots on the Peninsula that they could not shell, and, 'in fact, any strong force of Turks guarding the European side of the Narrows can then be starved out'.[70]

20 JUNE 1915, MALTA, NURSE LYDIA KING . . . DEAR DIARY

Arrived Malta 11 a.m. Started unloading patients at 2 p.m. I have such a nice boy, too sick to be moved, we have given him subcutaneous saline and everything. Finished unloading 6 p.m. and stayed with my patient and instead of dinner I relieved my feelings in my room. My patient died at 10.10 p.m. My nineteenth death in a fortnight, and such lovely boys. Am just heartily sick of the whole of the war.[71]

21 JUNE 1915, IN MELBOURNE, KEITH MURDOCH MAKES A MOVE

After nine months of working and festering in Melbourne as political correspondent for Sydney's evening paper *The Sun*, while the greatest story in the world – the war – is going on far away and covered by Charles Bean, the frustrated Keith Murdoch receives an interesting offer. The owner of his paper, Hugh Denison, has decided to bring back from London his star performer there, Campbell-Jones.

Would Keith like to fill his vacancy?

Perhaps. What he really wants to do is cover the war, a feeling exacerbated by the fact that yet another brother is about to join up. But at least this would get him closer to the action. And there is something more . . .

When he talks on the subject to his close friend, Labor Prime Minister Andrew Fisher, the Australian leader affirms his view that Keith is doing the right thing by not going into uniform, as he would 'make only an indifferent soldier',[72] and he gives him a task on the way over. The Prime Minister is now beyond frustrated at the lack of information coming from Gallipoli. No matter that he is the democratically elected leader of the Australian people, the British Government make no allowance for his rights to know the welfare of Australian troops, and his major source of information remains the heavily censored articles of Charles Bean. When Murdoch is travelling through the halls of power in London, he could be Prime Minister Fisher's eyes and ears on the ground on all matters affecting the troops. And could he go to Egypt on the way over, and hopefully to the Dardanelles from there, and write a report for him?

The Prime Minister has been worried sick about just how bad the situation is, and he fears for the welfare of the soldiers. Nominally, at the behest of the Defence Minister, Murdoch is to provide any suggestions for improvement in 'Arrangements for the receipt and delivery of letters, papers and parcels to and from members of the Australian Imperial Force',[73] but truly his brief will be much wider than that.

Yes, Prime Minister.

Murdoch soon decides it is precisely the kind of thing he would like to do, for though, as he writes in a letter to Prime Minister Fisher, he 'cannot overlook the fact that all the cabling and writing in the world is not going to win this war',[74] this will be something he really can do to help the war effort. His delight is manifold when Fisher also arranges a letter of introduction to the Commander-in-Chief of the Mediterranean Expeditionary Forces, General Sir Ian Hamilton, who will hopefully allow Murdoch to actually visit the Dardanelles to further his investigations.

Thrilled at the way things are turning out, Murdoch makes his preparations to leave.

Meanwhile, arriving back at Imbros, with an all-new wardrobe, writing materials and nothing less than a Parisian *cuisinier* in tow, Ellis Ashmead-Bartlett is also eager to show his fellow correspondents his new toy – a genuine movie camera, with which he can record events beyond writing word pictures.

Do you like it, Charles Bean?

The Australian correspondent, back at Imbros on one of his regular breaks, is not sure, reaching out his long fingers to touch the alien object, as if it is a boiling-hot potato, or a jam-tin bomb. What he is certain he does not like is word from Ashmead-Bartlett that he has been telling influential people in London that the whole Gallipoli campaign is 'going all wrong'. 'It seemed,' Bean confides in his diary, 'to be typically and exactly the thing that a War Correspondent ought not to do.'[75]

Of the Old School of journalism, proper and professional, Bean passionately believes that the role of a war correspondent, or any journalist for that matter, is to record faithfully what is occurring and not try to alter what is occurring. (Unless, of course, a man is wounded and under fire and you can scurry forward and save his life.) And though sometimes gutted by the way things have turned out, and the lives that have been lost, Bean still has faith that the campaign can be saved.

And so has General Hamilton, as it happens, the more so when informed that another two divisions – beyond the three already promised – will soon be on their way to him. Clearly, back in London, the Easterners are winning the debate, and from being the poor relation in the piece, Hamilton is now being flooded with resources – so many and so much it is decided to postpone for a couple of weeks the ANZAC breakout conceived at Birdwood's Headquarters. This initial plan comprised slipping out of Anzac Cove by night, travelling north along the virtually unprotected coast to Fisherman's Hut, sparsely held by either side in such rough country that the natural defences are already formidable, and attacking Chunuk Bair from the west, along the seaward ridges and slopes.

But now it is clear that, by early August, General Hamilton will have a total of 13 divisions to throw into the line, and so a much grander plan starts to take shape. Added to the ANZAC breakout will be the simultaneous landing of the IXth Corps, composed of two New Army Divisions plus corps troops, some 40,000 men in all, at Suvla Bay to establish a northern base. The bonus of a Suvla Base is that it will simply give Hamilton somewhere to store his new-found surfeit of soldiers. In subsequently taking the Anafarta Range to the north and east of Suvla Bay and pushing east across the Peninsula, the Allies can sever communication between the Turkish Army and Constantinople, while at the same time communication will be established with the ANZAC breakout's newly won northernmost positions on the Sari Bair Range, creating a front stretching south all the way from Suvla Bay to Gaba Tepe.

Let the Turks try to stop *that*.

LATE JUNE 1915, ANZAC COVE, A MESSAGE FROM ABOVE

Look, if it is not quite manna from heaven, it at least runs close, as on this day, some eight weeks after the Anzacs have first landed on Turkish shores, a German aeroplane flies overhead at an altitude just above rifle range, and drops leaflets on the Australian and New Zealand lines. Or at least it intended to. In fact, most of them flutter down into Turkish trenches, but never mind. For after realising the leaflets have been sent to the wrong address, many of the Turks wrap them around a stone, sometimes with a nasty message scrawled on it ('The old Turk,' Bean records, 'scribbled on the back of this in pencil some very filthy remarks about our wives and mothers')[76] and throw them over.

The leaflets promise the Anzacs excellent treatment and bounteous provisions if they'll do just one thing:

Come and surrender . . .

**On all fronts of this war, your own people
and your allies' situation is as hopeless as
on this Peninsula . . . your honour is safe!
Further fighting is mere stupid bloodshed![77]**

Of course, none of the Anzacs take them up on the offer, but at least for a few days the lucky ones have the rare luxury of toilet paper. (For his part, Captain Gordon Carter is amused by their presumption, though he writes to his parents, 'There is one thing to the credit of the Turk – he is a clean fighter. What prisoners I've seen have been fine stalwart fellows with good clean faces – they looked gentlemen.')[78]

28–30 JUNE 1915, BATTLESHIP HILL, TURKEY BROKEN AT THE NEK

Mustafa Kemal is convinced that there's a major Allied attack on the horizon. There is movement down in the Krithia region, and the enemy fire seems to be getting more and more intense in his sector. Typically, however, it is not enough for him simply to wait for the enemy to attack . . . his men must get in first, and they must do it quietly, under a veil of utmost secrecy.

In these latter days of June, as the weather gets hotter and the impetus is to have this whole affair over with, Mustafa frames an attack at the northern end of the Nek, knowing that if they can break through, they will be able to direct their fire right onto the principal Anzac anchorage at North Beach, as well as onto all the posts that line Monash Valley. The enemy's position would be untenable, and Mustafa Kemal is prepared to take mighty risks to achieve it – even sacrificing the cream of the accomplished 18th Regiment, which has just arrived to be positioned in front of Baby 700 and the Chessboard, a grid-like network of Turkish trenches opposite Pope's Hill.

On the night of 29 June, the last trace of sunlight is gone by 9.30 pm, and a huge gust of wind brings with it the rolling sound of thunder. At 9.55 pm, Colonel Mustafa – thrilled that General Enver himself happens to be here for the occasion – gives the word, sending the 18th Regiment written instructions to 'attack the enemy opposite your positions'.[79]

Those worthies say their prayers and steel themselves. The wind, thick with salt, is blowing off the Aegean, picking up any loose debris it can find on its ravenous path up to Russell's Top and tossing it over the Turks' newly dug trenches at the Nek, flinging it into the soldiers' faces. There is trouble in the air, menace and confusion, as the Turkish barrage begins, lobbing shells down on the Australian defenders – who happen to be Lieutenant-Colonel Alexander White's 8th Light Horse Regiment.

Unable to see whether the barrage is having any effect, the on-edge Turks continue to fire wildly, and are confused when they hear cheers. The Australians seem unaccountably to be enjoying the tumult, their cries being carried by the wind to bounce off the cliffs, somersault and soar up towards the heavens.

To add to the uproar of the Turkish artillery, now an Indian mountain battery sends star-shells at them, which soon set fire to the scrub near Lone Pine. The night is filled with explosions, flaring flames, choking smoke, billowing dust and yes . . . still cheers.

And yet one Turkish shell actually does land close to a bullseye, claiming 22 casualties in the 8th Light Horse Regiment, of whom seven are killed. (Among the wounded is none other than Colonel Alexander White, who takes a flesh wound to the skull when hit by a fragment of shell.)

Has such a disaster weakened the Australians' resolve in any manner? Has it *hell*. Though the losses are tragic, they are insignificant in terms of overall numbers, and so it is that the 8th Light Horse is still there in force as midnight of 29 June approaches and Mustafa's 18th Regiment is given the final order to attack.

The barrage suddenly stops, and the inevitable cry of *'Allah! Allah! Allah!'* rises up, followed by wave after wave of Turkish soldiers running down the slope from the Nek to Russell's Top, across the exceedingly narrow spine of land that connects them.

And therein lies the problem for the Turks. So narrow is the razor-back ridge that they have no capacity to outflank the Australians and instead must run tightly packed together – meaning that the 8th Light Horse just can't miss.

'Our men,' Trooper Ernie Mack would recall, 'sat right up on the parapets of our trenches and when not firing were all the time calling out for the Turks to come along and hooting and barracking them. In fact most of the chaps took [it] as a real good joke.'[80]

Yes, one or two Turks make it to the Australian trenches, but that is nothing that a few quick thrusts of the bayonet can't fix. And at another point, some 50 Turks actually occupy one of the saps and push forward but, again, they are soon forced out by a concerted drive of soldiers.

The most amazing thing is that this goes on for almost *two hours* before the Turkish 18th Regiment is defeated everywhere. By pursuing the sheer insanity of crossing this narrow bridge of land into massed Australian guns, a battalion and a half of the Ottoman's 18th Regiment is wiped out, with 260 dead,[81] while the Light Horse lose only seven men killed and 19 wounded.

This has been a bad blow for Colonel Mustafa – not helped by the fact that General Enver is still on the scene at Kemalyeri, from where he witnesses the devastation firsthand. No good news has come back from the front this night.

They have not taken Russell's Top. They have not pushed the enemy into the sea. Despite General Enver's assurance to the shattered and scattered surviving men of the 18th that their efforts had been 'most useful in engaging the attention of the English at a critical moment',[82] a question mark is placed firmly over Mustafa's judgement and ability to command the Ari Burnu sector.

—

The disaster notwithstanding, still the Turks keep pressing the Anzac lines in coming days, and though the battles at this time are not nearly as ferocious as early in the campaign, still the Australians and New Zealanders see a steady stream of dead and wounded coming back from the frontlines.

In one particular battle in early July, Trooper Bluegum again finds himself in the thick of it on Holly Ridge, at a point where the Turks land some 200 shells on their trenches in just a few hours. Most of the men keep their heads down, but one of their number, Sergeant Fred Tresilian, a Boer War veteran originally from down Wagga Wagga way, appears to relish it. '[Fred] seemed to love the firing-line like home,' Bluegum would record. 'He was quite fearless. Somehow he seemed to revel in the roar of battle.'[83]

And so it is on this occasion. When the Turks drop no fewer than a dozen shells right on the tiny ANZAC section of trenches, carnage results, as the parapet is blown apart, as is most of the trench itself. Those not killed are wounded, blinded, buried, choked, deafened or all of the above. One of the last is Trooper Bluegum, and when he can finally see and hear and breathe again, the first person he encounters is Sergeant Fred Tresilian, laughing merrily.

'Hello, Bluegum,' he says, easy as you please, 'not killed yet?'[84]

For his part, Bluegum is *not* surprised to see the Sergeant not killed yet, as despite having volunteered for some of the riskiest scouting and patrol work, he somehow seems to avoid all the bullets. But can it last?

Perhaps. And yet, only ten days later, when still one more battle breaks out, a bullet comes so close it actually nicks Tresilian's cheek.

He's done it again!

A short time later though a sniper's rifle cracks and a bullet comes and drops Tresilian dead.

Such is life, and death, at Gallipoli.

Chapter Fifteen

THE BATTLE IS NIGH

I stick to what I wrote to Wolfe Murray: the combination
of Stopford and Reed is not good; not for this sort of job.[1]
General Sir Ian Hamilton, Gallipoli Diary

Hamilton has not the strength to give those with whom
he is surrounded a straight out blow from the shoulder
– however much the situation demands it. To mix the
metaphor – he has an unlucky ability for gilding the
pill. He can't administer a pill unless it is golden . . .[2]
Charles Bean on General Hamilton

MID-JULY 1915, IMBROS, SHHHHHHHH, THE PLAN IS PERFECTED

That hush around General Hamilton in these dog days of mid-July? It's
the sound of fresh divisions *finally* starting to arrive, as he and his senior
staff work on the finer details of their secret plan to finally and properly
seize the Dardanelles – a plan so sensitive and so vital it must be kept
from getting out at all costs, and so is kept 'within a tiny circle'.[3]

The Commander of the Mediterranean Expeditionary Force has
accepted the logic of General Birdwood's plan, that with just one more
Division he could break out of Anzac and seize the heights of the Sari
Bair Range.

Not that General Hamilton is expecting it to be that easy.

'As to our tactical scheme for producing these strategical results,'

SARI BAIR RANGE

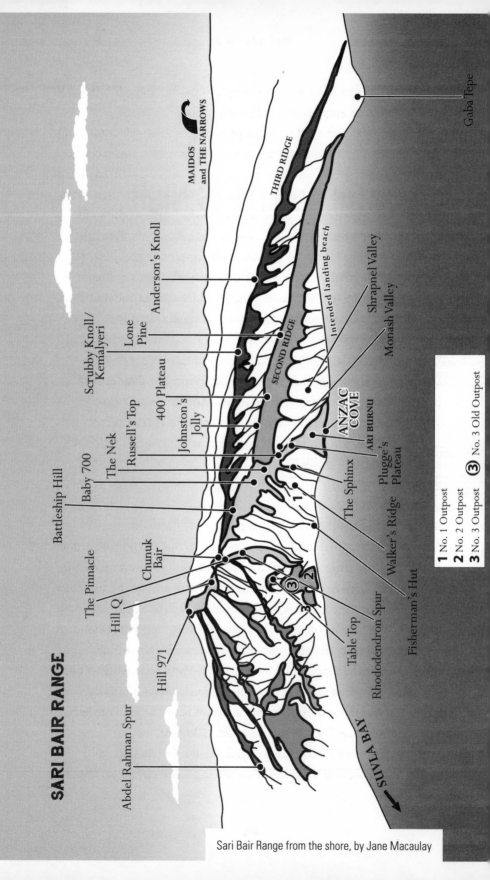

- SUVLA BAY
- Abdel Rahman Spur
- Hill 971
- Hill Q
- The Pinnacle
- Chunuk Bair
- Battleship Hill
- Baby 700
- The Nek
- Russell's Top
- Johnston's Jolly
- 400 Plateau
- Lone Pine
- Scrubby Knoll / Kemalyeri
- Anderson's Knoll
- MAIDOS and THE NARROWS
- THIRD RIDGE
- SECOND RIDGE
- Intended landing beach
- Shrapnel Valley
- Monash Valley
- ANZAC COVE
- ARI BURNU
- Plugge's Plateau
- The Sphinx
- Walker's Ridge
- Fisherman's Hut
- Rhododendron Spur
- Table Top
- Gaba Tepe

1 No. 1 Outpost
2 No. 2 Outpost
3 No. 3 Outpost
③ No. 3 Old Outpost

Sari Bair Range from the shore, by Jane Macaulay

he astutely notes in his diary, 'it is simple in outline though infernally complicated in its amphibious and supply aspects.'[4]

In short, a multi-faceted assault is planned, across a wide front, with each successive attack depending on the one next to it to succeed or, like the weakest link in the chain, the whole thing risks breaking down.

The French and British forces at Cape Helles will launch their attack so as to draw the attention and resources of the Turks to the south. It will be sustained for precisely as long as it takes to burn through the 4000 soldiers that GHQ has calculated as surplus to requirements – cheers, lads.[5] So, too, will the Australians make an attack at Lone Pine –'the crown of the 400 Plateau'[6] – the key post right in the middle of the ANZAC front. This heart-like crown is divided by Owen's Gully into two lobes: the northern Johnston's Jolly, and the southern Lone Pine.

There, where the trenches are anywhere from 50 to 100 yards apart, the plan is relatively simple. After a long bombardment, the Australians and New Zealanders will simply charge forward and take over the forward trenches. Once the Turks know that there is a serious attack here, they will inevitably call in forces from elsewhere, including from the peaks of the Sari Bair Range – the troops stationed around Chunuk Bair, Hill Q, Hill 971, Battleship Hill and Baby 700 – which is where the next part of the plan comes into play.

For, after Lone Pine is secured and the Turks from on high come forward, under the cover of darkness and distraction the Right Covering Force of the New Zealand Mounted Rifles Brigade are to stealthily make their way through the least defended part of the perimeter, at the far north, and knock out the thin defences leading up to the heights of the Sari Bair Range. In particular, they are to overwhelm the significant Turkish enclave known as Old Number Three Outpost, which stands guard over the entrance to Sazli Gully (the place Mustafa Kemal had pinpointed to his superiors just over a month beforehand). Altogether, the Right Covering Force is to be around 1900 men.[7]

A Left Covering force is, in principle, to do the same but will take a wider left hook, north from the Anzac Sector, and clear a path for an approach to Hill 971 via a small indent in the land called Aghyl Gully.

Shortly thereafter, two columns of troops, totalling 10,000 men, would also move out of the ANZAC perimeter. The Left Assault Column – commanded by Major-General Vaughan Cox with his 29th Indian Brigade and assisted by the newly promoted Brigadier-General John Monash with his 4th Brigade[8] – would first head north along the northern beach road and then turn right, trekking and fighting their way through the night, up Aghyl Gully then climbing and fighting all the way to the summits of Hill 971 and Hill Q before dawn. The Right Assault Column, all men of the Shaky Isles under Brigadier-General Francis Johnston (Commander of the New Zealand Infantry Brigade), will head east from the Number Two Outpost, following the route of the covering force before them, then break into two groups to trek and climb and fight their way to the summit of Chunuk Bair.

While all this is going on into the night, two new British Divisions will arrive on the shores of Suvla Bay, some four and a half miles to the north of Anzac Cove.

The actual landing spot is a large plain, dominated by a dried salt lake, flanked on three sides by hills beginning around three miles from the shore. The first of these British forces – 18,000 strong of the 11th Division – are to sweep south-east, across that plain and up to the surrounding ridges as swiftly as possible, to occupy the high ground leading up to the Anafarta villages and Sari Bair Range before daylight. 'Of first importance' will be the taking of Chocolate Hills and W Hills before daybreak,[9] which will hopefully lead on to the taking of the village of Big Anafarta.

At daybreak, they will be followed along the ridge line by two brigades – 8000 soldiers – who have landed after them. From here, if required, these troops will be in a position to advance along the eastern spurs of Hill 971, which would link them with elements of the Left Assault Column of the ANZAC breakout.

And then, the denouement. By dawn the following morning, the two columns atop Hill 971 and Chunuk Bair will be in position to

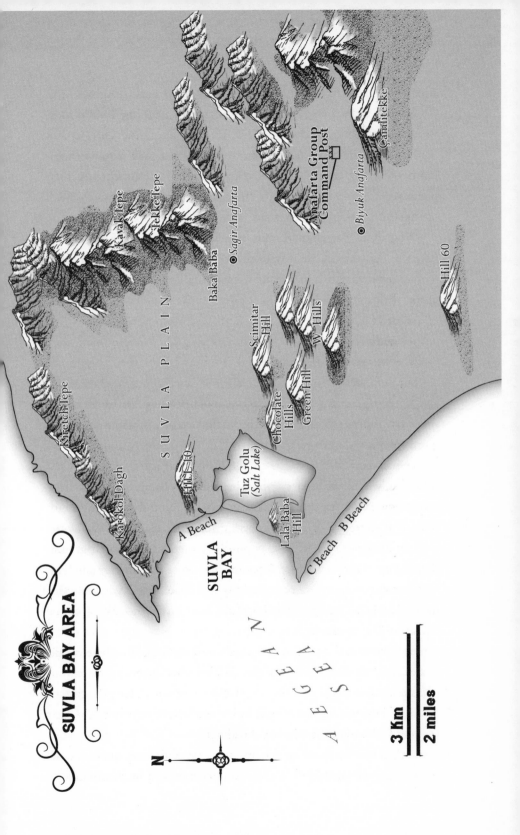

Suvla Bay area, by Jane Macaulay

attack the Turks dug in on Baby 700 *from behind*, and at this moment the men of the 8th and 10th Light Horse will attack the Nek in four waves of 150 soldiers each.

The Turks, attacked from in front and behind, will fall away, and Baby 700 will be captured. If the taking of Chunuk Bair from the rear is delayed for any reason, the attack on the Nek and Baby 700 will nevertheless proceed, acting as a feint if nothing else.

Oh, and, as Bean would note, 'simultaneously the 1st Light Horse Brigade, [which was] then holding Pope's and Quinn's, was to seize with its 1st Regiment a part of the Chessboard and with its 2nd a sector of the Turkish Quinn's'.[10]

All clear?

Not really.

Then let's go through it again.

And so General Hamilton and his senior officers do, again and again and again, trying to refine the plans and define the goals, to the point that every individual unit across the 90,000 soldiers involved would be given specific orders to go after clearly designated targets, and on a very strict timetable.

It really is dreadfully complicated, but, if all goes well, by the conclusion of the battle the Allies will be in control of all the high ground from Ejelmer Bay in the north through Chunuk Bair and along to Gaba Tepe. They will have finally secured the heights of the Sari Bair Range, which was their target on the day of the landing and was momentarily in their grasp, before Colonel MacLagan had taken the decision to reinforce the Second Ridge.

Having Suvla Bay will give the Allies their own port to get them through the winter, and if all goes really well they will be able to break free of the dreadful confines of the Gallipoli Peninsula and march on Constantinople.

True, there are naysayers to the plans within the tight circle, pointing out that 'the ground between Anzac and the Sari Bair crestline is worse than the Khyber Pass'[11] – as many British officers would know, as they had been there – but General Hamilton is not particularly concerned. It is the strong reckoning of both Generals Birdwood and Godley that their men can do it, and that is good enough for him. '[A]fter all,' Hamilton notes in his diary, 'is not "nothing venture nothing win" an unanswerable retort?'[12]

Not for the newly arrived Commander of the AIF 1st Division it isn't.

Major-General James Legge – a one-time brilliant barrister who had gone on to pioneer the Military Training Scheme – is convinced that in his sector the plan to attack Lone Pine will see the slaughter of many Australians for little gain. He makes no bones about saying this, just as he had been a critic of the whole landing at Gallipoli in the first place. He feels that the Turkish trenches at Lone Pine are far too heavily defended for the Anzacs to be able to seize them without suffering extraordinary losses.

But Birdwood insists. It is *because* Lone Pine is so key to the Turkish defences that he wants to attack it, because only an attack on such a crucial point would force the Turks to move their reserves there, leaving them unavailable to oppose the main attacks at Chunuk Bair and Hill 971.

Another critic is Colonel Cyril Brudenell White, Chief of Staff to Birdwood, who thinks the plan is fraught with danger from the first, and rather more delicately says so.

But what can Legge and Brudenell White do? A year earlier, to the day, the Australian Government had signed over control of Australian soldiers to the British Government and, *ipso facto*, their officers, so it really doesn't matter what some of the leading Australian officers on site think about the likely fate of their soldiers.

General Birdwood is the Commander of the Anzacs, and General Hamilton the Commander of all the forces on the Peninsula. They are English and they decide what happens to Australian forces. And this, make no mistake, is what both Generals Hamilton and Birdwood want, as with their staff they continue to refine the orders. With all the fresh divisions arriving in the Dardanelles, Hamilton is even starting to feel confident of a breakthrough. 'It seems likely,' he writes, 'that during the first week of August we may have 80,000 rifles in the firing line striving for a decisive result . . .'

How many are likely to be killed and wounded in such an attack?

'Quite impossible to foresee casualties,' he notes, 'but suppose for example, we suffered a loss of 20,000 men; though the figure seems alarming when put down in cold blood, it is not an extravagant proportion when calculated on basis of Dardanelles fighting up to date . . .'[13]

Exactly. When judged against the catastrophic casualty figures to date – the losses at the landing, or the three battles for Krithia – just how bad could the 'August Offensive', as it has become known, really be?

It is perhaps inevitable that, at this time, the ubiquitous Charles Bean gets wind of the whole plan. One day in mid-July, his brother Jack – who has just returned from hospital at Alexandria – has popped over to his dugout for a lunch of bread, tea and flies. Afterwards Charles accompanies him back to the 3rd Battalion HQ so he can write up his notes on what Jack's mob had done in the first three days after the landing. As they weave around groups of chattering men, Jack is impressed at his brother's apparent new-found popularity with the soldiers, who wave and nod with respect.

When they arrive at Jack's camp, Bean hears talk for the first time of a big attack to be launched in early August . . .

It worries him. For if he is hearing about it like this, so casually mentioned, with everyone living on top of everyone else, how long can it be before it is general knowledge and the enemy finds out too?

Of more concern to Birdwood than simple security, however, is the overall health of the veteran ANZAC troops, as no fewer than 200 men a day at Anzac Cove alone are now being evacuated through sickness, and those who remain are teetering on it. Oh yes, Birdwood knows all that, all right. As he walks around the trenches, he is frequently told by the men, 'No Turk is going to get past here – I'll see to that: but if you asked me to march a couple of miles after him, I just couldn't do it.'[14]

And there is also a problem with morale in certain sections, with the practice of 'malingering' – staying in hospital well past the point of recovery – on the rise.

Another sign is a warning from the Chief Staff Officer of the 1st Australian Division, Colonel White, that he has become aware of 'increases of wounded men sent down to the base hospitals with the remark "self-inflicted"'.[15] It is a real problem, and one getting worse with the passing weeks.

'They now knew,' Bean would record, 'that for them the prospect was one of battle after battle, in which, in the long run, there must almost certainly be one of two endings. They felt themselves penned between two long blank walls reaching perpetually ahead of them, from which there was no turning and no escape, save that of death or of such wounds as would render them useless for further service.'[16]

Battalion Commanders must be on the lookout for such cases – a wound to the left hand or left foot always being the most suspicious – and gather evidence so the soldiers who do it can be court-martialled.

And yet, for all the growing weakness of the Anzacs, it may be they are stronger in body and in spirit than their counterparts at Cape Helles. That, at least, is the impression of the Secretary of the Dardanelles Committee, Lieutenant-Colonel Maurice Hankey, sent by that Committee on a fact-finding mission.

Though General Hamilton has not seen a lot of him, Hankey has shown the General the copy of a personal cable he has sent to Lord Kitchener, where he has reported after his visit to Anzac, 'Australians are superbly confident and spoiling for a fight.'[17]

The Turks?

Well, from the ANZAC side of the trenches, there are clear signs that they, too, must be struggling, most particularly as it is noted that they 'occasionally held their hands above the parapet to be shot at',[18] presumably in order to be evacuated themselves. But there are other signs that, like the Anzacs, their spirit remains strong . . .

On one occasion, as detailed by Charles Bean, the Turks put a new spin on an old game that the two sides play daily. This version starts the same, with the Turks putting up a mock tin periscope, to draw useless Anzac fire. Once it is shot away, up comes one obviously made of cardboard. '[Our men] fired at it and missed,' Bean would recount. 'Someone else fired and missed again. Every time they missed the cardboard gave a little confident shake as a duck waggles its tail. The Turk in the trench was signalling a miss.'

At last, though, it is shot away, and the Anzacs wait to see what he will put up this time. It proves – and here's the innovation – to be 'a bit of shining tin this time . . . cut in the shape of a cross. Everybody knew what this ally of Germany meant by that, this Turk with the German officers in command and the German money at his back – it was a jeer at our religion and the religion of Germany; and the joke ceased at that instant as if it had been cut short by a chopper.'[19]

How *dare* he?

24 JULY 1915, ELLIS ASHMEAD-BARTLETT'S BLOOD BOILS

Is it sedition – 'conduct encouraging insurrection against the established order' – or not? It just might be, but Ellis Ashmead-Bartlett and his officer friends can barely help themselves.

After the correspondent spends a morning at Anzac Beach with his newly purchased cinematograph – capturing moving pictures of over 20 bathing soldiers being killed or wounded by shrapnel, 15 by just one shell – he returns to Imbros, where he dines with Lieutenant-Colonel Aubrey H. Herbert and, most pertinently, Colonel Leslie Wilson, an extremely well-connected Member of Parliament with the Conservative Party, who tells tale after tale of 'muddle, mismanagement and useless slaughter'.[20]

Other officers might feel the need to mute their criticisms of the Generals, but Wilson is too senior himself to care. On one recent occasion, he had been ordered to take a trench of such little consequence that he had vigorously protested, further pointing out that even if they captured it, it would prove impossible to hold. 'Time and time again I protested,' he tells his appalled dining companions, 'but finally received a definite order which had to be obeyed. We took it without much trouble and then got bombed out, exactly as I had predicted, losing three good officers and eighty men. Finally, I retired with only six survivors.'[21]

What follows is even more appalling, and hideously wasteful of British lives, as General Hunter-Weston – now known as 'the Giggling Butcher' to troops and officers alike – had then ordered a Marine battalion to take the same trench, only for exactly the same catastrophe to befall them! The whole thing had been entirely consistent with the daily shemozzle Wilson had experienced since arriving here. 'The orders issued to the 29th Division are seldom intelligible,' he declares, 'and always had to be changed, modified, or ignored. We can never get a definite objective for an attack, as the orders always end up with "Go as far as you can and then entrench".'[22]

Colonel Wilson's opinions of Hunter-Weston marry strongly with Ashmead-Bartlett's own passionately held views. 'After my first conversations with him,' Ashmead-Bartlett would later recount, 'he seemed to me not to have the smallest knowledge of war and to throw away many lives in the most wicked and reckless manner without having any clear idea in his mind of any objective.'[23]

Yes, there is the small mercy that, just in the last week, Hunter-Weston had gone back to England – whether sick from sunstroke, sacked or suffering some kind of breakdown like Carden is not known, though on her hospital ship Nurse Lydia King refers to him as a 'crotchety old man'[24] – but that is no solace for those thousands of men who now lie in their graves because of him. The problem is that Hamilton and his HQ staff still remain. Everywhere these men go, the diners on Imbros agree, there is never a good word said for any of them, and Sir Ian is criticised 'because he never visits the front-lines'.[25]

And what frustrates the English correspondent more than anything is that he cannot write the truth of the matter, as it will be instantly censored. 'I thought there were limits to human stupidity but now I know there are none,' he had confided to his diary the week before. 'The censorship has now passed beyond all reason.'[26]

Truly, he tells his companions, it does not matter how mild one's views, the censors will knock it out. There are *four* of them. And even the mild reports that do get through are delayed more than ever, Ashmead-Bartlett suspects, so that the words of Sir Ian Hamilton – who has now taken to writing *his own* despatches, which contain the most ghastly lies – are released well before the correspondent's reports.

In his last missive, Sir Ian had announced to the world that 5150 Turks had been killed and 15,000 wounded. How could he possibly know that?

Exactly! Ashmead-Bartlett's own estimate is about 40 per cent of that.

In the course of the conversation, Aubrey Herbert makes what Ellis judges to be 'the most serious of all' charges against him, that General Hamilton routinely leaves 'thousands of our wounded to perish in front of the lines after these attacks have failed instead of arranging for an armistice'.

The truth is that the British Generals aren't even close enough to negotiate an armistice with the eager Turks to gather in the wounded. For they are mostly on Imbros, where they 'have their dinners and their baths and apparently it never interferes with their night's rest the knowledge that hundreds of their fellow men are lying mutilated and unattended only a few yards away from our front lines crying for water suffering the agonies of the damned and knowing that their fate is a long slow lingering death from suppurating wounds or from thirst and starvation'.[27]

And yet still the fresh divisions continue to arrive from Great Britain, many of them in recent days. Well, the English journalist views them with nothing less than pity. Yes, back in London, he had rallied for more men to be sent, but that had been on the understanding they should land at Bulair – and now these Generals have swooped on the idea of new recruits to plan yet another slaughter. 'The sending of the 13th Division to Helles,' he had written in his diary, 'makes it look as if they intended that Achi Baba shall eat up this Division as well as so many others. The appetite of this mountain is insatiable.'[28]

The more Ashmead-Bartlett contemplates these fresh plans for useless slaughter, the more appalled he is: 'Thus we carry on at this hopeless game, ignoring all the strategical possibilities in the situation by persisting in these murderous frontal attacks on impregnable positions, losing tens of thousands of our best and bravest men without achieving any result or carrying us any nearer to our goal.'[29]

Well, it is clear to Ashmead-Bartlett and these senior officers. As a matter of urgency, Hamilton must be replaced and with him the entire cabal of incompetent senior officers around him, led by the execrable Braithwaite. If this is sedition, so be it.

LATE JULY 1915, THE WORD COMES THROUGH

At last!

For both Colonel Brazier and Lieutenant Throssell, it is the news they have long been waiting for. After months of waiting, of festering, they and 80 reinforcements from the 10th Light Horse are to go to Gallipoli, to rejoin the main body of the Regiment. With a song in their hearts, their eyes on the prize – *Gallipoli!* – they catch the train to Alexandria and are soon on the blue waters of the Mediterranean, heading north.

LATE JULY 1915, THE HEIGHTS OF ANZAC, NOT THE WAY WE DO IT IN FRANCE, OLD BOY

And here now is General Sir Frederick Stopford, the Commander of the three freshly arrived divisions of the IXth Corps, 61 years old and in poor health, come to survey for the first time the shores upon which his forces must shortly storm.

Despite a military career stretching back to the Grenadier Guards in 1871, the Egyptian and Sudan campaigns in the 1880s and the Ashanti Campaign of 1895, before rising to the lofty position of commanding the first home-defence army, he has never actually led men in battle.

Never mind.

On this hot morning, it is at Stopford's specific request that Birdwood takes him to the northern heights of Anzac Cove, from where he can best survey it. He needs to know just what his soldiers will be facing on first landing in terms of both natural and Turkish defences. The old man – and he looks old, make no mistake – surveys the scene for over a minute before giving his preliminary verdict. 'I like this,' he says, 'better than I thought I should.'

'Of course you do,' General Birdwood replies, 'and if you will take my advice I feel confident you will get right through. There are no continuous trenches – only short lengths. If you will land on a broad front, with every unit going forward at once, you will turn every existing trench. On the whole of that front we think there are no more than 1,000 men of the Turkish Gendarmerie. Land, as I did, just before dawn. The moon will be just right, and the men can't lose their way.'

At first, Stopford seems keen on this proposal, but then offers, 'My men have done no night work.'

'Nor had mine – and you have a week before you to practise them on the islands, where there is country very similar to this. Give them plenty of night practice, and make sure every officer knows his objective, and you can't fail!'[30]

'What about the preliminary bombardment?' one of Stopford's Brigadier-Generals, Hamilton Reed, VC, asks. 'We never attack without it in France.'

'In France, yes – but here, no. What have you to bombard? Your one great chance of success lies in surprise, which any bombardment would destroy.'[31]

Reed looks far from convinced. That is *not* the way they do it in France.

Having been briefed by General Hamilton on his desires, Birdwood tries to impress upon these senior officers the need to push quickly inland once the landing is done and secure the ridges – as the Turks will be certain to move their forces there quickly, just as had happened at Cape Helles and Anzac Cove – but they don't seem particularly convinced of that, either.

Hopefully it will all work out.

EARLY AUGUST 1915, ABOVE ANZAC COVE, SUSPICIONS ARE RAISED

Colonel Şefik, the 27th Regiment's Commander, is one of the first to notice it. Having been at the frontline since day one, he is well equipped to notice changes to the enemy's rhythms, and never has he seen activity like this. There is such an increase in traffic in Anzac Cove, with ever more men and munitions coming and going – but mostly coming – that it is ever more obvious the enemy is planning some kind of imminent major attack.

General Liman von Sanders for one is not surprised, having received a report a fortnight earlier that 'spoke of the concentration of 50,000 to 60,000 men on the island of Lemnos alone and gave the number of warships and transport vessels there as 140'.[32]

This had been followed up on 22 July with an even starker warning from German Field Army Headquarters: 'From reports received here it is probable that at the beginning of August a strong attack will be made on the Dardanelles, perhaps in connection with a landing in the Gulf of Saros or on the coast of Asia Minor. It will be well to economize ammunition.'[33]

Von Sanders tells all of his commanders on the Peninsula to 'be vigilant and ready to fight at any moment, above all, after midnight and at dawn'.[34] As to exactly where the enemy will strike, rumours swirl, and von Sanders and his senior officers shuffle their units accordingly, massing their troops, many newly arrived, at the spots where the invaders are most likely to try to break through or attempt a new landing. Structural defences are improved, including placing ever more heavy logs over the forward trenches, covered by a thick layer of dirt, as protection against a barrage – of course leaving loopholes in the parapets so the soldiers can continue to fire at the enemy trenches.

Colonel Fahrettin, General Esat's Chief of Staff, has noted that something strange is going on at the Old Number Three Outpost, which sits at the seaward end of one of the spurs above Sazli Gully between Anzac and Suvla Bay. At around 9 pm, regular as clockwork, an enemy ship has been shining its searchlight on, and shelling, this spot before directing similar fire to Table Top Hill just to the north. Colonel Fahrettin orders the men at the outpost – the majority of whom have taken to sheltering at the rear of the position during the attacks, leaving the trenches virtually unmanned – to be 'cautious and awake . . . It is clear that new enemy forces are on their way.'[35]

AFTERNOON, 5 AUGUST 1915, A MOB OF NEW ARRIVALS AT ANZAC

Abdul's at it again. Upon hearing the news that Warsaw has fallen to the might of the German Army, on this morning they put up placards in their front trenches reading, in 'French' and 'English', **WARCHEUVE EST TOMBE, LA CHUTE DE VARCHORD**, and **VARSAW ASH FALLIN**.[36]

'Well,' says one Anzac sentry, as he lines up his rifle on the poles supporting the notices, 'let's see if we can't make his notice fall too.'[37] Within seconds, the notices **ASH FALLIN** too!

And now the new recruits are arriving. For starters, there are the newly arrived British soldiers of the IXth Corps' 13th Division, now on loan to Birdwood's ANZAC, who've arrived at Anzac Cove for the August Offensive. Smuggled in on the nights of 3, 4 and 5 August, so as not to arouse the suspicion of the Turks, and secreted in freshly excavated catacombs, trenches and dugouts, they seem little more than boys, and weedy ones at that. 'Poor little chaps,' Bean writes, 'they struck me as wretched little specimens of men – dirty, skinny, rather spiritless.'[38] (Ashmead-Bartlett agrees, noting of other new 'Kitchener Mob' arrivals, 'This 11th Division of Kitchener's New Army does not impress one too favourably. Many of the men are a weedy-looking lot – thin, narrow-chested, and small.')[39]

The exception are the newly arrived Australian reinstoushments – clearly well fed from the comparatively sumptuous fare in the camps in Egypt – and frequently all but jumping out of their skin in their eagerness to see action, to be part of the war, to be blooded, to not miss out.

Answering to the latter description is Hugo Throssell, who, at last, joins the rest of the 10th Light Horse on Russell's Top and Walker's

Ridge, where he is immediately embraced by his brother Ric – promoted to *Sergeant*, now, if you please – and buried in the bear hugs, handshakes and back-slapping of so many of his comrades, whom he has not seen for nigh on three months. Some of them he barely recognises, and he is deeply grieved to note the ones who are missing. Still, the only person who may possibly outdo him in his enthusiasm to be here is the man over there puffing contentedly on his pipe, Colonel Noel Brazier, who has preceded Throssell by a few days – 'looking as fat as a whale and fit as a fiddle'.[40]

Only shortly after setting foot on the sacred shores, the Colonel hears that he has arrived just in time for a major action that the 10th Light Horse is to take part in.

Action, at last!

6 AUGUST 1915, ABOVE ANZAC COVE, PUMP PRIMED ON BIRDIE BULL

Something *is* going on, Mehmet!

From on high the Sari Bair Range, five transports are spotted off the beaches by the alert Turks and there is a mass of movement at the piers. Streams of donkeys burdened with ammunition boxes are soon seen trudging up the hills towards the frontlines, while the new troops beetle about below.

Turkish artillery opens fire onto the beach.

—

Down at the docks at Imbros, Ellis Ashmead-Bartlett is there as the newly arrived troops of the 11th Division pile into the new 'beetle' style lighters – self-propelled, armour-plated landing craft, each holding 500 men, and so-called because of being painted black and having ramp arms that look like antennae – that will carry them into Suvla Bay, 'a new battleground on bloodstained Gallipoli'.[41]

'To me it was a sad, almost pathetic spectacle,' writes the veteran correspondent. 'How few have any realisation whatsoever of what modern war is like? How many who are now embarking, without a thought to the future, will be dead before the sun rises again?'[42]

Who can begin the August Offensive by making the first diversionary attack on the heavily entrenched Turks at Cape Helles? None other than some of the remains of the 29th Division – the very force that have already been so devastated by their battles here, dating from their first landing from *River Clyde* on 25 April. Since that time, their casualty rate has been nearly 50 per cent, but that matters little. For it is as in days of yore:

> Once more unto the breach, dear friends, once more;
> Or close the wall up with our English dead![43]

Late in the afternoon, the whistle blows and they charge forth into withering fire laid down by four Turkish divisions. Twice the Allies secure some Ottoman trenches; twice the counter-attacks obliterate their gains.

Worse, for such a sacrifice, it entirely fails as a diversion. At Fifth Army HQ, General von Sanders receives a message that the enemy has 'failed to gain a foothold', and acts accordingly.[44] He leaves his troops exactly where they have been.

At Anzac Cove, the situation is primed. That morning, General Birdwood has injected his ANZAC forces with a good dose of 'Birdie Bull'. This day will see nothing less than our second advance on our way to Constantinople . . . The whole world has now heard of the action of the Australians and New Zealanders . . . and we therefore have to act up to an extraordinarily high standard to live up to our reputation.

They will advance on a wide front, Birdwood tells them, and must take the Turkish trenches and hold them against counter-attack.

Remember, men, the order of the day must be 'shove on and keep shoving on' until we are in complete

`possession of the heights above us, when we hope we`
`will have the Turks at our mercy.`

`We know that we have established a moral superi-`
`ority over the Turks . . . Though they are terrified`
`of the Australian and New Zealand soldiers in the`
`open . . .`[45]

The timing of the Lone Pine attack is particularly important. General Birdwood has scheduled it for 5.30 pm – several hours before General Stopford's forces make their landing at Suvla Bay – so that, 'getting the Turkish reserves deeply committed on my own front, the opposition at Suvla would be proportionately weakened'.[46]

The previous evening, some of the senior officers of the 1st Brigade's 3rd Battalion – who, like all in 1st Brigade, are thrilled they are now going to have the chance to prove themselves as the 3rd Brigade had done on the day of the landing, and the 2nd Brigade at Krithia – had discussed at what time on this day the men should have their rum issued. The Colonel had been strong: 'I believe the "issue" will be a good tonic to the men in their present condition, but I do not like the idea of giving it to them just before they go into action. We will have one "issue" in the morning, and the other after the fight is over.' This decision, Charles Bean would proudly note, 'is supported by the medical officer, Capt J. W. B. Bean, and was adopted for the 3rd Battalion'.[47]

That morning – in the first sign that they were about to go into action – soldiers had been issued with a white strip of calico together with a big white patch (remarkably similar to the white armbands previously forced onto those with VD). They had had to sew the strips onto the sleeves of their shirts at the level of their biceps, while the patch had been sewn onto their backs. It is hoped these will help to identify the Australians to each other when the fog of war is at its thickest.

Those men who can, nap. Others stare. Still others sharpen their bayonets with the fervour of those convinced it might be the difference between life and death. The sun shines hotly. The birds are singing. And there are even butterflies.

A few hundred yards away in his dugout, Bean is writing a letter to his parents, telling them that their beloved Jack will be going over the top at Lone Pine shortly:

> We hope that this will be the last big fight and finish the
> business but I rather doubt if we have anything like the
> numbers necessary to make it complete.[48]

The letter finished, Bean is quick to head to the trenches at Lone Pine, where Jack's 3rd Battalion are about to go into action. As he approaches, the great planned bombardment is underway, with both naval and land-based artillery pouring shells down on the Turkish positions. (Moving in towards her old familiar position opposite Gaba Tepe,[49] *Queen Elizabeth* is giving the Turks plenty of Old Harry with her roaring guns.) At the same time, the tunnels that the Diggers have forged in previous weeks even closer to the Turkish trenches are exploded in the hope that it will add to the dust and confusion that the Australians can charge into, as well as the resulting craters providing shelter for the lines of attack.

—

In the foremost Turkish trenches, carnage reigns . . . and rains.

The Turkish trench improvements are proving a diabolical failure. With direct hits, the heavy log roofs are caving in, crushing those below and blocking sections of soldiers off from each other. The few who survive are being 'made crazy by shells detonated in the tunnels'.[50] It is a disaster.

—

Even for the Australian soldiers who are 100 yards back from the barrage, it is hard to bear. By now, the shells are falling so thick and fast it is 'one continuous roar',[51] as it builds towards its planned climax at 5.30 pm.

The Turks, in turn, are dropping shells from field guns and howitzers on the Australian trenches. Many of the Allied reinforcements are desperately shaken by it, but the veterans such as Archie Barwick know to hold their breath as they hear the approaching shell roaring through the air and steady themselves for the coming shock as it explodes. Personally, Archie finds it 'a good plan to open your mouth & stand on your toes when you are expecting a high explosive to land near you, funny as it may seem, it takes a lot of the pressure off you'.[52]

In the trenches 50 yards back, Captain Gordon Carter, with the 1st Battalion, is moving into the reserve position, to follow up the initial assault. Carter is anxious, yes, but also experienced. He has no further doubts about himself, and knows that whatever happens he will be able to rise to it.

Right at the front, in the middle of the tumult, the 3rd Battalion's Private Cecil McAnulty, from Middle Park, Victoria, settles down in the few minutes he's got left before the action and dashes off a quick entry in his diary:

Am now sitting down waiting for the word and taking the chance to write these lines. Our artillery started to bombard their trenches at 4 and will continue till 5[53] when we make the rush. Their artillery are replying now and shells are beginning to rain down on us . . . The fumes are suffocating, the shrapnel is pouring all around us, getting chaps everywhere. This is hell waiting here.

The charge at Lone Pine that Cecil is waiting to take part in is intended to be overwhelming, each of the three battalions launching three waves of soldiers, 200 strong, from the bulge in the trenches right opposite Lone Pine that is the Pimple, almost simultaneously. The first wave will be coming at the Turks from shocking proximity, courtesy of the engineers having dug a secret tunnel that starts from the Pimple and then branches left and right, to form a frontline trench just 40 yards from the Turks. Once the soldiers in there pull away the sandbags and thin layer of earth above them, they will form the first attacking wave. Following fast on the heels of their subterranean mates, the second and third wave, equipped with picks and shovels (as well as rifles), will launch overland at the enemy, about 100 yards opposite, from the Pimple's main fire-trenches.

The tall, red-headed figure you can see there, now approaching? It is Charles Bean, arriving just in time to see the officers walking along the main fire-trench, giving the men their last-minute orders and tips. 'Look out for enemy wire . . .'

'They were chaffing one another,' Bean would recount, 'seemed quite eager to go out and do something . . . I saw not the slightest trace of nervousness. Men all had packs with some sort of tucker or nicknacks in.'[54] They appear like spectators waiting to see a football match.

'*Au revoir*,' says one soldier to his mate, 'meet you over there.'

'So long, Tom,' comes the reply, 'see you again in half-an-hour.'[55]

'Jim here?' asks another soldier, who has been searching from bay to bay of the trenches.

'Right,' a voice calls back.

'Bill, here.' Then Bill says to one of the adjacent soldiers, 'Can you find room for me beside Jim here? Him and me are mates an' we're going over together.'[56]

One soldier from the later lines suddenly comes forward, thrusts a sovereign into the hand of a man about to go and says, 'You go back there and take my place. My mate is here, and I've got to go with him!'[57]

Among them is Fighting Mac, the Salvation Army chaplain with the 4th Battalion – who had previously pulled so many of them out of the brothels and given such thunderingly inspiring sermons – the Reverend William McKenzie. 'Boys,' he says, 'I've preached to you, and I've prayed with you, do you think I'm afraid to die with you? I'd be ashamed to funk it when you're up against it right here.'[58]

A young officer crouching in the corner of the fire-step checks his wristwatch: '5.27. Prepare to go over the parapet.'[59]

Immediately the men in the frontline pull down the top bag of the parapet, to make it easier for them to climb up and over.

Now the officer takes his whistle in his hand. 'Prepare to jump out.'[60]

Now the men jostle a little, as they put their front foot on the fire-step, ready to launch:

I see you stand like greyhounds in the slips,
Straining upon the start. The game's afoot:
Follow your spirit, and upon this charge
Cry 'God for Harry, England, and Saint George!'[61]

– before the 'Starter's three short whistle blasts'.[62]

'!'

'!'

'!'

And now, in selected spots ahead of them, the ground erupts before the Turkish trenches and the men in the forward tunnels burst forth like escapees from a graveyard, closely followed by the next two overland lines.

With a roar, they are all up and over, charging forward, across a front some 200 yards wide, the sun immediately 'pouring golden rays over the ridges and parapets, and gilding the white armbands and the calico square on each man's back . . .'[63] Behind the men as they charge, Fighting Mac walks, carrying a spade with him. He will not kill, but maybe he can help.

Immediately, many of the charging men fall to the blizzard of Turkish bullets, but still the majority make it to their destination, only to scale the enemy parapets and look down to find they can't get into the front trenches, as the log roofs have fallen in. They have become a veritable bunker, with only the loopholes allowing air in and out. This brings a 'check' to the Anzacs' advance.

General 'Hooky' Walker cries out, 'My God, the boys have failed!'[64]

But then the Australians fire into the loopholes, while others try to lift the logs off and jump into the various gaps. Still others jump over the first trench and then down into the second Turkish trench and some of the open communication trenches behind, which will give them access to the first trench.

'No, no they haven't,' General Walker cries, 'I told you so!'[65]

Those first to drop into the openings face almost certain death, because the surviving Turks are waiting for them, but – as is the pattern – there are enough men following up, dodging a few blood-ied figures crawling back to the Australian trenches, that those first defenders are in turn swamped. Within a minute, the trenches at Lone Pine are filled with rolling balls of battle, bouncing back and forth and off into blind saps before bursting back again, a bloody trail marking their course.

—

For the Turkish soldiers of the 47th Regiment who are actually in the trenches facing the attack, the situation is horrifying.

'It was an extraordinary fire,' one officer would recall. 'They began to attack in waves . . . one wave would collapse on us like a wooden fence, and then a new wave would immediately appear . . . can you imagine our Mehmets letting them pass, a new calamity . . . would incessantly appear, and it would be felled.'[66]

So heavily are the Turks firing that many of their rifles are soon overheating, with the grease between the wooden and metal parts sizzling, and the mechanisms seizing up, momentarily allowing the Australians to charge forward with little fire on them. The battle soon becomes 'hand to hand',[67] bayonet to bayonet.

The Turkish 47th Regiment's 1st Battalion, which had started the battle with some 500 men, is down to 33, with 'no officers left', and no contact with regimental command. It's 'truly an apocalypse, an apocalypse indeed'.[68]

Watching events unfold from the east at Kemalyeri – the Turks' dire predicament discernible even behind the huge dust cloud that is the battlefield – Brigadier-General Esat orders Colonel Mustafa Kemal at Battleship Hill to have Major Zeki and his 1st Battalion of the 57th Regiment, which has stood in reserve, 'move at once to Lone Pine'.[69]

—

The tide of battle at Lone Pine continues to ebb and flow, crash and career, from trench to trench, leaving great gouts of blood in the now red clay as it goes.[70] In the murderous maze of trenches, one cannot be sure who is enemy and who countryman. At first, the Australians know not to attack anyone displaying a flash of white. But then the canny Turks start to strip the white off dead Australians and put it on themselves. And so the Diggers are ordered to remove their own. Screams, curses in different languages and universal death rattles fill the night.

Archie Barwick is right in the thick of it and will never forget how some of his comrades willingly go *to certain death*. As they chase one group of Turks round a little sap, the Turks disappear around a bend. All of the Australians know that the first man around the corner will die. But, as Archie would record, one of their number *threw himself fair at them & the six fired together & fairly riddled him with bullets. That was our chance & we [got] into them & it was all over in a few minutes*.[71]

Another group of Australian soldiers are feeling their way forward along a trench when they hear unidentifiable voices far ahead. Perhaps their own? Or Turks? One Australian soldier volunteers to go ahead.

A very short time later, he is back, and makes his report. 'They are Turks all right,' he says softly, 'and they got me in the stomach.'[72] With which, he continues to talk quietly for a few minutes before sitting down . . . and then lying down. And then he stops talking, and starts shaking . . . off this mortal coil . . . before suffering spasms of great agony. And now this mother's son is still.

—

From the Turkish side, Major Zeki and his battalion are the nearest available reserve and have been quickly called on. They march silently into Owen's Gully, just below the battle, and which in the last two months has been a safe zone for them, but . . . no more. As soon as his troops turn into the gully, they come under heavy fire from the enemy up ahead.

Scrambling on, leading his soldiers, Major Zeki meets a Battalion Commander of the 47th, who looks a frightened shadow of a man. Fresh from battle, he has fled down from the destruction above, shattered, scattered and scared.

'What has happened?' Major Zeki implores.

'We're lost, we're lost, we're lost,' the man mutters repeatedly, his tormented eyes darting all around, as he constantly looks over his shoulder to see if he is pursued, if the enemy have broken through yet.

'I want you to tell me what the situation is and what you wish me to do,' Zeki says firmly.

The Commander gathers himself just enough to say, 'The situation is critical. My whole battalion remained in shelter of the trenches after the bombardment. I'm waiting here for the remnants of it – I have no-one now under my command. If any survive, I'm here to stop them and take them under my command.'[73]

Looking around, Zeki appreciates the scale of damage that's already been done on Lone Pine. Looking at this shell-shocked commander, waiting here for troops that can surely never come, he resolves to seek out the 47th Regiment Commander, Major Tevfik.

'Where is the Commander of your regiment?'

'He has withdrawn into the zone of the 125th Regiment. He is at the rear shoulder of that hill, where he can see well what is happening.'[74]

Swiftly Major Zeki's troops move on.

—

Captain Gordon Carter and his men of the 1st Battalion also move forward, ready to make their assault. To Carter's amazement, when the time comes to charge over open ground, they suffer few casualties, as the Turkish fire has died down by now, and they are soon able to join their comrades pushing forward in the Turkish trenches, battling the Turks as they go and trying to ignore the puddles of Australian blood that abound. It is going to be a long night, for those that make it to sun-up.

Two hours after the attack at Lone Pine has begun, with the situation still not clear, Charles Bean, worried about Jack, decides to head to the northern section of the perimeter, where the Breakout is due to be made. On the way, he comes across some of Jack's comrades, who tell him that his brother has been shot once more! Mercifully, however, again it looks like he is going to live, as instead of a shot to the head, heart or abdomen – all of which are near-certain death sentences – he has suffered a shrapnel wound to his right hand and wrist, badly shattering them. The main thing is he has been safely evacuated to the beach.

Strange. In peacetime Australia, Charles Bean would have been devastated to hear such news. In wartime Gallipoli, there can be little doubt that Jack is one of the lucky ones, because it will get him out of the firing line, and Charles Bean is proud that the wound has come honourably.

By 8.30 pm, the situation at Lone Pine is partly stabilised, as the Australians are in possession of the first three rows of Turkish trenches, and have been able to place heavy sandbag walls between themselves and the now massing Turks on the other side, yet no one is under any illusions. Everyone knows the battle will continue as the Turks launch counter-attack after counter-attack, and the call for stretcher-bearers is heard throughout a black night now shattered by the roar of rifles and machine-guns, the screams of dying men, and the regular explosions of artillery shells and bombs.

Though pleased so far with what has been achieved, General Birdwood is shocked at the number of deaths: 'God forbid that I should ever again see such a sight as that which met my eyes when I went up there: Turks and Australians piled four and five deep on one another. The most magnificent heroism had been displayed on both sides.'[75]

(The danger of the position is emphasised for General Birdwood when he foolishly puts the top of his head above the parapet for the split instant necessary for a Turkish bullet to give him a new part in his hair. 'It was lucky,' he would reminisce ever afterwards, showing off his scar, 'that I am not a six-footer.')[76]

As to the carnage before him, Charles Bean feels the same as Birdwood. 'The dead lay so thick,' he would write later, 'that the only respect which could be paid to them was to avoid treading on their faces.'[77]

That rather wistful figure strolling along the beach at Imbros? It is General Hamilton, gazing contemplatively at the last of the departing flotilla bearing the 11th Division, gliding away in the gathering dusk, to soon be swallowed by the gloom. 'The empty harbour frightens me. Nothing in legend stranger or more terrible than the silent departure of this silent Army, K.'s new Corps, every mother's son of them, face to face with their fate.'[78]

Chapter Sixteen

'PUSH ON!'

The extreme difficulty of the ground which the Left
Assaulting Column [which included Monash's 4th
Brigade] was to traverse can hardly be exaggerated.
It is mad country . . . The 4th Brigade, through
no fault of its own, was unquestionably in the
worst state of all the ANZAC brigades.[1]
James Rhodes, Gallipoli

I am sorry, boys, but the order is to go.[2]
Colonel Brazier

6 AUGUST 1915, NORTHERN ANZAC, THE SILENT MARCH TO THE NORTH

As the bloody distraction at Lone Pine continues, the four columns of troops who have been secreted in the gullies and on the slopes of spurs hidden from the Turks at Anzac are finally ready to launch their left-hook advance. It is not going to be easy, as this is the roughest of terrain in the entire Anzac sector. In fact, its rambling ravines and steep cliffs provide such a strong natural defence, Turkish soldiers are only thinly scattered at fortified outposts and unconnected sections of trenches instead of forming a continuous frontline, as with the southern two-thirds of their Anzac front.

At 8.30 pm, the Right Covering Force – made up of men from the New Zealand Mounted Rifles Brigade – are the first to move out, and

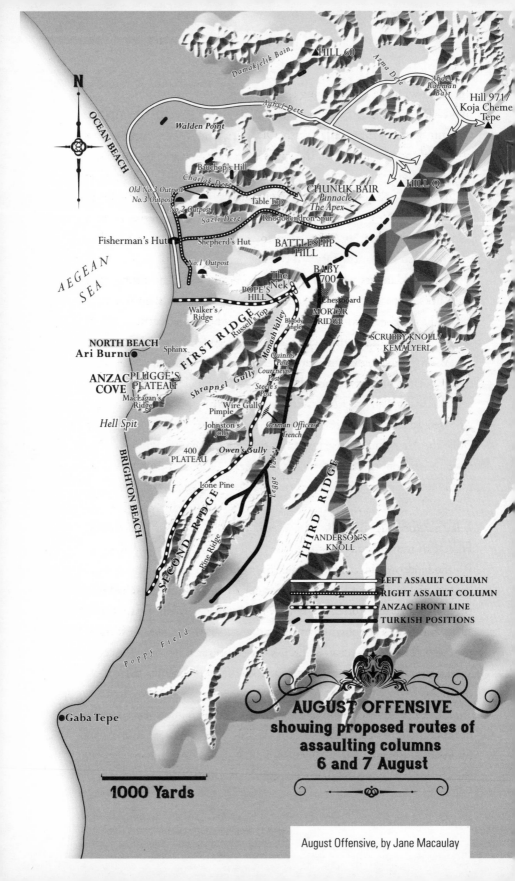

AUGUST OFFENSIVE, by Jane Macaulay

they start winding inland along the gullies just to the south like a silent snake. Their job is to clear the way for the much larger Right Assault Column and capture the Turkish Old Number Three Outpost, plus other high points that lie on the spurs on the way up to Chunuk Bair.

As they go – just as has happened every night for a while now at around 9 pm – the destroyer *Colne* sails close to the shore and begins to shell that Old Number Three Outpost. Used to it by now, the Turkish soldiers there retreat as per custom to their shelters at the rear, while only 40 or so stay in the forward trenches.

The Aucklanders who are assigned to attack this, the strongest of the Turks' outposts, arrive as the shelling pours down, their footsteps muffled by the bombardment. The ruse has worked perfectly.

As planned, the shelling ceases at exactly 9.30 pm, at which point it is the Aucklanders themselves who explode, charging forward with a cheer straight at the Outpost. Some of them veer off, hooking around to the rear to bayonet any resistant Turks, while throwing bombs after those who flee. In short order, 100 Turks lie dead and a few are taken prisoner, while the Aucklanders have lost only seven men with 15 wounded.

This section of the Right Covering Force has accomplished its mission. The other hills and posts are not yet taken, however. And though the New Zealanders are progressing towards the objective, any delay is worrying. Time is of the essence, so that the Right Assault Force can move through here in the dead of night on their way up to Rhododendron Ridge and Chunuk Bair beyond.

Just an hour after their Shaky Islander comrades have marched out, the Left Covering Force, made up of British soldiers, begins its own silent march further northward along the beach, with the same kind of task – to clear the way for the Left Assault Column.

A right hook, followed by a left hook. It *must* destroy the enemy defences!

It has already been a long day for General Otto Liman von Sanders, but it is about to become longer still. At around 9 pm, he receives a telephone call informing him that 'from the beach at Ari Burnu [Anzac] the enemy is moving northward along the coast . . .'[3]

Immediately he calls Colonel Fevzi at Saros, some 35 miles to the north-east, telling him to ready his battalion: 'Be prepared and make ready to march at once.'[4]

Around 9.30 pm, Bean is still eager to get to the northern section of the perimeter, where the true thrust of the night is due to take place. It is from here that General Godley is to command the Right and Left Assault Columns, who are about to start their advance to seize the high ground of the Sari Bair Range.

The Right Assault Column is made up of men of the New Zealand Infantry Brigade, under the overall command of Brigadier-General Francis Johnston, who . . . is a growing problem. Just how this alcoholic manages to access a seemingly never-ending supply of drink is never clear. What is apparent is that it now seems to be affecting his decision-making, or lack thereof.

'He sat for hours in absolute silence,' his staff officer, Brigade-Major Arthur Temperley, would later write of Johnston's behaviour over this time period, 'he was frequently barely coherent and his judgement and mind were obviously clouded.'[5]

And yet never do his men need more leadership than tonight. The job of the New Zealanders is to move up past the outposts already secured by their comrades of the Right Covering Force, and then on to Rhododendron Ridge and all the way to the heights of Chunuk Bair, likely against heavy resistance.

At their heart lies the Wellington Infantry Battalion, under the strong if gruff leadership of that fine officer from Taranaki, Lieutenant-Colonel William Malone. As he had recorded in his diary two days earlier, though, he is worried as to the state of his men's health. 'We are pleased to be moving, but the men are rundown and the reinforcement men are in a big majority, so I'm not too sanguine about what we can do.'[6]

And the men of the other battalions are in not much better shape. Their numbers are dangerously low, and many are sick and broken, any trace of their joy for life now lost from their vacant stares and shuffling gait.

Malone is aghast that Johnston would volunteer such men for this momentous task, even when Birdie himself has 'said the [New Zealand Infantry Brigade] had had so much hard work and had been so knocked about that it should not go out'.[7]

Beyond that, Johnston's whole manner worries Malone. 'He is too airy for me . . . He seems to think that a night attack and the taking of entrenched positions without artillery preparations is like "kissing one's hand". Yesterday he burst forth: "If there's any hitch I shall go right up and take the place myself." All, as it were, in a minute and on his own! He says, "There's to be no delay." He is an extraordinary man. If it were not so serious, it would be laughable. So far as I am concerned, the men, my brave gallant men, shall have the best fighting chance I can give them . . . No airy plunging . . .'[8]

Malone also fears deeply that his own fate may not be a happy one. Just an hour before he starts the night advance, he had written a letter to his beloved wife, Ida, in case anything should happen to him:

I expect to go through all right but, dear wife, if anything untoward happens to me, you must not grieve too much, there are our dear children to be brought up. You know how I love and have loved you.[9]

And now, as he is to move out, he cannot help but write once more, signing his letter:

My candle is all but burnt out and we will soon be moving. So good night, dearest one. With all my love. Your lover and husband. XXX.[10]

As Charles Bean arrives at General Godley's HQ at Number Two Outpost, the men of the Left Assault Column are on the move. They are being led out by Brigadier-General Monash's 4th Brigade, who are said to be 'the least healthy of all the Australian brigades'.[11]

As soldiers march by outside, all their bayonets 'wrapped in hessian to obviate glint' for when the sun rises[12] – *far and near, low and louder, on the roads of earth go by* – Bean lopes over to where Godley is standing and hears him ask one of his officers, 'Can I tell Army Corps that both the Brigades have cleared this place?'[13]

The officer goes outside to check, and comes back to report that the troops passing are those of Brigadier-General Monash, his stretcher-bearers, to be precise.

'Then I can say both Brigades are past here?'

'No, no, Sir, the Indian Brigade is only arriving.'

'What, are they behind Monash? Good God!'

'But that was the order they were told to go in, Sir.'[14]

Godley gives a small nod, as if to say 'very well then'.

Bean is stunned. This is the General in charge of the whole operation, and yet on something as basic as which order his troops are due to leave in, he is mixed up?

Bean needs a drink, and perhaps Godley does too, for the two share some of the General's whisky before Bean heads off into the darkness with the column of Indian soldiers, eager to catch up with Monash. As he goes, Godley calls after him in his plummy English accent, 'Tell him to hurry up.'[15]

The lanky journalist lets out a small, almost defeated sigh as he walks further into the darkness. Striding past the column of troops, whose movement is slowed by the gear on their backs, he has not gone far when he hears shots coming from a different direction, from a long way off.

From the direction of Suvla Bay?

Likely. The landing must have begun . . .

And then come more shots, from much nearer, as the Turks gather themselves to strike back at the columns of Anzacs heading up the gullies. As Brigadier-General Monash, with his troops up ahead, records, 'We had not gone half a mile when the black tangle of hills between the beach road and the main mountain-range became alive with flashes of musketry, and the bursting of shrapnel and star shell, and the yells of the enemy and the cheers of our men as they swept in, to drive in the enemy from molesting the flanks of our march.'[16]

As the firing goes on, Bean continues to move forward regardless, when suddenly he feels 'a whack, like a stone thrown hard, in the upper part of the right leg'.[17]

Has he been hit by a stray bullet or piece of shrapnel?

Very likely. But there doesn't seem to be any blood, so perhaps whatever it was has not penetrated – or maybe the whisky has numbed him to everything. And yet, a short time later when he again puts his right hand inside his pants, it comes away sticky and greasy. He *has* been hit, and the wound is bleeding profusely.

Very reluctantly – like brother Jack, aware that it could have been much worse – he leaves Monash and his men to their own devices and starts limping back, to either get to an aid post, where he can get some treatment, or to his dugout, which lies just near the Headquarters of ANZAC Commander General Birdwood.

10 PM, 6 AUGUST 1915, AND SO IT BEGINS AT SUVLA BAY

There are thousands of them.

Aboard a silent armada of ten destroyers with ten of the black 'beetle lighters' in tow, 11,000 soldiers of the first wave of General Stopford's 11th Division are now approaching the shores of Suvla Bay. The landing is under the control of Commander Edward Unwin of *River Clyde* infamy, and how can he not help but compare this time to the last? If only they had had these beetles at Cape Helles.

Still, despite there being a strong force now lining up on the destroyer to climb down into superb landing craft with drawbridges that will drop as soon as they hit the shore, there is some nervousness among these raw soldiers of Kitchener's all-volunteer New Army as to what to expect from their first action. Their anxiety is heightened, as one soldier would recall, by looking at his own ship's superstructure: 'There were patches on her squat funnels and bullet-holes on her bridges. And what were those dark stains upon her decks?'[18]

Now if the first of the 5000 British soldiers in the beetles don't quite 'storm ashore', at least they come on like a very strong breeze, and there is actually no reason to do anything else. Compared to what had been waiting for them at Cape Helles, the Turkish defences in these parts really are minimal. In fact, these men come 'ashore . . . on undefended beaches'.[19]

Atop the two hills overlooking Suvla Bay – Hill 10 at the east and Lala Baba at the south – the 1500-odd men of two Ottoman Gendarme Battalions first shoot up flares to illuminate those now crammed onto the beach and then open fire. Hill 10 pours down mortar shells, while those on Lala Baba fire their rifles.

Though Lala Baba falls quickly, Hill 10 does not. Like the mouse that scares the elephant, the Turks manage to keep up heavy fire on these strangely quiescent British troops, who display no dash, no daring, no derring-do. In the darkness, there is chaos on the heavily crowded beach as units are mixed up, and the shots that are fired by the few Turkish defenders all seem to find their mark. No one on the beach seems to know which hill they are meant to take and what their precise orders are. In the hurly-burly of it all, the general plan – to push east into the hills and then south to join hands with elements of the Left Assault Column trying to dominate the peaks of the Sari Bair Range – is lost sight of.

General Stopford? He is aboard his sloop, HMS *Jonquil*, somewhere well offshore. (In fact, far enough offshore that they can hear very little firing and assume that the forces have landed unopposed. General Stopford goes to sleep.)

———

As the beachhead at Suvla fills with more and more men, the Commander of the Bursa Gendarme Battalion rides up to Hill 10, from where, by field telephone, he begins to furnish Lieutenant-Colonel Wilmer, who commands all Turkish forces in the Suvla Bay area, with blow by blow descriptions of events as they unfold. Immediately Wilmer deploys two companies and a battalion to consolidate their position on the hill. He soon has about 3000 men to hold what looks like tens of thousands of men crowding onto the beach.[20]

Among the Turkish command elsewhere, things are frantic. Obviously what is needed are reinforcements to get to both Suvla Bay and Sari Bair. And quickly.

—

Meanwhile, the Wellington Mounteds of the Right Covering Force are winding their way carefully up Sazli Gully towards the Table Top. Their progress is steady but slow – certainly slower than headquarters' ludicrously optimistic timetable has allowed for. As surprise is of the essence, they are forbidden to fire their weapons. Slashing bayonets are the order of this murderous night against the Turks they come across, many of whom they find asleep before being sent to their eternal rest.

The close darkness, for all the problems it poses, is still welcome to the soldiers – especially now, as they find themselves climbing up a particularly hairy cliff. With any moonlight upon them at all, they would be easy pickings, clinging to the side of this razor-edged precipice with God knows how many Turks above ready to destroy them if only they spot them. Yes, the darkness brings solace, until suddenly . . . a flash! From above, a Turkish flare soars high across the sky in a graceful arc, briefly illuminating the soldiers' grim faces to each other as they hug the mountain, before it lands on the left of the ridge above them and sets fire to a knot of scrub, dried by the long summer days, and casts a dangerous glow that exposes their advance. Have they been spotted?

The men stiffen and hug the cliff even closer, their limbs frozen in awkward positions, waiting for a hail of fire. But still there is none.

As the fire dims, they start to climb once more, reaching the Table Top to find 'a small scrub-covered plateau about an acre in extent' virtually undefended.[21] The few Turkish soldiers who are found are quickly bayoneted.

As midnight approaches, the men have secured all the trenches on Table Top – 'the steepest of all the enemy's outposts'[22] – and now begin the long process of establishing small posts of soldiers along the ridge-line to secure it, all the way up to the head of the gully that leads to Rhododendron Ridge. So far, they have lost only four men, with nine wounded.

Their comrades in the main Right Assault Column, still below them, moving up along the Sazli Gully, are making slower progress . . . In the mess of ravines and clefts, not only do they encounter wire entanglements and small parties of Turks who have escaped the sweep done by the covering forces, but the long snake of troops also keeps breaking up at various points. Sections of men advance, before halting while men are sent back to get word from the main party. As one private recalls in a letter a month later, 'It was what we, in a joke, called a concertina march – moving and stopping – moving and stopping; oh, it was deadly.'[23]

Lieutenant-Colonel Malone, who had his doubts from the outset – 'I do feel the preparation as regards our Brigade anyway is not thorough'[24] – continues to coax his men forward.

On the cliff by Walker's Ridge, just near the Nek, sit two sets of brothers – Hugo and Ric Throssell – with their close friends, the Chipper brothers, Ross and Lindsay. All four had been at Prince Alfred College together, been farmers together, joined the 10th Light Horse together, and in just a few hours, they know, they will be jumping the bags together. Time for a slug or two of whisky, and a chat. Hugo, as is his way, has 'stole a bottle from Major Todd', and as the four settle down for what Hugo records as 'our 1st taste of whisky',[25] they watch the shadow of the warships down at Anzac Cove firing their guns onto the Turks . . . while talking about school days, the cricket and football matches . . . common friends . . . and the charge at dawn.

The mood is tense, but . . . companionable. If they are to go over the top, there is no one they would rather be going with. Finally, though, it is time. Just maybe, they can get some shut-eye before the charge. Together, they stand up, shake hands and wish each other all the best.

See you tomorrow morning. Hopefully. Brothers-in-arms, they take their leave.

—

At 1.45 am, as more and more reports stream in from Suvla and Anzac's northern sector, Liman von Sanders orders Colonel Fevzi of the Saros Group, who was warned some hours ago to ready his men, to force-march one of his regiments to Suvla Bay. *Çabuk!* Quickly!

If ever the British forces break through here, the results will be dire for the Turks.

—

In the Left Assault Column trying to get to Hill 971, Brigadier-General John Monash had known this would be a difficult exercise for his 4th Brigade, but not *this* difficult. In bright sunshine, with well-surveyed maps, it might – just might – be possible for healthy soldiers to traverse these endless gullies, the scrub, the hills, the cliffs, the slippery slopes upon which an acrobat would find it hard to stand. In the darkness, however, by the pale light of a partisan Turkish crescent moon that has now risen against them, with confused guides and officers, hopeless maps, and mostly sick soldiers carrying heavy packs and rifles, heading to a destination where, if they get there in time, their reward will probably be a fusillade of fire from on high, it is nigh on impossible. When the moon disappears behind the clouds, however, it gets even worse, and the men strike a pace slower than people shuffling towards a widow, outside a church, at a funeral.

As Monash will record in his diary, 'It was a black gloomy night and one could not see 10 yards ahead.'[26] They stumble, they stagger, they fall, they plummet, they curse and cry as at one point their native 'guides' – 'two Greek farmers who were supposed to know the country'[27] – even steer them into what one says is a short cut. And though it is a shorter route, it is also a blind, narrow ravine, where Turkish snipers fire at them from on high. Strong fire, too, which suggests their covering force has not done a thorough sweep of the area before them.

Some push on, but for many there is no way out but to go back the way they came and look for another way around. Whichever way they go, however, it seems there are pockets of Turks firing down on them. As one of Monash's Battalion Commanders would later recall, the men were clambering over 'rough broken stony ridges, densely covered with low prickly undergrowth, in which the Turks had taken cover and were obstinately disputing every yard of our advance'.[28]

Many of the 29th Indian Brigade too have lost their way. They are scattered in the deep gullies at the foot of Chunuk Bair and Hill Q, some far south of their intended route.

Those in the Right Assault Column are doing a little better, even as they continue to march like a rigid old concertina. They *must* get to the top of Chunuk Bair in time to attack the Turks on Baby 700 from behind, before the Light Horse hurl themselves at the Turks at dawn. All they can do is push on, hoping against hope that they can do it.

By 4 am, the most forward of the New Zealand infantry, the Otago men, emerge onto Rhododendron Ridge, which they know leads up to Chunuk Bair. Yes, those at the front are only half a mile away from the summit, which lies some 600 feet higher, but they needed to have been there an hour ago. Malone and his men, further back in the column, continue their own trudge upwards, hoping to reach the head of the gully before daybreak. Malone is beyond frustrated that they have not been able to move faster. Hopefully, there is still time to call off the Nek attack.

For their part, General Birdwood and Lieutenant-Colonel Andrew Skeen – the key architect of the whole plan – are worried. All night, they have been in touch with General Godley in Number Two Outpost by field telephone, and it is now obvious that Monash and the Indians remain far away from their objectives and will be unable to play a part in the dawn battles to come.

The New Zealanders, meanwhile, have 'by a heroic effort seized the lower part of Rhododendron'[29] but are still well away from taking

Chunuk Bair. This means that the key precondition for launching the attacks due at the Nek, Quinn's and Pope's has not been fulfilled, but Birdwood and Skeen – with General Godley at Divisional HQ pushing hard to *attack*, whatever the circumstances – decide to go ahead anyway. This despite the previous estimation of Birdwood and Skeen that 'an unaided attack' across the Nek would be 'almost hopeless'.[30]

It is now clear to those Anzacs who have survived the night at Lone Pine that the Turkish reinforcements are arriving en masse, as they can *see* the brutes streaming forward in Legge Valley, just as they will soon be apparently arriving in the trenches on Baby 700.

With no word that the attack on the Nek is to be called off, the senior officers of the 3rd Brigade review the plans once more. It is much like the attack made the day before at Lone Pine. From precisely 4 am, a thick naval bombardment will smash their machine-guns and force Johnny Turk to keep his head down. The instant the bombardment stops, at precisely 4.30 am, four successive waves of the Australian Light Horse – with 150 men in each wave – will charge from their own trenches to the defending Turks', just 30 yards away across no-man's-land. The Australians will have no bullets in the chambers, only bayonets and bombs, as the key is not to waste time firing but to get across the ground and *into 'em*.

There will be a gap of two minutes between each wave, and whenever Australian soldiers make it into the Turkish trenches, they are to put up marker flags to indicate which segments have been taken and how far the advance has got.

A simultaneous attack by the New Zealanders towards the rear of Baby 700, while other Australian forces attack from Pope's Hill, will ensure the fracturing of the focus of the Turkish defences – or it is *supposed* to, but it seems the New Zealanders are going to miss the party. True, there are other difficulties with the plan, and, as a matter of fact, Charles Bean would later say that sending men charging along that 40-yard-wide ridge, the Nek, and its sloping sides at trenches situated above them, 'was like attacking an inverted frying pan from its handle'.[31]

Unfortunately for the Light Horse, there is yet another obstacle. The Ottoman soldiers manning the Nek are the well-trained and disciplined men of Colonel Mustafa Kemal's 19th Division. Many of these men have been on the Peninsula since the beginning and, though battle weary, have formidable knowledge of the terrain – and a great eagerness to expel the invaders from their shores.

And they are ready. There will be no surprise.

At 1.10 am, Colonel Şefik had sent a 'secret' message to Blind Halis and the other Battalion Commanders to be ready for an attack:

```
The current situation is of the utmost
importance. The Officers request that
Commanders work tirelessly and observe with
extraordinary care . . . Be on extreme
alert.
Lt Col. Sefik
Commander 27th Regiment³²
```

At 4 am, just as planned, the barrage of shellfire starts to land on the Turkish trenches at the Nek, as the men of the 8th and 10th Light Horse Regiments steel themselves for what is to come, just 30 minutes hence. In the dimness of it all, they can just make out the Nek before them, its foremost trenches merely 50 yards away up a small slope, and behind that the hill of Baby 700, on which whole *tiers* of Turkish trenches are situated, all with guns aimed right at them.

Ideally, the barrage will make the bastards take cover, and yet, despite the bombardment – there is really not much to it, with one man noting in his diary that it is 'desultory' and a 'joke'³³ – there is no sense that the Turks are bothered by it at all. Far from it.

Instead, there is simply a constant rain of bullets on the parapets of the Australian trenches, from both rifles and machine-guns.³⁴ By Brigade-Major Jack Antill's count, 'there must have been a score or more of the latter in action at close quarters, indicating a sure knowledge of our plans'. It is obvious to him, and to others, that the projected attacks are 'foredoomed to failure',[35] and it seems madness to go on with them. And still the machine-guns remain intact, firing on the Australians at will, obviously unaffected by what had been the 'bombardment'.

And so, at least by Antill's later account, in this time 'two urgent telephone messages were sent to divisional headquarters describing the situation, which was stated to be a most serious development and urging the abandonment or postponement of the attack'.[36]

It is to no avail.

For the 'laconic reply' from Godley comes back: 'The attack must proceed according to plan.'[37]

And for the Bullant, that is that. Divisional HQ has given him an order, and it is for him to see it through. (Shades of Alfred, Lord Tennyson: 'Forward, the Light Brigade!/ Was there a man dismay'd?')

After this second refusal to change plans, the men must go out into that withering fire and face certain death. For the vast majority of them, General Hamilton's 'hourglass of eternity' again starts dropping grains of sand that hit like thunder, as every *second* brings them closer to the moment when the first wave must charge out into that fusillade of solid lead.

Can Colonel Alexander White ask his men of the 8th Light Horse Regiment – scheduled to be in the first wave – to go out into it and not go out himself? As the Commanding Officer, normally his role is to stay back, so he can best control his regiment as the fight develops.

But not this time.

This time, he comes to a key decision.

A little after 4.15 am, coatless and perhaps dazed by what he is about to do, he offers his hand to his Brigade-Major. 'Goodbye, Antill,' he says quietly.[38] Colonel White has decided he will personally lead the charge of his men.

Antill is stunned, admiring and disapproving all at once. Colonel White is still a young man, a good man, a married man with a young child. He has everything to live for. There is no expectation that he will lead the charge, and good military reasons for him not to go. And yet he insists, against all efforts from Antill and other senior officers to dissuade him.

Still the grains of sand in the eternity hourglass keep falling, and, with ten minutes to go, Colonel White moves among his brother officers, with his watch in his hand, encouraging them, but certainly not hiding what awaits. 'Men,' he tells them, 'you have ten minutes to live.'[39]

No one moves, no one complains, no one tries to dissuade him. They check their bayonets, look each other in the eyes, shake hands. They are going over the top. With eight minutes to go, Colonel White keeps moving down the line, checking that his men are also ready, calmly talking to as many of them as he can in the time that remains.

'How are you feeling?' he asks Trooper Dave McGarvie, above the constant shattering roar of the bombardment, and the rifle and machine-gun fire.

'We'll do our best, sir,' McGarvie replies.

'I'm sure you will.'[40]

The Colonel moves on.

And then it happens.

The shattering roar of the bombardment stops. In the words of the injured Charles Bean, now near the Sphinx on his way to his dugout at Anzac Cove, it is 'cut short as if by a knife'.[41]

Confused, Colonel White looks at his watch. It is only 4.23 am.

Among all the officers in the Australian trenches, there is confusion. All of them know that the bombardment should continue until 4.30 am, but now, unaccountably, it has stopped – with the sudden silence now broken only by scattered rifle shots from the Turks, hitting the very parapets that the Australians are about to climb over.

'What do you make of it?' Lieutenant Wilfred Robinson whispers to Major Tom Redford, a native of Warrnambool. 'There's seven minutes to go.'

'They may give them a heavy burst to finish,' Major Redford replies hopefully,[42] only to be ever more devastated with disappointment and frustration as every passing silent minute proves that hope to be without foundation.

There is all but equal amazement in the Turkish trenches. Having endured many bombardments like this, they know that, usually, no sooner has it ended than the charges begin.

But this time . . . *nothing?*

'Three minutes to go,' Colonel White tells his men quietly,[43] praying that the bombardment will resume. And yet all is near silence.

'Dawn was beginning to steal into the sky behind the Turkish position,' journalist Phillip Schuler will later report. 'A thin, waning moon shed but little light . . . From a forward observation station I noted the battle line spitting red tongues of flame all along to the Nek . . .'[44]

A message now comes to Colonel White from a Sergeant at the far end of the line, worried by the now unrelenting machine-gun fire atop his parapets: 'Does the order still hold good?'

Colonel White does not hesitate and sends back the message: 'Yes.'[45]

———

And now, with two minutes to go, first one, and then another, and then another Turk tentatively lifts his head above the parapet, like rabbits sniffing the wind.

For, unlike their fallen comrades at Lone Pine, who had been 'cooped up in dark trenches that could be demolished with high explosives and set on fire',[46] and with thanks to the prescience of their Regimental Commanders, their trenches are not closed over. (Other trenches with those coverings have frequently caved in and been set alight under the bombardment.)

And so, when there is still no reaction from the Australian trenches, and the mass of Turkish soldiers realise they can look over without having their heads blown off, a handful of them stand up, their rifles forward. Realising there is to be no fire upon them, a few even climb out and sit on the parapets, aiming their rifles forward, with bayonets fixed, allowing yet more Turkish soldiers to take their positions in the trenches and rest their own rifles on the seated men.

Soon the Turks are lined two deep between the machine-gunners

– now aiming their German-made, water-cooled Maxims at the top of the Australian parapet.

All up, some 200 Turkish soldiers are now in the front trench looking through their sights at the Australian trenches just 50 yards away. None are more eager than the survivors of Turkey's 18th Regiment, the same men who had charged across this ground, downhill, on the night of 29 June, to be decimated by these same soldiers who are lining up against them now. Now it is *their* turn, as the wave of Australians prepares to run at them, uphill.

The Turks fire off a few scattered shots, while all of the Turkish machine-guns – including the ones on the Chessboard and Baby 700 – also unleash a quick, chattering burst, just to make sure everything is in working order.

No man running into that solid wall of rifle and machine-gun muzzles could possibly last for long, and for many of the Turks it is inconceivable that the enemy will even try. (And it also seems strange that they are not calling out to their God, the way calling out to Allah is so ingrained on their own side of the trenches.)

Isn't it?

And yet the Turks are more than ready for whatever it is the Australians are about to throw at them, their fingers white on their triggers, just awaiting the last ounce of pressure to fire.

———

In the Australian trenches, the first wave of the 8th Light Horse Regiment are jostling forward in turn, getting into position, shaking each other by the hand, wishing each other luck, looking into each other's eyes, getting their feet onto the firing step. In many of the deepest parts of the trench, 'pegs had been driven into the wall for the men to hold, and niches cut for their feet, so that when the signal came they would be able to spring out in a flash'.[47] Right behind them are the soldiers of the second wave, ready to give them a 'leg-up'.

'Two minutes.'

Now the Turkish firing becomes even more intense, both from their machine-guns and from their three-inch field guns near Hill 60. The shells are now landing so thickly all around the Australians that not only is there a constant barrage of shrapnel overhead, but the salty and acrid fumes from the multiple explosions are so thick many begin to cough.

'One minute.'

No one speaks, bar muttered prayers.

As the second hand creeps towards the 12, the officer next to White brings the whistle up to his lips an instant after taking a long, deep breath. He is looking at White expectantly . . .

. . .

. . .

In the trenches, Major Tom Redford remarks quietly to Lieutenant Robinson, 'See you later, Robbie.'[48]

. . .

. . .

Colonel White's roar – 'Go!'[49] – hangs momentarily suspended, before the piercing whistle shatters the dawn, and up and over they *'GO!'*. As one, the first wave of men of the 8th Light Horse, 150 horse-less horsemen, charge forward, cheering and yelling as they go to . . . 'GIVE IT TO THEM, BOYS'[50] . . . only for those cheers to be drowned out by the instantaneous roars of 500 rifles and five machine-guns. The Turks are firing not only from the Nek but also from Baby 700, behind and above it, a fusillade so heavy and concentrated that the individual stutters combine into one almighty roar as the Maxim machine-guns grow red with rage.

'A thousand sticks rattled across a thousand sheets of corrugated iron at the rate of a thousand revolutions a minute,' as Colonel Noel Brazier would later put it, 'would hardly give a conception of what the sound of the guns was like.'[51]

At the time, the still bleeding Charles Bean is limping along some 600 yards downhill from the Nek, as he tries to get back to his dugout. At the battle's boom, he takes pause, as he hears 'a sudden roar of musketry and machine-gun fire, like the rush of water pouring over Niagara'.[52]

Watching on, Lieutenant-Colonel Şefik feels that 'because of the success their friends had achieved the day before [at Lone Pine], the Australians attacked with greater courage and recklessness . . . The short distance of ground between the two sides was once again covered with the dead bodies of Australia . . .'[53]

On, and on, and on.

'It was one continuous roaring tempest,' Bean would recount. 'One could not help an involuntary shiver – God help anyone that was out in that tornado. But one knew very well that men were out in it – the time put the meaning of it beyond all doubt.'[54]

John Monash and his soldiers of the 4th Brigade are also within earshot at the time, less than 2000 yards away, lost in the kind of steep, narrow gully that this part of the Gallipoli Peninsula so specialises in.

Even closer are Johnston and the men of the Right Assault Column. Of course, they are supposed to have already taken Chunuk Bair and by now be advancing south from there, along the crest of the range over Battleship Hill and towards Baby 700 from the rear. Alas, they have not yet taken that summit, and rather – at Johnston's order – are waiting, many of them slumped in the scrub taking rest and sucking on pebbles to wet their parched whistles.

How many could live in that roaring tempest?

Very, very few.

Most of the Australians, including Colonel White and Major Redford, are cut down within just 'ten paces' of the trenches[55] – as if, in the words of one eyewitness, 'the men's limbs had become string'[56] – their bodies and heads riddled with bullets, and still shaking long afterwards as yet more bullets thud into them.

As if that isn't enough, the Turks are also hurling bombs at them, and now Turkish shells are exploding over no-man's-land.

In the middle of all the carnage, Redford is still alive. Just as he lifts his noggin to look, however . . . another bullet hits him in the head. 'He died with a soft sigh and laid his head gently on his hands as if tired,'

Major William McGrath of the 8th Light Horse Regiment would later tell the others.[57]

Of the 150 Australian soldiers who have gone out, just one, Lieutenant Cyril Godfrey Marsh, a 22-year-old clerk from Victoria, manages to get close to the Turkish trenches, his body visible just before their parapet and the mass of guns that have brought him down. Well, maybe there is one more, though it will forever be unclear. But both at the time, and since, the reports are confused, with poor light, billowing smoke and raining destruction meaning there are few certainties beyond death for the vast majority.

Only in a small dip on the left-hand slope of the Nek are there Australian soldiers who have gone to ground in no-man's-land, not easily seen from the Turkish trenches. Of the rest, the luckiest are those who have been hit and only wounded as soon as they rose, falling straight back into the trenches. They are now joined by others who manage to crawl back – on their bellies, because all who get to their knees are instantly shot – who also fall back into the trenches. Everywhere now there is blood, screams, death rattles, spilling intestines, severed legs, men missing arms with blood pouring forth, cries of anguish, yelling, and still the noise of the bullets and exploding shells . . . all while the second wave starts to takes its place on the fire-step, trying not to put their feet on the dead and dying men who are now thick all around at the bottom of the trenches.

Stretcher-bearers! STRETCHER-BEARERS, NOW!

Who can stop it? Or at least who, with sufficient authority to actually make an impact, can *call* for it to be stopped?

Certainly not Colonel White, who now lies dead, his brain shattered.

By this time, a battery of French three-inch field guns – captured by the Turks from the Serbians in the Balkan War – is pouring shells at the rate of one every ten seconds into the no-man's-land of the Nek.[58]

The affair has taken on a mad, military momentum all its own. For, just as planned, less than two minutes later the whistles blow again, and out charges the second wave, led by Major Arthur Vivian Deeble – with not a single man wavering, though all know their likely fate.

Their only concession to what has happened to the first wave is that many of them now run doubled up, hoping to present a smaller target, their eyes fixed on the massed specks of flame coming from the many muzzles straight in front of them in the near-darkness, as bullets kick up spurts of dirt all around them.

If possible, this time the roar is even greater, the fire and bombs even more concentrated, the devastation even more catastrophic, as the few survivors hurdle the dead and dying and charge forward . . . until, following the lead of Major Deeble, who has miraculously survived, they throw themselves at 'the nearest depression in the ground',[59] as the bullets continue to whine over their heads. There are almost a dozen survivors near to Deeble, and to those who can hear him over the roar, the Major yells, 'Scratch a little cover and wait for the next line!'[60]

And yet, though the official brigade history will record, 'There was no hesitation or falter amongst our officers and men especially of the 8LH,' the fact remains, they 'were practically wiped out'.[61]

Again, it is not even certain that anyone made it to the Turkish trenches to strike a blow, although some would say that out on the right flank, carrying his yellow-and-red marker flag, Sergeant Roger Palmer – who had been wounded shortly after the landing but had escaped from the hospital and stowed away to rejoin the 8th Light Horse – did make it and was even able to wave his flag, before being cut down by a forest of bayonets.

Back in the Australian trenches, chaos reigns. More death, more destruction, more attempts to retrieve those who have been fearsomely wounded within a few yards and are incapable of getting back into the trenches themselves. Further out, some lucky ones are marginally protected by small folds in the ground, others shielded by the bodies of their dead comrades and even Turks killed as much as six weeks earlier. And yet they daren't move, for to do so would instantly bring trained fire upon them. All they can do is lie face-down and hope to be mistaken for the dead. To get up and keep charging would be completely pointless. (No less pointless than it had been to charge in the first place, across that open ground, into that mass of guns, but still . . .)

All around now, the earth is soaked with blood, and the air filled with bullets and shrapnel, wafting smoke and the sound of dying men. Is this not enough?

No. Not for the defenders. To make absolutely sure that there is no chance of any of the attackers getting through, two Turkish field guns from nearby Hill 60 are now brought into play, exploding shells and sending scything shrapnel all over no-man's-land. Many a man who has miraculously survived to this point is now no more than warm flesh getting colder by the second.

Those still surviving, somehow, wait – ready to rise again, should the third wave get to them and go forward from there.

Of the 300 men of the 8th Light Horse Regiment who had charged at the enemy over the last five minutes, there are just 90 left now unscathed. While only 13 would be immediately recorded as 'killed', the 3rd Light Horse Brigade Diary states, 'Probably all those marked "missing" – some 134 brave and true – "were all killed".'[62]

And now the men of the 10th Light Horse start to take their positions, coughing through the thick Lyddite fumes of the exploding shells and making their way forward to the starting line, past streams of their fearfully wounded comrades, and over the dead and dying in the clogged trenches, now muddy with blood. At least this delays their getting to the starting line, allowing a little precious time.

Through the fog, Colonel Brazier raises his periscope to see the devastation on an unimaginable scale. Dead men, dying men, everywhere, all 'lying prone in line in front of the trench about 10 yards away at most'.[63] And, needless to say, no evidence that he can see that any of the men have made it to the enemy trenches. It is hopeless, completely hopeless. And sheer insanity to send the men of the 10th Light Horse to add to the dead.

And there will be no relief from General Birdwood and Lieutenant-Colonel Skeen. When informed of the situation, Skeen comments, 'It is not the Light Horse I am anxious about. I think they will be all right. What I hope is that they will help the New Zealanders.'[64] Alas, the worthy New Zealanders at this point are still climbing towards Chunuk Bair.

One of the Wellington Mounteds, however, who had reached the heights of Table Top in the middle of the night and dug in, is in a position to see what is happening at the Nek, but powerless to do anything. He would write in his diary the next day, 'I saw the whole thing . . . and don't want to see another sight like it. They were fairly mown down by machine guns.'[65]

The appalled Brazier is contemplating just what he should do to stop this obscene and useless slaughter of his men, when he feels a presence at his shoulder. It proves to be a young staff officer from Brigade Headquarters, with a rather terse query.

'Why have you not sent your men over?'[66]

Brazier is equally terse in his reply. 'In view of the scene in front of the trenches and the fire of the enemy machine-guns not having been affected by our artillery,' he barks, 'I do not propose sending my men over until I have reported this fact to H.Q., and I have my orders confirmed.'[67]

And so the hell with it. On the spot, Brazier, who can be as prickly as barbed wire wrapped around a thorn bush, decides to go to Brigade HQ himself and ask General Hughes to call off the attack.

But when Brazier breathlessly arrives, Hughes is not there.

Hughes is not there!

Seeking to witness the charge from a different point, the General has gone across to a bombing emplacement, from where he can safely observe their progress. It leaves Brazier face to face with the man he hates with a passion, who is, nevertheless, the only man who can give the order he needs: Brigade-Major Jack Antill, the Bullant. He is alone.

In clipped tones, straining for calm, Brazier quickly relays what he has seen. 'Nearly all the 8th Regiment did not advance ten yards beyond the trenches. It is possible that they have all been killed . . .'

The Bullant barely blinks.

Brazier spits it out, his words military but his manner mutinous: 'Will you confirm the order to advance?'[68]

Ah, but Antill, out of his depth and desperately clinging to orders in the madness, will not buckle. 'There is a flag on the Turks' trenches,'

Antill insists,[69] before giving the command that makes Brazier red with rage. 'Push on and carry enemy's trenches!'[70]

Straining for control and only just managing it, Brazier implores Antill to listen. 'There is no flag now on the enemy's trenches,' he rasps. 'It is murder to push on!'

'Push on!' Antill roars.[71]

Exasperated, Brazier says, 'Will you please write it on the message . . .' He then adds, through gritted teeth, 'Don't forget I told you.'[72]

With ponderous tread, Lieutenant-Colonel Brazier trudges back to the frontline, where a small posse of officers and men await the decision, one that they know is a matter of life or death . . .

Their own.

'I am sorry, boys,' Brazier tells them heavily, upon arriving, 'but the order is to go.'[73]

The order is to go . . .

The order is to go . . .

And orders are orders.

They are the 10th Light Horse Regiment, you see? These are the orders they have been given to follow, and follow them they must. And they know what it means, all right.

Down in the frontline of the third group to charge, Trooper Harold Rush – a softly spoken farmer from Western Australia, just 23 years old – has fixed his bayonet, steeled himself and put one foot on the firing step ready to spring forward at the whistle. He has time for one last thing. Turning to his mate beside him, he offers his hand and says, 'Good-bye cobber, God bless you.'[74] His cobber takes his hand, and then the two turn, put their feet on the firing step, and start to pray together.[75]

Other men are equally looking each other in the eyes, embracing, shaking hands and wishing each other all the best. 'For bravery,' Brazier would record, 'each line was braver than that which went before. Death stared them in the face and not a man wavered.'[76]

Though Major Tom Todd will be in overall charge of this third wave, out on the right Hugo Throssell steadies and readies, addressing his own men. 'Boys. I am to lead you in a charge. It is the first time I have ever done such a thing, and if any man among you has any misgiving he may go with someone more experienced.'[77]

No one makes the slightest move. If Throssell is to lead them, not a man among them can ask for better than that.

They, too, ready themselves, with Lance-Corporal Sid Ferrier, a 36-year-old building contractor from Western Australia, placing himself right beside Throssell. This time, they will have to climb even more over the parapets, as there is the additional height of an entire layer of dead Australian soldiers that lies before them.

It is 4.45 am.

Now, from the Turkish lines, comes a strange . . . *pleading* . . . call. '*Dur! Dur! Dur!*'[78]

(Stop! Stop! Stop! Do not keep running into our guns, slaughtering yourselves.)

Too late. The whistle blows, and with a cheer for the ages . . . for all eternity . . . the vast wave of Australian humanity rolls out, eager to crash upon the enemy trenches, even as the five Turkish Maxim machine-guns start chattering at the oncoming wave, and some 500 Turkish soldiers all around keep loading again and again the five-bullet magazines into their Mausers and firing into the throng. They just cannot miss.

One more time, the Australian soldiers are cut to pieces, including Trooper Harold Rush and his cobber, shot dead within yards of their trench. If God has blessed either of them, it is not obvious.

In the later, famed words of Charles Bean, 'With that regiment went the flower of the youth of Western Australia, sons of the old pioneering families, youngsters – in some cases two or three from the same home . . .

'Men known and popular, the best loved leaders in sport and work in the West . . . rushed straight to their death.'[79]

Ric Throssell is one of many who goes down within the first few yards, shot through the chest, but still able to call out, 'I'm done – but keep on! Keep on! Keep the ball rolling!'[80]

And yet rare pockets of men from the third line, including those around Hugo Throssell, actually do make it over the first few yards . . .

As there are so few of them, the situation is clearly hopeless, and with another rare burst of sanity amid all the madness, Hugo Throssell shouts, 'Get down!' to the surviving chargers near him,[81] and is immediately obeyed as men hurl themselves to the earth. Miraculously, Throssell has done it at a point where a tiny bit of cover is afforded by a small hollow, which they throw themselves into, lying as flat as they possibly can as bullets whistle overhead. The luckiest ones – and they include Sid Ferrier – are able to get a little added shelter if they have come to ground behind a dead body, and those bodies continue to shake violently as bullets keep pouring in from Turkish gunners.

Still with spirit, Throssell calls out cheerily to those with him, above the ongoing roar of the machine-guns, 'A bob in, and the winner shouts!'[82]

Is he serious?

He's serious!

Well, there's nothing better to do. And so, just as they had done with their beloved drinking game, the soldiers around Throssell – even as the bullets buzz overhead and the shrapnel bursts – start to 'take a number' and try to 'sell a pony'.

But, as later recounted by Sergeant 'Big Mac' Macmillan, from Gippsland, 'I was just beginning to count when a shell came a bit too near. So we got the word to retire, and never knew on whom those drinks were.'[83]

It is a rare moment of levity, and a successful retreat from the carnage, as still out in no-man's-land scenes of agony continue all around.

Over on the left of the assault, Corporal Maitland Hoops hears a ragged voice calling him. It is his close mate, Geoff Howell, bleeding badly and in agony.

'Shoot me, please,' he begs Maitland. 'I am done.'[84]

Maitland cannot bring himself to do it, but, in any case, it is not long before a bullet hits Howell in the head, and he is mercifully no more.

Beside himself with both fury and misery, as the fourth line start steeling themselves to get ready to go over the top, Lieutenant-Colonel Brazier knows he must try once more to stop the charge – and it is all the more urgent when two notes come. One is from Major Tom Todd, the 45-year-old New Zealand-born accountant who has miraculously survived the third charge, and even been able to get this message through, written on the back of a scrap of pink paper, reporting the hideous situation he and the scattering of other survivors have found themselves in, and asking for further orders.

And the second message comes from Major Joe Scott, who is in charge of the fourth line from the far right flank, seeking confirmation of 'all the other reports and asking the advisability of pushing on'.[85]

Brazier goes looking for the only man who can call it off, now that Antill won't – 'as he had never left his trench'[86] – and that is the newly promoted Brigadier-General Frederic Hughes.

He finds Hughes in the bombing emplacement. Saluting, Brazier reports the gravity of the situation, that the first three waves have been massacred for no advance, and that Brigade-Major Antill has ordered them to 'Push on'. But he cannot hold himself in, imploring, in stark terms, for Hughes to call off the attack.

The truth of it, Sir, is that 'the whole thing is nothing but bloody murder'.[87]

In response, the General utters just four words: 'Try Bully Beef Sap.'[88]

Brazier is astounded. The General is referring to a trench off to the right that is likely the only trench within coo-ee that is more suicidal to attack than the Nek.

Can he be *serious?*

Desperately, Brazier tries to point out the insanity of such a move, but is at least relieved that Hughes is relenting on continuing the hopeless attack at the Nek. Brazier trudges back towards his men, entirely intent on doing nothing. At least the fourth line has been saved.

Meanwhile, the men of the fourth line, caught by the force of a military machine that seems to have no off button, move forward to take their place on the firing step, ready to go up and over. On the right flank, Major Joe Scott is waiting anxiously to find out what Colonel Brazier has achieved and in the meantime – because of the continuing roar of both guns and artillery – has instituted a system whereby the signal for his men to charge will be a wave of the hand, not a whistle.

The soldiers at this point are on a hair-trigger. Their heads are down, and many of them are praying, summoning their last reserves of courage. Their concentration is not on Major Scott but on the man beside them, and on their troop leaders. In that situation, it only needs one man to be confused, to charge, to pull that hair-trigger and the men beside him on both sides will also charge, starting a chain reaction.

And then it happens.

Lost in the fog of war, an officer who knows of Antill's second instruction to 'Push on!' but does not know of Brazier's attempt to get General Hughes to call it off arrives at 5.15 am on the right of the line and asks why they have not GONE OVER THE TOP?!?![89]

It is the way he says it.

Captain Andrew Rowan, a grazier from Western Australia, takes it as an order, and immediately waves his arm, before hopping the bags himself, to be shot in the head and fall back dead. But his final wave to the world is seen by Sergeant William Sanderson, who waves himself and also charges forward.[90] In an instant, half of the fourth wave is up and charging!

The chain reaction has exploded.

'By God I believe the right has gone on!' Major Scott cries,[91] before shouting at the other men to stop. It is too late for most.

The Turkish guns chatter. The Australian men fall.

And die.

The 'butcher's bill', when it finally becomes confirmed – at the moment, many are just 'missing' – is devastating. No fewer than 600 men had hopped the bags, of whom 234 had been killed and 138 wounded.[92]

And the Turks, who were meant to be wiped out by the attack? Well protected in their trenches, superbly armed and with more ammunition than they know what to do with, they have lost just a dozen men or so.

And there is no flag in their trenches. The sacrifice of so many men has achieved precisely . . . nothing.

Brazier returns to the centre of the line, only to hear that . . . most of the fourth line has gone! Their commander holds out little hope that any of them have survived. As Brazier later recalled, '[I] thought that only myself and my messengers were left.'[93]

When an officer of Royal Engineers, whose job today it is to blow up enemy trenches and tunnels, arrives to ask for further instructions – as they have received orders to keep the attack going – Brazier has a firm answer for him. Exhaustedly, no longer caring if he is court-martialled, but simply unwilling to waste another life uselessly, Colonel Brazier tells the officer that they are NOT to proceed, and he will answer for it personally.

Nigh speechless with fury and grief at the entirely needless slaughter of his men for absolutely no gain, Colonel Brazier can do nothing for now but wait and observe, 'a lonely sentinel watching with a periscope'.[94]

After half an hour, he sends a written message to Brigade HQ, notifying them 'that the trenches are empty, that if attacked the Turks can run right over the British troops and will H.Q. send up reinforcement and relief'.[95]

When the reply comes back, Brazier grabs the note with his dirt-encrusted hands and reads, 'Keep on observing.'[96]

But let Charles Bean have a final word: 'And as for the boys – the single-minded, loyal Australian country lads – who left their trenches in the grey light of that morning with all their simple treasures on their backs to bivouac in the scrub that evening – the shades of evening found them lying in the scrub with God's wide sky above them . . .'[97]

Chapter Seventeen
BATTLE FOR THE HEIGHTS

My candle is all but burnt out . . .[1]
Colonel William Malone, Commander Wellington Infantry
Battalion, writing to his wife before marching out to Chunuk Bair

All men, all creatures, suffer from tiredness. But men have
a mental force which allows them to go on without resting.[2]
Mustafa Kemal, Anafarta Group Commander,
on the battle at Chunuk Bair

DAWN, 7 AUGUST 1915, ABOVE SUVLA BAY, THE TRUTH DAWNS

He is a man with crystal-clear blue eyes, high cheekbones and an air
of great authority about him. He is Colonel Mustafa Kemal, standing atop Battleship Hill, gazing through his binoculars at the tumult
below. And he is in no doubt that his prediction has become a reality.
The invaders are trying to go from 'Anzac in the direction of Hill 971,
just as predicted all along'.[3]

(He had *told* them so.)

At least Kannengiesser's 9th Division has been despatched towards
the heights, which brings him some relief.

—

The sun is rising as Malone and his men, as well as the other New

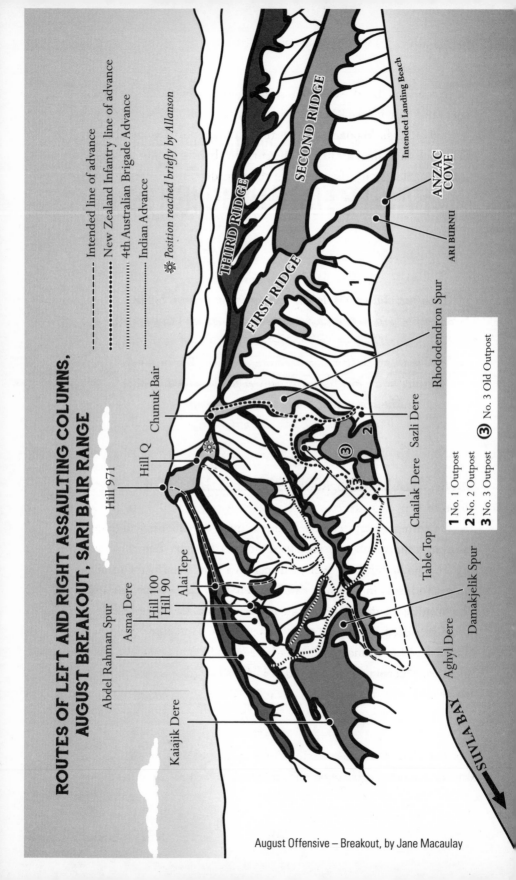

ROUTES OF LEFT AND RIGHT ASSAULTING COLUMNS, AUGUST BREAKOUT, SARI BAIR RANGE

—————— Intended line of advance

●●●●●●● New Zealand Infantry line of advance

∙∙∙∙∙∙∙∙∙ 4th Australian Brigade Advance

———————— Indian Advance

✳ *Position reached briefly by Allanson*

THIRD RIDGE

SECOND RIDGE

FIRST RIDGE

Intended Landing Beach

ANZAC COVE

ARI BURNU

Rhododendron Spur

Chunuk Bair

Hill Q

Hill 971

Abdel Rahman Spur

Asma Dere

Hill 100
Hill 90

Alai Tepe

Sazli Dere

Chailak Dere

Table Top

Damakjelik Spur

Aghyl Dere

Kaiajik Dere

1 No. 1 Outpost
2 No. 2 Outpost
3 No. 3 Outpost
③ No. 3 Old Outpost

SUVLA BAY

August Offensive – Breakout, by Jane Macaulay

Zealanders on hand, set about securing the ridgeline at the Apex, concealed just below Rhododendron Ridge, with Chunuk Bair just beyond on high. Malone presumes this is the spot from where they are to launch their final assault on the summit, but he cannot be sure as Johnston, along with the officers of the Brigade headquarters, has still not arrived to the head of their column, so he now sends word back to the Commander:

> *7th August*
> *OC N.Z. Inf Bde*
> *I am occupying a position nearly at the head of the gully. As it is day and I am not sure of my position, I am lining the crest of the surrounding ridges to ensure reasonable safety.*
> *I am reconnoitring forward and will act on further knowledge and report.*
> *W. G. Malone*
> *Lt. Col[4]*

A short time later, Johnston and his staff join them at the ridge. Johnston appears particularly dishevelled and inarticulate, brimming with fighting spirit – or some kind of spirit, for the smell of strong alcohol is apparent – yet somehow morose.

Though half of their men are dispersed and not ready for an attack, Johnston insists in his own impulsive way that the attack go ahead as per their instructions. The heights must be seized, regardless of delay.

But Malone, a man of 'inflexible resolution'[5] and convinced it will be an exercise in suicide, will not hear of it. Certainly not yet, when they know nothing of what lies before them.

—

As the New Zealanders vacillate, the relatively undefended heights above them are beginning to be reinforced.

Kannengiesser and his gaggle of senior officers, after riding hard from Kemalyeri, are forced to dismount for the final scramble up the steep, scree-strewn slope to the narrow, razor-edged plateau at Chunuk Bair. With the help of prickly bushes and rough grass, they pull themselves atop the comb's edge at around 6.30 am. Catching his breath, Kannengiesser looks through his binoculars across the rugged hills and out to the Aegean Sea, where the most amazing thing emerges from the rising mists . . .

Suvla Bay is full of ships! They count 'ten transports, six warships, and seven hospital ships'.[6] The warships are firing on Turkish positions on land, while the transports are disgorging ever more soldiers onto a shore that is already crowded with them.

'On land,' the German officer would later recount, 'we saw a confused mass of troops like a disturbed ant-heap, and across the blinding white surface of the dried salt sea we saw a battery marching in a southerly direction. With our few revolvers we could do nothing against it.'[7]

Returning his gaze to the slopes in front of him, he sees that it is just a confusion of valleys – obviously difficult country to traverse if the enemy is coming their way – but on the other hand he can see no Turkish defensive positions from this particular vantage point. In fact, the prevailing sense all around him is a certain 'peace and quiet'.[8]

Now concerned by the immensity of the ridge that he has been charged to defend, he begins 'a reconnaissance of the country so as to be able to receive the approaching regiments with final orders'.[9] In terms of existing defences, all he can find just down from the summit is one battery – whose commander is fast asleep – manned by 20 sleepy gunners.

Kannengiesser does not like it at all. The English are making for the heights of Sari Bair Range, and if they capture them the battle will be lost. And he has too few troops for the length of front he has to defend.

Immediately this moustachioed 47-year-old military professional – regarded by Colonel Kemal, a hard marker, as 'one of the most talented of all the German officers in our army'[10] – begins to dictate reports to his second-in-command. This worthy hurriedly translates them into Turkish for the benefit of the troops, while another Turkish officer keeps a lookout with his inevitable binoculars. (Like doctors with stethoscopes, Turkish officers must always have binoculars around their necks. And if they want to achieve the highest of ranks, a luxurious moustache is a near must.)

—

Tucked just behind the lip of Rhododendron Ridge, unseen by Kannengiesser, the New Zealand troops are, for the moment, safe. And yet Malone's instinct to keep his men right there until they are better supported on their flanks and have more situational understanding is now being overturned. For, once more, Johnston insists the men go forward and advance on the summit of Chunuk Bair, come what may.

So be it. The exhausted, thirsty and hungry men of the New Zealand Infantry Brigade begin a slow, single-file march forward. Onwards and upwards, ever upwards.

—

With the first rays of the sun now hitting the peaks, the Turkish officer with his binoculars is still standing atop Chunuk Bair, making a slow, sweeping scan, from left to right, of the rugged ground below.

Suddenly, he gives a start and jerks the binoculars back to a point he'd just passed over, trying to focus on something.

There!

From out of the dusky dimness just 500 yards below, struggling towards the light, he sees *Ingiliz* soldiers exhaustedly climbing, 'splendidly equipped with white bands on their left arms'.[11] And though they appear tired, this string of soldiers emerging from the valley below seems to never end. *Still* they keep coming.

The instant that the attention of Colonel Kannengiesser is drawn to it, the German officer immediately orders the nearest Turkish soldiers – the 20 that he'd found defending the Turkish battery – to open fire, but they refuse.

'We can only commence to fire,' the response comes, 'when we receive an order from *our* battalion commander.'[12]

Kannengiesser explodes. He runs over and jumps among them, and in a mixture of outraged German, what little Turkish he knows and international sign language for 'I will shoot you myself if you don't do as I say', manages to achieve the desired result.

The Turkish soldiers start firing down on the climbing soldiers below, and the exhausted New Zealanders immediately throw themselves to the ground like freshly scythed wheat. 'They gave me the impression,' the German Colonel would later say of the New Zealand soldiers, 'that they were glad to be spared further climbing.'[13]

—

Monash, meanwhile, is completely exhausted, as are his men, after the most frustrating night of their lives. In the darkness, trying to follow the impossible route, being fired upon by tireless pockets of Turks, they have failed to reach their objective of Hill 971, and for the moment can go little further.

For now, Monash orders his men to dig in on this east–west ridge, which, according to the rudimentary map he carries, seems to put them in good position to eventually launch an attack on their objective. (He is mistaken. They are in fact still 600 yards short of where he believes they have reached. But still the men work on, entrenching their positions in the wrong place.)

It's now approaching 8 am, and two companies of Colonel Kemal's 19th Infantry Division arrive just in time to help to defend Chunuk Bair. Kannengiesser now has some 250 soldiers. The New Zealanders have hunkered down, many retreating to the Apex as the two sides engage in a light skirmish, trying to determine the other's strength.

For Johnston down below, Malone's judgement is proved correct, but it is Brigade-Major Temperley who convinces him of the need to halt, as all who venture above the small bump of the Apex are immediately cut down by 'a storm of rifle and machine-gun fire from the crest'.[14]

Citing the suicidal nature of trying to advance, Temperley dashes off a message to Divisional Headquarters detailing their position and saying that *in view of the fact that we are absolutely unsupported on our right or left and can see no sign of movement of any troops we deemed it prudent to remain here and await a further advance.*[15] Brigadier-General Johnston approves the message and it is taken back by a runner.

The New Zealanders keep firing, with one of the thousands of bullets sent towards the summit being of particular significance . . .

—

Atop Chunuk Bair just after 9 am, Colonel Kannengiesser is starting to feel a little more in control. Reinforcements are arriving every minute, and their hold on the peak looks to be assured. Hunkered behind the crest of the ridge, he momentarily stands up to direct the amassing Turkish soldiers into better positions, when, just like the line in Rudyard Kipling's poem 'Gunga Din', 'a bullet come an' drilled the beggar clean'.

The German officer feels as if a jam-tin bomb has gone off in his heart, as a searing pain moves out from his centre and paralyses every limb. His legs are ripped out from underneath him as he reels backward and goes down hard.

The Turkish officers surrounding him look down at their stricken commander, mouths agape. In moments, Kannengiesser is scooped up by the tender yet strong hands of the stretcher-bearers and taken away to be looked after by the medics.

—

Alas for the New Zealanders, it does not affect the course of the battle. The Turks are attuned to the loss of troopers and officers alike, and the senior men at the command post act quickly, directing men down an ever-widening front as they stretch out along the main ridgeline of the range. They are the kings of the castle, and for the moment the New Zealanders are pinned down, only able to advance on the high ground with extreme difficulty and great loss.

Still, their fighting spirit is in marked contrast to what is happening at Suvla Bay.

For do the British even truly want to get off the beach?

To Private William Tope of the 12th Battalion, perched in one of the highest positions on the Anzacs' left flank and watching the beach at Suvla Bay through his telescope since dawn, it doesn't really seem so, despite the fact they now have 20,000 soldiers landed. Not only are they clearly not threatening any of the higher ground that surrounds Suvla Bay – even though they must surely know that Turkish reinforcements are on their way – but, as Tope keeps watching, stupefied, they form up on the beach, as he would recount, 'just as if they were on a parade ground in some English town. While they were there, there was shrapnel bursting over the top of them and, do you know, they wouldn't move . . . these little Englishmen were just standing there.'[16]

What is needed, of course, is strong leadership urging the men forward, but the man in charge of the whole exercise, Lieutenant-General Stopford, is well offshore aboard the HQ yacht *Jonquil* at this time, just waking up from his sleep on deck. It had been an uncomfortably hot night, and he found he slept better there.

As the morning wears on, it seems like the only thing keeping pace with the Turks blazing away at the Brits below is the sun blazing down on them all. It is going to be a long, hot day – all in a place where the water supply is dismal.

MID-MORNING, 7 AUGUST 1915, ANZAC COVE, COUNTING THE COST OF THE CARNAGE

And now, as water flows down a gully, and a rock falls down a hill, so too do the battles on high inevitably bring a bleeding stream of shockingly wounded men roughly tumbling down the slopes to the beach. There are men missing arms and jaws. Men with their hands over their abdomens trying to hold their intestines in place, as their very lives slip through their bloody fingers. Men with that glazed, haunted look of those who have realised that they really are . . . about . . . to . . . die.

Both Chipper brothers, Ross and Lindsay – who had been drinking whisky with the Throssell brothers just hours before – have already been shot dead. All around them in no-man's-land are dozens, *hundreds* of other dead, while there are also dozens of severely wounded men lying in the hot sun, including Ric Throssell, who has a bullet through the lungs and is coughing thick globs of bubbly blood. Not far away from Ric, but not daring to try to get to him, is his brother, Hugo, who is essentially untouched but equally forced to lie still. The one slim chance any of them have of surviving is to crawl back after nightfall, as any movement now will see a blizzard of bullets raking their tortured bodies.

'The summit of the Nek could be seen crowded with . . . bodies . . .' Charles Bean would record. 'At first here and there a man raised his arm to the sky, or tried to drink from his water-bottle. But as the sun of that burning day climbed higher, such movement ceased. Over the whole summit the figures lay still in the quivering heat.'[17]

A very few, who are near the parapet, are rescued by men throwing out grappling irons and dragging them in. One of these, Trooper Paul 'Ginty' McGinness of the 8th Light Horse Regiment, has an extraordinary if superficial wound, as a bullet had hit his ammunition belt and then ploughed across his skin from hip to hip.

Many die in the course of the morning. And for what? Certainly not for the achievement of the original objective – which was to act as a diversion, and draw troops away from Chunuk Bair and Hill 971, which are still held by the Turks. In fact, Turkish reserves are still streaming up to the peaks. A Turkish Commander has quickly and smoothly taken the wounded Kannengiesser's place, and though there is much confusion as men from disparate divisions become mixed up, he keeps it together and has enough soldiers to hold their line.

In fact, for those trying to take Chunuk Bair, the situation is so grim that the brooding discord between the New Zealand officers

– particularly between Lieutenant-Colonel Malone and Brigade-Major Temperley – is beginning to flare. Despite the message sent to Division Headquarters that they are best to hold off on an attack until night-time, Godley, completely out of touch with the field conditions, had responded at 9.30 am over the field telephone with something close to the highest order of insanity: 'Attack at once.'[18]

Obeying the order, now an officer lets out a cry: 'Come along lads!'[19] The dutiful military men begin their advance into the withering fire from on high. The sounds of rifles rollick down the hill, bringing tidings of death.

The Aucklanders lose '200 men in twenty minutes'.[20]

Johnston, 'watching from below, had seen platoon after platoon of Auckland fall as it passed The Apex'.[21] One chap would recall that Johnston 'stood on the crest of Rhododendron Ridge cheering his men on. [He] had to be removed by force.'[22] And still he orders that the advance must continue.

Malone is outraged. This is just the kind of wanton recklessness with men's lives he has come to most detest: innocent men served a veritable death sentence at the utterance of a fool and . . .

And here comes Brigadier-General Johnston now, to *order* Malone to send them over the top of the Apex, to follow up the disastrous attempt by the Aucklanders.

No.

Malone refuses. 'Stop where you are!' Malone yells to his soldiers, before turning to Johnston.[23] 'My men are not going over in daylight, but they'll go over at night time and they'll take that hill.'[24]

Brigadier-General Johnston is stunned. He opens his mouth to speak, but, before he can, Malone ensures that his own decision carries the day, by turning to his loyal men and saying, 'Wellington Battalion come away from the ridge.'[25]

In an instant – the time it takes to understand that their salvation from all but certain death has come from their beloved Colonel – his men retreat back down the slope. Now turning back to Johnston, Malone barks, 'I will take the risk and any punishment. These men are not going over until I order them to go. I'm *not* going to send them over to commit suicide.'[26]

This is war. Yes, Johnston has superior rank, but Malone is the true leader. Finally the Brigadier-General gives in to reality. He concedes they have no chance of taking Chunuk Bair in daylight and sends word back to Godley at Number Two Outpost.

General Godley, receiving the news, also concedes that there is 'no hope of the [Right Assault Column] being able to reach the crest of the range in full daylight'.[27]

They will attack tomorrow at dawn.

DUSK, 7 AUGUST 1915, SOMEWHERE BELOW HILL 971, THE IMPOSSIBLE MUST BE POSSIBLE

As the sun fades, bringing welcome relief to the parched soldiers of Monash's 4th Brigade – who have spent the day digging with their bayonets to gain shelter from Turkish fire – a supply of picks and shovels belatedly arrives at their frontline. The senior officers have not yet realised their error in defining their locality, and so the task of entrenching this point is actively renewed as the light begins to fade.

That afternoon, Monash has received orders that, like the New Zealanders over at Chunuk Bair, their advance is to be resumed at dawn, and Hill 971 is to be taken at daybreak.

Monash is . . . hesitant. His men are weary, he argues, his forces insufficient.

Unfortunately, his warning is not heeded, and now an officer passes Monash two messages from Godley down at Outpost Two: 'The G.O.C. wishes you to close the troops . . . well up the slopes towards the enemy during the preliminary bombardment of the position, so as to be ready to reach the crest as soon as the gun-fire stops to-morrow morning. The assault should be carried out with loud cheering.'[28]

Godley adds in his second message, 'I feel confident that, after to-day's rest, and starting comparatively fresh, your brigade will make a determined effort to capture the key of the positions . . .'[29]

Great that Godley is confident, because Monash certainly isn't. Still, ever resilient, he begins to formulate a plan.

They are to move out at 3 am.

PRE-DAWN, 8 AUGUST 1915, FROM DOWN UNDER TO UP ON CHUNUK BAIR

It has been a bitter battle, and it has been going for nigh on 24 hours, but now the remaining men of the New Zealand Infantry Brigade under Brigadier-General Johnston must pull out all stops. The previous day's slaughter above the Apex must be put behind them. As one man had recited to himself to help him try to get through the day, 'bullets now or shrapnel later . . . bullets now or shrapnel later . . . bullets now or shrapnel later . . .'[30] They have no choice but to get on with the job.

With so many men dead and injured, Godley has ordered two battalions of the New Army to reinforce the troops on the Apex. Also joining them, as reserves, are the Auckland Mounted Rifles and the Maori contingent, who have just arrived from the Table Top.

Colonel William Malone, true to his solemn words the day before, is preparing to lead his Wellingtons in one last assault for the summit. Resolute, but still doubtful that he will survive it, at 3 am he wakes his batman to pass on his wife's address in the luscious farmlands of Taranaki, in case of his death. Ashen-faced, Malone shakes his comrade's hand before saying, 'Good-bye.'[31]

His men form up for the attack, and pass through the Aucklanders, who are holding the line at the Pinnacle, before beginning the climb to Chunuk Bair. Quickly now, carefully, the Wellingtons pick their way over the corpses of the day before and push towards a summit, and . . .

And somehow their timing is perfect. For once, they commence their charge just as a barrage finishes, and it just so happens the Turkish resistance is minimal. As one soldier would recall, 'The Turks, there were pretty few of them there, they scooted, and there was one old fellow there – he had a beard – about 70 – he pulled his rifle on us . . . The poor old joker, somebody shot him.'[32]

It seems the shallow trenches on the summit had provided precious little protection from the shelling overnight, so Johnny Turk had abandoned them, retreating back to the more strongly held Hill Q, and those who remain are quickly quelled. Yes, it is 24 hours later than planned, but they are in possession of Chunuk Bair, and as the sun rises, they can even see the Promised Land, and more importantly the promised waters of the Narrows!

All of which is to the good. To the bad is the obvious difficulty there will be in holding Chunuk Bair, as the Turks now unleash hell to dislodge them, starting with heavy shelling that cuts a swathe not only through Malone's Wellingtons but also through the companies of the New Army troops of Britain there to support them.

Malone instructs them: Dig! Defend! Get ready for the Turkish troops that will soon be launched upon us!

And so the men occupy the Turks' trenches on the forward side of the ridge, while digging support trenches on the reverse side, sheltered from the Turkish artillery. The clay is almost rock hard, but the men try their best, racing the rising sun, which will lift the haze that hangs over them and expose them as even surer targets to the Turks spread above on Hill Q.

DIG, you noble bastards!

—

Monash's men are not so close to their objective.

The naval bombardment on Hill 971 ceases. And though 'according to Godley's order, the column should have been "ready to reach" Hill 971' by this stage, they are nowhere near it! In fact, as Bean would later note, 'The distance had been underestimated, the locality mistaken, and the start made hours too late . . .'[33]

They are wide of their mark. They are lost.

And now they are being fired upon by Turkish machine-guns that are well positioned above them: 'Being in no present danger, [the Turks] worked their guns with coolness and decisive effect . . .'[34]

Monash's men are scattered, confused and out of touch with their Commander. Their numbers are quickly decimated. The objective of Hill 971 – though lost at the inception of this ludicrous plan – is absolutely out of reach. The best they can do is hold onto the line they'd begun to entrench the day before.

—

Colonel Kemal has not slept. Dark purple stains lurk beneath his water-blue eyes, and his normally rigid back is slumped over, haunted by fatigue. Ever since the fading darkness of night began to threaten the Peninsula with a new day of bloodshed, he has been watching the enemy ships fire on the area between Battleship Hill and Chunuk Bair.

From all the reports he is receiving, it is obvious there is a great deal of confusion along the range near Chunuk Bair as to where the enemy will strike, who the commander is and what their next move should be. One report reads, 'We have men from the 14th, 64th and 25th and various . . . other regiments at the frontline. They are all mixed up . . . Most of the officers are martyred or wounded . . . In the name of the security of our homeland, I request that you send a determined and expert person to this sector.'[35]

Another Battalion Commander reports at 5.40 am, 'it is unclear whether the soldiers who have advanced towards Chunuk Bair and are consolidating their positions are friend or foe'.[36]

Colonel Kemal has little doubt. They are foe. And must be eliminated. Gazing hard through his binoculars at the peaks of the Sari Bair Range, hoping to sight them as dawn's fingers slowly curl around the summit, he feels very strongly 'the weight of responsibility . . . heavier than anything, even death'.[37]

—

At Lone Pine, meanwhile, the desperate fighting has now been going on without break, from trench to trench, backward and forward, to the left and right, and back again, and back and forth, each move paid for with blood, as both sides pour in battalion after battalion to either hold what has been won or counter-attack and win back what has been lost. Acts of extraordinary bravery are performed on both sides, few of which are subsequently acknowledged. The Anzacs will be awarded no fewer than seven Victoria Crosses for actions at Lone Pine alone, though none from the first few hours – for nearly all of the officers needed to vouch for early turns of bravery have been killed.

And, of course, the casualty rate is fearful.

As to Private Cecil McAnulty, who had written in his diary just before the battle 'hope to get through alright',[38] to his amazement he has survived so far, and now, despite the bullets and shrapnel still whizzing past, he takes the time to write a little more:

> I've pulled through alright so far, just got a few minutes to spare now. I'm all out, can hardly stand up. On Friday when we got the word to charge, Frank and I were on the extreme left of the charging party. There was a clear space of 100 yards to cross without a patch of cover. I can't realise how I got across it . . .
>
> We were right out in the open and all the Turkish machine-guns and rifles seemed to be playing on us and shrapnel bursting right over us. I yelled out to the other 4 chaps, 'This is only suicide, boys. I'm going to make a jump for it.' I thought they said alright we'll follow. I sprang to my feet in one jump[39]

These prove to be the last words he writes, and his body is found later.

—

At 5 pm on that sultry afternoon of 8 August, General Sir Ian Hamilton – alarmed at the lack of news from Suvla Bay – comes ashore at that spot, hoping against hope that at last the breakthrough they have been waiting for might have been achieved . . . only to come across a scene that completely staggers him.

Despite everything he has said to General Stopford of the need for speed, the need to get off the beach and capture the high ground so they are not trapped on the edges like the Anzacs had been once the Turkish reinforcements had arrived, he finds on the beach, as he would angrily report to Lord Kitchener, 'most of the troops strolling about as if it was a holiday'.[40]

The problem, Hamilton determines, lies not with the men but with their senior officers, who 'seem to have no drive or control over them, and, worst of all, they have been saturated with pamphlets and instructions about trench warfare, and their one idea is to sit down and dig an enormous hole to hide themselves in . . .'[41]

Most frustrating of all to General Hamilton is when he finds out that five battalions are being 'held up by a party of five or six hundred Turkish Gendarmerie'.[42]

In Hamilton's view, the Turks could be quickly put paid to with a bayonet charge, but their Commanding Officer, Major-General Frederick Hammersley, won't hear of it. For he is 'preparing a turning movement from the south in accordance with Stopford's order not to make frontal attacks'.[43]

Even more appalling, most of the soldiers really have been resting during the day, and intend to keep doing so. The next move planned by the senior officers is for an advance 'at dawn next morning'.[44]

Stupefied, Hamilton orders Commodore Keyes – who is equally aggrieved – to take him in his motorboat to *Jonquil*, where General Stopford has been based for all bar a couple of hours of the battle so far, so he can confront the man ultimately responsible.

Stopford, however, is quick to assure him. 'Everything is quite all right and going well,' he says.[45]

'And where are they now?' Hamilton asks, incredulous.

'There,' Stopford says, showing him the position on the map on the table. 'Along the foot of the hills.'

'But they held that line, more or less, yesterday.'

'Yes,' agrees Stopford, going on to explain that because the men had been tired out and he had not been able to keep the water and guns up to them the way he would have liked, he had decided not to attack the main ridge until the following morning, as that would likely be 'a regular battle'.[46]

'A regular battle is just what we are here for,' Hamilton would record as the words he *wants* to say, but he does not. That would be impolite. This is Stopford's show and, though Sir Ian is Commander-in-Chief, he simply does not believe in riding roughshod in that manner. He had not done it with General Hunter-Weston on the day of landing, nor in any of the Battles of Krithia, and he does not do it now. It is not in his nature.

But at least he allows himself to give Stopford some pepper. 'We must occupy the heights at once,' he says. 'It is imperative . . .'

Can't be done, says Stopford. One can't just rewrite orders willy-nilly like that. 'I agree with you in principle, as to the necessity of pushing on,' Stopford says, 'but there are many tactical reasons against it, especially the attitude of my Generals on shore who have told me that the men are too tired.'[47]

Stopford, too, does not like to ask his Generals to do something they don't want to, and presumably the Generals feel the same about their soldiers.

Desperate, Hamilton goes in search of Major-General Hammersley, whom he finds at the northern end of a small half-moon of a beach . . . only to hear more of the same. Too difficult to attack now, and much better to wait until daylight when it would all be so much easier.

Just for once, Hamilton insists. 'There has never been a greater crisis in any battle than the one taking place as we speak,' he says. 'It is imperative, absolutely imperative that we occupy the heights before the enemy bring back the guns and they receive the reinforcements that are marching at this very moment to their aid. This is not a guess. Our aeroplanes have spotted the Turks marching on us from the north.'[48]

Hammersley finally agrees to send the 32nd Brigade to the Sari Bair Range overnight, but that is as far as he will go.

'I fancy,' Hamilton would report witheringly afterwards, 'they were upset and tired by landing at night, and then thought they had done such a tremendous big thing advancing a couple of miles or so into the country that they might then rest on their oars.'[49]

For the moment, Hamilton returns to his command vessel, *Triad*, hopeful that the morrow will bring better things, but not yet insisting upon it.

Throughout the rest of the day, the Turks, with artillery positioned on Hill Q and Battleship Hill, continue pounding the New Zealanders and the British frontline atop Chunuk Bair, as well as launching attacks against them. Through it all, Colonel William Malone has been unceasing in his efforts to rally his men, to organise them, direct them, and even lead them in the many bayonet charges they are forced to perform, to keep waves of Turks away. When one of his fellow officers remonstrates, saying Malone should not be putting himself in such danger, Malone's answer is the measure of the man: 'You're only a kid – I'm an old man – get out yourself!'[50]

In the end, however, it is one of those things. Near dusk, at the end of a day when some hundreds of his own men lie dead and wounded all around him, a piece of shrapnel scythes cruelly through the air and in an instant a brave woman in Taranaki is a widow, though she doesn't know it yet, left to raise her three children on her own – just as Malone's five children from his previous marriage are left without a father. For he lies dead in a shallow trench, the men closest to him weeping over his bloodied corpse.

Compounding the tragedy is that Malone actually only had to survive a little longer to make it to safety. After sundown, the Wellingtons are relieved by soldiers from the Otago Battalion and the Wellington Mounteds. It is a measure of just how torrid their time atop Chunuk Bair has been that, of the Wellingtons' original contingent of 760 soldiers, less than 50 are still standing and unwounded.

But at least, at this time, as the sun goes down on 8 August, Chunuk Bair remains in the hands of the Allies.

—

It is going to take a massive effort to dislodge them. And quite a leader of men . . .

All day, Colonel Kemal has been at Battleship Hill receiving news riddled with 'discrepancies about whether the peak [of Chunuk Bair] has or has not been taken by the enemy'. The latest report says, 'the enemy continue to dig trenches at Chunuk Bair . . . The enemy soldiers are walking around the trenches and placing sand bags in them . . .'[51]

From his observations, though, one thing is blindingly clear on this evening of 8 August: 'Chunuk Bair is in a dangerous situation.'[52]

Yet again, just after 7 pm, the telephone rings. It is Liman von Sanders' Chief of Staff, who wishes to know what Colonel Mustafa Kemal thinks of the situation.

'There is one moment left to reclaim our position,' Kemal replies. 'If we lose that moment, we are faced with a general catastrophe.'[53]

He explains that, because of the nature and quantity of the enemy force that has landed at Suvla, it is necessary to ensure command and control in that sector by uniting the effort under a single commander.

'Is there no other solution?' the Chief of Staff asks.

And here is Mustafa Kemal's chance. 'There is no other option,' he says forcefully, 'but to assign all the available forces under my command.'

'Won't that be excessive?'

'It won't be enough,' Kemal says, before putting the phone down.[54]

Three hours hence, at 9.45 pm, he receives an order from General Esat: 'You are to take command of the Anafarta Group effective immediately. You are to proceed immediately to [the Group's Headquarters] and execute an attack by sunrise 9 August.'[55]

Though Mustafa has not slept for three days and three nights straight, and is in any case a sickly shadow of his former healthy self, his heart leaps. His desires have been realised. He is now in charge of no fewer than six divisions, and given the responsibility of winning back the day, and the night!

Within two hours, at 11.30 pm, under the cover of darkness, Colonel Kemal rides away from the Headquarters of the 19th Division, alive as never before. 'For four months,' he would recall, 'I had lived three hundred metres away from the firing line, breathing the fetid smell of corpses. Finally I was able to breathe clean air again.'[56]

PRE-DAWN, 9 AUGUST 1915, IF AT FIRST YOU DON'T SUCCEED, TRY, TRY AGAIN

Hammersley's 32nd Brigade?

As demanded by Sir Ian Hamilton, they actually do try to take the heights to the east of Suvla Bay, alas arriving at the highest ridge . . . some 30 minutes too late. For by the early hours of 9 August, the Turkish reserves have flooded the hills. Immeasurably aided by the advantage of height, and well-placed artillery, they are able to cut the 32nd Brigade to pieces, and force a rag-tag retreat. By the time the sun rises, two full Turkish Divisions, with artillery, are securely positioned atop the heights surrounding Suvla Bay, raining hell down upon the two British Divisions, who simply have not had the gumption to attack quickly enough.

Surely nothing else could go wrong for the British, on this whole disastrous venture at Suvla Bay? Yes, it could, and Ellis Ashmead-Bartlett is there to witness it. Though the naval artillery is showing every bit of ferocity that the troops are not, the same problem dogs them here as has happened at Anzac Cove and Cape Helles – when the Turkish artillery is positioned on the lee side of the hills, naval shells are simply incapable of knocking them out.

What the shells can do, however, in these dry conditions, is to start fires, and that is what happens at midday on 9 August, just as some British soldiers are at last making an attempt to reach the heights of Scimitar Hill, a lump of tactical importance east of the salt lake. Worse, a wind comes pouring down the hill, catches the flames and sends them straight at the climbing soldiers.

As Ashmead-Bartlett watches on, appalled, he sees wounded British soldiers, now burning, break cover from the flaming scrub beneath the lip of Scimitar Hill and crawl out into the open, where they are cut down by snipers and shrapnel. After the flames have passed on, all that remains are 'little mounds of scorched khaki . . . where another mismanaged soldier of the King had returned to mother earth'.[57]

The English correspondent keeps watching, powerless to do anything, bar chronicle the catastrophe.

Later that afternoon, he is joined by fellow journalist Henry Nevinson, who is feeling every bit as appalled as Ashmead-Bartlett by what he has seen. He has come from the far side of the Salt Lake and still can't quite fathom how it can all have gone so wrong. 'Our infantry,' Nevinson declares, 'are demoralised, weary, and absolutely refuse to advance. The muddle is beyond anything I have ever seen.'[58]

For his part, Ashmead-Bartlett is convinced it is yet more evidence that the problem lies not with the soldiers but with their officers. He has seen for himself, up close, just how badly organised the whole thing had been from first to last by the officers who were meant to be in charge. 'Confusion reigned supreme,' he would record in his diary. 'No one seemed to know where the headquarters of the different brigades and divisions were to be found. The troops were hunting for water, the staffs were hunting for their troops, and the Turkish snipers were hunting for their prey.'[59] In only the last of these do the hunters find what they are looking for in abundance.

Late that evening, Ashmead-Bartlett comes across Sir Ian Hamilton, standing all alone, on the north coast of Suvla Bay, not a staff officer or underling to be seen anywhere near. There is an unmistakable aspect to Hamilton, a paleness, an anxiety as he watches the billowing columns of smoke from the battle gone wrong, the battle he had staked his career on, now turning to ashes before his eyes. Just as he had feared, all the ranges around Suvla Bay are now held by whole divisions of Turkish reinforcements, which have arrived on this day. Hamilton had thrown a huge number of rifle men onto the frontline, but now there are none left to throw. The English General has squandered 9000 men in four days, with next to nothing to show for it, bar the squalid flats of Suvla Bay. And for all of the August Offensives, there are 25,000 casualties so far.

To Ashmead-Bartlett, it seems clear that the Commander-in-Chief has just realised at this hour 'that his final effort to reach the Narrows had failed'.[60]

Despite the Suvla Bay disaster and the debacle of Hill 971 (Monash alone has 'lost nearly 1,000'[61] and Bean later writes of the attempt as 'one of those "black days" which most deeply affect the spirits of soldiers'[62]), it remains possible that the August Offensive could be considered a success if it can hold on to just one last thing: the summit of Chunuk Bair. Magnificently, the New Zealanders had held onto it all through 9 August – despite continued attacks – and as dusk falls on this day they are relieved by soldiers of the 6th Loyal North Lancashires, who are part of Kitchener's New Army.

PRE-DAWN, 10 AUGUST 1915, THE DENOUEMENT

But can Chunuk Bair continue to be held?

Not if Colonel Kemal has anything to do with it. Fully aware of the strategic significance of this vantage point, he is prepared to sacrifice much to hold it. Even his life, if it comes to that.

The following morning, just before dawn, Colonel Kemal pulls back the flap of his tent and, as is his habit, looks first to the sky to determine the state of the heavens. They are sparkling, the stars like fireflies burning off the last of their lustre in the few minutes that remain before they must, alas, give way to the day.

Looking now before him, towards the network of shallow trenches nestled just below the crest of Chunuk Bair, he squints to properly discern the silhouettes of his men. Many are sitting alone smoking cigarettes, their thoughts with the prospect of violent death and the glories of the afterlife. Others are huddled in groups, whispering and checking their equipment. Some are assembled in a line, prostrating themselves to Allah. The Colonel sees others move purposefully, hunched over, keeping themselves small and inconspicuous to enemy observers. Few of them laugh or smile. All are fated to attack, with this charge forward at Chunuk Bair at the prow of an attack across nearly the entire line atop the Sari Bair Range. 'The dark curtain of night had been raised,' Mustafa Kemal would later recall. 'The moment for attack had come.'[63]

According to his plan, the Turks are going to go into the enemy trenches, just a stone's throw over the crest of the ridge – the Mehmets with their bayonets only, the officers with their swords – and sweep down on the enemy en masse.[64] The enemy may kill the first ones, but they will not kill us all. There is to be no bombardment beforehand. The invaders have become used to that. They expect a bombardment. Not this time. It will just be us, and our bayonets, and Allah. And we will charge in a full-frontal attack.

True, many of his officers think such a move is crazy, and are brave enough to say so, but for Mustafa Kemal the decision is not an intellectual but a visceral one, the sort of decision that comes 'from what we feel in the blood and the fiery moments of battle'.

Slowly, he rises out of his tent and stretches his aching, battle-worn limbs. Reaching into his right-hand breast pocket, he pulls out his trusty watch, which he has had since his days at the Ottoman War College – a gold-coloured watch with a plain white face marked with Roman numerals, which fits snugly in the palm of his hand. It is nearly 4.30 am. In a matter of minutes, the first dull glow of dawn will hit and they will be exposed to the enemy.

Without hesitation, he walks briskly to the front of his newly formed-up men and offers his final instructions. 'Soldiers,' he begins, in his richly resonant and confident voice. 'There is no doubt that we will defeat the enemy that stands before us . . . I will go ahead first. As soon as you see me raise my whip then you will all leap forward!'[65]

The word is spread around quickly, and all men, from every part of the front within seeing distance, turn to focus on their Commander. Now is the moment. Now is their time. They will know triumph, or they will know eternity, or they will know both – but whatever else, with this many men ready to sacrifice themselves for their country, for their god, defeat is not a possibility.

Colonel Kemal walks just 'five to ten steps' up the slope in the gloom, turns to his men, raises his whip . . . before dropping his arm.

In an instant, the first line of 300-odd Turkish soldiers bursts up, and over, running silently for the first few steps before uttering their earthly cry to those heavens above: '*Allah! Allah! Allah!*'

Behind them, in succession, come more and more waves of just as many men, fighting for their homeland.

So fast are they, so surprising is the attack, that many of the soldiers of the 6th Loyal North Lancashires, who have not quite heeded the warning to dig in and stay alert, go from a deep sleep to an eternal sleep in the time it takes to slip a Turkish 12-inch bayonet between their ribs. 'The enemy,' Mustafa Kemal would recount, 'could not even find time to use their weapons. It was an epic, throat to throat struggle . . .'[66]

Within minutes, the first line of the North Lancashires' defence is annihilated.

And after four hours of fighting, all the survivors of the British forces have retreated at full pelt from the southern end of the Anafarta Group's front. The Turks are once again in control of Chunuk Bair. It is then that the British start to rain continuous fire on the position, coming 'from ships and shore mortars and field guns'.[67]

Mustafa Kemal, in the thick of it with his men, looks out at the sea and traces an arc upwards with his eyes as 'shrapnel and pieces of steel poured down like rain from the sky'.[68] Within seconds, his surrounds are filled with the bodies of martyrs and the groans of the wounded.

In the middle of it all, Colonel Kemal is suddenly – *crack!* – hit by a piece of shrapnel in his chest. When he throws his hand to it, that hand comes away bloody.

'Sir,' the officer next to him says, 'you are shot.'

Kemal covers the officer's mouth with his hand. '*Sus,*' he hisses. 'Shut up.'[69]

With the officer now silent, Colonel Mustafa Kemal looks back down at his chest as his fingers fumble around the wound. But there's not a single piece of shrapnel embedded in his skin. His pocket watch, however, is smashed into pieces.[70]

It is extraordinary good fortune.

Despite the hail of fire that continues to rain down from the defiant

British forces, Chunuk Bair is lost. The simple plan and inspirational leadership of Colonel Mustafa Kemal has worked. As his Chief of Staff, Major Izzetin, would write in his diary that day, 'The crisis has been overcome. Kemal's energy and effectiveness have borne fruit.'[71]

The next morning, at 8.45 am, Colonel Kemal, with the strange sense of having an ache in his chest but a song in his heart, sits down in his headquarters and writes to General von Sanders:

> The enemy at Chunuk Bair and Rhododendron Ridge have been driven back.
>
> Commander of the Anafarta Group
> Mustafa Kemal[72]

11 AUGUST 1915, UPON THE AEGEAN SEA, THE BATTLE'S ROAR EBBS

Captain Gordon Carter is one of the lucky ones. Despite having been in almost continuous action over the last five days, and having seen so many bullets and bayonets take his comrades around him, somehow he is still – physically at least – unscathed. 'I am really very weak,' he writes in his diary, 'and seem to have hardly any flesh on me. No wonder the bullets miss me.'[73]

Mentally, like many of the other survivors, he is not so well, and every time he closes his eyes he comes to with a start, as he sees enormous Turks with bayonets coming straight for him, wanting to shoot him and stab him and choke him and kill his comrades and . . .

Oh. Just a nightmare.

And then he tries to sleep again, and the same thing happens. At least he is lucky now to be on a hospital ship heading back to Lemnos with many of the badly wounded men from his battalion. At last, it looks like he is going to be able to get some desperately needed rest.

Back at Anzac, finally, it is over. After five days of battle, Lone Pine is in Australian hands, its trenches occupied by Anzac boots – all at the cost of some 2000 Anzac lives, and more than three times that for the Turks. As one Australian soldier who has 'for four days . . . been dragging Turkish dead out of the captured trenches and burying them in large holes' writes of the Australian victory in a letter home, 'although not decisive, it finished very much to our advantage and "Jacko" the Turk is now in a very desperate position. He is like a dying donkey, his last kick is always his hardest.'[74]

And yet, the net result of the Anzacs now having Lone Pine is . . . not much.

Yes, it is an advantage to have it, which is to the good, but the maxim established by Sir John French a year earlier in France, regarding trench warfare, again holds true: with two forces of relatively equal strength, through massive effort and the loss of many lives, you can bend the enemy's trench, but not break it. At Lone Pine, the Pimple has simply become bigger and more bulbous.

Few are more appalled by the sheer waste of Australian lives than Charles Bean, particularly when it comes to what happened at the Nek. While admiring of the courage displayed – 'For sheer bravery, devoted loyalty, and that self-discipline which seldom failed in Australian soldiers, they stand alone in the annals of their country'[75] – their deaths had been pointless.

'Although at such crises in a great battle firm action must be taken, sometimes regardless of cost,' he would write many years later, 'there could be no valid reason for flinging away the later lines after the first had utterly failed. It is doubtful if there exists in the records of the A.I.F. one instance in which, after one attacking party had been signally defeated, a second, sent after it, succeeded without some radical change having been effected in the plan or the conditions.'[76]

He also reserves some criticism for 'the gallant [Lieutenant-Colonel] White': 'Acting as a sportsman rather than a soldier, by leading forward the first line deprived his regiment of the control which should have been exercised over its operations. Its morale did not require the stimulus of personal leadership; and had his protest been added to Brazier's, Antill might have discontinued the attack.

The most grievous result was the needless loss of lives precious to their nation.'[77]

For his part, rarely, if ever, has Ashmead-Bartlett been so angry, depressed and disillusioned all at once. A veteran of seven wars, including one he fought in, he has seen bad times before. But not like this. Not so many wasted lives for such little gain. Returning to Imbros, he hears for the first time what has happened at Cape Helles, where the attacks on Achi Baba have failed once more.

'Deathly depression reigns at Imbros,' he would record. 'The truth is now generally known that we have failed everywhere. The empty tents of the IXth Corps, glistening in the sun, have become tombstones of the dead; at night they appear ghostlike and deserted under the moonlight. Where is that mighty host which occupied them but five days ago?'[78]

Dead. Nearly all dead.

So, too, many of those who had gone into the attacks at Achi Baba and Anzac, with Ashmead-Bartlett recording, 'The 29th Division also suffered heavily, and our total casualties at Helles alone have not been under six thousand.'[79]

Anzac? Birdwood will soon tell him the truth: 'He said his total losses were 375 officers and 10,138 rank and file in the operations on the left and over 2,000 in the taking and holding of Lone Pine Plateau.'[80]

And so it goes on. Stark statistics, one after the other, confirm catastrophic losses on an unimaginable scale. The total casualties therefore cannot be much under 28,000 – an appalling total for the gains, which, as General Godley expressed it, amounted to some 500 acres of bad grazing ground.

Making matters worse for Ashmead-Bartlett is that, somehow, he has to write an account of the battle at Suvla Bay that will contain something of the truth, while still passing the censor: 'an almost impossible task. It is easy enough to write up a success, but it would defy the genius of Ananias to make a victory out of this affair, either at Helles, Anzac, or Suvla. We have landed again and dug another graveyard. That is all.'[81]

As to Charles Bean, he too does the best he can to give an honest account of what has happened at the 'Battle of Lonesome Pine', but the only way to get it through is to leave out the horror of what has occurred. In the final result, he manages to almost make it sound like this battle has bordered on victory: 'The position at the moment of writing is that we have given the Turks a heavy blow opposite part of the Australian line. The battle is still raging.'[82]

Of the Battle of the Nek, Bean does, however, manage to get it into print that 'extraordinarily Gallant Attempts of the Light Horse on the trenches opposite them were futile. The fighting has been tremendously intense, charge after charge being made.'[83]

Only General Hamilton has no such problems, as he puts out his own releases, subsequently run in the British press, trumpeting 'a successful attack' by the ANZAC troops who had made 'additional gains and further progress'.[84]

Of Suvla Bay, Special Correspondent General Hamilton reports that 'the new British artillery beat down row after row of Turkish trenches . . . and the Turks beat a hasty retreat'.[85] Never fear, the readers of the British Empire are told, 'the Turkish troops are getting very demoralised, and the whole population of Constantinople is pessimistic'.[86]

General Hamilton's press releases are used as the basis for euphoric reports carried around the world:

ON GALLIPOLI
SUVLA BAY LANDING
'MOST BRILLIANT FEAT'
GREAT FORCE
DISEMBARKED

'The most brilliant work yet carried out in the war,' is how the Athens correspondent of the 'Daily Chronicle' describes the recent landing of British troops at Suvla Bay, in Gallipoli (N.N.E. of the Australian positions at Gaba Tepe). He continues . . .

Compared with the landing at Gaba Tepe, the brilliance of the Suvla Bay achievement lies in another direction, though its immediate consequence was a fierce, long struggle, which brought out all that was best in the fighting qualities of the British troops...[87]

17 AUGUST 1915, CAIRO, KEITH MURDOCH CONFRONTS AND IS CONFRONTED

Keith Murdoch is shocked. To this point, he has devoured all the correspondents' accounts of the glories of Gallipoli, and yet, now he is here in Cairo, actually talking to the wounded soldiers who have been there, everything sounds so different.

After visiting the Australian training camp at Mena to try to get to the bottom of the mail problem, he has visited the hospitals too, where convalescing soldiers and officers tell of the shattering charges against chattering machine-guns that have cut Australians down like wheat, of the terrible mismanagement from first to last, of the lack of water, sanitation and supplies.

It all heightens his desire to see the situation for himself, and on this day he writes a letter:

***To the Commander in Chief, General Sir Ian Hamilton:

Dear Sir,

On the advice of Brigadier-General Legge I beg to request permission to visit Anzac.
    I am proceeding from Melbourne to London
. . . and at the Commonwealth Government's request am enquiring into mail arrangements, dispositions of wounded, and various other

matters in Egypt in connection with our
Australian Forces . . . I should like to go
across [to the Dardanelles] in only a semi-
official capacity, so that I might record
censored impressions in the London and
Australian newspapers I represent, but any
conditions you impose I should, of course,
faithfully observe . . .

   May I add that I had the honour of meeting
you at the Melbourne Town Hall . . .; also
may I say that my anxiety as an Australian
to visit the sacred shores of Gallipoli while
our army is there is intense . . .

I have the honour to be,
Sir,
Yours obediently,
(Sd.)
Keith A. Murdoch.[88]

General Hamilton reads the letter shortly before sending off a cable of his own to Lord Kitchener, advising that although, admittedly and unfortunately, his coup has so far failed,[89] he has worked out what *is* needed to finally triumph at the Dardanelles:

IF . . . THIS CAMPAIGN IS TO BE BROUGHT TO AN EARLY AND SUCCESSFUL CONCLUSION LARGE REINFORCEMENTS WILL HAVE TO BE SENT TO ME . . . OWING TO THE DIFFICULTY OF CARRYING ON A WINTER CAMPAIGN, AND THE LATENESS OF THE SEASON, THESE TROOPS SHOULD BE SENT IMMEDIATELY.[90]

Hamilton estimates that another 105,000 soldiers, or so, should do it.

19 AUGUST 1915, GALLIPOLI, FAIR DINKS

And now, here at last at Gallipoli are the first arrivals of the 17,000 men of the AIF's 2nd Australian Division, composed mostly of those who had joined up in the latter months of 1914 and first months of 1915. They are lauded by the press as men of a rather more substantial cut, incapable of just dropping everything and signing up like those gadabouts in the first lot, and, Charles Bean notes, 'a high proportion volunteered not so much from impetuosity of spirit as because of a reasoned patriotism. The newspapers, in the effort to encourage enlistment, pointed out that these men were perhaps more truly representative of Australia.'[91]

Oh, *really?*

When the men of the 1st Divvy are sent articles from home glorying in this very theme, they are thrilled to hear it and delighted that the 2nd Divvy have at last graced them with their presence. Of course, as detailed by Bean, they at once christen them 'the "Dinkum" that is, "the genuine" Australians'.[92]

And what an impression they make!

'These troops,' Bean records, 'came to the tired and somewhat haggard garrison of Anzac like a fresh breeze from the Australian bush.'

'Great big cheery fellows, whom it did your heart good to see,' wrote another Australian. 'Quite the biggest lot I have ever seen.'

Huge, healthy men of robust good spirits, strong of limb, clear of eye – just what the doctor ordered.

Careful, though . . .

Though it is tempting to throw such men straight onto the frontline to relieve the exhausted troops there now, or to launch them immediately into a battle planned for Hill 60, which is about to be launched, General Birdwood is careful not to do so. Instead, after bivouacking them for a short time at the foot of the Sphinx, he sends them up to Bauchop's Hill, where they can act as reserve to General Godley.

It would be madness to throw such fresh troops straight into a major battle, and even General Godley will not countenance it . . .

20 AUGUST 1915, NOT A RED LETTER DAY

Ever and always, it is the shining spot in the otherwise very dark lives of the Turkish soldiers at Gallipoli. In the midst of all the death and destruction, the fear and ferocious fighting, just occasionally a messenger arrives from their own villages – 'The messenger arrived! The messenger arrived!'[93] – bringing letters, food, gifts and news from home.

The soldiers crowd around the messenger. 'What of my family?'

My fiancée?

My children?

My parents?

And, of course, the messenger – usually an old man from home – does his best. But then the hardest part . . .

'Where is the son of Durmuş Kara Ali?' the messenger asks,[94] as he has a gift of a handkerchief for him, from his girl in the village.

'Blown to pieces by a bomb three days ago . . .'[95]

The messenger drifts off as, devastated, he tries to fathom how he is going to be able to break that news to the girl. The soldiers' eyes fill with tears.

There is similar angst in the Anzac lines. 'I've seen anxious troopers, with yearning eyes,' one soldier would record, 'hang round till the last letter and postcard were sorted – then wander away silently, and gaze dry-eyed over the blue Mediterranean. [All of them] would have given the world to be able to take a peep at the wife who scanned the casualty lists so eagerly as they appeared in the papers, and the kiddies who strutted round proudly, saying, "Daddy's gone to the war".'[96]

21 AUGUST 1915, MELBOURNE, A TELEGRAM ARRIVES

For those men and boys who don't go to war, this has to be the biggest bastard of a job left: delivering cables. Oh yes, it had been cushy enough early on, as it had mostly been standard fare of safe arrivals, babies born, engagements announced and the blessed news that 'I'll be home soon'. But ever since this business at the Dardanelles had descended into carnage, the telegraph boys have a new kind of cable to deliver. They are from the government, and always stamped *Personal Acknowledgment of Delivery*, meaning that it is the job of the boy to get the signature of the person to whom it is addressed. Pretty soon, everyone knows that **URGENT TELEGRAM** at the top is almost always a death sentence, because the news is invariably that a distant Australian soldier is either MISSING IN ACTION, seriously wounded or KILLED IN ACTION.

Sometimes it is all you can do to get the signature out of them, and the scenes you are in the middle of are terrible.

And so it is on this day, for Myrtle White . . .

Dear Madam,
It is my painful duty to have to inform you
the sad news of the death of your husband,
Lieutenant Colonel A. H. White, Commanding
Officer, 8th Light Horse Regiment . . . which
occurred in action at Gallipoli on the 7th
August 1915.
    I am instructed to convey to you the
sincere regret of the Minister for Defence
and the Commonwealth Government in the great
loss you and the Army have sustained by the
death of the gallant officer.
Yours faithfully
Capt.
Officer i/c Base Records[97]

Myrtle's grief is deeper than the ocean. To think of her beloved husband now dead in a ditch on the other side of the world is almost more than she can bear, but bear it she must, for the sake of their infant son, to begin with. In the tragic tradition of war widows through the ages, it is now she who must soldier on . . . alone.

In at least one instance on the Gallipoli Peninsula, at around this point in the campaign, a family member decides to do more than just grieve from afar. For the story will long be told how a Brigade Commander notices something strange about one of his soldiers in the trenches and takes a second look.

'How old are you?' he asks the soldier softly. 'Take off your cap.'

'Forty, sir.'

'No. Your real age.'[98]

There is a pause. A grimace. And then a confession.

'Sixty, sir!' the old man replies.

After both of his sons had been killed on the day of the landing, he had lied about his age, joined up and come looking for any trace of them . . .

Chapter Eighteen

THE BATTLE OF HILL 60

For connoisseurs of military futility, valour,
incompetence and determination, the attacks
on Hill 60 are in a class of their own.[1]
Robert Rhodes James

The Angel of Death is abroad throughout the land
. . . You can almost hear the beating of his wings![2]
John Bright, British Member of Parliament (1843–1889) and orator

23 AUGUST 1915, SLAUGHTER ON HILL 60

Shattered, missing limbs, their faces contorted into the grimaces of agony they wore when death overtook them . . . Hundreds of dead men, many disembowelled, now lie all over the lower reaches of Hill 60, clogging up the trenches, staring glassy-eyed at the weeping sun.

It had been a saga of devastation . . .

To begin with, Hill 60 is really just a scrubby lump of land rather than a hill, its tired summit just 60 feet above sea level. Charles Bean calls it 'little more than a swelling in the plain',[3] and it lies just a mile back from the beach that stretches between Suvla Bay and Anzac Cove.

Despite its diminutive stature, the capture of Hill 60 (along with Scimitar Hill and W Hills immediately to its north) will allow the Allied Anzac–Suvla line to push eastward into the Anafarta Range and, crucially, shorten that line. Turkish rifles currently outnumber the Allies' 75,000 to 50,000, so rounding off and contracting the Allied line is an important defensive strategy that will help secure the 'bridge' between the two bridgeheads – Suvla and Anzac – while limiting any immediate threat to the Allies' Suvla occupation. The problem remains, however, that the Turks hold the high ground and will fight to the death to keep it against those who would try to seize it from them.

Who can the Allies call on in their hour of desperate need?

Why, none other than the famous 29th Division. No matter that the 29th have been shot and shattered from ship to shore and back again so many times since their tragic landing from *River Clyde*. No matter that most of the fine soldiers who stood before King George in March stand no more, as no fewer than 30,000 men have now gone through their doomed ranks since the beginning of the campaign, only to be spat out the other side, either dead or wounded. No matter, even, that they can muster fewer than 7500 soldiers capable of holding a rifle. For their arrival on this battlefield, poised as they are to take Scimitar Hill on the left, lifts the army as one.

A couple of days earlier, on the afternoon of 21 August, 500 men of the AIF's 13th and 14th Battalions had been in the thick of the attack on Hill 60 . . . only to be decimated by machine-gun and artillery fire. The shelling had started another fire in the brush, and all those lying prone from wounds were incinerated. And yet more troops had gone to the heavily held position – including the 750 untried Dinkums of the 18th Battalion who have not been ashore a day.

Hence the dead . . .

Yes, General Godley really had intended to keep those huge-limbed, fresh and cheery-faced Australians in reserve, but then things had gone wrong, you see, with so many of the experienced troops killed that he simply had had to throw them in and hope for the best.

And then the next night, in desperation, Brigade-Major Guy Powles of the New Zealand Mounted Rifles had summoned the Commanding Officer of the 18th Battalion and advised his new colleague by the light of a candle, 'You are to assault with bomb and bayonet only.'

'But,' the Commander had interrupted, 'we have no bombs . . .?'

'You must do the best that is possible without them.'[4]

And so they had. But in the maelstrom the brave soldiers of the 18th – most of them from the Sydney inner-city suburbs of Annandale, Leichhardt and Marrickville – had simply been cut to pieces. Hamilton's report to the War Office after the initial battles of 21 and 22 August gives some clue as to how grim the situation is now:

```
The troops attacked with great dash and
stormed the lower slopes of the hill in spite
of strong entrenchments, but I regret to say
they were not able to attain their objective
nor even to consolidate the position gained
. . . Casualties not yet to hand, but I fear
they amounted to some 6,000 in all . . .⁵
```

When even Hamilton concedes that victory may not necessarily be just up the next hill, how bad must things be?

Very bad. The 29th Division has briefly held the crest of Scimitar Hill before being repelled with severe casualties, and the 11th Division has been unable to maintain a contiguous line in the first Turkish trenches on W Hills.

And yet Hamilton and Godley remain as intent as ever on securing Hill 60, come hell or high water. With the spirit most fervently displayed by General Hunter-Weston in months gone by, Godley continues to feed in whatever troops he can garner. They *must* have Hill 60.

25 AUGUST 1915, CAIRO, THE WORD COMES THROUGH AND THE WORD IS GOOD

He has the cable!

General Hamilton has graciously acceded to Keith Murdoch's request from Cairo to visit Anzac Cove. And yes, first he must sign the

War Correspondents' Declaration, but that is a mere formality. He puts his elegant signature on the standard form without a second thought:

> I, the undersigned, do hereby solemnly undertake to follow in every particular the rules issued by the Commander-in-Chief through the Chief Field Censor ... [not to] impart to anyone military information of a confidential nature ... unless first submitted to the Chief Field Censor.[6]

K. Murdoch

27 AUGUST 1915, THE WORD COMES THROUGH AND THE WORD IS BAD

After three weeks in the field without rest, at last the word comes through. The shattered survivors of Colonel Brazier's 10th Regiment of the Australian Light Horse – now only mustering 160 men from their original contingent of 500 – are to be relieved from defending Russell's Top. They do not have to be asked twice. Just after sunset on this coolish evening, they are relieved by some more of the Dinkums and set off with the slightest of skips in their otherwise delirious step. Once the Light Horsemen get close to the 'safety' of Table Top, where they are meant to rest, bullets are buzzing around like flies on a turd. They decide to push on.

Worse, at 9 pm the word comes back: 'Sling off your pack, and come forward with just your fighting gear and ammunition.'[7] The men look at each other, slack-jawed with disbelief, but do as asked. Within minutes, they receive a countermand: head towards Suvla Bay, to the south-western ramparts of Hill 60.

Again they follow orders, just as they follow directions, and soon come closer to Hill 60, all the time passing ever more wounded men coming back from the firing line – including soldiers of Monash's embattled 4th Brigade, who are another group on the lengthy list of troops who can't seem to gain a moment's relief.

'It can be easily understood,' Thomas Kidd would write in his diary, 'that we were not in very good fettle, although the men were all game enough for anything and had no time for grumblers.'[8]

Led by Brazier, the 10th Light Horse keep moving. Because the whole area has been dug out with sapping trenches, they are able to get within half a mile of Hill 60 without ever being seriously exposed to enemy fire. Then it becomes very tricky indeed. With a wretched squeal, one of the few mules they have goes down, but, mercifully, the rest get through to the trenches at the back of the hill. At 11.30 pm, the hardy South Australians of the 9th Light Horse show the 10th Light Horse how best to position themselves and give them fair warning that, come sun-up, there will likely be more shrapnel than they have ever seen before.

By the flickering light of exploding shells, the 10th Light Horse Regiment can now see just what they are truly facing. One man squints through the periscope to focus: the hill before them is covered in a fresh crop of corpses. The ones on top are the men of Monash's brigade, who have fallen just this afternoon. Lying underneath them are Indian, British and Gurkha soldiers, together with more from the New Zealand Mounted Rifle Brigade and the AIF's 5th Brigade, a terrifying testimony to all those who have tried to take the hill.

The 9th and 10th Light Horse Regiment, it seems, are the last two units that Godley has to throw into the fray.

—

Meantime atop Hill 60, such as it is, Colonel Halil and his 1350 Turkish soldiers remain under severe pressure. The enemy has captured trenches at the bottom of the hill's slopes and are now within 300 yards of the summit. What is also clear is that Colonel Mustafa Kemal wants those trenches cleared at any cost. In his breast pocket, Halil has the last message from him:

I am waiting for the following news from you: 'The enemy who

entered our trenches have been destroyed, our soldiers have taken the enemy's trenches.
Any other information you send me is unimportant.[9]

—

And so the 160 men of the 10th Light Horse settle down in the bitterly cold night, waiting for the warmth of the rising sun, while being entirely unsure whether for some of them – perhaps many of them? – it will be the last sunrise they will ever see.

Even as they are settling in, the fighting goes on, and just next to them, twice the men of the 9th Light Horse make charges, using 50 men in each wave. In their last charge, they are wiped out to a man.

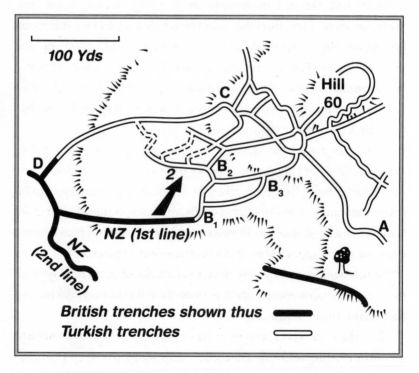

Allied and Turkish trench dispositions, Hill 60, 26 August 1915, after a map by C. E. W. Bean

28 AUGUST 1915, HILL 60, IN GODLEY WE TRUST

Sure enough, the following morning the shrapnel comes thick and fast, with one shell dropping right in the middle of the 10th Light Horse Regiment, but it miraculously fails to explode. Colonel Noel Brazier is not so lucky. Just after dawn, he is hit by a lead ball to his left eye, blinding him instantly. Though it looks like he will survive, he must be led away. Either way, his war is over. However, there is an upside, as he will later write: 'Got shrapnel bullet in left eye and good bye to Antill and two wars.'[10]

All the 10th Light Horse Regiment can do in the absence of an organised charge is dig themselves into their trenches more deeply, and this they do with some enthusiasm. At 3 pm that afternoon, however, word comes that General Godley has arrived and would like to see the 10th Light Horse Regiment's senior officers – a tad problematic as there are very few left.

In the end, the man who has taken over from Brazier, Major Jack Scott, an accountant from Katanning, Western Australia, summons Lieutenant Hugo Throssell, as well as a 33-year-old grazier by the name of Captain Phil Fry and 20-year-old Duntroon graduate Captain Horace Robertson, to join him in reporting to the General. Quickly, and staying low, they make their way to Godley's position, a safe distance back from the frontlines.

After they arrive, the General is not long in getting to the point: 'A most difficult and important piece of work has to be done and you have been selected for it. You must take and hold a trench, the possession of which is absolutely essential to a big operation. Once you have it, you must hold on to it like grim death. The trench is about 80 or 90 yards away from where we now stand, and the ground between is flat and clear.'[11]

Somehow, General Godley makes such light of it that, in spite of the yawning gap between their positions on the military hierarchy, Lieutenant Throssell just can't resist.

'Is it the only trench you want us to take?' he asks in the manner of a man heading off to the tobacconist and wondering if the General would really like only one cigar and not two.

'Only one,' General Godley replies quietly,[12] unaware that off to the side Captain Fry is winking at Hugo.

Very well then.

'I know you will get it,' Godley tells them. 'It's the holding that is the difficulty.'[13]

Indeed. Godley shows them the map, which they examine by the dull glow of his lantern.[14]

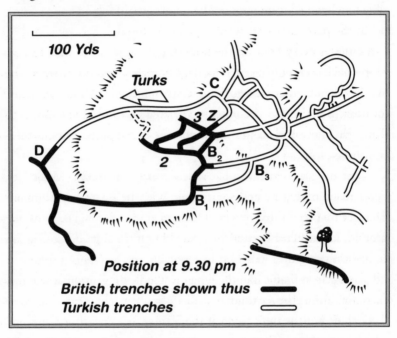

Allied and Turkish trench dispositions, Hill 60, pre-attack, 27 August 1915, after a map by C. E. W. Bean

Trenches and pockets thereof in close proximity are being held by a few lone survivors of the 9th Light Horse Regiment, together with some survivors of the New Zealand Mounted Rifles and the 18th Battalion – but Turks are holding trenches all around them. The job of the 10th Light Horse is to clean the Turks out of the nearby trenches and consolidate the position by digging trenches to connect those already held.

The officers take their leave, with one of them commenting to

Throssell that General Godley makes it sound 'as simple as going down to Claremont Show'.[15]

They are put in the hands of a Major, who takes them to the top of another nearby hill, where he can point out the particular trench on the south-western side of Hill 60 that they are asked to take. But it is difficult, all right. From where they stand, the whole thing looks to Throssell's eyes like a maze. 'The trenches were so close, it was impossible to tell which were ours and which were Turks.'[16]

In the particular trench they are asked to take, it is explained, for five minutes every hour on the hour, the Australians of the 9th Light Horse have been putting up pink flags to show the artillery where they are, in the hope that same artillery can lob some shells onto the Turks' location. But this has become problematic. In the last few hours, the Turks have cottoned on to the tactic and are now putting up pink flags they have captured.

Eager to get a closer look at just what they are facing, Major Jack Scott requests that he and some of the men be taken to reconnoitre. The fact that to do this they will have to cover 20 yards or so of open ground, unprotected by trench, means that it becomes perilously close to the last thing they will ever do.

The one-way traffic coming down is filled with grievously wounded men, for, just as the Australian artillery has been concentrating on the Turkish end of the trench, so are the Turks lobbing shells on this open area with, as Hugo Throssell would record, '75's falling around us'.[17]

When they come to a trench about as shallow as it is wide, well covered by a couple of snipers, the 10th lose no fewer than 11 men racing across 20 exposed yards before it is decided that – to limit the exposure – only squadron leaders should go to investigate. Throssell stays back.

After they return around 7 pm and make their report – it is every bit as grim as they had feared – Captain Fry decides Throssell should see the situation for himself and, just as it is going dark, they make a dash of death across the chain length of carnage, treading on dead and wounded men as they go.

'It was awful,' Lieutenant Throssell would recount, 'but we had to find out what was before us.'[18]

The answer is withering fire, plentiful bombs and a guarantee of suffering many casualties.

It is half-past nine before they get back to their men – in time to grab a bite to eat and a tot of rum against the biting cold. Between them, Captain Fry and Throssell have decided the best time for A & B (combined) Squadron to follow their orders will be at 11 that night. The officers – Scott, Fry and Robertson – go off to receive further instructions from General Godley. When they are not back by 11.30, the whole Regiment comes to the conclusion that it must be off for the night and . . .

And here they are now.

General Godley's 'instructions' are not really worthy of such a grandiose word. For he is of the strong opinion that the 10th Light Horse has what it takes to get the job done. The longer the Turks keep digging in and the Australians keep waiting, the harder it will be. So they must go now.

Tonight!

EARLY HOURS, 29 AUGUST 1915, HILL 60, 'OUT WITH THEM!'

The few men who have gone to sleep are roused and Major Scott issues his final instructions over the sounds of rifles cracking and bombs exploding within 50 yards. Thick palls of smoke drift over them.

We are going in at 1 am. We are going in hard and fast. We are going to take a hundred yards off them and kill whatever Turks we can find, and then we are going to get ready for the massive counter-attack we know is coming.

Now, you must divide up into three lines, fix bayonets and take 200 rounds of ammunition and three sandbags.

'The first line . . . ten time fuse bombs to each section of four men. The second line . . . no bombs, but each man . . . a pick or shovel.'[19]

At 1 am – we have synchronised watches – the 9th are going to take down their sandbag barrier and attack the Turks from their western end, while we of the A–B Squadron charge overland from Trench 3, straight at the Turks from an angle they are not expecting. Meanwhile, Squadron C will do the same from Trench 2. There will be no preliminary bombardment on them as this is to be a *surprise* attack.

Everyone clear?

Everyone seems to be, and so the preparations are made.

All set?

All set.

As they file into position through access Trenches 2 and 3, which are filled with New Zealanders, these good men roar their encouragement: 'Go it, boys! Into them! Give it to them! Down with them! Out with them!'[20]

As quickly as they can, the Australians move forward.

Just before 1 am, Hugo Throssell has the 24 C Squadron men he is in charge of in position – all of them looking rather ethereal in the thin moonlight. They wait for the shout to go up. Captain Phil Fry, who is to lead the first line, has done Lieutenant Throssell the great honour of choosing him to lead the second line.

Hugo is pleased. Phil Fry is a great bloke, and is so frequently and fervently on his knees praying that Hugo often tells him, 'Put in a word for me.'[21] There could be no better man to be following in.

It does not take long . . .

'The first line has charged!' calls out the biggest man of the 10th Regiment, the giant from Gippsland, Sergeant Macmillan,[22] with a force that only a man of six foot four inches can muster.

Throssell and his men scramble up and out of the trench, and are soon running as one, sprinting on an angle across the 60 yards that separate them from the Turk trenches visible there in the moonlight . . . as if it is a school carnival in Perth.

Away from the high walls of the trench and into the open air, as cold as a German's heart, the troopers of the 10th Light Horse Regiment keep running. Now, though bombs are bursting all around, for the

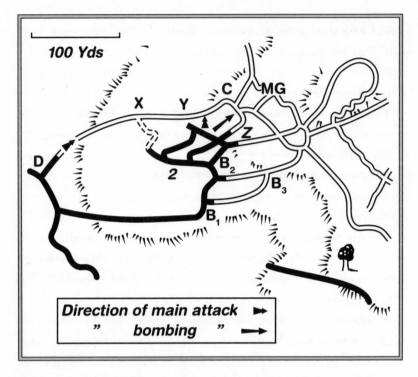

More accurate Allied and Turkish trench dispositions, Hill 60, compiled from aeroplane photographs taken in September and Turkish sources, after a map by C. E. W. Bean

most part they are not under heavy fire – certainly not as heavy as on the first line, who have made the mistake of cheering as they go.

The second line travels the ground quietly and quickly, with the notable exception of Throssell himself, who catches a foot and falls heavily, before getting up and instantly falling again. To his amazement, however, he is not hit and is soon fully back on his feet and jumping into the same Turkish trench in which his comrades are already unleashing hell.

The survivors of the first line have done their work well, after a series of vicious clashes as short as they are sharp and bloody. The trench is now substantially captured, with several Turks lying dead at the feet of the first line (side by side, in a curiously peaceful pose, with the bodies of Reynell's 9th Light Horse Regiment killed the night before). The rest of the Turks have fled.

And here now is the courageous Captain Fry, running back and forth along the parapet, 'heedless of his own danger, encouraging his men'.[23]

'Is that you, Throssell?' he shouts.

'Yes,' Hugo replies. 'What are you doing up there, Phil?'

'Just seeing all is right,' Fry replies before dropping into the trench.[24]

While Throssell's men are filling sandbags to build a barricade to block the trench and make good their claim to this section – meaning the only way the Turks can get to them now is to climb over it, in which case they will have their bloody heads blown off – Throssell instinctively moves forward of his men in the direction that the Turks have fled, knowing it can only be a matter of time before the bravest of them return around the doglegs.

And, sure enough – only an instant after he is positioned in what is effectively a blind no-man's-land facing the Turkish-held end of the trench – an enormous Turkish soldier comes around the corner, only for the West Australian to drive his bayonet[25] into him, ending his life in an instant. And here is another! And another! And one more! And . . . one . . . *more.*

Soon there are lots of them coming, and Throssell, closely supported by Corporal Ferrier and Sergeant Macmillan, turns into a whirling dervish with the bayonet. He yells to the others, who are doing the same, 'Stick it, boys! Stick it!'[26]

They stick it, and they stick it, and they stick it to them . . . and through them.

What does it do to a man to be in the fight of his life, in an enclosed space four feet wide, shooting at other humans who are shooting at you, thrusting your bayonet into another man's stomach, to see his intestines spilling out under the moonlight, to be conscious every second that if you don't kill your enemy he will kill you?

Throssell doesn't yet know.

But on this bloody night, in this ferocious battle, likely no one is more heavily engaged in the struggle than the West Australian. Amid all the screams, all the dead and dying men – including many of his fellow Australian soldiers – Throssell, 'fighting like a lion',[27] uses his rifle as club, gun and spear successively: smashing, shooting and grievously goring every Turkish soldier he can get to.

The Turks retreat under the onslaught, no doubt to gather themselves for another attack.

For the moment, the Australians are in control of the greater length of the trench, and it will now be for them to withstand the brutal counter-attack, which they have always known must come. The first thing is for the eight West Australians to familiarise themselves with the contours of the trench they have taken.

'Each of the sections is about five yards long, and a bend of about two feet,' Throssell would later explain. 'We occupied section A, section B was neutral territory, vacant except for the bodies of the Turks, and section C was occupied by the Turks.'[28]

Yes, cat and mouse, but who is the cat and who is the mouse?

Over the top of the newly constructed sandbag barricade, Throssell catches sight of the enemies' bayonet tips in a curiously flickering light. For the Turks have other ways of attacking, and on their own side the flares of matches soon illuminate their determined faces as they put flame to the fuses of their bombs.

From out of the dark, suddenly a strange fizzing sound comes from above, then a wobbling light. The lobbed Turkish bomb arcs over the barricade and lands near Throssell.

Fortunately, whoever threw it had been so concerned about not having it blow up in his own hands that there is plenty of time for Throssell to gather it up, wait a moment until it appears that the fuse has about three seconds to go, and then lob it back whence it came.

An explosion and some screams from the other side of the sandbag wall give fair indication that it has been on the mark, but still it does not stop more bombs from falling.

Quick!

Almost as if it is a sport, the men of the 10th Light Horse scoop the bombs up and endeavour to hurl them back before they explode. Sometimes they are quick enough to catch them midair and, returning service, have the satisfaction of seeing the flash of light and hearing the *whump* and screams from the other side. Sometimes the fuse is too short and those men who have not had time to throw themselves to the ground and trust to luck are killed or wounded.

'Well, it was a great game,' one of the soldiers would later recount, 'a kind of tennis over the traverse and sandbags but the prize every time was men's lives. But the boys played it as calmly as if we'd been playing with rubber balls over a net in a rose garden, with the girls looking on, and afternoon tea at the finish.'[29]

On both sides of the wall, all is madness and mayhem, *bloody* madness and mayhem. The Australians also throw their own bombs, which they have in plentiful supply, though they are 'careful to do [it] with a much shorter fuse',[30] only throwing after lighting and counting to three, so they cannot be sent back marked *return to sender*.

In the frenzy of the battle, Throssell is concerned that the whole trench is defended, not just his end, and shouts out to Sergeant Macmillan that he needs to speak to him.

Macmillan, known as Big Mac because, as Throssell says, 'The very sight of him puts courage into us,'[31] makes his way to his Commanding Officer, climbing over the dead and wounded to get there. As he approaches, Throssell shouts, 'Are they all right down your way?'[32]

Sergeant Macmillan affirms it, Throssell gives him some instructions – all without pausing in his own battles – and Big Mac makes his way back.

The key for Fry and Throssell is to keep the floor of the trench clear so that those bombs not caught can be quickly picked up. So if you're wounded, men, you can leave your equipment, rifles, ammunition, water bottles and tucker on top of the parapet for us on your way out.

They must also throw dead bodies out over the trenches, and that includes, as it turns out, some of the Australians of the 9th Battalion who had disappeared the night before. Most active is Captain Fry, who seems to be everywhere at once getting the men organised. He's so heedless of his own safety that his men practically have to force him to come down into shelter.[33]

For his part, Throssell keeps gathering and throwing, gathering and throwing, but he soon realises that more bombs are coming than he can cope with. He calls for another bomb thrower to replace the fallen.

And who is this?

Why, it is young Private Frank McMahon from Western Australia, only 19 years old, a nice kid, 'a fine type of young Australian'[34] but very wet behind the ears.

'What are you doing here, Mac?' Throssell asks.

'I heard you yelling for the bonny boys to come on,' McMahon replies, 'and I wanted to be in the show.'

'Well, have you ever thrown bombs?' Throssell asks.

'No,' he says, stepping up to the mark just when he is needed most, 'but I'll bloody soon learn.'[35]

As good as his word, young McMahon is soon hurling back bombs with the best of them, to the point that once he notices his jacket is getting in the way, so he quickly peels it off and gets on with the job. He joins the other men, including Sid Ferrier, Tommy Renton and Henry Macnee.

Setting to with a will, the men work feverishly in the confined space – just five yards long, four foot six inches deep, four feet wide, with a foot of earth as a parapet. It does not stop even when McNee is wounded twice in the head and in the hand, for he stays on. When Renton loses a leg, he reluctantly has to withdraw and be carried back, but still the others keep going in the now sticky trench. The leg is simply heaved over the side without ceremony. For every man who falls, another quickly comes forward. For all the gravity of the situation, still there is extraordinary levity on the Australian side – 'It was the best bit of sport I ever had in my life,' one soldier would recall[36] – with those surviving having many narrow escapes that cause high hilarity.

As the battle goes on, however, it becomes progressively more difficult to keep the trench floor clear of debris so they can move quickly, and so too do the Turks get better – or at least the smart ones have survived – at delaying the throw of their bombs until the fuse is near the end. And they're also trying a different kind of bomb.

The consequences are tragically inevitable.

Down, lads!

Out of the night comes a light that doesn't wobble. This one is not the size of a cricket ball but more like a big biscuit tin. It is so heavy that it doesn't go far, barely clearing the sandbags, but it explodes instantly.

It takes out the top half of the wall, and the Australians quickly retreat a little and build another one a few yards back. The expected counter-attack is not long in coming, culminating in another huge biscuit-tin bomb exploding, demolishing the wall.

Amid the carnage, Throssell picks himself up, dusts himself off and sees Big Mac slumped against the bottom bags with a bad wound in his leg, while Captain Phil Fry is lying on his back.[37]

'All right, Phil?' Throssell shouts.

When Phil doesn't answer, Throssell bends down and puts his hand under his friend's head to raise it a little, only to realise that the back of that head is not really there anymore.

With Phil dead, Lieutenant Hugo Throssell is left in charge, and he immediately orders two of his men – because just one could never do it – to drag Big Mac down the narrow sap and into the trenches proper till they can get him all the way to the main clearing station at the beach. (The only way they can move Mac is for the wounded soldier to propel himself with his one good leg. 'He talked calmly and encouraged bearers. Other men shot in hands, legs, head and injured by bombs remained and fought on.')[38]

Meanwhile, Throssell, who seems to have a charmed life as bombs burst all around without bringing him down, sends back orders for timber and iron to be sent forward so they can build some rough cover against the shrapnel. In short order, between gathering and throwing bombs, Throssell and his men are taking it in turns with the pick and shovel to get one piece of timber and latticework iron – the only things that have come – in place. To make up for what they lack, they stretch their great-coats over the lattice and hope that might do the trick.

The most amazing thing?

In the frenzy of it all, and despite the lack of any contact with the enemy that does not have a fuse attached to it, the two enemies seem to come to a tacit agreement whereby every now and then a mutual 'smoko' of five to ten minutes is unofficially declared. In that time, the Turks might throw only a bomb or two, and the Australians hurl it back without adding one of their own.

Now, if the darkest hour is just before the dawn, then surely dawn cannot be far away. So heavy are the Turkish attacks that twice Throssell and his men have to fall back by five yards at a time, getting the Australians in the next section to dismantle half the sandbag wall that separates them so they can quickly climb over before rebuilding it.

Both times, the inevitable cries of *'Allah! Allah! Allah!'* rise to a climax before the Turks attack again, coming from the scrub to the north-east and shooting and throwing a mass of bombs from afar.

A sudden stab of red-hot pain in the back of Throssell's neck tells him he has been hit. And yes, there is blood, but not bloody enough to bloody worry about. Clearly, just a flesh wound. Same with the piece of shrapnel that shortly afterwards goes through his shoulder, just as his torso becomes wet with blood. Still he keeps going, getting his men ready for what he knows is to come.

There, men, you can see the forest of bayonets rising from yonder Turkish trench. That is where they will charge from. We must hold our fire until I give the word. And, sure enough, some Turks emerge from their trench – and then more do. There are two waves of them racing up the slope from the north! To Throssell's eyes, they look fresh and unblooded, as if they have just arrived as reinforcements.

Right by Throssell in the trenches, Frank McMahon, the 19-year-old West Australian who has been such a warrior since coming forward, sights a German officer at a good distance behind a mass of Turks. The officer is throwing clods of earth at his men, trying to urge them forward. It is too good an opportunity to miss.

McMahon takes careful aim, as does Ferrier, and they fire simultaneously. The German officer drops on the instant, and of course both men claim the kill.

'It's been my ambition ever since I enlisted to get a German Officer,' McMahon announces, 'and now I am satisfied.'[39]

So enthused is he that he half-stands up to get another shot at any officer he can see . . . when his head suddenly snaps back and half-explodes. As he falls back, a Turkish bomb lands right on his torso, blowing him to pieces.

There is no time to grieve. With another collective cry of *'Allah! Allah! Allah!'*, the Turks are clearly preparing for a mass rush forward.

But Throssell has his own ideas. In his view, it is important that the Turks know that the *Australians* are now here, the ones he fancies the Turks fear most.

'Shout and yell, boys,' he calls to his men, 'and coo-ee like the devil.'[40] And so they do.

On Throssell's further orders, the surviving Australians of the 10th Light Horse wait until the Turks are just ten yards away before they stand, some on the parapet, and shout and cheer enough to make it sound like they are 300 strong in the dimness of it all.

As the Turks cry *'Allah! Allah! Allah!'*, they are met with equally passionate cries of 'Coo-ee! Coo-ee! COO-EEEEEEEE!'.

The competing cries fill the night.

'Allah!'

'Coo-ee!'

'ALLAH!'

'COO-EEEEEEE!'

And so it goes.

'We coo-eed until you'd have thought we were a mob of drunken bushmen riding home from town on a Saturday night,' one of the soldiers would recall.

And it works, too! Suddenly the Turkish charge falters about ten yards away from the Australians, and some even 'bolted back amongst the bushes'.[41]

Too late for the rest. The Australians now open fire at point-blank range until the carnage is catastrophic.

'We just blazed away until our rifles got red hot and the bolts jammed,' Throssell would recount, 'then we picked up the rifles left by the wounded and those killed. Twenty yards was about our longest range, and . . . I think I must have fired a couple of hundred, and when we were wondering how we could stand against such numbers, the Turks turned and fled.'[42]

Coo-EEE!

Ah, but there are plenty more where they came from, and within a few minutes another wave of Turks is coming at them, for much the same result, with the Australians again standing and firing in the last seconds when every bullet is guaranteed to take out a Turk – if not two. Again the charge is beaten back.

For the next mass attack, the Turks come at them from the rear and flank as well, and all the Australians can do this time is stand back to back in a rough circle and keep firing. For a third time, the attack is beaten off, *in extremis*, at which point one soldier is heard to mutter something about the advisability of 'retiring'.

The cry immediately goes up: 'Who said retire?'[43]

Which one of you BASTARDS was it?

No one will admit to it, which is likely a good thing under the circumstances, as there is genuine outrage at the very suggestion.

The loud row is perhaps even fortunate, as it may confuse the Turks as to just how many men they have left to face. It holds them up just long enough that, likely in the nick, a machine-gun arrives from the nearest New Zealand trench, borne by five of their brave soldiers and two Dinkums from the 18th Battalion. There is just enough time for them to set it up as the daylight starts to broaden.

Down at the beach at Anzac Cove, Sergeant Macmillan arrives on his stretcher in the grey dawn, whereupon General Birdwood catches sight of him and orders the stretcher-bearers to stop.

'How are they going on up there?' he asks.

'It's all right, sir,' Macmillan answers. 'Throssell's still on top.'[44]

Birdwood is seen to instantly straighten with the news, and even give a half-smile.

Up on Hill 60, when the Turks charge again, there is no need to wait until they are ten yards off. Instantly, the Australians bring their rifles and bomb-throwing arms to bear – between the Turks and the Australians, around 3500 bombs have been thrown on the night – and with the chattering New Zealand machine-gun doing its worst, the attack is beaten off once more.

'The trench,' Throssell would record, 'was ours.'

Still, they must keep busy. Throssell's immediate concern is to get material to fix more shrapnel shelters. He has just returned from doing exactly that, bearing wood and iron, when young Ferrier appears, normal except for the bloody stump from which his right arm had once hung. A bomb blew up just as he was about to throw it.

'Get the boys out of that,' Sid Ferrier says to Throssell, remarkably calmly, nodding towards the trench behind where the bomb throwing has started again. 'It's too hot altogether.'

Then Ferrier walks six yards before sitting down. In the absence of stretcher-bearers, someone gives him the all-purpose tot of rum, and he manages to get to the dressing station 300 yards away. What's left of his arm is amputated at the shoulder, and he is quickly evacuated to a hospital ship.

And what about you, Lieutenant Hugo Throssell? You now have blood all over you from seemingly a dozen wounds on your face, neck, torso and hands. One officer, Lieutenant Tom Kidd, would ever afterwards be struck by how amazing it was that Throssell could still be standing – let alone fighting – with so much blood pouring from his face and hands. 'You'd have thought by the look of them he had been killing pigs. Then, too, he had got a bullet through the neck on the right side, and his coat collar and shoulder was all blood from that, and his left shoulder had been torn with a bomb, and that was all blood too. In fact, he was just sweat and blood and dirt from head to foot, and, as though that were not enough, he was as lame as a cat from two other hits, one on the leg and the other on the foot.'[45]

Despite all that, still Throssell wants to get back to the battle, but this time a battalion doctor steps in and insists.

'With so many dead men lying around, Sir,' one of them says, 'you risk getting septic poisoning if you don't get your wounds dressed.'[46]

It is a reasonable point and, knowing the dangers of getting tetanus, which really is a death sentence, Throssell reluctantly accedes to it, retiring briefly to the dressing station. Among his other repairs, one of the **Australia** shoulder badges, 'twisted and broken, [that was] driven into his shoulder',[47] is removed.

Then he quickly returns to his men with more timber and iron that he has found, together with some periscopes. Yet the most senior doctor present takes only one look at him before immediately ordering him to retire and get straight onto a hospital ship, where he is soon placed into a bath in an effort to clean his many wounds, before being put to bed in clean sheets, wearing clean pyjamas. (He is, and make no mistake, not only one of the most courageous ones, but also the luckiest. Of the 24 men whom he had led in the charge at 1 am, he is one of only two left. Of the 160 men of the 10th Light Horse who'd started the action, there are less than a hundred able to continue the fight.)

The New Zealand Mounted Rifles have fared even worse, 'almost entirely consumed'.[48]

When Hugo awakes, it is to the vision of a woman with a beautiful face peering down upon him – a Red Cross nurse.

Up on Hill 60, though the Turks are still in control of its summit, its seaward slopes are secured by the Australian occupation of those high trenches, and the link between Suvla Bay and Anzac Cove is established – just.

The final epitaph for the effort is recorded in the diary of one of the troopers of the Auckland Mounted Rifles, James Watson, who had lost many of his own comrades in the battle:

We gained about 400 acres in four days fighting. 1000 men killed and wounded. Land is very dear here.[49]

And so with the conclusion of the Battle of Hill 60, the curtain is closed on the August Offensive. Despite the odd triumph here and there, in the final wash-up few are under the impression that it has been anything other than a colossal failure. For the first time, a creeping despair starts to show up among the Anzacs, particularly the veterans. While some of the new arrivals remain bright-eyed and bushy-tailed, still new enough to remain optimistic, for the old fellows – and they really do feel *old*, whatever the date on their birth certificate – there is no escaping the fact that after 18 weeks in this hell on earth they remain further from Constantinople than they had been on the first day, despite suffering 90,000 casualties, 23,500 of whom are beneath the sod, or still lying upon it.

And even those few men unmarked by bullets or shrapnel are mostly debilitated by disease. It is so bad that just under a hundred men a day have to be evacuated to Lemnos to receive treatment, and not all by chance. The problem of self-inflicted wounds is a continuing one.

'Main thing to do today,' Private Charles Bingham of the 1st Field Ambulance would write some time later, 'was the clearing out of all patients except for the few self-inflicted ones whom we keep here. You see anyone who wounds himself to get out of this awful place is not allowed to go, he may die here in hospital but he mustn't leave the Peninsula and quite right too I think.'[50]

For others, the problem is that they are too brave. A case in point is one of Queensland's finest, Private Bob Gray of the 9th Battalion, who is feeling so 'butcher's' – Digger shorthand for 'butcher's hook', as in *crook* – that he finally goes to see the doctor.

He had, after all, been wounded on the day of the landing and ignored treatment since. Now, it is 'again giving a little trouble', so maybe the doc, 'could advise a little treatment'?

Not really, no.

Upon examining Gray, the horrified doctor finds that, besides the inevitable dysentery, the soldier has 'a compound fracture of the arm, two bullets through his thigh, another through his diaphragm, liver, and side and there were adhesions to the liver and pleura'.[51]

Private Gray is immediately sent home to Australia.

Not that it stops him. He is no sooner discharged from hospital than, as a matter of urgency, he re-enlists so he can return to the front . . .

Another aching to return to the front is Captain Carter. From Imbros, he had been transferred to Alexandria and then Cairo, and things gradually got better to the point that on a good night he could actually sleep for several hours without killing any Turks at all. Strangely, the true worry is that he doesn't seem to worry anymore . . .

'It is pretty noticeable to me the small amount of feeling or senti-ment I have for anything,' he confides to his diary. 'Nothing astonishes me – and I don't feel sad or sorry about anything. It seems like being a sort of human machine. I heard that Price had died of wounds. I was very sorry indeed but it did not disturb me much mentally – though he practically lived with me in Gallipoli and I got very fond of him. It appears to be a mental deafness – so to speak – my brain seems dull to all sentiment.'[52]

All he knows is two things. He wants to see Nurse King – the two have exchanged letters and parcels but have not been able to meet, since she is still on her hospital ship – and he wants to get back to Anzac. But when he tries to check himself out of his hospital in Alexandria, the nurses insist that if he goes back too soon he will just get sick again and have to come back. Better that he gives it just a little bit longer, and he might be right as rain.

'I trust this hastiness to get back to a fight,' Captain Carter writes, 'does not last after peace is declared – if I ever get that far . . .'[53]

Chapter Nineteen

KEITH MURDOCH ARRIVES

He was a man of forceful personality, combining
keen love of power with an intense devotion
to his country and countrymen.[1]
Charles Bean on Keith Murdoch

There is nothing new in the present [censorship] situation
that should unduly depress our people [Australians] . . .
There is no better way of stimulating recruiting . . . than
the publication of the spirit-stirring stories, fresh and non-
controversial, of the gallant lads now fighting at Gallipoli.[2]
*Deputy Chief Censor Colonel W. H. Hall, defending the army against
those who say that censors are keeping the truth from Australia*

EARLY HOURS, 2 SEPTEMBER 1915, ON IMBROS, HAMILTON DROWNS

Hands are closing around General Ian Hamilton's throat and pushing him under the waters of the Dardanelles. He can't breathe, can't breathe, can't BREATHE, and though he tries to fight . . . slowly . . . slowly . . . slowly the fight begins to go out of him and . . . and . . . and . . .

And then he wakes up. It has just been a nightmare.

Or has it? Lost in that strange, sleepy netherworld where one is flooded with relief that it has only been a bad dream . . . but still haunted by the all-too-real emotions that have come with it, Ian Hamilton lies in his bed still shivering with the *horror* of it.

But is he alone? Is there not someone else in his tent too?

Barely able to breathe, he looks closely. There! There is someone in his tent. An assassin? A what?

Terrified, now wide awake, sort of, he carefully looks at the face of the intruder . . . only to be frustrated. For though he can discern the broad shape, he cannot distinguish any features of the face. In his entire life, he has never been so scared. And even when he fully wakes at dawn, and, of course, there is no one there, and no sign that anyone has been there, still he feels unsettled. Still he feels that someone has come in the night to do him down.

'For hours afterwards,' he would recount, 'I was haunted by the thought that the Dardanelles were fatal, that something sinister was a-foot, that all of us were pre-doomed.'[3]

Just a day later, there is a visitor . . .

General Hamilton? Keith Murdoch, the Australian correspondent, is here to see you.

After a long journey from Cairo, Keith Murdoch has arrived on Imbros and wishes to present his credentials to the Commander of the Mediterranean Expeditionary Forces, by whose sole leave he has been allowed to visit here, and thank him for 'having stretched a point in my favour by letting me see the Peninsula'.[4]

Upon meeting Murdoch, General Hamilton is half-impressed – finding him to be 'a sensible, well-spoken man with dark eyes who said that his mind was a blank about soldiers and soldiering' – but only half. For, as Hamilton also notes, the journalist 'made me uncomfortable by an elaborate explanation of why his duty to Australia could be better done with a pen than with a rifle'.[5]

Which brings Murdoch to the point. He needs to get to Gallipoli to see it for himself, and it is quickly arranged . . .

The journalist soon finds himself aboard a destroyer, gazing resolutely at the wonder before him – Anzac Cove. And oh, the tingling thrill when, just as he knows the soldiers had done on 25 April, he has to climb down the sides of the destroyer and into a boat that takes him to the shore – though in his case he actually lands on a sturdy wooden pier.

Now, just what Keith is expecting, he is not sure. Already, having visited the hospitals in Cairo to talk to dozens of wounded Diggers and officers, lying there among thousands of others with the most grisly wounds imaginable, he had been told something of the true grimness of the place . . . but nothing could prepare him for this.

The death. The destruction. The sheer *desolation* of the place. The bullets that have bloodied the trail of wounded men coming towards the very boat he has just got off. The shells that continue to fly overhead and burst close. The sense that at any moment they all risk being overwhelmed by just one more Turkish attack.

To get his bearings, Murdoch is more than somewhat dependent on finding the most experienced Australian correspondent on site, Charles Bean, and immediately seeks him out. The Melburnian is shocked to be weakly if warmly greeted by a suddenly much older-looking Bean, sick and lying grimly on his dugout bunk, struggling to get up to shake his hand, having been laid low for several days with the Gallipoli Gallop. By the dim illumination of the sole spirit lamp, the younger man gazes with wonder at his colleague's living circumstances, as Bean labours to get himself dressed.[6] One wall of the dugout is made of sandbags alone, while the other is black clay and has dirty clothes hanging from nails pounded into it. Bean does all his work on a desk made from packing cases, and sits on the same and . . .

And now Bean is ready, and they must go. Be careful to keep your head down, Keith, as this may be dangerous. Though still as weak as a kitten, Bean manages first of all to guide Murdoch – against the constant flow of stretcher-bearers carrying horribly wounded men the other way – to the high frontlines to get an overview of the layout of the whole campaign, as well as introducing him to several key officers, before leaving his intrepid visitor alone, so he can return to his sick bunk.

For the rest of the day, and indeed most of the next four days – with Bean joining for the final half-day on 6 September – Murdoch goes from trench to trench, post to post, keeping his head below the parapet and trying not to reel every time the endless shelling comes close, talking to as many soldiers and officers as he can to get a feel for the whole campaign.

And he is, frankly, appalled.

Here are his countrymen, living in thousands of tiny dugouts that are clinging to little more than a cliff face, as bullets and shells fly, and the supply line behind withers.

Men *live* like this? Fight and *die* like this?

It is not just the horrors of the frontline, the constant shooting and shelling, the dead and disfigured, the stench and flies – though all of that certainly shakes him. What angers Murdoch is the stories he hears of mismanagement, the sacrifice of Anzac lives by ordering rushes straight onto enemy machine-guns, when there had been no hope of success and an all but certain guarantee of death on a mass scale. He *weeps* as he surveys the ground at the Nek, 'where two of our finest Light Horse regiments were wiped out in ten minutes in an attempt to advance a few yards . . .'[7]

Gazing out on the killing fields of Lone Pine – now held by the Australians, at a cost of 2277 soldiers killed or wounded, causing a bump in the Turkish lines – he can scarcely credit the number of dead bodies he is seeing in no-man's-land. As arranged by the good old Bean, Murdoch talks extensively to General 'Hooky' Walker, as well as six senior Australian officers and one senior British officer. Everywhere – including at Suvla Bay, which he also briefly visits – is death, desolation and devastation, with an exhausted army holding on against a pressing foe, but for how long?

Certainly the journalist is impressed with the resilience and resourcefulness of the Anzacs, together with their courage. 'It is stirring,' he would record of his countrymen, 'to see them, magnificent manhood, swinging their fine limbs as they walk about Anzac. They have the noble faces of men who have endured. Oh, if you could picture Anzac as I have seen it, you would find that to be Australian is the greatest privilege that the world has to offer.'[8]

But admire the men as he does, his overwhelming sense is of the sheer, bloody futility of it all, the waste of human lives, when to his eyes there is little chance that they will ever be able to do anything more than cling to the cliffs, while regularly losing many of their numbers to bullets and sickness. How has it come to this? There, too, he is not long in getting an answer as he talks to soldiers, most of whom point accusatory fingers at GHQ, at General Hamilton and his senior staff.

The Australian officers, while they remain loyal to GHQ, make no bones about the fact that, as bad as it all is now, it is bound to get much worse when the winter comes. 'The winter campaign,' Murdoch would report the Australian officers telling him, 'is what we dread above all else, [as] many of our positions will become quite untenable.'⁹

After visiting Quinn's Post with Bean on the morning of 6 September – men LIVE and DIE like this? – Murdoch leaves Anzac Cove at midday and heads back to Imbros, his head and heart whirling with emotion. On the one hand, there really is a lot to admire in what the men have achieved, and in the calibre of some of the senior officers. Just that morning, at Lone Pine, General Walker had told him of how, 'I've come to believe in and love my men. I would not change my command for the world.'¹⁰

But on the other hand . . . for how long can they hang on? And even if they can, for what purpose? When you are paying a thousand lives to capture one hill, is it remotely realistic to think you could get all the way to Constantinople?

Are his impressions so bad, perhaps, because this is his first experience in the frontline of a war, and he simply doesn't know enough to realise that this is the way all wars are fought? That worry lasts no longer than his first conversation back at Imbros with the vastly experienced war correspondent Ellis Ashmead-Bartlett. The sophisticated Englishman – now situated in a large tent in a specially selected shady spot in a grove surrounded by hedges – is quick to tell the raw Australian that in his view things are every bit as bad as Murdoch thinks. What's more, he has said as much to influential people in London on a quick trip back there in June, after *Majestic* had been sunk. The problem the English journalist has now is that, this far away from London, he cannot reach the same people and, of course, all of the articles he writes and letters he sends must first pass the censor, meaning he can't be critical. And nor can any of the other journalists. But he has criticism a'plenty for General Hamilton and even more for his prig of a Chief of Staff, General Walter Braithwaite. Both men, he has long believed, must be sacked – which would make it easier for the brass to acknowledge the obvious, that the Peninsula must be evacuated.

Murdoch has been thinking along those lines, and to have such a senior correspondent agree with such vehemence turns his views into a passionate conviction. The two talk late into the night, and then the next day as well, and on again into the next night, trying to work out what to do.

Ultimately, Murdoch is insistent that the 'conspiracy of silence' must be broken.[11] 'Unless someone lets the truth be known at home,' he says, 'we are likely to suffer a great disaster.'

He is equally sure he is *not* that man. 'I have only been here for a short time,' Murdoch says, 'and I have only acquired a local knowledge of Anzac, so I do not feel that my word will carry sufficient weight with the authorities.'[12]

And as Ashmead-Bartlett has committed himself to his paper to stay here to cover the campaign, and cannot easily return to London to knock on doors once more, the obvious solution then beckons. '*You* must write an uncensored letter, telling the plain truth,' Murdoch says, 'which I will carry to London.'[13]

Ashmead-Bartlett demurs, preferring to coach Murdoch on all essential points of the disaster that is Gallipoli and the catastrophe it will become if the troops are still here in winter.

But Murdoch pleads that that is not enough: 'I want something definite under your signature.'

The Englishman continues to resist, but in the end Murdoch is so insistent, and persuasive, that he finally agrees. Some might say this will break the censorship rules – even though neither man has any intent of publishing the letter – but that is rather beside the point.

'The issue now,' Ashmead-Bartlett notes, 'is to try and save what is left of the army.'[14]

True, the classic role of a journalist is to chronicle the times, not attempt to be a directly involved player in them, but on this occasion both men have come to the conclusion that, whatever the public is told, they are beholden to bring to the attention of those who do make the ultimate decisions that Gallipoli is already a disaster, now heading to a catastrophe unless drastic action is taken – starting with the dismissal of General Hamilton.

But to whom should Ashmead-Bartlett write the letter?

The Englishman must, Murdoch suggests forcefully, 'write to Mr Asquith, as the head of the Government and, therefore, the person on whom primary responsibility for coming to a decision must fall'.[15]

And writing to Asquith helps them to get around the censorship rules, which are of course designed to keep the oft bitter truth from the public domain. Could anyone argue that the rules are intended to keep that same bitter truth from the most powerful political figure in the land, whose job it is to know the truth and so decide what must be done? Ashmead-Bartlett knows Asquith. Of course he can write to him, as one Englishman to another. And Murdoch is on a special commission from the Australian Prime Minister, to report on the Australian troops, so of course he can carry it.

And so, in his tent, as the Parisian *cuisinier* of Ashmead-Bartlett prepares the next sumptuous meal, the Englishman gets to work and begins to compose the letter, bashing out the words on his Empire typewriter perched atop the ammunition box he uses for a desk. The full facts, which he has long been aching to write, simply pour out of him, a torrent of truth that has at last burst its banks:

```
Our last great effort to achieve some definite
success against the Turks was the most ghastly and
costly fiasco in our history since the battle of
Bannockburn . . .
     Personally, I never thought the scheme decided
on by headquarters ever had the slightest chance
of succeeding, and all efforts now to make out that
```

it only just failed ... bear no relation to the real
truth ...

The army is in fact in a deplorable condition.
Its morale as a fighting force has suffered
greatly, and the officers and men are thoroughly
dispirited. The muddles and mismanagement eclipse
anything that has ever occurred in our Military
History. The fundamental evil at the present
moment is the absolute lack of confidence in all
ranks in the Headquarters Staff. The confidence
of the army will never be restored until a really
strong man is placed at its head ...

If we are to stay here for the winter let orders
be given for the army to start its preparations
without delay. If possible have the colonial troops
taken off the Peninsula altogether, because they
are miserably depressed since the last failure,
and with their active minds, and the positions
they occupy in civil life, a dreary winter in the
trenches will have a deplorable effect on what
is left of this once magnificent body of men, the
finest any Empire has ever produced.[16]

Finally finishing, he hands the letter to Keith Murdoch, together with
several letters of introduction he has written for him – including to
Harry Lawson, the proprietor of his paper, *The Daily Telegraph*, and
Chairman of the Newspaper Publishers' Association, which will hopefully allow Murdoch to meet the people he must in London, to tell the
truth about what is happening to the army in the Dardanelles. The two
journalists take their leave of each other with some emotion, fully aware
of the gravity of what they are doing, and unaware that some of their
conversation has been overheard by one of the other correspondents.
For if walls have ears, so too, sometimes, do the canvas flaps of tents ...

Shortly afterwards, on the morning of 8 September, Keith Murdoch walks up the gangplank of the destroyer that is to take him from Imbros back to Egypt, before he is due to take SS *Mooltan* on to London. Every now and then, like a best man fretting over the wedding ring before the marriage ceremony, he pats the inside pocket of his jacket to ensure that the precious letter is still safely there.

Only a short time later, General Hamilton receives a note from one of the other correspondents, who has got wind of some letter that Ashmead-Bartlett has apparently written to the proprietor of *The Daily Telegraph*, critical of the whole Gallipoli campaign and the way it is being run, and it seems Keith Murdoch is carrying it back to London. For 'the honour of my profession',[17] this correspondent feels he must bring it to General Hamilton's attention.

Hamilton is bemused. 'I had begun to wonder what had come over Mr Murdoch and now it seems he has come over me!'[18]

Nevertheless, the matter must be dealt with . . .

EVENING, 8 SEPTEMBER 1915, NO CRUELLER STROKE THAN THIS

Hugo Throssell's heart is breaking. On the hospital ship *Davannah* steaming west in the Mediterranean, they are just off the coast of Spain when one of his fellow troopers, Sid Ferrier – who had had his arm amputated straight after the battle of Hill 60 – starts ailing. Badly. It had seemed that with close medical attention, rest, a proper diet and no bombs incessantly landing all around, he had been getting better, just as they all had been. Hugo has been visiting him for a couple of hours a day, the two talking quietly of what they would do in London, and how it would be when they got back home . . . home to Australia. And after Hugo had told the doctor of Sid's extraordinary courage, the medico had taken a special interest in him thereafter. But, just a few days earlier, things had taken a severe turn for the worse, when the stump of Sid's arm became infected and turned a grisly, putrescent black. It's tetanus.

The doctors have been working on him since, and Sid's wonderful pluck has never deserted him – despite his sweating body being contorted into grotesque arching forms and going through severe spasms as the tetanus takes hold – but now, as the soft dusk of eventide creeps up on the ship, so too is it obvious that the darkness is coming for Sid, as Hugo stands over his dribbling and mostly unconscious form. Quietly, the doctor tells Hugo that at least he doesn't think Sid is suffering.

Now, though, Sid's breaths are coming in raspy form, with ever long pauses between. The end is nigh. Hugo leans in close as Sid gets out his last word on this earth . . .

'Mother . . .'

Shortly afterwards, Throssell writes to that good woman in Western Australia:

> *I cannot tell you how I feel about it, dear Mrs. Ferrier. I have seen many brave men in the last few months, and although there may be plenty of men just as brave, there never lived a <u>braver</u> man than your son.*[19]

The next morning, Hugo stands to attention beside Colonel Noel Brazier and the half a dozen soldiers of the 10th Light Horse as the chaplain conducts the funeral service on the deck. Brave Sid's body, wrapped in the Union Jack, lies on a slanting board before them. Out of respect, the ship's engines have been stopped, and the only sound apart from the chaplain's voice is the light whistle of the sea breeze through the superstructure.

As they commit Sid's eternal soul to the Lord and his body to the deep, all of them salute – some with the left hand, if the right has been amputated. Sid's body hits the water with a splash and then slips beneath the waves.

Ashes to ashes, dust to dust, Sid to the aquatic depths . . .

Back at Gallipoli, the battle goes on, both with the Turks and with the men of the 2nd Division, who remain eager, and sometimes too eager, to see action.

One Dinkum Captain is getting endless queries from his men.

'What the hell is the good of sitting here?' asks one, champing at the bit to get into action.

'Why can't we charge and blow the bastards out?' asks another.

The Captain is beaten in making his reply by an old hand, whose penchant for bravado and death-wish tomfoolery is long gone: 'Yer bastards put yer bloody head over parapet & get a little sudden death. You wouldn't get 5 bloody yards.'[20]

The younger Dinkums pipe down out of respect, but still their desire for the glory of battle rages.

17 SEPTEMBER 1915, A VERY STRANGE WELCOME – BIENVENUE EN FRANCE

Just after SS *Mooltan* docks by the quay in Marseilles – in a brief layover on his trip from Egypt to England – Keith Murdoch looks up to see two high-ranking British Army officers, with the two telltale red tabs on their collars, approaching him. They have just boarded the steamer and have been asking for him.

Keith Murdoch?

Yes.

'You have a letter from Mr Ashmead-Bartlett . . .'

'Yes . . .'

'You must hand it over to us.'[21]

'It is for the Prime Minister.'[22]

Still the officer asks him to hand it over.

Murdoch realises he has no choice, and he very reluctantly does so, along with his report on the postal-service arrangements – sadly, even before he has time to add a *PS* as to what's wrong with the mail service at Marseilles.

With a nod, the British Army officers allow him to continue his journey.

(Prime Minister Andrew Fisher, when he finds out what has occurred, is appalled. 'I have a strong and growing feeling,' he would later note publicly, 'that it was not a friendly action on the part of the [British] Government . . . to send a military officer to seize Mr Murdoch's belongings and examine them while he carried the credentials of the [Australian] Prime Minister and the Minister of Defence on a mission on which he had been dispatched because we could not get any information.' It is nothing less than 'an insult and an affront'.)[23]

The two British intelligence officers left in Murdoch's wake as he departs once more on SS *Mooltan* are stunned. They had been told the letter would be to Harry Lawson of *The Daily Telegraph*. And now they have intercepted a missive marked to the *Right Honourable H. H. Asquith, 10 Downing Street, London*.

And yet, while they are fearful as to just what it is they have done, General Hamilton is not, when he is informed of this fact by the War Office. Rather, he is bemused once more. And relieved. For Hamilton has complete confidence in Asquith. 'I do not for one moment believe Mr. Asquith would employ such agencies,' he writes in his diary, 'and for sure he will turn Murdoch and his wares into the wastepaper basket . . . Tittle-tattle will effect no lodgement in the Asquithian brain.'[24]

MID-SEPTEMBER 1915, AT *THE TIMES* IN LONDON, LORD NORTHCLIFFE PACES

Copy boy!

Newspaper offices of the world have a certain sameness about them: the smell of printer's ink, the endless clatter of typewriters, the sense that there is just too much news breaking in too little time to get it all down, and too little space to fit it all in.

And, ever and always, all of that is exacerbated when the proprietor of the paper is in the building – and never more so than when that proprietor is the irrepressible Lord Northcliffe, a man as quick to promote the worthy as he is to fire the lazy. He wants stories, he wants action, he wants circulation increases, he wants them NOW, and . . .

And, what?

Lord Northcliffe wants to see *you*, Herbert Campbell-Jones, Managing Editor of the United Cable Service, in his office upstairs, right now.

Campbell-Jones, an Australian who has been working and prospering on Fleet Street for the last three years – and whom Murdoch is coming to London to replace – does not tarry, and would write about the whole affair in Sydney's *Sun* newspaper some five years later.[25]

When he gets upstairs, Lord Northcliffe, a forthright man at the best of times, is 'walking up and down the room . . . like a caged lion', and he really wants to know, 'What can be done to save those poor fellows on Gallipoli? Can't you get the High Commissioner, Sir George Reid, to tell the Australian Government the truth?'[26]

From his own sources, Lord Northcliffe has heard just how grim the whole situation is and wishes to exert his influence to help alleviate it. 'Can't you persuade Mr. Fisher to insist upon knowing the whole facts?'[27]

Well, Lord Northcliffe, as it happens, at this very moment there is a first-class Australian journalist by the name of Keith Murdoch 'on his way to England, after visiting Gallipoli, [who] would be able to lay the whole situation directly before the Australian Government'.[28]

For the forces of Lord Northcliffe, of *sanity*, this is exactly what they have been looking for: a recent, credible witness affirming that the whole Gallipoli campaign is a debacle, with a fearless passion, untroubled by politics or his lowly position in the military hierarchy compared with those who are responsible for it all.

Aboard *Mooltan*, steaming through the impossibly blue and sparkling waters of the Mediterranean, Keith Murdoch remains entirely unintimidated by what has happened in Marseilles, and is in fact more galvanised by it than ever. It's proof of the venal nature of the authorities that he and the Diggers at Anzac Cove are up against. Sitting in his cramped, damp cabin, gently swaying left to right, he begins drafting his *own* letter to replace the one that has been confiscated. After all, he has been there, he has been tutored by Ashmead-Bartlett, he understands the basic situation and even some of the finer points. Into early adulthood, Murdoch had been a very bad stutterer, but with pen in hand he does not falter, as the words simply pour out of him.

Once arrived in London, on 20 September, he meets Herbert Campbell-Jones at *The Times* and shows the second incarnation of the letter to him.

'I have never perused any document more packed with scorching phrases, more brutal in its utter frankness,' Jones would report.[29] He encourages Murdoch to keep going on it, to refine, and keep refining, till he gets it absolutely right. Murdoch settles down to keep working on it, and the phrases continue to furiously flow for no fewer than 28 pages, some 8000 words in all.

It is addressed to the Australian Prime Minister Andrew Fisher, and he does not mince words, some of it echoing the lost letter of Ashmead-Bartlett: 'I now write of the unfortunate Dardanelles expedition . . . It is undoubtedly one of the most terrible chapters in our history . . .'[30] There is, he says, no respect whatsoever for General Hamilton and his senior staff, with their red lapel tabs and red bands around their caps, and no one even bothers to hide it. 'Australians,' he reports firmly, 'now loathe and detest any Englishman wearing red.'[31]

Murdoch, clearly having overcome his concern that he is too inexperienced to make judgements on matters military, and allowing himself to be swept up in journalistic euphemism, now says of General Birdwood that he has 'not the fighting quality nor the big brain of a great general'.[32]

In terms of damning allegations, Murdoch swears that not a few hundred yards from where 134 Australian soldiers with fever were dying of the heat for want of relief, he had seen English staff officers aboard the once transatlantic Royal Mail ship *Aragon* 'wallowing in ice'.[33] The British troops at Suvla Bay, he notes, are 'fresh, raw, untried troops under amateur officers . . .'[34] Truly, they are 'merely a lot of childlike youths without strength to endure or brains to improve their conditions'.[35]

And then there is the enemy. 'From what I saw of the Turk, I am convinced he is . . . a better man than those opposed to him.'[36]

And yes, there are many demonstrable errors of fact in the account

– the smallest of which is that there is no record of Keith Murdoch ever having *seen* any Turks, and certainly none up close – and much of the rhetoric is overblown. But the thrust is entirely consistent with the situation: the military leadership has completely lost the confidence of all those it would seek to lead. The situation is hopeless, and getting worse.

'I do not like to dictate this sentence, even for your eyes, but the fact is that after the first day at Suvla an order had to be issued to officers to shoot without mercy any soldier who lagged behind or loitered in an advance.'[37]

He goes on . . .

'I must leave this story, scrappy as it is, of the operations, to tell you of the situation and the problems that face us. I will do so with the frankness you have always encouraged. Winter is on us, and it brings grave dangers. We have about 105,000 men . . . on the Peninsula. About 25,000 of these are at Helles, 35,000 at Anzac, and the rest at Suvla . . . These are all that remain of fully 260,000 men. Nowhere are we protected from the Turkish shell . . .'[38]

'We have to face not only this menace, but the frightful weakening effects of sickness. Already the flies are spreading dysentery to an alarming extent, and the sick rate would astonish you. It cannot be less than 600 a day. We must be evacuating fully 1,000 sick and wounded men every day. When the autumn rains come and unbury our dead, now lying under a light soil in our trenches, sickness must increase. Even now the stench in many of our trenches is sickening . . .

'Supposing we lose only 30,000 during winter from sickness. That means that when spring comes we shall have about 60,000 men left. But they will not be an army. They will be a broken force, spent. A winter in Gallipoli will be a winter under severe strain, under shell-fire, under the expectation of attack, and in the anguish which is inescapable on this shell-torn spot.[39]

'The troops are trying to support their officers, but it is becoming ever more difficult.

'Sedition is talked round every tin of bully beef on the peninsula and it is only loyalty that holds the forces together . . .'[40]

These are, of course, explosive allegations, and Murdoch works on it again and again. A broad summation is that Prime Minister Fisher, who had promised to fight for Great Britain 'to the last man and last shilling',[41] may very well achieve at least the former if the troops are left there for the winter.

After finally completing the letter on the morning of 23 September, Murdoch accompanies Herbert Campbell-Jones to lunch with the venerable editor of *The Times*, Geoffrey Robinson, at the famous Simpson's-in-the-Strand. Over the next three hours – as the white-jacketed chefs carve the meat at the table, the hovering waiters pour the wine and Murdoch in turn pours out everything he has seen – the dismal prospects for all those who remain there once the winter comes are starkly presented.

As Murdoch continues to draw word pictures of what is happening at Gallipoli, as vivid as they are violent, Robinson is clearly moved. 'The lunch,' Campbell-Jones would later recount, 'which began with good humour and gaiety, finished with a sense of sombre disaster.'[42]

And yet, given the amount that needs to be done, there is little time for dwelling on doom. While Murdoch goes off to Australia's High Commission to cable his letter through to Prime Minister Fisher, Robinson makes arrangements to help Murdoch gain access to the most powerful people in the land.

For it fits exactly with what his proprietor, Lord Northcliffe, has been saying all along, the same Lord Northcliffe who, though momentarily absent on pressing business, has told the editor that he must do everything possible to help the Australian.

By late afternoon, the *Times'* editor has arranged for Murdoch to have breakfast the following morning with one of Lord Northcliffe's key allies on the issue, Sir Edward Carson – the Unionist Chairman of the British Cabinet's Dardanelles Committee – who listens carefully. That afternoon, Murdoch meets the most influential member of the War Cabinet after the Prime Minister, holder of the new portfolio of Minister of Munitions since May, Lloyd George.

This is typical of the Welshman, who has always pursued an

open-door policy, seeing anyone and everyone who he thinks may have something worthwhile to say, regardless of their background, where they went to school, and so on . . . No airs and graces for him, and as a matter of fact very little furniture either . . . as when Murdoch meets Lloyd George in the newly rented premises at 6 Whitehall Gardens on the afternoon of 24 September, the sparseness of the environment is surprising. Lloyd George has no time for anything not to do with winning the war. And it is at this meeting that the matter takes on a momentum that not even Murdoch could have imagined.

Upon hearing the contents of the letter, Lloyd George is certain of one thing: it needs a wider airing. Merely sending it to the Australian Prime Minister, as Murdoch had done the day before, is likely to achieve little in the short term. Listen, Mr Murdoch, it is your 'urgent duty . . . to place it at the disposal of the British Cabinet',[43] including British Prime Minister Herbert Asquith.

Stunned at the speed with which things are moving – Murdoch is a man who has been on Gallipoli for no more than four days, and *he* is now the expert being consulted by the British Cabinet Ministers and perhaps the Prime Minister himself? – the Australian tries to demur, saying, 'I do not think Mr Fisher would like me to do that at all.'[44]

But Lloyd George is at his persuasive best, insisting.

Murdoch finally agrees, and, after his departure, Lloyd George writes to Carson, describing the Australian as 'exceptionally intelligent and sane. That makes the account he gave me of his visit to the Dardanelles . . . disquieting . . .'[45] He goes on to say, 'I agree that Murdoch's report does not differ in essentials from that furnished to us by Colonel Hankey . . .'[46]

Another parenthesis here. For, to be sure, Murdoch is not the only one making this kind of report about the Dardanelles, nor making such accusations about General Hamilton. In fact, there have been many others, starting with Ashmead-Bartlett on his visit back to London in June. As to Hankey, his report had been submitted to the Committee three weeks before Murdoch's, and, though couched in far more careful language – 'The Government may well ask themselves whether they are justified in continuing a campaign which takes so tremendous a toll on the country in human life and material resources'[47] – the upshot had been much the same.

For Hankey makes no bones about it, and his thrust is clear: 'It is evident that every alternative must be examined before we are committed to so dangerous and speculative an operation as a winter campaign in the Gallipoli Peninsula.'[48]

More recently, Prime Minister Asquith's son, Arthur, serving at Cape Helles as a soldier, had written to his father, 'This Ian Hamilton is the limit, and it is so obvious to all out here what a terrible mess and massacre he has made of the expedition from the start. I don't believe he has ever been in any of the front trenches and I can honestly say I have never once seen any of his staff officers there.'[49]

As to General Sir Frederick Stopford – who had been dismissed by General Hamilton a fortnight after the debacle of Suvla Bay and sent home – he had no sooner returned to London than he began writing memos and telling all who would listen that the incompetence lay with General Hamilton and his most senior staff, 'making very serious charges about the general interference of G.H.Q. in the battle'.[50]

And in just the last week, one of those senior staff, the supremely well-connected Major Guy Dawnay, had also returned to the British capital, and he has been quietly letting the right people know that his superior officer is just not quite up to it. 'The salient fact,' Dawnay would later be quoted as saying, 'is that he was *no use*.'[51]

And yet, if such blows against Hamilton's standing have seriously weakened the Commander-in-Chief of the Mediterranean Expeditionary Force, it is now Keith Murdoch who is placed in the position to deliver the knockout blow, if he can manage it. Close parenthesis.

In fact, the Murdoch letter is discussed at the Dardanelles Committee meeting that afternoon of 24 September, with Sir Edward Carson informing his colleagues that he has met an Australian, 'Mulock', who, among other things, has given him 'an appalling account of the provisions made for the sick and wounded on the peninsula'.[52] Kitchener is interested enough to take down the Australian's name and address, and promises to see this 'Mulock' and talk it over with him.

The next day, Keith Murdoch indeed sends two copies of his Fisher letter to Lloyd George, so that the Munitions Minister may keep one and pass one on to the Prime Minister. For the latter, Murdoch attaches a covering note:

> *Victoria Embankment.*
> *September 24, 1915.*
> *The Right Honourable H. H. Asquith, P.C., M.P.,*
> *Prime Minister.*
>
> *Dear Sir,*
> *Mr. Lloyd George has suggested to me that I should place at your disposal whatever knowledge I gained of the Dardanelles operations while an Australian civilian representative there.*
> *I therefore take the liberty of sending to you a copy of a private letter I have addressed to Mr. Fisher, in conformance with his request that I should write him fully on the subject. . .*[53]

On receipt of the explosive letter, Prime Minister Asquith moves quickly. On his orders, copies of it are quickly made and then distributed to every member of the Cabinet's Dardanelles Committee. Read this, and *then* see if you can make an argument that everything is okay. (One wonders, in passing, what the British Cabinet Ministers make of Murdoch's descriptions of the British at Suvla as 'toy soldiers', and his assertion that, 'The physique of those at Suvla is not to be compared with that of the Australians. Nor is their intelligence.')[54]

For Murdoch, meanwhile, a bewildering array of meetings, lunches and dinners follows, as he talks with everyone from Foreign Minister Edward Grey to Conservative Party Leader Andrew Bonar Law; from Chancellor of the Exchequer Reginald McKenna to First Lord of the

Admiralty Arthur James Balfour in the company of Colonel Maurice Hankey – the last of whom 'objected to the tone' of the letter, if not its broad thrust.[55] Murdoch even meets Winston Churchill, who defends Hamilton, and describes Murdoch's letter as 'lurid',[56] but such has the star of the former First Lord of the Admiralty faded by this time, it really matters little what he thinks. Along with Kitchener, he is regarded as one of the principal architects of the whole debacle. Of course he has to defend the whole campaign.

On one point, Prime Minister Asquith is perfectly clear, at least the way Murdoch would tell it afterwards: 'Ashmead-Bartlett had a perfect right to communicate with me direct without the intervention of the army censor, and that is why on hearing that the War Office had retained possession of the letter, I immediately sent for it.'[57]

With so many copies of the explosive Murdoch letter now circulating, it is inevitable that Lord Northcliffe, now returned from his business trip, receives one. For the media baron who has so long run a campaign against Lord Kitchener – and lost no little bark from his shins and circulations from his mastheads in the process – the letter is manna from heaven.

Gallipoli vilification is his vindication! Here is a credible witness, just arrived from the Dardanelles, who is detailing just what a debacle Lord Kitchener – Northcliffe's sworn enemy – has presided over. The media baron immediately has copies of his own made, and passes them on to the editor of *The Times* and his key offsiders.

Hearing of it in turn, Keith Murdoch is suddenly alarmed at how such a sensitive document is now spreading like the plague. On the Monday morning, he dashes off a note to Lord Northcliffe:

My dear Lord Northcliffe,
I was most surprised last night to find that you had given my private letter to Mr Fisher to Mr Lovat Fraser to read and that it was to go on to Colonel Repington. MAY I BEG YOU TO SEE THAT IT GOES POSITIVELY NO FURTHER.[58]

Northcliffe replies, pointing out that he has only sent copies to the very tight circle within his paper who see all confidential documents, and, 'You will never hear of the document from them,' which is the good news. And yet, Lord Northcliffe adds, 'but I understand that the copy you sent to the Cabinet has apparently been shown to a newspaper editor. That is not my business, but, on the other hand, if I were in possession of the information you have, involving as it does the lives of thousands of your and of my compatriots, I should not be able to rest until the true story of this lamentable adventure was so well known as to force immediate steps to be taken to remedy the state of affairs.'[59]

In any case, even if Murdoch had wanted to, it is too late to get the genie back in the bottle. For that genie has turned into a cyclone, gathering strength, just as it gathers adherents who have long been saying what Murdoch is saying, and who now have the perfect person carrying the perfect document to create just the kind of storm required to blow down the existing structure.

The fact that this cyclone is blowing at a time when the British Government in general, and the British Generals specifically – and none more so than their chief, the Secretary for War, Lord Kitchener – are under pressure as never before is significant. For in France, the Battle of Loos, the British contribution to the major French offensive in Artois, has just taken place. Following a plan that Lord Kitchener has personally endorsed, using artillery shells that he has organised – which fail to make any impact on the barbed-wire defences – Loos has seen in the first instance 10,000 British soldiers trapped in open fields as withering machine-gun fire mows them down and a devastating barrage of shelling finishes the wounded. All for precious little gain of territory.

The first wave suffered 8000 casualties in less than four hours – and the British Army is on its way to suffering 16,000 dead and 44,000 wounded in the course of the one battle. (Twice the German rate of attrition.) The catastrophe is compounded when, for the first time, the British release canisters of poison gas . . . only for the wind to change, and another 2000 of their own men go down. All up, not even the censors will be able to keep the humiliating and appalling news from the public of what has happened to the first massed engagement of divisions of Kitchener's New Army.

'Never,' one German regimental history would rather blithely comment, 'had machine-guns such straightforward work to do, nor done it so effectively.'[60]

In Great Britain, there is a growing sense that there is extreme ineptitude in the highest reaches of the British military, and it is in this environment that Murdoch is circulating, confirming news that an even greater catastrophe waits for them unless they do something. Prime Minister Asquith, for one, wants Kitchener gone, and he would soon be saying out loud what many had thought for a long time, that Kitchener is 'an impossible colleague', whose 'veracity left much to be desired'.[61] Even Churchill has so lost faith that he is close to writing a letter to Asquith threatening his resignation if Kitchener is not removed from the War Office.

And Asquith wants to remove him, but the real question remains: how to do it? Despite everything, Kitchener remains so popular with the public it would be political suicide to simply dismiss him. For the moment, they must simply try to limit the damage he does.

MORNING, 26 SEPTEMBER 1915, ALEXANDRIA, A LOVELY SURPRISE

Captain Carter, please report to the office. There, at the military hospital by the harbour – almost a halfway house for those heading back to Gallipoli – Gordon Carter responds immediately, wrapping an overcoat around his pyjamas.

And suddenly, there she is. Nurse King. Come to see him. Her ship has come in. And it feels as if his has too. And, whatever else, his previous worry about having 'a mental deafness . . .' where 'my brain seems dull to all sentiment . . .' starts to dissipate. For in her presence, he feels a great deal indeed.

The two start to talk . . .

In fact, he takes her out to lunch, and, after one thing leads to another, he doesn't get back to his hospital until well after midnight, which is strictly against regulations. 'Nobody appeared to spot me but you can never tell . . .'[62]

Still. They can punish him if they like. He has seen Nurse King, and they have talked.

Soon, he must head back to Anzac.

28 SEPTEMBER 1915, IMBROS, THE AXE FALLS
A little odd?

On this morning, Ellis Ashmead-Bartlett is asked to go to see General Walter Braithwaite in his tent . . . only to find Braithwaite in the company of his son and another officer.

'Sit down,' Braithwaite commands, rather peremptorily.

This looks like it is going to be interesting.

'When I had a talk with you in June last,' Braithwaite begins, 'you promised not to criticise the leaders of the Army, the conduct of the campaign, or to break the regulations again.'

'I consented to certain things,' the English journalist allows, 'and as far as I knew I had kept my agreement.'

Braithwaite insists to differ. 'On September 8th you sent off an uncensored letter by Murdoch, who was leaving, addressed to Mr Asquith.'

'I did, and I considered I had a perfect right to address the Prime Minister direct.'

'You know you had not, and your letter has got Murdoch into serious trouble.'

'How did you find out I had sent this letter?'

Braithwaite declines to answer, only informing the veteran correspondent that the letter had been seized from Murdoch when he landed in Marseilles.

'Has it been passed on to the Prime Minister?' the journalist asks sharply.

Taken aback and suddenly uncertain, because Ashmead-Bartlett is not reacting in the shamefaced manner he had expected, Braithwaite can only get out 'I don't know . . .' before gathering himself once more, to say the thing he has called the correspondent to hear. 'As you have broken the rules of censorship, you will no longer be allowed to stay with the Army, and must sever your connection with it at once and return home.'

There. It is said. Ashmead-Bartlett has been kicked out. But again, the journalist surprises him. For, instead of vociferously arguing against any such drastic action, the younger man seems almost delighted. Leaping to his feet, he bursts out, 'May I leave at once? I have long been anxious to be relieved of my post, and have in fact applied . . . to be allowed to return.'[63]

What can Braithwaite say? Having kicked him out, the army can hardly hold the journalist at their leisure, and so Hamilton's Chief of Staff says yes, he may leave as soon as he can go.

Within hours, after saying goodbye to the few friends Ashmead-Bartlett can find, he takes his leave of GHQ 'without a single regret'. 'Never have I known,' as he would later recount his feelings at the time of departure, 'such a collection of unsuitable people to whom to entrust a great campaign, the lives of their countrymen, and the safety of the Empire.'[64]

London, ahead.

One who is appalled by what has happened to Ashmead-Bartlett is Charles Bean, now back at Imbros for some recuperative time. 'The little worm of a Press Officer who I think keeps a spy in our camp in the shape of one of the servants,' he records in his diary, 'seems to have found out that Murdoch was carrying the letter. A wire was sent home and M. was either searched or forced to give the letter up.'[65]

And yet neither Hamilton nor any of his staff will make any apology for it, with Hamilton's Chief of Intelligence even telling the Australian war correspondent that the days of his profession are coming to an end, as it is the role of the army itself to tell the public what is going on: 'In a properly organised nation the government does not need war correspondents – it simply tells the people what it thinks will conduce to winning the war. If truth is good for the winning of the war, it tells them the truth; if a lie is likely to win the war it tells them lies.'[66]

6–11 OCTOBER 1915, LONDON, NOT A MEETING OF MINDS

In London, however, the truth – at least after a fashion – is on the march, and gathering fresh adherents as it goes along.

At the Dardanelles Committee Meeting on 6 October, Murdoch's letter – now an official state document printed on that same duck-egg-blue stationery used for all documents of the Committee of Imperial Defence – is extensively discussed. Though Prime Minister Asquith is starting to have some doubts as to its veracity, noting it to be 'a rather bitter document, conspicuous for the omission of any praise for anyone or anything at the Dardanelles',[67] while Colonel Hankey has told him it is 'full of serious misstatements of fact', there is no getting around the point – as Bonar Law and Lloyd George point out – that its thrust is correct. In fact, as Lloyd George emphasises, 'stripped of all its journalism, it would be found to correspond fairly closely with Colonel Hankey's report'.[68]

What is also bringing matters to a head is the growing likelihood that Germany and Austria-Hungary will launch a full-blown invasion of Serbia from the north, while the pro-German Bulgarians declare war and attack from the east.

If Serbia falls, a direct overland train line between Germany and Turkey will effectively open, allowing the Ottomans to be suddenly flooded with first-class armaments and munitions. The French – who, it must be said, are losing interest in the Dardanelles – are convinced that French and British Divisions must be sent to Salonica, the long-time Ottoman port where the Young Turks Revolution began in 1908, and now a Greek port where the Allies already have a secure base. So insistent have the French been that the 10th Irish Division has already left Suvla Bay, following the French 2nd Division from Cape Helles on 28 September. So supportive is Lloyd George that he has been all for completely closing down at least the Suvla operation and sending 45,000 troops to Salonica.

The obvious complication, alas, is that if divisions are withdrawn from the Dardanelles and sent to Salonica, and the Dardanelles campaign fails, the Turkish troops would then be free to attack Greece from the east, as Germany attacked from the north, and Bulgaria from the north-east.

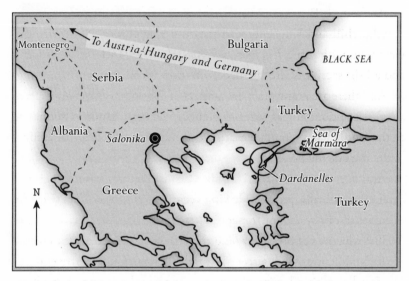

Salonica, 1915, by Jane Macaulay

Greece's pro-Entente Prime Minister Venizelos has just resigned – after being pushed to do so by Greece's pro-Central Powers King Constantine (his wife, Sophie of Prussia, is Kaiser Wilhelm's sister) – so there is a real risk that Greece will declare itself for Germany. Britain must prepare coercive measures, possibly including flooding Salonica with over 100,000 troops, in an attempt to encourage Greece to give up her neutrality, honour her pledge to help Serbia, and join the Entente along with her 600,000 troops.

Yes, it is as complicated as Chinese calculus . . .

'We are face to face with a most important decision,' says Foreign Secretary Sir Edward Grey. 'We must act on the presumption that Germany will open the road south to Constantinople within four weeks, and we must hear the naval and military opinion as to what is the proper strategical policy. Should it be (1) to force through the

Gallipoli Peninsula; (2) to abandon Gallipoli, with, perhaps, an attack on Alexandretta or (3) go to the assistance of Serbia?'[69]

For the first time, thus, at a formal meeting to discuss the policy of war, the possibility of abandoning Gallipoli is seriously discussed.

Abandon the Dardanelles?

Are you mad?

Churchill and Kitchener lead the outcry against it. It is their firm view that, with just a *few more divisions*, the Dardanelles can be won, and all the sacrifices already made will prove worth it.

And there are many practical matters to consider. Is evacuation even a realistic option? For, as Maurice Hankey had highlighted in his memo to the Dardanelles Committee, there are actually two issues at hand.

'Is it tactically possible?'

And . . .

'Is it politically possible, having regard to the place that prestige occupies in our system of Imperial Defence?'[70]

Just what loss of prestige would there be in the entire Muslim world of the Middle East having seen the mighty British Empire arrive in the Dardanelles with all guns blazing only now to be leaving behind its dead and its dignity to the 'unspeakable Turks', of all peoples.

It is almost unimaginable.

The argument becomes very heated, and, trying to re-impose control, Asquith decides – in a classic political move – to set up a weekend joint naval–military committee to 'examine the merits of the western and Gallipoli fronts'.[71] Even as that committee meets, however, the troops of Germany and Austria-Hungary do indeed attack, to be quickly ensconced in the Serbian capital, Belgrade.

It is time for bitter recriminations, and the meeting of the Dardanelles Committee at 10 Downing Street on 11 October is just the place to have them. For the situation is now as critical in the Balkans as it is in the Dardanelles, and whatever decision they make is going to alter the fate of nations.

The tone is set by a Cabinet paper that Lloyd George, furious about the fate of Serbia, circulates to his colleagues, for discussion on this day:

> The helplessness of the four Great Powers to save
> from destruction one little country after another
> that relied on their protection is one of the most
> pitiable spectacles of this war. The notion that we
> are satisfying the needs of this critical situation
> by making another attack on the Gallipoli
> peninsula is, to my mind, an insane one . . .[72]

Meanwhile, with winter now approaching, and no progress on the Peninsula, a decision has to be made. Do they stay or do they go? If they stay, they are going to need reinforcements to get through the season. If they are going to go, the organisation for that evacuation will have to begin immediately.

For those who wish them to stay, a fiery Sir Edward Carson, the Chair of the Dardanelles Committee, has a rather pertinent question as to what the forces are supposed to *do* at Gallipoli: 'Is it to hold and to prepare to resist the Bulgarians, Germans and Turks?'[73]

For his part, Sir Edward Grey is firm that whatever happens from here, Gallipoli *must* be evacuated. 'One way,' he says, 'is to advance and carry the Peninsula, and *then* leave, having saved our prestige, whatever the cost.'

Standing aghast at the notion of evacuation of any kind is, of course, Lord Kitchener. 'Abandonment,' he says, 'would be the most disastrous in the history of the Empire. We should lose about 25,000 men and many guns. Egypt will not stand for long. The troops along the canal would not be able to hold on.'

Equally typically, Kitchener's view outrages Lloyd George. 'If we abandon Serbia,' the Welshman thunders, 'the whole of the East will point to the way Britain abandons her friend and conclude that Germany is the country to be followed.'[74]

'A third alternative, to putting the troops in Salonica, or leaving them in Gallipoli,' posits Lord Curzon, 'would be to come to terms with the Turks?' How the mighty have fallen. Less than a year after the British gave the Turks a bloody nose through the might of the Imperial

Fleet, the unthinkable is now a possibility. 'It is now unavoidable,' Lord Curzon persists, 'that we should endeavour to make some arrangement with the Turks.'[75]

Well, they never. Of course, for the moment, Lord Curzon is shouted down, but, whatever else, it is indicative of the paralysis that these leaders of British military policy feel when it comes to knowing what to do about the Dardanelles and Salonica. In the end, it is an emasculated Winston Churchill who tries to boil it all down, putting before the Committee three basic options. (And certainly – *sniff* – 'making some arrangement with the Turks' is not one of them.) They are:

'1. Whether to send an army to Salonica to help the Serbians.

'2. To send a force to Gallipoli.

'3. Whether to abandon the whole proposition in Gallipoli.'

Prime Minister?

Asquith says he has an open mind, before saying it is 'out of the question' to abandon Gallipoli and to throw troops into Serbia.[76]

In the end, they decide they must send one of their most eminent soldiers – perhaps Lord Kitchener himself – to make a personal inspection of the Dardanelles and Salonica, and 'to consider and report as to which particular sphere and with what particular objective, we should direct our attention'.[77]

In the meantime, they will send 'an adequate substantial force', to be held for the moment in Egypt.[78]

The meeting breaks up amid some acrimonious feeling. Privately, Lloyd George remains furious with Churchill, who, he feels, 'will not acknowledge the futility of the Dardanelles campaign'.[79] His strong view is that Winston 'prevents the Prime Minister from facing the facts, by reminding him that he, too, is implicated in the campaign, and tells him that if the thing is acknowledged to be a failure, he as well as Churchill will be blamed'.[80] And when it comes to Kitchener, don't get him started! The Secretary for War is so wedded to the Dardanelles he has circulated a memorandum to the Dardanelles Committee advocating sending another 150,000 troops to Gallipoli. And all this while Serbia is suddenly being overrun by the Austro-Hungarians, Germans and Bulgarians for want of sufficient Allied troops at Salonica to stop them.

And yet, in the wake of such serious discussions, Lord Kitchener, for once, decides he really may need more information from his man on the ground, and cables General Hamilton in the Dardanelles accordingly:

WHAT IS YOUR ESTIMATE OF THE PROBABLE LOSSES WHICH WOULD BE ENTAILED TO YOUR FORCE IF THE EVACUATION OF THE GALLIPOLI PENINSULA WAS DECIDED UPON AND CARRIED OUT IN THE MOST CAREFUL MANNER? NO DECISION HAS BEEN ARRIVED AT YET ON THIS QUESTION OF EVACUATION, BUT I FEEL I OUGHT TO HAVE YOUR VIEWS. [81]

On its receipt, General Hamilton is stunned. 'If they do this they make the Dardanelles into the bloodiest tragedy of the world!' he notes in his diary. 'I won't touch it.'[82] And even to Kitchener, he is unaccustomedly blunt:

My opinion now is that it would not be wise to reckon on getting out of Gallipoli with less loss than that of half the total force . . .[83]

Fifty per cent! Kitchener is more implacably opposed than ever.

Matters become even more tense when, on 14 October, exactly as has been feared, Bulgaria joins the Central Powers – meaning that the supply chain between Germany and Turkey is now complete.

Greece? Nowhere to be seen. Despite its own treaty with Serbia, it fails to honour its obligations, fearing that to do so would see it invaded.

And yet, though the Dardanelles Committee meets again on the afternoon of the same day that Bulgaria declares war, still they are unsure what to do about Gallipoli – whether to stay or go.

But one thing is clear. The statement of Prime Minister Asquith that Sir Ian Hamilton 'had had very great chances, but had been uniformly unsuccessful, and had lost the confidence of the troops under him' is broadly agreed with by all present.[84] Consequently, they ask Lord Kitchener to do the honours, without delay . . .

Chapter Twenty

TO LEAVE, OR NOT TO LEAVE, THAT IS THE QUESTION

What makes the men growl is seeing immaculately
dressed British staff officers walking about washed
and shaved asking silly damned questions. I am fairly
convinced I am becoming a bit of a Socialist.[1]
Captain Bill Knox

Extraordinary friendly exchanges between the Turks and
our fellows this morning early. Some of our chaps ran
right over to the enemy trenches and exchanged bully,
jam, cigarettes etc. The whole business was wonderful and
proves how madly unnecessary this part of the war is.[2]
Lieutenant Thomas E. Cozens

NIGHT, 15 OCTOBER 1915, IMBROS, DO NOT GO GENTLE INTO THAT GOOD NIGHT

One cannot knock on a tent, no matter how grandiose it is, and so
the only thing the messenger can do is call softly in the night, until
General Hamilton responds – which does not take long, as he has only
just turned in.

A cable for you, Sir . . .

By the light of the lantern that the messenger offers, the General
sees that the cable is from Lord Kitchener, marked Secret and Personal.

Suspecting all too well what it is going to say and that, far from secret, it will more than likely be in the headlines back home, Hamilton tells the young fellow that he will read it the following morning.

Sure enough, the cable from Kitchener is as he expected:

THE WAR COUNCIL HELD LAST NIGHT DECIDED THAT THOUGH THE GOVERNMENT FULLY APPRECIATE YOUR WORK . . . THEY, ALL THE SAME, WISH TO MAKE A CHANGE IN THE COMMAND WHICH WILL GIVE THEM AN OPPORTUNITY OF SEEING YOU.[3]

Kitchener goes on to explain that his position will be taken by the former Commander of the Third Army in France, General Sir Charles Monro, currently serving on the Western Front.

Hamilton has a miserable breakfast, and then returns to read Kitchener's cable again. Is the fact that he has been replaced by Monro – a noted 'Westerner', always eager to pour resources into killing Germans in France and Belgium, rather than Turks in the Dardanelles – a sign of Kitchener's waning influence in the realms of real power? Probably.

Hamilton's answer is for Kitchener to come out to the Dardanelles and run the campaign himself, and the dismissed General fully intends to try to convince him to do exactly that. With the sort of pull that Kitchener would have on munitions and reinforcements, he could finally make the whole thing happen and could 'bring off the coup right away'.[4] With Kitchener in command, Hamilton has no doubt: 'In one month from to-day, our warships will have Constantinople under their guns.'[5]

At tea that afternoon with Braithwaite – who has also been recalled – and others who appear equally depressed, Hamilton tries to cheer them up. 'My credit with Government is exhausted; clearly I can't screw men or munitions out of them. The new Commander will start fresh with a good balance of faith, hope and charity lodged in the Bank of

England. He comes with a splendid reputation, and if he is big enough to draw boldly on this deposit, the Army will march; the Fleet will steam ahead; what has been done will bear fruit, and all our past struggles and sacrifices will live.'[6]

As to his own fate, the old soldier is sanguine, and realistic: '[The fact is] I have not succeeded and there is nothing more to be said.'[7]

The following day, 17 October, Hamilton leaves Gallipoli forever, close to a broken man. He has done his best and been found wanting. Bean, who remains an admirer of Sir Ian Hamilton as a man if not as a General, is there at the melancholy adieu. To him, Hamilton looks 'very haggard – almost broken up'.[8]

The ghastly weather, a cold drizzle that chills everyone on the Peninsula to the marrow of their bones, matches Hamilton's mood, and, after this long day of emotional farewells, he boards HMS *Chatham* and immediately heads below, even as he can hear the anchor chains grinding and the screws beginning to turn, and feels the small shudder a ship gives just before it gets underway.

General Hamilton is just settling down when a message comes from the skipper, asking would he please come topside once more, as Admiral de Robeck begs the pleasure of his company on the quarter-deck. Reluctantly, General Hamilton agrees, and he arrives in time to look out and see *Chatham* steering a corkscrew course – threading in and out among the warships at anchor. As they pass each one, the decks are crowded, and as Hamilton would record, '[we were] sent . . . on our way with the cheers of brave men . . .'[9]

22 OCTOBER 1915, CHURCHILL'S LAST HURRAH AT CHARING CROSS

All aboooooooard! Just after 6 am, the steam train bearing General Sir Charles Monro and his senior staff on the first leg of their journey towards the Dardanelles lurches forward the first inch of its trip to the Channel, where a fast ship awaits.

Truthfully, Monro is feeling more than a little under the weather after a big farewell the night before, and things are not improved by 'the appalling smell of beer exhaled by our servants who had spent the night "celebrating"'.[10]

Worse still? Suddenly there is a commotion, a flurry of activity bursting forth along the platform, scattering people and porters like chickens before a fox. One does not tarry before a 'Gentleman' on a mission, and least of all when the said gentleman with the bow tie and bowler hat is Winston Churchill.

For it is he, and, huffing and puffing like the steam train itself, he throws a sheaf of papers through the window at Monro, and shouts, 'Don't forget, if you evacuate it will be the biggest disaster since Corunna!'[11]

LATE OCTOBER 1915, GALLIPOLI, HUNKERING DOWN

After his victory for the ages atop Chunuk Bair back in August, Colonel Mustafa Kemal has remained at the front, though tensions between him and the leadership – particularly the German leadership of Liman von Sanders – are worse than ever.

What's more, on 20 September, Kemal had fallen ill, with what the doctor thought was malaria. It appears that his endless months at the front are beginning to wear him down at last, draining the vigour out of his watery blue eyes and crumpling his once handsome posture, much to the frustration of his ever-active mind. For the first time, he starts to think seriously of returning to Constantinople . . .

30 OCTOBER 1915, A WHIRLWIND HITS THE PENINSULA

It is typical of General Sir Charles Monro. No nonsense, straight to the point, get the job done, what!

Another man taking over such a command might ease his way into the job and bit by bit come to understand its contours. But not this 55-year-old graduate of the Royal Military Academy Sandhurst, a professional soldier all his life, eager to get to the task that has been set for him by the Dardanelles Committee, to determine the advisability of evacuation – not that he tells anyone that.

Only 36 hours after arriving at Imbros, Monro boards a destroyer and visits, in just the one day – in fact, in no more than six hours – all of Cape Helles, Anzac Cove and Suvla Bay, firing off questions to the cabal of senior officers in each spot, who are of course on hand to greet him. True, the angle of his questioning seems more aligned with that of a man seeking answers that will buttress his already strong opinions on the matter, rather than seeking to shed light – but questions they are.

He seeks to know the attacking ability, if any, that remains in the men in charge, the security of their supply lines and the state of their stores, their ability to withstand the winter, the state of their troops, and their estimation of the state of the enemy troops – their capability and intentions.

He is appalled, though not particularly surprised, by the answers. Everyone is exhausted, morale is low, sickness is endemic – 500 evacuations a day over the last month – supplies are spasmodic and both sides appear to be essentially spent in terms of mounting the force necessary to strike a serious blow on their enemy.

Surely, nowhere can things be grimmer than here at Anzac Cove? One glance shows an entire army clinging to the cliffs for dear life, and a pall of exhaustion, desiccation and devastation hanging over the entire place. 'Like Alice in Wonderland,' Monro comments to Aspinall beside him. 'Curiouser and curiouser.'[12]

Cognisant of his instructions to check the dugouts and trenches for how well they would stand up to the German modern armaments (including howitzers and heavy shells) now believed to be on their way to Turkey, he is blunt, telling Birdwood that, on the Western Front, 'nothing less than from twelve to sixteen feet of head-cover was considered sufficient; and for safety every deep shelter must have several exits'.[13] Anzac would never withstand serious German shelling.

But then he sees Suvla Bay and the whole setup is even worse. At least at Anzac, there is a sense of aggression against the Turks. Though there have been no major actions since the battle of Hill 60, small-scale trench warfare has continued, and Birdwood has particularly pushed the tunnelling to undermine the enemy at Posts including Pope's, Quinn's and Courtney's. The most ambitious of all is a 60-foot tunnel to be dug beneath the Nek, large enough to accommodate troops two abreast that would emerge behind the enemy's trenches. Mining and counter-mining, explosion and counter-explosion of tunnel galleries has become the order of the day. That notwithstanding, the general feeling is one of exhaustion and ennui.

And there are people in London, who haven't seen this, who think it is feasible that an army clearly so exhausted can hang on through winter? That they can maybe even break out and make their way to Constantinople after everything they've been through? Not even the Generals on site appear to believe that, having given Monro a formal paper on his arrival advising that it would take no fewer than 400,000 men to get through to the Narrows, and that no attack could begin until the spring.

Yes, *400,000* men! Men who should be in France killing Germans, not here in the Dardanelles wasting their time and losing their lives uselessly. It is not only a nonsense, but an obvious nonsense.

Lord Kitchener receives Monro's report the following day at the War Office:

AFTER AN INSPECTION OF THE GALLIPOLI PENINSULA I HAVE ARRIVED AT THE FOLLOWING CONCLUSIONS: THE TROOPS ON THE PENINSULA – WITH THE EXCEPTION OF THE AUSTRALIAN AND NEW ZEALAND CORPS – ARE NOT EQUAL TO A SUSTAINED EFFORT OWING TO THE INEXPERIENCE OF THE OFFICERS, THE WANT OF TRAINING OF THE MEN, AND THE DEPLETED CONDITION OF MANY OF THE UNITS.
WE MERELY HOLD THE FRINGE OF THE SHORE, AND ARE CONFRONTED BY THE TURKS IN VERY FORMIDABLE ENTRENCHMENTS WITH

ALL THE ADVANTAGES OF POSITION AND POWER
OF OBSERVATION . . .
     ON PURELY MILITARY GROUNDS,
THEREFORE, IN CONSEQUENCE OF THE GRAVE
DAILY WASTAGE OF OFFICERS AND MEN
WHICH OCCURS, AND OWING TO THE LACK
OF PROSPECT OF BEING ABLE TO DRIVE THE
TURKS FROM THEIR ENTRENCHED LINES,
I RECOMMEND THE EVACUATION OF THE
PENINSULA.[14]

As simple as that. Perhaps the Anzacs might be able to hold on over the winter, but that is it. Much better to acknowledge the reality that they are wasting their time here. Far better to get them back to Egypt – at least, as many as can be safely evacuated – and have them recuperate so they can live to fight another day.

And yet, if Kitchener is astounded to receive such a clear-cut call for evacuation, it is as nothing to his reaction a short time later, when, in a follow-up cable, Monro gives his estimate as to how many men might be lost in evacuating: between 30 and 40 per cent. Yes, that is a little better than the forecast by Hamilton, but that had been a man arguing the virtues of the status quo and trying to hold onto his job. This estimate, presumably, is a cold-eyed calculation: 40,000 men, or thereabouts, consigned to their death or capture if they pull out.

Kitchener is implacably opposed and sends a cable to Birdwood:

I ABSOLUTELY REFUSE TO SIGN ORDERS FOR
EVACUATION, WHICH I THINK WOULD BE THE
GRAVEST DISASTER AND WOULD CONDEMN A
LARGE PERCENTAGE OF OUR MEN TO DEATH
OR IMPRISONMENT.[15]

But for most members of the Cabinet, Monro's views carry weight. He is an officer of undoubted military expertise, with no investment in staying, because he had no part in the decision to go in the first place. He has looked, he has calculated, and he has . . . decided. (By any estimation, the embittered Winston Churchill's summation that 'he came, he saw, he capitulated' is grossly unfair.)[16]

So, from this point, the decision to evacuate should be straightforward – particularly when Ellis Ashmead-Bartlett, now returned to London, starts giving lectures, covered by the newspapers, where he talks openly about the Dardanelles disaster. 'In his opinion,' notes *The Times*, 'it would have been much wiser never to have landed at Anzac . . . and [he] pointed out what we should have to face if we were obliged to stay on the Peninsula during the winter.'[17]

But, in fact, despite the formal advice to get out of the Dardanelles, and the growing outcry at what is happening there, the resistance to leaving remains formidable. For look there!

Even all these months on, the idea of storming the Dardanelles with the Fleet, supported by the army, *still* has not died. And the man promoting it door to door in London is none other than Commodore Roger Keyes. A devotee, back in March, to the idea that forcing the Dardanelles was sound – it was just that the execution lacked vigour – he feels the same now, though with even more passion. On his side, Keyes has the strong support of Admiral Wemyss, and the two push hard on the plan they have worked out together: just like March, but more so!

What they must do, you see, is attack at the darkest hour just before a dawn, further clouded by the smokescreen they will lay down, and then simply charge at the minefields and the Narrows – minesweepers and destroyers to the fore. Yes, in this way they will lose some vessels, maybe many, but the point is that some are bound to get through! And, once through, all the old rules would apply. Wave one Union Jack in the Sea of Marmara and the Turkish war would be over!

Excellent.

Kitchener loves this revisitation of the old plan from the first, embracing it in the way a drowning man embraces a lifebuoy when his ship is sinking.

Such Kitchener enthusiasm drives the likes of Lloyd George to distraction – as Minister for Munitions, Lloyd George has come to see up close the level of Kitchener's incompetence in everything to do with modern warfare – to the extent that, on 28 October, the Welshman leads a delegation of Cabinet Ministers who dine with Prime Minister Asquith to urge him to outright sack the Secretary for War, and to hell with the political consequences!

As to Keyes' plan, they point out the obvious: the Imperial Fleet, with French assistance, had tried forcing the Narrows on naval power alone six months earlier and it had not worked. Why on earth would they revisit it?

Prime Minister Asquith couldn't agree more. As to getting rid of Kitchener, leave it with him . . .

1 NOVEMBER 1915, MONTAZA BEACH, EGYPT, NOTE FROM ANOTHER WORLD

It is a strange circumstance indeed that such a message should wash up on one of the few Mediterranean shores where it will attract immediate attention, but this appears to be the case. For in the bottle is a scrap of paper and on it is scrawled a note:

> *Am prisoner about 2 miles from where we landed between the dried lake and the other.*
>
> *ERC Adams 8 AIF*[18]

It is the first sign of life of Edgar Adams, who had gone missing on the afternoon of the 25 April landing and had not been heard from since. Once advised by cable that he is alive – *he is alive!* – there is great rejoicing in the Adams household in Mildura.

EARLY NOVEMBER 1915, GALLIPOLI, COMETH THE COLD

Trooper Bluegum, who has now been at Anzac Cove for well over five months, puts it typically well: 'Days dragged drearily on. Pessimism peeped into the trenches. Later in the solitude of the dug-out pessimism stayed an unwelcome guest, and would not be banished. All the glorious optimism of April, the confidence of May, June and July had gone, and the dogged determination of August, September and October was fast petering out.'[19]

A low, slow malaise starts to settle over the Anzacs, above and beyond the general sickness they have all been struggling with for so long. As winter starts to approach, a general sense of hopelessness deepens, and while the wild birds far above are clearly flying south for the warmer climes, the men must stay. Now, night after night, the creeping cold comes up from the depths of the Dardanelles, steals across the ravaged landscape and settles in the trenches, where it stealthily begins turning flesh to ice, lays siege to the soul and seeps into the marrow of men's bones. On a bad night, it is *cold* . . . so freezing cold, so catastrophically cold that, as the running joke among the Diggers goes, instead of blowing out the candle in your dugout at night, you actually have to knock the flame off with the butt of your .303. So cold that Trooper Bluegum and his comrades frequently fire 'five rounds rapid' for the simple pleasure of 'hugging the rifle barrel'.[20] Warmth!

In early autumn, the tepid sunlight of dawn had managed to chase the cold away again, at least a little, but now, as the season progresses, the 'sun' is that in name only, and the best you can hope for is a general numbness to relax the cold's agonising grip, as the brass monkeys scamper hither and thither.

The temperature is dropping, the wind is blowing like a bastard and winter is grabbing the Dardanelles by the throat. Can men even live in an open trench in winter in Turkey? It is debatable, and orders go out for materials from Egypt to help to cover those trenches.

In fact, that cover might be useful for more than keeping out the cold when the expected munitions of Germany arrive, and the Diggers will likely be facing 'modern bombardment',[21] under more high-explosive heavy howitzer shells than ever.

Aware of this, Lord Kitchener has already instructed Birdwood, 'you should study very carefully and carry out defensive works and communication trenches on the lines of those that have successfully resisted German artillery in France, so as to be prepared to resist increased bombardment of your positions. My advice is dig.'[22]

Now there's something that had not previously occurred to them.

In the meantime, the problem of self-inflicted wounds among the Anzacs is now so bad – soldiers prepared to do anything just to get away from this infernal place – that Birdwood posts a new rule. From now on, if a soldier is suspected of such a thing, he will not be sent to the hospitals of Great Britain, Malta or Egypt but will go no further than the toxic tent hospitals of Lemnos.[23]

And maybe that helps. But one machine-gunner thwarts Birdwood anyway, by putting an instantaneous fuse bomb under his pillow and blowing his brains out. 'Strain evidently too much for him,' his mate records in his diary. 'Traces of doubtful syphilis.'[24]

Many others continue to be killed in battle, with Private Charles Bingham, of the 1st Field Ambulance – a gentle man of impeccable manners, who had seen little of the rough side of life before joining up – recording how a particular Captain of the Royal Garrison Artillery had come in with his brain spilling out of his shattered skull, with no fewer than three wounds in his chest and two in his stomach from shrapnel. How do you even *begin*? All they can do is dress his wounds the best they can, pushing his brains back into his skull and putting a bandage around it, and then Bingham and a comrade carry him to a tent, where they have no choice but to leave him, while they concentrate on helping men who *might* be saved.

'We heard the death rattle in his throat but oh it seems awful for civilised men to leave him by himself to die like a dog. Flies just eating him. I put a cloth over his face and eyes to keep them off but I looked back an hour later and someone had removed it. I mention this to show just how human life is valued here. Some mother perhaps is worrying her heart out for him too . . .'[25]

Of course, the Turks, French and British are suffering similarly. For those who stick it out on both sides of no-man's-land, the knowledge that they are all in the same wretched boat continues to, somehow – through an affinity of abysmal-ness – bring a strange air of fraternity to the two sides, all while they continue to try to kill each other.

Sergeant Cuthbert Finlay would later tell of another odd truce at Quinn's at this time, how one morning he and his fellow Diggers noticed Turkish heads coming above the parapet and signalling them, before again a parcel is thrown over containing cigarettes and a note in bad French that translates to, **Have these with pleasure, our heroic enemies. Send milk.**[26]

Well, one thing leads to another, and before long the soldiers from both sides have once more emerged from their trenches to shake hands, communicate the best they can, exchange mementoes – but, alas, no milk – and get a look at each other before, again, the war calls.

'The Turks and ourselves intermingled in No Man's Land for about a quarter-hour,' Finlay would tell Bean, 'and then "finis" was announced. A few shots were fired towards the sky and everything went on as usual.'[27]

Back to the business.

3 NOVEMBER 1915, LONDON, HOW THE MIGHTY HAVE FALLEN

For Lloyd George, it is something, anyway. On this day, he receives a handwritten letter from Prime Minister Asquith that helps to mollify him a little:

10 Downing Street Whitehall 3rd November

My dear Lloyd George,
. . . What I wanted you to know before tomorrow's Cabinet was that, in view of the conflicting opinions now to hand of Monro and the other generals in regard to the future of the Dardanelles, I arranged today that [Kitchener] should proceed without delay

... to Alexandria, and after visiting Gallipoli and Salonica, and conferring with all our military and diplomatic experts in that quarter of the world, advise us as to our strategy in the Eastern Theatre. In the meantime, I propose to take over the [War Office] ... We avoid by this method of procedure the immediate supersession of K. as War Minister, while attaining the same result ...

Yours very sincerely,
HHA[28]

Lloyd George must concede the brilliance of the manoeuvre. For while many in the Cabinet agree with him that Lord Kitchener must go, to the British public he remains a hero and for the moment probably *is* unsackable. By sending 'K.' to Gallipoli to see for himself, it serves both purposes: informing him of the situation and getting him away from the War Office for a precious month, allowing some level of organisation to be imposed.

4 NOVEMBER 1915, ANZAC COVE, GETTING OUT OF THE KITCHENER

All these months in, it takes a bit to stun 'Birdie', but the mixed signals and conflicting assertions he is getting from the seemingly ever more erratic Secretary for War are verging on the simply ludicrous.

Yet more cables come from Kitchener, changing his position each time: from staying, to landing elsewhere, to forcing the Fleet through, to replacing Monro, to evacuation. All of that on *just this one day*. And to add to it, Lord K. is 'coming out at once to see things for himself ...'[29] General Birdwood reels, though maintaining a calm exterior.

For his part, whatever Kitchener's own confused state of mind, there is one thing he is certain of: he does not wish to be sacked in his absence from London. It is for this reason that he carefully packs away into his baggage before departure the official seals of the War Office, without which orders are null and void.

Two days later, on 6 November, Birdwood gets a solid intimation of the way London's thoughts are turning when he receives a cable from Prime Minister Asquith, telling him to prepare IN CONCERT WITH THE NAVAL AUTHORITIES AND YOUR STAFF . . . IN THE UTMOST SECRECY A COMPLETE PLAN FOR EVACUATION IF AND WHEN IT SHOULD BE DECIDED UPON.[30]

1.40 PM, 13 NOVEMBER 1915, ANZAC COVE, THE GREAT MAN STEPS ASHORE

It couldn't be, could it? Not Great Britain's most famous military man – in fact, the most famous military man in the world – stepping ashore here at Anzac Cove? Well, there is *someone* large and ungainly getting out of a picket boat on the pier at North Beach, just come from the destroyer *La Foray* offshore, and Birdie seems to be fussing all around him. The soldiers look closer . . .

It is! The same walrus moustache, the same imperious air, the same red hatband and baleful glare that has stared down on potential recruits all over the British Empire – it is Field Marshal Lord Kitchener!

After all the cables, all the reports, all the endless hand-wringing and discussions, the great man has come to have a look at the situation himself. As he steps from the small boat that is ferrying him, he is accompanied, of course, by his faithful Aide-de-Camp Captain Oswald FitzGerald, who *never* leaves his side. For such an occasion as this, however, there are also many Generals of his senior staff jockeying for position around him. Of course, such a well-uniformed entourage arriving attracts a great deal of attention, and of course the soldiers instantly recognise the towering and beribboned Lord Kitchener with the greying temples in the middle of the throng.

Private Reginald Scott Gardiner is, if you can believe it, just *two yards away* from where the good Lord first sets foot on land, and will report to his mother in a letter, 'He is very tall and broad, with bushy moustache, and red face . . .'[31]

And they run from everywhere, the interaction between this most supreme of British officers and the many men he has caused to be in this most godforsaken of places carefully recorded by Charles Bean, who watches closely. 'The tall red cap,' the Australian journalist would record in his diary that night, 'was rapidly closed in amongst them – but they kept a path and as the red cheeks turned and spoke to one man or another, they cheered him – they, the soldiers – no officers leading off or anything of that sort. It was a purely soldiers' welcome.'[32]

And yes, the Lord their saviour, maybe, is even able to rise magnificently to the occasion. 'The King,' he says with some warmth, 'asked me to tell you how splendidly he thinks you have done.'[33]

Hurrah!

'You have done very well indeed,' he confirms, 'better even than I thought you would.'[34]

For the next two hours, Kitchener, still accompanied by his doting entourage, strides around this most perilous of domains, this small 400 acres that has been paid for so heavily with blood, and carefully examines what he can see of the Turkish lines. As has happened at the beach, he creates quite a sensation in the trenches, as the men recognise him and cheer him as he strides forward, likely touched by their acclaim but not particularly showing it.

Still, almost like a royal visit, he does stop here and there to chat to the men, saying how 'proud and pleased' he is by their efforts, and asking them to hang on 'a little while longer'.[35]

In one trench, General Birdwood borrows one of the Diggers' periscopes and holds it momentarily above the parapet, at which point a shot rings out and the instrument is shattered. 'The chap can shoot the eye out of a mosquito,' the Digger drawls, and now holds his hat on the end of a rifle to demonstrate further. This time, nothing, but not to worry. 'If I had my head in it,' he says cheerfully to Lord Kitchener, 'he would drill a hole in it!'

The entourage moves on, with Lord Kitchener remarking, 'Thank you very much, we can find our way now, thanks.'[36]

Surprisingly – given that he has the air of a man who knows all there is to know – he even asks a few questions as he continues to make his way around. And the more he inspects the situation, the more obvious it becomes to him that he is standing in the middle of military hell on earth – where there is no spot secure from artillery, where the enemy has all the advantages of numbers, supply, observation *and* height. After surveying the whole thing intently, Kitchener puts his hand on Birdwood's arm and says with some feeling, 'Thank God, Birdie, I came to see this for myself. You were quite right. I had no idea of the difficulties you were up against. I think you have all done wonders.'[37] (It is the same unexpected kind of warmth the Secretary for War had displayed when they had met at Mudros. The normally undemonstrative Kitchener, at least with fellow officers, had leaned in and squeezed Birdwood's arm, saying, 'I can't tell you how glad I am to have you with me again, Birdie, and be away from all those bloody politicians.')[38]

And then, with as little ceremony as the way he arrived, Lord Kitchener, with his entourage, returns to the pier at North Beach and is taken off through the now heavy swell on the small lighter that awaits.

Though on the subject of possible evacuation he remains non-committal, upon returning to the flagship *Lord Nelson* later that afternoon and having more discussions, it would seem, at least to General Birdwood, that, 'Kitchener had begun to dislike the idea of evacuation less than formerly.'[39]

That may just be Birdie's hope getting the better of him, however, as Kitchener's visit coincides with the formation of a 'small committee of naval and military officers working at Mudros',[40] including Lieutenant-Colonel Cecil Aspinall, who are already busy drawing up a broad master plan for evacuation.

Two days later, Kitchener sends a cable:

KITCHENER TO PRIME MINISTER ASQUITH: TO GAIN WHAT WE HOLD, HAS BEEN A MOST

REMARKABLE FEAT OF ARMS. THE COUNTRY
IS MUCH MORE DIFFICULT THAN I IMAGINED,
AND THE TURKISH POSITIONS . . . ARE
NATURAL FORTRESSES WHICH, IF NOT TAKEN
BY SURPRISE AT FIRST, COULD BE HELD
AGAINST VERY SERIOUS ATTACK BY LARGER
FORCES THAN HAVE BEEN ENGAGED . . .
. . . EVERYONE HAS DONE WONDERS
. . .

   AS REGARDS EVACUATION OF GALLIPOLI,
WE DO NOT CONSIDER THAT ANY DECISION
CAN BE WISELY COME TO UNTIL WE KNOW
OF THE COERCIVE MEASURE TO BE TAKEN
AGAINST GREECE.[41]

15 NOVEMBER 1915, LONDON, AN EASTERNER HEADS TO THE WESTERN FRONT

Winston Churchill has had enough.

When Prime Minister Asquith profits by Kitchener's absence to form a smaller, five-member War Committee, which excludes the two principal architects of the Dardanelles disaster – Churchill and Lord Kitchener – the erstwhile First Lord of the Admiralty tenders his resignation to Asquith on the same day: 'Knowing what I do about the present situation, and the instrument of executive power, I could not accept a position of general responsibility for war policy without any effective share in its guidance & control . . .

'I therefore ask you to submit my resignation to the King. I am an officer, and I place myself unreservedly at the disposal of the military authorities, observing that my regiment is in France.'[42]

Four days after his resignation is accepted, Churchill pauses only to take a parliamentary Parthian shot at Jacky Fisher for having thwarted him in his magnificent plans for the Dardanelles. 'I did not receive from the First Sea Lord,' he gravely tells the House, 'either the clear

guidance before the event, or the firm support after, which I was entitled to expect. If the First Sea Lord had not approved the operations, if
he believed they were unlikely to take the course that was expected of
them, if he thought they would lead to undue losses, it was his duty to
refuse consent. No one could have prevailed against such a refusal. The
operation would never have been begun . . .'

His advice now to the government is consistent with what he has
been saying all along: do nothing on the Western Front that costs more
in Allied lives than the enemy's. And in the meantime, 'in the East,
take Constantinople, take it by ships if you can; take it by soldiers if
you must; take it by whichever plan, military or naval, commends itself
to your military experts, but take it, and take it soon, and take it while
time remains'.[43]

With which, Winston takes his hat, his coat and his umbrage and
shortly afterwards a ticket for the Western Front, where he is promoted
to the rank of Lieutenant-Colonel and placed in command of the 6th
Battalion of the Royal Scots Fusiliers.

17 NOVEMBER 1915, BACK AT GALLIPOLI, A HARBINGER OF HELL?

And isn't that just the experience of mankind through the ages? No
matter the advances in weaponry, the leaps of lethalness that every generation must face, still nature is capable of generating a fury that truly
defines the word, making man's attempts to match it appear puny. So
it is on this afternoon as a storm hits the Dardanelles, of such power in
its wind, rain, thunder, lightning and COLD that it is nigh *biblical* in
proportions.

Oh, repent ye sinners, and shelter from His wrath if you can, as
most damaging of all are the enormous breakers that pick up vessels
and hurl them on the shore, holing their hulls, shattering their sterns
and bows on the rocks and – most worryingly of all – washing away all
but one of the piers that are the lifeline for all at Anzac Cove.

Walking among the piles of debris on the beach the next morning,
'just lined with wrecks of punts and tugs etc, and also mules and ponies

in all directions',[44] Charles Bean – who has turned 36 on this day – comes across Commander George Gipps, who tells him they have just 40 hours' water left at Anzac.

'How do you think we're going to get on in the winter?' Bean asks.

Gipps is incredulous. 'The winter!' he exclaims. 'I think we're within two days of a disaster.'[45]

Inevitably, the talk among both the senior military officer corps and the correspondents turns to evacuation – whether it is first even possible, and, if that, advisable. 'The result of all this will be, probably, a sort of Crimea,' Bean writes in his diary. 'I think we can hang on, in a sort of way – but at the cost of the utmost suffering to which our past trials have not been a fleabite by comparison.'[46]

Even to those who advocate evacuation most passionately, however, it is obvious that the key must be secrecy. Under no circumstances must the Turks get wind that they are even thinking of it, for forewarned would be forearmed, and the Turks being ready to pounce at the first sign of their leaving would lead to certain catastrophe at the point when they no longer have the men to resist. *Secrecy*, above all.

18 NOVEMBER 1915, THE LORDS BREAK THEIR SILENCE

Great Britain's magnificent House of Lords – boasting some 600 years of history, secure in the knowledge that the power of the sun that never sets on the British Empire is always at high noon here at the heart of the Houses of Parliament – is, nevertheless, troubled. For decades, nay *centuries*, the great affairs of the day discussed in this great chamber have traditionally been all about how to maximise the success already achieved. But of late, where the news from just about every military front is bad, and the suspicion has grown that the problem lies not with the Empire itself but the way His Majesty's Government administers it, the venerable Baron Ribblesdale, politician and huntsman, who had lost his last son and heir at Gallipoli just six weeks earlier, can bear it no longer.

Rising from his seat, this epitome of an English aristocrat gazes momentarily at his fellow Lords, all of them seated in an elongated semicircle before the throne, which perches upon a raised platform at the far end of the chamber, before his clipped Oxford tones ring out across the august assembly. 'I turn for a moment to the Dardanelles,' he begins. 'It is common knowledge, I believe, that Sir Charles Monro, who was sent out the other day to the Dardanelles, has reported in favour of withdrawal from the Dardanelles and adversely to the continuance of winter operations there . . . Perhaps his decision was not one that the Government liked very much. I would ask, has Lord Kitchener been sent out to give a second opinion on the Dardanelles, or has he gone out to act and to withdraw the Expedition?'[47]

For many, including Malcolm Ross, New Zealand's official war correspondent, these remarks are flippant to a fault, and their publication cause a measure of despair. As Ross later writes, 'One read in the papers speeches of Members of [the British] Parliament asking light-heartedly why the forces were not withdrawn from the Dardanelles, as if it were a process of merely picking up baggage and walking off. People talking like that could not have the faintest conception of the conditions under which we [have] been holding on . . .'[48]

It surely won't be long before the Turks and the Germans get wind of this . . .

22 NOVEMBER 1915, A BREAKTHROUGH AT MUDROS

After long discussion, Lord Kitchener cables the Prime Minister from Mudros:

OUR OFFENSIVE ON THE PENINSULA HAS UP
TO THE PRESENT HELD UP THE TURKISH
ARMY, BUT WITH GERMAN ASSISTANCE,
WHICH IS NOW PRACTICALLY AVAILABLE, OUR
POSITIONS THERE CANNOT BE MAINTAINED
AND EVACUATION SEEMS INEVITABLE . . .
[IF WE PULL OUT,] THE EVACUATION OF
SUVLA AND ANZAC SHOULD BE PROCEEDED

WITH, WHILE CAPE HELLES COULD AT ALL EVENTS BE HELD FOR THE PRESENT.[49]

Of course, eight months earlier, this would have been enough. On matters military, Kitchener commanded, others obeyed. But not now. So reduced are his stocks that, while his view is to be taken into account, the decision remains one for the Cabinet to make, and this will require further deliberation.

At least, however, Kitchener's view is in accord with that of many other significant figures. Prime Minister Asquith, as he advises the War Committee, 'feels bound to advise the evacuation of the Gallipoli Peninsula on military grounds, notwithstanding the grave political disadvantages which may result from this decision'.[50]

For when it comes to making a sane decision, do they have a *choice*? It is now obvious to most of them – led by the outraged Lloyd George and Bonar Law – that to leave the forces they have now on the Gallipoli Peninsula, unaided, would see them simply hold their position at best, and lose it at worst. To have them break through the Turkish positions would require more troops and resources of artillery and ammunition than Great Britain actually has to spare. Nowhere is the position worse than at Anzac, where the Commanders on the ground had told Kitchener that keeping the supply lines open during the forecasted harsh winter was expected to be more than problematic.

They *must* be evacuated.

Against that, from back at Mudros, Commodore Keyes and Admiral Wemyss have been arguing as furiously as ever that the whole battle *still* can be won, by forcing the Narrows, at which point the troops at Gallipoli could triumphantly march on Constantinople.

But make no mistake, Admiral Wemyss makes clear to the Admiralty in a cable:

GENERAL MONRO PLACES THE PROBABLE LOSSES AT 30 PERCENT: I DO NOT THINK HE EXAGGERATES. I AM, HOWEVER,

STRONGLY OF THE OPINION SUCH A DISASTER SHOULD NOT BE ACCEPTED WITHOUT AN EFFORT BEING MADE TO RETRIEVE OUR POSITION. I CONSIDER THAT A COMBINED ATTACK BY NAVY AND ARMY WOULD HAVE EVERY PROSPECT OF RECEIVING DECISIVE RESULTS.[51]

Wemyss and Keyes are supported in London by the likes of the Lord Keeper of the Privy Seal, Lord Curzon, who is insistent that any evacuation would condemn to death half the troops, and he refuses to countenance it, whatever Kitchener says. 'I wish to draw it in no impressionist colours,' he writes, in a paper soon circulated to Cabinet, 'but as it must in all probability arise. The evacuation and the final scenes will be enacted at night. Our guns will continue firing until the last moment . . . but the trenches will have been taken one by one, and a moment must come when a final *sauve qui peut* takes place, and when a disorganized crowd will press in despairing tumult on to the shore and into the boats. Shells will be falling and bullets ploughing their way into the mass of retreating humanity . . . Conceive the crowding into the boats of thousands of half-crazy men, the swamping of craft, the nocturnal panic, the agony of the wounded, the hecatombs of slain. It requires no imagination to create a scene that, when it is told, will be burned into the hearts and consciences of the British people for generations to come.'[52]

These prove to be merely his opening remarks . . .

And then there are their French allies – backed by the Russians – who fervently want Salonica reinforced to assist France's retreating army in Serbia and protect the other Balkan states.

For the moment, thus, Cabinet decides to overrule the recommendations of both Kitchener and the War Committee, and postpone a final decision until after the Anglo-French War Conference at Calais on 4 December 1915. The British hope they can convince the French to abandon the Salonica campaign altogether. But, yes, in the meantime, it is only prudent to have those on the Gallipoli Peninsula *prepare* to get out, so that if evacuation does happen, all can be ship-shape and with ships waiting.

The main thing from now is to get it underway and ensure that, as the War Committee has decided, 'Every possible precaution is to be taken to preserve secrecy, upon which the feasibility of the operation so largely depends.'[53] The greatest challenge will obviously be to keep the evacuation secret from the many watching Turkish eyes, and get as many men off before the Turks become aware and likely launch their final assault.

How to accomplish that?

The key job of forming up the plans for the evacuation of the Anzacs falls to the recently promoted Brigadier-General Brudenell White, a clear thinker and an excellent organiser who is General Godley's right-hand man at Anzac.

On the same day that Kitchener had sent his cable to London, General Birdwood had sent his own cable to Brudenell White at Anzac Cove, noting that, while Birdie personally remains against evacuation, MY VIEWS UNLIKELY TO BE ACCEPTED . . . INFORM GENERAL GODLEY AND START FUTURE PLANS ACCORDINGLY.[54]

Brudenell White, the Australian soldier whose curriculum vitae boasts graduation from the prestigious British Army Staff College of Camberley, England, does exactly that, initially working off the sketchy plan that had been provided three weeks earlier by Lieutenant-Colonel Cecil Aspinall and his committee. It is no small job . . .

Two massive armies are so very close to each other, in a perpetual death grip, and yet somehow a plan must be formulated to shift no fewer than 83,000 soldiers contained across Suvla Bay and Anzac Cove – not to mention huge quantities of munitions, guns, animals and stores – out from under the noses of the Turks, without them being aware. And, yes, Brudenell White is firm from the beginning: Anzac and Suvla *must* be evacuated simultaneously, as doing one before the other would obviously alert the enemy.

Though there had been no detail to the plan, Lieutenant-Colonel

Aspinall's solution to the problem – working it out at Port Mudros with senior army and naval officers, much of it during the visit of Lord Kitchener – had been to carry it out in three stages, and with this Brigadier-General Brudenell White broadly agrees. (Though he strongly disagrees with Aspinall's notion that the men could come off during the day, as requested by the navy, for ease of operations. This would alert the enemy, and the evacuation would be ruined. As Brudenell White is clear from the start, 'It is upon the existence of perfectly normal conditions that I rely for success.')[55]

Now, a classic military evacuation would see frontline troops retreating through the second and third lines, and setting up a new line, before the second and third lines do the same successively and successfully, until fully detached from the enemy. But, as Brudenell White is quick to note, and Bean to chronicle, at Anzac Cove there is never a possibility of this because 'the centre of the enemy's line, at the Nek, is within 800 yards of the chief embarkation point at North Beach'.[56]

Given that the enemy only has to push a short way forward to Russell's Top and they will have clear vision to the beach – together with line of fire artillery – the only way here is going to be to hold the frontline to the last, and keep the enemy ignorant that all behind have gone, before letting the frontline make good their escape.

To the meticulous Brudenell White, one thing is obvious from the first. Things must continue to appear normal, however many men are taken off, and they must conjure an image of 'going to Winter Quarters'.[57] Following this line of reasoning, Brudenell White starts spending hours every day, and well into the wee hours, sitting at his desk at ANZAC HQ – with his braces and tie on, his pipe hanging out the right-hand side of his mouth – filling out page after page in his notebook with highly detailed plans.

As all of Anzac has to be evacuated simultaneously with Suvla, he liaises constantly with the Chief of Staff of IXth Corps, Brigadier-General Hamilton Reed, who has carriage of the evacuation there. And it will take a great deal of persuasion, and even intervention from Birdwood, who is also finally able to get Lieutenant-General

Julian Byng to agree to maintain the Suvla frontline to the end – even though they are more able to keep pulling back – so as not to forewarn the Turks of their evacuation.

Brudenell White quickly establishes that, in the preliminary stage – lasting for a fortnight or so and starting immediately – the back areas of Anzac, well behind the frontlines, could be gradually thinned of all the sick and wounded, so as not to arouse suspicion. This would bring the Anzac Cove troops from around 42,000 down to 36,000. Even if the evacuation does not go ahead, this thinning would be no more than prudent, as Anzac moves into defensive mode to get through the winter, requiring fewer men.

Then, in the intermediate stage, they could take the numbers at Anzac down to around 22,000 over ten days or so. And finally, the key will be to get the remaining men on the frontline out over just two nights, requiring the navy to provide three times its usual number of vessels in attendance, constantly ferrying the soldiers to troopships offshore. Following the plan, the HQ staff of each unit will be withdrawn on the first of the two nights, leaving behind just one s officer with a couple of signallers. On the key final night, the men will be withdrawn in three successive instalments, 'A', 'B' and 'C', with the machine-gunners of 'C' last, the 'Die Hards' (as they become known) to beat them all.

Now, in this final stage, it will obviously be the equivalent of holding off a rolling boulder of granite with nothing more than a balloon, but Brudenell White has a curious confidence about him, and at least projects the feeling that it can be done without losing anywhere near the number of casualties that have been estimated. If, at the end, their foothold is held by the 'bravest and the steadiest men',[58] it may even be possible to pull off a coup, and get most of the men off without mishap.

The numbers will at first be thinning and then falling away to a mere skeleton crew, but it must *look* to the Turks as if they are all there, as strong as ever, that nothing at all has changed in the daily goings-on the Turks have been observing for so long. And in the early stages no one must know, not even those who are being evacuated, for if the Turks get word of it, the whole thing will be impossible.

Now, how to make it appear that the Allies are there in force, firing as strongly as ever and ready to devastate any Turk who ventures across no-man's-land – even when most of the men will be long gone? This is where – almost immediately, in the first two days of deliberations – Brudenell White achieves a conceptual breakthrough. 'We will,' he quietly tells his closest colleagues, 'school the Turk to silence . . .'[59]

And that school will open for three days, starting tomorrow.

24 NOVEMBER 1915, DARDANELLES, THE 'SILENCE RUSE' IS LAUNCHED[60]

Something is going on. But what?

The newly promoted Major Gordon Carter, back with his men for the last month – 'I got a nasty shock to find that I hardly knew any of the officers'[61] – is convinced that, whatever is going on, it is on the quiet. As a matter of fact, *everything* is now on the quiet. For he has just received a very strange order from ANZAC HQ. From tonight, at 6 pm, and for the next two days and nights, *no one* at Anzac Cove is to move out of their trenches, fire rifles or machine-guns, throw biscuit-tin bombs or shout out. If you're going to snore, do it quietly.

Everybody is to stay silent, on pain of punishment. (And, at Gallipoli, they don't muck around. In July, an Australian Digger had been court-martialled and sentenced to death for falling asleep on duty – as a warning to all that the crime was serious – even if the sentence had been commuted to a long spell in military prison.)

Everything is to be made to appear as if the Anzacs are hunkering down, bunkering down, for the winter – and in giving this impression, the weather is certainly cooperative, as things become ever colder. In the meantime, however, other Brudenell White plans are being put into play, with company after company of soldiers being evacuated from Anzac Cove at night and not replaced.

During the day, there is normal boat traffic to and from the Cove and to the newly reconstructed piers, and the numbers of soldiers in the frontlines is as strong as ever.

24–25 NOVEMBER 1915, LONE PINE, ALL QUIET ON THE EASTERN FRONT

At 4.35 in the morning on Lone Pine ridge, Lieutenant Mehmed Fasih opens his eyes. He is exhausted, but, as a dutiful soldier, he knows he must resist the temptation to sleep.

After crawling out of his tent, he goes about his morning ablutions and then sits down with a hot Turkish coffee to write his first report of the day: '*Vukuat yok. 800 mermi, 6 bomba sarfolunmuş.* – No incidents. Eight hundred bullets, six bombs used.'

Continuing about his day, the Lieutenant visits his Commanders, chats, smokes, has more coffee, drops in on his men in their trenches. It seems nothing is amiss, and yet still something is gnawing at him, as if something is out of kilter . . .

It is 8 pm that night before it . . . clicks. 'There is an exceptional silence on the front-line tonight,' he writes in his diary. 'Such a situation is really quite strange. It's as if the watch has been stopped.'[62] It is all . . . strangely alarming. Before retiring for the night, he notes yet again, 'The silence of the enemy continues.'[63]

The front remains eerily quiet overnight, and the only thing being thrown by the enemy is 'bully beef cans full of jam'.[64] (Which, at least, the Turks far prefer to bully beef itself.)

The next morning, Mehmed Fasih emerges from his tent and pauses. It is not simply that his boots have crunched on frost for the first time in this campaign; it is that he can *hear* it. His every exhalation is a bloom of white as the night has brought a frozen change, and all is so quiet it gives 'the full meaning of silence'.[65] Hugging his coat tightly around his torso, Fasih contemplates the horror of the winter months to come in this terrible place and heads off to a meeting with his Battalion Commander, where they talk about what everyone in the Turkish trenches is now talking about – quietly – the enemy's lack of action.

Fasih and his Commander are puzzled, agreeing that it's 'excessive. The only sounds that can be heard are coming from our side.'[66] To add to the mystery, Fasih has been given reports that the enemy have removed the barbed wire from in front of their trenches: 'Battalion commander really is dumbfounded.'

After some discussion, the two men walk around to the trenches to gauge the mood. 'The rank and file, especially the ones who have been at the front-line for a while, can hardly contain their curiosity. They are walking out into the open and firing their weapons. Nothing! They are observing the enemy. Nothing!'[67]

Later in the morning, Lieutenant Mehmed Fasih is sitting down to read the newspaper when his Regiment Commander arrives.

'The silence,' the Commander says, 'do not be duped by it.'[68]

At that moment, Mehmed Fasih has a thought. 'What if we send out one of our reconnaissance men?' he offers. The two men sit down to consult further on the matter. They decide to send out a volunteer to recon the enemy's trenches and get some idea of what the hell is going on.

That evening at 6 pm, Mehmed Fasih hands out the orders to his reconnaissance men and lets the most game among them do the duty of going forward:

> Soldiers are to observe the line ... Meanwhile, one soldier from the 8th Company's reconnaissance arm is to advance safely. If needed, others from the 8th Company will reinforce their comrade. Each soldier is to be issued two bombs. Once you have arrived close to the enemy trenches you are to listen. If you hear something you are to go closer. If possible you are to enter their trenches. You are to search the trench thoroughly and ascertain whether there is dynamite in the trenches, bringing back a token, a loophole or what not.[69]

For his part, Lieutenant George Stanley McIlroy is at Lone Pine on this day, the second day of the ruse. It is in a part of the trenches where, as he would write, 'it would have been possible, although distinctly inadvisable to lean over and shake hands with Abdul'.[70] So close, in fact, and in a pre-dawn so silent, the Anzacs can hear the approaching Turks before they can see them.

There! The Australian sentry on duty first sees a head, and then a shoulder, appear over the top of the trench, and then a full figure crawling towards the Australian lines. The whisper goes down: 'Hey! Corp! Is that a bloody live target?'[71]

It is quickly decided that the still approaching figure does come 'within the meaning of the Act'.

And so, as the figure keeps approaching the loophole, clearly with intent of peeking inside, the Australians place the muzzle of a rifle at the other end.

Of course, the Turk never knows what hits him, as the bullet instantly kills him. The most amazing thing, though, is that because the discharge of the gun has been muffled further by a blanket around the other end, a *second* Turk appears and crawls forward, 'to see what held his "cobber" gazing spellbound into the loophole'.

This fellow puts his eye to the next loophole along . . .

'But as neither he nor his cobber had any inclination to return and report to their comrades, no doubt, the latter suspected there was a catch in it, and things soon settled down again to an unbroken silence.'[72]

A similar scene takes place at Quinn's. There, just after dawn, four Turks even venture out into no-man's-land, and could have been shot easily by the Australian machine-gunner secreted at an enfilading angle at Steele's. But the Turks are deliberately even allowed to pull back a couple of the screens that have prevented bombs landing in the trenches, and it is only when they throw bombs and one of them actually jumps into the darkened trench that muted reply is made, and the others hunted off.

But still, for the Turks watching, such a muted reply seems strange. There are some Anzacs there, but how many? The Turks appear to be almost *worried* for them, and later in the day a message wrapped to a rock is thrown into Quinn's:

My dear Australian, how do you?
We hope that you are in good
health. Always the best. Reply if
you please.

Soldas Turgo[73]

The '*Soldas Australos*' do not reply, recognising that the note is less an enquiry as to their health and more a query whether they are at home.

On the morning of the third day of silence on the front, a freezing wind lashes the side of Lieutenant Mehmed Fasih's tent, some of the tranquillity of the previous days is lost, and he can't bring himself to get up. Not just yet.

His men had escaped the fate of their other curious comrades, having returned safely in the night with news that 'there were men guarding the front of the trenches and there were sounds of talking coming from the trenches',[74] so they had not proceeded any closer. After lying in until 7.30 am, Mehmed Fasih decides to read the newspaper. Granted, it is eight days old, but still . . .

Straightening it out before him, he is met with an extraordinary report: 'The issue of an English evacuation from Chanak is being debated in the House of Lords . . .'[75] Excitedly, he reads on about Monro's report to Kitchener, savouring particularly the words 'it is impossible, unthinkable for the English to continue to keep its force [on the Peninsula]'.[76]

Müjde! Good news! Still, wary of his enemy, whom he has grown to know, and who have pursued all manner of means to survive and make ground, he remains unconvinced. Mehmed Fasih puts down the paper and jots in his diary, 'I guess the result of all this discussion will become clear later down the line.'[77]

His superiors, including General Enver in Constantinople and

Liman von Sanders here on the Peninsula, are also circumspect about these public declarations of Britain's war strategy, so there is no way these men can easily believe that the Britons would be so imprudent. Surely this is yet another ruse, a campaign of misinformation . . . but then again, the winter is coming and it is clear from their vantage points that their enemy is suffering.

As for the other Ottoman and German brass, who have already seen the report, there are mixed feelings and long debates about what this really means. Colonel Kannengiesser, for one, does not believe the English capable of swallowing such a large dose of pride. 'Rumours and suggestions that the enemy were going to evacuate Gallipoli naturally swarmed around us,' he would later recall. 'I personally did not believe in such a possibility because, taking into account the English character, I considered it out of the question that they would give up such a hostage of their own free will and without a fight.'[78]

Major Zeki agrees. 'After the fighting at Hill 60 the papers and news agencies began to talk about evacuation,' he would later recall to Charles Bean. 'There was a doubt in the air; some thought you were going, some that you would attack, some that you would go on as we saw you digging, digging for the winter. The general view was that you would leave the peninsula.'[79]

Colonel Mustafa Kemal is very strongly of the view that they will leave. As early as October, he had written in a letter to his friend in Constantinople, 'The enemy facing us is now exhausted. Hopefully, he will soon be driven away entirely. In any case, the country is safe at this position.'[80] And later he recalled, 'I had realized that the enemy was about to withdraw, and so I had proposed an offensive. But they turned it down.'[81]

Though upset that, once again, his advice is not heeded by his superiors, Colonel Mustafa Kemal is not *quite* at the end of his tether with both General Enver and General Liman von Sanders, but he can certainly see it from here. His health, too, is getting worse by the day and the revered Commander thinks seriously about returning to Constantinople.

AFTERNOON, 26 NOVEMBER 1915, AT ANZAC, A SPY FROM ON HIGH

Everybody out!

Turkish plane coming this way, at a very low altitude. Manfully resisting the impulse to try to shoot it down with rifle and machine-gun fire as they usually do, the Anzacs do as Brigadier-General Brudenell White has specifically instructed:

```
In case of appearance of hostile aircraft,
men must come out of their dug-outs and show
themselves.⁸²
```

That evening, the word goes out. Everyone is to stand to on the front trenches, because it is a near certainty that the Turks will send out patrols tonight to find out what is going on.

Sure enough, in the wee hours that night, curiosity really does get the better of the Turks, as the vigilant Anzacs see a few tentative souls coming forward from the Turkish trenches. The Anzacs resist the impulse to shoot, hoping that more will gather. It works. After the first Turks appear and are not shot at, then more come, and all together they start walking towards the Australians and New Zealanders.

Steady, men. Steady . . . Steady . . . Steady . . .

And *now*.

'Then, of course,' one private would recount, 'everybody opened fire, and that was that. The Turks, of course, realised they had been tricked.'⁸³

Hopefully, now, the brutes have learned their lesson. Just because things are quiet, it doesn't meant that the Anzacs have *gorn*. The Turks better keep their bloody heads down.

As it happens, however, within hours everyone will be doing exactly that. On the morning of 27 November, another howling and horrifying storm hits the Dardanelles, the worst in these parts for 40 years. The wind howls, the seas rear up, the thunder and lightning flashes, before hail pelts down as never before. A few old villagers, who had refused to leave their lifelong homes nearby, would declare 'that they had never lived through' such a storm.[84] In fact, 'storm' does not quite do the phenomenon justice. For after the hail then comes the rain for the next 24 hours.

But this is not rain like they know in Australia and New Zealand. This is not just pouring rain, this is *lashing* rain, stinging rain, freezing and flooding rain that turns into a howling blizzard that would not only wake the dead but in many cases also begins to wash them away – with the rain gushing down the hills of both Anzac Cove and Suvla Bay, dislodging corpses and sweeping them into the trenches.

Oh the horror, as the soldiers on the lower slopes are suddenly engulfed with this flood of rotting corpses, in a torrent so strong that several Diggers drown. The only way to survive is to immediately get up and out of those trenches. It means that suddenly, on both sides of a watery no-man's-land, shivering blue-faced soldiers arise to stare at each other.[85]

While even the Turks are shocked by the ferocity of the storm, at least they are locals, with a better reckoning of local conditions, and at least they have the high ground, meaning the flooding debris rushes more from them than upon them.

And then comes an icy cyclone that would blow a dog off a chain and does in fact blow many tethered donkeys into the sea, and the suddenly snarling Aegean roars up like an enraged lion to, once more, effortlessly destroy one pier and badly damage another.

Under such conditions, as Birdwood would describe it, 'no boat could get near any of the beaches',[86] and such small boats as are anchored near the shore soon end up as wreckage on the beaches. What on earth would they do if such a wind hit during the evacuation, if it happens?

Even through such weather, however, Brudenell White and the group of officers now brainstorming around him remain hard at work, as the winds howl all around. And their persistence is bearing fruit. Brudenell White is deeply satisfied with the outcome of his 'silence ruse', which has worked like a charm. As he would later recall, 'the enemy displayed marked uneasiness and eventually reconnoitred our line in several places, suffering many casualties'.[87]

And now, just five days after receiving confirmation that the evacuation is to go ahead, he despatches his carefully calibrated operational timetable to ANZAC HQ, outlining the next two stages:

First Stage: Wherein everything surplus to actual requirement to resist attack is removed;
Wherein time is not a vital factor;
For which adequate transport is provided to enable full advantage to be taken of every hour of fine weather.
Second Stage: The removal, from ANZAC and SUVLA as a whole, in two (2) nights of all remaining personnel and the destruction of guns and stores likely to be of use to the enemy.[88]

It then goes on to outline the precise logistics of achieving this ambitious plan. By Brudenell White's meticulous estimation, the next stage should 'begin at once'. And within 'ten working days'[89] they could reduce their numbers at Anzac Cove to 22,000.[90]

Brudenell White knows there will be many objections to his plan, but he is adamant that it is the only way to slip off the Peninsula with as few casualties as possible.

28 NOVEMBER 1915, ANZAC, A VISITATION FROM THE HEAVENS

Strange. Very strange. Private John Cargill from Redfern in Sydney is asleep in his trench just down from Quinn's when it happens. After being stirred awake by something unknown, he looks up and sees strange white flakes floating down.

What the *hell* is that? It looks sort of like frost. But as far as he knows, frost always comes out of the ground, not the sky.

It is curious enough that he nudges his cobber Otty awake. 'Hey,' he says to the native-born Englishman, 'I didn't know that frost came out of the [sky].'

''Course it don't, you mug,' Otty replies derisively, 'that's snow.'

'Snow?'

Snow.

Private Cargill has heard of snow. And this it? Bonza! And yet, when he makes to jump out of the trench to get a better look at it and maybe make a snowball, Otty grabs him.

'No, stay here,' he says, 'it'll be there in the morning. If you get up now, you won't be able to get back into your bunk again.'

'Oh, all right.'[91]

As it turns out, however, Cargill is one of the few who doesn't get up, as many other Anzacs who are similarly seeing snow for the first time are soon up and chiacking, making snowballs and throwing them at each other, even as a full-blown blizzard begins to rage.

Snow! Real snow!

In the morning, the previous ugliness of the trenches – corpses, skeletons, shrapnel, discarded ammunition boxes, rubbish and latrines – is now covered with what Banjo Paterson might have called 'the vision splendid of a snow-covered field extended'. White snow!

The wonder of it all does not last long, for what comes with it, of course, is a cold more terrible than they have already experienced, and soon enough up by Anzac's side, *'where the hills are twice as steep and twice as rough . . . the man that holds his own is good enough'*.

It is so cold that the water in their water bottles freezes, as it does in the water cans, meaning the cooks have a hard time, having to melt the water they need for cooking. So cold that many of the rifles have frozen mechanisms and no longer work. Within 24 hours, men are reporting to casualty stations with ghostly-white, frostbitten feet that are soon to turn black as the flesh dies, and still the mercury falls – and more and more men with it.

At Hill 60, Major Cecil Allanson's 1/6th Ghurkha Rifles are positioned with little shelter and feel the full brunt of the frozen winds. 'The cold was just intense,' the Major would recall, 'and I have never seen such courage as I saw through this blizzard. Men found at the parapet facing the Turk with glassy eyes and stone dead, who gave up their lives rather than give in. Imagine the death of slow, accepted torture. It is, at such periods, and at such periods only, that one really does not seem afraid of death.'[92]

Perhaps the Anzacs might have been able to withstand it better if they had been issued with winter kit, but that has not been organised yet. Still broadly in their summer clothes, in mostly exposed trenches, they shiver in their shorts, aghast, as icicles form on the ceilings of their dugouts. Tarpaulins and tents collapse under the weight of snow, rations are washed away and ruined, and their hands, not to mention their whole bodies, are so cold they are incapable of anything bar the most basic motions. This includes Charles Bean, who, in his dugout, is so cold he cannot write. He must get up and walk for fear of freezing to death.

Down on the exposed plains of Suvla Bay, it is all much worse. There, in far more open country, where the ground is so rocky that many have not been able to dig trenches and so escape the wind that way, it freezes them clear to the bone . . . and deeper still. Overall, some 200 drown or die of exposure, while there are a staggering 5000 cases of frostbite at Suvla alone. And on the calendar, at least, winter has not yet begun.

As the storm persists, Brudenell White and his cabal of senior officers, still working practically around the clock on their evacuation plans, become more and more concerned: how on earth would they get currently some 83,000 men off Suvla and Anzac if such a storm should hit again? The vessels would not be able to get close to the shore, and even if they did, there would be no piers left for the men to board them from.

Nevertheless, such an experience certainly galvanises the Allied leadership when it comes to the impossibility of holding on in these parts through the winter. 'Though I had so much disliked the idea of evacuation when it was first mooted,' General Birdwood would record, 'I now threw myself into the project with all my heart.'[93]

Further helping to concentrate their minds on the need to get out is that, from late November, it is obvious that the much feared modern heavy shells from Germany and Austria – just like those used in France on the Western Front with such devastating effect – have started to arrive.

Private George Scott is with his mates in a spot called Victoria Gully – never before touched by shellfire – when he suddenly gets wind of a two-up game up the way. George loves two-up and heads off just 30 seconds or so before a shell from a newly arrived Austrian howitzer battery lands fair among them. He rushes back to find all his mates killed, bar Sergeant Jack Herbert, who is just alive. 'They've got me downstairs, Scottie,' he whispers with his dying breath. 'No more fun for me!'[94]

Major Cecil Allanson is similarly hit shortly afterwards and comes to, blinded, in a hospital ship, aware he is being given the last sacrament. A short time later, he is just about able to speak and whispers a question to the person in the next bed: 'Am I dying, as I have just been given the last rites?'

'Be of good cheer,' the voice comes back. 'I have also been given them, and I only have jaundice . . .'[95]

But there is no denying the increasingly heavy and accurate fire descending upon them. Clearly the road – and, more pertinently, the railway line – from Berlin to Constantinople is now open, and hell is rushing their way. Unless, of course, they are no longer here . . .

All they need is the say-so from London and they could swing into operation. It is with this in mind that on 1 December a frustrated General Monro, in Mudros, sends a cable to the War Office:

EXPERIENCE OF RECENT STORMS INDICATES THAT THERE IS NO TIME TO LOSE. GENERAL BIRDWOOD TELEGRAPHED YESTERDAY THAT IF EVACUATION IS TO BE MADE POSSIBLE IT IS ESSENTIAL TO TAKE ADVANTAGE OF EVERY FINE DAY FROM NOW. IF DECISION CANNOT BE REACHED VERY SHORTLY, IT MAY BE EQUIVALENT TO DECIDING AGAINST EVACUATION.[96]

At Anzac Cove, morale continues to fall . . .

The shells continue to strike with ever greater power and frequency, and one day at this time Charles Bingham and his mates in the 1st Field Ambulance note, as a shell bursts nearby, 'the body of a man going up in the air, arms and legs spread out. He must have gone fully 50 feet up and landed and lay where he was quite dead I believe . . . There were arms and legs and entrails all over the place, one leg was found near the beach and the head right up on top of the hill.'[97]

There is only so much more he can bear. 'If only I can see dear old home again,' he writes in his diary, 'I would die quite content, but it's a chance only. Things here aren't as cheerful as could be and I pray to God that he will spare me to get away from it without being a coward.'[98]

Chapter Twenty-One

GO GENTLE INTO THAT GOOD NIGHT

[Brudenell] White's strength was normally clothed
with such charm and consideration for others that it
was pleasure for most men, high or low, to deal with
him. When to such a character are added powers
of thought and action such as White possessed, the
devotion of other men spontaneously flows to it.
Charles Bean[1]

7 DECEMBER 1915, LONDON, DISCRETION IS THE BETTER PART OF VALOUR

In the weeks since the powers in London received first Monro's and then
Kitchener's recommendations to evacuate the Gallipoli Peninsula, the
debate has been intense between the 'Stayers' and the 'Evacuationists',
with the fault line between tracing a remarkably similar divide between
the Easterners and Westerners of old.

Yes, the War Committee had officially advised on 23 November
that the evacuation go ahead on 'military grounds', but the Stayers,
led by the likes of Admiral Wemyss and Commodore Keyes, as well as
politicians such as Lord Curzon, had strongly disagreed.

According to the Stayers, the way forward is for four British divisions in Salonica to be sent to Gallipoli to make a further push in the
hope of a breakthrough. Even Lord Kitchener, despite his own advice to

the government in favour of evacuation, is entertaining this idea.

A great obstacle to this plan – not at all untypically for the British when it comes to foreign policy, and in fact a tradition to rival plum pudding – is the French. Those in power in Paris refuse to abandon the Salonica campaign and the embattled Serbs. What's more, there's talk of them moving their troops *from* the Dardanelles *to* Egypt!

The British are hamstrung. With their available manpower, it is not possible to pursue winter campaigns in both the Balkans and the Dardanelles. Yet if they stay at the Dardanelles, they may well risk their alliance with France . . .

It is every bit as unimaginable as the thought of trying to hold onto the Dardanelles without them is horrifying.

As the first week of winter comes to an end, the British Cabinet meets on this day, and immediately afterwards Prime Minister Asquith pens a letter to King George to inform His Majesty of the decision:

> In view of the opinions given by Generals Monro and Birdwood [about] the prospects of a reinforced attack from Suvla, it is felt that there was no alternative but to proceed as quickly as possible with the evacuation of the positions at Suvla and Anzac, that at Helles being for the present at any rate retained.[2]

(Indeed, the simultaneous evacuation of Helles has been discussed over the weeks but, not only are there not enough boats at hand, thanks to the storms the piers there are in a shambles. Helles can freeze over, but it will still have to wait.)

9.30 AM, 8 DECEMBER 1915, MUDROS, PULLING OUT ALL THE STOPS

Birdwood has no sooner received news of the evacuation than he sends one of his own to inform Godley – who has just been promoted to lead Anzac – who passes the message on to the man with the plan, Brigadier-General Brudenell White:

Intermediate period is to commence at once.[3]

For the mastermind, this cable means he can now begin with the real work. Within the hour, at Anzac, Brudenell White sends out the first of many daily orders to come, detailing to Divisional Commanders how many guns and men are to head to the beach *that night* for evacuation to winter headquarters. But, against any of them being taken prisoner, Brudenell White tells all bar his most intimate staff that the reason they're leaving is 'to minimize water and supply difficulties'[4] over the coming winter months, and instructs them to tell others the same. The reductions over the last fortnight have seen the troops at Anzac Cove fall from 41,700 down to 36,000.

The subtractions had started with the barest trickle of sick and wounded, a trickle that in previous days had turned into a rivulet. With the order from London, the rivulet becomes a river, a full flow of men coming down from the higher reaches of the trenches.

And, just to keep the Turks guessing, they continue to maintain periods of complete silence in different trenches night after night so that, come the time, the Turks really will be properly schooled not to associate that silence with an evacuation . . .

'We put it down to your wanting a quiet period [after the blizzard] to dig out your front trenches also,' Major Zeki would later recount. 'We were, however, ordered to send out patrols and get into your trenches. Every unit had to send a patrol, but every patrol reported your line held.'[5]

10 DECEMBER 1915, DARDANELLES, EAST IS EAST, WEST IS WEST, AND ONE MAN HEADS NORTH

After more than ten exhausting months on the Peninsula, fighting tooth and nail, heart and soul – and putting his own life on the line countless times – Colonel Mustafa Kemal is near the point of collapse.

He must leave for Constantinople to recuperate. Astride his horse, he looks out over this bloodied land with powerful emotions. In his time here, he has earned the kind of reputation that can only be 'earned on the battlefield',[6] something he hopes will allow him to accomplish even greater things. And yet it has come only with the sacrifice of tens of thousands of young, courageous men who have brought these invading armies to their exhausted knees. With a strong sense of both pride and sorrow, he rides away . . .

12 DECEMBER 1915, GALLIPOLI, THE WORD SPREADS

Among the Anzacs, of course, this kind of secret cannot be kept for long.

For have yers *heard*?

An evacuation. They're going to pull us out. Get us back to Cairo.

As this second freezing week of December comes to a close, the word inevitably spreads like wildfire – the only warm thing going – up the tracks, along the trenches, down the gullies to Anzac Cove. It swirls around the thousands of crosses in the cemeteries, heading all the way up to Quinn's Post, Russell's Top and places beyond.

Or is it just one more furphy?

Among the lower ranks, no one is sure, but mostly the stunned men refuse to believe it can be true. Many don't *want* to believe it, feeling very strongly that after so many of their mates had been cut down to win this land with blood, it is simply incomprehensible that they would give it back to the Turks.

Soon enough, however, there is no denying it. First the men see materiel being shifted from the frontlines down towards the beaches, where obviously a lot of work is being done on the piers. Then more and more of the heavy guns and cases of ammunition start coming down the hills. The real key, though, is that the ranks start to thin, and even newly arrived reinforcements are suddenly sent back to Alexandria with no explanation. The normal trickle of men returning to Gallipoli, having recovered from wounds, also ceases.

It is appalling.

Around Trooper Bluegum, the attitude is clear: *We're damned if we'll evacuate. We are going to see this game through.*[7]

Adding to that feeling is the contemplation of just how impossible it would be to withdraw without the action turning into a Turkish turkey shoot as the Diggers flee their guns.

'It seemed,' our favourite Trooper would write, 'that the job of getting out was fraught with more potentialities of disaster than the job of getting in. The landing on April 25 was responsible for some slaughter. The evacuation, we reckoned, would be carnage.'[8]

On the other hand, it explains why their ranks have been so clearly thinning in recent weeks, and as the freezing conditions continue to grip them by their extremities, thoughts of the warmth in Egypt are not altogether unattractive. It also explains why the quarter-master staff have suddenly loosened up . . . Those who had once guarded supplies like they were the crown jewels act like they have suddenly found Christ, transformed into inordinately generous souls.

One young soldier marvels at his new gumboots . . . that he never even signed for! Stretcher-bearer Charles Bingham is equally amazed: 'We could take anything we wanted out of the store . . .'[9] And he and three of his mates do just that. They walk into their camp's store and take an entire case of pineapple rings and Ideal milk. Retreating to a quiet spot, they sit down and eat the pineapple till they feel sick, burping from indigestion. Never mind, though. There are also more five-gram tablets of bicarbonate soda than they know what to do with, and after taking those, they sit down and have *another* feast.

And yet even when it becomes official on 14 December and the men are all told that it is *on*, they are also told in strictest terms that not even the word 'evacuation' can be mentioned.

Night after night it goes on . . .

Company after company descend the newly widened tracks, often down steps cut into the frozen soil to make it easier for heavy traffic, carrying their rifles with butt plates covered in cloth, with whatever supplies they can carry and whatever animals they can lead, and walk onto piers covered with several layers of blankets to deaden the noise. From there, they climb onto the ten 'motorised lighters', barges and small boats that will take them to the three ferry ships for troops (plus one for animals, one for guns, one for vehicles) just offshore from just after dusk to just before dawn.

With the rising sun, the Turkish observers can see just the same numbers of men disembarking from barges, and just the same number of donkeys hauling boxes of supplies on high. What they don't know is that the sole job of those men disembarking is to do this every morning for nearly two weeks straight, and the boxes being hauled by the donkeys have nothing in them. Those massive piles of stores down by the beach? Yes, some of them are real, marked for destruction when the time comes to go, as they simply can't get all of them away in time, but many of them are dummy stores – no more than piles of empty boxes held down by tarpaulins. Every day, the Anzac becomes more facade than force.

For the same reason, those remaining soldiers light extra cooking fires to cover for those who are gone, and those in the ever thinner frontline trenches are wanton in their waste of ammunition to keep up the impression that they are there in great numbers.

It's all in keeping with Brudenell White's plan to create an illusion of normality, 'that we should do our utmost to avoid alarming the enemy in any way'.[10]

Charles Bean, of course, chronicles the ongoing evacuation in minute detail. And no matter that on 13 December an order goes out that from noon that day no further mail is to be sent or received; the next night Charles Bean writes to his parents for later posting, 'I want to see the end of Anzac. I don't want actually to be in the last lot to leave the beach, because the risk of being killed or cut off is too great . . . It is an adventure – no one can foretell the ending. It depends largely on the weather. Tonight we have ideal conditions – a cloudy sky covering the half moon; but a very smooth sea.

'There are three more nights to go . . .'[11]

It will, Bean knows, be touch and go. Although all has gone extraordinarily well so far, the truth is that with just one mistake, one slip by one man, the Turks would become aware of what is happening and the inevitable result would be the catastrophic overwhelming of the troops who remain. The Allies are getting to the precarious point where the ranks are so thin that even a small probe by the Turks would break through. Winston Churchill, following events from afar in France, predicts disaster in these final days. 'The hour of Asquith's punishment and K's exposure draws nearer,' he writes with some fervour to his wife, Clementine.[12]

On the night of 15 December, no fewer than 2662 soldiers and officers are in the process of being removed from Anzac while supplies are stacked up on the beach, ready to be destroyed with fire or acid if, as now seems likely, the men won't be able to manage to remove them. With only restless sleep possible on this night, Bean constantly rises from his bunk to peer into the darkness, the landscape flickeringly illuminated by a moon obscured by scudding clouds, and the regular explosion of shells. As time hangs ever heavier, he constantly looks at his watch by the light of a struck match, just as he had done when this all began. A cold wind is starting to blow – 'the waterproof sheet at the door of my dugout began to fidget to and fro in the gusts'[13]– and the clouds are getting bigger and blacker. It is a real worry, for if the bad weather returns, the whole evacuation program will be shot. As might they be. From Anzac Cove, he hears the hoots of a steamer. Offshore he can see a hospital ship, hovering, waiting, almost *expecting* trouble. Down on the beach, the incinerators are burning brighter than usual.

Bean goes back to his bunk, but the sound of the flapping sheet and the terror of it all makes sleep impossible. His hands and the soles of his feet are tingling, just as they used to before he went out to bat in a big cricket match. After everything they have gone through, this rising gale looks likely 'to stop everything for a week! For two weeks! It would perhaps make a shambles of our piers, like that other gale did. They would take weeks to rebuild, and would the Turks with their great new howitzers let us do it?'[14]

Finally, though, the weather calms and things return to their normal, frigid, calm state and that – normal – is all that counts.

'During the last week at Anzac,' Bean would record, 'almost every thought and action was tested by the rule of "normality". Too much activity was regarded with as much general disfavour as too little.'[15]

Yes, totally abnormal things are happening, like the dumping of lots of extra ammunition and the like into latrines or the sea, but it's all happening at night. And there are one or two abnormal things happening in the day, like 'improving defences by erecting barbed-wire entanglements',[16] but they are calculated exceptions to the rule.

Another real problem now beckons for Brudenell White – the tightly coiled spring, driving the clockwork operations all around – who is still ensconced in Anzac HQ, just back from the beach, sleeping very little and sending out a constant stream of precise instructions.

He must decide just who is going to man the trenches to the last – the most precarious position of the lot – when those remaining have every chance of being wiped out by overwhelming numbers of Turks flooding down the hills against all but no resistance.

The problem is not that no one wants to do it. It is that nigh everyone does. Though swamped by volunteers, Brudenell White proceeds by a simple rule: he wants the best, most capable men to be last off, the ones deemed most likely to perform well in a rear-guard action, remain calm and deadly, and allow as many of their comrades to get away as possible. It will be the responsibility of each Company commander to select those men – a skeleton crew of perhaps as few as six soldiers holding the line where 100 once stood, but maintaining the same responsibilities and using the same structures of command and communications as previously.

With those Die Hards, Brudenell White decides to leave a strong representation of stretcher-bearers and medical staff. If fighting does break out – which is, after all, likely – they will be needed in numbers.

With the 1st Field Ambulance, Charles Bingham is not positive he wants that honour. 'We are it seems to be left to the last,' he writes in his diary, 'and I don't suppose any of us will get off as we will be all blown to pieces by the howitzers and shrapnel shells. It's awful but we must do our duty.'[17]

In the meantime, the key remains to maximise visibility, to make it *appear* as though the Allies are still 40,000 strong.

With this in mind, Brudenell White sends out orders that each remaining Battalion must be as visibly active as possible and interpret these orders as they see fit.

Many choose to have men loitering about, gazing at the sky. Some men have different ideas. Why not a cricket game? If you could ignore the mortar shells and rifle fire from the Turks, it might jolly well be possible. And so they do.

In mid-afternoon on 17 December, it is a tentative group that sets up stumps on the pockmarked patch of ground known as Shell Green. Now, just what the Turks in the trenches above make of the strange spectacle is unclear – grenade-throwing practice perhaps? – but from the point of view of the men of the Light Horse, the main thing is that for the moment the Turks hold their fire and simply watch. Still, after three hours the Turks have had enough and start to send down some mortar fire to clear the Australians out. Whatever strange thing they are doing must be stopped!

Does the mortar fire stop the cricket cold? Not on your nelly. As recorded by Brigadier-General Granville Ryrie, 'The game continued anyway, just to let them see we were quite unconcerned . . . and when the shells whistled by we pretended to field them. The men were wonderfully cheerful and seemed to take the whole thing as a huge joke.'[18]

Charles Bean, watching closely, is particularly impressed, not simply with Major George Macarthur Onslow's batting under some pressure – less from the bowling than the mortars – but with the overall cool of the cricketers.

The Turks, however, decide they are less than impressed by the invaders' insistence on continuing this strange practice and unleash doubly heavy salvos of mortar fire.

The game is reluctantly called off. A draw? Happily, there is no record of any player having to *retire hurt* or worse.

That happiness over, tension returns. Tomorrow, everyone now knows, the final stage of the evacuation will begin, with all of the remaining soldiers – some 20,000 at Anzac, with the same number at Suvla – due to be taken off in just two nights.

The night of 17 December is perfect – calm and misty – and the lighters continue to go back and forth, taking men away. Bean stays up until 1 am, going over the timetable for the following day's events that Brudenell White has very kindly allowed him to be privy to before dropping off to sleep.

Just after 2.30, however, he awakens once more. Something is happening. *What is it?*

Voices. Whose?

English. Provincial.

'*Coom* along an' help General Lesslie, boys,' a voice is saying over the ongoing pounding of Beachy Bill to the south. 'An' doan' tarry now.'[19]

But it is not just that. There is a strange glow filling the sky from the direction of North Beach. There is an enormous fire in their lines – a real worry, as that is out of the ordinary and therefore suspicious. Ever the chronicler, Bean rises to record the event, taking his camera to the spot where an enormous dump of tinned beef ration and oil has been set alight by person or persons unknown. All around it, men are furiously trying to put the fire out, the glare of the flames illuminating their desperate faces and the silhouette of the hills behind. Others are wetting down adjacent stacks, trying to prevent them from going up, too.

'Oil drums burst with terrific force,' Trooper Bluegum records.[20]

With each explosion, the men glance nervously to the brooding hills. It is staggering that the Turks have not been alerted that things are out of the ordinary. In the distance, the voices of British sailors can be heard bawling orders to soldiers embarking on the piers.

'God,' Bean would note in his diary, 'has blessed the British navy with much courage and little brains.'[21]

Mercifully, the fire is broadly under control within an hour and, somehow, the Turks *still* have not twigged.

In his own dugout, Private Charles Bingham is feeling dreadful. Along with his mates who have also been selected to stay behind to help deal with the likely carnage, the best they can hope for is to be captured and hopefully survive the rest of the war as prisoners.

'This suspense is awful,' he confides to his diary. 'I suppose that we will all be in Constantinople soon, if the shells don't get us. I am going to try and be brave but it's hard to be left.'[22]

18 DECEMBER 1915, ANZAC COVE, THE END OF THE BEGINNING, AND THE BEGINNING OF THE END

On this, the day when the final part of the evacuation is due to begin, General Birdwood decides to put out a Special Army Order to his men:

Remember that in the final retirement silence is essential ... Those left in the front line to the last will, in their turn, quietly and silently leave their trenches, passing through their comrades in the covering positions to their place of embarkation in the same soldierly manner in which the troops have effected their various magnificent landings on the shores of this peninsula during the last eight months.

To withdraw in the face of the enemy in good order, and with hearts full of courage and confidence for the future, provides a test of which any soldiers in the world may be justly proud, and that the 9th and 'Anzac' Corps will prove themselves second to none as soldiers of the Empire, I have not the slightest doubt.

W. R. BIRDWOOD, Lieut.-General Commanding Dardanelles Army.[23]

Among the first to leave at his scheduled time is Charles Bean, who walks with heavy heart amid the cold and clinging mist that lies upon the pier, and climbs onto the beetle that is to take him to the cruiser *Grafton*.

He has been here from the first, seen such courage, so many deaths, so much pain, such sorrow, such staggering heroism.

And now, after a long battle that, in his eyes, had so completely absorbed 'the people's energies, so completely concentrated and unified their effort, that . . . in those days Australia became fully conscious of itself as a nation . . .'[24] they are leaving? It simply does not seem *right*.

And he means it. It will ever after be his proclaimed view that, 'In no unreal sense it was on the 25th of April, 1915, that the consciousness of Australian nationhood was born.'[25]

He gazes back at that receding shore now with great emotion.

'So I have left old Anzac,' he writes in his diary. 'In a way I was really fond of the place.'[26]

His emotion aside, Anzac Cove looks completely normal, 'with incinerator first going dreamily and the big fire still smoking'.[27] Amazingly, it seems the Turks *still* don't know that half of the Anzacs have now gone, just as has happened at Suvla Bay. And the second half should be off in the next two days.

Aboard the ship, Bean chats to the captain of *Grafton*, who proves to be the son of the great English cricketer W. G. Grace, meaning he is the very chap whose brother had once beaten Bean out for a spot in the 1st XI at good old Clifton College in England. Of course, to the sound of Beachy Bill still giving old Harry to those at Anzac, they chat cricket over a cup of tea . . .

NIGHT, 18 DECEMBER 1915, ANZAC, DRAWING THE CURTAIN

Now, following Brudenell White's minutely calibrated plan, landmines have been buried just below the surface along the most obvious paths for any pursuing flood of Turks. For the Anzacs themselves, long trails of sugar and flour show retreating troops the zigzagging route they must follow to avoid detonating those mines.

To the soldiers' amazement, when they get to the beach, instead of the rickety piers that have long been there, somehow, magically, in just the last few days, solid new piers have been built to enable them to embark quickly on the lighters. 'No sooner had each party arrived on the beach,' one soldier would recount to his parents, 'than they were aboard the steam and motor lighters and away to the troop ships which were lying close and handy.'[28]

Out on the *Grafton*, Charles Bean keeps glancing nervously towards the beaches, half-expecting to see huge explosions and hear the shattering roar of a full-blown Turkish attack, but there is nothing, absolutely nothing. All is as it ever was.

'The rattle from Anzac is like a low crackling fire. That at Suvla like a kettle of water boiling.'[29]

Dotted in the darkness, to the fore of the hills, lightly silhouetted by the rising moon, Bean can see through his binoculars the odd pinprick of cooking fires – the majority of which, he knows, have no one sitting around them.

Movement to his right – it is an unlit destroyer, stealthily gliding towards the shore, ready to load yet more soldiers from the endless lighters.

All seems to be going according to plan.

After asking that he be woken if such an attack eventuates – the ship is going to stay close to Anzac Cove – Bean goes to bed and is relieved to wake the following morning, knowing that his uninterrupted sleep means that all must have gone well.

Better still, this Sunday morning has dawned sparkling and clear. To this point, the weather has been extraordinarily kind, and yet the men have remained conscious that if the storms they experienced in November return, the weather will be a more fearful opponent than the Turks. But can it hold for another 24 hours? And can they get through this day with the Turks none the wiser before the last 10,000 soldiers – holding Anzac from Hill 60 in the north to the Second Ridge in the south – evacuate that night?

19 DECEMBER 1915, ALL ABOARD!

At Anzac Cove, there is great tension in the air among the Die Hards, but so too is there an overwhelming sense of sadness. As the day warms to get *well* above freezing point, many of the soldiers are seen to visit the graveyards that abound all around Anzac. Quietly, intently, they tidy up the plots by neatly arranging stones; they replace the old biscuit box crosses with constructions of solid wood, carefully carving names that will last the years; they plant sprigs of wattle that will bloom into life next spring. Finally, they bow their heads and say their prayers for the departed souls of loved mates gone to God.

And here is General Birdwood, on this last bright morning of the Gallipoli campaign, landing on the pier for a final look around – no matter that the pier is then and there under rifle fire from the enemy. When he had taken leave of his family nearly a year before to take command of Anzac, his four-year-old daughter had kissed him goodbye and asked, 'Do you think Daddy, they will kill you at the war?'[30] and he had always laughed about it, feeling sure that he would survive to kiss her again. He confidently sets foot on the pier and . . . immediately goes down!

His staff rush over, only to find he is dead . . . relieved to be entirely okay.

'Matting,' he would later explain, 'had been laid on the landing-stage to ensure silence, when the men embarked, and as I stepped ashore I caught my foot in this and fell flat . . .'[31]

He quickly heads ashore to less exposed positions, doing everything he can to ensure that all is in order and nothing more can be done.

'I was sad,' he would recall, 'but I had pride in the knowledge of the fine deeds that my men had done [here].'[32]

As he passes a cemetery, an Australian soldier salutes him and says, 'I hope they won't hear us going down to the beaches.'[33]

Brudenell White has, effectively, thought of that too.

Remaining troops on the frontlines ensure that the floors of their trenches are ripped up to be as soft as a freshly ploughed field so that when they leave, the noise of their boots – which are in turn wrapped 'with bed-socks, bags, shirts, sleeves, anything at all, to hush the sound of the marching to the beach'[34] – will be absorbed.

For the most part, the day proceeds according to plan, with the exception that one group of soldiers assigned to break up jars of rum and pour them into the Aegean just can't help themselves and, in the end . . . practically have to be poured into their boats themselves.

Most worryingly, after a long, tense afternoon, there comes a horrifying report that enemy troops are on the march north from Cape Helles, but nothing seems to come of it.

Ah, but the Turks are starting to notice that something is going on, all right. The sounds of a heavy bombardment coming from Cape Helles is one indication. Given recent form, 'something unusual might be occurring at Anzac and Suvla'.[35] And there is something else, too.

Just before the sun goes down, they can see an unusually high number of steamers coming from Imbros, perhaps as many as 35. Is this to be *another* landing?

Everyone must be on full alert.

Just before 4 pm, Brudenell White sits, sipping afternoon tea with a handful of other officers in a little dugout just back from the beach at Anzac Cove. They take their final sips before hopping up, placing their knives and forks in their pockets – nothing is to be left behind – and gathering around an old kerosene tin. Without a word, one of the officers takes 'an opened bottle of whisky and breaks it across the kerosene tin'.[36] And with that, it is time.

They pace down to the shore to have one last look around.

It's 'all ready'.[37]

Brudenell White heads back up to the almost emptied HQ and sits somewhat nervously at his table. Taking pencil in hand, he begins to write the first of a series of notes about the night's proceedings. He plans on staying on the ground until the last of his men come down safely from the trenches above. And if he's going to do that, with all the waiting it will entail, he may as well have something to occupy himself with. Lighting his pipe and letting it hang in its usual place out the right side of his mouth, he begins to write:

'We have finished our high teas, and the sun is going down . . . it is all very still. It has been flat and calm all day and there is not a ripple on the water and that means a good deal to us . . . Last night we saw away 9,900 . . .'[38]

The sun sets at 5 pm, and just 30 minutes later the first of the final three lots of troops due to come off tonight – this one dubbed 'A' section, 4000 soldiers strong – starts to leave their trenches and make their way to the piers far below.

With just a handful of men holding what had been held by tens of thousands, the air is thick with tension. All are aware of just how vulnerable they are. Anxiously, they wait for the partial protection of darkness to fall and the near-full moon to rise to give them the illumination they need. When at last it does, one of the Die Hards, Major Gordon Carter, notes the moon is 'very bright with a fine rainbow round it for half an hour or so',[39] even as a low mist gathers on the beach, making the most perfect shroud imaginable for the cutters and motor lighters now gathering there.

As the men start to embark, HMS *Grafton* hovers just off North Beach, ready to provide covering fire on specific targets should the troops be heavily pursued and need support. Charles Bean *lifts up his eyes unto the hills*, looking for some sign of abnormality, of alarm . . . but so far, mercifully, nothing.

Thousands of Indians, Gurkhas, Norfolk Yeomanry, Suffolk Yeomanry, Welch Horse and Anzacs continue to stream, mostly to the North Beach piers – and in lesser numbers to the ones at Anzac Beach – and from there onto the motor lighters and barges, and away to the larger vessels offshore. From the dot of 8.30 pm onwards, the next 4000 soldiers begin to descend – floating phantoms in the night, the ghosts of Gallipoli gliding silently through the soft, aching light. Again, no alarm is sounded and the entirety of this 'B' Section is away by 11.30.

A breeze caresses from the north, the only movement of nature on an otherwise completely still night. On the Aegean Sea, just offshore, the vessels continue gliding on dark glass.

Staggeringly, there are now fewer than 1500 men holding the 11,000 yards of the Anzac frontline – with, in fact, just one per 20 yards manning a gun or moving around firing other guns, while the rest of the Diggers make their final preparations for departure. This includes shooting most of those horses and donkeys that cannot be embarked, to prevent the Turks having use of them.

At least one notable animal is spared, however. Archie Barwick will ever after recall his last vision of Anzac from the departing boat: Simpson's donkey, 'little Murphy . . . standing on a little rise overlooking the cemetery. It was a pity they could not have brought him off, he was such a pet too.'[40]

The cruiser *Chatham* is chugging slowly up and down the coast just off Anzac and Suvla. On the bridge, Birdwood and Wemyss have their glasses trained on the coast, trying to get some idea of how the evacuation is proceeding.

Of course, they can see very little, but that in itself is encouraging – every hour that passes without the sounds of the Turkish Army falling upon the thin ranks of the Anzacs, or in the first instance sending a rain of shells onto the beaches and piers, is a great hour.

And those Anzacs are busy, all right. Over the last few weeks, some of the soldiers, with ingenuity that would do Lance-Corporal William Beech and his periscope proud, have worked out a way to have their rifles fire long after they have gone. The best method, invented by Lance-Corporal Bill Scurry, involves filling a kerosene can with water and then puncturing the can so that it slowly drips into a second can.[41] At a certain point, when the second can – attached by string to the trigger of the rifle – has sufficient weight, it will topple and the rifle will fire. Another way is to have two pieces of string attached to a weight, with the short string wrapped around a candle. When the candle burns down, it burns the string too, meaning the weight – with the longer piece of string attached to the trigger – drops, thus firing the rifle.

All the various systems are put into play as the Diggers continue destroying the supplies that they won't be able to take with them. Captain Aubrey Wiltshire records, 'Into our latrine pit we threw 70,000 rounds SAA, 1500 grenades and bombs. The enemy are welcome to this if they like to clean it.'[42]

Many of them also put final touches to their endlessly diverse farewell messages to the Turks, written on whatever pieces of cardboard or paper they can find:

Au revoir, Abdul. See you later on.[43]

Good-bye, Mahomet. Better luck next time.[44]

Abdul, you're a good clean fighter and we bear you no ill-will.[45]

Merry Christmas, Abdul; you're a good sport anyhow, but the Hun is a fair cow.[46]

And yes, of course, there is the odd aggressive message as well, in one case mixed with an unspeakably crude drawing of Kaiser Bill and the Sultan above the scrawled words *Abdul: you silly c--!*[47]

There is also the odd booby trap, with cans of food that have been punctured the day before to ensure they have gone off and will make anyone who eats them sick.

But for the most part, the tone of the Digger farewell is friendly, in the manner of one of two brothers who have fought each other to a bloodied standstill, before one reaches out to the other and gives him an exhausted pat on the back – that's enough now, mate.

Among Trooper Bluegum's fellow Diggers, they leave boxes of cigarettes, tins of jam, pouches of tobacco.

And they might have even left the Turks some cases of rum, too, but after one too many cases of drunkenness, 'the order had gone out that all liquor except that in the casualty clearing stations should be poured out on the ground or into the sea'.[48] A pity.

Still, in the absence of rum, many of them do what they can.

In one dugout, the Diggers go to the effort of setting up a gramophone, 'so as soon as they touched it, it would play *The Turkish Patrol . . .*'[49]

In another nearby dugout, the men go to a similar effort, albeit with a twist . . .

'A light horseman set up a table for four,' Bluegum would recount. 'There was jam, bully beef, biscuits and cheese. And a note: "There are no booby traps in this dug-out". It was almost true. He had added black powder from cartridges to the packet of tobacco he left behind.'[50]

Someone is in for a non-lethal surprise.

Soon enough, though, it is time. Time to prepare for the last phase of the entire operation to be put into action as the 1500 Die Hards to beat them all – 'C' section – get ready to leave their posts, with the first due to depart at 1.30 am.

Their boots covered with 'socks, moccasins, bits of underpants, sleeves of shirts and all manner of things',[51] they quickly move from gun to gun and either fire them or set off the mechanism that will make most of them fire in the next 30 minutes, and some as long as 45 minutes hence.

Nervous?

Rather. In the delicate diary words of Captain Aubrey Wiltshire, the tension of leaving 'caused excessive secretions and the rear trenches and dugouts were systematically fouled . . .'[52]

And now it really is time. It is an extraordinary thing for many of these Diggers, on this clear, freezing night, to turn their backs on the trenches that so many of their mates have given their lives to defend, turn their backs on their foes to face the calm, moonlit waters of the Aegean far below. But so they do, to the minute.

Those on the far north and far south of the perimeter, in staggered sequence, start following the white powder lines and drain straight down the hill some 1500 yards to the piers, where cutters wait to whisk them away.

In the near distance, there is the exchange of musketry fire here and there along the line, while from further away comes the occasional belch of a blast from Beachy Bill, providing odd comfort – for all is sounding as it usually does at this time of night. And from the far south, at Cape Helles, comes the rolling roar of a fierce exchange of artillery fire, but this, too, is as planned by Brudenell White – their brethren there are trying to shift the Turkish focus to them, away from Anzac Cove.

The mood, however, remains on a knife's edge for the first of these Die Hards. For the first time in eight months, there is a breach in the Anzac line, with nothing between them and 80,000 Turks but a skeleton crew of soldiers softly padding down the slopes. At all times, they are expecting to hear shouts of discovery from behind, followed by the inevitable cries of '*Allah! Allah! Allah!*' as the heathen hordes fall upon them.

But to their considerable surprise there is no attack. They are not followed.

Yet.

At least not by the Turks . . .

'Tread softly, boys,' one soldier comments as they steal down the hill, 'and don't let them hear us deserting them.'[53]

This genuine worry of what their dead mates would think of what they are doing is a common emotion, most particularly as they pass the graveyards.

'I am sure,' another soldier would record of his thoughts, 'that they will turn in their graves and wonder where we are when the Turks begin to walk over them.'[54]

The Die Hards keep descending as post after post continues to be abandoned, but . . .

But where the bloody hell is *Fred*? High in the hills west of Chunuk Bair at Durrant's Post, Private Fred Pollack of the 13th Battalion has gone missing. A rough-and-ready bloke from Sydney, Fred had been so exhausted by the sheer tension of the last 48 hours that he was given permission to have a kip in a nearby dugout, just down from the front trenches. But now at 2 am, when it's time to scarper and his mates go to get him, he is not there. *Fred is not there!* He must have meant a different dugout.

In an agony of worry, unable to shout his name as that might alarm the Turks, his mates race from dugout to dugout, but Fred is not to be found. Finally, their Captain orders them to abandon the search. Fall in. Get down. Down to the beaches. They obey orders. *Bloody Fred!*

Gazing shoreward, Charles Bean keeps consulting his watch and his copy of the timetable, marking off company after company who he knows are leaving post after post. Intermittent fire comes from the Turkish trenches, and the first of the self-activated Anzac rifles fire back.

As Bean sips a delightful cup of hot cocoa on the bridge with Captain Grace, he knows soon enough that only the centre is manned now. At 2.40 am, Lone Pine, and the spirits of 1000 dead Australian soldiers, is abandoned by the 37 men of 24th Battalion, with Courtney's going five minutes later, followed by Quinn's and Pope's at 2.55 am.

Russell's Top, opposite the Nek, is the last occupied frontline post.

It has been so hard-won, with so many Australian lives lost there that it is hard to leave, but, at exactly 3.14 am, the raggedy remnant of the 20th Battalion, those phantoms of the trenches, turn on their padded heels and walk away . . .

Quickly and quietly now, lads. In the near distance, shots ring out spasmodically as the self-firing rifles do their work. These last men head towards the beaches, following the instructions that have been so minutely worked out for them. At successive points, they pull rolls of barbed wire across the paths behind them, as well as activating booby traps and lighting fuses. Clouds obscure the moon and the mission becomes so much darker.

Ah, but there are still a few men left behind, back from the Nek, who have been given an alternative route to descend to avoid such obstacles, given one last task before departure. For, of course, how else could such a monumental battle for the ages finally end?

Not with a whimper, but with a bang.

Over the last weeks, three tunnels between Russell's Top and the Nek have been packed with a total of three and a half tons of high explosive. The largest charge – weighing two tons – is located at the end of a tunnel directly beneath the Turkish frontline at the Nek.

The men of the Rear Party, who are charged with setting off the mines, are sitting atop Russell's Top now. Their commander is Major Richard Fitzgerald, who is 'calm and collected' and focuses on keeping his men cheerful. At 1 am, the group had feasted on the now plentiful supplies; 'The meal consisted of sardines, biscuits, pineapple and mock cream soup in that order! After we had finished the table was left laid for the Turks, with a note written by Major Fitzgerald, which reads:

Good-bye, Jackie, will see you later. You are a good fighter, but we don't like the company you keep.[55]

And now, nigh on 3.30 am, the men of the Rear Party just have to wait for the word to come through that the rest of the 20th Battalion is clear and that the first of them are piling onto the piers and getting into the evacuation vessels. It is coming time; they'll soon have to blow the bastard.

High in the hills, the rhythm of gunfire slows as most of the self-activating rifles stop firing. The Turks continue to respond with a few desultory shots, and then there is . . . silence. In the Turkish trenches, puzzlement rises.

It's time.

Time to fire the Parthian shot to beat them all.

Satisfied that all the men are now clear down at the North Beach pier, the man that Brudenell White has designated as Rear Guard Commander, Newcastle's own Colonel John Paton, makes the call.

Moments later, high in the hills, Major Fitzgerald puts the field telephone down and gives the order 'to fire the mines . . . [but] not until he had got on top of the dugout to see the effect'.[56]

Lieutenant James Caddy slowly, carefully pushes down the plunger before him. On the instant, the electric circuit connected to the detonator, which is some 100 yards away at the end of the tunnel that finishes under the Turkish trenches at the Nek, is completed.

For . . . THAR she blows! At first, there is a rumble like an earthquake, and then a huge pillar of flame shoots skyward at the Nek, illuminating all the hills around . . . and goes long enough that Bean notes how its 'brilliant glare [is] reflected on the under-surface of two clouds of dust and smoke'.[57]

Lieutenant Caddy would later recall, 'The ground vibrated, there was a dull roar and two large craters were formed . . . Immediately afterwards, heavy rifle fire opened up along the whole of the enemy line.'[58]

For the first time in eight months, there is no one there to make reply. The Turks try again, with many other long bursts. One very stray bullet, flying far from home, hits a Light Horseman in the retreating boats. Mercifully, he is only lightly wounded.

And then . . . still nothing.

—

Up in the Turkish frontlines, chaos reigns. Yes, the Turks know that there have been two mighty explosions beneath their trenches at the Nek – and they have likely lost 70 men[59] – but when all the men from nearby trenches rush forward, as they have been trained to do to stem the breach, there is nothing coming back. No bullets, no bombs, nothing. Is this another ruse designed to bring them forward en masse, only to be killed? They proceed slowly. Still, there is no fire upon them.

—

Halfway down the hill ahead of them, two figures are fleeing. Judging discretion to be the better part of valour, Lieutenant Caddy and his sergeant are making good their escape. It is time to get back to the beach, at all pace. A bob in, and the winner shouts!

All up, the explosions have been nigh on enough to wake the dead . . . and really do wake one other person.

High in the hills, a man wakes more abruptly than at any time in his life, the tons of high explosive having been detonated just a short distance from him.

Who am I? Where am I? What is *happening?*

Oh . . . *Gawd.*

I am Private Fred Pollack of the 13th Battalion, and the last thing

I remember is receiving permission to have a bit of a kip in a nearby dugout, with my mates assuring me they would wake me when it came time to pull out. And now they're not bloody well here.

I charge along the trenches but find them empty, too. Oh Gawd, oh Gawd, oh *Gawd*! Am I really the last bastard left at Anzac Cove, while everyone else has gone? Me and tens of thousands of Turks?

Oh, *Gawd*.

A fire to port! From the decks of *Grafton*, Charles Bean suddenly sees what could be mistaken for a giant, mad firefly buzzing along the shores of Suvla, but it is in fact a bobbing torch flame, held by a man running along the beach and setting fire to flammable material soaked in kerosene, nestled among the reserve stores stacked up on the shore, put aside in case the evacuation was delayed.

The piles flare instantly. Fires in the night!

Tearing down the hill, Fred, a long way from Sydney Town, makes it to the beach, hoping, praying to find someone still there – a movement, a light, a boat!

Suddenly, however, he sees what may be a lantern or the like at North Pier.

Fred charges towards it along the rough sands of the beach. It is just before 4 am.

Colonel John Paton is preparing to get the last lighters away. With the explosion in the hills, it can only be a matter of minutes before this beach will be swarming with Turks. All of the departing men are gazing into the heavy shadows to look for attackers.

There! From the north, a figure is charging at them from the edge of darkness. In an instant, the Australians reach for their guns.

Coo-ee.

It proves to be the infinitely relieved Fred Pollack, who hurls himself into one of the last departing lighters. Saved![60]

And so is Private Charles Bingham, amazed that all of his worst fears have *not* been realised. And now that it is all happening, his whole outlook has changed, as recorded in his diary: 'It is an honour to be last here I feel now.'[61]

Brigadier-General Cyril Brudenell White, too, has stayed to the last, aboard one of the lighters waiting to take the men away.

'It has been a continuous stream for the last 20 minutes but now it is dying down. The gaps between the little groups and then between the single men grow wider and then the trickle stops. The enemy machine guns are going hard on Russell's Top now. They did not know what to make of the mine, but the bullets go into our parapets in front of the empty trenches or over our heads and into the sea.'[62]

The evacuation of Suvla Bay has gone equally well, with no fatalities.

Still, Colonel Paton doesn't leave; he's concerned that there may be other stragglers. And so he waits, together with several others. They continue to peer into the darkness, but by ten past four, with still no sign of anyone else to come, Colonel Paton barks a command.

A sailor slips the mooring rope before, with a running jump, he leaps onto the steamboat, the last man to leave.

The terse wireless message goes out: evacuation completed.[63]

The relief is overwhelming. Bean is standing next to a naval officer when the message is handed to him. That officer now turns, proffers his hand in the moonlight and says quietly to Bean, 'Thank God.'[64]

—

Allah be praised.

Extraordinarily, on the Turkish side, all these months on, Private Âdil, the 17-year-old shepherd who had been in the trenches on the First Ridge on the morning of 25 April and among the first to fire on the approaching Anzacs, is *still* here.

And he is as confused as everyone else. The heavy fog that now rolls in is in sympathy with the Turks' lack of understanding.

'We had no idea,' Âdil will later recount. 'All the gun noises had stopped . . .'[65]

They send out a scout, who carefully makes his way forward. He comes back and tells them the blessed news.

'*Gittiler!* – They've gone!'[66]

Similar scenes are taking place everywhere in the area.

———

And . . . *fire!*

From the waters off Gallipoli, the guns of the covering squadron pour salvo after salvo upon the old Anzac positions, to blow up the stores and mule carts and slow the Turkish brutes down in their descent from the hills. In fact, the Turks are obliged to take shelter in the very trenches they have been shelling for the last eight months.

For the moment, many of the Royal Navy cruisers and destroyers, secure with their precious cargo below decks, stay just beyond the range of the Turkish guns. The officers keep their binoculars trained on the shore, eager to see what will happen. Just after dawn, their reward is to see Turkish soldiers charge down the hillside and onto the beaches, where their first target is the few unburned piles of stores. Like mad things, they find anything edible and start gorging themselves. The ships send some shells upon them as a chaser.

This vision of their enemies on the shore, while they are on ships headed away, is for many of the soldiers and officers the first gut realisation that they have actually done it: they have survived Gallipoli.

Around the ships, cheers ring out as men clap each other's backs and furiously pump each other's hands. In this moment, there are no Generals, Colonels, Sergeants or Privates – they are just Anzacs, men who have got clean away. They have done it! Brudenell White notes proudly, '. . . Anzac is deserted now . . .'[67]

Some men cry. Far on the northern horizon, black clouds are gathering, clouds that will soon unleash torrents upon *torrents* of rain and such howling wind that the piers will be washed away.

The Die Hards stare to the last, gazing back to the sacred shores, so confidently stormed eight months earlier, now drenched in the blood of half a million men, with some 135,000 buried in shallow graves.

For this, too, is the rule in these parts . . . The Emperors, Sultans,

Kings, Presidents, Prime Ministers and Warlords send their soldiers and sailors, the battle breaks out, and the Dardanelles exacts its deadly toll. So it has been for centuries. So it is now.

The tides of war that have flooded them forth to this place are now receding, and the survivors are as relieved as they are surprised to be alive to see the day – while desperately aware of just how many they are leaving behind.

And so they continue to gaze back until, with the fog, the dawn, the distance, the Dardanelles quickly fade from view, gone . . . but never forgotten.

EPILOGUE

> When peace comes, and we are free to move about the
> country, no doubt the tourist of the future will come
> to inspect these parts . . . I suppose that some day, on
> some high plateau overlooking Anzac beach, there will
> be a noble memorial erected by the people of Australia,
> to honour the memory of their fallen dead, who lie
> peacefully sleeping in the little valleys all around.[1]
> *Colonel John Monash, 18 June 1915, while*
> *sitting in his dugout at Anzac Cove*

> We had nothing against them. He was fighting. Johnny
> Turk was fighting for his country and we was fighting
> for our country. No, there was nothing personal, no.[2]
> *Private Jack Nicholson to the ABC in 1980*

> We didn't hate the enemy . . . Their duty was to come here
> and invade, ours was to defend. No, I never hated them,
> never. And now my friends we're brothers and I want to
> send my regards to all of them, my regards to the Anzacs.[3]
> *Turkish Private Âdil to the ABC in 1985*

So successful was the withdrawal from Anzac Cove and Suvla Bay and
so dire the winter on the Dardanelles that, on 27 December 1915, the
British Cabinet committed to getting out of Cape Helles as well. Using
similar methods, Cape Helles was successfully evacuated on the early
morning of 8 January 1916.

With that last man off, so ended the whole ill-fated Dardanelles
campaign, which extracted a devastating human toll all round:[4]

Australia	8709 dead; 19,441 wounded
New Zealand	2721 dead; 4752 wounded
Britain	21,255 dead; 52,230 wounded
France	9829 dead; 17,175 wounded
India	1358 dead; 3421 wounded
Newfoundland	49 dead; 93 wounded
Total Allies	43,921 dead; 97,112 wounded
Turkey	86,692 dead; 164,617 wounded

With so many dead – and with such an exotic location for the Allies' campaign, silently gliding in the dark to an unknown shore, gripping the popular imagination – it is not surprising that the first anniversary of the landing was strongly commemorated.

At his camp by the Suez Canal in Egypt, Brigadier-General John Monash declared a special holiday for his troops. They solemnly began the day with a remembrance ceremony of the Gallipoli landing a year earlier, and it finished with most of the 15,000 Diggers, many of them three sheets to the wind, swimming naked in the Canal. (And so began, perhaps, another tradition of the anniversary: reverence followed by revelry.)

In London, no fewer than 2000 Australian and New Zealand troops – referred to in the papers as 'the knights of Gallipoli'[5] – marched through the streets.

In Australia, on what had already officially been named 'Anzac Day', there was an equal mix of pride for what had been accomplished and grief for those lost, as so many families around the country marked the anniversary of the beginning of the campaign that had taken their loved ones.

One newspaper, *The Queenslander*, captured the mood when it noted, 'a sob seemed to shake the community on Tuesday as it stepped forward and placed a simple flower on the graves of the gallant men slain on the heights of Gallipoli'.[6]

The crowds were huge, the tone sanguine. 'The dominant note,' *The*

Queenslander observed, 'was one of mourning – it could not have been otherwise – but mingled with it, and breaking through like sunlight glinting through the rain clouds which gathered and yielded soft showers during the day, was the feeling of triumph and pride that Australia has such worthy sons.'[7] (And, yes, in the afternoon, heavy drinking and two-up were the order of the day.)

In Sydney, a march was held, with thousands of returned soldiers forming up in the Domain and parading down Macquarie Street, as the Governor-General took the salute, and 'at 9 am, every train and tram was brought to a standstill for one minute, and cheers were given for the King, the Empire, and the Anzacs'.[8]

Those returned soldiers too ill to march were carried in motor cars, and some of them were cared for by nurses. Many of them would never walk again, but at least on this day they were heartily cheered by the large crowds. A similar commemorative ceremony was held in Sydney for 'Lone Pine Day' on 8 August. 'The sight was an impressive one. Many of the men were battle scarred, several had lost limbs, and one man was blind and had to link arms with a comrade. But all marched with heads proudly erect, confident, and satisfied with duty nobly done.'[9]

It was a tradition that soon grew, most particularly from the mid-1920s onwards, when organised marches and dawn services took hold.

In the years since, Australia as a whole has been extremely proud of the legend of Gallipoli, so proud that our people – characteristically irreverent when it comes to just about everything else – to this day regard Anzac Day with a naturally bowed head.

On this subject, Christopher Bantick wrote a fascinating piece for *The Australian* in 2010, noting that while 'there were astounding feats of bravery at the Gallipoli landing in 1915 . . . the legend that arose from them is indeed mythical . . . Why Australia craved such a legend of its own lies in its lack of foundation myths. There was no battle for independence, as in the US, no civil war as there had been in England and no revolution as in France.'[10]

And woe betide any who would not treat the saga with the same veneration.

A case in point is what happened in 1926 when Brigadier-General Cecil Aspinall, the British staff officer turned historian,[11] sent his first draft chapters about the Gallipoli landing – set to be published as part of the British Official History – to Australia for comment. Counter to the stories of bravery and daring that had sparked the growing legend of Anzac Day in Australia, the Englishman wrote that, on the day of the first landing at Gallipoli, many Australians had displayed outright cowardice: 'For many the breaking point had now been passed, and numbers of unwounded men were filtering back to the beach [in an] endless stream . . . the gullies in the rear were choked with stragglers and men who had lost their way . . .'[12]

Aspinall maintained that, after a relatively easy landing, 'confusion amongst the Australian forces prevented a coordinated attack "which could scarcely have failed" to win the day'.[13]

Now, no matter that in his diary entry on the day Charles Bean himself had noted that the number of *stragglers . . . began to reach* *serious fair proportions*[14] and in his post-war account he had allowed that some of the Australian soldiers of 'weaker fibre'[15] had indeed found shelter in the gullies. Bean, upon reading the draft chapters, could not abide Aspinall's rendition of the Australians' performance on that day.

As documented by Thomson, it was Bean who blew the shrill and angry whistle. Immediately, he circulated Aspinall's account among former AIF Commanders, 'one of whom feared that the manuscript would persuade civilian leaders that "most of the leaders were inept daunted men and that a large proportion of the glory of Anzac is mere propaganda"'.[16]

It *must* be removed!

But Aspinall would not back off, and on first hearing the news that it even *might* be deleted, he wrote in a memo, 'This chapter was a difficult one to write because the truth about the Australians has never yet been told and in its absence a myth has sprung up that the Anzac troops did magnificently against amazing odds. If this is omitted there is nothing of the truth left . . .'[17]

Australia most certainly did not see it that way. Getting wind of

Aspinall's claims of 'stragglers and shirkers', not heroes and warriors born, Sydney's *Daily Guardian* exploded in outrage, referring to the allegation as 'The Vilest Libel of the War'.[18] And Prime Minister Billy Hughes was equally appalled, personally and on behalf of the nation, fulminating to the press, 'Australia's sons acquitted themselves like heroes and with heroism unsurpassed in the history of the world.'[19]

Hughes went on, telling *The Brisbane Courier*, 'I can only say that the man who wrote them has been guilty of an infamous libel on men, the glory of whose deeds will live forever . . . Why the British Government chose such a one to write the story of the war passes human comprehension.

'One thing is certain, that the man who said eight thousand Australians were skulking on the beach, was not on that beach . . . Certainly when this immortal exploit was taking place, he was probably in a very safe place, miles and miles away.'[20]

(A fairly accurate assessment, as it turned out, as on the day Aspinall had been secure aboard *Queen Elizabeth*, on Hamilton's staff, helping to preside over the whole catastrophe. And of the sources cited by him for the claim, the only person actually there at the time was Colonel Ewen MacLagan, who was flat out on the Second Ridge for most of the day, and nowhere near the safe gullies.)

Prime Minister Hughes went on, giving fair warning, 'If these infamous statements are published under the authority of the British Government, how can Australians listen patiently to talking about standing shoulder to shoulder with men who slandered them in this fashion?'[21]

Not surprisingly, with threats like that, and with agitation by both Prime Minister Hughes and Charles Bean, the offending passages were dropped from the final publication.

For what it's worth, my own view is that, however many men might have given in to civilian sanity and sought shelter on the first day – as I frankly suspect I might have, had I been present – there can be no doubt that the overall effort of the Australians as part of the Anzacs in Gallipoli, from the first day to the last, really was an extraordinary one.

Beyond debate regarding its enduring legend and legacy, however, there were many important lessons for the Australian military to come from Gallipoli. The most important one was best enunciated by Lieutenant-General Sir Thomas Blamey, when, in the Second World War, before the battle of Tobruk, he strongly cautioned against plans to put Australian troops again under British command: 'Past experience has taught me to look with misgiving on a situation where British leaders have control of considerable bodies of first-class Dominion troops while Dominion commanders are excluded from all responsibility in control, planning and policy.'[22] Never again would Australia cede control of its army or navy to Great Britain.

Many other lessons were elucidated by subsequent inquiries into just how the whole Dardanelles campaign had gone so wrong. On 23 August 1916 in London, a Royal Commission into the Dardanelles began. No fewer than 200 witnesses were called to give sworn testimony over the ensuing 12 months.

They included all of the leading political, military and even journalistic figures of the day who had either played a significant role in the Dardanelles campaign or been able to observe it closely. All of Herbert Asquith, Winston Churchill, Sir Ian Hamilton, John de Robeck, Roger Keyes, Sir Frederick Stopford and Sir John Fisher gave their considered accounts, together with the likes of Keith Murdoch and Ellis Ashmead-Bartlett.

The Commission's two reports were scathing in their conclusions:

- . . . sufficient consideration was not given to the measures necessary to carry out such an expedition with success.[23]
- . . . the difficulties of the operations were much underestimated. At the outset all decisions were taken and all provisions based on the assumption, that, if a landing were effected, the resistance would be slight and the advance rapid.[24]
- . . . the plan of attack from Anzac and Suvla in the beginning of August was open to criticism.[25]
- There was no meeting of the War Council between March

19th and May 14th. Meanwhile important land operations were undertaken. We think that before such operations were commenced the War Council should have carefully reconsidered the whole position. In our opinion the Prime Minister ought to have summoned a meeting of the War Council for that purpose.[26]

The most staggering thing about the whole outcome of the findings of the Dardanelles Commission? Despite the fact that it had comprehensively demonstrated that the plan to force the Dardanelles was fraught from the first, that the Turks had shown beyond doubt that when their minefields were intact, their batteries manned and their ammunition supplies strong, it was close to impossible for even a powerful fleet to force its way through the Straits, *still* in late 1918 there were those in the highest echelons of the British military establishment who were intent on giving it another go.

They were led by the completely unstoppable and recently promoted Rear-Admiral Roger Keyes, who by this time was in command of the Dover Patrol, responsible for keeping the English Channel clear of German naval vessels. And he was strongly backed by his great supporter, Admiral Rosslyn Wemyss, who had become First Sea Lord in December 1917.

Extraordinarily, at the time the Turks surrendered – on 30 October 1918 at a signing in Mudros Harbour, just 12 days before the Armistice with Germany – the Cabinet had approved the plans of Keyes and Wemyss to attack the Dardanelles again!

Mercifully, under the terms of the Treaty of Mudros, the Dardanelles was placed under international control with the Turkish affirmation, under the later Treaty of Sèvres, that the Dardanelles would remain open 'both in peace and war, to every vessel of commerce or of war and to military and commercial aircraft, without distinction of flag'.[27] On 12 November 1918, a squadron of British destroyers sailed through on their way to Constantinople, the guns of the forts lying mute and impotent above them.

As to many of the major players in the campaign, the virtues or otherwise of their roles at Gallipoli – for good or bad – would stay with them for a long time, including well beyond death.

Lord Kitchener's reputation never recovered from the shambles of an operation that he had overseen from the start. After his return from the Dardanelles in late November 1915, 'Lord K.' was forced to succumb to the humiliation of having one Major-General Sir William Robertson imposed upon him as Chief of the Imperial General Staff, effectively to oversee his every move. No more could Kitchener behave like an aristocrat who was answerable to no one, least of all the Cabinet.

On 5 June 1916, Lord Kitchener found himself on HMS *Hampshire*, travelling to the Russian port of Archangel, with a mission of negotiating with the Tsar's government ways to better coordinate the Allies' military operations. *Hampshire* had two escort ships, *Unity* and *Victor*, which, alas, received orders from Captain Saville of *Hampshire* to return to Scapa Flow because they had fallen behind in the bad weather and it was considered unlikely that enemy submarines would be active in such conditions.

Hampshire continued alone, soon finding itself just off the Orkneys (an archipelago in northern Scotland) in a Force 9 gale and . . . a minefield. The mines had been laid three days earlier by a German submarine, *U-75*, and had already claimed a British ship, *Crown*. Shortly before 7.30 pm, *Hampshire*, with 655 men on board, suddenly hit a mine and was quickly on its way to the bottom, taking Lord Kitchener and all bar 12 sailors with it. Captain FitzGerald was close by his side to the end.

One survivor reported that Kitchener met his death with typical dignity and resolution to the last. The news of his demise hit Great Britain, and indeed the British Empire, like a thunderclap. 'Never,' his biographer Sir George Arthur would insist, 'since man has made the lightning his messenger, did the passing of an individual so profoundly move humanity as a whole. For an instant a hush seemed to fall alike on soldier and citizen, on camp and council-chamber . . .'[28]

The Memorial Service for Lord Kitchener was held in a packed St Paul's Cathedral, and was presided over by the Archbishop of

Canterbury. When Their Majesties the King and Queen arrived in an open carriage with an escort of Life Guards, they were saluted by a group of Australian and New Zealand soldiers, who, though so badly wounded in Gallipoli they had to be accompanied by their carers, had been released from hospital for the occasion, so they could pay their deepest respects to Lord Kitchener.

(I know.)

Captain Oswald FitzGerald's body was washed ashore in Great Britain, and he was quietly buried in Eastbourne, Sussex.

Winston Churchill, of course – the other principal architect of the Dardanelles campaign – was far more fortunate, and managed to not only outlast the most fierce opprobrium for his part in the affair but also go on to become Britain's most famous Prime Minister. After serving with some distinction as an officer in France, Churchill returned to England and parliament in June 1916, and, under the Prime Ministership of David Lloyd George in 1917, once again became Minister of Munitions. Throughout the 1920s and 1930s, Churchill's career waxed and waned, but of course it prospered as never before shortly after the Second World War broke out – vindicating his warnings about the danger of an Adolf Hitler-led Germany over the previous seven years. He took over the Prime Ministership from Neville Chamberlain, retaining it till just after the end of that war. He regained the position in 1951, retired in 1955 and died in 1965.

Herbert Asquith resigned on 5 December 1916, after losing the confidence of the public, the press and his fellow politicians over his lack of dynamism in his conduct of the war so far. Though he remained in the Commons and leader of the Liberal Party, he never again held office. He died on 15 February 1928.

The man selected to provide that dynamism was Lloyd George, and one of his first moves was to make Lord Northcliffe his 'Director of Propaganda' – a role in which the pressman prospered. On the day of Armistice, 11 November 1918, Northcliffe resigned, and went back to exclusively running his tabloid newspapers, before dying in August 1922 of a blood infection.

Among Lord Northcliffe's closest confidants at the time of his death – even though he had returned to Australia – was Keith Murdoch, who had become so enamoured of the Lord and his methods that he was soon to become known as 'Lord Southcliffe'. Lionised for his intervention in the Gallipoli campaign, Murdoch had become close to many key figures in England's ruling class, made regular visits to the Western Front and continued to rise in journalism – before returning to Melbourne early in 1921 to take a position as Editor-in-Chief of the Melbourne evening *Herald*. That paper became a stunning success, in part because Murdoch followed much the same model of tabloid journalism he had learned firsthand from his inspiration, Lord Northcliffe. By both covering and *generating* political controversy, and always putting it on the front page, as well as providing heavy celebrity coverage, he lifted circulation by 50 per cent in just his first four years.

Just like Northcliffe, Murdoch also aspired to own the newspapers, and in 1928 he became Managing Director of the company that owned the paper *The Herald & Weekly Times*, the same year that the 42-year-old married the 19-year-old Melbourne beauty Elisabeth Joy Greene. In short order – and even while Murdoch bought the exceedingly dull *Adelaide Register* before turning it into a tabloid, and then took over *The Adelaide Advertiser* and *The Adelaide News* – the couple had one son and three daughters.

Keith Murdoch's key breakthrough came in 1948, when he persuaded the *Herald* board to sell to him its holdings in *The Adelaide News*, and when he died in 1952, this was the key asset of his estate – allowing his dream to be fulfilled. For, from the moment of establishing his family and having a son, Murdoch had been obsessed with training that son, Rupert, so he could take charge of the family business and make a success of it.

He did.

The rights and wrongs of 'the Murdoch letter' would be heatedly discussed for a century and counting . . . Though there would be many critics, led by General Hamilton, who were scathing in the accusations of dishonour levelled at Murdoch for breaching the censorship regulations, Keith Murdoch was an ardent defender of his own actions. In response to the Hamilton criticisms, he said simply, 'I had a perfectly clear conscience as to what I did. I went to London and I hit Sir Ian Hamilton as hard as I could. I thought the vital thing was to get a fresh mind on the spot. The British Cabinet confirmed this view by recalling him within a week of my report being discussed by it . . .

'I broke no censorship pledge . . . I wrote nothing for publication without censorship. I wrote a report for the Prime Minister of my own country, and received his thanks, and also the thanks of the succeeding Prime Minister.'[29]

He had already been backed up by former Australian Prime Minister Andrew Fisher, who, upon being installed as one of those presiding on the Dardanelles Commission, had explained to his fellow Commissioners that Murdoch had visited the Dardanelles at *his* behest, and that the correspondent's first loyalty – strange as it might seem to them – was to Australia. You see, gentlemen, Australia has a 'separateness' from Britain, and as a 'self-governing Dominion',[30] sometimes its interests would be different from Great Britain's.

The controversy would rumble on, however, and other writers – particularly the most esteemed contemporary writer of the lot, Les Carlyon – have strongly downplayed the significance of the letter, maintaining Murdoch was little more than a pawn in the grand power play of others.

Again, for what it's worth, I most respectfully disagree with Les, and cite the words of Charles Bean in 1958: 'Keith felt that the Australians were being sacrificed . . . and he wrote his letter with the sledgehammer phrases – often massive over-statements – which were typical of his writing in controversy. But there was much truth behind them – the troops had no great confidence in Hamilton; he had not the crude strength for such an enterprise . . . Murdoch's letter was, I should say, the main agent in bringing about Hamilton's fall.'[31]

With Hamilton's fall, and Monro's fresh eyes on site, the evacuation that would save so many Australian lives became all the more likely.

Rupert Murdoch has himself been a great defender of the faith, noting, 'My father's letter from Gallipoli to Fisher was a highly emotional, important and nationalistic piece of reporting.'[32]

Charles Bean? His time at Gallipoli and then the Western Front as a war correspondent, filling 226 notebooks along the way, would form the foundation stone for his work for the next 23 years, as he compiled 12 volumes of the *Official History of Australia in the War of 1914–1918*, of which he wrote the first six, with the 12th and final volume being published in 1942.

A significant part of that was his return to Gallipoli in January 1919, leading the Australian Historical Mission, to gather facts and increase Australian understanding of the lie of the land from the other side of the trenches. At the Nek, they had to tread lightly, around and over the bones of the Light Horsemen who lay there still. (In some of the lesser known spots of Gallipoli, human bones from 1915 can still be seen today – though their provenance is not certain.) In 1946, Bean released a separate, single-volume account of the war titled *Anzac to Amiens*, and in 1957 published *Two Men I Knew*, about the founders of the AIF, William Bridges and Cyril Brudenell White.

Beyond his writings, Bean's other great legacy, of course, is the Australian War Memorial. While covering the devastating battles of the Australians on the Western Front, he conceived the notion that, like the British and Canadians particularly, Australia should have an institution filled with relics, photos and records to commemorate the Australian wartime experience – and suggested as much to the Federal Government in November 1916. Bean was its first Director,[33] put enormous energy into laying its historical foundation stones, and could take a deep bow when it opened its doors on 11 November 1941.

Surprisingly, for one who was such a devotee of the British Empire, Charles Bean more than once declined a knighthood. He died aged 88 on 30 August 1968, survived by his wife, Ethel, a one-time Queanbeyan nurse, and their daughter and grandson.

Ellis Ashmead-Bartlett also attracted a great deal of notoriety for his part in the Dardanelles campaign – most particularly its ending – and on the strength of it was able to take a lecture tour of England

and Australia before returning to cover the continuing fighting on the Western Front. Strangely, in a brief belief that the sword might be mightier than the pen after all, following the conclusion of the Great War he went to Hungary to fight with an anti-Bolshevik faction, before returning to England to be elected to parliament. He stood on the side of the Conservatives and became the Member for Hammersmith North. He died in Lisbon in 1931 aged just 50.

Sir Ian Hamilton, in whom Kitchener and Churchill had invested such high hopes, never saw active service again. Bloodied but unbowed, believing himself unfairly maligned, Sir Ian continued to keep busy with service to many military institutions and veteran organisations – and, in an effort to restore his reputation, wrote and published his *Gallipoli Diary* in 1920. Based on his diary of the time – and notwithstanding accusations that he coloured it brightly for publication – it gave a great insight into his thoughts, feelings and motivation throughout the whole tumultuous campaign, albeit retrospectively. He was a driving force and Vice-President of the Anglo-German Association, established in 1928, devoted to promoting Germany in Great Britain, and declared himself a great admirer of Adolf Hitler.

Tragically, his one son, Harry, who was a graduate of Sandhurst, was killed in North Africa in 1941 by the forces of one and the same. Hamilton died in London in October 1947, at the age of 94.

Lieutenant-General William Birdwood continued to lead the Anzacs on the Western Front in France, before leaving them to first become Aide-de-General to the King, and then Commanding Officer of the Fifth Army in May 1918. Visiting Australia in 1919, he was greeted, he would recount, by a 'poster depicting a huge hand – the hand of one of my diggers – held out to welcome a small figure, representing myself, with the words "PUT IT RIGHT THERE, BIRDIE"'.[34]

Shortly afterwards, he was created a baronet, before heading back to India, where he became Commander-in-Chief of the Indian Army in 1925. Though coveting the role of Governor-General of Australia, such a position was not to be his, and he returned to England in 1930, where he was elected to the Mastership of Peterhouse, Cambridge, in 1931. Birdie returned to Turkey in May 1936, along with Sir Roger Keyes. While walking around the old positions at Gallipoli, he 'was able to see for the first time from the enemy's point of view . . . I marvelled to think how we had ever been allowed to land and retain our positions for all those long months.'[35] Though Mustafa Kemal was unavailable, Birdwood did see the former 3rd Corps and Northern Group Chief of Staff, Fahrettin. As recounted in Birdwood's book *Khaki and Gown*, among other things that Sir William asked him were, 'What had Kemal to say about our evacuation?'

'Kemal,' Fahrettin replied, 'had left the Peninsula before you evacuated, but when he heard the news he said, "Had I been there, and had the British got away without loss, as they did, I would have blown out my brains."'[36]

In 1938, Sir William was created, if you please, 'Baron Birdwood of Anzac and Totnes', living the rest of his years quietly until dying on 17 May 1951.[37]

The body of Sir William Bridges was the only one returned to Australian shores from Gallipoli, just as his horse, Sandy, was the only one of 136,000 Australian horses to return. After a funeral in Melbourne on 2 September 1915 – some 15 weeks after Sir William had died – he was finally buried at Duntroon, the establishment at which he had the honour of being the first Commanding Officer.

John Monash, of course, went on to cover himself in glory at the Western Front. He didn't just bend the German line, he broke it. He was of the new scientific breed of generals, and his battles were regarded as models of innovative tactics. He held the view that warfare was essentially a problem in engineering, of mobilising resources, like the conduct of a large industrial undertaking.

So successful was Monash that he was installed as Commander-in-Chief of all 150,000 Australians serving on the Western Front and was described by no less than Field Marshal Bernard Montgomery as 'the best general on the western front in Europe . . .'[38] Returning to Australia after the war, he became one of the most prominent and important leaders in the country, though likely not to the extent he should have been because of a certain anti-Semitism.

From 1925, he led Melbourne's Anzac Day march, while the cause closest to his heart was the Shrine of Remembrance, for which he was the prime mover.

So beloved a figure was he that not only did he do much to quell the anti-Semites but also, when he died in 1931, his soldiers and their families, and the Australian people, turned out in droves, a quarter of a million strong, as his flag-laden coffin was pulled on a gun-carriage through the streets of Melbourne.

Nor did Cyril Brudenell White ever quite receive the credit he deserved for the genius of his evacuation plan – though Charles Bean once described him as 'the greatest man it has been my fortune to intimately know'.[39] He remained, nevertheless, a respected figure for the rest of his life. Returning to Australia in June 1919, not long after being knighted, Sir Cyril became Chief of the General Staff. His first peacetime task was sitting on a committee that considered the future organisation of the Australian Military Forces, before he retired four years later to chair a variety of prestigious public and private institutions, while also engaging his passion for farming. He returned to the fray in 1939 at the outbreak of the Second World War, to again become Chief of the General Staff, in March 1940.[40]

At the age of 63, this man who had saved countless lives through the brilliance of his evacuation plan and the energy which he put into its execution, died tragically in a plane crash near Canberra in August 1940, which also saw the death of three Federal Cabinet Ministers. Sir Robert Menzies would later note, 'Of all the men who have served Australia in the military sphere, he is the one to whom my memory will turn in my last days as the very model of everything that an Australian should be.'[41]

Amen.

After Colonel Ewen MacLagan's service in Gallipoli – he had been evacuated sick in August – he went on to serve in France, most notably commanding the Australian 4th Division with great success at the Battle of Hamel in 1918. MacLagan retired from the military in 1925 and lived quietly thereafter, passing away at his daughter's home in Scotland on 24 November 1948. His finest epitaph is Sir John Monash's description: 'In appearance and in temperament he is every inch a soldier . . . Although not Australian born he was whole-heartedly Australian . . . He never failed in performance and invariably contrived to do what he had urged could not be done . . .'[42]

As recounted by Peter Burness in his book *The Nek: A Gallipoli Tragedy*, Colonel Noel Brazier 'lived out his life on his property in Kirup, in the south-west of Western Australia, part of which was broken up for soldier-settlement'.[43] He never overcame his bitterness towards the Bullant and to General Hughes for what had happened at the Nek, and was likely still mourning his lost men on the day he died, aged 80, in 1947.

The Bullant, Brigade-Major Jack Antill, went to his own grave in 1937 at the age of 71, denying any responsibility, to the end, for the death of so many on what Throssell called that 'fool charge'[44] at the Nek.

Of the men of the lower ranks who fought on the frontlines, the fate of Hugo Throssell is the one that moves me most. After being taken to an English hospital to recover from his wounds, he was awarded the Victoria Cross, the only Light Horseman to be so honoured. He then returned to his regiment in Egypt, where he was promoted to Captain and, in April 1917, during the 2nd Battle of Gaza, again displayed his extraordinary fearlessness, even after being wounded. Alas, when the survivors of the 10th Light Horse formed up for the inevitable roll call, it was found that Hugo's brother Ric – who, as ever, had been fighting side by side with him – was missing. As detailed in John Hamilton's great book, *The Price of Valour*, even though under enemy fire, Hugo moved out onto the battlefield among the devastation, whistling the very tune they had most loved when growing up together, the one taught them by their father. If only Ric is still alive, he will surely hear it during the rare lulls in the roar, and wave a hand, so Hugo can find him . . .

. . .?

. . .?

But there was nothing. Just so many groaning, dying men, so much blood and gore, so many entrails uselessly spilling out into the desert sands and men crying out for their mothers, their wives, their God, for release from this agony.

Hugo Throssell never did find him. What could he do but keep doing what he had been doing all along? He buried his grief and kept fighting. Upon his return to Perth in December 1918, Hugo was feted as a glorious Western Australian soldier who had won the Victoria Cross, but by now he wanted no part of it.

Eager for a new life, only three months after the Armistice he married a wonderful woman he had met in London, Katharine Susannah Prichard, a noted Australian author. They settled on a 40-acre mixed farm at Greenmount, 14 miles east of Perth, and in 1922 had one son, whom they named Ric.

It was not long before Hugo became involved in politics. Katharine was already a founding member of the Communist Party of Australia, while, despite his own blue-blood background, Hugo was soon speaking out against war, and up for the rights of workers and returned soldiers. He refused to attend Anzac Day on the grounds that it glorified war. Beyond his farming, he also did some work as a real-estate agent, as well as for Western Australia's Department of Agriculture. After a foray into gold prospecting in the early 1930s proved fruitless, the full weight of the Depression came down upon both Australia and Hugo, and while Katharine was on a six-month trip to Russia doing research for her soon-to-be-published polemical pamphlet 'The Real Russia', Hugo made a bad business decision that lost him money he did not quite have.

By 19 November 1933, it had all come to a head. Hugo Throssell, war hero, peace activist, husband, father, son, put a gun to his temple and pulled the trigger – choosing to share the fate of so many of his comrades at Gallipoli two decades earlier.

At the back of the will he had written the day before was a note:

I have never recovered from my 1914–18 experiences and with this in view I appeal to the State to see my wife and child get the usual war pension. Sgt. Hugo Throssell. No man could have a truer mate.[45]

He was buried with full military honours in Karrakatta Cemetery, Perth. (Mercifully, his wife and child did get the pension.)

Vale, Hugo. What a man you were. I weep.

His Victoria Cross, so hard won at Hill 60, was donated in 1983 by his son, Ric – also a peace activist – to the People for Nuclear Disarmament, who in turn sold it to the RSL, who presented it to the Australian War Memorial.

The other most notable of the nine Australian Victoria Cross recipients at Gallipoli was the then Private Albert Jacka, who left the Peninsula as Company Sergeant-Major. His fame grew exponentially from the moment that he earned a Military Cross on 7 August 1916 for his actions at Pozières. He went on to be awarded a bar for his Military Cross on 8 April 1917 thanks to his service at Bullecourt – freeing some Australians taken prisoner and, together with them, forcing 50 Germans to surrender. This was described by Charles Bean as 'the most dramatic and effective act of individual audacity in the history of the A.I.F.'[46] and by now his entire 14th Battalion were proud to call themselves 'Jacka's Mob'. His Commanding Officer, Brigadier-General Charles Brand, would later say of him that 'Captain Jacka was a super-soldier, a born leader, with an instinct to do the right thing in a critical situation. A company under his leadership was as good as an additional battalion.'[47]

In Australia, the face of Jacka featured large on recruitment posters beckoning Australian men to come to war.

Though his war finished when he was gassed near Villers-Bretonneux, Jacka returned to Australia as a hero and loved every moment of it, attending every Anzac Day march, front and centre, and being very active in returned soldiers' matters besides. Throughout the 1920s, he worked in a business importing electrical goods with two former brothers-in-arms and married before becoming the Mayor of St Kilda in 1930. Alas, the effects of being gassed never quite left him, and, together with the effects of kidney disease, he died in January 1932. Such was his enduring fame that he was given a state funeral, with 6000 people filing past his coffin – subsequently borne by eight fellow Victoria Cross winners before he was laid beneath the sod at St Kilda Cemetery, with full military honours.

Even in death, the VC winner was so beloved by Jacka's Mob that, on the anniversary of his death, survivors would gather at his grave to pay homage, tell yarns, drink and carry on in a manner that would have pleased him. In 1941, the 'pilgrimage was led by 100 former members of the 14th Battalion'.[48]

The rather more humble Trooper Bluegum never did make it back to Jean – or, as far as I know, the woman he met in Cairo, the 'queen' who 'moved amongst the revellers'.[49] Though he survived all of Gallipoli, Sinai and Palestine, Oliver Hogue died of influenza in London on 3 March 1919. I dips me lid, again, Bluegum. Great book.

Ellis Silas was far more longer lived than most of his comrades. After continuing his convalescence in England, he was discharged from the AIF as medically unfit in October 1916, shortly before publishing his diary and sketchbook, *Crusading at Anzac*. After returning to Australia in 1921, he based himself in Sydney and continued his career as an artist, before returning to England in 1925 and marrying two years later. The rest of his life was filled with sketching, painting and writing, and he died in London on 2 May 1972, close to 60 years after he had felt every day was likely to be his last, at Gallipoli.

Despite the message in the bottle to indicate he had been taken prisoner and was alive, Private Edgar Adams was never heard from again. An enquiry to the Turkish equivalent of the Red Cross produced no information, and though it appears the Turks tried to help, they claimed to have no record of him as a POW. In the course of writing this book, I heard one story from an Australian who had worked as a contractor in the Dardanelles in the 1960s, who claimed he had heard stories of old Australian soldiers still living among the locals, and I couldn't help but wonder . . . and yet, of course, we'll never know.

Major Gordon Carter and Nurse Lydia King? I do know. After Gordon's successful evacuation, they finally met up again for just a few minutes on 2 January 1916 at Tel-el-Kebir Railway Station in Egypt, as Gordon was still stationed there, and Lydia was on her way back to Australia with a tragic shipload of wounded soldiers. They next met on 12 May 1916 in Cairo when she got back, and had a long lunch with a bottle of bubbly. He proposed less than a month later, on 11 June 1916, and they married on 31 January 1917 in Southall, England, just before Gordon headed for the Western Front.

Their first son, Edward Carter, was born nine months after Armistice Day 11 November 1918 and is my 'Uncle Ted', of Tamworth. Still alive and going strong, he is one of the last Rats of Tobruk left standing! Gordon went on to a successful engineering career, which included involvement in building the Sydney Harbour Bridge. When my parents bought their farm at Peats Ridge in 1948, it was Gordon who visited and advised my father how to properly build the irrigation dam. Together, he and Lydia raised five children, of whom one died in her infancy, and another, John, disappeared while flying for the RAF over the English Channel on 1 April 1944. Gordon died on 11 July 1963; Lydia a decade later, on 18 September 1972.

Trooper Paul 'Ginty' McGinness – one of those men of the 8th Light Horse Regiment who was saved, *in extremis* – became of major Australian significance when he and fellow Gallipoli veteran Hudson Fysh went on to establish Qantas. Through much of 1920s Australia, the aviation world was filled with Gallipoli veterans, and their numbers included none other than Charles Kingsford Smith.

From the moment the *AE1* was last sighted – south-west of Duke of York Island off New Britain at 3.20 on the afternoon of 14 September 1914 – to the present day, there has not been the slightest sign of it. Not a bubble to the surface, not the tiniest skerrick of debris washed up on the shore – though as this book goes to press in mid-September 2014, the most serious and sophisticated search yet is about to be undertaken.

AE2 lies, of course, where it sank on 30 April 1915, on the floor of the Sea of Marmara, though it was not until 1998 that a Turkish marine engineer, Selçuk Kolay, at last located it, lying in mud at a depth of 72 metres, after a search lasting just under four years. Since that time, there have been grand plans to bring it to the surface again, but the technical, financial and political difficulties are many.

Dacre Stoker, on the other hand, proved nigh on unsinkable. He was released from his time as a POW in December 1918, but he received a great shock upon his return to England, when he found that the wife he had been pining for while imprisoned, the one he thought would be waiting for him, had in fact had a child to another man while he had been away. They were divorced within months.

For his bravery in forcing the Narrows on 25 April 1915, he was awarded the Distinguished Service Order (DSO) – a far lesser honour than the Victoria Cross awarded to the other three Allied submarine captains, one of whom had failed to get through, and the other two only having accomplished it once Stoker had proved it could be done.

For a brief time, he returned to the submarine service, but his passion had gone, and he left the Royal Navy in 1921, before embarking on an entirely different path in life, finding great success as an actor, writer and producer. His book *Straws in the Wind*, about his adventures on *AE2*, came out in 1925, and was a critical and commercial success. But his greatest triumph was on the stage and screen, where he frequently played the role of a military officer.

In 1925, he got remarried to a talented young English actress, Dorothie Pidcock, and the two lived happily ever after, or at least for the next 41 years. Fred and Elizabeth Brenchley's book, *Stoker's Submarine*, quotes veteran Tudor Jenkins, writing about the submarine captain in the London *Evening Standard* in 1965, on the 50th anniversary of the landing. 'Now a spry 80,' Jenkins wrote, 'he lives in Chelsea. I asked him whether he sometimes wondered whether it would not have been better if his message to de Robeck had not got through? "Maybe an immediate evacuation would have saved those terrible casualties," Stoker replied.'[50]

The Brenchleys also quote from a letter that Stoker wrote to *AE2* crew member Cecil Bray in the mid-1960s: 'The receipt of our signal stopped the Anzacs being withdrawn that night,' he told Bray. 'What a tragedy that campaign failed. It would have altered all history. No Russian revolution and possibly no communism.'

Dacre Stoker died on 2 February 1966. He, too, was a great.

Stoker's closest equivalent in this saga – a veritable lone wolf, seeking to sow havoc in enemy waters – was the admirable Karl von Müller, of *Emden* fame. Müller spent most of the rest of the Great War in a POW camp for German officers in the English Midlands. He was the ringleader of 21 of them escaping via a tunnel to briefly breathe the air of liberty once more, before being quickly recaptured. Falling ill in 1918, he was repatriated back to Germany just before the end of the war as part of a humanitarian prisoner exchange. Retiring from the navy within months of the war's conclusion, he briefly served as a politician, before dying on 11 March 1923.

Müller's one-time offsider, Kapitänleutnant Hellmuth von Mücke, returned to Germany a hero, having led his men to safety over nearly 7000 miles. He wrote two books on the saga, both of which sold well. Like Müller, von Mücke became involved in German politics after the war, and though he started out as a Conservative, by the end of the 1920s he was an outspoken pacifist. Through the 1930s, he was such a vociferous critic of Adolf Hitler that he was briefly imprisoned in 1936, and then again briefly at the beginning of the Second World War. A notable peace activist after the war, he died on 30 July 1957.

With the Ottoman surrender, General Liman von Sanders, then in Constantinople after unsuccessfully leading the Ottoman Army in Syria, gave himself up, and for his trouble the British imprisoned him on suspicion of war crimes for the next six months before releasing him in August 1919. He returned to Germany a respected figure in a devastated nation. Shortly after penning his memoirs, *Five Years in Turkey*, he died, aged 74, in Munich in 1929.

While the Dardanelles campaign, overall, is remembered in Germany, Great Britain and France, and revered in Australia and New

Zealand, it is in Turkey itself that it achieves its greatest significance, changing an entire nation. The day the Turks would choose to commemorate it, however, would not be the day of the landing but, rather, a month earlier, 18 March, when they had successfully beaten back the Fleet from entering the Dardanelles. This day would ever after be known as '*Çanakkale Deniz Zaferi*'[51] or 'The Çanakkale Naval Victory'.

Just after the Ottomans surrendered in October 1918, under the sheer weight of Allied arms pressing them on all sides, two key leaders of the Turkish Government, General Enver and Talaat, were among those who, on 3 November, fled across the Black Sea on board a German battleship to exile in Berlin.

Talaat stayed in Germany, living quietly under an assumed name, while Enver went on to Moscow. They were both soon condemned to death, *in absentia*, by a British court in Constantinople, for the Armenian genocide. The intent of both men was to rise again, ideally in a newly established Turkish state that could strike back at the Allies. But things would prove difficult . . .

On 15 March 1921, Talaat was just leaving his house in the affluent Berlin suburb of Charlottenburg when he felt a tap on his shoulder. It was the hand of the young Armenian man Soghomon Tehlirian, who had been lucky to escape the Armenian massacre of 1915, though his beloved mother, father and sisters had not. Left for dead, taken in by a Kurdish family, he had escaped through Persia and, by a long and circuitous route, made his way to Germany to start a new life. Two weeks earlier, Tehlirian had awoken from a nightmare: the vision of the corpse of his beloved mother, standing up before him, looking him in the eyes and saying, 'You know Talaat is here and yet you do not seem to be concerned. But you seem quite heartless and are not my son.'[52]

A cry in the night. He can bear it no more.

Now, as Talaat turns, Tehlirian points his nine-millimetre German automatic pistol straight at the Turk's forehead. It is *not* a shot heard around the world. In fact, it is not even heard by Talaat. For, after Tehlirian pulls the trigger, the bullet shreds Talaat's brain before the sound can reach him. He falls to the ground, blood gushing from his head.

After a cursory two-day trial, Soghomon Tehlirian was found innocent by a German court on grounds of temporary insanity due to the traumatic experience he had gone through during the genocide. In the course of the trial, an exchange took place:

Presiding Justice: What did you think of what you had done?
Tehlirian: I felt a great satisfaction.
Presiding Justice: How do you feel about it now?
Tehlirian: Even today, I feel a great sense of satisfaction.[53]

The fate of Enver was similar, even if what actually happened is less clear-cut. The upshot was the same: in fact, many shots from the Red Army all over his body on 4 August 1922, after the Russians perceived that Enver had double-crossed them.

No less than Vladimir Lenin had sent Enver to the 'Turkestan Autonomous Soviet Socialist Republic' in Central Asia to suppress the revolt there against the Bolsheviks, only to find that the Turk had colluded with the locals to rise against them! The most compelling account of his death is that, when the Russians came for him, Enver gripped his Koran and charged straight for them, firing all the while, before being cut down . . . and then having his head cut off for good measure. He was 40 years old.

The Ottoman victory at Çanakkale turned out to be the making of Mustafa Kemal. After recovering from his poor health in Constantinople, he was sent to various garrisons throughout the Empire. He was at the head of Seventh Army in Palestine during the final Allied offensive, which was the decisive blow that defeated the Turks in 1918.

Unhappy with the peace settlement imposed upon the Turks by the victorious Allies, Mustafa Kemal began and led the 'Turkish Nationalist Movement', which ultimately waged the Turkish War of Independence. In 1921, Mustafa Kemal established a provisional government in the central Anatolian town of Ankara, away from the occupied Constantinople.

The following year, the Ottoman Sultanate was formally abolished, and, in 1923, Turkey became a secular republic under the terms of the Treaty of Lausanne, the peace treaty that finally ended the state of war that had existed between the Turks and the Allies since 1914. The Turkish National Movement culminated in the Grand National Assembly, and Mustafa Kemal became the new republic's first President.

Once in office, President Mustafa Kemal launched a drive for modernity in all things, to convert the new, constitutional Republic of Turkey into a secular, modern nation-state. During his 15-year presidency, a range of sweeping reforms were introduced in every field. It started with a new constitution, which borrowed heavily from established European codes. He also introduced language reform, which saw the official script changed from Arabic to Latin. He implemented broad education reforms, many of which were aimed at secularising society and lessening the influence of religion in public life. His government nationalised industry, established a banking system, introduced reforms to encourage equal opportunity for women, and brought in a number of other measures designed to build a new nation-state for the Turks.

In 1934, a law was introduced requiring all citizens to adopt a surname, à la the Europeans. Mustafa Kemal, never one to hide his light under a bushel, agreed with the Grand National Assembly that he be given the surname 'Atatürk', as in, 'Father of the Turks'.

His triumph at Gallipoli of course remained the foundation of his legend, and yet, despite the ferocity with which he had fought the invaders, he evinced no hatred for them after the war was over, and in 1935 penned words that became famous: 'Those heroes that shed their blood and lost their lives . . . You are now lying in the soil of a friendly country. Therefore rest in peace. There is no difference between the Johnnies and the Mehmets to us where they lie side by side now here in this country of ours . . . you, the mothers, who sent their sons from faraway countries wipe away your tears; your sons are now lying in our bosom and are in peace. After having lost their lives on this land they have become our sons as well.

'Today we honour the men who fought on both sides at Gallipoli.

We honour the countries from which they came, but above all we honour the spirit of peace and friendship which has proved to be an enduring legacy of the Gallipoli conflict.'[54]

Those magnificent words are now inscribed on a monument not quite as John Monash had predicted, 'on some high plateau overlooking Anzac beach,'[55] but in fact right by the beach itself, honouring all who fought in this extraordinary campaign.

In 1990, for the 75th anniversary of the Gallipoli landing, the government of Australian Prime Minister Bob Hawke flew 58 Diggers back to the fatal shore. In April 2014, I was sitting beside him at a lunch for the Australian Republican Movement, and he told me that it was the most moving moment of his time in office when the old Diggers arrived at Gallipoli and gingerly climbed off their bus to be cheered to the echo by the 4000-strong crowd of Australians, including many young backpackers, who had gathered for the occasion. And then when the Diggers had shuffled forward to meet a similar number of old Turkish soldiers waiting to greet them.

It was just as in days of yore, as had happened on 24 May 1915, during the first armistice.

Tentatively at first, and then with growing confidence, the Anzacs and Turks rise from their trenches and slowly walk towards each other, scarcely believing that this is possible, that they could really be upright in no-man's-land without being shot to pieces.

These men from countries on opposite sides of the planet continue to walk towards each other – over the corpses of their fallen friends, their brothers, the enemies who they have shot – until they are face to face.

'The two groups came together on the very spot where they had fought for their lives,' Mr Hawke said, 'shook hands, embraced, and clapped each other on the back. There was no rancour and many tears, and not just from the crowd. It was a truly wonderful thing to see.'[56]

Two of those men – Jack Ryan, 95, from Australia, and Hüseyin Kaçmaz, 97, from Turkey – were featured in an article, with photograph, in *The Sydney Morning Herald*, as they kissed each other on the cheek, hugged . . . and wept.

Jack Ryan and Hüseyin Kaçmaz embracing at the 1990 75th anniversary of the Gallipoli landing (AP Photo via AAP/Burhan Ozbilici)

(Me? I should like to think that, later on, they exchanged cigarettes, had a cup of tea, and for once the Australians might have had something better than bully beef to offer and, at last, some milk to lend.)

At the midday commemoration at Lone Pine a few hours later, when Prime Minister Hawke noted that, 'We do not come here to glorify war,' the veterans 'wept silently but called "Hear, hear".'

And some wept openly . . .

'Of course I cried,' veteran George Abraham, DCM, 92, told *The Herald*. 'Did you? Yes? It's good that so many young people did. It shows me the spirit is still there . . .'[57]

And so it is to this day.

We will remember them. On both sides.

NOTES AND REFERENCES

BACKGROUND AND ACKNOWLEDGEMENTS

1. Keating, *Major Speeches of the First Year*, Speech at Ela Beach, Port Moresby, 25 April 1992, p. 57.
2. Keating, 'We Are Too Wise to be Cannon Fodder Again', *The Sydney Morning Herald*, 11 November 2013, www.smh.com.au.

PROLOGUE: A NATION IS BORN

1. Bean, *Official History of Australia in the War of 1914–1918*, Vol. I, pp. 11–12.
2. Laseron, Diary, 23 December 1914, ML MSS 1133, p. 2, www.acmssearch.sl.nsw.gov.au.
3. Derham, *The Silence Ruse*, p. 1.
4. *The Bulletin*, 5 January 1901, p. 10.
5. Ibid.
6. *The Sydney Morning Herald*, 6 January 1910, p. 7.
7. Ibid., 23 December 1909, p. 6.
8. Ibid., 6 January 1910, p. 7 (reported speech changed to direct speech).
9. Ibid.
10. Ibid.
11. Ibid., 22 December 1910, p. 6.
12. For the full text of Kitchener's report to the government, see Kitchener, 'Australian Defence', *The Western Mail* (Perth), 26 February 1910, p. 44, http://trove.nla.gov.au.
13. *The Barrier Miner*, 'The Defence Act', 19 April 1912, p. 2, http://trove.nla.gov.au.
14. McEwan, '"Smelly" – The Lee-Enfield Rifle', *The Gallipoli Gazette*, Vol. 43, No. 1, 2013, p. 6.
15. *The Advertiser* (Adelaide), 23 March 1914, p. 17.
16. Ibid.
17. His full last name is Sinclair-MacLagan, but, in keeping with Bean, only MacLagan is used throughout.
18. Hogue, *Trooper Bluegum at the Dardanelles*, p. 70, https://archive.org.

19. Carlyle, *Memoirs of the Life and Writings of Thomas Carlyle*, p. 311.
20. Turfan, *Rise of the Young Turks*, p. 209.
21. Ibid.
22. Ibid., p. 211.

CHAPTER ONE: A REAL WAR

1. Glenny, *The Balkans*, p. 22.
2. *The Argus*, 'In Australia', 21 August 1914, p. 8 (quote corrected to match the original), http://trove.nla.gov.au.
3. Ibid.. 'Austrian Tragedy', 1 July 1914, p. 15, http://trove.nla.gov.au.
4. Ibid.
5. Alington, *The Lamps Go Out*, p. 39.
6. Churchill, Randolph, *Winston S. Churchill*, Vol. II, *Companion*, Pt III, p. 1989.
7. *The New York Times*, New York Times Current History, p. 209, www. gutenberg.org.
8. Based on Cunneen, *Kings' Men*, p. 116.
9. Ibid., p. 110.
10. *Daily Herald* (Adelaide), 'A Whirlwind of Words', 31 July 1914, p. 5, http://trove.nla.gov.au.
11. Ibid.
12. *The Labor Call*, 6 August 1914, p. 4.
13. *The Evening News* (Sydney), 'References by Mr Cook', 1 August 1914, p. 8, http://trove.nla.gov.au.
14. *The Colac Herald*, 'Prime Minister at Colac', 3 August 1914, p. 2, http://trove.nla.gov.au.
15. Scott, John, *Vickers*, p. 111.
16. Kautsky, *Outbreak of the World War*, p. 529.
17. A curiosity of the document is its condition that, if Russia intervenes on the side of Serbia in the dispute with Austria-Hungary, thereby activating Germany's alliance with Austria-Hungary, then Turkey agrees to join the war on the side of Germany against Russia. The curiosity is that Russia *had already* mobilised its forces and just the previous day Germany *had* moved to support Austria-Hungary and declared war on Russia.
18. Djemal Pasha, *Memories of a Turkish Statesman*, pp. 113–14, https://archive.org.
19. Horne, *Source Records of the Great War*, Vol. I, pp. 377–8.
20. Ibid., pp. 370–1.
21. Cassar, *Kitchener's War*, p. 20 (reported speech changed to direct speech).

22. Scott, Ernest, *Official History of Australia in the War of 1914–1918*, Vol. XI, p. 8.

23. The Governor-General to the Secretary of State, Telegram No. 13, 3 August 1914 (received 6.30 pm), *Correspondence Regarding the Overseas Assistance Afforded to His Majesty's Government by His Majesty's Overseas Dominions*, p. 4.

24. *Daily Mail*, 3 August 1914, p. 4.

25. Butler, Daniel A., *Shadow of the Sultan's Realm*, p. 71.

26. Hayman and Hayman, *Great Britain and the European Crisis*, p. 95, http://books.google.com.au.

27. Bethmann-Hollweg, speech at the Reichstag, 4 August 1914, *Berliner Tageblatt*, 5 August 1914, p. 5.

28. *Berliner Tageblatt*, 5 August 1914, p. 3.

29. Brock and Brock, *Margot Asquith's Great War Diary 1914–1916*, p. 108.

30. *The Times*, 5 August 1914, p. 9.

31. Pilot Robinson's story seems to be the only reference to consular officials aboard SS *Pfalz*. How he knew they were such is unknown.

32. I record my deep thanks to Keith Quinton, author and researcher, Australian Army History Unit, Fort Queenscliff.

33. *The Bathurst Times*, 5 August 1914, p. 2.

34. Stoker, *Straws in the Wind*, p. 61.

35. Ibid.

36. Hough, *Death of the Battleship*, p. 13, http://books.google.com.au.

37. Stoker, p. 61.

38. Scott, Ernest, Vol. XI, pp. 13–14.

39. Bean, *Anzac to Amiens*, p. 22.

40. *The Argus*, 8 August 1914, p. 16.

41. McCarthy, *Gallipoli to the Somme*, p. 79.

42. Since 1997, spelled Kosciuszko.

43. In the First World War, the AIF uses the term 'brigade' to describe a formation of four infantry battalions. The Light Horse uses 'brigade' to describe a formation of three regiments – a regiment is like a battalion but smaller. The 1st Division AIF has three brigades, the 1st, 2nd and 3rd Brigades. The four battalions in each of these brigades are further divided into a headquarters company and four other companies, A, B, C and D. 1st Brigade: 1st, 2nd, 3rd, 4th Battalions all from New South Wales; 2nd Brigade: 5th, 6th, 7th, 8th Battalions all from Victoria; 3rd Brigade: 9th Battalion from Queensland, 10th from South Australia, 11th from Western Australia, 12th from Tasmania (half), Western Australia and South Australia.

44. *The Sydney Morning Herald*, 6 August 1914, p. 6.
45. *The Dominion* (Wellington), 6 August 1914, p. 6.
46. *The New Zealand Herald*, Vol. LI, Issue 15680, 6 August 1914, p. 9.
47. *The Nelson Evening Mail*, Vol. XLV, 5 August 1914, p. 5.
48. Voltaire, *Candide*, p. 124.
49. Hough, *The Great War at Sea*, p. 84.
50. Çulcu, *Ikdam Gazetesi'nde Çanakkale Cephesi I. Cilt (The Çanakkale Front According to Ikdam Newspaper, Vol. I)*, p. 50.
51. Ibid., p. 51.
52. Ibid., p. 52
53. Beşikçi, *The Ottoman Mobilization of Manpower in the First World War*, p. 111.
54. *The Times*, 20 August 1914, Issue 40610, p. 5.
55. Kannengiesser, *The Campaign in Gallipoli*, p. 25.
56. Cemil to Enver, 3 August 1914, in Aksakal, *The Ottoman Road to War in 1914*, p. 103. Enver's request to send the two warships to Constantinople had been taken up very quickly by the Germans, as it assured their strong hand in the Black Sea. Germany's Navy Ministry gave Souchon orders to head to Istanbul as early as 3 August (Aksakal, p. 110).
57. Kannengiesser, p. 25.
58. Ibid., pp. 25–6.
59. Ibid., p. 26.
60. Ibid.
61. Ibid.
62. Çulcu, p. 56.
63. James, Robert R., *Gallipoli*, p. 9.
64. Morgenthau, *Ambassador Morgenthau's Story*, p. 71, https://archive.org.

CHAPTER TWO: GETTING STARTED

1. Bean, *Official History of Australia in the War of 1914–1918*, Vol. I, p. 93.
2. Ibid., Vol. II, p. 31.
3. *The Courier* (Ballarat), 13 August 1914, p. 4.
4. Erickson, *Ordered to Die*, p. 15.
5. Erickson, *Gallipoli*, p. 30.
6. Housman, *A Shropshire Lad*, p. 39, http://books.google.com.au.
7. Schuler, *Australia in Arms*, p. 21, https://archive.org.
8. Hoddinott, Typed Manuscript, AWM MSS0791, p. 39.
9. McLaglen, *Bayonet Fighting for War*, p. 12, http://www.scribd.com.
10. Hogue, *Trooper Bluegum at the Dardanelles*, p. 258, https://archive.org.

11. Rule, E. J., 'Capt. Albert Jacka: Seventh Anniversary of Death', *Reveille*, 1 January 1939, pp.12–13.
12. Sandford, *Key to Infantry Training*, p. 8.
13. Howard, *On Three Battle Fronts*, pp. 13–14.
14. Silas, Diary, August 1914, p. 1, MLMSS 1840, http://acms.sl.nsw.gov.au.
15. *New-York Tribune*, 24 August 1914, p. 1.
16. *Daily Mail*, 8 September 1914, p. 4.
17. Morgenthau, *Ambassador Morgenthau's Story*, p. 81, https://archive.org.
18. Moorehead, *Gallipoli*, p. 25.
19. Aksakal, *The Ottoman Road to War in 1914*, p. 135.
20. Usedom, 'Despatches from Admiral von Usedom to the Kaiser about the defences of the Dardanelles, and naval operations before and after the British landings' (translation), NA CAB 45/215, p. 4.
21. Fisher, Letter to the Chief of the Imperial General Staff, Churchill to General Sir Charles Douglas (C.I.G.S.), 1 September 1914, Appendix (A1), NA CAB 19/28.
22. *The Oamaru Mail*, 19 June 1917, p. 6.
23. Memorandum by Major-General Callwell, Director of Military Operations, Appendix (A2), NA CAB 19/28, p. 235. Following the war, Callwell returned to his previous career as a journalist and writer. His post-war work included *The Dardanelles*, written in 1919.
24. *The Northern Miner*, 'Proclamation', 3 December 1914, p. 4, http://trove.nla.gov.au.
25. *The Argus*, 'German New Guinea', 14 September 1914, p. 8, http://trove.nla.gov.au.
26. Stoker, *Straws in the Wind*, p. 68.
27. Wheat, Narrative, 1914–1918, ML MSS 3054, Item 3, p. 2.
28. Mango, *Atatürk*, p. 126.
29. Mustafa Kemal (Atatürk) to Salih (Bozuk), undated, 1914, Atatürk, *Atatürk'ün Bütün Eserleri* (*Collected Works of Atatürk*), p. 207.
30. Mustafa Kemal (Atatürk) to a friend, 17 September 1915, ibid., p. 201.
31. Mustafa Kemal (Atatürk) to Salih (Bozuk), undated, 1914, ibid., p. 207.
32. White's Light Horse Regiment was originally numbered the 6th; however, following reorganisation in October, it was renumbered the 8th and became part of the 3rd Light Horse Brigade, along with the 9th Light Horse Regiment (South Australia) and 10th Light Horse Regiment (Western Australia).
33. Still, the 4th Light Horse Regiment (Victoria), 6th Light Horse and 7th Light Horse (New South Wales) never wore the emu plume.
34. Aitken, *Wartime*, Winter 2001, pp. 50–3.

35. Ibid., p. 50.
36. Hogue, *Love Letters of an Anzac*, p. 9.
37. *The Sydney Morning Herald*, 'Breast Forward', 6 November 1914, p. 6, http://trove.nla.gov.au.
38. Hogue, *Love Letters of an Anzac*, p. 17.
39. Ibid., p. 18 (reported speech changed to direct speech).
40. Ibid.
41. French, *1914*, p. 144.
42. French, Third Despatch (Aisne), 8 October 1914, www.1914-1918.net.
43. French, *1914*, p. 144.
44. *Financial Times*, 20 September 1914, p. 3.
45. French, *1914*, p. 145.
46. Ibid.
47. Massie, *Castles of Steel*, p. 427.
48. Churchill to Fisher, Letter, 23 December 1914, Gilbert, *Winston S. Churchill*, Vol. III, *Companion*, Pt I, p. 327.
49. Fisher, *Fear God and Dread Nought*, p. 166.
50. *The Sydney Morning Herald*, 10 August 1914, p. 8.
51. Hogue, *Trooper Bluegum at the Dardanelles*, p. 24, https://archive.org.
52. Jose, *Official History of Australia in the War of 1914–1918*, Vol. IX, p. 152.
53. *Mercury* (Hobart), 22 September 1914, p. 5.
54. *The Sydney Morning Herald*, 'The Navies: Marauding Emden', 23 September 1914, p. 11, http://trove.nla.gov.au.
55. *The Sydney Morning Herald*, 22 September 1914, p. 7.
56. Jose, Vol. IX, p. 157.
57. Morgenthau, p. 107, https://archive.org.
58. Carden to Admiralty, Telegram, 27 September 1914, NA ADM 137/96.
59. Morgenthau, p. 110, https://archive.org.
60. Ibid., p. 106.
61. Ibid.
62. Ibid., p. 107.
63. For further reading, see McCarthy, *Gallipoli to the Somme*, p. 76.
64. *The Sydney Morning Herald*, 28 September 1914, p. 8.
65. Bean, *Official History of Australia in the War of 1914–1918*, Vol. I, p. 92.
66. *The Truth* (Melbourne), 'A Military Camp Sensation: Salacious She and the Soldiers', 10 October 1914, p. 5, http://trove.nla.gov.au.
67. Ibid.
68. Ibid.
69. *The Argus*, 'City Disturbance', 12 October 1914, p. 8, http://trove.nla.gov.au.

70. Ibid.
71. Clark, *A History of Australia*, p. 386.
72. *The Argus*, 'City Disturbance', 12 October 1914, p. 8, http://trove.nla. gov.au.
73. Ibid.
74. The actual quote is, 'as Lord Chesterfield said of the Generals of his day, "I only hope when the enemy reads the list of their names, he trembles as I do."' Duke of Wellington, *Supplementary Despatches*, p. 582.
75. *The Journal of the Royal Australian Armoured Corps Association*, 'The Mounted Soldiers of Australia', December 2007, No. 452, p. 3.
76. For further reading, see Browning and Gill, *Gallipoli to Tripoli*, p. 95.
77. For further reading, see Burness, *The Nek*.
78. Brazier, Diary, 26 September 1914, AWM 1DRL/0147.
79. Caulfield, *The Unknown Anzacs*, p. 11.
80. Frame, *The Shores of Gallipoli*, p. 74.
81. Jackh, *The Rising Crescent*, p. 117.
82. Talaat Pasha, *Posthumous Memoirs*, p. 8, https://ia600309.us.archive. org/19/items/PoshumousMemoirsOfTalaatPasha/collection.pdf.
83. Horne, *Source Records of the Great War*, Vol. II, p. 398 (reported speech changed to direct speech).
84. Morgenthau, p. 128, https://archive.org.
85. Ilhan, *Gelibolu*, p. 55.

CHAPTER THREE: FAREWELL TO AUSTRALIA

1. Gorman, Johnson and Braddock, *With the Twenty-Second*, p. vii.
2. The convoy will pick up the Japanese warship *Ibuki* and two more transports in two days' time off Fremantle, bringing the total number of transports to 38 and escorts to four.
3. Paterson, A. B., *The Sydney Morning Herald*, 'The Transports', 8 December 1914, p. 8, http://trove.nla.gov.au.
4. Ibid.
5. Ibid. This author is tragically proud of being the only Wallaby ever to be sent from the field for violence against the All Blacks. I am told by my friend Wayne Shelford, the former All Black captain, a very proud Maori, that those words actually translate to 'Forever and ever, be strong'.
6. Ibid.
7. Cochrane, *Simpson and the Donkey*, p. 71.
8. Slade to Churchill, 30 October 1914, Minute, NA ADM 137/96.
9. 'Report of the Committee Appointed to Investigate the Attacks on and

the Enemy Defences of the Dardanelles Straits, Section IX Summary',
NA ADM 186/600, p. 23.

10. Bilgin, *Çanakkale Savaşı Günlüğü*, p. 73.
11. Some sources indicate that the bombardment lasted for 17 minutes,
while yet others claim 20 minutes.
12. Bilgin, p. 73.
13. The Honourable Sir Thomas Mackenzie, 'Supplementary Report', in
'The Final Report of the Dardanelles Commission', p. 93.
14. Asquith, *H. H. Asquith Letters to Venetia Stanley*, Letter No. 202,
4 November 1914, p. 309. On the afternoon of 4 November, the
Ottoman Ambassador in London, Tevfik Pasha, acting under
instructions from Constantinople, called on Grey and asked for his
passports. The following day, Britain and France declared war on Turkey.
15. Venning, 'The Priapic PM who Wrote Love Letters to his Mistress as
he Sent a Generation Off to Die in the Trenches', *Daily Mail*, 27 April
2012, www.dailymail.co.uk.
16. Ibid.
17. Asquith's replacement in 1916, Lloyd George, was the same regarding
women. Kitchener said he avoided telling military secrets to the
Cabinet, as they would all tell their wives, apart from Lloyd George,
who would tell someone else's wife.
18. These figures are according to Butler, Arthur G., *Official History of the
Australian Army Medical Services*, pp. 34, 37.
19. Langford, Diary, undated, AWM 3DRL/7454, p. 6.
20. *The London Gazette*, 5 November 1914, No. 28963, p. 8997, www.
thegazette.co.uk.
21. Bean, War Diary, October–December 1914, AWM 38, 3DRL606/1/1,
p. 6.
22. *Kan-Karroo Kronikle*, 4 November 1914, Vol. 1, No. 3, AWM 073952,
p. 3.
23. The islands, which Australia has been controlling since 1955, were sold
to Australia in 1978 by John Cecil Clunies-Ross, who was later forced
into bankruptcy by the Australian Government, impelling him to leave
the islands forever.
24. Jose, *Official History of Australia in the War of 1914–1918*, Vol. IX,
p. 180.
25. Lochner, *Die Kaperfahrten des kleinen Kreuzers Emden*, p. 295.
26. Jose, Vol. IX, p. 180.
27. Bean, *Official History of Australia in the War of 1914–1918*, Vol. I,
pp. 105–6.
28. Like *Emden*, *Sydney* was a light cruiser, albeit a heavy one: 5400 tons

as against the 4000 tons of *Emden*. *Sydney* also had bigger guns and a faster top speed: 26 knots versus 24 knots. The faster ship dictates the range at which the fight takes place. As you get the upper hand, you close the range and come in for the kill.

29. Raeder, *Der Krieg zur See, 1914–1918*, p. 68, https://archive.org.
30. *The Sydney Morning Herald*, 30 December 1914, p. 10.
31. Much of this description draws heavily from Banjo Paterson's firsthand account: *The Sydney Morning Herald*, 'The *Sydney*'s Fight', 30 December 1914, http://trove.nla.gov.au.
32. Paterson, 'The *Sydney*'s Fight', *The Sydney Morning Herald*, 30 December 1914, p. 10, http://trove.nla.gov.au. Though in Banjo Paterson's original account, the word 'blanky' was used instead of 'bloody', I have used what I believe the lad actually said, unburdened by the need to shield sensitive readers.
33. This dialogue and order of procedure is a reconstruction arrived at by consulting with military historian and author Greg Blake.
34. Jose, Vol. IX, p. 198.
35. Ibid.
36. *Mirror* (Perth), 'Hell on the *Emden*!', 23 November 1935, p. 22, http://trove.nla.gov.au (reported speech changed to direct speech).
37. The shells are filled with a high explosive consisting chiefly of picric acid.
38. Paterson, 'The *Sydney*'s Fight', *The Sydney Morning Herald*, 30 December 1914, p. 10, http://trove.nla.gov.au.
39. Bean, *Official History of Australia in the War of 1914–1918*, Vol. I, p. 106.
40. Coe, Diary, 9 November 1914, AWM 2DRL/491, p. 25.
41. Raeder, p. 80.
42. *Royal Australian Navy: Australians in World War I.*
43. Bean, *Official History of Australia in the War of 1914–1918*, Vol. I, p. 107.
44. Ernie Boston (aboard HMAS *Sydney* escorting the Anzacs of Gallipoli), Track 2, Sailah, *Stories from Gallipoli*, ABC Audio.
45. Bean, *Official History of Australia in the War of 1914–1918*, Vol. I, p. 107.
46. Hoddinott, Typed Manuscript, AWM MSS0791, p. 43.
47. *The Sydney Morning Herald*, 1 January 1915, p. 3.
48. Stoker, *Straws in the Wind*, p. 76.
49. Horne, *Source Records of the Great War*, Vol. III, p. 401.
50. The original 'Mussulmans' has been changed here to 'Muslims' for the modern English reader.

51. Horne, Vol. II, pp. 398–400.
52. Paterson, 'The First Force', *The Sydney Morning Herald*, 12 January 1915, p. 9, http://trove.nla.gov.au.
53. Coe, Diary, 29 November 1914, AWM 2DRL/491, p. 26.
54. Lord Northcliffe to Lord Murray of Elibank, Letter, 1 December 1914, Churchill, Randolph, *Winston S. Churchill*, Vol. II, *Companion*, Pt I, p. 288.
55. Coe, Diary, 1 December 1914, AWM 2DRL/491, p. 79.
56. Ibid.
57. Bean, *Official History of Australia in the War of 1914–1918*, Vol. I, p. 113 (reported speech changed to direct speech).
58. Paterson, 'The First Force', *The Sydney Morning Herald*, 12 January 1915, p. 9, http://trove.nla.gov.au.
59. Drane, *Complete Anzac Gallipoli War Diary*, 15 December 1914, http://bushroots.com.
60. Paterson, 'The First Force', *The Sydney Morning Herald*, 12 January 1915, p. 9, http://trove.nla.gov.au.
61. Coe, Diary, 2 December 1914, AWM 2DRL/491, p. 77.
62. Langford, Diary, 1 December 1914, AWM 3DRL/7454, pp. 22–3.
63. The Grand Fleet was the main fleet of the British Navy during the First World War.
64. Hogue, *Trooper Bluegum at the Dardanelles*, p. 37, https://archive.org.
65. *The Chronicle* (Adelaide), 'With our Troops in Egypt', 23 January 1915, p. 42, http://trove.nla.gov.au.
66. Barwick, Diary, undated, AWM F940.26093 B296d, p. 16.
67. Coe, Diary, 2 December 1914, AWM 2DRL/491, p. 44.
68. Barwick, Diary, undated, AWM F940.26093 B296d, p. 16.
69. Forrest, War Diary, 9 December 1914, p. 11.
70. *The Advertiser* (Adelaide), 'Russian Successes', 20 January 1915, p. 7, http://trove.nla.gov.au.
71. McCarthy, *Gallipoli to the Somme*, p. 88.
72. Bean, *Official History of Australia in the War of 1914–1918*, Vol. I, p. 115.

CHAPTER FOUR: A MAN WITH A PLAN

1. Gilbert, *Winston S. Churchill*, Vol. III, *Companion*, Pt I, p. 344.
2. Rayment, Diary, undated, AWM PR91/042, p. 31.
3. Coe, Diary, undated, AWM 2DRL/491, pp. 2–3.
4. Caulfield, *The Unknown Anzacs*, p. 28.
5. Bean, *Official History of Australia in the War of 1914–1918*, Vol. I, p. 126.

6. Laugesen, *Glossary of Slang and Peculiar Terms in Use in the A.I.F. 1921–1924*, http://andc.anu.edu.au/australian-words.

7. McMullen, *Pompey Elliott*, p. 100.

8. Forrest, War Diary, 9 December 1914, p. 10, www.amosa.org.au.

9. Langford, Diary, undated, AWM 3DRL/7454, p. 32.

10. Hogue, *Trooper Bluegum at the Dardanelles*, p. 51, https://archive.org.

11. Drane, *Complete Anzac Gallipoli War Diary*, January 1915, http://bushroots.com.

12. Silas, *Crusading at Anzac*.

13. Hogue, *Trooper Bluegum at the Dardanelles*, p. 36, https://archive.org.

14. Seal, *The Lingo*, p. 57.

15. Barwick, Diary, undated, AWM F940.26093 B296d, p. 9.

16. Hartnett, 'With the "Boys": A Soldier's Life', *The Gundagai Independent and Pastoral, Agricultural and Mining Advocate*, 20 April 1915, p. 2, http://trove.nla.gov.au.

17. Robertson, *Anzac and Empire*, pp. 43–4.

18. Henry John Frederick Coe to his Parents, Letter, 26 December 1914, AWM 2DRL/491, p. 2.

19. Ibid., 30 January 1915, AWM 2DRL/491, p. 1.

20. Serle, *John Monash*, p. 209.

21. Bean, *Official History of Australia in the War of 1914–1918*, Vol. I, pp. 117–18.

22. *Reveille*, 1 February 1936, Vol. 9, No. 6, p. 3 (reported speech changed to direct speech).

23. Ibid. There are many claimants to the story of the origin of Anzac. This is the one I find most credible.

24. Healy, *More Lives Than One*, p. 212, http://books.google.com.au.

25. Knightley, *Australia*, p. 64, http://books.google.com.au.

26. Gum trees had been cultivated in the area, and particularly southern Turkey, from the 1830s to combat swamps and malaria. The locals called eucalyptus 'the malaria tree'.

27. Smythe to Family, Letter, 27 December 1914, www.smythe.id.au.

28. Bean, War Diary, 1 January 1915, AWM 38, 3DRL606/2/1, p. 4.

29. McCarthy, *Gallipoli to the Somme*, pp. 91–2.

30. *The Advertiser* (Adelaide), 22 January 1915, p. 6.

31. Richards, *Wallaby Warrior*, p. 21.

32. Hogue, *Trooper Bluegum at the Dardanelles*, p. 57, https://archive.org.

33. Silas, Diary, 30 December 1914, ML MSS 1840, http://acms.sl.nsw.gov.au.

34. Ibid., 13 May 1915, p. 62.

35. Stoker, *Straws in the Wind*, p. 77.

36. Serle, pp. 206–7.

37. Jacka, Diary, Pt 4, 1 October 1914–18 December 1915, AWM MSS143A.
38. Moorehead, *Gallipoli*, p. 37.
39. *The Labor Call*, 6 August 1914, p. 4.
40. Secretary's Notes of a Meeting of the War Council held at 10 Downing Street, 25 November 1914, NA CAB 42/1/4, p. 3.
41. Marder, *From the Dreadnought to Scapa Flow*, p. 202.
42. James, Robert R., *Gallipoli*, p. 4.
43. Churchill, Winston, *The World Crisis*, Vol. II, p. 201.
44. Gilbert, Vol. III, *Companion*, Pt I, p. 344.
45. Hankey, *The Supreme Command*, pp. 265–6.
46. Rowse, *The Later Churchills*, p. 408.
47. Churchill to Carden, Telegram, 3 January 1915, Gilbert, Vol. III, *Companion*, Pt I, p. 367.
48. Carden to Churchill, Telegram, 5 January 1915, Gilbert, Vol. III, *Companion*, Pt I, p. 380.
49. Secretary's Notes of a Meeting of the War Council held at 10 Downing Street, 13 January 1915, NA CAB 42/1/6, p. 8.
50. Churchill, Winston, Vol. II, p. 119.
51. The Turks dusted off their 350-year-old bronze gun, the Great Turkish Bombard (later named the 'Dardanelles Gun'), for use against Duckworth's fleet. Cast in 1464, it could be unscrewed into two pieces for portability despite the fact it weighed 18.5 tons. It fired up to 24-inch stone balls. The gun was presented to Queen Victoria during her 1866 visit and, reputedly the oldest gun in existence, it is now displayed along with other big guns at the Royal Armouries Museum, Fort Nelson, Portsmouth, in the south of England.
52. French, *1914*, p. 316.
53. Secretary's Notes of a Meeting of the War Council held at 10 Downing Street, 13 January 1915, NA CAB 42/1/6, p. 8.
54. Asquith, *H. H. Asquith Letters to Venetia Stanley*, Letter No. 258, 13 January 1915, p. 375.
55. Secretary's Notes of a Meeting of the War Council held at 10 Downing Street, 13 January 1915, NA CAB 42/1/6, p. 8.
56. Fisher, *Fear God and Dread Nought*, p. 142.
57. Asquith, Margot, Diary, 10 January 1915, in Gilbert, Vol. III, *Companion*, Pt I, p. 400.
58. Ibid.
59. Asquith, Margot, Diary, 19 February 1915, ibid., p. 524.
60. Butler, Arthur G., *Official History of the Australian Army Medical Services*, pp. 73–4.

61. *The New Partridge Dictionary of Slang and Unconventional English*, p. 1736.
62. Richards, *Wallaby Warrior*, p. 19.
63. King, Lydia K., Diary, 13 January 1915, AWM 3DRL 6040.
64. Ibid.
65. Mango, *Atatürk*, p. 142.
66. Ibid., p. 143.
67. Iğdemir, pp. 35–6.

CHAPTER FIVE: 'THE FATAL POWER OF A YOUNG ENTHUSIASM'

1. Bean, *Official History of Australia in the War of 1914–1918*, Vol. I, p. 201.
2. Churchill, Winston, *The World Crisis*, Vol. II, p. 122.
3. Asquith, Herbert Henry, *Memories and Reflections*, p. 59.
4. Secretary's Notes of a Meeting of the War Council held at 10 Downing Street, 28 January 1915, at 11.30 am, NA CAB 42/1/26, p. 6.
5. Stoker, *Straws in the Wind*, p. 86.
6. Bean, *Official History of Australia in the War of 1914–1918*, Vol. I, p. 136.
7. *The Argus*, 4 March 1915, p. 9.
8. Bean, *Official History of Australia in the War of 1914–1918*, Vol. I, p. 130.
9. Ibid.
10. *Clunes Guardian and Gazette*, 12 March 1915, p. 3.
11. Brazier, Diary, undated 1915, AWM 1DRL/0147.
12. Bean, *Official History of Australia in the War of 1914–1918*, Vol. I, p. 138.
13. *The Advertiser* (Adelaide), 22 January 1915, p. 6.
14. Based on McCarthy, *Gallipoli to the Somme*, p. 97.
15. *The Essendon Gazette and Keilor, Bulla and Broadmeadows Reporter*, 29 April 1915, p. 3, http://trove.nla.gov.au.
16. Mulvey, Letter, 14 March 1915, AWM 2DR/0233, p. 15. NB: The author of this letter wrote 'Y.M.C.C.' (Young Men's Christian Council), but I have changed it to 'Y.M.C.A.' to make it recognisable to the reader.
17. Carter, Letters, Mena Camp, 7 February 1915, AWM 1 DRL 192.
18. McCarthy, p. 94.
19. 'The First Report of the Dardanelles Commission', p. 30.
20. Ibid.
21. Hart, 'Gallipoli: The War at Sea – An Overview', p. 4, archive.iwm.org.uk.

22. 'The First Report of the Dardanelles Commission', p. 31.
23. *Sunday Times*, 21 February 1915, p. 9.
24. Bonham Carter, *Winston Churchill As I Knew Him*, p. 361.
25. Secretary's Notes of a Meeting of the War Council held at 10 Downing Street, 24 February 1915, NA CAB 42/1/42, p. 4.
26. Ibid.
27. Ibid.
28. Ibid.
29. Gilbert, *Winston S. Churchill*, Vol. III, p. 303.
30. Ibid.
31. Secretary's Notes of a Meeting of the War Council held at 10 Downing Street, 24 February 1915, NA CAB 42/1/42, p. 5.
32. Churchill, Winston, Vol. II, p. 201.
33. Birdwood, *Khaki and Gown*, p. 250.
34. Ibid.
35. King, Lydia K., Diary, 27 March 1915, AWM 3DRL/6040, p. 13.
36. Carden to Churchill, Telegram, 4 March 1915, Gilbert, Vol. III, *Companion*, Pt I, p. 625.
37. Secretary's Notes of a Meeting of the War Council held at 10 Downing Street, 3 March 1915, NA CAB 42/2/3, p. 1.
38. Birdwood, *Khaki and Gown*, p. 250.
39. Kitchener to Birdwood, Telegram, 4 March 1915, Gilbert, Vol. III, *Companion*, Pt I, p. 633.
40. 'The First Report of the Dardanelles Commission', p. 33.
41. Birdwood to Kitchener, Telegram, 6 March 1915, Gilbert, *Winston S. Churchill*, Vol. III, *Companion*, Pt I, p. 643.
42. Hamilton, John, *The Price of Valour*, p. 80.
43. Şimşek and Güner, *Mayın Grup Komuntanı Binbaşı Nazmi Bey'in Günlüğüyle Çanakkale Deniz Savaşları*, p. 23.
44. Secretary's Notes of a Meeting of the War Council held at 10 Downing Street, 10 March 1915, NA CAB 42/2/5, p. 2.
45. Holland and Jordan, *The Story Behind the Monument*, p. 12.
46. Ibid., p. 51.
47. Gilbert, *Winston S. Churchill*, Vol. III, *Companion*, Pt I, pp. 677–8.
48. Hamilton, Ian, *Gallipoli Diary*, Vol. I, p. 3, https://openlibrary.org/books.
49. Ibid., p. 6.
50. Ibid., p. 7.
51. Ibid., p. 14.
52. Stoker, p. 91.
53. Ibid., p. 92.

54. Hamilton, Ian, *Gallipoli Diary*, Vol. I, p. 15, https://openlibrary.org/books.
55. Ibid., p. 16.
56. Ibid.
57. Howard, Michael, 'Churchill and the First World War', in Blake and Louis, *Churchill*, p. 138.
58. Hargrave, *The Suvla Bay Landing*, p. 30.
59. Dover: Lock and Key of the Kingdom, 'Admiral Sir Roger Keyes', http://www.dover-kent.co.uk.
60. Keyes, *The Naval Memoirs of Admiral of the Fleet*, p. 212.
61. Gilbert, *Winston S. Churchill*, Vol. III, *Companion*, Pt I, p. 687.

CHAPTER SIX: TESTING THE WATERS

1. Stevenson, *Lloyd George*, 4 April 1915, p. 40.
2. Morgenthau, *Ambassador Morgenthau's Story*, p. 217, https://archive.org.
3. Ibid., p. 218.
4. Ibid., p. 220.
5. Ibid.
6. Shakespeare, *Julius Caesar*, p. 66.
7. Keyes to de Robeck, Holographs, 15 March 1915, *The Keyes Papers*, p. 108.
8. 'The First Report of the Dardanelles Commission', p. 36.
9. Aspinall-Oglander, *Military Operations*, Vol. I, pp. 101–2.
10. Liddell Hart, *A History of the First World War*, pp. 168–9.
11. *The Nineteenth Century and After*, Vol. 106, p. 83.
12. Âdil, Selahattin in Martı, *Çanakkale Hatiraları (Çanakkale Memoirs)*, Vol. I, p. 130.
13. Ibid.
14. Örnek and Toker, p. 7.
15. Hart, 'Gallipoli: The War at Sea – An Overview', p. 34, http://archive.iwm.org.uk.
16. Morgenthau, p. 222, https://archive.org. This scene is reconstructed from Morgenthau's diary, as the Ambassador had seen a drill just three days earlier and penned his thoughts as to what the actuality would be like.
17. Örnek and Toker, p. 8.
18. Churchill, Winston, *The World Crisis*, Vol. II, pp. 225–6.
19. Hart, p. 34, http://archive.iwm.org.uk.
20. Massie, *Castles of Steel*, p. 461.
21. Hamilton, Ian, *Gallipoli Diary*, Vol. I, p. 36, https://openlibrary.org/books (in a letter Hamilton wrote to Kitchener; original: 'The

Irresistible, the *Ocean* and the *Bouvet* are gone! The *Bouvet*, they say, just slithered down like a saucer slithers down in a bath. The *Inflexible* and the *Gaulois* are badly mauled.').

22. Ibid., p. 31.
23. Ibid., pp. 32–3.
24. Ibid., p. 33.
25. Ibid., p. 34.
26. Refik, *Çanakkale'nin Ruh Portresi* (*A Portrait of Çanakkale's Spirit*), p. 32.
27. Ibid.
28. Ibid., p. 33.
29. Örnek and Toker, p. 12.
30. Âdil, Selahattin in Martı, Vol. I, p. 135.
31. Şimşek and Güner, *Mayın Grup Komutanı Binbaşı Nazmi Bey'in Günlüğüyle Çanakkale Deniz Savaşları*, p. 96.
32. Ibid.
33. Erickson, *Gallipoli*, p. 21.
34. Şimşek and Güner, *Mayın Grup Komutanı Binbaşı Nazmi Bey'in Günlüğüyle Çanakkale Deniz Savaşları*, p. 96.
35. Wester-Wemyss, *The Navy in the Dardanelles Campaign*, p. 41.
36. Marder, *From the Dreadnought to Scapa Flow*, p. 249.
37. Hamilton, Ian, *Gallipoli Diary*, Vol. I, p. 37, https://openlibrary.org/books.
38. Ibid., p. 39.
39. Ibid., p. 40.
40. Morgan, *Churchill*, p. 489.
41. Wester-Wemyss, pp. 41–2.
42. Hamilton, Ian, *Gallipoli Diary*, Vol. I, p. 41, https://openlibrary.org/books (reported speech changed to direct speech).
43. Ibid., p. 45.
44. Ibid., p. 41.
45. Ibid., p. 40.
46. Wester-Wemyss, p. 44.
47. Hamilton, Ian, *Gallipoli Diary*, Vol. I, p. 49, https://openlibrary.org/books.
48. *The Argus*, 'Weeding Out Process', 21 January 1915, p. 7, http://trove.nla.gov.au.
49. Bean, *Official History of Australia in the War of 1914–1918*, Vol. I, p. 210.
50. James, Lawrence, *Churchill and Empire*, p. 114.
51. Nevinson, *The Dardanelles Campaign*, p. 62.

52. Drummond, *The Art of Decision Making*, p. 206.
53. Churchill, Winston, Vol. II, p. 232.
54. Ibid., Vol. II, p. 234.
55. Ibid.
56. Ibid.
57. Ibid., Vol. II, p. 249.
58. Ibid.
59. 'The First Report of the Dardanelles Commission', p. 43.
60. Churchill, Winston, Vol. II, p. 229.
61. Kannengiesser, *The Campaign in Gallipoli*, p. 21.
62. Sanders, *Five Years in Turkey*, p. 58.
63. Ibid., pp. 58–9.
64. Prigge, *Liman von Sanders Paşa'nin Emir Subayı Binbaşı Erich R. Prigge'nin Çanakkale Savaşı Günlüğü* (*Çanakkale War Diary of Major Erich Prigge, Liman von Sanders' Aide-de-Camp*), p. 51.

CHAPTER SEVEN: THE SKY LOWERS

1. Laffin, *Damn the Dardanelles*, p. 41.
2. Hamilton, Ian, *Gallipoli Diary*, Vol. I, p. 80, https://openlibrary.org/books.
3. Tragically, Rupert Brooke died just two evenings before the landing, after a brief illness.
4. Prigge, *Liman von Sanders Paşa'nin Emir Subayı Binbaşı Erich R. Prigge'nin Çanakkale Savaşı Günlüğü* (*Çanakkale War Diary of Major Erich Prigge, Liman von Sanders' Aide-de-Camp*), p. 51.
5. Sanders, *Five Years in Turkey*, p. 59.
6. Ibid., p. 61.
7. Mango, *Atatürk*, p. 145.
8. Aker, S., 'Çanakkale-Arıburnu Savaşları ve 27. Alay (Çanakkale-Arıburnu Battles and the 27th Regiment)', in Martı, *Çanakkale Hatiraları* (*Çanakkale Memoirs*), Vol. I, p. 232.
9. 3rd Brigade War Diary, April 1915, AWM4, 23/3/2, p. 19.
10. Ibid.
11. Masefield, *Gallipoli*, p. 41, https://openlibrary.org/books.
12. 'The First Report of the Dardanelles Commission', p. 37.
13. *The Courier-Mail* (Brisbane), 'War Letters of Sir John Monash', p. 13, http://trove.nla.gov.au.
14. Mücke, *Ayesha*, p. 167, https://openlibrary.org/books.
15. Ibid., p. 172.
16. Bean, *Official History of Australia in the War of 1914–1918*, Vol. I, p. 213.

17. Hogue, *Trooper Bluegum at the Dardanelles*, p. 51, https://archive.org.
18. Ibid., p. 59.
19. Bean, War Diary, 2 April 1915, AWM38, 3DRL606/3/1, p. 25.
20. Caulfield, *The Unknown Anzacs*, p. 38.
21. Hogue, *Trooper Bluegum at the Dardanelles*, p. 51, https://archive.org.
22. Knightley, *Australia*, p. 64.
23. Bean, War Diary, 2 April 1915, AWM38, 3DRL606/3/1, p. 27.
24. Fewster, 'The Wazza Riots, 1915', *Journal of the Australian War Memorial*, No. 4, April 1984, p. 50.
25. Downing, *Digger Dialects*, p. 41. The translation is reinforcements.
26. Bean, War Diary, 2 April 1915, AWM38, 3DRL606/3/1, p. 29 (reported speech changed to direct speech).
27. Hogue, *Trooper Bluegum at the Dardanelles*, p. 61, https://archive.org.
28. 'Report of Proceedings of Court of Inquiry, 3 August 1915, Reporting on the Disturbance in Cairo on the Night of 31st July 1915', AIF HQ Egypt, Central Registry, 1914–1918, AWM 80i5/2023.
29. *The Truth* (Melbourne), 'The Red Plague', 31 July 1915, p. 1, http://trove.nla.gov.au.
30. Herbert Gordon Carter to Mr H. J. Carter, Letter, 15 April 1915, AWM 1DRL/192, p. 15.
31. King, Lydia K., Diary, AWM 3DRL/6040.
32. Silas, Diary, Mitchell Library, ML MSS 1840, p. 35, http://acms.sl.nsw.gov.au.
33. Rayment, Diary, undated, AWM PR91/042, p. 40.
34. *The Courier-Mail* (Brisbane), 'War Letters of Sir John Monash', 13 November 1934, p. 13, http://trove.nla.gov.au.
35. Barwick, Diary, ML MSS 1493/1/Box 1/Item 1 (No. a3226047), p. 89, www.acmssearch.sl.nsw.gov.au.
36. McCarthy, *Gallipoli to the Somme*, p. 102.
37. King, Lydia K., Diary, 3 April 1915, AWM 3DRL/6040, p. 14.
38. *The Courier-Mail* (Brisbane), 'War Letters of Sir John Monash', 13 November 1934, p. 13, http://trove.nla.gov.au.
39. Hurst, *Game to the Last*.
40. *The Courier-Mail* (Brisbane), 'War Letters of Sir John Monash', 13 November 1934, p. 13, http://trove.nla.gov.au.
41. Muir, Diary, 11 April 1915, AWM RCDIG0000428, p. 10.
42. McCarthy, p. 107.
43. Bean, War Diary, 11 April 1915, AWM38, 3DRL606/3/1, p. 57.
44. Hamilton, Ian, *Gallipoli Diary*, Vol. I, p. 98, https://openlibrary.org/books.
45. Ibid., p. 97.

46. Ibid., p. 99.
47. Ibid.
48. Ibid., p. 30.
49. Ibid.
50. Ibid.
51. Ibid., p. 31.
52. McCarthy, p. 107.
53. Aspinall-Oglander, *Military Operations*, Vol. I, p. 110.
54. Williams, *The Battle of Anzac Ridge*, p. 57.
55. Hamilton, Ian, *Gallipoli Diary*, Vol. I, p. 27, https://openlibrary.org/books.
56. *Reveille*, April 1936, p. 64.
57. Carter, Diary, 11 April 1915, AWM 3DRL/6418, p. 103.
58. Ibid., 13 April 1915, AWM 3DRL/6418, p. 105.
59. Ibid., 14 April 1915, AWM 3DRL/6418, p. 104.
60. Lt Hasan Ethem Mülazim to his Mother, 17 April 1915, 'Last Letter of a Turkish Martyr Killed in the Gallipolian War', 17 April 1915, *The Gallipolian*, No. 76, Winter 1994, p. 6.
61. Hamilton, Ian, *Gallipoli Diary*, Vol. I, p. 119, https://openlibrary.org/books.
62. McCarthy, p. 108.
63. Ibid.
64. Ibid.
65. Ibid.
66. Sari Bair Range is the collective name for the three main ridges and their numerous spurs, gullies and other geological features. The three main ridges are: First Ridge (Sari Bair, or Main Ridge), which runs almost perpendicular to the coast from Plugge's Plateau north-east to end at Hill 971; Second Ridge (Bolton's Ridge), which runs approximately north–south and parallel to the coast from Baby 700 to 400 Plateau; and Third Ridge (Gun's Ridge), which originates at Chunuk Bair and also runs south parallel to the coast, ending at Gaba Tepe. The name Sari Bair, meaning Yellow Slope, actually denotes in Turkish the cliffs at 'the Sphinx'. This name was misappropriated by the British and used to denote the First Ridge running north-east from Plugge's to Hill 971.
67. Masefield, p. 42, https://openlibrary.org/books.
68. Stoker, *Straws in the Wind*, p. 100.
69. Ibid.
70. Masefield, p. 42, https://openlibrary.org/books.
71. Barwick, Diary, ML MSS 1493/1/Box 1/Item 1 (No. a3226047), p. 89,

www.acmssearch.sl.nsw.gov.au (reported speech changed to direct speech).

72. Ibid., p. 96.
73. Masefield, p. 43, https://openlibrary.org/books.
74. Ibid., p. 45.
75. Ibid., p. 46.
76. Richards, *Wallaby Warrior*.
77. McCarthy, p. 112.
78. Belford, 'Eleven-Legs', p. 64.
79. Hamilton, Ian, *Gallipoli Diary*, Vol. I, pp. 120–1, https://openlibrary. org/books.
80. Ibid., p. 123, https://openlibrary.org/books.

CHAPTER EIGHT: THE LANDING ('*SILAH BAŞINA!* – TO ARMS!')

1. Stead, 'The Eastern Ogre; or St George to the Rescue', *The Review of Reviews*, Vol. 14, October 1896, p. 358.
2. Hamilton, Ian, *Gallipoli Diary*, Vol. I, p. 125, https://openlibrary.org/ books.
3. Bean, *Official History of Australia in the War of 1914–1918*, Vol. II, p. 910.
4. Henderson, Letter, 24 April 1915, AWM RCDIG0000999, p. 1.
5. Annear, War Service Record, NAA 3033933, p. 22.
6. Bean, *Official History of Australia in the War of 1914–1918*, Vol. I, p. 244.
7. DeWeerd, *President Wilson Fights His War*, p. 110.
8. Bean, *Official History of Australia in the War of 1914–1918*, Vol. I, p. 244.
9. Ashmead-Bartlett, *The Uncensored Dardanelles*, p. 45, https:// openlibrary.org/books.
10. Ashmead-Bartlett, Diary, 22 April 1915, p. 31, http://acms.sl.nsw.gov. au.
11. Başkanlığı, *Armenian Activities in the Archive Documents 1914–1918*, pp. 128–9, www.ata-a.org.au.
12. Davidson, *The Incomparable 29th and the 'River Clyde'*, p. 43, www.gutenberg.org.
13. Knaggs, Diary, 24 April 1915, AWM PR85/096, p. 5.
14. Stoker, *Straws in the Wind*, p. 105.
15. Ibid., p. 106.
16. Ibid.
17. King, Jonathan, *Gallipoli Diaries*, p. 19.

18. The Men of Anzac, *The Anzac Book*, p. 15.
19. Travers, *Gallipoli*, p. 70.
20. Ashmead-Bartlett, *The Uncensored Dardanelles*, p. 45, https://openlibrary.org/books.
21. The Men of Anzac, p. 1.
22. Ashmead-Bartlett, *The Uncensored Dardanelles*, p. 45, https://openlibrary.org/books.
23. Winter, *25 April 1915*, p. 94.
24. Ibid., p. 92.
25. Aker, S., 'Çanakkale-Arıburnu Savaşları ve 27. Alay (Çanakkale-Arıburnu Battles and the 27th Regiment)', in Martı, *Çanakkale Hatiraları (Çanakkale Memoirs)*, Vol. I, p. 202. I have added the exclamation mark, on the grounds that, under the circumstances, I cannot believe he said it any other way!
26. Ibid.
27. Ibid., pp. 202–3.
28. Stoker, p. 107.
29. Broadbent, *Gallipoli*, p. 55.
30. Bell, 'History of the Ninth Battalion AIF', SLQ OM64-5/517 26.
31. Winter, p. 92.
32. *The Advertiser* (Adelaide), 'Australians Win Imperishable Fame', 8 May 1915, p. 15, http://trove.nla.gov.au.
33. Ashmead-Bartlett, *The Uncensored Dardanelles*, p. 46, https://openlibrary.org/books.
34. Bean, *Official History of Australia in the War of 1914–1918*, Vol. I, p. 249.
35. Margetts to his Parents, 23 May 1915, AWM 1DRL/0478, Item 2, p. 2.
36. Stoker, p. 58.
37. No Standard Operations Procedure for E Class submarines has survived from this time. The information given regarding the operations of the *AE2*, including the dialogue used and ordering procedures, is a verbal reconstruction arrived at by subject-matter consultant Hugh Dolan, and as a result of extensive conversations with officers formerly serving Australian Oberon and Collins Class submarines.
38. Bean, *Official History of Australia in the War of 1914–1918*, Vol. I, p. 252.
39. Ibid.
40. Winter, p. 94.
41. Ibid., p. 95.
42. Örnek and Toker, *Gallipoli*, p. 19.
43. Bean, *Official History of Australia in the War of 1914–1918*, Vol. I, p. 254.

44. This hope is recorded in Norris, War Narrative ('There and Back'), 11 April 1914–18 November 1916, ML MSS 2933/Item 3, p. 29.

45. Aker, S., 'Çanakkale-Arıburnu Savaşları ve 27. Alay (Çanakkale-Arıburnu Battles and the 27th Regiment)', in Martı, Vol. I, p. 203.

46. Winter, p. 95.

47. For several reasons – companies of battalions being landed in different locations, unsynchronised watches, the exigencies of war and the fact that war diaries and memoirs were written in retrospect – it is difficult to determine the precise landing time of the first Anzacs, and indeed all three AIF Brigades more broadly. For example, the 3rd Brigade's landing times differ between the Brigade and Battalion War Diaries: the 9th Battalion does not give a landing time, the 10th Battalion records 4.15 am, 11th Battalion 4.30 am, and 12th Battalion 4.10 am. Charles Bean records the time of the first landing as 4.30 am (*Official History of Australia in the War of 1914–1918*, Vol. I, p. 253). As a solution, I have used the 3rd Brigade War Diary landing times as a guide to when its battalions *began to land*. As such, the first battleship tows land *from* 4.15 am (3rd Brigade War Diary, April 1915, AWM 4, 23/3/2, p. 19).

48. Bean, *Official History of Australia in the War of 1914–1918*, Vol. I, p. 255.

49. 10th Infantry Battalion War Diary, 25 April 1915, AWM4 23/27/2, pp. 2–4.

50. *The Register* (Adelaide), 'Thirteenth Anniversary', 25 April 1928, p. 10, http://trove.nla.gov.au.

51. Cameron, *25 April 1915*, p. 58.

52. Beevor, Diary, April 1915, AWM MSS0761, p. 11. There is no specific date given for this entry. It is assumed that it was written some time after the landings in April.

53. Ibid., p. 12.

54. Ibid.

55. Bean, *Official History of Australia in the War of 1914–1918*, Vol. I, p. 256.

56. *The West Australian*, 'The Australians at Gallipoli', 13 July 1915, p. 9, http://trove.nla.gov.au.

57. *The Register* (Adelaide), 'Thirteenth Anniversary', 25 April 1928, p. 10, http://trove.nla.gov.au.

58. *The Advertiser* (Adelaide), 'The War: Letters from the Front', 7 July 1915, p. 13, http://trove.nla.gov.au.

59. Ataksor, *Çanakkale Raporu (Çanakkale Report)*, p. 120.

60. Beevor, Diary, April 1915, AWM MSS0761, p. 13.

61. Ibid (reported speech changed to direct speech).
62. Ibid., pp. 13–14.
63. Ibid., p. 14.
64. Ibid.
65. *Mercury* (Hobart), 3 July 1915, p. 5.
66. Ibid.
67. Örnek and Toker, p. 19.
68. Hogue, *Trooper Bluegum at the Dardanelles*, p. 74, https://archive.org.
69. Winter, p. 94.
70. Aker, S., '*Çanakkale-Arıburnu Savaşları ve 27. Alay* (Çanakkale-Arıburnu Battles and the 27th Regiment)', in Martı, Vol. I, pp. 214–15.
71. Ibid., p. 215.

CHAPTER NINE: 'MIDST THE THUNDER AND TUMULT

1. Silas, Diary, 5 May 1915, ML MSS 1840, p. 55, http://acms.sl.nsw.gov.au.
2. Stoker, *Straws in the Wind*, p. 109.
3. Beevor, Diary, April 1915, AWM MSS0761, p. 14.
4. Ibid.
5. Ibid. (past tense changed to present tense).
6. This is my assumption, based on expert medical advice, as to what such a hard blow to the head would do to a soldier in this circumstance.
7. Hamilton, Ian, *Gallipoli Diary*, Vol. I, p. 128, https://openlibrary.org/books.
8. Ibid.
9. Ibid.
10. Ibid., pp. 128–9.
11. Ibid., p. 129.
12. Gunner Bill Greer, 1st Battery, Australian Field Artillery, Track 2, in Sailah, *Stories from Gallipoli*, ABC Audio.
13. The sunrise was at 5.24 am on the morning of 25 April 1915 (www.sydneyobservatory.com.au/2012/the-moon-and-the-sun-and-the-landing-at-anzac-cove-on-25-april-1915).
14. Bean, War Diary, 25 April 1915, AWM38, 3DRL606/5/1, April–May 1915, p. 20.
15. Cameron, *25 April 1915*, p. 34.
16. *The Register* (Adelaide), 'Thirteenth Anniversary', 25 April 1928, p. 10, http://trove.nla.gov.au.
17. *Mercury* (Hobart), 3 July 1915, p. 5.
18. It has proved difficult to match records at the Australian War Memorial

with Oliver Hogue's recollection, but the closest fit is Edwin Haskins Burne.

19. Hogue, *Trooper Bluegum at the Dardanelles*, p. 67, https://archive.org.

20. Firkins, *The Australians in Nine Wars*, p. 40.

21. Eşref, R., 'Anafarta Kumandanı Mustafa Kemal ile Mülakat (Interview with Mustafa Kemal, Commander of the Anafarta Group)', in Martı, *Çanakkale Hatiraları (Çanakkale Memoirs)*, Vol. III, p. 21.

22. Ibid.

23. Ibid. (reported speech changed to direct speech).

24. Örnek and Toker, *Gallipoli*, p. 22.

25. Sabri, *Seddülbahir'in Ilk Şanlı Müdafaası (The First Glorious Defence of Seddülbahir)*, p. 4.

26. Örnek and Toker, p. 23.

27. Sabri, p. 4.

28. Aker, S., 'Çanakkale-Arıburnu Savaşları ve 27. Alay (Çanakkale-Arıburnu Battles and the 27th Regiment)', in Martı, Vol. I, p. 216 (reported speech changed to direct speech).

29. Ibid., p. 220.

30. Ibid., p. 221.

31. It is in fact 590 feet high.

32. Charles Bean, interview with Brigadier-General J. W. McCay, Notebook, 1920, AWM38, 3DRL 606/28A/1, p. 4, www.awm.gov.au.

33. Ibid.

34. Ibid. Major Walter Cass, Brigade-Major of the 2nd Brigade, who 'distinctly remembers' hearing this key conversation, later recalled a slightly different version. According to his recollection, after landing, he and Colonel McCay had met MacLagan by chance on the beach. Here MacLagan had said, 'Well McCay, the position is this, I've gone to the left following the enemy instead of to the right. If you can change your plans and go to the right then it will settle the difficulty and things will be alright . . .': Cass, 'Early Events of the 2nd Infantry Brigade at Anzac, 25/04/1915', AWM 3DRL 8042, Item 6.

35. Aker, S., 'Çanakkale-Arıburnu Savaşları ve 27. Alay (Çanakkale-Arıburnu Battles and the 27th Regiment)', in Martı, Vol. I, pp. 226–7.

36. Hamilton, Ian, *Gallipoli Diary*, Vol. I, p. 133, https://openlibrary.org/books.

37. Carlyon, *Gallipoli*, p. 204.

38. Hamilton, Ian, *Gallipoli Diary*, Vol. I, pp. 133–4, https://openlibrary.org/books.

39. McCarthy, *Gallipoli to the Somme*, p. 116.

40. This is consistent with the formulaic manner of speaking for both the

Royal Navy and the Australian Navy at the time.

41. Stoker, *Straws in the Wind*, p. 108.

42. This is consistent with the formulaic manner of speaking for both the Royal Navy and the Australian Navy at the time.

43. No Standard Operations Procedure for E Class submarines has survived from this time. The information given regarding the operations of the *AE2*, including the dialogue used and ordering procedures, is a verbal reconstruction arrived at by subject-matter consultant Hugh Dolan, and as a result of extensive conversations with officers formerly serving Australian Oberon and Collins Class submarines.

44. As above.

45. Stoker, p. 111.

46. Ibid.

47. Verbal reconstruction (see note above).

48. Stoker, p. 112.

49. Knaggs, Diary, 25 April 1915, AWM PR85/096, p. 5 (reported speech changed to direct speech).

50. Verbal reconstruction (see note above).

51. Knaggs, Diary, 25 April 1915, AWM PR85/096, p. 5 (reported speech changed to direct speech).

52. Verbal reconstruction (see note above).

53. As above.

54. Stoker, p. 112.

55. Ibid., p. 113.

56. Wheat, narrative, ML MSS 3054, Item 3, p. 15.

57. Knaggs, Diary, 25 April 1915, AWM PR85/096.

58. Stoker, p. 113.

59. Verbal reconstruction (see note above).

60. Bean, *Official History of Australia in the War of 1914–1918*, Vol. I, p. 392.

61. Ibid., p. 393.

62. Corbett, *History of the Great War*, www.naval-history.net.

63. Ashmead-Bartlett, *The Uncensored Dardanelles*, p. 48, https://openlibrary.org/books.

64. Bean, *Official History of Australia in the War of 1914–1918*, Vol. I, p. 318.

65. Derham, *The Silence Ruse*, p. 8.

66. Bean, *Official History of Australia in the War of 1914–1918*, Vol. I, p. 366.

CHAPTER TEN: BETWEEN THE DEVIL AND THE DEEP BLUE SEA

1. Richards, Thomas James, Diary, 11 June 1915, AWM 2DRL/0786, p. 59.
2. Hogue, *Trooper Bluegum at the Dardanelles*, p. 167, https://archive.org.
3. Eşref, R., 'Anafarta Kumandanı Mustafa Kemal ile Mülakat (Interview with Mustafa Kemal, Commander of the Anafarta Group)', in Martı, *Çanakkale Hatiraları (Çanakkale Memoirs)*, Vol. III, p. 24.
4. Ibid.
5. Ibid. (reported speech changed to direct speech).
6. Ibid. (reported speech changed to direct speech).
7. Ibid., p. 25.
8. Fenwick, *Gallipoli Diary*, p. 7.
9. Kemalyeri, M., 'Çanakkale Ruhu Nasıl Doğdu (How the Spirit of Çanakkale was Born)', in Martı, Vol. III, p. 301.
10. Ibid., p. 302.
11. Ibid., p. 303.
12. Ibid., p. 304.
13. Ibid.
14. Eşref, R., 'Anafarta Kumandanı Mustafa Kemal ile Mülakat (Interview with Mustafa Kemal, Commander of the Anafarta Group)', in Martı, Vol. III, p. 28.
15. This order was found on the body of a dead Turkish soldier (Mango, *Atatürk*, pp. 146–7).
16. Dolan, *Gallipoli Air War*, p. 113.
17. McCarthy, *Gallipoli to the Somme*, p. 117.
18. Bean, *Two Men I Knew*, p. 60.
19. Ibid., p. 61.
20. McCarthy, p. 118.
21. Derham, *The Silence Ruse*, p. 9.
22. Bean, *Official History of Australia in the War of 1914–1918*, Vol. I, p. 393.
23. Ibid., p. 314.
24. Due to extremely effective Turkish fire, no Allied troops or equipment were landed between 12 pm and 4.30 pm.
25. Reynolds, Diary, 25 April 1915, AWM RCDIG0001013, p. 54.
26. Cameron, *Shadows of Anzac*, p. 16.
27. Carter, Diary, 25 April 1915, AWM 3DRL/6418, p. 115.
28. Herbert Gordon Carter to Mr and Mrs H. J. Carter, Letter, 30 April 1915, AWM 1DRL/192, p. 17.
29. Ibid.
30. Carter, Diary, 25 April 1915, AWM 3DRL/6418, p. 116.

31. King, Lydia K., Diary, 25–26 April 1915, AWM 3DRL/6040, p. 19.
32. Beevor, Diary, April 1915, AWM MSS0761, p. 19.
33. Ibid., pp. 20–1.
34. Williams, *The Battle of Anzac Ridge*, p. 111.
35. Fenwick, p. 8.
36. Bean, *Official History of Australia in the War of 1914–1918*, Vol. I, p. 568.
37. Silas, Diary, 25 April 1915, pp. 33–4, ML MSS 1840, http://acms.sl.nsw.gov.au.
38. Ibid., p. 35.
39. Ibid., p. 36.
40. Bean, *Official History of Australia in the War of 1914–1918*, Vol. I, p. 464.
41. Cavalier, Ronald, Letter, 25 April 1915, AWM PR86/287, p. 2.
42. 4th Battery Australian Field Artillery War Diary, 25 April 1915, AWM RCDIG1018662, Item 13/66/7, p. 4.
43. Kemalyeri, M., 'Çanakkale Ruhu Nasıl Doğdu (How the Spirit of Çanakkale was Born)', in Martı, Vol. III, pp. 308–9.
44. Cameron, *Shadows of Anzac*, p. 88.
45. Bean, *Bean's Gallipoli*, p. 87. As luck would have it, the bullet lodged in his backside.
46. 3rd Infantry Battalion War Diary, 25 April 1915, AWM4 23/20/2, pp. 2–3.
47. Bean, War Diary, 1 January 1915, AWM38, 3DRL606/25/1, p. 46.
48. Stoker, *Straws in the Wind*, pp. 119–20.
49. Ibid., p. 119.
50. Ibid., p. 120.
51. Ashmead-Bartlett, *The Uncensored Dardanelles*, p. 48, https://openlibrary.org/books.
52. Ibid., p. 49.
53. Ibid., pp. 49–50.
54. These figures are rough estimates and vary according to different sources. According to Peter Williams, Turkish casualties on the Anzac front were 4000 on the first day. Combined with the casualties at Cape Helles, Williams estimates 6000 Turkish casualties (Williams, p. 146).
55. Hamilton, Ian, *Gallipoli Diary*, Vol. I, p. 143, https://openlibrary.org/books.
56. Ashmead-Bartlett, *The Uncensored Dardanelles*, p. 50, https://openlibrary.org/books.
57. Ibid.
58. Aker, S., 'Çanakkale-Arıburnu Savaşları ve 27. Alay (Çanakkale-

Arıburnu Battles and the 27th Regiment)', in Martı, Vol. I, p. 202.

59. Hamilton, Ian, *Gallipoli Diary*, Vol. I, p. 142, https://openlibrary.org/books.
60. Ibid.
61. Ibid., p. 143.
62. Bean, *Official History of Australia in the War of 1914–1918*, Vol. I, p. 460.
63. Hamilton, Ian, *Gallipoli Diary*, Vol. I, p. 144, https://openlibrary.org/books.
64. Keyes, *The Keyes Papers*, p. 128.
65. Brodie, *Forlorn Hope 1915*, p. 71, http://books.google.com.au.
66. Hamilton, Ian, *Gallipoli Diary*, Vol. I, p. 144, https://openlibrary.org/books.
67. Frame, *The Shores of Gallipoli*, p. 110.

CHAPTER ELEVEN: 'ANGIN' ON, LIKE CATS TO A CURTAIN

1. Cavill, *Imperishable Anzacs*, p. 93.
2. King, Jonathan, *Gallipoli Diaries*, 2008, p. 62.
3. Hill, William John Rusden, Letter from the Front, 29 August 1915, ML DOC 2480, p. 3.
4. Aitken, James Murray, Diary, 29 April 1915, AWM 1DRL/0013, p. 20.
5. Fahrettin, 'Fahrettin Altay', in Martı, *Çanakkale Hatiraları (Çanakkale Memoirs)*, Vol. II, p. 22.
6. Bean, War Diary, 25 April 1915, AWM38, 3DRL606/5/1, p. 37.
7. Ibid., p. 38.
8. Hamilton, Ian, *Gallipoli Diary*, Vol. I, p. 145, https://openlibrary.org/books.
9. Ibid.
10. Silas, Diary, 26 April 1915, ML MSS 1840, p. 37, http://acms.sl.nsw.gov.au.
11. Ibid.
12. Caulfield, *The Unknown Anzacs*, p. 74.
13. Carter, Diary, 26 April 1915, AWM 3DRL/6418, p. 117.
14. Carter, Herbert Gordon to Mr and Mrs H. J. Carter, Letter, 1 May 1915, AWM 1DRL/192, p. 20.
15. Ibid.
16. Hamilton, Ian, *Gallipoli Diary*, Vol. I, p. 146, https://openlibrary.org/books.
17. Ibid.
18. Ibid., p. 148.

19. Carlyon, *Gallipoli*, p. 222.
20. Bean, *Official History of Australia in the War of 1914–1918*, Vol. I, p. 511.
21. Ibid., p. 515.
22. Ibid., p. 516.
23. Ibid., p. 524.
24. Barwick, Diary, undated, ML MSS 1493/1/Box 1/Item 1, p. 110, http://acms.sl.nsw.gov.au.
25. Ibid., pp. 110–11.
26. Ibid., pp. 111–12.
27. Bean, *Official History of Australia in the War of 1914–1918*, Vol. I, p. 520.
28. Ibid., p. 521.
29. Hogue, Letters relating to Oliver 'Trooper Bluegum' Hogue, 1915–1927, undated, AWM RCDIG 0000997, p. 3.
30. House of Representatives, *Official Hansard*, No. 17, Thursday 29 April 1915, p. 2724.
31. Ibid., Friday 30 April 1915, p. 2814.
32. Ibid.
33. Dülger, *AE2 Denizalti Gemisini Nasil Batirdim* (*How I Sunk the AE2 Submarine*), p. 19.
34. Stoker, *Straws in the Wind*, p. 137.
35. Knaggs, Diary, 30 April 1915, AWM PR85/096, p. 8 (reported speech changed to direct speech).
36. Ibid (reported speech changed to direct speech).
37. Ibid (reported speech changed to direct speech).
38. Stoker, p. 137.
39. The AE2 Commemorative Foundation website, http://ae2.org.au.
40. Tenses changed, from Stoker's account of his thoughts at the time.
41. Stoker, p. 138 (reported speech changed to direct speech).
42. Knaggs, Diary, 30 April 1915, AWM PR85/096, p. 8 (reported speech changed to direct speech).
43. Dülger, p. 44.
44. The final words of Lieutenant Geoffrey Haggard RN as he opened the vents to flood *AE2*'s ballast tanks were provided by subject-matter expert Hugh Dolan. Haggard recalled these words to his daughter years after this event.
45. Dülger, p. 45.
46. Ibid., p. 46.
47. Bean, *Official History of Australia in the War of 1914–1918*, Vol. I, p. 532.

48. Ibid., p. 539.

49. For further reading, see Mango, *Atatürk*.

50. Eşref, R., '*Anafarta Kumandanı Mustafa Kemal ile Mülakat* (Interview with Mustafa Kemal, Commander of the Anafarta Group)', in Martı, Vol. III, pp. 33–4.

51. Ibid., p. 37.

52. Ibid., p. 36.

53. Bean, *Official History of Australia in the War of 1914–1918*, Vol. I, p. 599.

54. Hogue, *Trooper Bluegum at the Dardanelles*, p. 74, https://archive.org.

55. Ibid., pp. 76–7.

56. Ibid., p. 77.

57. Ibid., p. 79.

58. Ibid., p. 81.

59. McCarthy, *Gallipoli to the Somme*, p. 196.

60. Bean, *Official History of Australia in the War of 1914–1918*, Vol. I, p. 273.

61. Monash, John to Hannah Monash, 18 July 1915, Sir Monash Papers, SLV, MS 13875, Box 4083/1, p. 99.

62. Silas, Diary, 2 May 1915, ML MSS 1840, p. 47, http://acms.sl.nsw. gov.au.

63. Ibid., p. 48.

64. Ibid., p. 49.

65. Ibid.

66. Ibid.

67. Ibid., p. 50.

68. Ibid.

69. *The Australian National Review*, 1 August 1937, Vol. 2, No. 8, p. 93.

70. Simpson, John (aka John Simpson Kirkpatrick), Service Record, NAA B2455, p. 74.

71. It is likely that Simpson had more than one donkey.

72. Walsh, 'Kirkpatrick, John Simpson (1892–1915)', http://adb.anu. edu.au.

73. Cochrane, *Simpson and the Donkey*, p. 71.

74. Silas, Diary, 2 May 1915, ML MSS 1840, p. 50, http://acms.sl.nsw. gov.au.

75. Harvard Citation of song's source: Latimer, Harrison (vocalist) and Francis, W. W. (composer), 'Australia Will Be There: Australia's War Song', Regal, United Kingdom, 1915, http://trove.nla.gov.au, seen in Hamilton, John, *Goodbye Cobber, God Bless You*, p. 55.

76. 'Anaesthesia and the Wounded at ANZAC, Gallipoli, WWI', in

Cooper, et al., 'Proceedings of the 8th International Symposium on the History of Anaesthesia'.

77. Carter, Diary, 2 May 1915, AWM 3DRL/6418, p. 122.
78. King, Lydia K., Diary, between 29 April and 5 May 1915, AWM 3DRL/6040, p. 21.
79. McCarthy, p. 131.
80. Ibid.
81. Bean, War Diary, 3 May 1915, AWM38, 3DRL606/7/1, p. 3.
82. Ashmead-Bartlett, *The Uncensored Dardanelles*, p. 84, https:// openlibrary.org/books (reported speech changed to direct speech).
83. Ibid. (reported speech changed to direct speech).
84. Ibid. (reported speech changed to direct speech).
85. Aspinall-Oglander, *Military Operations*, Vol. I, p. 335.

CHAPTER TWELVE: ANZACS TO THE FORE

1. *The West Australian*, 'The Australians at Gallipoli', 13 July 1915, p. 8, http://trove.nla.gov.au.
2. *The Sydney Morning Herald*, 'Mr Ashmead Bartlett's Story', 8 May 1915, p. 13, http://trove.nla.gov.au.
3. Ibid., p. 12.
4. *Kalgoorlie Miner*, 7 September 1915, p. 6.
5. Paterson, *Song of the Pen*, p. 371.
6. McAnulty, Diary, 8 June 1915, AWM 1DRL/0422, p. 6.
7. Ibid., p. 2.
8. McLarty, Letter, 11 August 1915, AWM 3DRL/3339, p. 2.
9. Malone, *No Better Death*, p. 181.
10. Bean, *Official History of Australia in the War of 1914–1918*, Vol. II, p. 19 (reported speech changed to direct speech).
11. Hamilton, Ian, *Gallipoli Diary*, Vol. I, p. 211, https://openlibrary.org/books.
12. Bean, *Official History of Australia in the War of 1914–1918*, Vol. II, p. 4.
13. Bean, War Diary, 5 May 1915, AWM38, 3DRL606/7/1, p. 25.
14. Bean, *Official History of Australia in the War of 1914–1918*, Vol. II, p. 22.
15. Ibid., p. 23.
16. Malone, 8 May 1915, p. 182.
17. Ibid., p. 183.
18. Hamilton, Ian, *Gallipoli Diary*, Vol. I, p. 211, https://openlibrary.org/books.
19. Bean, *Official History of Australia in the War of 1914–1918*, Vol. II, p. 31.

20. Bean, *Gallipoli Correspondent*, p. 91.
21. McCarthy, *Gallipoli to the Somme*, p. 139.
22. Bean, War Diary, 8 May 1915, AWM38, 3DRL606/7/1, p. 50.
23. Ibid.
24. Ibid.
25. Ibid., p. 53.
26. Ashmead-Bartlett, *The Uncensored Dardanelles*, p. 84.
27. Hamilton, Ian, *Gallipoli Diary*, Vol. I, p. 213, https://openlibrary.org/books.
28. Ibid., p. 104.
29. Gunner Bill Greer, 1st Battery, Australian Field Artillery, Track 4, Sailah, *Stories from Gallipoli*, ABC Audio.
30. Bean, War Diary, 8 May 1915, AWM38, 3DRL606/7/1, p. 50.
31. Bean, *Bean's Gallipoli*, p. 119.
32. Bean, *Gallipoli Mission*, p. 298.
33. Hamilton, Ian, *Gallipoli Diary*, Vol. I, pp. 209–10, https://openlibrary.org/books.
34. Mackenzie, *Gallipoli Memories*, p. 152.
35. Ashmead-Bartlett, *The Uncensored Dardanelles*, p. 92, https://openlibrary.org/books.
36. Ibid., p. 93.
37. Ibid., p. 101.
38. Olden, *Westralian Cavalry in the War*, p. 29.
39. Bean, *Official History of Australia in the War of 1914–1918*, Vol. II, p. 91.
40. Hamilton, Ian, *Gallipoli Diary*, Vol. I, pp. 258–9, https://openlibrary.org/books.
41. Berrie, *Under Furred Hats (6th ALH Regt)*, pp. 20–2.
42. Hogue, *Trooper Bluegum at the Dardanelles*, p. 61, https://archive.org.
43. Ibid.
44. Throssell, Diary, 19 May 1915, AWM PR85/361.
45. Hamilton, John, *The Price of Valour*, p. 89.
46. Brazier, Diary, 16 May 1915, AWM 1DRL/0147.
47. Hogue, *Trooper Bluegum at the Dardanelles*, p. 85, https://archive.org.
48. It is not confirmed that these names were called out during this roll call. However, they are the names of soldiers from the 16th Battalion who are listed on the Commonwealth War Graves website (www.cwgc.org) as being killed on 9 May 1915.
49. Silas, Diary, 11 May 1915, ML MSS 1840, p. 60, http://acms.sl.nsw.gov.au.
50. Mustafa Kemal to Enver, 3 May 1915, Atatürk, *Atatürk'ün Bütün Eserleri (Collected Works of Atatürk)*, p. 369.

51. *The Washington Post*, 12 May 1915, p. 1.
52. Bean, *Official History of Australia in the War of 1914–1918*, Vol. I, p. 289.
53. Ibid., p. 118 (reported speech changed to direct speech).
54. Churchill, Winston, *The World Crisis*, Vol. II, p. 346.
55. Ibid.
56. Ibid. (reported speech changed to direct speech).
57. Pollock, *Kitchener*, p. 295.
58. *The Times*, 14 May 1915, p. 8.
59. Ibid., p. 9.
60. Gilbert, *Winston S. Churchill*, Vol. III, *Companion*, Pt II, p. 885.
61. Secretary's Notes of a Meeting of the War Council held at 10 Downing Street, 14 May 1915, NA CAB 42/2/19, p. 3.
62. Ibid.
63. Massie, *Castles of Steel*, p. 484.
64. Ibid.
65. Aspinall-Oglander, *Military Operations*, Vol. I, p. 365.
66. Hamilton, Ian, *Gallipoli Diary*, Vol. I, p. 230, https://openlibrary.org/books.
67. Ibid., pp. 231–2.
68. Hart, 'Gallipoli: The War at Sea – An Overview', http://archive.iwm.org.uk, p. 276.
69. Gorman, Johnson and Braddock, *With the Twenty-Second*, p. vii.
70. George Ivan Smith, Pacific Director of the BBC, 1941–1946, reported anecdote, http://1914-1918.invisionzone.com. In the letter to the *Guardian* recounting this episode, there is '*****' where the word 'bastard' appears, but that is my best estimation of what was likely said. It also has this occurring on the day of the landing, which does not make sense, whereas about a month in is far more likely.
71. Kennedy, *The Whale Oil Guards*, p. 14.
72. Derham, *The Silence Ruse*, p. 13.
73. Bean, *Two Men I Knew*, p. 74.
74. Benson, *The Man with the Donkey*, p. 45.
75. Derham, p. 14.
76. Bean, *Official History of Australia in the War of 1914–1918*, Vol. II, p. 130.
77. Churchill, Winston, Vol. II, p. 359.
78. Riddell, *Lord Riddell's War Diary*, p. 93.
79. Churchill, Winston, Vol. II, p. 362.
80. *The Sydney Morning Herald*, 15 May 1915, p. 14.
81. McCarthy, p. 191.
82. Ibid., p. 150.

83. Ibid.
84. Bean, *Official History of Australia in the War of 1914–1918*, Vol. II, p. 200.
85. Ibid.
86. Silas, Diary, 16 May 1915, p. 63, ML MSS 1840, http://acms.sl.nsw.gov.au.
87. Ibid.
88. Ibid., 17 May 1915, p. 64.
89. Ibid., 22 May 1915, p. 72.
90. John Monash to Hannah Monash, 22 June 1915, Sir Monash Papers, SLV, MS 13875, Box 4083/1, p. 87.
91. Wodehouse, *Blandings Castle*, p. 29.
92. Hamilton, Ian, *Gallipoli Diary*, Vol. I, p. 235, https://openlibrary.org/books.

CHAPTER THIRTEEN: THE TURKISH OFFENSIVE

1. Ashmead-Bartlett, *The Uncensored Dardanelles*, p. 126, https://openlibrary.org/books.
2. Mackenzie, *Gallipoli Memories*, pp. 80–1.
3. Bean, *Official History of Australia in the War of 1914–1918*, Vol. II, p. 133.
4. Ibid., p. 138.
5. Ibid.
6. Ibid., p. 139. It is normal for a third or so of any large force (such as the corps-sized force that was defending Anzac) to have jobs that do not put them in the trenches with a rifle.
7. Ibid., p. 137.
8. Hogue, *Trooper Bluegum at the Dardanelles*, p. 92, https://archive.org.
9. Ibid.
10. McCarthy, *Gallipoli to the Somme*, p. 148.
11. Ibid.
12. Bean, *Official History of Australia in the War of 1914–1918*, Vol. II, p. 140.
13. Ibid., p. 138.
14. Barwick, Diary, 22 August 1914–September 1915, ML MSS 1493/1/Box 1/Item 1, p. 127.
15. Laffin, *Damn the Dardanelles*, p. 81.
16. This quote comes from an interview conducted by historian Dr Peter Williams with a 12th Australian Infantry Battalion veteran, in Hobart, 1980.

17. Hogue, *Trooper Bluegum at the Dardanelles*, p. 115, https://archive.org.
18. Ibid., p. 75.
19. Bean, *Official History of Australia in the War of 1914–1918*, Vol. II, p. 149 (reported speech changed to direct speech).
20. Bean, 'Albert Jacka', *Reveille*, 31 January 1932, p. 2.
21. Bean, *Official History of Australia in the War of 1914–1918*, Vol. II, p. 150.
22. Jacka, Diary, 19 May 1915, AWM MSS143A, Pt 4, p. 10 (or at least the reverse side of p. 5, as Jacka has marked it in his diary).
23. Bean, *Official History of Australia in the War of 1914–1918*, Vol. II, p. 143.
24. Dolan, *Gallipoli Air War*, p. 198.
25. Ibid.
26. Kemal, Mustafa to Corinne Lütfü, 3 July 1915, in Atatürk, *Atatürk'ün Bütün Eserleri (Collected Works of Atatürk)*, p. 228.
27. Mülazim, Lt Hasan Ethem to his Mother, 17 April 1915, 'Last Letter of a Turkish Martyr Killed in the Gallipolian War', *The Gallipolian*, No. 76, Winter 1994, p. 6.
28. Hogue, *Trooper Bluegum at the Dardanelles*, p. 95, https://archive.org (reported speech changed to direct speech).
29. Ibid.
30. Bean, *Official History of Australia in the War of 1914–1918*, Vol. II, p. 160.
31. Butler, Arthur G., *Official History of the Australian Army Medical Services, 1914–1918*, p. 159.
32. *The Sunday Times* (Perth), 16 April 1916, p. 1S.
33. 3rd Australian Field Ambulance War Diary, May 1915, AWM4 26/46/5, p. 9. NB: In the original cable, it says 'Shrapnel Valley', but as I have used 'Shrapnel Gully' throughout, for consistency I do so here too.
34. Hogue, *Trooper Bluegum at the Dardanelles*, p. 117, https://archive.org.
35. Adams, Diary, 19 May 1915, AWM RCDIG0000862, p. 61.
36. Ibid. (reported speech changed to direct speech).
37. King, Lydia K., Diary, 21 May 1915, AWM 3DRL/6040, p. 23.
38. Bean, *Official History of Australia in the War of 1914–1918*, Vol. II, p. 162.
39. Ibid.
40. For their parts, the Turks were horrified when the Allies bombed their hospitals and mosques in those first days in April – including the entire hospital at Maidos (which had Allied wounded as well), despite being clearly marked.
41. Bean, *Official History of Australia in the War of 1914–1918*, Vol. II, p. 162.
42. Harry Benson, Track 5, Sailah, *Stories from Gallipoli*, ABC Audio.

43. Editorial, *The Times*, 19 May 1915, p. 9.
44. Bean, *Official History of Australia in the War of 1914–1918*, Vol. II, p. 251.
45. Ibid.
46. Ibid.
47. Benson, *The Man with the Donkey*, p. 43.
48. Bean, Despatch, *Commonwealth Government Gazette*, No. 7, 13 January 1916, p. 92.
49. Ibid.
50. Ashmead-Bartlett, *The Uncensored Dardanelles*, pp. 106–7, https://openlibrary.org/books.
51. Ashmead-Bartlett, Diary, ML A1583, p. 65, http://acms.sl.nsw.gov.au.
52. Ashmead-Bartlett, *The Uncensored Dardanelles*, pp. 106–7, https://openlibrary.org/books.
53. *Daily Mail*, 21 May 1915, p. 4.
54. Pound and Harmsworth, *Northcliffe*, p. 478.
55. In today's Saudi Arabia.
56. Mücke, *Ayesha*, p. 223, https://openlibrary.org/books. Though in his account, von Mücke has this number at 30, he has made a mistake in his mathematics, as his party was 49 strong when setting out, and, as three men were killed along the way, only 46 were to make it into Constantinople.
57. Lochner, *Die Kaperfahrten des kleinen Kreuzers Emden (The Naval Boardings of the Small Cruiser Emden)*, p. 393.
58. Örnek and Toker, *Gallipoli*, p. 40.
59. Fahrettin, 'Fahrettin Altay', in Martı, *Çanakkale Hatiraları (Çanakkale Memoirs)*, Vol. II, p. 29.
60. For further reading, see Cameron, *Shadows of Anzac*.
61. Carlyon, *Gallipoli*, p. 287.
62. McAnulty, Diary, 10 June 1915, AWM 1DRL/0422, p. 6.
63. Ibid., p. 7. The 6th Light Horse wore wallaby fur around their hat, instead of the emu plume.
64. Hogue, *Trooper Bluegum at the Dardanelles*, p. 114, https://archive.org.
65. Mackenzie, p. 83.
66. Hamilton, Ian, *Gallipoli Diary*, Vol. I, p. 249, https://openlibrary.org/books.
67. Hogue, *Trooper Bluegum at the Dardanelles*, p. 116, https://archive.org.
68. Bean, *Gallipoli Mission*, p. 58.
69. Fahrettin, 'Fahrettin Altay', in Martı, *Çanakkale Hatiraları (Çanakkale Memoirs)*, Vol. II, p. 30.
70. Cicognani, Diary, 1 November 1914–September 1915, ML MSS 1238, p. 39, http://acms.sl.nsw.gov.au.

71. Bean, *Gallipoli Correspondent*, p. 117.
72. For further reading, see Fahrettin, 'Fahrettin Altay', in Martı, *Çanakkale Hatiraları (Çanakkale Memoirs)*, Vol. II, p. 29.
73. Herbert, *Mons, Anzac and Kut*, p. 119 (reported speech changed to direct speech).
74. The correct spelling for this saying in Modern Turkish is '*Uğurlar ola. Güle güle gideceksiniz, güle güle geleceksiniz.*'
75. Herbert, p. 119.
76. Ashmead-Bartlett, *The Uncensored Dardanelles*, p. 110, https://openlibrary.org/books.
77. Howard, Michael, 'Churchill and the First World War', in Blake and Louis, *Churchill*, p. 138.
78. James, Lawrence, *Churchill and Empire*, p. 115.
79. Ibid.
80. Thomas, *Raiders of the Deep*, p. 64.
81. No record of this, but it is the standard instruction in such cases.
82. No record of this, but it is the standard instruction in such cases.
83. Czech-Jochberg, *Die Verantwortlichen im Weltkrieg (The Responsible Ones in a World War)*, p. 96.
84. Thomas, p. 64.
85. Ibid.
86. Birdwood, *Khaki and Gown*, p. 267.
87. Thomas, p. 64.
88. Moorehead, *Gallipoli*, p. 176.
89. Hamilton, Ian, *Gallipoli Diary*, Vol. I, p. 247, https://openlibrary.org/books.
90. Fenwick, *Gallipoli Diary*, p. 20.
91. *The West Australian*, 'Invented in the Trenches', 12 August 1915, p. 8, http://trove.nla.gov.au.
92. Seal, Graham, *Great Anzac Stories*, p. 39.
93. Broadbent, *The Boys Who Came Home*, p. 87.
94. Birdwood, *Khaki and Gown*, p. 270 (reported speech changed to direct speech).
95. Ibid. (reported speech changed to direct speech).
96. For further reading, see Bull, *Battle Tactics*.
97. John Cargill, Track 7, Sailah, *Stories from Gallipoli*, ABC Audio.
98. Cameron, *Sorry, Lads, But the Order Is to Go*, p. 156.
99. Hogue, *Trooper Bluegum at the Dardanelles*, p. 168, https://archive.org.
100. Ibid.
101. Monash, John to Hannah Monash, 24 May 1915, Sir Monash Papers, SLV, MS 13875, Box 4083/1, p. 67.

102. Ibid.
103. McLarty, Letter, 11 August 1915, AWM 3DRL/3339, p. 2.
104. Ashmead-Bartlett, *The Uncensored Dardanelles*, p. 114, https://openlibrary.org/books.
105. Ibid.
106. Ibid., p. 118.
107. Keyes, *The Keyes Papers*, p. 147.
108. Hamilton, Ian, *Gallipoli Diary*, Vol. I, p. 263, https://openlibrary.org/books.
109. Birdwood, *In My Time*, p. 34.
110. Carter, Diary, 1 June 1915, AWM 3DRL/6418, p. 152.
111. Bean, *Official History of Australia in the War of 1914–1918*, Vol. II, p. 208.
112. Ibid., p. 210.
113. Ibid., p. 211.
114. Monash, *War Letters of General Monash*, pp. 41–2.
115. *The Courier-Mail* (Brisbane), 16 November 1934, p. 16.
116. Hogue, *Trooper Bluegum at the Dardanelles*, p. 168, https://archive.org.
117. Ibid., pp. 166–7.
118. Ibid., p. 147.

CHAPTER FOURTEEN: SUMMER SETS IN

1. Kinloch, *Echoes of Gallipoli*, p. 161.
2. Kent, *Trench and Troopship*, p. 52.
3. James, Robert R., *Gallipoli*, p. 222.
4. McAnulty, Diary, 14 June 1915, AWM 1DRL/0422, p. 8.
5. McLarty, Letter, 7 July 1915, AWM 3DRL/3339, p. 1.
6. Butler, Arthur G., *Official History of the Australian Army Medical Services, 1914–1918*, p. 238.
7. Idriess, *The Desert Column*, p. 55.
8. Hamilton, Ian, *Gallipoli Diary*, Vol. I, p. 386, https://openlibrary.org/books.
9. McLarty, Letter, 7 July 1915, AWM 3DRL/3339, p. 1.
10. Flockart to his Mother, Letter, 27 May 1915, AWM 1DRL/0296, p. 2.
11. McCarthy, *Gallipoli to the Somme*, p. 184.
12. Fullerton, Diary, undated, AWM 1DRL/0302, p. 1.
13. Jack Nicholson, Track 4, Sailah, *Stories from Gallipoli*, ABC Audio.
14. Örnek and Toker, *Gallipoli*, p. 52.
15. Flockart, Letter, 28 May 1915, AWM 1DRL/0296, pp. 2–3.
16. Caulfield, *The Unknown Anzacs*, p. 155.

17. Kent, p. 70.
18. Hoddinott, Typed Manuscript, AWM MSS0791, p. 39.
19. Seal, G., *Inventing Anzac*, p. 28.
20. Edwards, Diary, 13 July 1915, AWM PR/192, p. 34.
21. Tiddy, Diary, 10 August 1915, AWM PR86/272, p. 18.
22. John Monash to Hannah Monash, 18 July 1915, Sir Monash Papers, SLV, MS 13875, Box 4083/1.
23. *The West Australian*, 'The Australians at Gallipoli', 13 July 1915, p. 8, http://trove.nla.gov.au.
24. McLarty, Letter, 11 August 1915, AWM 3DRL/3339, p. 1.
25. Gallipoli Slang, http://user.online.be/~snelders/slang.html.
26. Ekins, *War Wounds*, p. 53.
27. Churchill, Winston, *The World Crisis*, Vol. II, p. 390.
28. 'The Final Report of the Dardanelles Commission', p. 26.
29. Dardanelles Committee Meeting, 25 June 1915, NA CAB 42/3/5.
30. 'The Mounted Soldiers of Australia', from the TV series *Australians at War*, www.lighthorse.org.au.
31. *The Sunday Times* (Perth), 26 December 1915, p. 20.
32. Hamilton, John, *The Price of Valour*, p. 140.
33. Ashmead-Bartlett, *The Uncensored Dardanelles*, p. 122, https://openlibrary.org/books.
34. Ashmead-Bartlett, Diary, ML A1583, pp. 93–94, http://acms.sl.nsw.gov.au.
35. Ibid., p. 94.
36. Ashmead-Bartlett, *The Uncensored Dardanelles*, p. 123, http://acms.sl.nsw.gov.au.
37. Ibid., p. 124.
38. Ibid., p. 21.
39. Ibid., p. 125.
40. Ibid.
41. Ibid.
42. Ibid., 'Memorandum on Gallipoli', p. 128.
43. Ibid, 'Memorandum on Gallipoli'.
44. Ibid., 'Memorandum on Gallipoli', p. 129.
45. Ibid.
46. Ibid., p. 130.
47. Ibid. Kitchener is referring here to Hill 971, the highest peak of the Sari Bair Range.
48. Ibid., p. 131.
49. Ibid.
50. Ibid.

51. Ibid.
52. Ibid.
53. Tehlirian, Trial Transcripts, 16 April 1921, 3rd State Court, Criminal Department, Berlin, www.cilicia.com/armo_tehlirian.html.
54. Fenwick, *Gallipoli Diary*, p. 85.
55. Bean, *Bean's Gallipoli*, p. 161.
56. Kent, p. 52.
57. *Daily Mail*, 7 August 1915, p. 10.
58. In his diaries, Bean regularly alternates between calling his brother – Captain John Willoughby Butler Bean – Jack and Jock. He actually calls his brother Jock in this instance, but for ease of narrative I have used Jack throughout.
59. McCarthy, p. 156.
60. Hogue, *Trooper Bluegum at the Dardanelles*, p. 146, https://archive.org.
61. Tiddy, Diary, 6 June 1915, AWM PR86/272, p. 11.
62. Birdwood, *Khaki and Gown*, pp. 262–3.
63. Alexander Hay Borthwick, Letter, 27 June 1915, AWM PR01729, p. 1.
64. Hogue, Letters relating to Oliver 'Trooper Bluegum' Hogue, 24 July 1915, AWM RCDIG 0000997, p. 18.
65. Paşa, Mustafa Kemal, 'Anafartalar Hatiraları (Anafarta Memoirs)', in Martı, *Çanakkale Hatiraları (Çanakkale Memoirs)*, Vol. I, p. 43.
66. Ibid., p. 47.
67. Ibid., p. 48. Turkish historians have dubbed this now famous conversation 'The Sazlıdere Discussion'.
68. Birdwood, *Khaki and Gown*, p. 268.
69. Hamilton, Ian, *Gallipoli Diary*, Vol. I, p. 330, https://openlibrary.org/books.
70. Ibid.
71. King, Lydia K., Diary, 20 June 1915, AWM 3DRL/6040, p. 25.
72. Kitson, *Patriots Three*, www.abc.net.au/radionational.
73. Murdoch's instructions from Australian Acting Secretary of Defence Thomas Trumble, 2 July 1915, Appendix to Hamilton, Ian, Memorandum on Murdoch Letter, 26 November 1915, NA CAB 42/5/23, p. 12.
74. Murdoch, Letter to Andrew Fisher, 21 June 1915, NLA, MS 2823, Series 2, Folder 1, Box 2, p. 3.
75. Bean, *Gallipoli Correspondent*, p. 138.
76. Bean, War Diary, 25 June 1915, AWM 3DRL606/9/1, p. 20.
77. World War I propaganda leaflets and papers dropped from aircraft over Gallipoli and Palestine, 1917, ML, Strongroom, SAFE 1/213.
78. Herbert Gordon Carter to Mr and Mrs H. J. Carter, Letter, 26 June 1915, AWM 1DRL/192.

79. Atatürk, *Atatürk'ün Bütün Eserleri (Collected Works of Atatürk)*, p. 390.
80. Hart, 'Gallipoli: The War at Sea – An Overview', p. 202, http://archive. iwm.org.uk.
81. Ibid.
82. Bean, *Official History of Australia in the War of 1914–1918*, Vol. II, p. 316.
83. Hogue, *Trooper Bluegum at the Dardanelles*, p. 234, https://archive.org.
84. Ibid.

CHAPTER FIFTEEN: THE BATTLE IS NIGH

1. Hamilton, Ian, *Gallipoli Diary*, Vol. I, p. 5, https://openlibrary.org/books.
2. Bean, *Gallipoli Correspondent*, p. 169 (Diary, 17 October 1915).
3. Ibid., p. 329.
4. Ibid., p. 330.
5. See Aspinall-Oglander, *History of the Great War, Military Operations Gallipoli*, p. 142.
6. Bean, *Official History of Australia in the War of 1914–1918*, Vol. I, p. 339.
7. Kinloch, *Echoes of Gallipoli*, p. 188.
8. At the formation of the AIF, the Brigade Commanders were graded as Colonels. On 1 July 1915, they were regraded as Brigadier-Generals in order to align their ranks with that of their British counterparts. This new seniority was then backdated to the point at which they took command of the brigade. Brigadier-General was a temporary rank, and only lasted as long as the officer was serving in that capacity. I have chosen to use 'Colonel' up until 1 July, after which I refer to these officers (Monash, MacLagan, Johnston, etc.) as 'Brigadier-General'.
9. Hart, 'Gallipoli: The War at Sea – An Overview', p. 346.
10. Bean, *Official History of Australia in the War of 1914–1918*, Vol. II, p. 607.
11. Hamilton, Ian, *Gallipoli Diary*, Vol. I, p. 331, https://openlibrary.org/books.
12. Ibid.
13. Ibid., Vol. II, pp. 16–17.
14. Birdwood, *Khaki and Gown*, p. 268.
15. Stanley, *Bad Characters*, pp. 49–50.
16. Bean, *Official History of Australia in the War of 1914–1918*, Vol. II, p. 427.
17. Hamilton, Ian, *Gallipoli Diary*, Vol. II, p. 37, https://openlibrary.org/books. Bean has this telegram as: 'Australians are superbly dug in and

spoiling for a fight.' (Bean, *Official History of Australia in the War of 1914–1918*, Vol. II, p. 429.)

18. *The Times*, 20 October 1915, p. 6.

19. Ibid.

20. Ashmead-Bartlett, *The Uncensored Dardanelles*, p. 162, https:// openlibrary.org/books.

21. Ibid. (reported speech changed to direct speech).

22. Ibid. (reported speech changed to direct speech).

23. Ashmead-Bartlett, Diary, 24 July 1915, ML A1583, http://acms.sl.nsw. gov.au.

24. King, Lydia K., Diary, 23 July 1915, AWM 3DRL/6040, p. 27.

25. Ashmead-Bartlett, Diary, 24 July 1915, ML A1583, http://acms.sl.nsw. gov.au.

26. Ibid., 18 July 1915.

27. Ibid., 24 July 1915.

28. Ibid., 14 July 1915.

29. Ashmead-Bartlett, *The Uncensored Dardanelles*, p. 158, https:// openlibrary.org/books.

30. Birdwood, *Khaki and Gown*, p. 269.

31. Ibid.

32. Sanders, *Five Years in Turkey*, p. 79.

33. Ibid., p. 81.

34. James, Robert R., *Gallipoli*, p. 253.

35. Fahrettin, Altay Paşa, 'Fahrettin Altay', in Martı, *Çanakkale Hatiraları (Çanakkale Memoirs)*, Vol. II, p. 34.

36. Bean, *Official History of Australia in the War of 1914–1918*, Vol. II, p. 524. According to Bean's interview with Zeki Bey (Bean, *Gallipoli Mission*, p. 183), this happened at Anzac. And it was ordered by Mustafa Kemal.

37. Bean, *Official History of Australia in the War of 1914–1918*, Vol. II, p. 524.

38. McCarthy, *Gallipoli to the Somme*, p. 299.

39. Ashmead-Bartlett, *The Uncensored Dardanelles*, p. 167, https:// openlibrary.org/books.

40. Hamilton, John, *The Price of Valour*, p. 112.

41. Ashmead-Bartlett, *The Uncensored Dardanelles*, p. 177, https:// openlibrary.org/books.

42. Ibid.

43. Shakespeare, *King Henry the Fifth*, Act III, Scene I, p. 39, http://books. google.com.au.

44. Erickson, *Gallipoli*, p. 140.

45. 3rd Australian Light Horse Brigade War Diary, August 1915, AWM4 10/3/7, p. 82.
46. Birdwood, *Khaki and Gown*, p. 273.
47. Bean, *Official History of Australia in the War of 1914–1918*, Vol. II, p. 502.
48. McCarthy, p. 180.
49. *The West Australian*, 'With the Australians', 26 August 1915, p. 7, http://trove.nla.gov.au.
50. Çelik, 'Gallipoli: The August Offensive', www.awm.gov.au.
51. Barwick, Diary, ML MSS 1493/1/Box 1/Item 1, p. 146, www.acmssearch.sl.nsw.gov.au.
52. Ibid., p. 147.
53. It is of interest that the private is unaware of the actual time of battle commencement: 5.30 pm.
54. Bean, *Bean's Gallipoli*, p. 182.
55. Bean, *Official History of Australia in the War of 1914–1918*, Vol. II, p. 502.
56. McCarthy, p. 170.
57. Birdwood, *Khaki and Gown*, p. 272.
58. *Port Lincoln Times*, 'Visit of Salvation Army Chief', 19 August 1932, p. 7, http://trove.nla.gov.au.
59. *The West Australian*, 'With the Australians', 26 August 1915, p. 7, http://trove.nla.gov.au.
60. Bean, *Official History of Australia in the War of 1914–1918*, Vol. II, p. 503.
61. Shakespeare, *King Henry the Fifth*, Act III, Scene I, p. 40, http://books.google.com.au.
62. 2nd Infantry Battalion War Diary, August 1915, AWM4, 23/19/6, p. 5.
63. Bean, *Anzac to Amiens*, pp. 45–6.
64. Barwick, Diary, ML MSS 1493/1/Box 1/Item 1, p. 151, www.acmssearch.sl.nsw.gov.au.
65. Ibid., p. 151.
66. Oral, *Gallipoli 1915*, p. 244.
67. Ibid.
68. Ibid., p. 245.
69. Bean, *Gallipoli Mission: Supplementary Material*, 'The Turkish Side at Lone Pine', p. 184.
70. The Turkish name for Lone Pine is Kanlı Sırt, which means 'Bloody Ridge'. It was so named to commemorate this brutal battle.
71. Barwick, Diary, ML MSS 1493/1/Box 1/Item 1, p. 153, www.acmssearch.sl.nsw.gov.au.

72. Bean, *Official History of Australia in the War of 1914–1918*, Vol. II, p. 508.
73. Bean, *Gallipoli Mission: Supplementary Material*, 'The Turkish Side at Lone Pine', p. 185.
74. Ibid. (reported speech changed to direct speech).
75. Birdwood, *Khaki and Gown*, p. 273.
76. Ibid., p. 267.
77. Bean, *Official History of Australia in the War of 1914–1918*, Vol. II, p. 532.
78. Hamilton, Ian, *Gallipoli Diary*, Vol. II, p. 54, https://openlibrary.org/books.

CHAPTER SIXTEEN: 'PUSH ON!'

1. James, Robert R., *Gallipoli*, p. 237.
2. Brazier, Comments, Official History 1914–1918 War Records of Charles E. W. Bean, Correspondence 1926–31, AWM 3DRL 7953/27, Pt 3, Ch. XVIII.
3. Sanders, p. 83 (past tense changed to present tense).
4. Ibid.
5. Pugsley, *Gallipoli*, p. 278.
6. Malone, *No Better Death*, p. 294.
7. Ibid.
8. Ibid., pp. 294–5.
9. Ibid., p. 297.
10. Ibid., p. 299.
11. Travers, *Gallipoli*, p. 124.
12. Hart, 'Gallipoli: The War at Sea – An Overview', p. 303.
13. Bean, *Gallipoli Correspondent*, p. 146.
14. Ibid.
15. Ibid.
16. Monash, Diary, 6 August 1915, SLV, MS 13875, Box 4083/1, p. 103.
17. Bean, *Bean's Gallipoli*, p. 186.
18. Juvenis, *Suvla Bay and After*, p. 7.
19. Erickson, *Gallipoli*, p. 157.
20. Ibid.
21. Bean, *Official History of Australia in the War of 1914–1918*, Vol. II, p. 571.
22. Ibid., p. 572.
23. Pugsley, p. 276.
24. Malone, p. 295.

25. Throssell, Katharine Susannah Prichard's Papers, 7 August 1915, NLA MS 6201, Folder 7.
26. Monash, Diary, 6 August 1915, SLV, MS 13875, Box 4083/1, p. 103.
27. Ibid.
28. Bean, *Official History of Australia in the War of 1914–1918*, Vol. II, p. 591.
29. Ibid., p. 606.
30. Ibid.
31. Hamilton, John, *Goodbye Cobber, God Bless You*, p. 243.
32. Ataksor, *Çanakkale Raporu (Çanakkale Report)*, pp. 286–7.
33. Raynell, Diary, 10 August 1915, AWM PR86/388, p. 30.
34. Antill, Comments, Official History 1914–1918 War Records of Charles E. W. Bean, Correspondence 1926–31, AWM 3DRL 7953/27, Pt 3, Ch. XVIII.
35. Ibid.
36. Ibid.
37. Ibid.
38. Hamilton, John, *Goodbye Cobber, God Bless You*, p. 285.
39. Schuler, *Australia in Arms*, p. 241, https://archive.org.
40. Hamilton, John, *Goodbye Cobber, God Bless You*, p. 285.
41. Bean, *Official History of Australia in the War of 1914–1918*, Vol. II, p. 612.
42. Ibid., p. 613.
43. Brazier, Comments, Official History 1914–1918 War Records of Charles E. W. Bean, Correspondence 1926–31, AWM 3DRL 7953/27, Pt 3, Ch. XVIII.
44. Schuler, p. 238.
45. Ibid., p. 241 (reported speech changed to direct speech).
46. Danışman, *Gallipoli 1915 Day One Plus*, p. 73.
47. Bean, *Official History of Australia in the War of 1914–1918*, Vol. II, p. 612.
48. Cameron, *Sorry, Lads, But the Order Is to Go*, p. 183.
49. Bean, *Official History of Australia in the War of 1914–1918*, Vol. II, p. 613.
50. Simpson, Cameron Victor, *Maygar's Boys*, p. 279.
51. Brazier, Letter to C. E. W. Bean, 7 March 1924, AWM 38 DRL 8042, Item 25, p. 1.
52. McCarthy, *Gallipoli to the Somme*, p. 174.
53. Aker, S., 'Çanakkale-Arıburnu Savaşları ve 27. Alay (Çanakkale-Arıburnu Battles and the 27th Regiment)', in Martı, *Çanakkale Hatiraları (Çanakkale Memoirs)*, Vol. I, pp. 287–8. There were, in fact, no New Zealanders involved in this action.

54. *The West Australian*, 'The Dardanelles', 28 September 1915, p. 5, http://trove.nla.gov.au.

55. Bean, *Official History of Australia in the War of 1914–1918*, Vol. II, p. 614.

56. Ibid.

57. Redford, Diary, undated addendum, AWM PR85/064. This quote comes from an addendum to Major Thomas Redford's personal diary. There is a brief introduction in the typed transcript of the diary by a person identified only as 'W. H. C.' W. H. C. notes, 'The rest of the diary [that is, those entries after his entry on the morning of 7 August at 4 am], which includes a description of the assault on the Nek and the death of Major Redford, was completed in a different handwriting. At no stage does the new diarist reveal his identity, but I believe he was Major William McGrath, 8th Light Horse Regiment, who enlisted on 23 September 1914 and returned to Australia on 3 July 1919.' I have gone with this conclusion.

58. For further reading, see *The West Australian*, 28 September 1915, p. 5.

59. Deeble, Major J., Acting Commander 8th Light Horse Brigade, Report, 7 August 1915, in 3rd Australian Light Horse Brigade War Diary, AWM4 10/3/7, Appendix X, p. 84.

60. Ibid. (reported speech changed to direct speech).

61. 3rd Australian Light Horse Brigade War Diary, 7 August 1915, AWM4 10/3/7.

62. Statistics of Casualties, Russell's Top, 7 August 1915, in 3rd Australian Light Horse Brigade War Diary, 7 August 1915, AWM4 10/3/7.

63. Brazier, Letter to C. E. W. Bean, 7 March 1924, AWM 38 DRL 8042, Item 25, p. 2.

64. Bean, *Official History of Australia in the War of 1914–1918*, Vol. II, p. 607.

65. Pugsley, p. 280.

66. Brazier, Comments, Official History 1914–1918 War Records of Charles E. W. Bean, Correspondence 1926–31, AWM 3DRL 7953/27, Pt 3, Ch. XVIII (reported speech changed to direct speech).

67. Brazier, Letter to C. E. W. Bean, 7 March 1924, AWM 38 DRL 8042, Item 25, p. 2 (reported speech changed to direct speech). Another version of this quote is in Brazier, Comments, Official History 1914–1918 War Records of Charles E. W. Bean, Correspondence 1926–31, AWM 3DRL 7953/27, Pt 3, Ch. XVIII.

68. Brazier, Letter to C. E. W. Bean, 7 March 1924, AWM 38 DRL 8042, Item 25, p. 3 (reported speech changed to direct speech).

69. Brazier, Comments, Official History 1914–1918 War Records of

Charles E. W. Bean, Correspondence 1926–31, AWM 3DRL 7953/27, Pt 3, Ch. XVIII (reported speech changed to direct speech).

70. 10th Australian Light Horse Regiment War Diary, 7 August 1915, Russell's Top, AWM4 10/15/4.

71. Brazier, Comments, Official History 1914–1918 War Records of Charles E. W. Bean, Correspondence 1926–31, AWM 3DRL 7953/27, Pt 3, Ch. XVIII (reported speech changed to direct speech).

72. Brazier, Letter to C. E. W. Bean, 7 March 1924, AWM 38 DRL 8042, Item 25, p. 4. When it came to compiling the official history of the war, Bean asked for Antill's comments about that day at the Nek. In his recollections, Antill wrote, 'The statement that "the brigade major had just heard that a red and yellow flag had been seen upon the parapet. It was essential, he said, to support the men who had already got across and he ordered the attack to proceed" is baseless – an invention of some individual, and entirely contrary to fact.' (Brazier, Comments, Official History 1914–1918 War Records of Charles E. W. Bean, Correspondence 1926–31, AWM 3DRL 7953/27, Pt 3, Ch. XVIII). Bean's assessment of this was, 'Antill's comments are worthless: he says he never heard of a flag appearing in the Turkish trenches – actually he was the first man who, three or four days later, gave me an account of the incident! . . . many of his facts seem to me to have been invented in the intervening years.' (Bean to Sir J. Edmunds, 17 June 1931, Official History 1914–1918 War Records of Charles E. W. Bean, Correspondence 1926–31, AWM, 3DRL 7953/27, Pt 3, Ch. XVIII.)

73. Brazier, Comments, Official History 1914–1918 War Records of Charles E. W. Bean, Correspondence 1926–31, AWM 3DRL 7953/27, Pt 3, Ch. XVIII.

74. *The Canberra Times*, 25 April 1986, p. 8.

75. For further reading, see Hamilton, John, *Goodbye Cobber, God Bless You*, p. 309.

76. Brazier, Comments, Official History 1914–1918 War Records of Charles E. W. Bean, Correspondence 1926–31, AWM 3DRL 7953/27, Pt 3, Ch. XVIII.

77. *The West Australian*, 'The Story of Hill 60', 22 November 1915, p. 8, http://trove.nla.gov.au.

78. Örnek and Toker, *Gallipoli*, p. 94.

79. Bean, *Official History of Australia in the War of 1914–1918*, Vol. II, p. 618.

80. Hamilton, John, *The Price of Valour*, p. 143.

81. *The West Australian*, 'The Story of Hill 60', 22 November 1915, p. 8, http://trove.nla.gov.au.

82. Burness, *The Nek*, p. 116.
83. Hamilton, John, *The Price of Valour*, p. 140.
84. Browning and Gill, *Gallipoli to Tripoli*, p. 115 (reported speech changed to direct speech).
85. Brazier, Letter to C. E. W. Bean, 7 March 1924, AWM 38 DRL 8042, Item 25, p. 4.
86. Brazier, Comments, Official History 1914–1918 War Records of Charles E. W. Bean, Correspondence 1926–31, AWM 3DRL 7953/27, Pt 3, Ch. XVIII.
87. Brazier, Letter to C. E. W. Bean, 7 March 1924, AWM 38 DRL 8042, Item 25, p. 4.
88. Ibid.
89. Bean, *Official History of Australia in the War of 1914–1918*, Vol. II, p. 619.
90. For further reading, see Burness, *The Nek*, pp. 114–15.
91. Bean, *Official History of Australia in the War of 1914–1918*, Vol. II, p. 619.
92. The Australian troops were essentially sent on a suicide mission at the Nek that morning. The troops came to place the blame on Godley, and renamed the Nek 'Godley's Abattoir'. The Turks, on the other hand, subsequently called the area Cesarettepe, meaning Bravery or Courage Hill.
93. Brazier, Comments, Official History 1914–1918 War Records of Charles E. W. Bean, Correspondence 1926–31, AWM 3DRL 7953/27, Pt 3, Ch. XVIII.
94. Ibid.
95. Brazier, Letter to C. E. W. Bean, 7 March 1924, AWM 38 DRL 8042, Item 25, p. 5 (tenses changed).
96. Brazier, Comments, Official History 1914–1918 War Records of Charles E. W. Bean, Correspondence 1926–31, AWM 3DRL 7953/27, Pt 3, Ch. XVIII.
97. *The West Australian*, 28 September 1915, p. 5.

CHAPTER SEVENTEEN: BATTLE FOR THE HEIGHTS

1. Malone, *No Better Death*, p. 299.
2. Mango, *Atatürk*, p. 152.
3. Kemal, Mustafa, 'Anafartalar Hatiraları (Anafarta Memoirs)', in Martı, *Çanakkale Hatiraları (Çanakkale Memoirs)*, Vol. I, p. 52.
4. Pugsley, *Gallipoli*, p. 277.
5. Ibid., p. 275.
6. Kannengiesser, *The Campaign in Gallipoli*, p. 205.

7. Ibid.
8. Ibid.
9. Ibid., p. 206.
10. Kemal, Mustafa, 'Anafartalar Hatiraları (Anafarta Memoirs)', in Martı, Vol. I, p. 53.
11. Kannengiesser, p. 207.
12. Ibid.
13. Ibid.
14. Pugsley, pp. 279–280.
15. Ibid. (tenses changed).
16. Broadbent, *The Boys Who Came Home*, p. 227.
17. Bean, *Official History of Australia in the War of 1914–1918*, Vol. II, p. 633.
18. Travers, *Gallipoli*, p. 126.
19. Bean, *Official History of Australia in the War of 1914–1918*, Vol. II, p. 639.
20. Ibid., p. 640.
21. Ibid., p. 641.
22. Pugsley, p. 283.
23. Carlyon, *Gallipoli*, p. 417.
24. Pugsley, p. 283.
25. Ibid.
26. Ibid.
27. Bean, *Official History of Australia in the War of 1914–1918*, Vol. II, p. 645.
28. Ibid., p. 654.
29. Ibid., pp. 654–5.
30. Pugsley, p. 284.
31. Malone, p. 311.
32. Pugsley, p. 286.
33. Bean, *Official History of Australia in the War of 1914–1918*, Vol. II, p. 659.
34. Ibid.
35. Kemal, Mustafa, 'Anafartalar Hatiraları (Anafarta Memoirs)', in Martı, Vol. I, p. 55.
36. Ibid.
37. Ibid., p. 58.
38. McAnulty, Diary, 6 August 1915, AWM 1DRL/0422, p. 38.
39. Ibid., 8 August 1915, pp. 38–9.
40. Arthur, *Life of Lord Kitchener*, p. 163.
41. Hamilton, Ian B. M., *The Happy Warrior*, pp. 379–80.

42. Arthur, p. 163.
43. Hamilton, Ian B. M., p. 368.
44. Arthur, p. 163.
45. Hamilton, Ian, *Gallipoli Diary*, Vol. II, p. 62, https://openlibrary.org/ books (reported speech changed to direct speech).
46. Ibid.
47. Ibid., p. 63 (reported speech changed to direct speech).
48. Ibid., p. 65 (reported speech changed to direct speech).
49. Arthur, p. 164.
50. Bean, *Official History of Australia in the War of 1914–1918*, Vol. II, p. 677.
51. Kemal, Mustafa, 'Anafartalar Hatiraları (Anafarta Memoirs)', in Martı, Vol. I, p. 60.
52. Ibid. (tenses changed).
53. Ibid.
54. Ibid.
55. Ibid., p. 62.
56. Ibid.
57. Ashmead-Bartlett, *The Uncensored Dardanelles*, p. 189, https:// openlibrary.org/books.
58. Ibid.
59. Ibid., p. 190.
60. Ibid.
61. Monash, Diary, 16 August 1915, SLV, MS 13875, Box 4083/1, p. 104.
62. Bean, *Official History of Australia in the War of 1914–1918*, Vol. II, p. 663.
63. Kemal, Mustafa, 'Anafartalar Hatiraları (Anafarta Memoirs)', in Martı, Vol. I, p. 88.
64. For further reading, see Eşref, R., 'Anafarta Kumandanı Mustafa Kemal ile Mülakat (Interview with Mustafa Kemal, Commander of the Anafarta Group)', in Martı, Vol. III, p. 51.
65. Kemal, Mustafa, 'Anafartalar Hatiraları (Anafarta Memoirs)', in Martı, Vol. I, p. 89.
66. Ibid.
67. Cameron, *Sorry, Lads, But the Order Is to Go*, p. 332.
68. Kemal, Mustafa, 'Anafartalar Hatiraları (Anafarta Memoirs)', in Martı, Vol. I, p. 89.
69. Eşref, R., 'Anafarta Kumandanı Mustafa Kemal ile Mülakat (Interview with Mustafa Kemal, Commander of the Anafarta Group)', in Martı, Vol. III, p. 52.
70. This story is told in Atatürk, *Atatürk'ün Bütün Eserleri* (*Collected Works*

of Atatürk), p. 427. He later gave his smashed watch to Otto Liman von Sanders as a memento. In return, Liman von Sanders bequeathed Mustafa Kemal his own watch, which bore his ancestral family crest.

71. Mango, p. 152.
72. Atatürk, *Atatürk'ün Bütün Eserleri* (*Collected Works of Atatürk*), p. 259.
73. Carter, Diary, 11 August 1915, AWM 3DRL/6418, p. 223.
74. McLarty, Letter, 11 August 1915, AWM 3DRL/3339, p. 1.
75. Bean, *Official History of Australia in the War of 1914–1918*, Vol. II, p. 631.
76. Ibid.
77. Ibid., pp. 631–2.
78. Ashmead-Bartlett, *The Uncensored Dardanelles*, p. 196, https://openlibrary.org/books.
79. Ibid.
80. Ibid., p. 202.
81. Ibid., p 197.
82. *The West Australian*, 26 August 1915, p. 7, http://trove.nla.gov.au.
83. Ibid.
84. Younger, *Keith Murdoch*, p. 58.
85. Ibid.
86. *The Advertiser* (Adelaide), 'Russians Fighting Valorously', 19 August 1915, p. 7, http://trove.nla.gov.au.
87. *The Argus*, 24 August 1915, p. 7.
88. Hamilton, Ian, *Gallipoli Diary*, Vol. II, pp. 266–7, https://openlibrary.org/books.
89. Ibid., p. 114.
90. Ibid., pp. 116–17.
91. Bean, *Official History of Australia in the War of 1914–1918*, Vol. II, p. 419.
92. Ibid., p. 420.
93. Münim, Mustafa, '*Cepheden Cepheye* (From Front to Front)', in Martı, Vol. III, p. 429.
94. Ibid.
95. Ibid. (reported speech changed to direct speech).
96. Hogue, *Trooper Bluegum at the Dardanelles*, p. 239, https://archive.org.
97. White, War Record, NAA, B2455, Item 36/45.
98. McCarthy, *Gallipoli to the Somme*, p. 192.

CHAPTER EIGHTEEN: THE BATTLE OF HILL 60

1. James, Robert R., *Gallipoli*, p. 309.

2. Hogue, *Trooper Bluegum at the Dardanelles*, p. 173, https://archive.org.
3. Bean, *Official History of Australia in the War of 1914–1918*, Vol. II, p. 724.
4. Ibid., p. 740 (reported speech changed to direct speech).
5. Hamilton, Ian, *Gallipoli Diary*, Vol. II, p. 135, https://openlibrary.org/books.
6. Hamilton, Ian, Memorandum on Murdoch Letter, 26 November 1915, Committee of Imperial Defence, NA CAB 42/5/23, p. 12.
7. Sweetman, 'Lieutenant Hugo Throssell VC, 10th Australian Light Horse, AIF', www.thefreelibrary.com (reported speech changed to direct speech).
8. Kidd, Diary, 28 August 1915, AWM PR82/137, p. 5.
9. Kemal, Mustafa, '*Anafarta Hatiraları* (Anafarta Memoirs)', in Martı, *Çanakkale Hatiraları* (*Çanakkale Memoirs*), Vol. I, p. 105.
10. Browning and Gill, *Gallipoli to Tripoli*, p. 142.
11. *The West Australian*, 'The Story of Hill 60', 22 November 1915, p. 8, http://trove.nla.gov.au.
12. Sweetman, 'Lieutenant Hugo Throssell VC, 10th Australian Light Horse, AIF', www.thefreelibrary.com.
13. Bean, *Official History of Australia in the War of 1914–1918*, Vol. II, p. 756.
14. Ibid., p. 753.
15. Sweetman, 'Lieutenant Hugo Throssell VC, 10th Australian Light Horse, AIF', www.thefreelibrary.com.
16. Ibid.
17. Ibid.
18. Ibid.
19. Kidd, Diary, 29 August 1915, AWM PR82/137, pp. 9–10.
20. *The West Australian*, 19 May 1916, p. 6.
21. Hamilton, John, *The Price of Valour*, p. 74. (reported speech changed to direct speech).
22. *The West Australian*, 29 May 1916, p. 6 (reported speech changed to direct speech).
23. Sweetman, 'Lieutenant Hugo Throssell VC, 10th Australian Light Horse, AIF', www.thefreelibrary.com.
24. *The West Australian*, 29 May 1916, p. 6.
25. There are differing accounts of whether he shot or bayoneted the five Turks. I have concluded that he mostly used the bayonet.
26. *The West Australian*, 'The Story of Hill 60', 22 November 1915, p. 8, http://trove.nla.gov.au.
27. Kidd, Diary, 29 August 1915, AWM PR82/137, p. 17.

28. Sweetman, 'Lieutenant Hugo Throssell VC, 10th Australian Light Horse, AIF', www.thefreelibrary.com.
29. *The West Australian*, 29 May 1916, p. 6.
30. Bean, *Official History of Australia in the War of 1914–1918*, Vol. II, p. 759.
31. *The West Australian*, 29 May 1916, p. 6.
32. *The West Australian*, 'The Story of Hill 60', 22 November 1915, p. 8, http://trove.nla.gov.au.
33. Bean, *Official History of Australia in the War of 1914–1918*, Vol. II, p. 758.
34. *The West Australian*, 29 May 1916, p. 6.
35. Ibid. In the original account, it has the word 'bally' instead of 'bloody' – reflecting the sensibilities of the time.
36. *The West Australian*, 'The Story of Hill 60', 22 November 1915, p. 8, http://trove.nla.gov.au.
37. *The West Australian*, 29 May 1916, p. 6.
38. Kidd, Diary, 29 August 1915, AWM PR82/137, p. 20.
39. Sweetman, 'Lieutenant Hugo Throssell VC, 10th Australian Light Horse, AIF', www.thefreelibrary.com (reported speech changed to direct speech).
40. *The West Australian*, 29 May 1916, p. 6.
41. Ibid.
42. Sweetman, 'Lieutenant Hugo Throssell VC, 10th Australian Light Horse, AIF', www.thefreelibrary.com (reported speech changed to direct speech).
43. Bean, *Official History of Australia in the War of 1914–1918*, Vol. II, p. 760.
44. Sweetman, 'Lieutenant Hugo Throssell VC, 10th Australian Light Horse, AIF', www.thefreelibrary.com (reported speech changed to direct speech).
45. *The West Australian*, 29 May 1916, p. 6.
46. Sweetman, 'Lieutenant Hugo Throssell VC, 10th Australian Light Horse, AIF', www.thefreelibrary.com (reported speech changed to direct speech).
47. Harding, Bruce, *They Dared Mightily*, p. 50.
48. Bean, *Official History of Australia in the War of 1914–1918*, Vol. II, p. 761.
49. Watson, Diary, 30 August 1915, National Army Museum, New Zealand, 1999.3061, p. 3.
50. Bingham, Charles, Diary, 2 December 1915, Private Collection of the Bingham Family.
51. Bean, *Official History of Australia in the War of 1914–1918*, Vol. II, p. 374.

52. Carter, Diary, 30 August 1915, AWM 3DRL/6418, p. 242.
53. Ibid., 3 September 1915, p. 246.

CHAPTER NINETEEN: KEITH MURDOCH ARRIVES

1. Bean, *Official History of Australia in the War of 1914–1918*, Vol. II, p. 781.
2. Younger, *Keith Murdoch*, p. 63.
3. Hamilton, Ian, *Gallipoli Diary*, Vol. II, p. 163, https://openlibrary.org/books.
4. Ibid., pp. 164–5 (reported speech changed to direct speech).
5. Ibid., p. 241.
6. Keith Murdoch's Gallipoli letter to Andrew Fisher is available to read online at the National Library of Australia, http://nla.gov.au/nla.ms-ms2823-2-1, or in hardcopy: Murdoch, Keith, *The Gallipoli Letter*, Allen & Unwin, Sydney, 2010.
7. Thompson, Jack (Preface), in Murdoch, *The Gallipoli Letter*, p. xii.
8. Murdoch, *The Gallipoli Letter*, p. 57.
9. Ashmead-Bartlett, *The Uncensored Dardanelles*, p. 239, https://openlibrary.org/books (reported speech changed to direct speech).
10. Bean, War Diary, 6 September 1915, AWM38, 3DRL606/10/1, p. 124 (tenses and pronouns changed).
11. Moorehead, *Gallipoli*, p. 259.
12. Ashmead-Bartlett, *The Uncensored Dardanelles*, p. 239, https://openlibrary.org/books (reported speech changed to direct speech).
13. Ibid. (reported speech changed to direct speech).
14. Ashmead-Bartlett, *The Uncensored Dardanelles*, p. 239, https://openlibrary.org/books.
15. Ibid.
16. Ashmead-Bartlett to Asquith, Letter, 8 September 1915, in Ashmead-Bartlett, Diary and Papers, ML A1583, Mitchell Library, SLNSW, http://acms.sl.nsw.gov.au, pp. 245–50.
17. Hamilton, Ian, *Gallipoli Diary*, Vol. II, p. 190, https://openlibrary.org/books (reported speech changed to direct speech).
18. Ibid.
19. Throssell, Hugo to Mrs Alicia Jane Ferrier, 4 March 1916, Papers of Hugo Vivian Hope Throssell, AWM 1DRL/0581, p. 2.
20. Wiltshire, Diary, 7 September 1915, ML MSS 3058/Box 1/Item 2, p. 30, http://acms.sl.nsw.gov.au.
21. *The Sun* (Sydney), 23 May 1920, p. 3.
22. Transcript of Keith Murdoch's Evidence before Dardanelles

Commission, 5 February 1917, in Murdoch, Papers of Sir Keith Arthur Murdoch, NLA, MS 2823, Series 2, Folder 3, p. 859.

23. Younger, p. 72.
24. Hamilton, Ian, *Gallipoli Diary*, Vol. II, p. 227, https://openlibrary.org/books.
25. *The Sun* (Sydney), 23 May 1920, p. 3.
26. Ibid.
27. Ibid.
28. Ibid.
29. Ibid.
30. Murdoch, Keith Arthur to Andrew Fisher ('The Gallipoli Letter'), 23 September 1915, in Murdoch, Papers of Sir Keith Arthur Murdoch, NLA, MS 2823, Series 2, Folder 1, p. 1.
31. Ibid., p. 13.
32. Ibid., p. 18.
33. Ibid., p. 21.
34. Ibid., p. 4.
35. Ibid., p. 17.
36. Ibid., p. 23.
37. Ibid., p. 17.
38. Ibid., p. 9.
39. Ibid., pp. 13–14.
40. Ibid., p. 19.
41. *Daily Herald* (Adelaide), 'A Whirlwind of Words', 31 July 1914, p. 5, http://trove.nla.gov.au.
42. *The Sun* (Sydney), 23 May 1920, p. 3.
43. Transcript of Keith Murdoch's Evidence before Dardanelles Commission, 5 February 1917, in Murdoch, Papers of Sir Keith Arthur Murdoch, NLA, MS 2823, Series 2, Folder 3, p. 861.
44. Ibid. (reported speech changed to direct speech).
45. Colvin, *The Life of Lord Carson*, p. 85.
46. Ibid., p. 87.
47. Roskill, *Hankey*, p. 207.
48. Situation in Dardanelles: Memorandum by Secretary After Personal Visit, Pt IV, 'Remarks on Future Policy', 30 August 1915, in Lloyd George, Lloyd George Papers, United Kingdom Parliamentary Archives, LG/D/23/4/8, p. 2.
49. Copy of Letter from the Dardanelles, in ibid.
50. Moorehead, *Gallipoli*, p. 253.
51. James, Robert R., *Gallipoli*, p. 318.
52. Dardanelles Committee Meeting, 24 September 1915, NA CAB 42/3/30, p. 7.

53. Murdoch, Keith to H. H. Asquith, Letter, 25 September 1915, appended to Murdoch, Keith to Andrew Fisher ('The Gallipoli Letter'), 23 September 1915, in Murdoch, Papers of Sir Keith Arthur Murdoch (1886–1952), NLA, MS 2823, Series 2, Folder 1.

54. Murdoch, Keith to Andrew Fisher ('The Gallipoli Letter'), 23 September 1915, in Murdoch, Papers of Sir Keith Arthur Murdoch (1886–1952), NLA, MS 2823, Series 2, Folder 1, pp. 16–18.

55. Transcript of Keith Murdoch's Evidence before Dardanelles Commission, 5 February 1917, in Murdoch, Papers of Sir Keith Arthur Murdoch, NLA, MS 2823, Series 2, Folder 3, p. 862.

56. Ibid., p. 863.

57. Ashmead-Bartlett, *The Uncensored Dardanelles*, p. 252, https://openlibrary.org/books.

58. Murdoch, Keith to Lord Northcliffe, Note, 27 September 1915, in Northcliffe, Northcliffe Papers, Vol. XXVII, British Library, MS 62179.

59. Lord Northcliffe to Keith Murdoch, 30 September 1915, in ibid.

60. Ellsworth-Jones, *We Will Not Fight*, p. 57.

61. Woodward, *Field Marshal Sir William Robertson*, p. 20.

62. Carter, Diary, 26 September 1915, AWM 3DRL/6418, p. 269.

63. Ashmead-Bartlett, *The Uncensored Dardanelles*, p. 247, https://openlibrary.org/books.

64. Ibid.

65. Bean, *Gallipoli Correspondent*, p. 161.

66. McCarthy, *Gallipoli to the Somme*, p. 187.

67. Dardanelles Committee Meeting, 6 October 1915, NA CAB 42/4/3, p. 5.

68. Ibid.

69. Dardanelles Committee Meeting, 7 October 1915, NA CAB 42/4/4, p. 4.

70. Situation in Dardanelles: Memorandum by Secretary After Personal Visit, Pt IV Remarks on Future Policy, 30 August 1915, in Lloyd George, Lloyd George Papers, United Kingdom Parliamentary Archives, LG/D/23/4/8, p. 3.

71. Gilbert, *Winston S. Churchill*, Vol. III, p. 548.

72. Lloyd George, *War Memoirs*, p. 298, https://archive.org.

73. Dardanelles Committee Meeting, 11 October 1915, NA CAB 42/4/6, p. 5.

74. Ibid., p. 6.

75. Ibid., p. 9.

76. Gilbert, *Winston S. Churchill*, Vol. III, p. 550.

77. Dardanelles Committee Meeting, 11 October 1915, NA CAB 42/4/6, p. 15.
78. Ibid.
79. Gilbert, *Winston S. Churchill*, Vol. III, p. 551.
80. Ibid.
81. Hamilton, Ian, *Gallipoli Diary*, Vol. II, p. 249, https://openlibrary.org/books.
82. Ibid.
83. Ibid., p. 253.
84. Dardanelles Committee Meeting, 14 October 1915, NA CAB 42/4/9, p. 4.

CHAPTER TWENTY: TO LEAVE, OR NOT TO LEAVE, THAT IS THE QUESTION

1. King, Jonathan, *Gallipoli Diaries*, 2008, p. 293.
2. Cozens, Diary, 19 October 1915, AWM 2DRL/0002, p. 10.
3. Hamilton, Ian, *Gallipoli Diary*, Vol. II, p. 272, https://openlibrary.org/books.
4. Ibid., p. 274.
5. Ibid.
6. Ibid., p. 275.
7. Birdwood to Brudenell White (reported speech changed to direct speech), in Derham, *The Silence Ruse*, p. 19.
8. Bean, *Gallipoli Correspondent*, p. 169.
9. Hamilton, Ian, *Gallipoli Diary*, Vol. II, p. 277, https://openlibrary.org/books.
10. Hart, 'Gallipoli: The War at Sea – An Overview', p. 397, http://archive.iwm.org.uk.
11. Ibid., p. 398.
12. Aspinall-Oglander, *Military Operations*, Vol. II, p. 402.
13. Bean, *Official History of Australia in the War of 1914–1918*, Vol. II, p. 839.
14. Aspinall-Oglander, *Military Operations*, Vol. II, p. 402.
15. Churchill, Winston, *The World Crisis*, Vol. II, p. 491.
16. Ibid.
17. *The Times*, 28 October 1915, p. 7.
18. Williams, *The Battle of Anzac Ridge*, p. 135.
19. Hogue, *Trooper Bluegum at the Dardanelles*, p. 267, https://archive.org.
20. Ibid., p. 269.
21. Bean, *Official History of Australia in the War of 1914–1918*, Vol. II, p. 849.
22. Ibid., p. 838.

23. For further reading, see Stanley, Peter, *Bad Characters: Sex, Crime, Mutiny, Murder and the Australian Imperial Force.*

24. Wiltshire, Diary, 1 October 1915, ML MSS 3058/Box 1/Item 3, p. 9, http://acms.sl.nsw.gov.au.

25. Bingham, Charles, Diary, 5 November 1915, Private Collection of the Bingham Family.

26. Finlay to Director, Australian War Memorial, 9 December 1929, AWM 1DRL/0284.

27. Ibid.

28. Herbert H. Asquith to Lloyd George, 3 November 1915, in Lloyd George, Lloyd George Papers, United Kingdom Parliamentary Archives, LG/D/18/2/12, pp. 1–4.

29. James, Robert R., *Gallipoli*, p. 328.

30. Bean, *Official History of Australia in the War of 1914–1918*, Vol. II, p. 853.

31. Gardiner to his Mother, Letter, 20 November 1915, in Gardiner, Extracts of Letters from Reginald Scott Gardiner to his Mother, 1914–1915, AWM 1DRL/0304, p. 10.

32. Bean, *Frontline Gallipoli*, p. 176.

33. Birdwood, *Khaki and Gown*, p. 280.

34. Bingham, Diary, 13 November 1915, Private Collection of the Bingham Family.

35. Cameron, *Gallipoli*, p. 203.

36. Ibid., p. 204.

37. Birdwood, *Khaki and Gown*, p. 280.

38. Cassar, *Kitchener's War*, p. 252.

39. Birdwood, *Khaki and Gown*, p. 281.

40. Bean, *Official History of Australia in the War of 1914–1918*, Vol. II, p. 853.

41. Kitchener to Asquith, Telegram, 15 November 1915, War Committee Meeting, 23 November 1915, NA CAB 42/5/20, pp. 14–15.

42. Gilbert, *Winston S. Churchill*, Vol. III, p. 564.

43. Ibid., pp. 566–7.

44. Bingham, Diary, 18 November 1915, Private Collection of the Bingham Family.

45. Bean, *Bean's Gallipoli*, p. 231.

46. Bean, War Diary, 18 November 1915, AWM38, 3DRL606/20/1, p. 67.

47. Debate in the House of Lords, *Hansard*, 18 November 1915, Vol. 20, p. 409, http://hansard.millbanksystems.com.

48. Ross, 'The Secret Operations', *The Evening Post* (Wellington, New Zealand), 31 December 1915, p. 7, http://paperspast.natlib.govt.nz.

49. Kitchener to Asquith, Telegram, 22 November 1915, Mediterranean

Expeditionary Force War Diary, AWM4 1/4/8, Pt 2, p. 45.

50. War Committee Meeting, 23 November 1915, p. 10, NA CAB 42/5/20.

51. James, Robert R., *Gallipoli*, p. 336.

52. Curzon, Memorandum, 25 November 1915, Cabinet Papers, NA CAB 37/138/12, p. 7.

53. War Committee Meeting, 23 November 1915, NA CAB 42/5/20, p. 10.

54. Bean, *Official History of Australia in the War of 1914–1918*, Vol. II, p. 842.

55. Ibid., p. 861.

56. Ibid., p. 858 (tenses changed).

57. Derham, p. 20.

58. Moorehead, *Gallipoli*, p. 283.

59. Derham, p. 21.

60. Brudenell White dubbed this the 'silence ruse'. The troops called it the 'silent stunt'. Charles Bean also called it the 'Silent Battle'.

61. Carter, Herbert Gordon to Mr and Mrs H. J. Carter, Letter, 26 October 1915, AWM 1DRL/192, p. 28.

62. Bey, *Çanakkale 1915 Kanlısırt Günlüğü* (*Çanakkale 1915 Lone Pine Diary*), p. 140.

63. Ibid., p. 141.

64. Ibid.

65. Ibid., p. 142.

66. Ibid.

67. Ibid.

68. Ibid., p. 143 (reported speech changed to direct speech).

69. Bey, pp. 143–4.

70. Cameron, *Gallipoli*, p. 231.

71. Ibid. NB: I have added the word 'bloody', as the most likely word to have actually been said.

72. Ibid.

73. Bean, *Official History of Australia in the War of 1914–1918*, Vol. II, pp. 843–4.

74. Bey, p. 145.

75. Ibid.

76. Ibid.

77. Ibid.

78. Kannengiesser, p. 245.

79. Bean, *Gallipoli Mission*, p. 248.

80. Kemal, Mustafa to Salih (Bozok), 11 October 1915, in Atatürk, *Atatürk'ün Bütün Eserleri* (*Collected Works of Atatürk*), p. 272.

81. Mango, *Atatürk*, p. 155.

82. White, Brudenell, 'Note on the Withdrawal of Anzac', AWM 3DRL/1400, Series 4, Wallet 3, p. 4.
83. Carlyon, *Gallipoli*, p. 520.
84. Kannengiesser, p. 239.
85. For further reading, see James, Robert R., *Gallipoli*, p. 335.
86. Birdwood, *Khaki and Gown*, p. 284.
87. White, Brudenell, 'Note on the Withdrawal of Anzac', AWM 3DRL/1400, Series 4, Wallet 3, p. 4.
88. 'Selected Excerpts of the Original Evacuation', in Derham, p. 272.
89. Ibid.
90. Ibid., pp. 273–4.
91. John Cargill, Track 7, Sailah, *Stories from Gallipoli*, ABC Audio.
92. Cameron, *Gallipoli*, p. 233.
93. Birdwood, *Khaki and Gown*, p. 286.
94. Hart, 'Gallipoli: The War at Sea – An Overview', p. 412.
95. Ibid. (reported speech changed to direct speech).
96. James, Robert R., *Gallipoli*, p. 336.
97. Bingham, Diary, 7 December 1915, Private Collection of the Bingham Family.
98. Ibid., 29 November 1915.

CHAPTER TWENTY-ONE: GO GENTLE INTO THAT GOOD NIGHT

1. McCarthy, *Gallipoli to the Somme*, p. 78.
2. Asquith, Prime Minister to King George V, Letter, undated, R/256, NA CAB 37/139/17, pp. 2–3. I presume this letter was written some time after the Cabinet meeting on 7 December and before orders to evacuate were sent out the following morning.
3. Bean, *Official History of Australia in the War of 1914–1918*, Vol. II, p. 863.
4. Ibid., p. 864.
5. Bean, *Gallipoli Mission*, p. 244.
6. Kemal, Mustafa to Hilda Christianus, 6 June 1915, in Atatürk, *Atatürk'ün Bütün Eserleri* (*Collected Works of Atatürk*), p. 225.
7. Hogue, *Trooper Bluegum at the Dardanelles*, p. 271, https://archive.org.
8. Ibid., p. 272.
9. Cameron, *Gallipoli*, p. 257.
10. Bean, *Two Men I Knew*, p. 113.
11. McCarthy, *Gallipoli to the Somme*, p. 198.
12. Gilbert, *Winston S. Churchill*, Vol. III, p. 608.
13. Bean, War Diary, night of 15 December 1915, AWM38 3DRL606/21/1, p. 74.

14. Bean, *Bean's Gallipoli*, p. 249.
15. Bean, *Official History of Australia in the War of 1914–1918*, Vol. II, p. 884.
16. Ibid., p. 898.
17. Bingham, Diary, 15 December 1915, Private Collection of the Bingham Family.
18. Ryrie, Granville to Mrs Granville Ryrie, 23 December 1915, AWM PR84/193, pp. 202–3.
19. Bean, *Bean's Gallipoli*, p. 252.
20. Hogue, *Trooper Bluegum at the Dardanelles*, p. 275, https://archive.org.
21. Bean, *Bean's Gallipoli*, p. 253.
22. Bingham, Diary, 5 November 1915, Private Collection of the Bingham Family.
23. Derham, *The Silence Ruse*, p. 33 (Special Army Order, Headquarters Dardanelles Army, 18 December 1915).
24. Bean, *Official History of Australia in the War of 1914–1918*, Vol. I, Preface, p. xlviii (tenses changed).
25. Ibid., Vol. II, p. 910.
26. Bean, *Bean's Gallipoli*, p. 254.
27. Ibid., p. 255.
28. Steel, Arthur Valentine (1st Battalion AIF), Letter to Marie and George Steel, January 1916, courtesy of Steel family of Wangaratta, with thanks. And I thank them for allowing me to publish it.
29. Bean, War Diary, 18 December 1915, AWM38, 3DRL606/23/1, p. 34.
30. Birdwood, *Khaki and Gown*, p. 240.
31. Ibid., p. 289.
32. Ibid.
33. Moorehead, *Gallipoli*, p. 288.
34. Steel, Arthur Valentine (1st Battalion AIF), Letter to Marie and George Steel, January 1916, courtesy of Steel family of Wangaratta, with thanks. And I thank them for allowing me to publish it.
35. Bean, *Official History of Australia in the War of 1914–1918*, Vol. II, p. 899. So, at least, did Zeki Bey tell Bean after the war.
36. White, Brudenell, 'ANZAC 4pm 19th–4am 20th December 1915', 20 December 1915, in Papers of General Sir Cyril Bingham Brudenell White, AWM 3DRL/1400, Series 4, Wallet 3, p. 2.
37. Ibid.
38. Ibid., p. 1.
39. Carter, Diary, 19–20 December 1915, AWM 3DRL/6418, p. 354.
40. Caulfield, *The Unknown Anzacs*, p. 161.
41. For further reading, see Bean, *Official History of Australia in the War of 1914–1918*, Vol. II, p. 883.

42. Wiltshire, Diary, 20 December 1915, ML MSS 3058/Box 1/Items 2–4, p. 19, http://acms.sl.nsw.gov.au.
43. Hogue, *Trooper Bluegum at the Dardanelles*, p. 278, https://archive.org.
44. Ibid.
45. Ibid.
46. Ibid.
47. Wiltshire, Diary, 20 December 1915, ML MSS 3058/Box 1/Items 2–4, p. 19, http://acms.sl.nsw.gov.au.
48. Bean, *Official History of Australia in the War of 1914–1918*, Vol. II, p. 870.
49. Barwick, Diary, ML MSS 1493/1/Box 1/Item 1, p. 262, http://acms.sl.nsw.gov.au.
50. Serle, *John Monash*, p. 250.
51. Dolan, *Gallipoli Air War*, p. 358.
52. Wiltshire, Diary, 20 December 1915, ML MSS 3058/Box 1/Item 4, p. 17, http://acms.sl.nsw.gov.au.
53. Hogue, *Trooper Bluegum at the Dardanelles*, p. 278, https://archive.org.
54. Steel, Arthur Valentine (1st Battalion AIF), Letter to Marie and George Steel, January 1916, courtesy of Steel family of Wangaratta, with thanks. And I thank them for allowing me to publish it.
55. Caddy, 'Last Shot on Anzac', *Reveille*, Vol. VI, No. 4, 1 December 1932, p. 38.
56. Ibid.
57. Bean, *Official History of Australia in the War of 1914–1918*, Vol. II, pp. 895–6.
58. Caddy, 'Last Shot on Anzac', *Reveille*, Vol. VI, No. 4, 1 December 1932, p. 38.
59. Colonel Zeki later told Charles Bean that the last Turks to die at Anzac were the 70 men sitting atop this explosion on the Nek.
60. For further reading, see Bean, *Official History of Australia in the War of 1914–1918*, Vol. II, p. 896.
61. Bingham, Diary, 2 December 1915, Private Collection of the Bingham Family.
62. White, Brudenell, 'ANZAC 4pm 19th–4am 20th December 1915', 20 December 1915, in Papers of General Sir Cyril Bingham Brudenell White, AWM 3DRL/1400, Series 4, Wallet 3, p. 14.
63. Bean, War Diary, 20 December, AWM38 3DRL606/22/1, p. 46.
64. McCarthy, p. 204.
65. Broadbent, *The Boys Who Came Home*, p. 127.
66. Ibid.
67. White, Brudenell, 'ANZAC 4pm 19th–4am 20th December 1915',

20 December 1915, in Papers of General Sir Cyril Bingham Brudenell White, AWM 3DRL/1400, Series 4, Wallet 3, p. 14.

EPILOGUE

1. Monash, John to Hannah Monash, 18 June 1915, Sir Monash Papers, SLV, MS 13875, Box 4083/1, p. 86.
2. Jack Nicholson, Track 5, Sailah, *Stories from Gallipoli*, ABC Audio.
3. Broadbent, *The Boys Who Came Home*, p. 130.
4. Ekins, *Gallipoli Strengths and Casualties*.
5. Australian War Memorial, 'The Anzac Day Tradition', www.awm. gov.au.
6. *The Queenslander*, 29 April 1916, p. 36.
7. Ibid.
8. *The Bathurst Times*, 26 April 1916, p. 2.
9. *The Farmer & Settler*, 8 August 1916, p. 2.
10. Bantick, 'What Lies Beneath a National Legend', *The Australian*, 24 April 2010, p. 5, www.theaustralian.com.au.
11. By this time, his name had become Aspinall-Oglander – courtesy of marrying Florence Joan Oglander of the famous Isle of Wight dynasty in 1927.
12. Thomson, 'History and "Betrayal": The Anzac Controversy', *History Today*, 1 January 1993, Vol. 43, Issue 1, p. 8.
13. Ibid.
14. Bean, War Diary, 25 April 1915, AWM38, 3DRL606/5/1, p. 37.
15. Bean, *Official History of Australia in the War of 1914–1918*, Vol. I, p. 462.
16. Thomson, *History Today*, 1 January 1993, Vol. 43, Issue 1, p. 9.
17. Ibid., p. 10.
18. *Daily Guardian* (Sydney), 7 October 1927; *Daily Express*, 8 October 1927, in Bean, War Records of Charles E. W. Bean, AWM 3DRL 7953, Item 29, 3.
19. O'Neill, Margot, 'Legend of Gallipoli', *Lateline*, 23 April 2001, http:// www.abc.net.au/lateline/stories/s281842.htm.
20. *Brisbane Courier*, 8 October 1927, p. 17.
21. Ibid.
22. Hetherington, *Blamey, Controversial Soldier*, p. 133.
23. 'The Final Report of the Dardanelles Commission', HMSO, p. 86.
24. Ibid.
25. Ibid., p. 87.
26. 'The First Report of the Dardanelles Commission', HMSO, p. 43.

27. Osmańczyk, *Encyclopedia of the United Nations and International Agreements*, p. 2107.

28. Arthur, *Life of Lord Kitchener*, p. 355.

29. *The Herald* (Melbourne), 18 May 1920, in Murdoch, Papers of Sir Keith Arthur Murdoch (1886–1952), NLA, MS2823, Series 2, Folder 3.

30. Andrews, Eric M., *The Anzac Illusion*, p. 119. NB: Fisher did not sign off on the Dardanelles Commission's final report because his duties as High Commissioner of Australia prevented him giving adequate time to the investigation.

31. Younger, *Keith Murdoch*, p. 74.

32. Lisners, *The Rise and Fall of the Murdoch Empire*, p. 92.

33. Albeit in an Acting Director role.

34. Perry, W., 'Field Marshal Lord Birdwood of Anzac', *Sabretache*, Vol. 29, February–March 1988, No. 1, p. 8.

35. Birdwood, *Khaki and Gown*, p. 296.

36. Ibid.

37. For further reading, see James, Robert R., 'Birdwood, William Riddell, first Baron Birdwood (1865–1951)', *Oxford Dictionary of National Biography*, May 2009, www.oxforddnb.com.

38. Montgomery, *A History of Warfare*, p. 494.

39. Bean, *Two Men I Knew*, p. xi.

40. For further reading, see Hazlehurst, Cameron, *Ten Journeys to Cameron's Farm*, pp. 139–160.

41. Derham, *The Silence Ruse*, p. viii.

42. Hill, A. J., 'Sinclair-Maclagan, Ewen George (1868–1948)', http://adb. anu.edu.au.

43. Burness, *The Nek*, p. 144.

44. Hamilton, John, *The Price of Valour*, p. 121.

45. Throssell, Hugo, Papers, NAA, PP645/1, M5273, p. 76.

46. Bean, *Official History of Australia in the War of 1914–1918*, Vol. III, p. 720.

47. *The Advertiser* (Adelaide), 'Jacka, V.C. Dead', 18 January 1932, p. 9, http://trove.nla.gov.au.

48. *Reveille*, 'Visit to V.C.'s Grave', February 1941, p. 11.

49. Hogue, *Trooper Bluegum at the Dardanelles*, p. 57, https://archive.org.

50. Brenchley and Brenchley, *Stoker's Submarine*, p. 81.

51. Beşikçi, *The Ottoman Mobilization of Manpower in the First World War*, p. 11.

52. Tehlirian, Soghomon, Trial Transcripts, 16 April 1921, 3rd State Court, Criminal Department, Berlin, www.cilicia.com/armo_tehlirian.html.

53. Ibid.

54. Cranston, 'Turkey, Australia Come Together for Dedications', *The Canberra Times*, 26 April 1985, p. 15, http://trove.nla.gov.au.

55. Monash, John to Hannah Monash, 18 June 1915, Sir Monash Papers, SLV, MS 13875, Box 4083/1, p. 86.

56. *The Sydney Morning Herald*, 27 April 1990, p. 5.

57. Ibid.

BIBLIOGRAPHY

Initials used:

ADM	Admiralty
AWM	Australian War Memorial, Canberra
HMSO	His Majesty's Stationery Office, Kew, London
ML	Mitchell Library, Sydney
NA	National Archives, Kew, London
NAA	National Archives of Australia, Canberra
SLQ	State Library of Queensland, Brisbane
SLNSW	State Library of New South Wales, Sydney

BOOKS

Aksakal, Mustafa, *The Ottoman Road to War in 1914: The Ottoman Empire and the First World War*, Cambridge University Press, Cambridge, 2008

Alington, Argentine F., *The Lamps Go Out: 1914 and the Outbreak of War*, Faber & Faber, London, 1962

Anderson, Fay and Trembath, Richard, *Witnesses to War: The History of Australian Conflict Reporting*, Melbourne University Press, Melbourne, 2011

Andrews, Eric M., *The Anzac Illusion: Anglo-Australian Relations During World War I*, Cambridge University Press, Cambridge, 1993

Anonymous ('By a British Officer Who Has Served in It'), *The German Army from Within*, Hodder and Stoughton, London, 1914

Arthur, Sir George, *Life of Lord Kitchener*, Vol. III, Macmillan and Co., London, 1920

Aspinall-Oglander, Cecil F., *History of the Great War, Military Operations Gallipoli*, Vol. II, Imperial War Museum, London, 1992

——, *Military Operations: Gallipoli*, Vol. I, William Heinemann, London, 1929

——, *Military Operations: Gallipoli*, Vol. II, William Heinemann, London, 1932

Asquith, Herbert H., *H. H. Asquith Letters to Venetia Stanley*, Brock, Eleanor and Brock, Michael (eds), Oxford University Press, Oxford, 1982

——, *Memories and Reflections, 1852–1927*, Vol. II, Cassell & Co., London, 1928

Ataksor, Halis, *Çanakkale Raporu (Çanakkale Report)*, Timaş Yayınları, Istanbul, 2008

Atatürk, Mustafa Kemal, *Atatürk'ün Bütün Eserleri (Collected Works of Atatürk)*, Vol. I, '1903–1915', Kaynak Yayınları, Istanbul, 1998

Bayur, Yavuz H., *Türk Inkilâbı Tarihi (History of the Turkish Revolution)*, Vol. II, Türk Tarih Kurmu Basım Evi, Ankara, 1945

Bean, Charles E. W., *Anzac to Amiens: A Shorter History of the Australian Fighting Services in the First World War*, Australian War Memorial, Canberra, 1946

——, *Bean's Gallipoli: The Diaries of Australia's Official War Correspondent*, Fewster, Kevin (ed.), 3rd ed., Allen & Unwin, Sydney, 2007

——, *Frontline Gallipoli: C. E. W. Bean, Diaries from the Trenches*, Fewster, Kevin (ed.), Allen & Unwin, Sydney, 1990

——, *Gallipoli Correspondent: The Frontline Diary of C. E. W. Bean*, Fewster, Kevin (ed.), Allen & Unwin, Sydney, 1983

——, *Gallipoli Mission*, 1st ed., Australian War Memorial, Canberra, 1952

——, *Official History of Australia in the War of 1914–1918*, Vol. I, 'The Story of ANZAC from the Outbreak of War to the End of the First Phase of the Gallipoli Campaign, 4 May 1915', 11th ed., Angus & Robertson, Sydney, 1933

——, *Official History of Australia in the War of 1914–1918*, Vol. II, 'The Story of ANZAC from 4 May 1915 to the Evacuation of the Gallipoli Peninsula', 6th ed., Angus & Robertson, Sydney, 1938

——, *Official History of Australia in the War of 1914–1918*, Vol. III, 'The Australian Imperial Force in France, 1916', 12th ed., Angus & Robertson, Sydney, 1941

——, *Two Men I Knew: William Bridges and Brudenell White, Founders of the A.I.F.*, Angus & Robertson, Sydney, 1957

Belford, Walter C., *'Eleven-Legs': Being the Story of the 11th Battalion (AIF) in the Great War of 1914–1918*, Imperial Printing Company, Perth, 1940

Benson, Irving, *The Man with the Donkey: John Simpson Kirkpatrick, The Good Samaritan of Gallipoli*, Hodder and Stoughton, London, 1965

Berrie, George L., *Under Furred Hats (6th ALH Regt)*, Naval & Military Press, London, 2009

Beşikçi, Mehmet, *The Ottoman Mobilization of Manpower in the First World War*, Brill, Boston, 2012

Bey, Mehmed Fasih, *Çanakkale 1915 Kanlısırt Günlüğü: Mehmed Fasih Bey'in Günlüğü* (*Çanakkale 1915 Lone Pine Diary: Mehmed Fasih Bey's Diary*), Denizler Kitabevi, Istanbul, 2006

Bilgin, Ismail, *Çanakkale Savaşı Günlüğü* (*Çanakkale War Diary*), Timaş Yayınları, Istanbul, 2009

Birdwood, William R., *Khaki and Gown: An Autobiography*, Ward, Lock & Co., London, 1941

——, *In My Time: Recollections and Anecdotes*, Skeffington, London, 1945

Blake, Robert and Louis, William R. (eds), *Churchill*, Oxford University Press, Oxford, 2002

Bonham Carter, Violet, *Winston Churchill As I Knew Him*, Eyre & Spottiswoode and Collins, London, 1965

Brenchley, Fred and Brenchley, Elizabeth, *Stoker's Submarine: Australia's Daring Raid on the Dardanelles on the Day of the Gallipoli Landing*, HarperCollins, Sydney, 2001

Broadbent, Harvey, *The Boys Who Came Home: Recollections of Gallipoli*, ABC Books, Sydney, 1990

——, *Gallipoli: The Fatal Shore*, Penguin, Melbourne, 2005

Brock, Eleanor and Brock, Michael (eds), *Margot Asquith's Great War Diary 1914–1916: The View from Downing Street*, Oxford University Press, Oxford, 2014

Browning, Neville and Gill, Ian, *Gallipoli to Tripoli: History of the 10th Light Horse Regiment A.I.F. 1914–1919*, Hesperian Press, Perth, 2012

Bull, Stephen, *Battle Tactics: Trench Warfare*, Casemate, Havertown (PA), 2003

Burness, Peter, *The Nek: A Gallipoli Tragedy*, Pen and Sword Military, Barnsley, 2013

Butler, Arthur G., *Official History of the Australian Army Medical Services, 1914–1918*, Vol. I, Pt I, 2nd ed., Australian War Memorial, Canberra, 1938

Butler, Daniel A., *Shadow of the Sultan's Realm: The Destruction of the Ottoman Empire and the Creation of the Modern Middle East*, Potomac Books, Washington DC, 2011

Cameron, David W., *25 April 1915: The Day the Anzac Legend was Born*, Allen & Unwin, Sydney, 2007

——, *Gallipoli: The Final Battles and Evacuation of Anzac*, Big Sky Publishing, Sydney, 2011

——, *Shadows of Anzac: An Intimate History of Gallipoli*, Big Sky Publishing, Sydney, 2013

——, *Sorry, Lads, But the Order Is to Go: The August Offensive, Gallipoli 1915*, UNSW Press, Sydney, 2009

Carlyle, Thomas, *Memoirs of the Life and Writings of Thomas Carlyle*, Shepherd, Richard Herne and Williamson, Charles Norris (eds), Vol. 2, W. H. Allen, London, 1881

Carlyon, Les, *Gallipoli*, Pan Macmillan, Sydney, 2001

Cassar, George H., *Kitchener's War: British Strategy from 1914 to 1916*, Brassey's, Washington DC, 2004

Caulfield, Michael, *The Unknown Anzacs: The Real Stories of our National Legend*, Hachette, Sydney, 2013

Cavill, Harold W., *Imperishable Anzacs: A Story of the Famous First Brigade, from the Diary of Private Harold Walter Cavill*, Williams Brooks, Sydney, 1916

Churchill, Randolph, *Winston S. Churchill*, Vol. II, *Companion*, Pt I, '1901–1907', Heinemann, London, 1966

——, *Winston S. Churchill*, Vol. II, *Companion*, Pt III, '1911–1914', Heinemann, London, 1969

Churchill, Winston, *The World Crisis*, Vols I, II, Thornton Butterworth, London, 1923

Clark, Charles M. H., *A History of Australia*, Vol. V, 'The People Make Laws (1888–1915)', Melbourne University Press, Melbourne, 1981

Clews, Graham T., *Churchill's Dilemma: The Real Story Behind the Origins of the 1915 Dardanelles Campaign*, Praeger Publishers, Santa Barbara (CA), 2010

Cochrane, Peter, *Simpson and the Donkey: The Making of a Legend*, Melbourne University Press, Melbourne, 1992

Colvin, Ian, *The Life of Lord Carson*, Vol. III, Victor Gollancz, London, 1936

Correspondence Regarding the Overseas Assistance Afforded to His Majesty's Government by His Majesty's Overseas Dominions, T. Fisher Unwin, London, 1914

Çulcu, Murat, *Ikdam Gazetesi'nde Çanakkale Cephesi (The Çanakkale Front According to Ikdam Newspaper)*, Vol. I, Kaptan Yayıncılık, Istanbul, 2004

Cunneen, Christopher, *Kings' Men: Australia's Governors-General from Hopetoun to Isaacs*, Allen & Unwin, Sydney, 1983

Czech-Jochberg, Erich, *Die Verantwortlichen im Weltkrieg (The Responsible Ones in a World War)*, K. F. Koehler, Leipzig, 1932

Danışman, H. Basri, *Gallipoli 1915 Day One Plus . . . 27th Ottoman Inf. Regt. vs. ANZACS: Based on Account of Lt. Col. Şefik Aker Commander of 27th Inf. Regt*, Denizler Kitabevi, Istanbul, 2007

Derham, Rosemary, *The Silence Ruse: Escape from Gallipoli – A Record and Memory of the Life of General Sir Brudenell White*, Oryx Publishing, Melbourne, 2000

DeWeerd, Harvey A., *President Wilson Fights His War: World War I and the American Intervention*, Macmillan, New York, 1968

Dolan, H., *Gallipoli Air War: The Unknown Story of the Fight for the Skies over Gallipoli*, Pan Macmillan, Sydney, 2013

Downing, Walter H., *Digger Dialects: A Collection of Slang Phrases Used by the Australian Soldiers on Active Service*, Lothian Book Publishing Company, Melbourne, 1919

Drummond, Helga, *The Art of Decision Making: Mirrors of Imagination, Masks of Fate*, John Wiley & Sons, New York, 2002

Dülger, Bahadır, *AE2 Denizalti Gemisini Nasil Batirdim (How I Sunk the AE2 Submarine)*, Millet Yayını, Istanbul, 1947

Ekins, Ashley, *Gallipoli Strengths and Casualties*, AWM, Canberra, 2014

——, *War Wounds: Medicine and the Trauma of Conflict*, Stewart, Elizabeth (ed.), Exisle Publishing, Wollombi (NSW), 2011

Ellsworth-Jones, Will, *We Will Not Fight: The Untold Story of the First World War's Conscientious Objectors*, Aurum Press, London, 2007

Erickson, Edward J., *Defeat in Detail: The Ottoman Army in the Balkans, 1912–1913*, Praeger Publishers, Westport (CT), 2003

——, *Gallipoli: The Ottoman Campaign*, Pen and Sword Military, Barnsley, 2010

——, *Ordered to Die: A History of the Ottoman Army in the First World War*, Greenwood Press, Westport (CT), 2000

Fenwick, Percival, *Gallipoli Diary: 24 April–27 June*, David Ling, Auckland, 2000

Firkins, Peter C., *The Australians in Nine Wars: Waikato to Long Tan*, McGraw-Hill, New York, 1972

Fisher, John A., *Fear God and Dread Nought: The Correspondence of Admiral of the Fleet Lord Fisher of Kilverstone*, Vol. III, 'Restoration, Abdication, and Last Years, 1914–1920', Marder, Arthur (ed.), Jonathan Cape, London, 1952

Frame, Tom, *The Shores of Gallipoli: Naval Dimensions of the Anzac Campaign*, Hale & Iremonger, Sydney, 2000

Freely, John, *The Western Shores of Turkey: Discovering the Aegean and Mediterranean Coasts*, Tauris Parke, London, 2004

French, John D. P., *1914*, Constable and Company, London, 1919

Gilbert, Martin, *Winston S. Churchill*, Vol. III, '1914–1916', Heinemann, London, 1971

——, *Winston S. Churchill*, Vol. III, *Companion*, Pt I, 'Documents, July 1914–April 1915', Heinemann, London, 1972

——, *Winston S. Churchill*, Vol. III, *Companion*, Pt II, 'Documents, May 1915–December 1916', Heinemann, London, 1972

Glenny, Misha, *The Balkans: Nationalism, War, and the Great Powers, 1804–2011*, updated ed., Penguin Books, New York, 2012

Gorman, Eugene, Johnson, Carl and Braddock, Kristine (eds), *With the Twenty-Second: A History of the Twenty-Second Battalion, A.I.F.*, revised edition, Jenkin Buxton Printers & Inhouse Research and Publications, Melbourne, 2001

Hamilton, Ian B. M. (Sir Hamilton's nephew), *The Happy Warrior: A Life of General Sir Ian Hamilton*, Cassell, London, 1966

Hamilton, John, *Goodbye Cobber, God Bless You*, Pan Macmillan, Sydney, 2004

——, *The Price of Valour*, Pan Macmillan, Sydney, 2012

Hanioğlu, M. Şükrü, *Atatürk: An Intellectual Biography*, Princeton University Press, Princeton, 2011

Hankey, Lord Maurice P. A., *The Supreme Command: 1914–1918*, Vol. I, George Allen & Unwin, London, 1961

Harding, Bruce, *They Dared Mightily*, AWM, Canberra, 1963

Hargrave, John, *The Suvla Bay Landing*, MacDonald, London, 1964

Hazlehurst, Cameron, *Ten Journeys to Cameron's Farm: An Australian Tragedy*, ANU Press, Canberra, 2013

Herbert, A., *Mons, Anzac and Kut*, Edward Arnold, London, 1919

Hetherington, John, *Blamey, Controversial Soldier: A Biography of Field Marshal Sir Thomas Blamey, GBE, KCB, CMG, DSO, ED*, AWM, Canberra, 1973

Hogue, Oliver ('Trooper Bluegum'), *Love Letters of an Anzac*, 3rd ed., Andrew Melrose Ltd, London, 1916

Holland, Chris and Jordan, Tony, *The Story Behind the Monument: The 29th Division in Warwickshire and North Oxfordshire, January–March 1915*, Stretton Millennium History Group, Coventry, 2005

Horne, Charles F. (ed.), *Source Records of the Great War*, Vols I–III, National Alumni, Cambridge University Library, Cambridge, 1923

Hough, Richard A., *The Great War at Sea: 1914–18*, Oxford University Press, Oxford, 1983

Howard, Fred, *On Three Battle Fronts*, Vechten Waring Company, New York, 1918

Hurst, James, *Game to the Last: The 11th Australian Infantry Battalion at Gallipoli*, Big Sky Publishing, Sydney, 2011

Idriess, Ion L., *The Desert Column*, Angus & Robertson, Sydney, 1932

Iğdemir, Uluğ, *Atatürk'ün Yaşamı (Life of Atatürk)*, Vol. I, 1881–1918, Turk Tarih Kurumu Basımevi, Ankara, 1980

Ilhan, Mehdi and Yumuşak, Ibrahim (eds), *Gelibolu: Tarih, Efsane ve Ani (Gallipoli: History, Legend and Memory)*, Istanbul Medeniyet University, Istanbul, 2012

Jackh, Ernest, *The Rising Crescent: Turkey Yesterday, Today, and Tomorrow*, Farrar & Rinehart, New York, 1944

James, Lawrence, *Churchill and Empire: Portrait of an Imperialist*, Weidenfeld & Nicolson, London, 2013

James, Robert R., *Gallipoli*, Pimlico, London, 1999

Jose, Arthur W., *Official History of Australia in the War of 1914–1918*, Vol. IX, 'The Royal Australian Navy, 1914–1918', Bean, Charles E. W. (ed.), 9th ed., Angus & Robertson, Sydney, 1941

Juvenis (pseud.), *Suvla Bay and After*, Hodder and Stoughton, London, 1916

Kannengiesser, Hans, *The Campaign in Gallipoli*, Major C. J. P. Ball (trans.), Naval & Military Press, East Sussex, 2011

Kautsky, Karl, *Outbreak of the World War*, Montgelas, Max and Schucking, Walther (eds), Oxford University Press, New York, 1924

Keating, Paul, *Major Speeches of the First Year*, Australian Labor Party, Canberra, 1993

Kennedy, John J., *The Whale Oil Guards*, James Duffy and Co., Dublin, 1919

Kent, D. (ed.), *Trench and Troopship: The Experiences of the Australian Imperial Force, 1914–1919*, Hale and Iremonger, Sydney, 1999

Keyes, Sir Roger, *The Keyes Papers*, Vol. I, '1914–1918', Allen & Unwin for the Navy Records Society, Sydney, 1979

——, *The Naval Memoirs of Admiral of the Fleet: The Narrow Seas to the Dardanelles, 1910–1915*, Thornton Butterworth, London, 1934

King, Jonathan, *Gallipoli Diaries: The Anzacs' Own Story Day by Day*, 2nd ed., Kangaroo Press, Sydney, 2003

——, *Gallipoli Diaries: The Anzacs' Own Story Day by Day*, 2nd ed., Simon & Schuster, Sydney, 2008

Kinloch, Terry, *Echoes of Gallipoli: In the Words of New Zealand's Mounted Riflemen*, Exile Publishing, Auckland, 2005

Laffin, John, *Damn the Dardanelles: The Story of Gallipoli*, Osprey, London, 1980

Liddell Hart, Basil H., *A History of the First World War*, Pan Books, London, 1973

Lisners, John, *The Rise and Fall of the Murdoch Empire*, John Blake Publishing, London, 2013

Lochner, R. K., *Die Kaperfahrten des kleinen Kreuzers Emden: Tatsachenbericht (The Naval Boardings of the Small Cruiser Emden: A Factual Report)*, Wilhelm Heyne Verlag, Munich, 1979

Mackenzie, Compton, *Gallipoli Memories*, Cassell & Co., London, 1929

Malone, William G., *No Better Death: The Great War Diary and Letters of William G. Malone*, Crawford, John and Cooke, Peter (eds), Reed Books, Auckland, 2005

Mango, Andrew, *Atatürk: The Biography of the Modern Founder of Turkey*, The Overlook Press, New York, 2000

Marder, Arthur, *From the Dreadnought to Scapa Flow: The Royal Navy in the Fisher Era, 1904–1919*, Vol. II, 'The War Years: To the Eve of Jutland', Oxford University Press, London, 1965

Martı, Metin (ed.), *Çanakkale Hatıraları (Çanakkale Memoirs)*, Vols I–III, Arma Yayınları, Istanbul, 2005

Massie, Robert K., *Castles of Steel: Britain, Germany and the Winning of the Great War at Sea*, Random House, New York, 2004

McCarthy, Dudley, *Gallipoli to the Somme: The Story of C. E. W. Bean*, John Ferguson, Sydney, 1983

McMullen, Ross, *Pompey Elliott*, Scribe, Melbourne, 2008

The Men of Anzac, *The Anzac Book*, 3rd ed., AWM, University of New South Wales Press, Sydney, 2010

Monash, John, *War Letters of General Monash*, Angus & Robertson, Sydney, 1935

Montgomery, Bernard, *A History of Warfare: Field-Marshal Viscount Montgomery of Alamein*, World Publishing Company, London, 1968

Moorehead, Alan, *Gallipoli*, Wordsworth Editions, Hertfordshire, 1998

Morgan, Ted, *Churchill: Young Man in a Hurry, 1874–1915*, Simon & Schuster, New York, 1984

Murdoch, Keith, *The Gallipoli Letter*, Allen & Unwin, Sydney, 2010

Nevinson, Henry W., *The Dardanelles Campaign*, Nisbet & Co., London, 1918

The New Partridge Dictionary of Slang and Unconventional English, Vol. II, Dalzell, Tom and Victor, Terry (eds), Routledge, Oxford, 2006

Olden, Arthur C. N., *Westralian Cavalry in the War: The Story of the Tenth Light Horse Regiment, A.I.F., in the Great War, 1914–1918*, Alexander McCubbin, Melbourne, 1921

Oral, H., *Gallipoli 1915: Through Turkish Eyes*, Türkiye İş Bankası Kültür Yayınları, Istanbul, 2007

Örnek, Tolga and Toker, Feza, *Gallipoli: The Front Line Experience*, 2nd ed., Currency Press, Sydney, 2006

Osmańczyk, Edmund J., *Encyclopedia of the United Nations and International Agreements*, Vol. III, 'N to S', Mango, Anthony (ed.), Routledge, New York, 2003

Paterson, Andrew B., *Song of the Pen, A. B. 'Banjo' Paterson: Complete Works 1901–1941*, Campbell, Rosamund, Harvie, Philippa (eds), Lansdowne Press, Sydney, 1983

Pelvin, Richard, *Royal Australian Navy*, Department of Veterans Affairs, Canberra, 2011

Pollock, J., *Kitchener: Comprising The Road to Omdurman and Saviour of the Realm*, Constable, London, 2001

Pound, Reginald and Harmsworth, Geoffrey, *Northcliffe*, Cassell, London, 1959

Prigge, Erich R., *Liman von Sanders Paşa'nin Emir Subayı Binbaşı Erich R. Prigge'nin Çanakkale Savaşı Günlüğü (Çanakkale War Diary of Major Erich Prigge, Liman von Sanders' Aide-de-Camp)*, Timaş Yayınları, Istanbul, 2011

Pugsley, Christopher, *Gallipoli: The New Zealand Story*, Reed Publishing, Auckland, 1998

Refik, I., *Çanakkale'nin Ruh Portresi (A Portrait of Çanakkale's Spirit)*, Albatros Yayınları, Turkey, 1998

The Returned Soldiers Association, *ANZAC Memorial*, 2nd ed., Sydney, 1917

Richards, Tom, *Wallaby Warrior: The World War I Diaries of Australia's Only British Lion*, Growden, Greg (ed.), Allen & Unwin, Sydney, 2013

Riddell, George A., *Lord Riddell's War Diary*, Ivor Nicholson and Watson, London, 1933

Robertson, John, *Anzac and Empire: The Tragedy and Glory of Gallipoli*, Hamlyn Australian, Melbourne, 1990

Roskill, Stephen W., *Hankey: Man of Secrets*, Vol. I, '1877–1918', St Martin's Press, New York, 1970

Rowse, Alfred L., *The Later Churchills*, Macmillan, London, 1958

Royal Australian Navy: Australians in World War I, Department of Veterans Affairs, Canberra, 2011

Sabri, Mahmut, *Seddülbahir'in Ilk Şanlı Müdafaası: 26 Alay III Tabur'un Muharebesi (The First Glorious Defence of Seddülbahir: Battle of the 3rd Battalion, 26th Regiment)*, Yeni Anadolu Matbaası, Konya, 1933

Samson, Charles R., *Fights and Flights*, Ernest Benn, London, 1930

Sanders, Liman von, *Five Years in Turkey*, The United States Naval Institute, Annapolis, 1927

Sandford, A. H., *Key to Infantry Training*, Critchely Parker, 1915

Scott, Ernest, *Official History of Australia in the War of 1914–1918*, Vol. XI, 'Australia During the War', Bean, Charles E. W. (ed.), 7th ed., University of Queensland Press, Brisbane, 1941

Scott, John D., *Vickers: A History*, Weidenfeld & Nicolson, London, 1962

Seal, Graham, *Great Anzac Stories: The Men and Women Who Created the Digger Legend*, Allen & Unwin, Sydney, 2013

——, *Inventing Anzac: The Digger and National Mythology*, University of Queensland Press, Brisbane, 2004

——, *The Lingo: Listening to Australian English*, UNSW Press, Sydney, 1999

Serle, Geoffrey, *John Monash: A Biography*, Melbourne University Press, Melbourne, 1985

Shakespeare, William, *Julius Caesar*, Macmillan and Co., London, 1890

Silas, Ellis, *Crusading at Anzac: Pictured and Described by Signaller Ellis Silas, A Soldier–Artist Serving with the Australian Imperial Forces*, 2nd ed., The British-Australasian, London, 1916

Simpson, Cameron V., *Maygar's Boys: A Biographical History of the 8th Light Horse Regiment AIF 1914–19*, Just Soldiers, Military Research & Publications, Melbourne, 1998

Şimşek, Erdoğan and Güner, Aynur (eds), *Mayın Grup Komuntanı Binbaşı Nazmi Bey'in Günlüğüyle Çanakkale Deniz Savaşları*, Deniz Basımevi, Istanbul, 2010

Stanley, Peter, *Bad Characters: Sex, Crime, Mutiny, Murder and the Australian Imperial Force*, Murdoch Books, Sydney, 2010

Stevenson, Frances, *Lloyd George: A Diary*, Taylor, Alan J. P. (ed.), Hutchinson & Co., London, 1971

Stoker, Henry G., *Straws in the Wind*, Herbert Jenkins, London, 1925

Thomas, Lowell J., *Raiders of the Deep*, William Heinemann, London, 1928

Travers, Tim, *Gallipoli: 1915*, Tempus, Stroud, 2001

Turfan, M. Naim, *Rise of the Young Turks: Politics, the Military and the Ottoman Collapse*, I.B. Taurus and Co., London, 2000

Turkish General Staff, *Osmanlı Imparatorluğu'nun Siyasi ve Askeri Hazırlıkları ve Harbe Girişi* (*Ottoman Empire's Politics, Military Preparations and Entry to War*), Vol. I, '*Birinci Dünya Harbinde Turk Harbi* (The Turkish War in WWI)', Genelkurmay Basımevi, Ankara, 1970

Tyquin, M. B., *Neville Howse: Australia's First Victoria Cross Winner*, Oxford University Press, Melbourne, 1999

Voltaire, *Candide*, Boni and Liveright Inc., New York, 1918

Wellington, Arthur Duke of, *Supplementary Despatches, Correspondence and Memoranda of Field Marshal Arthur Duke of Wellington, K.G.*, Vol. 6, Wellington, Duke of (son) (ed.), John Murray, London, 1860

Wester-Wemyss, R. E., *The Navy in the Dardanelles Campaign*, Hodder and Stoughton, London, c.1924

Williams, Peter D., *The Battle of Anzac Ridge: 25 April 1915*, Australian Military History Publications, Sydney, 2007

Winter, Denis, *25 April 1915: The Inevitable Tragedy*, University of Queensland Press, Brisbane, 1994

Wodehouse, P. G., *Blandings Castle, and Elsewhere*, Jenkins, London, 1957

Woodward, David R., *Field Marshal Sir William Robertson: Chief of the Imperial General Staff in the Great War*, Greenwood Publishing Group, Westport (CT), 1998

Younger, R. M., *Keith Murdoch: Founder of a Media Empire*, HarperCollins, Sydney, 2003

MAGAZINES AND JOURNALS
Aitken, Peter, '"Kangaroo Feathers" and the Mystique of the Light Horse', *Wartime*, No. 14, Winter 2001

The Australian National Review, Vol. 2, No. 8, 1 August 1937

Bean, Charles E. W., 'Albert Jacka', *Reveille*, 31 January 1932

——, Despatch, *Commonwealth Government Gazette*, No. 7, 13 January 1916

Caddy, J. P., 'Last Shot on Anzac', *Reveille*, Vol. VI, No. 4, 1 December 1932

Fewster, Kevin, 'The Wazza Riots, 1915', *Journal of the Australian War Memorial*, No. 4, April 1984

The Journal of the Royal Australian Armoured Corps Association, 'The Mounted Soldiers of Australia', December 2007, No. 452

McEwan, B., '"Smelly" – The Lee-Enfield Rifle', *The Gallipoli Gazette*, Vol. 43, No. 1, 2013

Mülazim, Lt Hasan Ethem, 'Last Letter of a Turkish Martyr Killed in the Gallipolian War', 17 April 1915, *The Gallipolian*, No. 76, Winter 1994

Perry, W., 'Field Marshal Lord Birdwood of Anzac', *Sabretache* (The Journal and Proceedings of the Military History Society of Australia), Vol. 29, February–March 1988, No. 1

Reveille, 'Visit to V.C.'s Grave', February 1941

Rule, E. J., 'Capt. Albert Jacka: Seventh Anniversary of Death', *Reveille*, 1 January 1939

Stead, William Thomas (ed.), 'The Eastern Ogre; or St George to the Rescue', *The Review of Reviews*, Vol. 14, October 1896, Office of the Review of Reviews, London

Thomson, Alistair, 'History and "Betrayal": The Anzac Controversy', *History Today*, 1 January 1993, Vol. 43, Issue 1

NEWSPAPERS
For newspaper articles accessed online, see section below.

The Advertiser (Adelaide)

The Argus

The Bathurst Times

Brisbane Courier

The Bulletin
The Canberra Times
Clunes Guardian and Gazette
The Courier (Ballarat)
The Courier-Mail (Brisbane)
Daily Guardian (Sydney)
Daily Mail
The Dominion (Wellington)
The Farmer & Settler
Financial Times
Kalgoorlie Miner
The Labor Call
Mercury (Hobart)
The Nelson Evening Mail
New-York Tribune
The New Zealand Herald
The Nineteenth Century and After
The Oamaru Mail
The Queenslander
Reveille
The Sun (Sydney)
The Sunday Times
The Sunday Times (Perth)
The Sydney Morning Herald
The Times
The Washington Post
The West Australian

ONLINE ARTICLES, PAPERS AND RESOURCES

The Advertiser (Adelaide), 'Australians Win Imperishable Fame', 8 May 1915,
        Trove, National Library of Australia, http://trove.nla.gov.au
——, 'Jacka, V.C. Dead', 18 January 1932, Trove, National Library of
        Australia, http://trove.nla.gov.au
——, 'Russian Successes', 20 January 1915, Trove, National Library of
        Australia, http://trove.nla.gov.au
——, 'Russians Fighting Valorously', 19 August 1915, Trove, National
        Library of Australia, http://trove.nla.gov.au
——, 'The War: Letters from the Front', 7 July 1915, Trove, National
        Library of Australia, http://trove.nla.gov.au
AE2: The Silent Anzac, AE2 Commemorative Foundation, http://ae2.org.au

The Argus, 'Austrian Tragedy', 1 July 1914, Trove, National Library of Australia, http://trove.nla.gov.au

——, 'City Disturbance', 12 October 1914, Trove, National Library of Australia, http://trove.nla.gov.au

——, 'German New Guinea', 14 September 1914, Trove, National Library of Australia, http://trove.nla.gov.au

——, 'In Australia', 21 August 1914, Trove, National Library of Australia, http://trove.nla.gov.au

——, 'Weeding Out Process', 21 January 1915, Trove, National Library of Australia, http://trove.nla.gov.au

Ashmead-Bartlett, Ellis, Diary and Papers, ML A1583, Mitchell Library, SLNSW, http://acms.sl.nsw.gov.au

——, *The Uncensored Dardanelles*, Hutchinson & Co., London, 1920, Open Library, 14 August 2012, https://openlibrary.org/books

Australian War Memorial, 'About the Australian War Memorial', www.awm.gov.au

——, 'The Anzac Day Tradition', www.awm.gov.au

Bantick, Christopher, 'What Lies Beneath a National Legend', *The Australian*, 24 April 2010, www.theaustralian.com.au

The Barrier Miner, 'The Defence Act', 19 April 1912, Trove, National Library of Australia, http://trove.nla.gov.au

Barwick, Archibald, Diary, ML MSS 1493/1/Box 1/Item 1, Mitchell Library, SLNSW, http://acms.sl.nsw.gov.au

Başkanlığı, Türkiye Cumhuriyet Genelkurmay, *Armenian Activities in the Archive Documents 1914–1918*, Vol. I, '1914–1915', Genelkurmay Basımevi, Ankara, 2005, Australian Turkish Advocacy Alliance, www.ata-a.org.au

Bean, Charles E. W., Notebook, 1920, Official History, 1914–18 War: Records of C. E. W. Bean, Official Historian, AWM38, 3DRL 606/28A/1, Australian War Memorial, www.awm.gov.au

Brodie, Charles G., *Forlorn Hope 1915: The Submarine Passage of the Dardanelles*, Frederick Books, London, 1956, Google Books, 31 July 2010, http://books.google.com.au

Çelik, Kenan, 'Gallipoli: The August Offensive – A Turkish View of the August Offensive', 2000, Australian War Memorial, www.awm.gov.au

The Chronicle (Adelaide), 'With our Troops in Egypt', 23 January 1915, Trove, National Library of Australia, http://trove.nla.gov.au

Cicognani, Harry Claude, Diary, ML MSS 1238, Mitchell Library, SLNSW, http://acms.sl.nsw.gov.au

The Colac Herald, 'Prime Minister at Colac', 3 August 1914, Trove, National Library of Australia, http://trove.nla.gov.au

Corbett, Julian S., *History of the Great War: Naval Operations*, Vol. 2 (Pt 2 of 2 online), 'December 1914 to Spring 1915', Longmans, Green & Co., London, 1921, Naval-History.Net, 22 February 2013, www. naval-history.net

The Courier-Mail (Brisbane), 'War Letters of Sir John Monash', 13 November 1934, Trove, National Library of Australia, http://trove. nla.gov.au

Cranston, Frank, 'Turkey, Australia Come Together for Dedications', *The Canberra Times*, 26 April 1985, Trove, National Library of Australia, http://trove.nla.gov.au

Daily Herald (Adelaide), 'A Whirlwind of Words', 31 July 1914, Trove, National Library of Australia, http://trove.nla.gov.au

Davidson, George, *The Incomparable 29th and the 'River Clyde'*, Howse, Jeannie and Clarke, David (transcribers), James Gordon Bisset, Aberdeen, 1919, Project Gutenberg, 5 May 2008, www. gutenberg.org

Debate in the House of Lords, *Hansard*, 18 November 1915, Vol. 20, *Hansard* 1803–2005, UK Parliament, http://hansard. millbanksystems.com

Dover: Lock and Key of the Kingdom, 'Admiral Sir Roger Keyes', www. dover-kent.co.uk

Drane, T. E., *Complete Anzac Gallipoli War Diary*, Bushroots, 20 April 2009, http://bushroots.com

The Evening News (Sydney), 'References by Mr Cook', 1 August 1914, Trove, National Library of Australia, http://trove.nla.gov.au

Forrest, Frederick E., War Diary, 19 October 1914–8 September 1917, Army Museum of South Australia, www.amosa.org.au

French, Sir John, Third Despatch (Aisne), 8 October 1914, The Long, Long Trail: The British Army in the Great War of 1914–1918 – for Family Historians, www.1914-1918.net

Gallipoli Slang, http://user.online.be/~snelders/slang.html

Hamilton, Ian, *Gallipoli Diary*, Vols I, II, Edward Arnold, London, 1920, Open Library, 14 April 2010, https://openlibrary.org/books

Hart, Peter, 'Gallipoli: The War at Sea – An Overview', The Joint Imperial War Museum/Australian War Memorial Battlefield Study Tour to Gallipoli, September 2000, Imperial War Museum, 2001, http:// archive.iwm.org.uk

Hartnett, Mr, 'With the "Boys": A Soldier's Life', *The Gundagai Independent and Pastoral, Agricultural and Mining Advocate*, 20 April 1915, Trove, National Library of Australia, http://trove.nla.gov.au

Hayman, Christy and Hayman, Lilly, *Great Britain and the European Crisis:*

Correspondence, and Statements in Parliament, 1914, Google Books, 3 July 2013, http://books.google.com.au

Healy, Tim, *More Lives Than One: My Days of Hazard*, D. Appleton-Century Company, incorporated, New York/London, 1944, Google Books, 18 October 2007, http://books.google.com.au

Hill, A. J., 'Sinclair-Maclagan, Ewen George (1868–1948)', Australian Dictionary of Biography, National Centre of Biography, Australian National University, 1988, http://adb.anu.edu.au

Hogue, Oliver, *Trooper Bluegum at the Dardanelles*, Andrew Melrose Ltd, London, 1915, Internet Archive, 6 September 2008, https://archive. org

Hough, Richard A., *Death of the Battleship*, Macmillan, 1963, Google Books, 4 September 2007, http://books.google.com.au

Housman, Alfred E., *A Shropshire Lad*, Branden Books, Wellesley (Mass), 1896, Google Books, http://books.google.com.au

James, Robert R., 'Birdwood, William Riddell, first Baron Birdwood (1865–1951)', *Oxford Dictionary of National Biography*, Oxford University Press, 2004, online edition, May 2009, www.oxforddnb. com

Keating, Paul, 'We Are Too Wise to be Cannon Fodder Again', *The Sydney Morning Herald*, 11 November 2013, www.smh.com.au

Kitchener, Lord, 'Australian Defence', *The Western Mail* (Perth), 26 February 1910, Trove, National Library of Australia, http://trove.nla.gov.au

Kitson, Jill, *Patriots Three: Billy Hughes, Lloyd George and Keith Murdoch during World War I*, ebook ed., ABC Books, Sydney, 2005, ABC Radio National, www.abc.net.au/radionational

Knightley, Phillip, *Australia: A Biography of a Nation*, Vintage, London, 2001, Google Books, http://books.google.com.au

Laseron, Charles F., Diary, ML MSS 1133, Mitchell Library, SLNSW, www. acmssearch.sl.nsw.gov.au

Laugesen, Amanda (ed.), *Glossary of Slang and Peculiar Terms in Use in the A.I.F. 1921–1924*, Australian National Dictionary Centre, Australian National University, 30 May 2011, http://andc.anu.edu. au/australian-words

Lloyd George, David, *War Memoirs*, Vol. I, Odhams Press, London, 1939, Internet Archive, 21 May 2005, https://archive.org

The London Gazette, 5 November 1914, No. 28963, www.thegazette.co.uk

Masefield, John, *Gallipoli*, Macmillan, New York, 1916, Open Library, 16 December 2011, https://openlibrary.org/books

McLaglen, Captain Leopold, *Bayonet Fighting for War*, Harrison and Sons, London, 1915, Scribd, http://www.scribd.com

Mirror (Perth), 'Hell on the *Emden*!', 23 November 1935, Trove, National
    Library of Australia, http://trove.nla.gov.au

Morgenthau, Henry, *Ambassador Morgenthau's Story*, Doubleday, Page, New
    York, 1918, Internet Archive, 4 August 2010, https://archive.org

'The Mounted Soldiers of Australia', from the TV series *Australians at War*,
    The Australian Light Horse Association, www.lighthorse.org.au

Mücke, Hellmuth von, *Ayesha*, Verlag August Scherl, Berlin, 1915, Open
    Library, 8 January 2011, https://openlibrary.org/books

The New York Times, *New York Times Current History: The European War
    from the Beginning to March 1915*, Vol. 1, No. 2, Project Gutenberg,
    2005, www.gutenberg.org

The Northern Miner, 'Proclamation', 3 December 1914, Trove, National
    Library of Australia, http://trove.nla.gov.au

O'Neill, Margot, 'Legend of Gallipoli', *Lateline*, 23 April 2001, www.abc.
    net.au/lateline/stories/s281842.htm

Pasha, Djemal, *Memories of a Turkish Statesman: 1913–1919*, George H.
    Doran Company, New York, 1922, Internet Archive, 14 April
    2010, https://archive.org

Pasha, Talaat, *Posthumous Memoirs*, p. 8, https://ia600309.us.archive.org/19/
    items/PoshumousMemoirsOfTalaatPasha/collection.pdf

Paterson, A. B., 'The First Force', *The Sydney Morning Herald*, 12 January
    1915, Trove, National Library of Australia, http://trove.nla.gov.au

———, 'The *Sydney*'s Fight', *The Sydney Morning Herald*, 30 December 1914,
    Trove, National Library of Australia, http://trove.nla.gov.au

Port Lincoln Times, 'Visit of Salvation Army Chief', 19 August 1932, Trove,
    National Library of Australia, http://trove.nla.gov.au

Raeder, Erich, *Der Krieg zur See, 1914–1918: Der Kreuzerkrieg in den
    ausländischen Gewässern, Bd. II: Die Tätigkeit der kleinen Kreuzer
    'Emden', 'Königsberg' und 'Karlsruhe'*, Mittler & Sohn, Berlin, 1923,
    Internet Archive, 6 February 2013, https://archive.org

The Register (Adelaide), 'Thirteenth Anniversary', 25 April 1928, Trove,
    National Library of Australia, http://trove.nla.gov.au

Ross, Malcolm, 'The Secret Operations', *The Evening Post* (Wellington, New
    Zealand), 31 December 1915, Papers Past, National Library of New
    Zealand, http://paperspast.natlib.govt.nz

Schuler, Phillip F. E., *Australia in Arms: A Narrative of the Australasian
    Imperial Force and Their Achievement at ANZAC*, T. Fisher Unwin,
    London, 1916, Internet Archive, 1 August 2012, https://archive.org

Shakespeare, William, *King Henry the Fifth*, 7th ed., The Princess's Theatre,
    London, 1859, Google Books, 25 October 2007, http://books.
    google.com.au

Silas, Ellis, Diary, Mitchell Library, SLNSW, ML MSS 1840, http://acms. sl.nsw.gov.au

Smith, George Ivan, Pacific Director of the BBC, 1941–1946, reported anecdote, The Great War Forum, http://1914-1918.invisionzone. com

Smythe, Herbert 'Bert' Andrew, Reg. No. 1175, Letter to Family, 27 December 1914, Smythe Family Website, 2013, www.smythe.id.au

Sweetman, John R., 'Lieutenant Hugo Throssell VC, 10th Australian Light Horse, AIF', 2001, The Free Library, www.thefreelibrary.com

The Sydney Morning Herald, 'Breast Forward', 6 November 1914, Trove, National Library of Australia, http://trove.nla.gov.au

——, 'Mr Ashmead Bartlett's Story', 8 May 1915, Trove, National Library of Australia, http://trove.nla.gov.au

——, 'The Navies: Marauding Emden', 23 September 1914, Trove, National Library of Australia, http://trove.nla.gov.au

——, 'The Transports', 8 December 1914, Trove, National Library of Australia, http://trove.nla.gov.au

Tehlirian, Soghomon, Trial Transcripts, 16 April 1921, 3rd State Court, Criminal Department, Berlin, Cilicia.com, www.cilicia.com/ armo_tehlirian.html

Toye, Richard, *Lloyd George and Churchill: Rivals for Greatness*, Pan, Kindle edition, Amazon, 2012, www.amazon.com

The Truth (Melbourne), 'A Military Camp Sensation: Salacious She and the Soldiers', 10 October 1914, Trove, National Library of Australia, http://trove.nla.gov.au

——, 'The Red Plague', 31 July 1915, Trove, National Library of Australia, http://trove.nla.gov.au

Venning, Annabel, 'The Priapic PM who Wrote Love Letters to his Mistress as he Sent a Generation Off to Die in the Trenches', *Daily Mail*, 27 April 2012, www.dailymail.co.uk

Walsh, G. P., 'Kirkpatrick, John Simpson (1892–1915)', Australian Dictionary of Biography, National Centre of Biography, Australian National University, 1983, http://adb.anu.edu.au

The West Australian, 'The Australians at Gallipoli', 13 July 1915, Trove, National Library of Australia, http://trove.nla.gov.au

——, 'The Dardanelles', 28 September 1915, Trove, National Library of Australia, http://trove.nla.gov.au

——, 'Invented in the Trenches', 12 August 1915, Trove, National Library of Australia, http://trove.nla.gov.au

——, 'The Story of Hill 60', 22 November 1915, Trove, National Library of Australia, http://trove.nla.gov.au

———, 'With the Australians', 26 August 1915, Trove, National Library of
    Australia, http://trove.nla.gov.au
Westbrook, F. E., 'On Our Critic's Apologies', *The Essendon Gazette and
    Keilor, Bulla and Broadmeadows Reporter*, 29 April 1915, Trove,
    National Library of Australia, http://trove.nla.gov.au
Wiltshire, A. R. L., Diary, ML MSS 3058/Box 1/Items 2–4, Mitchell
    Library, SLNSW, http://acms.sl.nsw.gov.au

PAPERS, DIARIES, CORRESPONDENCE, REPORTS AND MANUSCRIPTS

2nd Infantry Battalion War Diary, AWM4 23/19/6
3rd Australian Field Ambulance War Diary, AWM4 26/46/5
3rd Australian Light Horse Brigade War Diary, AWM4 10/3/7
3rd Brigade War Diary, AWM4 23/3/2
3rd Infantry Battalion War Diary, AWM4 23/20/2
4th Battery Australian Field Artillery War Diary, AWM RCDIG1018662,
    Item 13/66/7
10th Australian Light Horse Brigade War Diary, AWM4 10/15/4
10th Infantry Battalion War Diary, AWM4 23/27/2
Adams, John, Diary, AWM RCDIG0000862
Aitken, James Murray, Diary, AWM 1DRL/0013
Annear, W. R., War Service Record, NAA 3033933
Antill, J. M., Comments, Official History 1914–1918 War Records of
    Charles E. W. Bean, Correspondence 1926–31, AWM 3DRL
    7953/27, Pt 3, Ch. XVIII
Asquith, Prime Minister to King George V, Letter, undated, R/256, NA
    CAB 37/139/17
Barwick, Archibald, Diary, undated, AWM F940.26093 B296d
Bean, Charles, War Diary, AWM38, 3DRL606/1/1, 3DRL606/2/1,
    3DRL606/3/1, 3DRL606/5/1, 3DRL606/7/1, 3DRL606/9/1,
    3DRL606/10/1, 3DRL606, 3DRL606/21/1, 3DRL606/22/1,
    3DRL606/23/1, 3DRL606/25/1
———, War Records of Charles E. W. Bean, AWM 3DRL 7953
Beevor, Miles, Diary, AWM MSS0761
Bell, James, 'History of the Ninth Battalion AIF', manuscript, SLQ, OM64-
    5/517 26
Bingham, Charles, Diary, Private Collection of the Bingham Family
Borthwick, Alexander Hay, Letters and Postcard, AWM PR01729
Branches and Services: General Staff, April–July 1916, NA WO 95/4
Brazier, Noel, Comments, Official History 1914–1918 War Records of

Charles E. W. Bean, Correspondence 1926–31, AWM 3DRL
7953/27, Pt 3, Ch. XVIII
——, Diary, AWM 1DRL/0147
——, Letter to C. E. W. Bean, 7 March 1924, AWM 38 DRL 8042,
Item 25
Carden to Admiralty, Telegram, 27 September 1914, NA ADM 137/96
Carter, Herbert Gordon, Diary, AWM 3DRL/6418
——, Letters, Mena Camp, AWM 1DRL/192
Cass, Walter E. H., 'Early Events of the 2nd Infantry Brigade at Anzac,
25/04/1915', AWM38, 3DRL8042, Item 6
Cavalier, Ronald, Diary/Letter, AWM PR86/287
Coe, Henry J. F., Diary, AWM 2DRL/491
Coe, Henry J. F. to his Parents, Letter, 26 December 1914 and 30 January
1915, AWM 2DRL/491
Cooper, M. G. et al. (eds), 'Proceedings of the 8th International Symposium
on the History of Anaesthesia', Australian Society of Anaesthetists,
Sydney, 2014
Cozens, Thomas E., Diary, AWM 2DRL/0002
Curzon, Lord, Memorandum, 25 November 1915, Cabinet Papers, NA CAB
37/138/12
Dardanelles Committee Meeting, 25 June 1915, NA CAB 42/3/5
——, 24 September 1915, NA CAB 42/3/30
——, 6 October 1915, NA CAB 42/4/3
——, 7 October 1915, NA CAB 42/4/4
——, 11 October 1915, NA CAB 42/4/6
——, 14 October 1915, NA CAB 42/4/9
Edwards, R. A., Diary, AWM PR/192
Finlay to Director, Australian War Memorial, 9 December 1929, AWM
1DRL/0284
'The First Report of the Dardanelles Commission', HMSO, London, 1917
'The Final Report of the Dardanelles Commission', HMSO, London, 1919
Fisher, John Arbuthnot, Letter to the Chief of the Imperial General Staff,
Churchill to General Sir Charles Douglas (C.I.G.S.), 1 September
1914, Appendix (A1), NA CAB 19/28
Flockart, Robert Pearce, Letters, 27 May 1915, 28 May 1915, AWM
1DRL/0296
Fullerton, Alexander Young, Diary, AWM 1DRL/0302
Gardiner, Reginald Scott, Extracts of Letters from Reginald Scott Gardiner
to his Mother, 1914–1915, AWM 1DRL/0304
Hamilton, Ian, Memorandum on Murdoch Letter, 26 November 1915,
Committee of Imperial Defence, NA CAB 42/5/23

Henderson, Alan Dudley, Letter, AWM RCDIG00000999

Hill, William John Rusden, Letter from the Front, ML DOC 2480

Hoddinott, Rupert Uriah, Typed Manuscript, AWM MSS0791

Hogue, Oliver, Letters relating to Oliver 'Trooper Bluegum' Hogue,
      1915–1927, AWM RCDIG 0000997

House of Representatives, *Official Hansard*, No. 17, Thursday 29 April
      1915

——, No. 17, Friday 30 April 1915

Jacka, Albert, Diary, AWM MSS143A, Pt 4

Kan-Karroo Kronikle, 4 November 1914, Vol. 1, No. 3, AWM 073952

Kidd, Thomas A., Diary, AWM PR82/137

King, Lydia K., Diary, AWM 3DRL/6040

Kitchener to Asquith, Telegram, 15 November 1915, War Committee
      Meeting, 23 November 1915, NA CAB 42/5/20

Knaggs, Albert E., Diary, AWM PR85/096

Langford, Percival, Diary, AWM 3DRL/7454

Lloyd George, David, Lloyd George Papers, United Kingdom Parliamentary
      Archives, LG/D/18/2/12, LG/D/23/4/8

Margetts, Ivor Stephen, Diary, AWM 1DRL/0478

McAnulty, Cecil Anthony, Diary, AWM 1DRL/0422

McLarty, Hector Roy, Letters, 7 July 1915, 11 August 1915, AWM
      3DRL/3339

Mediterranean Expeditionary Force War Diary, AWM4 1/4/8, Pt 2, AWM4
      1/4/9, Pt 1

Monash, John, Diary, Sir Monash Papers, SLV, MS 13875, Box 4083/1

——, Sir Monash Papers, SLV, MS 13875, Box 4083/1

Muir, Frederick W., Diary, AWM RCDIG0000428

Mulvey, Frederick, Letter, 14 March 1915, AWM 2DR/0233

Murdoch, Keith A., Papers of Sir Keith Arthur Murdoch (1886–1952),
      NLA, MS 2823, Series 2, Folders 1 and 3

Norris, Sam, War Narrative ('There and Back'), Mitchell Library, SLNSW,
      ML MSS 2933/Item 3

Northcliffe, Lord, Northcliffe Papers, Vol. XXVII, British Library, MS
      62179

Rayment, George L., Diary, AWM PR91/042

Raynell, Carew, Diary, AWM PR86/388

Redford, Thomas H., Diary, AWM PR85/064

'Report of the Committee Appointed to Investigate the Attacks on and the
      Enemy Defences of the Dardanelles Straits, Section IX Summary',
      NA ADM 186/600

'Report of Proceedings of Court of Inquiry, 3 August 1915, Reporting on

the Disturbance in Cairo on the Night of 31st July 1915', AIF HQ
Egypt, Central Registry, 1914–1918, AWM 80i5/2023

Reynolds, Herbert V., Diary, AWM RCDIG0001013

Richards, Thomas J., Diary, AWM 2DRL/0786

Ryrie, Granville to Mrs Granville Ryrie, 23 December 1915, AWM
PR84/193

Secretary's Notes of a Meeting of the War Council held at 10 Downing
Street, 25 November 1914, NA CAB 42/1/4

——, 28 January 1915, NA CAB 42/1/26

——, 24 February 1915, NA CAB 42/1/42

——, 3 March 1915, NA CAB 42/2/3

——, 10 March 1915, NA CAB 42/2/5

——, 14 May 1915, NA CAB 42/2/19

Simpson, John (aka John Simpson Kirkpatrick), Service Record, NAA
B2455

Slade, Admiral Sir Edmond John to Winston Churchill, minute, 30 October
1914, NA ADM 137/96

Steel, Arthur Valentine (1st Battalion AIF), Letter to Marie and George
Steel, January 1916, courtesy of Steel family of Wangaratta

Throssell, Hugo, Diary, AWM PR85/361

——, Katharine Susannah Prichard's Papers, NLA MS 6201, Folder 7 (War
Diary)

——, Papers, NAA, PP645/1, M5273

——, Papers of Hugo Vivian Hope Throssell, AWM 1DRL/0581

Tiddy, Henry J., Diary, AWM PR86/272

Usedom, Admiral von, 'Despatches from Admiral von Usedom to the Kaiser
about the defences of the Dardanelles, and naval operations before
and after the British landings' (translation), NA CAB 45/215

War Committee Meeting, 23 November 1915, NA CAB 42/5/20

Watson, James W., Diary, National Army Museum, New Zealand,
1999.3061

Wellington Battalion War Diary, AWM4 Subclass 35/20; AWM4, 35/20/1,
RCDIG1001245

Wheat, John H., War Diary/Narrative, 1914–1918, ML MSS 3054, Item 3

White, Alexander Henry, War Record, NAA, B2455, Item 36/45

White, Brudenell, 'Note on the Withdrawal of Anzac', AWM 3DRL/1400,
Series 4, Wallet 3

——, Papers of General Sir Cyril Bingham Brudenell White, AWM
3DRL/1400, Series 4, Wallet 3

OTHER

Latimer, Harrison (vocalist) and Francis, W. W. (composer.), 'Australia Will Be There: Australia's War Song', Regal, United Kingdom, 1915, http://trove.nla.gov.au

Sailah, Steve, *Stories from Gallipoli*, ABC Audio, Sydney, 2013

World War I propaganda leaflets and papers dropped from aircraft over Gallipoli and Palestine, 1917, ML, Strongroom, SAFE 1/213

INDEX

Listings of illustrations and maps are in italics